50% OFF CSET Multiple Subjects Test Prep Course!

Dear Customer,

We consider it an honor and a privilege that you chose our CSET Multiple Subjects Study Guide. As a way of showing our appreciation and to help us better serve you, we have partnered with Mometrix Test Preparation to offer you **50% off their online CSET Multiple Subjects Prep Course.** Many CSET courses are needlessly expensive and don't deliver enough value. With their course, you get access to the best CSET prep material, and **you only pay half price**.

Mometrix has structured their online course to perfectly complement your printed study guide. The CSET Multiple Subjects Prep Course contains **in-depth lessons** that cover all the most important topics, over **700 practice questions** to ensure you feel prepared, more than **1350 flashcards** for studying on the go, and over **380 instructional videos**.

Online CSET Multiple Subjects Prep Course

Topics Covered:

- Reading, Language, and Literature
    - Foundations of Grammar
    - Style and Form
- History and Social Science
    - United States History
    - U.S. Government and Citizenship
- Science
    - Physical, Earth, and Space Sciences
- Mathematics
    - Algebra and Functions
    - Measurement and Geometry
- Physical Education and Human Development
    - Health, Wellness, and Fitness
- Visual and Performing Arts
    - Elements and Appreciation of Art

And More!

Course Features:

- CSET Multiple Subjects Study Guide
    - Get access to content from the best reviewed study guide available.
- Track Your Progress
    - Their customized course allows you to check off content you have studied or feel confident with.
- 5 Full-Length Practice Tests
    - With 700+ practice questions and lesson reviews, you can test yourself again and again to build confidence.
- CSET Multiple Subjects Flashcards
    - Their course includes a flashcard mode consisting of over 1350 content cards to help you study.

To receive this discount, visit them at www.mometrix.com/university/csetms/ or simply scan this QR code with your smartphone. At the checkout page, enter the discount code: **TPBCSETMS50**

If you have any questions or concerns, please contact Mometrix at support@mometrix.com.

SCAN HERE

 in partnership with

FREE Test Taking Tips Video/DVD Offer

To better serve you, we created videos covering test taking tips that we want to give you for FREE. **These videos cover world-class tips that will help you succeed on your test.**

We just ask that you send us feedback about this product. Please let us know what you thought about it—whether good, bad, or indifferent.

To get your **FREE videos**, you can use the QR code below or email freevideos@studyguideteam.com with "Free Videos" in the subject line and the following information in the body of the email:

    a. The title of your product

    b. Your product rating on a scale of 1-5, with 5 being the highest

    c. Your feedback about the product

If you have any questions or concerns, please don't hesitate to contact us at info@studyguideteam.com.

Thank you!

SCAN HERE

CSET Multiple Subject Test Prep
CSET Study Guide and Practice Exam for California Teachers
[5th Edition]

Joshua Rueda

Interested in buying more than 10 copies of our product? Contact us about bulk discounts:
bulkorders@studyguideteam.com

ISBN 13: 9781637753705

Table of Contents

Welcome

Dear Reader,

Welcome to your new Test Prep Books study guide! We are pleased that you chose us to help you prepare for your exam. There are many study options to choose from, and we appreciate you choosing us. Studying can be a daunting task, but we have designed a smart, effective study guide to help prepare you for what lies ahead.

Whether you're a parent helping your child learn and grow, a high school student working hard to get into your dream college, or a nursing student studying for a complex exam, we want to help give you the tools you need to succeed. We hope this study guide gives you the skills and the confidence to thrive, and we can't thank you enough for allowing us to be part of your journey.

In an effort to continue to improve our products, we welcome feedback from our customers. We look forward to hearing from you. Suggestions, success stories, and criticisms can all be communicated by emailing us at info@studyguideteam.com.

Sincerely,
Test Prep Books Team

FREE Videos/DVD OFFER

Doing well on your exam requires both knowing the test content and understanding how to use that knowledge to do well on the test. We offer completely FREE test taking tip videos. **These videos cover world-class tips that you can use to succeed on your test.**

To get your **FREE videos**, you can use the QR code below or email freevideos@studyguideteam.com with "Free Videos" in the subject line and the following information in the body of the email:

> a. The title of your product
> b. Your product rating on a scale of 1-5, with 5 being the highest
> c. Your feedback about the product

If you have any questions or concerns, please don't hesitate to contact us at info@studyguideteam.com.

1

Quick Overview

As you draw closer to taking your exam, effective preparation becomes more and more important. Thankfully, you have this study guide to help you get ready. Use this guide to help keep your studying on track and refer to it often.

This study guide contains several key sections that will help you be successful on your exam. The guide contains tips for what you should do the night before and the day of the test. Also included are test-taking tips. Knowing the right information is not always enough. Many well-prepared test takers struggle with exams. These tips will help equip you to accurately read, assess, and answer test questions.

A large part of the guide is devoted to showing you what content to expect on the exam and to helping you better understand that content. In this guide are practice test questions so that you can see how well you have grasped the content. Then, answer explanations are provided so that you can understand why you missed certain questions.

Don't try to cram the night before you take your exam. This is not a wise strategy for a few reasons. First, your retention of the information will be low. Your time would be better used by reviewing information you already know rather than trying to learn a lot of new information. Second, you will likely become stressed as you try to gain a large amount of knowledge in a short amount of time. Third, you will be depriving yourself of sleep. So be sure to go to bed at a reasonable time the night before. Being well-rested helps you focus and remain calm.

Be sure to eat a substantial breakfast the morning of the exam. If you are taking the exam in the afternoon, be sure to have a good lunch as well. Being hungry is distracting and can make it difficult to focus. You have hopefully spent lots of time preparing for the exam. Don't let an empty stomach get in the way of success!

When travelling to the testing center, leave earlier than needed. That way, you have a buffer in case you experience any delays. This will help you remain calm and will keep you from missing your appointment time at the testing center.

Be sure to pace yourself during the exam. Don't try to rush through the exam. There is no need to risk performing poorly on the exam just so you can leave the testing center early. Allow yourself to use all of the allotted time if needed.

Remain positive while taking the exam even if you feel like you are performing poorly. Thinking about the content you should have mastered will not help you perform better on the exam.

Once the exam is complete, take some time to relax. Even if you feel that you need to take the exam again, you will be well served by some down time before you begin studying again. It's often easier to convince yourself to study if you know that it will come with a reward!

Test-Taking Strategies

1. Predicting the Answer

When you feel confident in your preparation for a multiple-choice test, try predicting the answer before reading the answer choices. This is especially useful on questions that test objective factual knowledge. By predicting the answer before reading the available choices, you eliminate the possibility that you will be distracted or led astray by an incorrect answer choice. You will feel more confident in your selection if you read the question, predict the answer, and then find your prediction among the answer choices. After using this strategy, be sure to still read all of the answer choices carefully and completely. If you feel unprepared, you should not attempt to predict the answers. This would be a waste of time and an opportunity for your mind to wander in the wrong direction.

2. Reading the Whole Question

Too often, test takers scan a multiple-choice question, recognize a few familiar words, and immediately jump to the answer choices. Test authors are aware of this common impatience, and they will sometimes prey upon it. For instance, a test author might subtly turn the question into a negative, or he or she might redirect the focus of the question right at the end. The only way to avoid falling into these traps is to read the entirety of the question carefully before reading the answer choices.

3. Looking for Wrong Answers

Long and complicated multiple-choice questions can be intimidating. One way to simplify a difficult multiple-choice question is to eliminate all of the answer choices that are clearly wrong. In most sets of answers, there will be at least one selection that can be dismissed right away. If the test is administered on paper, the test taker could draw a line through it to indicate that it may be ignored; otherwise, the test taker will have to perform this operation mentally or on scratch paper. In either case, once the obviously incorrect answers have been eliminated, the remaining choices may be considered. Sometimes identifying the clearly wrong answers will give the test taker some information about the correct answer. For instance, if one of the remaining answer choices is a direct opposite of one of the eliminated answer choices, it may well be the correct answer. The opposite of obviously wrong is obviously right! Of course, this is not always the case. Some answers are obviously incorrect simply because they are irrelevant to the question being asked. Still, identifying and eliminating some incorrect answer choices is a good way to simplify a multiple-choice question.

4. Don't Overanalyze

Anxious test takers often overanalyze questions. When you are nervous, your brain will often run wild, causing you to make associations and discover clues that don't actually exist. If you feel that this may be a problem for you, do whatever you can to slow down during the test. Try taking a deep breath or counting to ten. As you read and consider the question, restrict yourself to the particular words used by the author. Avoid thought tangents about what the author *really* meant, or what he or she was *trying* to say. The only things that matter on a multiple-choice test are the words that are actually in the question. You must avoid reading too much into a multiple-choice question, or supposing that the writer meant something other than what he or she wrote.

3

5. No Need for Panic

It is wise to learn as many strategies as possible before taking a multiple-choice test, but it is likely that you will come across a few questions for which you simply don't know the answer. In this situation, avoid panicking. Because most multiple-choice tests include dozens of questions, the relative value of a single wrong answer is small. As much as possible, you should compartmentalize each question on a multiple-choice test. In other words, you should not allow your feelings about one question to affect your success on the others. When you find a question that you either don't understand or don't know how to answer, just take a deep breath and do your best. Read the entire question slowly and carefully. Try rephrasing the question a couple of different ways. Then, read all of the answer choices carefully. After eliminating obviously wrong answers, make a selection and move on to the next question.

6. Confusing Answer Choices

When working on a difficult multiple-choice question, there may be a tendency to focus on the answer choices that are the easiest to understand. Many people, whether consciously or not, gravitate to the answer choices that require the least concentration, knowledge, and memory. This is a mistake. When you come across an answer choice that is confusing, you should give it extra attention. A question might be confusing because you

 do not know the subject matter to which it refers. If this is the case, don't eliminate the answer before you have affirmatively settled on another. When you come across an answer choice of this type, set it aside as you look at the remaining choices. If you can confidently assert that one of the other choices is correct, you can leave the confusing answer aside. Otherwise, you will need to take a moment to try to better understand the confusing answer choice. Rephrasing is one way to tease out the sense of a confusing answer choice.

7. Your First Instinct

Many people struggle with multiple-choice tests because they overthink the questions. If you have studied sufficiently for the test, you should be prepared to trust your first instinct once you have carefully and completely read the question and all of the answer choices. There is a great deal of research suggesting that the mind can come to the correct conclusion very quickly once it has obtained all of the relevant information. At times, it may seem to you as if your intuition is working faster even than your reasoning mind. This may in fact be true. The knowledge you obtain while studying may be retrieved from your subconscious before you have a chance to work out the associations that support it. Verify your instinct by working out the reasons that it should be trusted.

8. Key Words

Many test takers struggle with multiple-choice questions because they have poor reading comprehension skills. Quickly reading and understanding a multiple-choice question requires a mixture of skill and experience. To help with this, try jotting down a few key words and phrases on a piece of scrap paper. Doing this concentrates the process of reading and forces the mind to weigh the relative importance of the question's parts. In selecting words and phrases to write down, the test taker thinks about the question more deeply and carefully. This is especially true for multiple-choice questions that are preceded by a long prompt.

9. Subtle Negatives

One of the oldest tricks in the multiple-choice test writer's book is to subtly reverse the meaning of a question with a word like *not* or *except*. If you are not paying attention to each word in the question, you can easily be led astray by this trick. For instance, a common question format is, "Which of the following is...?" Obviously, if the question instead is, "Which of the following is not...?," then the answer will be quite different. Even worse, the test makers are aware of the potential for this mistake and will include one answer choice that would be correct if the question were not negated or reversed. A test taker who misses the reversal will find what he or she believes to be a correct answer and will be so confident that he or she will fail to reread the question and discover the original error. The only way to avoid this is to practice a wide variety of multiple-choice questions and to pay close attention to each and every word.

10. Reading Every Answer Choice

It may seem obvious, but you should always read every one of the answer choices! Too many test takers fall into the habit of scanning the question and assuming that they understand the question because they recognize a few key words. From there, they pick the first answer choice that answers the question they believe they have read. Test takers who read all of the answer choices might discover that one of the latter answer choices is actually *more* correct. Moreover, reading all of the answer choices can remind you of facts related to the question that can help you arrive at the correct answer. Sometimes, a misstatement or incorrect detail in one of the latter answer choices will trigger your memory of the subject and will enable you to find the right answer. Failing to read all of the answer choices is like not reading all of the items on a restaurant menu: you might miss out on the perfect choice.

11. Spot the Hedges

One of the keys to success on multiple-choice tests is paying close attention to every word. This is never truer than with words like *almost*, *most*, *some*, and *sometimes*. These words are called "hedges" because they indicate that a statement is not totally true or not true in every place and time. An absolute statement will contain no hedges, but in many subjects, the answers are not always straightforward or absolute. There are always exceptions to the rules in these subjects. For this reason, you should favor those multiple-choice

questions that contain hedging language. The presence of qualifying words indicates that the author is taking special care with his or her words, which is certainly important when composing the right answer. After all, there are many ways to be wrong, but there is only one way to be right! For this reason, it is wise to avoid answers that are absolute when taking a multiple-choice test. An absolute answer is one that says things are either all one way or all another. They often include words like *every*, *always*, *best*, and *never*. If you are taking a multiple-choice test in a subject that doesn't lend itself to absolute answers, be on your guard if you see any of these words.

12. Long Answers

In many subject areas, the answers are not simple. As already mentioned, the right answer often requires hedges. Another common feature of the answers to a complex or subjective question are qualifying clauses, which are groups of words that subtly modify the meaning of the sentence. If the question or answer choice describes a rule to which there are exceptions or the subject matter is complicated, ambiguous, or confusing, the correct answer will require many words in order to be expressed clearly and accurately. In essence, you should not be deterred by answer choices that seem excessively long. Oftentimes, the author of the text will not be able to write the correct answer without offering some qualifications and modifications. Your job is to read the answer choices thoroughly and completely and to select the one that most accurately and precisely answers the question.

13. Restating to Understand

Sometimes, a question on a multiple-choice test is difficult not because of what it asks but because of how it is written. If this is the case, restate the question or answer choice in different words. This process serves a couple of important purposes. First, it forces you to concentrate on the core of the question. In order to rephrase the question accurately, you have to understand it well. Rephrasing the question will concentrate your mind on the key words and ideas. Second, it will present the information to your mind in a fresh way. This process may trigger your memory and render some useful scrap of information picked up while studying.

14. True Statements

Sometimes an answer choice will be true in itself, but it does not answer the question. This is one of the main reasons why it is essential to read the question carefully and completely before proceeding to the answer choices. Too often, test takers skip ahead to the answer choices and look for true statements. Having found one of these, they are content to select it without reference to the question above. The savvy test taker will always read the entire question before turning to the answer choices. Then, having settled on a correct answer choice, he or she will refer to the original question and ensure that the selected answer is relevant. The mistake of choosing a correct-but-irrelevant answer choice is especially common on questions related to specific pieces of objective knowledge.

15. No Patterns

One of the more dangerous ideas that circulates about multiple-choice tests is that the correct answers tend to fall into patterns. These erroneous ideas range from a belief that B and C are the most common right answers, to the idea that an unprepared test-taker should answer "A-B-A-C-A-D-A-B-A." It cannot be emphasized enough that pattern-seeking of this type is exactly the WRONG way to approach a multiple-choice test. To begin with, it is highly unlikely that the test maker will plot the correct answers according to some predetermined pattern. The questions are scrambled and delivered in a random order. Furthermore, even if the test maker was following a pattern in the assignation of correct answers, there is no reason why the test taker would know which pattern he or she was using. Any attempt to discern a pattern in the answer choices is a waste of time and a distraction from the real work of taking the test. A test taker would be much better served by extra preparation before the test than by reliance on a pattern in the answers.

Introduction

Function of the Test

The California Subject Examinations for Teachers (CSET) Multiple Subjects Exam is for educators in California who wish to receive credentialing to teach elementary or special education. Required by the state of California, the exam is broken up into three subtests and tests applicants on their knowledge of (1) Reading, Language, Literature, History, and Social Science; (2) Science and Mathematics; and (3) Physical Education, Human Development, and Visual and Performing Arts. In the year 2014, 7,168 applicants attempted to pass the test. Out of this number, 5,223 passed, a rate of 73 percent.

Test Administration

The exam is offered in testing centers across California. Those interested in the test should go to the CSET website www.ctcexams.nesinc.com/about_CSET.asp and search for a testing center near their area. The CSET Multiple Subjects Exam is available year-round by appointment, Monday through Saturday, but excludes some holidays. The three subtests can be taken altogether or separately. Be sure to register at the program website before scheduling your appointment to take the Multiple Subjects Exam I, II, and III.

If you fail one of the subtests, you can take that subtest again until you pass. There is no limit on retesting. However, you must redo the registration on the exam's website. The validity of score for the subtests is good for five years, which means you must earn certification within five years of passing the exam(s).

Test Format

The CSET Multiple Subjects subtests are computer-based exams broken into three separate parts. Subtest I and II allow three hours per subtest, while Subtest III lasts two hours and fifteen minutes. Taking all three subtests in a single session would take five hours, although you would be given the freedom to work on the subtests in any order you decide. Any break taken for any subtest remains part of the allotted testing time.

All three subtests consist of multiple-choice questions as well as constructed-response questions. A summary of the sections of the CSET Multiple Subjects Exam is as follows:

Section	Subjects	Multiple-Choice	Constructed Response	Time
Subtest I	Reading, Language, and Literature	26	2	180 minutes
	History and Social Science	26	2	
Total:		52	4	
Subtest II	Science	26	2	180 minutes
	Mathematics	26	2	
Total:		52	4	
Subtest III	Physical Education	13	1	135 minutes
	Human Development	13	1	
	Visual and Performing Arts	13	1	
Total:		39	3	

Scoring

Scores on the CSET Multiple Subjects Exam are converted to a scale of 100 to 300. The passing score for each subtest is a score of 220. If you choose to take the computer-based test, your score should show immediately after the test. Official scores are sent out from twenty to forty-five days after the test. You can choose who receives the scores.

Recent/Future Developments

Per their website, the CSET Multiple Subjects Subtest II has been redesigned to match the Next Generation Science Standards (NGSS). The first test administration for this development is August 7, 2017, and registration is currently open.

Study Prep Plan for the CSET

1 **Schedule -** Use one of our study schedules below or come up with one of your own.

2 **Relax -** Test anxiety can hurt even the best students. There are many ways to reduce stress. Find the one that works best for you.

3 **Execute -** Once you have a good plan in place, be sure to stick to it.

One Week Study Schedule		
Day 1	Reading, Language, and Literature
Day 2	Practice Questions for Subtest I
Day 3	Mathematics
Day 4	Practice Questions for Subtest II
Day 5	Visual and Performing Arts
Day 6	Practice Questions for Subtest III
Day 7	Take Your Exam!

Two Week Study Schedule			
Day 1	Reading, Language, and Literature	Day 8	Science
Day 2	Non-Written Communication	Day 9	Living and Nonliving Components in Environments
Day 3	History and Social Sciences	Day 10	Practice Questions for Subtest II
Day 4	Civil War and Reconstruction	Day 11	Visual and Performing Arts
Day 5	Practice Questions for Subtest I	Day 12	Physical Education
Day 6	Mathematics	Day 13	Practice Questions for Subtest III
Day 7	Linear and Quadratic Equations and Inequalities	Day 14	Take Your Exam!

One Month Study Schedule					
Day 1	Reading, Language, and Literature	Day 11	Answer Explanations for Subtest I	Day 21	Answer Explanations for Subtest II
Day 2	Language Development and Acquisition	Day 12	Mathematics	Day 22	Visual and Performing Arts
Day 3	Language and Linguistics: Assessment	Day 13	Linear and Quadratic Equations and Inequalities	Day 23	Visual Arts
Day 4	Stages of the Writing Process	Day 14	Representational Systems	Day 24	Health and Physical Fitness
Day 5	Non-Written Communication	Day 15	Making Inferences and Justifying Conclusions from Samples...	Day 25	Physical Growth and Development
Day 6	Reading Literature	Day 16	Science	Day 26	Social Aspects of Physical Education
Day 7	History and Social Sciences	Day 17	Structure of Living Organisms and Their Function	Day 27	Social Development
Day 8	Early Exploration, Colonial Era, and the War for Independence	Day 18	Living and Nonliving Components in Environments	Day 28	Practice Questions for Subtest III
Day 9	Civil War and Reconstruction	Day 19	The Solar System and the Universe	Day 29	Answer Explanations for Subtest III
Day 10	Practice Questions for Subtest I	Day 20	Practice Questions for Subtest II	Day 30	Take Your Exam!

Build your own prep plan by visiting:

testprepbooks.com/prep

As you study for your test, we'd like to take the opportunity to remind you that you are capable of great things! With the right tools and dedication, you truly can do anything you set your mind to. The fact that you are holding this book right now shows how committed you are. In case no one has told you lately, you've got this! Our intention behind including this coloring page is to give you the chance to take some time to engage your creative side when you need a little brain-break from studying. As a company, we want to encourage people like you to achieve their dreams by providing good quality study materials for the tests and certifications that improve careers and change lives. As individuals, many of us have taken such tests in our careers, and we know how challenging this process can be. While we can't come alongside you and cheer you on personally, we can offer you the space to recall your purpose, reconnect with your passion, and refresh your brain through an artistic practice. We wish you every success, and happy studying!

11

Reading, Language, and Literature

Language and Linguistics: Language Structure and Linguistics

Fundamental Components of Human Language

Among all languages, it is important to have fundamental structure to clearly communicate. There needs to be a logical way to organize words within a sentence so that people can read, speak, and listen in a meaningful way. There are four components of language structure:

- Morphology
- Semantics
- Syntax
- Phonology

Morphology

Morphology is the study of words. It explores how words are formed using morphemes (words or parts of words that contain their own meanings), as well as their relationship with other words within a language. For example, look at the word *cupcake*. The beginning and ending sounds *c* and *silent e* do not have meaning on their own. However, when combined with other morphemes, this compound word takes on a whole new meaning. Each word, *cup* and *cake,* has independent meanings. When you combine them, a new word, *cupcake,* takes on a completely independent definition.

Morphology examines root words, affixes (prefixes and suffixes), and stems. Not only does it analyze each part of words, morphology also looks at how words are used. Morphology can often answer how words are pronounced or the context in which words are used.

Derivatives and Borrowings

Derivatives are words that are formed from other words, otherwise known as **root words**. Word derivatives add morphemes, or affixes, to the beginning or ending of root words to create new words with new meanings. Below are some of the commonly used derivatives in the English language:

Root Word	Affix	Derivative
favor	-able	favorable
bare	-ness	bareness
child	-like	childlike
boast	-ful	boastful
whole	-some	wholesome
seven	-th	seventh
west	-ward	westward
north	-ern	northern
health	-y	healthy

Remember, sometimes the spelling of the root word changes once the affix is added to form the derivative. For example, by adding the affix *-iation* to the root word *affiliate*, first drop the *e*, and then add the *-iation,* to form *affiliation*.

12

Borrowings, otherwise referred to as **loanwords,** are words that are borrowed and incorporated into one's own language originating from a different language. It is not as though the borrowed words are returned like a library book; however, these words tend to relate strongly to the language loaning the words as opposed to the language borrowing the words. For example, the English word *music* is a borrowed word from the French word *musique*. The Spanish word *chofer* is borrowed from the French word *chauffeur*.

The following table lists some of the borrowed words from the Germanic Period, Old English Period, Middle English Period, Early Modern English Period, and the Modern English Period:

Germanic Period	
Language	**Borrowed Word Examples**
Latin	butere (butter), sacc (sack), win (wine)
Old English Period	
Language	**Borrowed Word Examples**
Latin	cest (chest), maegester (master), tigle (tile), circul (circle)
Celtic	brocc (badger), cumb (combe, valley)
Middle English Period	
Language	**Borrowed Word Examples**
French	attorney, baron, boil, crime, question, special
Scandinavian	cake, lump, skirt, ugly, want
Early Modern English Period	
Language	**Borrowed Word Examples**
Arabic	alcove, algebra, orange, sugar, zero
Greek	critic, data, pneumonia, tragedy
Latin	area, compensate, dexterity, vindicate
Modern English Period	
Language	**Borrowed Word Examples**
Dutch	booze, bow, scum, uproar
French	ballet, cabernet, brigade, battalion
German	dunk, hamburger, pretzel, strudel
Italian	balcony, grotto, regatta, zucchini
Russian	icon, vodka
Scandinavian	ski, slalom, smorgasbord
Spanish	alligator, coyote, ranch, tornado
Yiddish	bagel, kosher, oy vey

Word borrowing occurred frequently throughout history. Historical events and trends influence which languages influence one another.

Semantics

Semantics studies the meanings of words, phrases, sentences, and texts. Semantics can be divided into two major categories: lexical semantics and phrasal semantics.

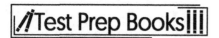

Lexical semantics not only studies individual words, but it also analyzes affixes, compound words, and phrases, whereas phrasal semantics studies the meaning of phrases and words. It looks at word meanings as opposed to how words are used. Lexical semantics compares and contrasts linguistic semantics structures across languages.

Syntax

Syntax refers to the arrangement of words, phrases, and clauses to form a sentence. Generally, sentences are formed using a very simple pattern: Subject + Verb + Object. For example, in "The boy ran down the street," the subject is "The boy," the verb is "ran," and the object is "the street." Syntax provides a set structure to sentences in a language. It provides an order to this sentence to make its meaning clear to the reader. Syntax can create a mood for a reader or express an author's purpose.

Knowledge of syntax can also give insight into a word's meaning. Here is an example of how the placement of a word can impact its meaning and grammatical function:

- The development team has reserved the conference room for today.

- Her quiet and reserved nature is sometimes misinterpreted as unfriendliness when people first meet her.

In addition to using *reserved* to mean different things, each sentence also uses the word to serve a different grammatical function. In sentence A, *reserved* is part of the verb phrase *has reserved*, indicating the meaning "to set aside for a particular use." In sentence B, *reserved* acts as a modifier within the noun phrase "her quiet and reserved nature." Because the word is being used as an adjective to describe a personality characteristic, it calls up a different definition of the word—"restrained or lacking familiarity with others." As this example shows, the function of a word within the overall sentence structure can allude to its meaning.

Pragmatics

Pragmatics is the study of what words mean in certain situations. It helps to understand the intentions and interpretations of intentions through words used in human interaction. Different listeners and different situations call for different language and intonations of language. When people engage in a conversation, it is usually to convey a certain message, and the message (even using the same words) can change depending on the setting and the audience. The more fluent the speaker, the more success she or he will have in conveying the intended message.

The following methods can be used to teach pragmatics:

- When students state something incorrectly, a response can be given to what they intended to say in the first place. For instance, if a student says, "That's how it didn't happen." Then the teacher might say, "Of course, that's not how it happened." Instead of putting students on defense by being corrected, this method puts them at ease and helps them learn.

- Role-playing conversations with different people in different situations can help teach pragmatics. For example, pretend playing can be used where a situation remains the same but the audience changes, or the audience stays the same but the situations change. This can be followed with a discussion about how language and intonations change too.

- Different ways to convey a message can be used, such as asking vs. persuading, or giving direct vs. indirect requests and polite vs. impolite messages.

14

- Various non-verbal signals can be used to see how they change pragmatics. For example, students can be encouraged to use mismatched words and facial expressions, such as angry words while smiling or happy words while pretending to cry.

Phonemic Awareness

A phoneme is the smallest unit of sound in a given language and is one aspect under the umbrella of skills associated with phonological awareness. A child demonstrates phonemic awareness when identifying rhymes, recognizing alliterations, and isolating specific sounds inside a word or a set of words. Children who demonstrate basic phonemic awareness will eventually also be able to independently and appropriately blend together a variety of phonemes.

Some classroom strategies to strengthen phonemic awareness may include:

- Introduction to nursery rhymes and word play
- Introduces speech discrimination techniques to train the ear to hear more accurately
- Repeated instruction connecting sounds to letters and blending sounds
- Use of visual images coupled with corresponding sounds and words
- Teaching speech sounds through direct instruction
- Comparing known to unfamiliar words
- Practicing pronunciation of newly introduced letters, letter combinations, and words
- Practicing word decoding
- Differentiating similar sounding words

Instruction of phonemic awareness includes recognizing, blending, segmenting, deleting, and substituting phonemes.

Phoneme Recognition
Phoneme recognition occurs when students recognize that words are made of separate sounds and they are able to distinguish the initial, middle, and final phonemes within words. Initial awareness of phonemes should be done in isolation and not within words. Then, phoneme awareness can be achieved through shared readings that are supplemented with identification activities, such as the identification of rhyming words.

Blending
Sound blending is the ability to mix together two or more sounds or phonemes. For example, a **consonant blend** is a combination of two or more consonants into a single sound such as /cr/ or /sp/. Blending often begins when the teacher models the slow pronunciation of sound parts within a word. Students are to do likewise, with scaffolding provided by the teacher. Eventually, the pronunciation rate is increased, so that the full word is spoken as it would be in normal conversation.

Segmenting
Sound segmentation is the ability to identify the component phonemes in a word. Segmentation begins with simple, single-syllable words. For instance, a teacher might pronounce the word *tub* and see if students can identify the /t/, /u/, and /b/ sounds. The student must identify all three sounds in order for sound segmentation to be complete.

Deleting

Sound deletion is an oral activity in which one of the phonemes of a spoken word is removed. For example, a teacher may say a word aloud and then ask students to say the word without a specific sound (e.g., "What word would be formed if cat is said without the /c/ sound?"). With repetition, deletion activities can improve phoneme recognition.

Substituting

Like deletion, **substitution** takes place orally and is initiated through modeling. However, instead of deleting a phoneme or syllable, spoken words are manipulated via the substitution of one phoneme for another (e.g., "What word would be formed if we change the /b/ in bun to /r/?").

Phonological Awareness vs. Phonemic Awareness

Phonological awareness is the recognition that oral language is made of smaller units, such as syllables and words. **Phonemic awareness** is a type of phonological awareness. Phonemic-aware students recognize specific units of spoken language called phonemes. **Phonemes** are unique and easily identifiable units of sound. Examples include /t/, /b/, /c/, etc. It is through phonemes that words are distinguished from one another.

Phonology

Phonology is the study of how speech sounds in a language are organized to make words. These patterns of sounds also include the study of phonemes (single units of sounds), syllables (vowel sounds heard within a word), stress or accent (emphasis on a sound or syllable within a word), and intonation (variation of tone or pitch in words). Despite their differences, phonology and phonetics (the study of isolated sounds in words) are often confused. Remember, phonology studies how sounds change in syllables, words, and sentences, as opposed to phonetics, where the focus is on a single speech sound.

Phonemes, Syllables, Onsets, and Rimes

A **phoneme** is commonly referred to as a sound or a group of sounds that differentiate one word from another in a spoken language. Phonemes are language-specific sound units that do not carry inherent meanings, but are simply known as the smallest unit in a language. For example, there are phonemes unique to the English

language that do not necessarily exist in other spoken languages. In English, although there are only twenty-six letters, there are forty-four phonemes:

Forty-Four Phonemes in English			
Consonant Sounds		**Vowel Sounds**	
/b/	boy	/a/	bat
/d/	desk	/e/	head
/f/	fall	/i/	dish
/g/	game	/o/	rock
/h/	hand	/u/	muck
/j/	joy	/a/	bake
/k/	king	/e/	meet
/l/	life	/i/	like
/m/	map	/o/	moat
/n/	nail	/yoo/	cube
/p/	park	/e/	alarm
/r/	run	/oo/	doom
/s/	sock	/oo/	nook
/t/	tail	/ou/	mouse
/v/	veil	/oi/	toy
/w/	water	/o/	call
/y/	yawn	/u/	herd
/z/	zebra	/a/	hair
/ch/	chalk	/a/	star
/sh/	shallow		
/th/	thorn		
/hw/	whale		
/zh/	leisure		
/ng/	sing		

Mastery of all forty-four phonemes in oral and written communication is a strong predictor of future reading readiness.

Syllables are defined as one complete unit of pronunciation. Every syllable contains only one vowel sound that can be created by one or more than one vowel. Syllables can consist of vowels that stand alone or combine with consonants. The study of syllables and how they operate help children to become stronger readers and will aid in spelling proficiency. Educators will often introduce new words that contain more than one syllable by teaching children to say and write the syllable. Segmenting a word into its individual syllables, as well as blending syllables into whole words, allows children to see the key parts of a word and provides opportunities for them to strengthen their reading skills.

In the English language, there are six different types of syllables, four of which are syllable combinations:

- Closed syllables: syllables that end in a consonant, as in *bat*, or *it*

- Open syllables: syllables that end with a vowel, as in *he*, *she*, or *we*

- Vowel-consonant-e syllables: syllables that end with a silent *e*, as in *ate*, *wife*, or *mile*

17

- Vowel team syllables: syllables that work in combination to create a new sound, as in *mouth* or *join*

- Consonant + le syllables: syllables that contain a consonant and end with an *le*, as in *turtle*

- R-Controlled syllables: syllables that contain a vowel followed by the letter *r*, where the *r* controls how the vowel is pronounced, as in *bird* or *word*

A word is broken up into two pieces: onset and rime. The **onset** is the initial phonological unit of any word, whether it is a consonant or a consonant cluster. The **rime** is the string of letters that follows the onset, usually consisting of a vowel or variant vowels along with one or more consonants. Many words in the English language share common features or patterns. These **word families** often share the same letter combinations that form the same or similar sounds. When introducing word families, educators will often initiate activities involving onsets and rimes to help children accurately recognize, read, and spell simple words. The study of onsets and rimes has shown to improve a child's overall literacy skills, increase reading fluency, and strengthen spelling skills. The following word family list illustrates words separated into onset and rime:

Word	Onset	Rime
sun	s	Un
sunny	s	unny
sunshine	s	unshine

Terminology Associated with Phonics

In understanding and working with phonics, there are specific terms and concepts it is vital to understand. Phonics itself teaches language and reading skills by focusing on letters and their specific sounds as well as the sounds made by common letter combinations. With the ability to recognize the patterns and combinations, early readers can begin to decode unfamiliar words.

Specific vocabulary includes:

Digraph—Two letters that, when combined, make a singular sound. Examples of digraphs include: *sh*, *th*, *ch*, and *ph*.

Grapheme—A grapheme is a symbol that is written that represents a sound (phoneme). In other words, it can be one or more written letters that represent a singular sound. For example, both the letter *s* and the letter combination *igh* (as in *sigh*) are graphemes.

Morpheme—This refers to the smallest unit of meaning in a word. Morphemes are further broken down into root words and affixes. For example, *at* is a root word, and it can't be broken down further without changing the meaning. Affixes include suffixes and prefixes; they can ascribe meaning as well. For example, both *un* and *s* add meaning to a word and are considered morphemes.

Onset—This refers to the first consonants or consonant blends in a word. For example, in the word *game*, the letter *g* is the onset; in the word *brake*, the letters *br* are the onset.

Phoneme—This refers to the smallest distinct unit of sound in a language. For example, the *b* in the word bat is a phoneme. It has a distinct sound all on its own.

Rime—These are the letters and sounds that follow the onset and can be a mix of vowels and consonants. For example, as noted above, in the word *game*, *g* is the onset, and so *ame* is the rime. In the word *brake*, *br* is the onset and *ake* is the rime.

Schwa—The schwa is a vowel sound sometimes created in the unstressed syllable of a word and typically makes a "uh" sound. For example, in the word *bacon*, the *o* is a schwa.

Vowel digraph—A vowel digraph is two letter vowels that create one sound. For example, the *ie* in a word like *thief*.

Alphabetic Principle

The **alphabetic principle** is the understanding of the names and sounds produced by letters, letter patterns, and symbols printed on a page. Through the alphabetic principle, students learn letter-sound correspondence, phonemic awareness, and the application of simple decoding skills such as the sounding out and blending of letter sounds. Since reading is essentially the blending together of multiple letter sounds, the alphabetic principle is crucial in reading development.

As with the instruction of letter recognition, research has revealed the following sequence to be effective in the teaching of the alphabetic principle:

- Letter-sound relationships need to be taught explicitly and in isolation. The rate at which new letter-sound correspondences can be presented will be unique to the student group. The order in which letters are presented should permit students to read words quickly. Therefore, letter-sound pairs that are used frequently should be presented before letter-sound pairs with lower utility. Similarly, letter-sound pairs that can be pronounced in isolation without distortion (f, m, s, r) should be presented first. Instruction of letters that sound similar should not be presented in proximity.

- Once single-letter and sound combinations are mastered, consonant blends and clusters (*br, cr, gr*) can be presented.

Although there is no formally established order for the introduction of letter-sound correspondences, educators are encouraged to consider the following general guidelines, but they should also keep in mind the needs, experiences, and current literacy levels of the students.

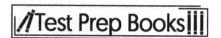

The following is intended as a general guide only:

1. a	10. s	19. w
2. m	11. g	20. k
3. t	12. h	21. x
4. p	13. i	22. v
5. o	14. f	23. y
6. n	15. b	24. z
7. c	16. l	25. j
8. d	17. e	26. q
9. u	18. r	

As a generally accepted rule, short vowels should be introduced ahead of long vowels, and uppercase letters should be mastered before the introduction of their lowercase counterparts.

Identifying Parts of Speech

Nouns

A noun is a person, place, thing, or idea. All nouns fit into one of two types, common or proper.

A **common noun** is a word that identifies any of a class of people, places, or things. Examples include numbers, objects, animals, feelings, concepts, qualities, and actions. *A, an,* or *the* usually precedes the common noun. These parts of speech are called **articles**. Here are some examples of sentences using nouns preceded by articles.

> *A* building is under construction.

> *The* girl would like to move to *the* city.

A **proper noun** (also called a **proper name**) is used for the specific name of an individual person, place, or organization. The first letter in a proper noun is capitalized.

> "My name is *Mary*."

> "I work for *Walmart*."

Nouns sometimes serve as adjectives (which themselves describe nouns), such as "hockey player" and "state government."

An abstract noun is an idea, state, or quality. It is something that can't be touched, such as happiness, courage, evil, or humor.

A concrete noun is something that can be experienced through the senses (touch, taste, hear, smell, see). Examples of concrete nouns are birds, skateboard, pie, and car.

A collective noun refers to a collection of people, places, or things that act as one. Examples of collective nouns are as follows: team, class, jury, family, audience, and flock.

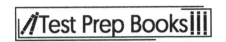

Pronouns

A word used in place of a noun is known as a **pronoun**. Pronouns are words like *I, mine, hers,* and *us.*

Pronouns can be split into different classifications (see below) which make them easier to learn; however, it's not important to memorize the classifications:

- Personal pronouns: refer to people, places, things, etc.
- First person: we, I, our, mine
- Second person: you, yours
- Third person: he, them
- Possessive pronouns: demonstrate ownership (mine, his, hers, its, ours, theirs, yours)
- Interrogative pronouns: ask questions (what, which, who, whom, whose)
- Relative pronouns: include the five interrogative pronouns and others that are relative (whoever, whomever, that, when, where)
- Demonstrative pronouns: replace something specific (this, that, those, these)
- Reciprocal pronouns: indicate something was done or given in return (each other, one another)
- Indefinite pronouns: have a nonspecific status (anybody, whoever, someone, everybody, somebody)

Indefinite pronouns such as *anybody, whoever, someone, everybody*, and *somebody* command a singular verb form, but others such as *all, none,* and *some* could require a singular or plural verb form.

Antecedents

An **antecedent** is the noun to which a pronoun refers; it needs to be written or spoken before the pronoun is used. For many pronouns, antecedents are imperative for clarity. In particular, many of the personal, possessive, and demonstrative pronouns need antecedents. Otherwise, it would be unclear who or what someone is referring to when they use a pronoun like *he* or *this.*

Pronoun reference means that the pronoun should refer clearly to one, clear, unmistakable noun (the antecedent).

Pronoun-antecedent agreement refers to the need for the antecedent and the corresponding pronoun to agree in gender, person, and number. Here are some examples:

The *kidneys* (plural antecedent) are part of the urinary system. *They* (plural pronoun) serve several roles.

The kidneys are part of the *urinary system* (singular antecedent). *It* (singular pronoun) is also known as the renal system.

Pronoun Cases

The subjective pronouns —*I, you, he/she/it, we, they,* and *who*—are the subjects of the sentence:

They have a new house.

The objective pronouns—*me, you* (*singular*)*, him/her, us, them,* and *whom*—are used when something is being done for or given to someone; they are objects of the action:

The teacher has an apple for *us.*

21

The possessive pronouns—*mine, my, your, yours, his, hers, its, their, theirs, our,* and *ours*—are used to denote that something (or someone) belongs to someone (or something):

> It's *their* chocolate cake.

> It's *my* chocolate cake!

One of the greatest challenges and worst abuses of pronouns concerns *who* and *whom.* Just knowing the following rule can eliminate confusion. *Who* is a subjective-case pronoun used only as a subject or subject complement. *Whom* is only objective-case and, therefore, the object of the verb or preposition:

> *Who* is going to the concert?

> You are going to the concert with *whom*?

Hint: When using *who* or *whom,* think of whether someone would say *he* or *him.* If the answer is *he,* use *who.* If the answer is *him,* use *whom.* This trick is easy to remember because *he* and *who* both end in vowels, and *him* and *whom* both end in the letter *M.*

Verbs

A verb is the part of speech that describes an action, state of being, or occurrence.

A **verb** forms the main part of a predicate of a sentence. This means that the verb explains what the noun (which will be discussed shortly) is doing. A simple example is *time flies*. The verb *flies* explains what the action of the noun, *time,* is doing. This example is a *main* verb.

Helping (auxiliary) verbs are words like *have, do, be, can, may, should, must,* and *will.* "I *should* go to the store." Helping verbs assist main verbs in expressing tense, ability, possibility, permission, or obligation.

Particles are minor function words like *not, in, out, up,* or *down* that become part of the verb itself. "I might *not.*"

Participles are words formed from verbs that are often used to modify a noun, noun phrase, verb, or verb phrase:

> The *running* teenager collided with the cyclist.

Participles can also create compound verb forms:

> He is *speaking.*

Verbs have five basic forms: the *base* form, the *-s* form, the *-ing* form, the *past* form, and the **past participle** form.

The *past* forms are either *regular* (*love/loved; hate/hated*) or *irregular* because they don't end by adding the common past tense suffix "-ed" (*go/went; fall/fell; set/set*).

Verb Forms

Shifting verb forms entails **conjugation,** which is used to indicate *tense, voice,* or *mood.*

Verb tense is used to show when the action in the sentence took place. There are several different verb tenses, and it is important to know how and when to use them. Some verb tenses can be achieved by changing the form of the verb, while others require the use of helping verbs (e.g., *is, was,* or *has*).

Present tense shows the action is happening currently or is ongoing:

> I walk to work every morning.

> She is stressed about the deadline.

Past tense shows that the action happened in the past or that the state of being is in the past:

> I walked to work yesterday morning.

> She was stressed about the deadline.

Future tense shows that the action will happen in the future or is a future state of being:

> I will walk to work tomorrow morning.

> She will be stressed about the deadline.

Present perfect tense shows action that began in the past, but continues into the present:

> I have walked to work all week.

> She has been stressed about the deadline.

Past perfect tense shows an action was finished before another took place:

> I had walked all week until I sprained my ankle.

> She had been stressed about the deadline until we talked about it.

Future perfect tense shows an action that will be completed at some point in the future:

> By the time the bus arrives, I will have walked to work already.

Voice

Verbs can be in the active or passive voice. When the subject completes the action, the verb is in **active voice**. When the subject receives the action of the sentence, the verb is in **passive voice**.

Active:

> Jamie ate the ice cream.

Passive:

> The ice cream was eaten by Jamie.

In active voice, the subject (*Jamie*) is the "do-er" of the action (*ate*). In passive voice, the subject *ice cream* receives the action of being eaten.

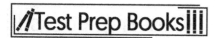
While passive voice can add variety to writing, active voice is the generally preferred sentence structure.

Mood

Mood is used to show the speaker's feelings about the subject matter. In English, there is *indicative mood,* *imperative mood,* and **subjunctive mood**.

Indicative mood is used to state facts, ask questions, or state opinions:

> Bob will make the trip next week.

> When can Bob make the trip?

Imperative mood is used to state a command or make a request:

> Wait in the lobby.

> Please call me next week.

Subjunctive mood is used to express a wish, an opinion, or a hope that is contrary to fact:

> If I were in charge, none of this would have happened.

> Allison wished she could take the exam over again when she saw her score.

Adjectives

Adjectives are words used to modify nouns and pronouns. They can be used alone or in a series and are used to further define or describe the nouns they modify:

> Mark made us a delicious, four-course meal.

The words *delicious* and *four-course* are adjectives that describe the kind of meal Mark made.

Articles are also considered adjectives because they help to describe nouns. Articles can be general or specific. The three articles in English are: a, an, and the.

Indefinite articles (a, an) are used to refer to nonspecific nouns. The article *a* proceeds words beginning with consonant sounds, and the article *an* proceeds words beginning with vowel sounds:

> A car drove by our house.

> An alligator was loose at the zoo.

> He has always wanted a ukulele. (The first u makes a y sound.)

Note that *a* and *an* should only proceed nonspecific nouns that are also singular. If a nonspecific noun is plural, it does not need a preceding article:

> Alligators were loose at the zoo.

The **definite article (the)** is used to refer to specific nouns:

> The car pulled into our driveway.

24

Note that *the* should proceed all specific nouns regardless of whether they are singular or plural:

> The cars pulled into our driveway.

Comparative adjectives are used to compare nouns. When they are used in this way, they take on positive, comparative, or superlative form.

The **positive** form is the normal form of the adjective:

> Alicia is tall.

The **comparative** form shows a comparison between two things:

> Alicia is taller than Maria.

Superlative form shows comparison between more than two things:

> Alicia is the tallest girl in her class.

Usually, the comparative and superlative can be made by adding *–er* and *–est* to the positive form, but some verbs call for the helping verbs *more* or *most*. Other exceptions to the rule include adjectives like *bad*, which uses the comparative *worse* and the superlative *worst*.

An adjective phrase is not a bunch of adjectives strung together, but a group of words that describes a noun or pronoun and, thus, functions as an adjective. *Very happy* is an adjective phrase; so are *way too hungry* and *passionate about traveling*.

Adverbs

Adverbs have more functions than adjectives because they modify or qualify verbs, adjectives, or other adverbs as well as word groups that express a relation of place, time, circumstance, or cause. Therefore, adverbs answer any of the following questions: *How, when, where, why, in what way, how often, how much, in what condition*, and/or *to what degree. How good looking is he? He is <u>very</u> handsome.*

Here are some examples of adverbs for different situations:

- how: quickly
- when: daily
- where: there
- in what way: easily
- how often: often
- how much: much
- in what condition: badly
- what degree: hardly

As one can see, for some reason, many adverbs end in *-ly.*

Adverbs do things like emphasize (*really, simply,* and *so*), amplify (*heartily, completely,* and *positively*), and tone down (*almost, somewhat,* and *mildly*).

Adverbs also come in phrases:

> The dog ran as <u>though his life depended on it.</u>

Prepositions

Prepositions are connecting words and, while there are only about 150 of them, they are used more often than any other individual groups of words. They describe relationships between other words. They are placed before a noun or pronoun, forming a phrase that modifies another word in the sentence. **Prepositional phrases** begin with a preposition and end with a noun or pronoun, the *object of the preposition. A pristine lake is <u>near the store</u> and <u>behind the bank.</u>*

Some commonly used prepositions are *about, after, anti, around, as, at, behind, beside, by, for, from, in, into, of, off, on, to,* and *with.*

Complex prepositions, which also come before a noun or pronoun, consist of two or three words such as *according to, in regards to,* and *because of.*

Conjunctions

Conjunctions are vital words that connect words, phrases, thoughts, and ideas. Conjunctions show relationships between components. There are two types: coordinating and subordinating.

Coordinating conjunctions are the primary class of conjunctions placed between words, phrases, clauses, and sentences that are of equal grammatical rank; the coordinating conjunctions are *for, and, nor, but, or, yet,* and *so.* A useful memorization trick is to remember that all the first letters of these conjunctions collectively spell the word fanboys.

> I need to go shopping, *but* I must be careful to leave enough money in the bank.

> She wore a black, red, *and* white shirt.

Subordinating conjunctions are the secondary class of conjunctions. They connect two unequal parts, one **main** (or **independent**) and the other **subordinate** (or **dependent**). I must go to the store *even though* I do not have enough money in the bank.

> *Because* I read the review, I do not want to go to the movie.

Notice that the presence of subordinating conjunctions makes clauses dependent. *I read the review* is an independent clause, but *because* makes the clause dependent. Thus, it needs an independent clause to complete the sentence.

Interjections

Interjections are words used to express emotion. Examples include *wow, ouch,* and *hooray.* Interjections are often separate from sentences; in those cases, the interjection is directly followed by an exclamation point. In other cases, the interjection is included in a sentence and followed by a comma. The punctuation plays a big role in the intensity of the emotion that the interjection is expressing. Using a comma or semicolon indicates less excitement than using an exclamation mark.

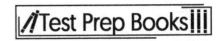

Clauses

Clauses contain a subject and a verb. An **independent clause** can function as a complete sentence on its own, but it might also be one component of a longer sentence. **Dependent clauses** cannot stand alone as complete sentences. They rely on independent clauses to complete their meaning. Dependent clauses usually begin with a subordinating conjunction. Independent and dependent clauses are sometimes also referred to as **main clauses** and **subordinate clauses**, respectively. The following structure highlights the differences:

> Apiculturists raise honeybees because they love insects.

Apiculturists raise honeybees is an independent or main clause. The subject is *apiculturists*, and the verb is *raise*. It expresses a complete thought and could be a standalone sentence.

Because they love insects is a dependent or subordinate clause. If it were not attached to the independent clause, it would be a sentence fragment. While it contains a subject and verb—*they love*—this clause is dependent because it begins with the subordinate conjunction *because*. Thus, it does not express a complete thought on its own.

Another type of clause is a **relative clause**, and it is sometimes referred to as an *adjective clause* because it gives further description about the noun. A relative clause begins with a *relative pronoun*: *that, which, who, whom, whichever, whomever,* or *whoever*. It may also begin with a *relative adverb*: *where, why,* or *when*. Here's an example of a relative clause, functioning as an adjective:

> The strawberries that I bought yesterday are already beginning to spoil.

Here, the relative clause is *that I bought yesterday*; the relative pronoun is *that*. The subject is *I*, and the verb is *bought*. The clause modifies the subject *strawberries* by answering the question, "Which strawberries?" Here's an example of a relative clause with an adverb:

> The tutoring center is a place where students can get help with homework.

The relative clause is *where students can get help with homework*, and it gives more information about a place by describing what kind of place it is. It begins with the relative adverb *where* and contains the noun *students* along with its verb phrase *can get*.

Relative clauses may be further divided into two types: essential or nonessential. **Essential clauses** contain identifying information without which the sentence would lose significant meaning or not make sense. These are also sometimes referred to as **restrictive clauses**. The sentence above contains an example of an essential relative clause. Here is what happens when the clause is removed:

> The tutoring center is a place where students can get help with homework.

> The tutoring center is a place.

Without the relative clause, the sentence loses the majority of its meaning; thus, the clause is essential or restrictive.

Nonessential clauses—also referred to as **non-restrictive clauses**—offer additional information about a noun in the sentence, but they do not significantly control the overall meaning of the sentence. The following example indicates a nonessential clause:

> New York City, which is located in the northeastern part of the country, is the most populated city in America.

> New York City is the most populated city in America.

Even without the relative clause, the sentence is still understandable and continues to communicate its central message about New York City. Thus, it is a nonessential clause.

Punctuation differs between essential and nonessential relative clauses, too. Nonessential clauses are set apart from the sentence using commas whereas essential clauses are not separated with commas. Also, the relative pronoun *that* is generally used for essential clauses, while *which* is used for nonessential clauses. The following examples clarify this distinction:

> *Romeo and Juliet* is my favorite play *that Shakespeare wrote*.

The relative clause *that Shakespeare wrote* contains essential, controlling information about the noun *play*, limiting it to those plays by Shakespeare. Without it, it would seem that *Romeo and Juliet* is the speaker's favorite play out of every play ever written, not simply from Shakespeare's repertoire.

> *Romeo and Juliet*, *which Shakespeare wrote*, is my favorite play.

Here, the nonessential relative clause—"which Shakespeare wrote"—modifies *Romeo and Juliet*. It doesn't provide controlling information about the play, but simply offers further background details. Thus, commas are needed.

Phrases

Phrases are groups of words that do not contain the subject-verb combination required for clauses. Phrases are classified by the part of speech that begins or controls the phrase.

A **noun phrase** consists of a noun and all its modifiers—adjectives, adverbs, and determiners. Noun phrases can serve many functions in a sentence, acting as subjects, objects, and object complements:

> *The shallow yellow bowl* sits on the top shelf.

> Nina just bought *some incredibly fresh organic produce*.

Prepositional phrases are made up of a preposition and its object. The object of a preposition might be a noun, noun phrase, pronoun, or gerund. Prepositional phrases may function as either an adjective or an adverb:

> Jack picked up the book *in front of him*.

The prepositional phrase *in front of him* acts as an adjective indicating which book Jack picked up.

> The dog ran into the back yard.

The phrase *into the backyard* describes where the dog ran, so it acts as an adverb.

Verb phrases include all of the words in a verb group, even if they are not directly adjacent to each other:

> I *should have woken up* earlier this morning.

> The company *is* now *offering* membership discounts for new enrollers.

This sentence's verb phrase is *is offering*. Even though they are separated by the word *now*, they function together as a single verb phrase.

Sentence Structure

All sentences contain the same basic elements: a subject and a verb. The **subject** is who or what the sentence is about; the **verb** describes the subject's action or condition. However, these elements, subjects and verbs, can be combined in different ways. The following graphic describes the different types of sentence structures.

Sentence Structure	Independent Clauses	Dependent Clauses
Simple	1	0
Compound	2 or more	0
Complex	1	1 or more
Compound-Complex	2 or more	1 or more

A **simple sentence** expresses a complete thought and consists of one subject and verb combination:

> The children ate pizza.

The subject is *children*. The verb is *ate*.

Either the subject or the verb may be **compound**—that is, it could have more than one element:

> *The children and their parents* ate pizza.

> The children *ate pizza and watched a movie*.

All of these are still simple sentences. Despite having either compound subjects or compound verbs, each sentence still has only one subject and verb combination.

Compound sentences combine two or more simple sentences to form one sentence that has multiple subject-verb combinations:

> *The children ate pizza,* and *their parents watched a movie.*

This structure is comprised of two independent clauses: (1) *the children ate pizza* and (2) *their parents watched a movie.* Compound sentences join different subject-verb combinations using a comma and a coordinating conjunction.

> I called my mom, *but* she didn't answer the phone.

> The weather was stormy, *so* we canceled our trip to the beach.

A **complex sentence** consists of an independent clause and one or more dependent clauses. Dependent clauses join a sentence using **subordinating conjunctions**. Some examples of subordinating conjunctions are *although*, *unless*, *as soon as*, *since*, *while*, *when*, *because*, *if*, and *before*.

> I missed class yesterday *because* my mother was ill.

> *Before* traveling to a new country, you need to exchange your money to the local currency.

The order of clauses determines their punctuation. If the dependent clause comes first, it should be separated from the independent clause with a comma. However, if the complex sentence consists of an independent clause followed by a dependent clause, then a comma is not always necessary.

A **compound-complex sentence** can be created by joining two or more independent clauses with at least one dependent clause:

> After the earthquake struck, thousands of homes were destroyed, and many families were left without a place to live.

The first independent clause in the compound structure includes a dependent clause—*after the earthquake struck*. Thus, the structure is both complex and compound.

Sentence Types

There isn't an overabundance of absolutes in grammar, but here is one: every sentence in the English language falls into one of four categories:

- Declarative
- Imperative
- Interrogative
- Exclamatory

Declarative sentences are the most common type, probably because they are comprised of the most general content, without any of the bells and whistles that the other three types contain. They are, simply, declarations or statements of any degree of seriousness, importance, or information. A Declarative sentence is a simple statement that ends with a period:

> The price of milk per gallon is the same as the price of gasoline.

An **imperative** sentence is a command, instruction, or request that ends with a period. Imperative sentences often seem to be missing a subject. The subject is there, though; it is just not visible or audible because it is *implied*. Look at the imperative example sentence:

> Buy the milk when you fill up your car with gas.

You is the implied subject, the one to whom the command is issued. This is sometimes called *the understood you* because it is understood that *you* is the subject of the sentence.

Interrogative sentences—those that ask questions—are defined as such from the idea of the word *interrogation*, the action of questions being asked of suspects by investigators. Although that is serious business, interrogative sentences apply to all kinds of questions.

Will you buy the milk?

To exclaim is at the root of **exclamatory** sentences. These are made with strong emotions behind them. The only technical difference between a declarative or imperative sentence and an exclamatory one is the exclamation mark at the end. The example declarative and imperative sentences can both become an exclamatory one simply by putting an exclamation mark at the end of the sentences.

The price of milk per gallon is the same as the price of gasoline!

Buy the milk when you fill up your car with gas!

After all, someone might be really excited by the price of gas or milk, or they could be mad at the person that will be buying the milk! However, as stated before, exclamation marks in abundance defeat their own purpose! After a while, they begin to cause fatigue! When used only for their intended purpose, they can have their expected and desired effect.

Language and Linguistics: Language Development and Acquisition

Language Development Stages

There are many factors that influence a child's language acquisition, such as a child's physical age, level of maturity, home and school experiences, general attitudes toward learning, and home languages. However, a child's **language acquisition** progresses through the following generalized stages:

Stage	Examples	Age
Preproduction	does not verbalize/ nods yes and no	zero to six months
Early production	one to two word responses	six to twelve months
Speech emergence	produces simple sentences	one to three years
Intermediate fluency	simple to more complex sentences	three to five years
Advanced fluency	near native level of speech	five to seven years

While this applies to language acquisition in one's home language, the very same stages apply to English language learners (ELLs). Since effective communication in any given language requires much more than a mere collection of vocabulary words that one can accurately translate, paying particular attention to each stage in language acquisition is imperative. In addition to vocabulary knowledge, language acquisition involves the study and gradual mastery of intonation, a language's dialects—if applicable—and the various nuances in a language regarding word use, expression, and cultural contexts. With time, effort, patience, and effective instructional approaches, both students and educators will begin to see progress in language acquisition.

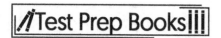

Second language acquisition does not happen overnight. When educators take the time to study each stage and implement a variety of effective instructional approaches, progress and transition from one stage to the next will undoubtedly be less cumbersome and more consistent. In the early stages of language acquisition, children are often silently observing their new language environment. At these early stages, listening comprehension should be emphasized with the use of read alouds, music, and visual aids. Educators should be mindful of their vocabulary usage by consciously choosing to speak slowly and to use shorter, less complex vocabulary. Modeling during these beginning stages is also very effective. If the educator has instructed the class to open a book for instance, they can open a book as a visual guide. If it is time to line up, the educator can verbally state the instruction and then walk to the door to begin the line.

During the **pre-production stage**, educators and classmates may assist ELLs by restating words or sentences that were uttered incorrectly, instead of pointing out errors. When modeling the correct language usage instead of pointing out errors, learners may be less intimidated to practice their new language.

As students progress into the **early production stage**, they will benefit from exercises that challenge them to produce simple words and sentences with the assistance of visual cues. The educator should ask students to point to various pictures or symbols and produce words or sentences to describe the images they see. At the early production and speech emergent stages, ELL students are now ready to answer more diverse questions as they begin to develop a more complex vocabulary. Working in heterogeneous pairs and small groups with native speakers will help ELL students develop a more advanced vocabulary.

At the **beginning and intermediate fluency stages**, ELLs may be asked questions that require more advanced cognitive skills. Asking for opinions on a certain subject or requiring students to brainstorm and find ways to explain a given phenomenon are other ways to strengthen language proficiency and increase vocabulary.

When a child reaches the **advanced fluency stage**, he or she will be confident in social and academic language environments. This is an opportune time to introduce and/or increase their awareness of idiomatic expressions and language nuances.

Language Acquisition and Vocabulary Development for Diverse Learners

Examples of Commonly Used Research-Based Strategies

For the vast majority of people, native language acquisition comes about naturally in childhood. From the time they are born, babies are usually surrounded by the language use of their parents or caregivers. The human brain is hardwired to learn language, meaning that babies do not have to put conscious effort into unraveling the intricacies of grammar or pronunciation; it is something that happens automatically as they are exposed to language. Furthermore, caregivers do not have to formally teach first language skills to babies.

First language acquisition in infancy and early childhood passes through several predictable stages. Babies begin by crying to express a range of emotions like hunger or discomfort. By the time they are two months old, they then begin cooing to convey other emotions, such as happiness and satisfaction. In later months, infants start to experiment with different sounds like babbling and gurgling by repeating simple syllables like "goo goo goo" and "ma ma ma" and show signs of comprehending certain full words. A baby's first word often occurs around one year of age, and for the next six months, the baby can conduct simple communication through one-word expressions like "Daddy," "milk," and "cat."

After they reach eighteen months, young children begin to use two- and three-word utterances to express more complex meaning, such as "Mommy go?" "Don't want to!" and "Where juice?" By the time they are two

and a half years old, toddlers enter the telegraphic stage of language where they begin using the grammatical structure of their native language, although not without some problems. A common error is "I goed to school," instead of "I went to school." However, even though young children do make mistakes in their language usage, it is nevertheless remarkable that they achieve functional mastery of a language in such a short amount of time, generally without any formal instruction.

Although acquisition of a first language is largely a natural process of childhood development, **second language acquisition** in older children or adults is quite different. This is partially linked to the critical period hypothesis, which states that language acquisition only occurs readily and naturally during the first few years of life; language acquisition that happens later, perhaps after puberty, is much more difficult and less successful. Children who are not exposed to any language before the age of five or so will have extreme difficulty learning a language later. This seems to indicate that the brain is primed to learn language from birth, but this readiness quickly diminishes after the critical period has been passed.

Although scientists continue to debate the exact significance of a critical period on second language development, learning a second language later in life clearly presents different challenges than learning a first language. In linguistics, *L1* refers to a speaker's native language and *L2* refers to a second language.

L2 acquisition follows different stages from that of L1. L2 acquisition begins with **preproduction**, also known as the **silent stage**, during which the learner is exposed to the new language, but lacks the skills to communicate and may only use body language or other non-verbal expressions. During the early production stage, the L2 learner begins using simple expressions and has limited comprehension ability.

Next is **speech emergence**—the low-intermediate stage. At this point, the language learner can form simple sentences although he or she makes frequent errors in grammar and usage. L2 learners then pass to **intermediate fluency**, where they begin to gain skills in academic or idiomatic language, demonstrate a much higher level of comprehension, and make fewer mistakes in their expressions.

Finally, the learner reaches **advanced fluency**, exhibiting near-native expressive and comprehensive skills. It is worth noting that even with near-native skills, after many years of advanced fluency, L2 learners may continue to speak with a different accent or use certain idiosyncratic expressions that are markedly different from native speakers. Nevertheless, they are certainly fluent.

In 2013, the Census Bureau reported that one in five Americans are speaking a language other than English at home, so language arts instructors will encounter a mixture of native speakers and second language learners in the classroom. In both cases, though, certain goals and strategies remain the same. The purpose of a language arts class is not to teach students language from scratch, but rather to further develop their preexisting knowledge and increase their awareness of how to use language for more effective and meaningful communication.

As the early stages of both L1 and L2 acquisition show, learners need language input before they can achieve language output. Providing students with a variety of language resources, both formally and informally, can give them valuable exposure to new means of expression. In class, this exposure can include daily assignments, a classroom library, or a bulletin board with news for students. Educators can also get students in the habit of accessing resources outside of the classroom such as visiting the school or public library, watching, reading, or listening to the news, or reading informally from magazines, blogs, or other sources of interest.

This exposure also relates to two different forms of vocabulary acquisition—through incidental learning or direct instruction. **Incidental learning** occurs when students naturally encounter new vocabulary in context

33

during daily life whereas **direct instruction** occurs through structured lessons and assignments in an academic setting.

In vocabulary development in particular, when it comes to direct instruction, there are several approaches to teaching new words to students. One is the **three-tier approach**, which states that vocabulary can be classified into three levels:

- Tier one—the most basic means of expression, e.g., *eat, school,* and *happy*
- Tier two—general academic words, e.g., *interpret, analyze, develop*
- Tier three—highly-specific words, e.g., *electromagnetic, genocide, sociolinguistic*

Tier three words should be taught within the subjects that they are directly related to rather than in a language arts class. Instead, language arts instruction should focus on tier two words that are broadly applicable to a range of subjects and, therefore, more practical for students.

Another theory of vocabulary development is learning language through chunks or groups of related words. By learning words in context along with other connected words, students are better able to connect vocabulary to areas of prior knowledge and more effectively store new words in their long-term memory. Students also gain a more complete set of tools with which to form new expressions, rather than simply learning new words in isolation. Learning in **semantic chunks**—clusters of five to ten words forming a connected phrase or sentence—is particularly useful for L2 learners in gaining familiarity with how to manipulate vocabulary and combine words to build meaning.

Vocabulary learning can also be conducted through a variety of media, combining visual, auditory, and active cues. One strategy is known as the **total physical response**, where students learn to associate a word with a certain physical reaction. For example, in response to the word **circumference**, students might use their finger to draw a circle in the air. Students can also watch videos related to the vocabulary topic they are learning about or look at visual representations of new words through a picture dictionary. By activating different styles of learning, instructors can provide students with more opportunities to acquire new language skills.

Evaluating the Effectiveness of Specific Strategies

New research on teaching strategies is emerging all the time, and it is important for instructors to stay abreast of new developments while evaluating when and how to implement any changes in their classroom. Instructors should also consider the pros and cons of different approaches to teaching.

In terms of encouraging students to seek outside language resources (noted the section above), the effectiveness differs greatly depending on students' background and home life. Students who must work after school to support themselves or their families may not have much time to stop by the public library or to read for leisure; in this case, instructors need to maximize in-class instruction time. According to another strategy, the three-tier approach, tier two words are most important in a language arts classroom. However, some L2 students in the early production or intermediate fluency stages may lack basic tier one skills and struggle with understanding more advanced academic vocabulary.

Also, the integrated approach to learning vocabulary in a group of related words calls on instructors to present words as they are actually used in context, which might involve using some tier three words related to specific fields of study. Is it more effective to focus only on having a broad base of general vocabulary or to spend some time building skills in different specialized areas? This question might be answered differently depending on the needs of students in class.

34

As they experiment with the effectiveness of new methods of instruction, educators can also move beyond outdated learning practices. Assignments such as getting a list of words to look up in the dictionary are not generally considered effective methods. As discussed earlier, words contain a multitude of meanings that take on importance dependent on context; simply memorizing words outside of context, then, does not provide long-term benefits to students' productive language skills.

Instructor-centered models of learning have also been overturned by more recent pedagogical research. While instructors are a valuable resource of providing information and modeling language use for students, educators simply supply the input while students still need a chance to produce output. This means giving students ample opportunity to practice and apply new vocabulary, calling on students' prior knowledge when introducing new vocabulary, and demonstrating how students can use language skills outside of the classroom.

Interpreting Research and Applying it to Particular Instructional Challenges Related to Language

For instructors, pedagogical research is only as valuable as its real-life application in the classroom. Educators need to be able to use research-based strategies to tackle issues that arise while teaching.

One challenge may be the gap that exists between students who come to class with a high degree of literacy and language skills and students who have had fewer opportunities to develop those skills before entering the classroom. For example, some students have no access to a computer or the Internet at home or have a limited/nonexistent home library. Closing the gap through basic media literacy—perhaps in collaboration with a school media specialist—can empower students to know how to access language resources through the library, Internet, or other sources and how to utilize these resources for both learning and leisure. The concept of vocabulary development through incidental learning holds that students will benefit from any reading material, so instructors can encourage students to pursue their own interests through reading if they seem disinterested in textbook offerings. Asking students to keep a personal reading log or daily journal can encourage them to make reading and writing part of their everyday lives.

Another common problem in language instruction is students forgetting new vocabulary as soon as they learn it. Repetition and reinforcement is key to creating lasting knowledge. Also, as many studies point to the importance of learning vocabulary in context, utilizing contextual learning strategies can help students build onto prior knowledge rather than treat every new word as something strange and unfamiliar. This can be done by prompting students for what they already know when a new concept is introduced in class, introduce possible unfamiliar words that they might encounter in a text, and encourage them to use context clues as they read to make logical guesses about how unknown words are connected to known ones. These strategies further empower learners to utilize the knowledge that they already possess.

Incorporating multimedia resources can also be a powerful tool for providing meaningful instruction for students with a variety of learning styles. If students struggle to remember new vocabulary words, strategies such as total physical response or recognizing a picture associated with the word can provide students with different tools to secure information in their long-term memory.

In terms of research specific to L2 learning, knowledge of the stages of development can help instructors handle frustrations that may arise during second language learning. For example, teachers may worry that students understand nothing during the silent period, but students are absorbing the basic linguistic information that they will need to start forming utterances. Rather than giving up and getting discouraged from the start, instructors can continue providing basic communication information that students will be ready to use within the first few weeks or months of being exposed to a new language.

Features of Exceptional Language Development

Some students may display special features that identify their language development as being exceptional. These students are learning a second language easier and at a quicker pace than their peers. It is important to identify these special features in order to adjust the learning plan to work better for these students.

One such special feature that may identify exceptional language development is when the student is speaking earlier and with more complexity than their peers. This includes speaking without pauses and having a larger vocabulary.

Another identifying factor of gifted language development is exceptional reading. Reading earlier and at a more advanced level shows that the student has a strong grasp of the language. Students with advanced language development may also exhibit an avid enjoyment of reading.

It is important to distinguish these features of advanced development from those of interlanguage effects. This is when the student is able to fill in the gaps of learning a new language with knowledge from their native language. Interlanguage effects can cause advanced development in some areas and delays in others. Looking for these potential delays and understanding the student's language history can help distinguish whether they have exceptional language development.

Language and Linguistics: Literacy

Developing Language Literacy Skills

It is believed that literacy development is the most rapid between birth and 5 years of age. From birth until around 3 months, babies start to recognize the sounds of familiar voices. Between 3 months and 6 months, babies begin to study a speaker's mouth and listen much more closely to speech sounds. Between 9 months and 12 months, babies can generally recognize a growing number of commonly repeated words, can utter simple words, respond appropriately to simple requests, and begin to attempt to group sounds.

In the toddler years, children begin to rapidly strengthen their communication skills, connecting sounds to meanings and combining sounds to create coherent sentences. The opportunities for rich social interactions play a key role in this early literacy development and help children to understand cultural nuances, expected behavior, and effective communication skills. By age 3, most toddlers can understand many sentences and can begin to generalize by placing specific words into categories. In the preschool years, children begin to develop and strengthen their emergent literacy skills. It is at this stage that children will begin to sound out words, learn basic spelling patterns, especially with rhyming words, and start to develop their fine motor skills. Awareness of basic grammar also begins to emerge with oral attempts at past, present, and future verb tenses.

English Literacy Development

English language literacy can be categorized into four basic stages:

- Beginning
- Early Intermediate
- Intermediate
- Early Advanced

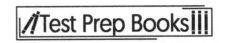

Beginning Literacy

This stage is commonly referred to as **receptive language development**. Educators can encourage this stage in literacy development by providing the student with many opportunities to interact on a social level with peers. Educators should also consider starting a personal dictionary, introducing word flashcards, and providing the student with opportunities to listen to a story read by another peer, or as a computer-based activity.

Early Intermediate Literacy

When a child begins to communicate to express a need or attempt to ask or respond to a question, the child is said to be at the early intermediate literacy stage. Educators should continue to build vocabulary knowledge and introduce activities that require the student to complete the endings of sentences, fill in the blanks, and describe the beginning or ending of familiar stories.

Intermediate Literacy

When a child begins to demonstrate comprehension of more complex vocabulary and abstract ideas, the child is advancing into the intermediate literacy stage. It is at this stage that children are able to challenge themselves to meet the classroom learning expectations and start to use their newly acquired literacy skills to read, write, listen, and speak. Educators may consider providing students with more advanced reading opportunities, such as partner-shared reading, silent reading, and choral reading.

Early Advanced Literacy

When a child is able to apply literacy skills to learn new information across many subjects, the child is progressing toward the early advanced literacy stage. The child can now tackle complex literacy tasks and confidently handle much more cognitively demanding material. To strengthen reading comprehension, educators should consider the introduction to word webs and semantic organizers. Book reports and class presentations, as well as continued opportunities to access a variety of reading material, will help to strengthen the child's newly acquired literacy skills.

Stages of Early Orthographic Development: Learning to Spell

Orthography is the representation of the sounds of a language by written or printed symbols. Learning to spell is a highly complex and cumulative process with each skill building on the previously mastered skill. This is considered **orthographic development.** It is imperative for educators to ensure that each skill is taught in sequential steps in order for children to develop spelling capabilities.

Emergent Spelling: Pre-Communicative Writing Stage

Children may be able to accurately identify various letters of the alphabet but will likely not be able to associate them to their corresponding sounds. Children may be able to string together letter-like forms or letters without a connection to specific phonemes (the smallest units of sound in a given language). Nearing the end of this phase, children progress from writing in all directions to writing in standard convention from left to right.

Letter Name-Alphabetic Stage

At this stage, children begin to understand unique letter-sound correspondence and can begin to differentiate between various consonant sounds. Children may even be able to connect two and three letters together in an attempt to spell a word, but the letters they use will generally only consist of consonants. Most show a clear preference for capital letters.

Within-Word Pattern Stage

With a strengthening ability to recognize and apply letter-sound correspondence, children in this spelling stage can use their understanding of phonics to attempt full words that incorporate vowels. With repeated and consistent exposure and practice, children start to focus on letter combinations, spelling patterns, consonant blends, and digraphs. In this stage, students are becoming aware of homophones and experiment with vowel sound combinations.

Syllables and Affixes Stage

Just as the name suggests, children at this stage are focused on syllables and combining them to form words. Children begin to develop a deeper understanding of the need for vowels to appear in each syllable, and words begin to readily resemble the proper conventions of English spelling to them.

Derivational Relations Stage

In this stage, students learn how spelling relates to meaning. Generalizations about spelling patterns and rules of spelling start to be more readily applied, which allows the child to attempt the spelling of unfamiliar words. Children begin learning about root words and consonant and vowel alterations. It is during this stage that children begin to accumulate a much greater vocabulary base.

Effective Teaching Strategies for Spelling

There are several effective strategies that educators can introduce to facilitate each developmental spelling stage. Strategies focused on alphabetic knowledge, including letter-sound games, are of primary importance in the beginning stages. As spelling skills strengthen, educators may choose to introduce word families, spelling patterns, and word structures. There is some controversy surrounding allowing children to use invented spelling in their writing. Research indicates that, provided there is spelling instruction taking place, allowing invented spelling supports growth in the areas of phonemic awareness, phonics, and general spelling skills.

Phonological and Phonemic Awareness

Phonological and phonemic awareness do not require written language because phonemic awareness is based entirely upon speech. However, phonological and phonemic awareness are the prerequisites for literacy. Thus, experts recommend that all kindergarten students develop phonemic awareness as part of their reading preparation.

Age-appropriate and developmentally appropriate instruction for phonological and phonemic awareness is key to helping children strengthen their reading and writing skills. Phonological and phonemic awareness, or PPA, instruction works to enhance correct speech, improve understanding and application of accurate letter-to-sound correspondence, and strengthen spelling skills. Since skill-building involving phonemes is not a natural process, PPA instruction is especially important for children who have limited access and exposure to reading materials and who lack familial encouragement to read. Strategies that educators can implement include leading word and sound games, focusing on phoneme skill-building activities, and ensuring all activities focus on the fun, playful nature of words and sounds instead of rote memorization and drilling techniques.

Once students are able to recognize phonemes of spoken language, phonics can be implemented in grades K–2. **Phonics** is the direct correspondence between and blending of letters and sounds. Unlike phonemic awareness, phonics requires the presence of print. Phonics often begins with the alphabetic principle, which teaches that letters or other characters represent sounds. Students must be able to identify letters, symbols, and individual sounds before they can blend multiple sounds into word parts and whole words. Thus, phoneme

awareness and phonics predict outcomes in word consciousness, vocabulary, reading, and spelling development.

Research has shown that phonics and sight-word instruction is best accomplished using the following steps:

- Step 1: Phonics instruction should begin with **consonant sounds**. Consonant sounds block the flow of air through the mouth. Consonants can form either continuous or stop sounds. **Continuous sounds** are those that can be said for a long period of time, such as /mmm/. **Stop sounds** are said in short bursts, such as /t/.

- Step 2: Teach the following common and regular letter combinations:

  - **Consonant digraphs:** Consonant digraphs are combinations of two or three consonants that work together to make a single sound. Examples of consonant digraphs are *sh, ch*, and *th.*

  - **Consonant blends:** Consonant blends are sometimes referred to as **consonant clusters**. Consonant blends occur when two or three consonant sounds are blended together to make a single consonant sound. Unlike consonant digraphs, each letter in a consonant blend is identifiable. Examples of consonant blends are *gl, gr, pl, sm*, and *sp.*

  - **Vowel digraphs: Vowel digraphs** are sets of two vowels that spell a single sound. Examples of vowel digraph pairs are *ow, ie, ae, ou, ei, ie*, and *oo.*

  - **Diphthongs:** Diphthongs are the sounds created by letter/vowel combinations. Examples of diphthongs are *ow* as in town or cow and *igh* as in high or tight.

  - **R- and l- controlled vowels:** These are words in which a vowel sound is controlled by an r, l, or ll following it. Examples include *car, girl, old,* or *call.*

- Step 3: Teach common **inflected morphological units**, which include word parts such as affixes or root words. Examples of morphological units that could be presented at this time are suffixes such as *-ed, -er, -est, -ing,* and *-s.*

- Step 4: Present common word patterns of increasing difficulty. **Word patterns** are made of sequences (or patterns) of vowels (V) and consonants (C). Examples include VC (*ear, egg, eat*, etc.), CVC (*cat, bat, map*, etc.), CCVC (*stop, frog, spot*, etc.), CVVC (*head, lead, dead*, etc.), CVCe (*same, make, pale*, etc.), etc.

- Step 5: Teach identification of **vowel-consonant patterns** and **multisyllabic-word syllabication**.

- Step 6: Discuss why some words are irregular, meaning that they are not decodable. Students may struggle decoding some words because the sounds of the letters found within the words do not follow predictable phonics patterns.

- Step 7: Time should be allotted for the instruction of common irregular sight words that are not readily decodable. However, this is usually not done until students are able to decode words that follow predictable phonic patterns at a rate of one letter-sound per second. Irregular sight words need to be gradually introduced. Words that are visually similar should not be shown in proximity to one another. The irregular words need to be practiced until students can read them with

39

automaticity. New words are not introduced until the previous sets are mastered. The words are continuously reintroduced and reviewed thereafter.

- Step 8: When students first begin reading, they may be able to decode some words that have not yet been introduced to them merely by using letter-sound correspondences. The instruction of irregular words should be applied to these words as well.

Phonics instruction should begin with the decoding of simple syllable patterns, such as *am* and *map*. Upon mastery of simple patterns, more complex patterns can be introduced, such as *tape* or *spot*. The following characteristics are present in an effective phonics program:

- The goal and purpose are clarified at the beginning of each lesson.

- Visual and concrete material, such as letter cards and dry-erase boards, are used.

- Direct instruction of letter sounds is provided through a series of mini lessons.

- Direct instruction in the decoding of letter sounds found in words is provided, such as sounding out letters and blending sounds into words.

Students partake in guided and independent practice during which immediate feedback is provided. Activities such as word reading and word sorts, which incorporate previously taught spelling patterns, can reinforce explicit phonics instruction.

Effective phonics programs allow students to apply new phonics skills in a broad range of reading and writing contexts.

The following strategies can be used to develop phonological and phonemic awareness in students that struggle with reading, disabled learners, special-needs students, English Language Learners (ELLs), speakers of nonstandard English, and advanced learners:

- Differentiated instruction for struggling readers, disabled students, or students with special needs should include the re-teaching and/or emphasis of key skills, such as blending and segmenting. Such instruction should be supported through the employment of a variety of concrete examples that explain a concept or task. Teaching strategies of such concepts or tasks should utilize visual, kinesthetic, and tactile modalities, and ample practice time should be allotted.

- Instruction of phonological and phonemic awareness can also be differentiated for ELLs and speakers of nonstandard English. Most English phonemes are present in other languages. Therefore, teachers can capitalize on the transfer of relevant knowledge, skills, and phonemes from a student's primary language into the English language. In this way, extra attention and instructional emphasis can be applied toward phonemes and phoneme sequences that are nontransferable between the two languages.

- Advanced learners benefit from phonological and phonemic instruction with greater breadth and depth. Such instruction should occur at a faster pace and expand students' current skills.

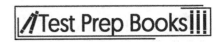

Common Morphemes

Morphemes are defined as the smallest unit of a word that has meaning. The morpheme must not be able to be broken into smaller units with the same meaning, and it maintains that meaning despite its context.

Morphemes can be further categorized as base or root morphemes and affixes. **Base or root morphemes** give the word their primary meaning and are also called **free morphemes** because they can stand alone and have a specific meaning. For example, *cat* is a base morpheme. It cannot be broken down and it provides the primary meaning. However, if we add the letter *s*, *cats*, *s* is a morpheme in that it is now the smallest unit of the word that provides a plural meaning.

The other category of morphemes is **bound morphemes**, which are affixes. Bound morphemes must be connected to another word and do not hold meaning on their own. In the above example, *s* has meaning but cannot stand alone. It must be bound to the free morpheme, *cat*.

The most **common prefixes** in English are:

- *re-: recount, recover, redress*
- *dis-: disown, discover, dismount*
- *over-: overjoyed, overcome, overworked*
- *un-: uncover, unjust, uncomfortable*
- *mis-: mistake, misrepresent, mishap*
- *out-: outtake, outcropping, outspoken*

The most **common suffixes** in English are:

- *-tion: action, publication, attention*
- *-ity: disparity, clarity, compatibility*
- *-er: leaner, cleaner, meaner*
- *-ness: kindness, darkness, fierceness*
- *-ism: Marxism, capitalism, socialism*
- *-ment: shipment, fragment, argument*
- *-ant: descendant, distant, miscreant*
- *-ship: relationship, friendship, leadership*
- *-age: patronage, baggage, package*
- *-ery: nursery, battery, misery*

Teaching morphemes is essential in having students learn how to break down words for reading and comprehension. Because the meaning of many affixes does not change, regardless of the root word they are attached to, once students recognize them and their meaning, they are better able to break the word down for pronunciation, identify the root, and decode meaning, which all contributes to their reading fluency and overall comprehension skills.

Having students learn to break words down into morphemes will help them realize that unfamiliar words contain parts that are familiar. Exercises should include this type of activity.

Another breakdown activity involves giving students complex words that contain multiple morphemes (a root or base and affixes). After breaking down the complex words, have the students research the etymology.

Students can also work with word lists and sort words by base or root words and affixes. Similarly, they can work with morpheme cards and put words together using affixes to create new words as a word building exercise, almost like the game *Boggle*.

Decoding

While reading has much to do with conceptual knowledge of English and awareness of the structures and rules of the language, recognizing word patterns can also help students see basic English principles. Being able to recognize familiar word patterns essentially helps students decode the pronunciation and even the meaning of unfamiliar words by recognizing core linguistic components.

Strategies

The ability to break apart a word into its individual phonemes is referred to as **segmenting**. Segmenting words can greatly aid in a child's ability to recognize, read, and spell an entire word. In literacy instruction, **blending** is when the reader connects segmented parts to create an entire word. Segmenting and blending practice work together like pieces of a puzzle to help children practice newly-acquired vocabulary. Educators can approach segmenting and blending using a multi-sensory approach. For example, a child can manipulate letter blocks to build words and pull them apart. An educator may even ask the child to listen to the word being said and ask him or her to find the letter blocks that build each phoneme, one at a time:

/m/ /u/ /g/

/b/ /a/ /t/

/r/ /u/ /n/

Once children are able to blend and segment phonemes, they are ready for the more complex skill of blending and segmenting syllables, onsets, and rimes. Using the same multi-sensory approach, children may practice blending the syllables of familiar words on a word wall, using letter blocks, paper and pencil, or sounding them out loud. Once they blend the words together, students can then practice segmenting those same words, studying their individual syllables, letters, and sounds. Educators may again read a word out loud and ask children to write or build the first syllable, followed by the next, and so on. The very same practice can be used to identify the onset. Children can work on writing and/or building this sound followed by the word's rime. Word families and rhyming words are ideal for this type of exercise so that children can more readily see the parts of each word. Using words that rhyme can turn this exercise into a fun and engaging activity.

Once children have demonstrated the ability to independently blend and segment phonemes, syllables, onsets, and rimes, educators may present a more challenging exercise that involves substitutions and deletions. As these are more complex skills, children will likely benefit from repeated practice and modeling. Using word

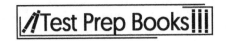

families and words that rhyme when teaching this skill will make the activity more enjoyable, and it will also greatly aid in a child's overall comprehension.

Substitution and Deletion Using Onset and Rime				
Word	**Onset Deletion**	**Rime Deletion**	**Onset Substitution**	**Rime Substitution**
Run	un	r	Fun	rat
Bun	un	b	Gun	bat
Sun	un	s	Nun	sat
Substitution and Deletion Using Phonemes				
Word		**Phoneme Substitution**		**Phoneme Deletion**
Sit		sat		si
Bit		bat		bi
Hit		hat		hi
Substitution and Deletion Using Syllables				
Word		**Syllable Substitution**		**Syllable Deletion**
cement		lament or, cedar		ce
moment		statement, or motive		mo
basement		movement, or baseball		base

Structural Analysis

Reading competence of multisyllabic words is accomplished through phonics skills that are accompanied by a reader's ability to recognize morphological structures within words. **Structural analysis** is a word recognition skill that focuses on the meaning of word parts, or morphemes, during the introduction of a new word. Therefore, the instruction of structural analysis focuses on the recognition and application of morphemes. **Morphemes** are word parts such as base words, prefixes, inflections, and suffixes. Students can use structural analysis skills to find familiar word parts within an unfamiliar word in order to decode the word and determine the definition of the new word. Identification and association of such word segments also aids the proper pronunciation and spelling of new multisyllabic words.

Similarly, learning to use phonics skills with more difficult words depends on a reader's ability to notice syllable structures within words that have more than one syllable. **Syllabic analysis, or syllabication, is a skill that teaches students how to analyze words and separate them into syllables. Syllables** are phonological units

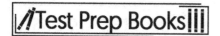
that contain a vowel sound. Teaching students how to break apart multisyllabic words into morphological and phonological units can greatly help them not to be intimidated by long words, since these tools will help them use syllable types to make longer words seem like a series of smaller words. The identified syllables can then be blended, pronounced, and/or written together as a single word. This helps students learn to decode and encode the longer words more accurately and efficiently with less anxiety. Thus, syllabic analysis leads to the rapid word recognition that is critical in reading fluency and comprehension.

Comprehension

Comprehension is defined as the level of understanding of content that a child demonstrates during and after the reading of a given text. Comprehension begins well before a child is able to read. Adults and educators can foster comprehension by reading aloud to children and helping them respond to the content and relate it to their prior knowledge. Throughout the reading process, the child asks and answers relevant questions confirming their comprehension and is able to successfully summarize the text upon completion.

Since reading comprehension encompasses several cognitive processes, including the awareness and understanding of phonemes, phonics, and the ability to construct meaning from text, educators should employ reading comprehension strategies prior to, during, and after reading.

Word Recognition and Analysis

Word recognition is the ability to correctly and automatically recognize words in or out of context. Word recognition is a prerequisite for fluent reading and reading comprehension. Phonics skills, syllabic skills, structural analysis, word analysis, and memorization of sight words lead to word recognition automaticity. Phonics and decoding skills aid the analysis of new words. Word analysis is the ability to recognize the relationships between the spelling, syllabication, and pronunciation of new and/or unfamiliar words. Having a clear understanding of word structure, orthography, and the meaning of morphemes also aids in the analysis of new words. However, not all words follow predictable patterns of phonics, morphology, or orthography. Such irregular words must be committed to memory and are called sight words.

Spelling and Vocabulary Development

Decoding and encoding are **reciprocal phonological skills**, meaning that their steps are opposite of each other.

Decoding is the application of letter-sound correspondences, letter patterns, and other phonics relationships that help students read and correctly pronounce words. Decoding helps students to recognize and read words quickly, increasing reading fluency and comprehension. The steps of the decoding process are as follows:

- The student identifies a written letter or letter combination.

- The student makes correlations between the sound of the letter or sounds of the letter combination.

- The student understands how the letters or letter combinations fit together.

- The student verbally blends the letter and letter combinations together to form a word.

Encoding is the spelling of words. In order to properly spell words, students must be familiar with letter/sound correspondences. Students must be able to put together phonemes, digraphs or blends, morphological units, consonant/vowel patterns, etc. The steps of encoding are identified below:

- The student understands that letters and sounds make up words.
- The student segments the sound parts of a word.
- The student identifies the letter or letter combinations that correspond to each sound part.
- The student then writes the letters and letter combinations in order to create the word.

Because the stages of decoding and encoding are reciprocal skills, phonics knowledge supports the development of reading and spelling. Likewise, the development of spelling skills reinforces phonics and decoding. In fact, the foundation of all good spelling programs is alignment with reading instruction and students' reading levels. Phonics instruction begins with simple syllable patterns and then progresses toward more complex patterns, the sounds of morphemes, and strategies for decoding multisyllabic words. Through this process, new vocabulary is developed. Sight word instruction should not begin until students are able to decode target words with automaticity and accuracy. Spelling is the last instructional component to be introduced.

Spelling development occurs in stages. In order, these stages are the pre-phonetic stage, the semiphonetic stage, the phonetic stage, the transitional stage, and the conventional stage. Each stage is explained below. Ways in which phonics and vocabulary development fit into the spelling stages are discussed. Instructional strategies for each phase of spelling are suggested.

Spelling development begins with the **pre-phonetic stage**, which is marked by an incomplete understanding of the alphabetic principle and letter-sound correspondences. During this stage, students participate in pre-communicative writing, which appears to be a jumble of letter-like forms rather than a series of discrete letters. Students' precommunicative writing samples can be used as informal assessments of their understanding of the alphabetic principle and knowledge of letter-sound correspondences.

Pre-phonetic stage of spelling development

45

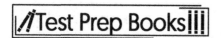
The pre-phonetic stage is followed by the **semiphonetic stage**, in which students understand that letters represent sounds. The alphabetic principle may be understood, but letter recognition may not yet be fully developed. In this stage, single letters may be used to represent entire words (e.g., *U* for *you*). Other times, multiple syllables within words may be omitted. Writing produced by students in this stage is still virtually unreadable. Teachers may ask students to provide drawings to supplement their writing to better determine what a student intended to write.

Semiphonetic stage of writing

The third stage in spelling development is the phonetic stage. In this stage, students have mastered letter-sound correspondences. Although letters may be written backward or upside down, phonetic spellers are able to write all of the letters in the alphabet. Because phonetic spellers have limited sight vocabulary, they will often spell irregular words incorrectly; however, these incorrectly spelled words may phonetically sound like the spoken word. Additionally, student writing becomes systematic. For example, students are likely to use one letter to represent a digraph or letter blend (e.g., *f* for /ph/).

Phonetic stage of writing

Spelling instruction of common consonant patterns, short vowel sounds, and common affixes or rimes can begin during the phonetic stage. Thus, spelling instruction during the phonetic stage coincides with the instruction of phonics and phonemic awareness that also occurs during this stage of development.

Word walls are advantageous during the phonetic stage because they provide visual groupings of words that share common consonant-vowel patterns or letter clusters. Students are encouraged to add words to each group. As a result, word walls promote strategic spelling, vocabulary development, common letter combinations, and common morphological units.

The transitional stage of spelling occurs when a student has developed a small sight vocabulary and a solid understanding of letter-sound correspondences. Thus, spelling dependence on phonology decreases. Instead, dependence on visual representation and word structure increases. As sight word vocabulary increases during the transition stage, the correct spelling of irregular words will also increase. However, students may still struggle to spell words with long vowel sounds.

Transitional stage of spelling

Differentiation of spelling instruction often begins during the transitional stage. Instruction ought to be guided by data collected through informal observations and assessments. Depending on individual needs, lessons may include sight word recognition, morphology, etymology, reading, and writing. Students can begin learning about homophones during the transitional stage. Homophones are words that sound the same but have different spellings and meanings (e.g., *their* and *there*). Additionally, students should be expected to begin writing full sentences at the transitional stage. Writing reinforces phonics, vocabulary, and correct spelling of words.

The **conventional stage** comes last, occurring after a student's sight word vocabulary is well developed and the student is able to read fluently with comprehension. By this stage, students know the basic rules of phonics. They are able to deal with consonants, multiple vowel-consonant blends, homophones, digraphs, and irregular spellings. Due to an increase in sight word recognition at this stage, a conventional speller is able to recognize when a word is spelled incorrectly.

It is at the conventional spelling stage that spelling instruction can begin to focus on content-specific vocabulary words and words with unusual spellings. In order to further reinforce vocabulary development of such content-specific words and apply phonic skills, students should be encouraged to use the correct spelling of such words within various writing activities.

For even the best conventional spellers, some words will still cause consistent trouble. Students can keep track of words that they consistently spell incorrectly or find confusing in word banks so they can isolate and eventually eliminate their individualized errors. Students can use their word banks as references when they come across a word with which they struggle. Students may also spend time consciously committing the words in their banks to memory through verbal or written practice.

Fluency

When children are able to read fluently, they read with accuracy, a steady and consistent speed, and an appropriate expression. A fluent reader can seamlessly connect word recognition to comprehension, whether reading silently or aloud. In other words, reading fluency is an automatic recognition and accurate interpretation of text. Without the ability to read fluently, a child's reading comprehension will be limited. Each time a child has to interrupt their reading to decode an unfamiliar word, comprehension is impaired.

There are a number of factors that contribute to the success of reading fluency. It is important that students have many opportunities to read. Access to a variety of reading genres at appropriate reading levels and effective reading fluency instruction also play important roles in how successful children will become fluent readers. The key is to have children repeat the same passage several times in order to become familiar with the words in the text and increase their overall speed and accuracy. Poems are an effective choice when teaching fluency, since they are usually concise and offer rhyming words in an entertaining, rhythmic pattern. Some other instructional strategies to consider include:

- Modeling reading fluency with expression
- Tape-assisted reading
- Echo reading
- Partner reading
- Small group and choral reading

Role of Automaticity

Automaticity is a student's ability to quickly recognize familiar words and read them. However, the ability to do this does not create a fluent reader. Automaticity does not equal fluency. In fact, the ability to recognize words simply means they can be read quickly and individually, but not necessarily in the phrases or sections that connect them to other words and attribute meaning to them.

Automaticity is the first step in developing fluency, though. Fluency involves a student's ability to read with speed, accuracy, and appropriate expression. Obviously, a student must be able to read words easily and quickly to be able to move into the next stages of reading, and for that reason, fluency comes with familiarity.

To develop skills in fluency, it is best to start with a text that the student is familiar with and is at their reading level. Students are then able to focus more on building reading speed and understanding meaning than on learning individual words or sounding them out.

A popular method for improving fluency relies fairly heavily on automaticity in that it asks students to read the same passage repeatedly. First, the passage is read, fluently, by the teacher, and then the student is asked to read the passage. Not only does the student read the same passage, but they do so aloud to receive feedback while reading. Teachers can correct pronunciation and address issues related to phonemic awareness. Additionally, playing recordings of fluent readers reading the passage or pairing students with more fluent readers may work. Again, the idea here is that automaticity is gained through multiple readings of a passage, and the student can then move on to reading fluently.

There is currently no research that fully supports independent reading as a viable strategy to build fluency based on automaticity. Automaticity and fluency are developed the more a student reads; therefore, silent reading may also help develop both skills.

Indicators of Reading Fluency

Accuracy refers to the frequency of pronunciation errors a student might make when reading. When students make frequent pronunciation errors while reading, guess at the pronunciation of unknown words, or ignore words altogether, they are showing signs of **dysfluency**. Reading accurately requires the reader to read words correctly with minimal to no errors. When errors do occur, readers who read with accuracy are generally able to self-correct and continue reading without interrupting the flow of the reading.

Rate refers to a student's ability to recognize words automatically without having to spend any time on decoding them. This manifests in their ability to read texts at a steady and consistent rate. Both accurate reading and reading at a consistent rate greatly strengthen a reader's overall reading comprehension.

Prosody refers to appropriate expression when reading—showing emotions, such as excitement, panic, or sorrow that accurately matches the intended emotions of the text. Readers may be able to read texts with accuracy and at a steady and consistent rate, but if they are unable to vocalize any expression in their reading or if the expression used does not match the intended expression of the text, their overall comprehension will be negatively affected. Readers who engage in an emotional or personal level with the text will experience greater reading comprehension and fluency.

Factors Affecting Comprehension

Phonics and Sight Words

Word recognition occurs when students are able to recognize and read a word automatically and correctly. Phonics and sight word instruction help with the promotion of accurate and automatic word identification and recognition. Once students are able to readily identify and recognize words, then they can focus on the meaning of the text and development of reading comprehension skills.

Phonics instruction stresses letter-sound correspondences and the manipulation of phonemes. Through phonics instruction, students discover the different sounds of a spoken language and how a written language's letters and symbols relate to one another. It is through the application of phonics principles that students are able to decode words. When a word is decoded, the letters that make up the printed word are translated into sounds. When students are able to recognize and manipulate letter-sound relationships of single-syllable words, then they are able to apply such relationships to decode more complex words. In this way, phonics aids reading fluency and reading comprehension.

Sight words, sometimes referred to as high-frequency words, are words that are used often but may not follow the regular principles of phonics. Sight words may also be defined as words that students are able to readily recognize and read without having to sound them out. Students are encouraged to memorize words by sight so their reading fluency is not deterred through the frequent decoding of regularly- occurring irregular words. In this way, sight word recognition aids reading fluency and reading comprehension.

Vocabulary Knowledge

Vocabulary knowledge is an indicator and predictor of comprehension. If students find a match between a word within a text and a word that they've learned through listening and speaking, they are likelier to recognize and understand the meaning of the word in the written context. As the students will spend less time decoding and interpreting the word, they are likelier to read fluently and with comprehension. In contrast, if students cannot connect a written word to a word within their speaking or listening vocabulary, their fluency and comprehension may be interrupted. This proves to be true even if the student is able to correctly pronounce the word.

Interrelationship Between Word Analysis Skills, Fluency, and Reading Comprehension

These three concepts—word analysis skills, fluency, and reading comprehension—are interconnected and inter-reliant. Word analysis refers to a student's ability to identify and define words; comprehension refers to the student's ability to then understand those words. Without analysis and comprehension, students can't read fluently. Conversely, if a student can recognize words and read fluently, this also suggests a higher level of comprehension. However, if a student can successfully decode with fluency but reads aloud without expression, there may be issues of comprehension. Rather than being a linear connection, the three concepts are more interrelated like a triangle.

Word analysis skills, which should be considered as contributing to comprehension, include identification of morphemes, recognition of common affixes, knowledge of root words and their etymology, sight recognition, and recognition of homographs. All these skills lend themselves to a student's ability to see a word and effortlessly recognize how it is pronounced or read. Even if a student can successfully use these strategies, if a text is well above their standard reading level, their **fluency** level may decrease. The same is true if the text is simple, in that fluency (and comprehension) will naturally increase. Increases in word analysis skills contribute to automaticity and fluency.

Comprehension skills, which then contribute to fluency, include background knowledge, vocabulary, sentence structure, syntax, reasoning, and knowledge of genre and style. A student's ability to bring this knowledge to reading demonstrates an increasingly strategic reader. That said, research suggests that comprehension and fluency share a bidirectional relationship in that each can contribute to the other; so, as a student gains word analysis skills and comprehension, fluency should naturally follow, and, as suggested, fluency can then increase comprehension.

Language and Linguistics: Assessment

Impact of Language Development and Language Differences

There is a direct connection between language development and literacy. In their early years, a child develops speech and language. Children are taught to read later. They then use their skills of literacy to further their education in all topics. This means that language development is the foundation for success in academia.

Becoming competent in a language requires a strong understanding of grammar, vocabulary, structure, and sociolinguistic purpose. This allows the student to communicate effectively in social settings and during formal academic instruction. Students who do not fulfill language competency will struggle to understand instruction. They may also find it difficult to communicate potential struggles.

Language difference is when a student speaks a language that differs from the one used by those around them, whether in an academic setting or otherwise. This should not be confused with language disorder. The student can communicate effectively with speakers of their language but struggle to do so in the new language that is being taught. As mentioned in the previous paragraph, this will lead to problems in developing the ability to read.

When helping students develop literacy, it is imperative to apply this knowledge. Looking for gaps in language development can explain difficulties in the processes of learning to read and reading to learn. Weak language comprehension should be addressed in order to improve literacy education.

A student who has weak language comprehension may struggle to understand what they are reading. They cannot understand what the language is saying or what certain words mean. As a result, they may avoid reading or doing work that is in the language they do not understand. Taking note of these difficulties during developing literacy can bring awareness to the foundational issue of limited language comprehension.

Assessment of Phonological and Phonemic Awareness

Entry-level assessments, progress monitoring, and summative assessments need to be administered in order to determine students' phonological and phonemic awareness.

The Yopp-Singer Test of Phonemic Segmentation

The **Yopp-Singer Test of Phonemic Segmentation** is an oral entry-level or summative assessment of phonemic awareness during which a teacher reads twenty-two words aloud one at a time to a single student. The student is to break each word apart by stating the word's sounds in the order that they are heard, and the teacher records the student's responses. Correctly segmented letter sounds are circled and incorrect responses are noted. If a student does well, then he or she is likely to do well in other phonemic areas. Upon poor student performance, the sound(s) with which a student struggles should be emphasized and/or retaught shortly after the time of the assessment.

After the Yopp-Singer Test, the blending of words, syllabification, and/or onset-rime identification should be assessed. The last set of phonological and phonemic skills to be assessed is composed of isolation, blending, deletion, and substitution.

Recognizing Rhyme Assessment
Word awareness, specifically awareness of onset-rime, can be assessed as a progress-monitoring activity. During this assessment, the teacher says two words. Students are to point their thumbs up if the words rhyme and down if the words do not rhyme. Immediate feedback and remediation are provided if the majority of the students respond incorrectly to a word pair.

Isolation or Matching Games
Games can be used to identify initial, medial, and final phonemes. During a phoneme-isolation activity, the teacher says one word at a time. The student is to tell the teacher the first, medial, or last sound of the word. During phoneme-matching activities, a teacher reads a group of words. The student is to say which two words from the group begin or end with the same sound. A similar activity can be completed to assess deletion and/or substitution (e.g., "What word would result if we replaced the /c/ of *cat* with an *h*?"). In this way, teachers can assess if **remediation** or extra instruction on initial, medial, or final phonemes is required and develop lessons accordingly.

Phoneme Blending Assessment
In this assessment, a teacher says all the sounds within a word and a student listens to the teacher and is asked for the word that they hear when the sounds are put together quickly. This skill will be needed when students learn letter-sound pairs and decipher unknown words in their reading. Thus, mastery of this assessment can be used as an indicator to the teacher that the students are ready to learn higher-level phonological and/or phonemic tasks.

Please note that student results should be recorded, analyzed, and used to determine if students demonstrate mastery over the assessed skill and/or identify the needs of students. If mastery is not demonstrated, then the assessments should be used to determine exactly which letter-sound combinations or other phonemes need to be remediated. Any of the strategies earlier addressed (rhyming, blending, segmenting, deleting, substituting) can be used for such purposes.

Fluency
Assessment of fluency must include entry-level assessments, progress monitoring, and summative assessments of accuracy, rate, and prosody. The results should be analyzed and interpreted in order to adjust instruction and provide struggling readers with proper interventions. Regular assessments also help teachers to construct differentiated instruction in order to address the fluency needs of advanced learners.

Running records, widely used fluency assessments, allow teachers to document error patterns in reading accuracy as students read benchmark books. As the student reads aloud, the teacher holds a copy of the same text and records any omissions, mispronunciations, and substitutions. With this information, teachers can determine which fluency strategies a student does or doesn't employ.

Rate
Assessment of reading rate often begins with sight-word reading automaticity. Automaticity assessment may also include the decoding of non-words in order to determine if a student is able to decode words using sound-syllable correspondence.

Among the most commonly used measurements of reading rate is oral contextual timed reading. During a **timed reading**, the number of errors made within a given amount of time is recorded. This data can be used to identify if a student's rate is improving and if reading rate falls within the recommended fluency rates for the student's grade level. If a student's reading rate is below average, any of the previously identified research-based, systematic, explicit strategies that improve fluency with respect to rate may be applied.

One common timed assessment for reading accuracy is the **WCPM**, the words-correct-per-minute assessment. The teacher presents an unfamiliar text to a student and asks the student to read aloud for one minute. As the student reads, the teacher records any omissions, mispronunciations, or substitutions. These errors are subtracted by the total number of words in the text to determine a score, which is then compared to oral reading fluency norms. With this assessment, teachers can select the appropriate level of text for each student.

Recommended Reading Fluency Rates		
Grade	**Semester**	**Correct Words Per Minute**
First Grade	Winter	38
	Spring	40–60
Second Grade	Fall	55
	Winter	73–79
	Spring	81–93
Third Grade	Fall	79
	Winter	83–92
	Spring	100–115
Fourth Grade	Fall	91–99
	Winter	98–113
	Spring	106–119
Fifth Grade	Fall	105
	Winter	109–118
	Spring	118–128

Prosody

In order to assess prosody, a teacher listens for inflection, expression, and pauses as the student reads a connected text aloud. The Integrate Reading Performance Record Oral Reading Fluency Scale designed by the National Assessment of Educational Progress (NAEP) is also used to assess prosody. Students at levels 3 and 4 are considered fluent in prosody, while students at levels 1 and 2 are considered to be non-fluent:

- Level 4: Reads mainly in large phrase groups. The structure of the story is intact and the author's syntax is consistent, even if there are some deviations from the text. Most of the story is read with expression.

- Level 3: Reads mainly in three- or four-word phrase groups. Majority of phrasing is appropriate and preserves syntax of the author. Little expression is present with interpreting the text.

- Level 2: Reads two-word phrases with some three- or four-word groupings. Word-by-word reading may occur. Some word groupings may seem awkward, indicating that the student is not paying attention to the larger context.

- Level 1: Reads word-by-word. Some occasional two-or-three word phrases may be present, but they are not frequent or they don't preserve meaningful syntax.

Writing

The following are examples of assessment practices that help drive instruction and strengthen a student's understanding and application of writing skills for different types of writing.

Effective writing assessments:

- Rating scales and rubrics
- Student logs: student evaluation of writing exercises
- Small groups and peer evaluations
- POWER method: Plan, Organize, Write, Edit, Rewrite (self-assessment)
- Standardized and diagnostic assessments
- Formative assessments
- Summative assessments

It is almost as important to provide feedback and evaluate a student's skill level as it is to teach. Most classes utilize both formative and summative assessments as a grading template. Although assessment and grading are not the same thing, assessments are often used to award a grade. A **formative assessment** monitors the student's progress in learning and allows continuous feedback throughout the course in the form of homework and in-class assignments, such as quizzes, writing workshops, conferences, or inquiry-based writing prompts. These assessments typically make up a lower percent of the overall grade. Alternatively, a **summative assessment** compares a student's progress in learning against some sort of standard, such as against the progress of other students or by the number of correct answers. These assessments usually make up a higher percent of the overall grade and come in the form of midterm or final exams, papers, or major projects.

One evidence-based method used to assess a student's progress is a rubric. A **rubric** is an evaluation tool that explicitly states the expectations of the assignment and breaks it down into different components. Each component has a clear description and relationship to the assignment as a whole. For writing, rubrics may be **holistic,** judging the overall quality of the writing, or they can be **analytic,** in which different aspects of the writing are evaluated (e.g., structure, style, word choices, and punctuation).

Rubrics can be used in all aspects of a curriculum, including reading comprehension, oral presentations, speeches, performances, papers, projects, and listening comprehension. They are usually formative in nature but can be summative depending on the purpose. Rubrics allow instructors to provide specific feedback and allow students to understand the expectations for an assignment.

An example of an analytic rubric is displayed below:

Name _____   Date _____

Essay Rubric	4 Mastery	3 Satisfactory	2 Needs Improvement	1 Poor
Writing Quality	-Excellent usage of voice and style -Outstanding organizational skills -Wealth of relevant information	-Style and voice of essay was interesting -Mostly organized -Useful amount of information	-Inconsistent style and voice -Lacked clear organization -Small amount of useful information	-No noticeable style or voice -Virtually no organization -No relevant information
Grammar Conventions	-Essentially no mistakes in grammar -Correct spelling throughout	-Minor amount of grammar and spelling mistakes	-Many errors in grammar conventions and spelling	-Too many grammatical errors to understand the meaning of the piece

Another research-proven strategy is **conferencing,** in which students participate in a group discussion that usually involves the teacher. Students learn best when they can share their thoughts on what they've read or written and receive feedback from their peers and instructors. For writing, conferencing is frequently done in the revision stage. Through discussion, students are also able to enhance their listening and speaking skills. Conferences can be done in a one-on-one setting, typically between a student and instructor, or in a small group of students with guidance from the instructor. They are useful in that they provide an atmosphere of respect where a student can share their work and thoughts without fear of judgment. They increase motivation and allow students to explore a variety of topics and discussions. Conferences also allow the instructor to provide immediate feedback or prompt students for deeper explanations of their ideas. The most successful conferences have these characteristics:

- Have a set structure
- Focus on only a few points—too many are confusing or distracting
- Are solution based
- Allow students to both discuss their thoughts/works and receive/provide feedback for others
- Encourage the use of appropriate vocabulary
- Provide motivation and personal satisfaction or pleasure from reading and writing
- Allow a time where questions can be asked and immediately answered

Rubrics and conferencing are both methods that provide useful **feedback,** one of the most important elements in the progress of a student's learning. Feedback is essentially corrective instruction delivered in writing, either verbally or non-verbally.

Assessment Methods and Instruments for Developing Abilities

Listening

Listening skills are foundational for a strong education. Developing listening abilities requires assessment methods and instruments to ensure success. One instructional method is to engage the listeners with participation. This could be through various activities or simply by allowing them to ask questions during active listening. Having listeners summarize or answer questions about what they have heard will help them stay alert and focused.

Speaking

Speaking skills are vital for communication. There are numerous assessment methods and instruments to help develop strong speaking skills. Reading aloud, giving presentations, and encouraging effective communication are all assessment methods for speaking skills. Eye contact should be part of strong speaking. Having a student repeat what has been said to them can help them develop speaking skills as well as the aforementioned listening skills.

Reading Comprehension

Reading skills can be developed and assessed in a multitude of ways. Assessments that ask for a student's understanding of a passage can help show the student's reading level. This could be through drawing the story, predicting what will happen next, or summarizing the text as a whole. Reading aloud helps develop reading skills and speaking skills, as mentioned earlier. Giving students a chance to read texts that may be above their level is a good way to see which portion of their development needs work. This could include comprehension, vocabulary, or ease of reading.

Comprehension is important because it provides meaning to reading and listening. Assessment of comprehension ensures that the student understands what they have read or heard. This can happen by asking the student to create a timeline that shows an order of events. This works for stories or historical accounts. Multiple-choice or fill-in-the-blank assessments test if the student can provide answers to contextual questions. Students may be asked to make connections between multiple texts or real life to show that they are understanding common themes.

Vocabulary

A strong vocabulary is necessary to enrich and improve a student's overall reading comprehension and writing ability. Vocabulary development can be assessed in a number of ways. Asking students to use new vocabulary in a writing assignment, scheduling multiple-choice exams, and giving assignments that ask for synonyms and antonyms of various words are all good options for assessing a student's vocabulary development. These assessments will show the student's strengths and weaknesses.

Spelling Conventions

Spelling conventions should be assessed to make sure that the student is properly understanding how to handle unfamiliar words. This helps with improving writing and creating stronger descriptions. To assess progress with spelling conventions, it is important to read vocabulary words aloud and have the student spell them on paper. Other assessment methods may include unscrambling words or matching words to the spelling convention they follow.

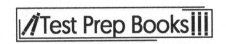

Interrelated Abilities

There are many interrelated abilities among these subjects. All of these skills contribute to English literacy. A student might use many of the same abilities to develop their listening, speaking, reading, comprehension, vocabulary, and spelling skills. This includes the ability to gather information and make inferences. When learning all of these skills, a student will also use their abilities for critical thinking and communication. These interrelated abilities will develop in addition to the skills mentioned and help the learning process.

Non-Written and Written Communication: Conventions of Language

English Grammar and Conventions

Sentence Structure

A **sentence** is a set of words that make up a grammatical unit. The words must have certain elements and be spoken or written in a specific order to constitute a complete sentence that makes sense:

- A sentence must have a **subject** (a noun or noun phrase). The subject tells whom or what the sentence is addressing (i.e., what it is about).

- A sentence must have an **action** or **state of being** (*a* verb). To reiterate: A verb forms the main part of the predicate of a sentence. This means that it explains what the noun is doing.

- A sentence must convey a complete thought.

The four types of sentence structure are simple, compound, complex, and compound-complex.

A **simple sentence** has one independent clause. Simple sentences do not necessarily have to be short sentences. They just require one independent clause with a subject and a predicate. For example:

Thomas marched over to Andrew's house.

Jonah and Mary constructed a simplified version of the Eiffel Tower with Legos.

A **compound sentence** has two independent clauses. A conjunction—*for, and, nor, but, or, yet, so*—links them together. Note that each of the independent clauses has a subject and a verb. Compound sentences do not have dependent clauses. For example:

We went to the fireworks stand, and we bought enough fireworks to last all night.

The children sat on the grass, and then we lit the fireworks one at a time.

A **complex sentence** has one independent clause and one or more dependent clauses.

Because she slept well and drank coffee, Sarah was quite productive at work.

Although Will had coffee, he made mistakes while using the photocopier.

A **compound-complex sentence** has at least three clauses, two of which are independent and at least one that is a dependent clause.

> It may come as a surprise, but I found the tickets, and you can go to the show.

> While trying to dance, I tripped over my partner's feet, but I regained my balance quickly.

An effective writer—one who wants to paint a vivid picture or strongly illustrate a central idea—will use a variety of sentence structures and sentence lengths. A reader is more likely to be confused if an author uses choppy, unrelated sentences. Similarly, a reader will become bored and lose interest if an author repeatedly uses the same sentence structure. Good writing is fluent. It flows. Varying sentence structure keeps a reader engaged and helps reading comprehension. Consider the following example:

> The morning started off early. It was bright out. It was just daylight. The Moon was still in the sky. He was tired from his sleepless night.

Then consider this text:

> Morning hit hard. He didn't remember the last time light hurt this bad. Sleep had been absent, and the very thought of moving towards the new day seemed like a hurdle he couldn't overcome.

Note the variety in sentence structure. The second passage is more interesting to read because the sentence fluency is more effective. Both passages paint the picture of a central character's reaction to dawn, but the second passage is more effective because it uses a variety of sentences and is more fluent than the first.

Errors in Standard English Grammar, Usage, Syntax, and Mechanics
Sentence Fragments
A complete sentence requires a verb and a subject, and it must express a complete thought. Sometimes, the subject is omitted in the case of the implied *you*, used in sentences that are the command or imperative form—e.g., "Look!" or "Give me that." It is understood that the subject of the command is *you*, the listener or reader, so it is possible to have a structure without an explicit subject. Without these elements, though, the sentence is incomplete—it is a **sentence fragment.** While sentence fragments often occur in conversational English or creative writing, they are generally not appropriate in academic writing. Sentence fragments often occur when dependent clauses are not joined to an independent clause:

Sentence fragment:

> Because the airline overbooked the flight.

The sentence above is a dependent clause that does not express a complete thought. What happened as a result of this cause? With the addition of an independent clause, this now becomes a complete sentence:

Complete sentence:

> Because the airline overbooked the flight, several passengers were unable to board.

Sentences fragments may also occur through improper use of conjunctions:

> I'm going to the Bahamas for spring break. And to New York City for New Year's Eve.

58

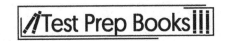

While the first sentence above is a complete sentence, the second one is not because it is a prepositional phrase that lacks a subject [I] and a verb [am going]. Joining the two together with the coordinating conjunction forms one grammatically-correct sentence:

> I'm going to the Bahamas for spring break and to New York City for New Year's Eve.

Run-ons

A **run-on** is a sentence with too many independent clauses that are improperly connected to each other:

> This winter has been very cold some farmers have suffered damage to their crops.

The sentence above has two subject-verb combinations. The first is "this winter has been"; the second is "some farmers have suffered." However, they are simply stuck next to each other without any punctuation or conjunction. Therefore, the sentence is a run-on.

Another type of run-on occurs when writers use inappropriate punctuation:

> This winter has been very cold, some farmers have suffered damage to their crops.

Though a comma has been added, this sentence is still not correct. When a comma alone is used to join two independent clauses, it is known as a **comma splice**. Without an appropriate conjunction, a comma cannot join two independent clauses by itself.

Run-on sentences can be corrected by either dividing the independent clauses into two or more separate sentences or inserting appropriate conjunctions and/or punctuation. The run-on sentence can be amended by separating each subject-verb pair into its own sentence:

> This winter has been very cold. Some farmers have suffered damage to their crops.

The run-on can also be fixed by adding a comma and conjunction to join the two independent clauses with each other:

> This winter has been very cold, so some farmers have suffered damage to their crops.

Parallelism

Parallel structure occurs when phrases or clauses within a sentence contain the same structure. Parallelism increases readability and comprehensibility because it is easy to tell which sentence elements are paired with each other in meaning.

> Jennifer enjoys cooking, knitting, and to spend time with her cat.

This sentence is not parallel because the items in the list appear in two different forms. Some are **gerunds,** which is the verb + ing: *cooking, knitting*. The other item uses the **infinitive** form, which is to + verb: *to spend*. To create parallelism, all items in the list may reflect the same form:

> Jennifer enjoys cooking, knitting, and spending time with her cat.

All of the items in the list are now in gerund forms, so this sentence exhibits parallel structure. Here's another example:

> The company is looking for employees who are responsible and with a lot of experience.

59

Again, the items that are listed in this sentence are not parallel. "Responsible" is an adjective, yet "with a lot of experience" is a prepositional phrase. The sentence elements do not utilize parallel parts of speech.

> The company is looking for employees who are responsible and experienced.

"Responsible" and "experienced" are both adjectives, so this sentence now has parallel structure.

Dangling and Misplaced Modifiers

Modifiers enhance meaning by clarifying or giving greater detail about another part of a sentence. However, incorrectly-placed modifiers have the opposite effect and can cause confusion. A **misplaced modifier** is a modifier that is not located appropriately in relation to the word or phrase that it modifies:

> Because he was one of the greatest thinkers of Renaissance Italy, John idolized Leonardo da Vinci.

In this sentence, the modifier is "because he was one of the greatest thinkers of Renaissance Italy," and the noun it is intended to modify is "Leonardo da Vinci." However, due to the placement of the modifier next to the subject, John, it seems as if the sentence is stating that John was a Renaissance genius, not Da Vinci.

> John idolized Leonard da Vinci because he was one of the greatest thinkers of Renaissance Italy.

The modifier is now adjacent to the appropriate noun, clarifying which of the two men in this sentence is the greatest thinker.

Dangling modifiers modify a word or phrase that is not readily apparent in the sentence. That is, they "dangle" because they are not clearly attached to anything:

> After getting accepted to college, Amir's parents were proud.

The modifier here, "after getting accepted to college," should modify who got accepted. The noun immediately following the modifier is "Amir's parents"—but they are probably not the ones who are going to college.

> After getting accepted to college, Amir made his parents proud.

The subject of the sentence has been changed to Amir himself, and now the subject and its modifier are appropriately matched.

Inconsistent Verb Tense

Verb tense reflects when an action occurred or a state existed. For example, the tense known as **simple present** expresses something that is happening right now or that happens regularly:

> She *works* in a hospital.

Present continuous tense expresses something in progress. It is formed by to be + verb + -ing.

> Sorry, I can't go out right now. I *am doing* my homework.

Past tense is used to describe events that previously occurred. However, in conversational English, speakers often use present tense or a mix of past and present tense when relating past events because it gives the

60

narrative a sense of immediacy. In formal written English, though, consistency in verb tense is necessary to avoid reader confusion.

> I traveled to Europe last summer. As soon as I stepped off the plane, I feel like I'm in a movie! I'm surrounded by quaint cafes and impressive architecture.

The passage above abruptly switches from past tense—*traveled, stepped*—to present tense—*feel, am surrounded*.

> I *traveled* to Europe last summer. As soon as I *stepped* off the plane, I *felt* like I was in a movie! I *was surrounded* by quaint cafes and impressive architecture.

All verbs are in past tense, so this passage now has consistent verb tense.

Split Infinitives

The **infinitive form** of a verb consists of "to + base verb"—e.g., to walk, to sleep, to approve. A **split infinitive** occurs when another word, usually an adverb, is placed between *to* and the verb:

> I decided *to simply walk* to work to get more exercise every day.

The infinitive *to walk* is split by the adverb *simply*.

> It was a mistake *to hastily approve* the project before conducting further preliminary research.

The infinitive *to approve* is split by *hastily*.

Although some grammarians still advise against split infinitives, this syntactic structure is common in both spoken and written English and is widely accepted in standard usage.

Subject-Verb Agreement

In English, verbs must agree with the subject. The form of a verb may change depending on whether the subject is singular or plural, or whether it is first, second, or third person. For example, the verb *to be* has various forms:

> I <u>am</u> a student.

> You <u>are</u> a student.

> She <u>is</u> a student.

> We <u>are</u> students.

> They <u>are</u> students.

Errors occur when a verb does not agree with its subject. Sometimes, the error is readily apparent:

> We is hungry.

Is is not the appropriate form of *to be* when used with the third person plural *we*.

> We are hungry.

61

This sentence now has correct subject-verb agreement.

However, some cases are trickier, particularly when the subject consists of a lengthy noun phrase with many modifiers:

> Students who are hoping to accompany the anthropology department on its annual summer trip to Ecuador needs to sign up by March 31st.

The verb in this sentence is *needs*. However, its subject is not the noun adjacent to it—Ecuador. The subject is the noun at the beginning of the sentence—students. Because *students* is plural, *needs* is the incorrect verb form.

> *Students* who are hoping to accompany the anthropology department on its annual summer trip to Ecuador *need* to sign up by March 31st.

This sentence now uses correct agreement between *students* and *need*.

Another case to be aware of is a **collective noun**. A collective noun refers to a group of many things or people but can be singular in itself—e.g., family, committee, army, pair team, council, jury. Whether or not a collective noun uses a singular or plural verb depends on how the noun is being used. If the noun refers to the group performing a collective action as one unit, it should use a singular verb conjugation:

> The family is moving to a new neighborhood.

The whole family is moving together in unison, so the singular verb form *is* is appropriate here.

> The committee has made its decision.

The verb *has* and the possessive pronoun *its* both reflect the word *committee* as a singular noun in the sentence above; however, when a collective noun refers to the group as individuals, it can take a plural verb:

> The newlywed pair spend every moment together.

This sentence emphasizes the love between two people in a pair, so it can use the plural verb *spend*.

> The council are all newly elected members.

The sentence refers to the council in terms of its individual members and uses the plural verb *are*.

Overall, though, American English is more likely to pair a collective noun with a singular verb, while British English is more likely to pair a collective noun with a plural verb.

Capitalization

Here's a non-exhaustive list of things that should be capitalized:

- The first word of every sentence or quotation
  - The realtor showed them the house.
  - Robert asked, "When can we get together for dinner again?"
- The first word of every line of poetry

62

- The first letter of proper nouns and words derived from them

  - We are visiting Germany in a few weeks.

  - We will stay with our German relatives on our trip.

- Holidays (Valentine's Day)

- The days of the week and months of the year (Tuesday, March)

- The first word, last word, and all major words in the titles of books, movies, songs, and other creative works, but not the articles, conjunctions, or prepositions: (In the novel, To Kill a Mockingbird, note that a is lowercase since it's not a major word, but to is capitalized since it's the first word of the title.)

- Titles when preceding a proper noun (President Roberto Gonzales, Mrs. McFadden, Sir Alec Guinness). When simply using a word such as president or secretary, though, the word is not capitalized.

- Capitalize familial relationships when referring to a *specific* person:

  - I worked for my Uncle Steven last summer.

  - Did you work for your uncle last summer?

- Capitalize directional words that are used as names, but not when referencing a direction:

  - The North won the Civil War.

  - After making a left, go north on Rt. 476.

  - She grew up on the West Coast.

  - The winds came in from the west.

- Seasons—spring, fall, etc.—are not capitalized.

Punctuation

Commas

A **comma** (,) is the punctuation mark that signifies a pause—breath—between parts of a sentence. It denotes a break of flow. As with so many aspects of writing structure, authors will benefit by memorizing all of the different ways in which commas can be used so as not to abuse them.

In a complex sentence—one that contains a subordinate (dependent) clause or clauses—the use of a comma is dictated by where the subordinate clause is located. If the subordinate clause is located before the main clause, a comma is needed between the two clauses.

I will not pay for the steak, *because I don't have that much money.*

63

Generally, if the subordinate clause is placed after the main clause, no punctuation is needed.

I did well on my exam because I studied two hours the night before.

Notice how the last clause is dependent because it earlier independent clauses to make sense.

Use a comma on both sides of an interrupting phrase.

I will pay for the ice cream, *chocolate and vanilla*, and then will eat it all myself.

The words forming the phrase in italics are nonessential (extra) information. To determine if a phrase is nonessential, try reading the sentence without the phrase and see if it's still coherent.

A comma is not necessary in this next sentence because no interruption—nonessential or extra information—has occurred. Read sentences aloud when uncertain.

I will pay for his chocolate and vanilla ice cream and then will eat it all myself.

If the nonessential phrase comes at the beginning of a sentence, a comma should only go at the end of the phrase. If the phrase comes at the end of a sentence, a comma should only go at the beginning of the phrase.

Other types of interruptions include the following:

- Interjections: Oh no, I am not going.
- Abbreviations: Barry Potter, M.D., specializes in heart disorders.
- Direct Addresses: Yes, Claudia, I am tired and going to bed.
- Parenthetical Phrases: His wife, lovely as she was, was not helpful.
- Transitional Phrases: Also, it is not possible.

The second comma in the following sentence is called an Oxford comma.

I will pay for ice cream, syrup, and pop.

It is a comma used after the second-to-last item in a series of three or more items. It comes before the word *or* or *and*. Not everyone uses the Oxford comma; it is optional, but many believe it is needed. The comma functions as a tool to reduce confusion in writing. So, if omitting the Oxford comma would cause confusion, then it's best to include it.

Commas are used in math to mark the place of thousands in numerals, breaking them up so they are easier to read. Other uses for commas are in dates (*March 19, 2016*), letter greetings (*Dear Sally,*), and in between cities and states (*Louisville, KY*).

Apostrophes
This punctuation mark, the apostrophe ('), is a versatile little mark. It has a few different functions:

- Quotes: Apostrophes are used when a second quote is needed within a quote:

    In my letter to my friend, I wrote, "The girl had to get a new purse, and guess what Mary did? She said, 'I'd like to go with you to the store.' I knew Mary would buy it for her."

64

- Contractions: Another use for an apostrophe in the quote above is a contraction. *I'd* is used for *I would*. The basic rule for making contractions is one area of spelling that is pretty straightforward: combine the two words by inserting an apostrophe (') in the space where a letter is omitted. For example, to combine *you* and *are*, drop the *a* and put the apostrophe in its place: *you're*.

  he + is = he's

  you + all = y'all (informal but often misspelled)

- Possession: An apostrophe followed by the letter s shows possession (*Mary's* purse). If the possessive word is plural, the apostrophe generally just follows the word.

  The trees' leaves are all over the ground.

Ellipses

An **ellipsis** (…) is used to show that there is more to the quoted text than is necessary for the current discussion. Writers use them in place of words, lines, phrases, list content, or paragraphs that might just as easily have been omitted from a passage of writing. This can be done to save space or to focus only on the specifically relevant material:

> Exercise is good for some unexpected reasons. Watkins writes, "Exercise has many benefits such as…reducing cancer risk."

In the example above, the ellipsis takes the place of the other benefits of exercise that are more expected.

The ellipsis may also be used to show a pause in sentence flow:

> "I'm wondering…how this could happen," Dylan said in a soft voice.

Semicolons

The **semicolon** (;) might be described as a heavy-handed comma. Take a look at these two examples:

> I will pay for the ice cream, but I will not pay for the steak.
> I will pay for the ice cream; I will not pay for the steak.

What's the difference? The first example has a comma and a conjunction separating the two independent clauses. The second example does not have a conjunction, but there are two independent clauses in the sentence, so something more than a comma is required. In this case, a semicolon is used.

Two independent clauses can only be joined in a sentence by either a comma and conjunction or a semicolon. If one of those tools is not used, the sentence will be a run-on. Remember that while the clauses are independent, they need to be closely related in order to be contained in one sentence.

Another use for the semicolon is to separate items in a list when the items themselves require commas:

> The family lived in Phoenix, Arizona; Oklahoma City, Oklahoma; and Raleigh, North Carolina.

Colons

In a sentence, **colons** are used before a list, a summary or elaboration, or an explanation related to the preceding information in the sentence:

There are two ways to reserve tickets for the performance: by phone or in person.

One thing is clear: students are spending more on tuition than ever before.

As these examples show, a colon must be preceded by an independent clause. However, the information after the colon may be in the form of an independent clause or in the form of a list.

The meal includes the following components:

- Caesar salad
- spaghetti
- garlic bread
- cake

Colons can also be used to introduce an appositive:

The family got what they needed: a reliable vehicle.

While a comma is more common, a colon can also precede a formal quotation:

He said to the crowd: "Let's begin!"

The colon is used after the greeting in a formal letter:

Dear Sir:
To Whom It May Concern:

In the writing of time, the colon separates the minutes from the hour (*4:45 p.m.*). The colon can also be used to indicate a ratio between two numbers (*50:1*).

Hyphens

The **hyphen** (-) is a small dash mark that can be used to join words to show that they are linked.

Hyphens can connect two words that work together as a single adjective (a compound adjective):

honey-covered biscuits

Some words always require hyphens even if not serving as an adjective:

merry-go-round

Hyphens always go after certain prefixes like *anti-* & *all-*.

Hyphens should also be used when the absence of the hyphen would cause a strange vowel combination (*semi-engineer*) or confusion. For example, *re-collect* should be used to describe something being gathered twice rather than being written as *recollect*, which means to remember.

Parentheses and Dashes

Parentheses are half-round brackets that look like this: ( ). They set off a word, phrase, or sentence that is an afterthought, explanation, or side note relevant to the surrounding text but not essential. A pair of commas is often used to set off this sort of information, but parentheses are generally used for information that would

not fit well within a sentence or that the writer deems not important enough to be structurally part of the sentence.

> The picture of the heart (see above) shows the major parts you should memorize.
> Mount Everest is one of three mountains in the world that are over 28,000 feet high (K2 and Kanchenjunga are the other two).

See how the sentences above are complete without the parenthetical statements? In the first example, *see above* would not have fit well within the flow of the sentence. The second parenthetical statement could have been a separate sentence, but the writer deemed the information not pertinent to the topic.

The **em-dash** (—) is a mark longer than a hyphen used as a punctuation mark in sentences and to set apart a relevant thought. Even after plucking out the line separated by the dash marks, the sentence will be intact and make sense.

> Looking out the airplane window at the landmarks—Lake Clarke, Thompson Community College, and the bridge—she couldn't help but feel excited to be home.

The dashes use is similar to that of parentheses or a pair of commas. So, what's the difference? Many believe that using dashes makes the clause within them stand out while using parentheses is subtler. It's advised to not use dashes when commas could be used instead.

Quotation Marks
Quotation marks ("") are used in a number of ways. Here are some instances where quotation marks should be used: to indicate a quote that was taken from somewhere else, either from a verbal or written source...

- Dialogue for characters in narratives. When characters speak, the first word should always be capitalized, and the punctuation goes inside the quotes. For example:

  Janie said, "The tree fell on my car during the hurricane."

- Around titles of songs, short stories, essays, and chapter in books

- To emphasize a certain word

- To refer to a word as the word its

Usage

There are conventions in English that are considered the correct form of the language. However, there are certain facets of communication that rely on preferred usage of these conventions. This varies based on the speaker and audience. For example, the use of the Oxford comma is debated. Its use depends on the type of publication, formality of the text, and preference of the writer. This is a stylistic preferred usage of the comma. Preferred usage can extend to spelling, pronunciation, and grammar.

Its and It's
These pronouns are some of the most confused in the English language as most possessives contain the suffix –'s. However, for *it*, it is the opposite. *Its* is a possessive pronoun:

> The government is reassessing *its* spending plan.

It's is a contraction of the words *it is*:

> *It's* snowing outside.

Saw and Seen

Saw and **seen** are both conjugations of the verb *to see*, but they express different verb tenses. *Saw* is used in the simple past tense. *Seen* is the past participle form of *to see* and can be used in all perfect tenses.

> I seen her yesterday.

This sentence is incorrect. Because it expresses a completed event from a specified point in time in the past, it should use simple past tense:

> I *saw* her yesterday.

This sentence uses the correct verb tense. Here's how the past participle is used correctly:

> I *have seen* her before.

The meaning in this sentence is slightly changed to indicate an event from an unspecific time in the past. In this case, present perfect is the appropriate verb tense to indicate an unspecified past experience. Present perfect conjugation is created by combining *to have* + past participle.

Then and Than

Then is generally used as an adverb indicating something that happened next in a sequence or as the result of a conditional situation:

> We parked the car and *then* walked to the restaurant.

> If enough people register for the event, *then* we can begin planning.

Than is a conjunction indicating comparison:

> This watch is more expensive *than* that one.

> The bus departed later *than* I expected.

They're, Their, and There

They're is a contraction of the words *they are*:

> *They're* moving to Ohio next week.

Their is a possessive pronoun:

> The baseball players are training for *their* upcoming season.

There can function as multiple parts of speech, but it is most commonly used as an adverb indicating a location:

> Let's go to the concert! Some great bands are playing *there*.

Insure and Ensure

These terms are both verbs. *Insure* means to guarantee something against loss, harm, or damage, usually through an insurance policy that offers monetary compensation:

> The robbers made off with her prized diamond necklace, but luckily it was *insured* for one million dollars.

Ensure means to make sure, to confirm, or to be certain:

> *Ensure* that you have your passport before entering the security checkpoint.

Accept and Except

Accept is a verb meaning to take or agree to something:

> I would like to *accept* your offer of employment.

Except is a preposition that indicates exclusion:

> I've been to every state in America *except* Hawaii.

Affect and Effect

Affect is a verb meaning to influence or to have an impact on something:

> The amount of rainfall during the growing season *affects* the flavor of wine produced from these grapes.

Effect can be used as either a noun or a verb. As a noun, *effect* is synonymous with a result:

> If we implement the changes, what will the *effect* be on our profits?

As a verb, *effect* means to bring about or to make happen:

> In just a few short months, the healthy committee has *effected* real change in school nutrition.

Conventions of Spelling

Conventions of spelling are important to learn for written communication. There are a number of generally accepted rules that guide the process. These rules should be used as a reference when there is doubt regarding how a word should be spelled.

Before referencing the conventions of spelling, the difference between vowels and consonants must be known. The vowels are *A, E, I, O, U,* and sometimes *W* and *Y*. The consonants are all the other letters not included in the vowel list. It is vital to know what letters belong in the vowel category. Some of the conventions of spelling reference what to do in the situation based on whether there is a vowel or consonant.

One convention of spelling is that the letter *I* comes before *E*. For example, this is seen in the words *fiery* and *piece*. There are two main exceptions to this rule. One exception is when the *I* and *E* follow the letter *C*, such as in the word *receive*. The second exception is when *I* and *E* make an A sound, such as in the word *neighbor*. There are words that do not obey this convention, such as the word *leisure,* but otherwise it is the standard.

69

Another convention of spelling is that most singular words are pluralized by adding the letter *S*. For example, think of the word *dog*. To pluralize this singular word, spell it as *dogs*. However, if a word ends in *S*, *CH*, *SH*, *Z*, or *X*, add the letters *ES* to pluralize it. For example, think of the word *bush*. To pluralize this word, spell it as *bushes*.

A third convention of spelling says to drop the final vowel when the word ends in a vowel and the suffix begins with a vowel. Think of the word *arguable*. This is a combination of the word *argue* and the suffix *- able*. Because the word ends in a vowel and the suffix begins with a vowel, drop the final vowel in the word, which is *E*. The word then becomes *arguable*.

The conventions of spelling also address words that are considered homophones and homographs. The spelling of a word may or may not change its meaning, depending on whether it is a homophone or homograph. Homophones are two or more words that sound the same but are spelled differently and have different meanings, such as *knight* and *night*. Homographs are words that are spelled the same but are pronounced differently and mean different things. The word *bass* is an example of this. It may refer to a type of instrument or a type of fish, depending on the context.

Non-Written and Written Communication: Stages of the Writing Process

Current trends in education have recognized the need to cultivate writing skills that prepare students for higher education and professional careers. To this end, writing skills are being integrated into other subjects beyond the language arts classroom. The skills and strategies used in language arts class, then, should be adaptable for other learning tasks. In this way, students can achieve greater proficiency by incorporating writing strategies into every aspect of learning.

To teach writing, it is important that teachers know the writing process. The five components of the writing process are as follows:

- **Pre-writing**: The drafting, planning, researching, and brainstorming of ideas

- **Writing**: The part of the project in which the actual, physical writing takes place

- **Revising**: Adding to, removing, rearranging, or re-writing sections of the piece

- **Editing**: Analyzing and correcting mistakes in grammar, spelling, punctuation, formatting, and word choice

- **Publishing**: Distributing the finished product to the teacher, employer, or other students

Pre-Writing Strategies

Planning is the precursor to writing. This brainstorming stage is when writers consider their purpose and think of ideas that they can use in their writing. Graphic organizers are excellent tools to use during the planning stage. Graphic organizers can help students connect the writing purpose to supporting details, and they can help begin the process of structuring the writing piece. Brainstorming can be done independently, in partners, or as a whole-class activity.

70

Outlining

An *outline* is a system used to organize writing. When planning, outlining is important because it helps readers organize important information in a logical pattern using Roman numerals. Usually, outlines start out with the main idea(s) and then branch out into subgroups or subsidiary thoughts or subjects. Not only do outlines provide a visual tool for writers to reflect on how events, characters, settings, or other key parts of the text or passage should relate to one another, but they can also lead writers to a creating a stronger conclusion. The sample below demonstrates what a general outline looks like:

I.   Main Topic 1
    a. Subtopic 1
    b. Subtopic 2
        1. Detail 1
        2. Detail 2
II.   Main Topic 2
    a. Subtopic 1
    b. Subtopic 2
        1. Detail 1
        2. Detail 2

Creating an outline that identifies the **main ideas** as well as the **supporting details** is a helpful strategy in the pre-writing stage. Most outlines will include a title that reveals the topic of the text and is usually a single phrase or word, such as "whales." If the passage will be divided up into paragraphs, or the paragraphs into sections, each paragraph or section will have its own main idea. These "main ideas" are usually depicted in outlines as roman numerals. Next, writers use supporting details in order to support or prove the main ideas. The supporting details should be listed underneath each main idea in the outline. For example:

Title: Whales

I. Killer whales

    a. Highly social

    b. Apex predator

II. Humpback whales

    a. Males produce "song"

    b. Targeted for whaling industry

III. Beluga whales

    a. Complex sense of hearing

    b. Slow swimmers

Graphic Organizers

Ideas from a text can also be organized using graphic organizers. A **graphic organizer** is a way to simplify information and take key points from the text. A graphic organizer such as a timeline may have an event listed

71

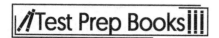

for a corresponding date on the timeline while an outline may have an event listed under a key point that occurs in the text. Each reader needs to create the type of graphic organizer that works the best for him or her in terms of being able to recall information from a story. Examples include a **spider-map**, which takes a main idea from the story and places it in a bubble with supporting points branching off the main idea. An **outline** is useful for diagramming the main and supporting points of the entire story, and a **Venn diagram** classifies information as separate or overlapping.

Note-Taking

Before tackling a writing project, it is helpful to practice prewriting strategies. This helps to organize the writing, clarify the content it will contain, and determine how information is prioritized. Note-taking is one prewriting strategy that can be used.

It is important to take notes whether the source of the information is a lecture, textbook, or something else. The notes taken should be clear, organized, and relevant to the writing. This allows an easily navigable resource for the writing.

While note-taking, a few habits should be developed to help the writing process. The notetaker should use headings to denote where information is located. Bullets can help break up information into individual points. In addition, information can be color coded based on topic or importance. These tips will help organize the notes for later reference when writing.

Revising and Editing

Writing is a multi-step process in which a writer must consider the message and the audience. Likewise, revisions should focus on specific areas. If revision requirements are too vague or all requirements are combined into one task, writers can become confused and overwhelmed. Breaking up revisions into specific categories will help writers to recognize, understand, and correct specific errors.

As writers begin writing their first draft of a writing piece, they need to continuously revise and edit their work. **Revisions** take place during and after the writing process. As writers revise their writing, they are encouraged to frequently refer back to the planning stage. This helps ensure that they are staying focused and are remaining on topic. During the revising and editing stage, writers should reread their work several times and focus on one aspect of their writing each time.

For example, the first review may be to examine the writing content, while the second review may focus on spelling, grammar, and punctuation. Another task should focus on language usage, wherein writers consider the writing style chosen and evaluate whether or not this style is appropriate for delivering the intended message to the intended audience. The writing structure is another area of focus that allows the writer to evaluate the introduction, body, and conclusion. Does the writing clearly introduce the topic, does the body gradually strengthen the writer's point of view with relevant and reliable sources and examples, and does the conclusion restate the writer's message in a concise and effective manner?

Another helpful strategy during this stage is to display any graphic organizers used during the planning stage and read the work aloud to another person to receive constructive feedback and to welcome other perspectives and ideas. This person can refer to the planning stage as the writer reads and can make connections as to whether or not the writer has stayed on topic.

Organization

Good writing is not merely a random collection of sentences. No matter how well written, sentences must relate and coordinate appropriately with one another. If not, the writing seems random, haphazard, and disorganized. Therefore, good writing must be organized, where each sentence fits a larger context and relates to the sentences around it.

Logical Sequence

Even if the writer includes plenty of information to support their point, the writing is only coherent when the information is in a logical order. First, the writer should introduce the main idea, whether for a paragraph, a section, or the entire piece. Second, they should present evidence to support the main idea by using transitional language. This shows the reader how the information relates to the main idea and to the sentences around it. The writer should then take time to interpret the information, making sure necessary connections are obvious to the reader. Finally, the writer can summarize the information in a closing section.

Though most writing follows this pattern, it isn't a set rule. Sometimes writers change the order for effect. For example, the writer can begin with a surprising piece of supporting information to grab the reader's attention, and then transition to the main idea. Thus, if a passage doesn't follow the logical order, don't immediately assume it's wrong. However, most writing usually settles into a logical sequence after a nontraditional beginning.

Introductions and Conclusions

Examining the writer's strategies for introductions and conclusions puts the reader in the right mindset to interpret the rest of the text. Look for methods the writer might use for introductions such as:

- Stating the main point immediately, followed by outlining how the rest of the piece supports this claim.

- Establishing important, smaller pieces of the main idea first, and then grouping these points into a case for the main idea.

- Opening with a quotation, anecdote, question, seeming paradox, or other piece of interesting information, and then using it to lead to the main point.

Whatever method the writer chooses, the introduction should make their intention clear, establish their voice as a credible one, and encourage a person to continue reading.

Conclusions tend to follow a similar pattern. In them, the writer restates their main idea a final time, often after summarizing the smaller pieces of that idea. If the introduction uses a quote or anecdote to grab the reader's attention, the conclusion often makes reference to it again. Whatever way the writer chooses to arrange the conclusion, the final restatement of the main idea should be clear and simple for the reader to interpret. Finally, conclusions shouldn't introduce any new information.

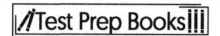

Propositions and Support

Proposition

The **proposition** (also called the **claim** since it can be true or false) is a clear statement of the point or idea the writer is trying to make. The length or format of a proposition can vary, but it often takes the form of a **topic sentence**. A good topic sentence is:

- Clear: does not weave a complicated web of words for the reader to decode or unwrap

- Concise: presents only the information needed to make the claim and doesn't clutter up the statement with unnecessary details

- Precise: clarifies the exact point the writer wants to make and doesn't use broad, overreaching statements

Look at the following example:

> The civil rights movement, from its genesis in the Emancipation Proclamation to its current struggles with de facto discrimination, has changed the face of the United States more than any other factor in its history.

Is the statement clear? Yes, the statement is fairly clear, although other words can be substituted for "genesis" and "de facto" to make it easier to understand.

Is the statement concise? No, the statement is not concise. Details about the Emancipation Proclamation and the current state of the movement are unnecessary for a topic sentence. Those details should be saved for the body of the text.

Is the statement precise? No, the statement is not precise. What exactly does the writer mean by "changed the face of the United States"? The writer should be more specific about the effects of the movement. Also, suggesting that something has a greater impact than anything else in US history is far too ambitious a statement to make.

A better version might look like this:

> The civil rights movement has greatly increased the career opportunities available for Black Americans.

The unnecessary language and details are removed, and the claim can now be measured and supported.

Support

Once the main idea or proposition is stated, the writer attempts to prove or **support** the claim with text evidence and supporting details.

Take for example the sentence, "Seat belts save lives." Though most people can't argue with this statement, its impact on the reader is much greater when supported by additional content. The writer can support this idea by:

- Providing statistics on the rate of highway fatalities alongside statistics for estimated seat belt usage.

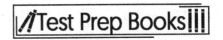

- Explaining the science behind a car accident and what happens to a passenger who doesn't use a seat belt.

- Offering anecdotal evidence or true stories from reliable sources on how seat belts prevent fatal injuries in car crashes.

However, using only one form of supporting evidence is not nearly as effective as using a variety to support a claim. Presenting only a list of statistics can be boring to the reader, but providing a true story that's both interesting and humanizing helps. In addition, one example isn't always enough to prove the writer's larger point, so combining it with other examples is extremely effective for the writing.

Another key aspect of supporting evidence is a *reliable source*. Is the source well known and trustworthy? Is there a potential for bias? For example, a seat belt study done by a seat belt manufacturer may have its own agenda to promote.

Focus

Good writing stays focused and on topic. Let's go back to the seat belt example. If the writer suddenly begins talking about how well airbags, crumple zones, or other safety features work to save lives, they might be losing focus from the topic of "safety belts."

Focus can also refer to individual sentences. Sometimes the writer does address the main topic, but in a confusing way. For example:

> Thanks to seat belt usage, survival in serious car accidents has shown a consistently steady increase since the development of the retractable seat belt in the 1950s.

This statement is definitely on topic, but it's not easy to follow. A simpler, more focused version of this sentence might look like this:

> Seat belts have consistently prevented car fatalities since the 1950s.

Providing adequate information is another aspect of focused writing. Statements like "seat belts are important" and "many people drive cars" are true, but they're so general that they don't contribute much to the writer's case. When writing, avoid these kinds of unfocused statements.

Transitions

Transitions are the glue that holds the writing together. They function to purposefully incorporate new topics and supporting details in a smooth and coherent way. Usually, transitions are found at the beginnings of sentences, but they can also be located in the middle as a way to link clauses together. There are two types of clauses: independent and dependent as discussed in the language use and vocabulary section.

Transition words connect clauses within and between sentences for smoother writing. "I dislike apples. They taste like garbage." is choppier than "I dislike apples because they taste like garbage." Transitions demonstrate the relationship between ideas, allow for more complex sentence structures, and can alert the reader to which type of organizational format the author is using.

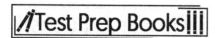
Transition words can be categorized based on the relationships they create between ideas:

- **General order**: signaling elaboration of an idea to emphasize a point—e.g., *for example, for instance, to demonstrate, including, such as, in other words, that is, in fact, also, furthermore, likewise, and, truly, so, surely, certainly, obviously, doubtless*

- **Chronological order**: referencing the time frame in which the main event or idea occurs—e.g., *before, after, first, while, soon, shortly thereafter, meanwhile*

- **Numerical order/order of importance**: indicating that related ideas, supporting details, or events will be described in a sequence, possibly in order of importance—e.g., *first, second, also, finally, another, in addition, equally important, less importantly, most significantly, the main reason, last but not least*

- **Spatial order**: referring to the space and location of something or where things are located in relation to each other—e.g., *inside, outside, above, below, within, close, under, over, far, next to, adjacent to*

- **Cause and effect order**: signaling a causal relationship between events or ideas—e.g., *thus, therefore, since, resulted in, for this reason, as a result, consequently, hence, for, so*

- **Compare and contrast order**: identifying the similarities and differences between two or more objects, ideas, or lines of thought—e.g., *like, as, similarly, equally, just as, unlike, however, but, although, conversely, on the other hand, on the contrary*

- **Summary order**: indicating that a particular idea is coming to a close—e.g., *in conclusion, to sum up, in other words, ultimately, above all*

Sophisticated writing also aims to avoid overuse of transitions and ensure that those used are meaningful. Using a variety of transitions makes the writing appear more lively and informed and helps readers follow the progression of ideas.

The writer should act as a guide, showing the reader how all the sentences fit together. Consider the seat belt example again:

> Seat belts save more lives than any other automobile safety feature. Many studies show that airbags save lives as well. Not all cars have airbags. Many older cars don't. Air bags aren't entirely reliable. Studies show that in 15% of accidents, airbags don't deploy as designed. Seat belt malfunctions are extremely rare.

There's nothing wrong with any of these sentences individually, but together they're disjointed and difficult to follow. The best way for the writer to communicate information is through the use of transition words. Here are examples of transition words and phrases that tie sentences together, enabling a more natural flow:

- To show causality: *as a result, therefore,* and *consequently*
- To compare and contrast: *however, but,* and *on the other hand*
- To introduce examples: *for instance, namely,* and *including*
- To show order of importance: *foremost, primarily, secondly,* and *lastly*

Here is an update to the previous example using transition words. These changes make it easier to read and bring clarity to the writer's points:

> Seat belts save more lives than any other automobile safety feature. Many studies show that airbags save lives as well; however, not all cars have airbags. For instance, some older cars don't. Furthermore, air bags aren't entirely reliable. For example, studies show that in 15% of accidents, airbags don't deploy as designed, but, on the other hand, seat belt malfunctions are extremely rare.

Also, be prepared to analyze whether the writer is using the best transition word or phrase for the situation. Take this sentence for example: "As a result, seat belt malfunctions are extremely rare." This sentence doesn't make sense in the context above because the writer is trying to show the contrast between seat belts and airbags, not the causality.

Point of View

Point of view is another important writing device to consider. In fiction writing, point of view refers to who tells the story or from whose perspective readers are observing the story. In nonfiction writing, the point of view refers to whether the author refers to himself or herself, their readers, or chooses not to refer to either. Whether fiction or nonfiction, the author carefully considers the impact the perspective will have on the purpose and main point of the writing.

- **First-person point of view**: The story is told from the writer's perspective. In fiction, this would mean that the main character is also the narrator. First-person point of view is easily recognized by the use of personal pronouns such as *I, me, we, us, our, my*, and *myself*.

- **Third-person point of view**: In a more formal essay, this would be an appropriate perspective because the focus should be on the subject matter, not the writer or the reader. Third-person point of view is recognized by the use of the pronouns *he, she, they*, and *it*. In fiction writing, third-person point of view has a few variations.

  - **Third-person limited point of view** refers to a story told by a narrator who has access to the thoughts and feelings of just one character.

  - In **third-person omniscient point of view**, the narrator has access to the thoughts and feelings of all the characters.

  - In **third-person objective point of view**, the narrator is like a fly on the wall and can see and hear what the characters do and say but does not have access to their thoughts and feelings.

- **Second-person point of view**: This point of view isn't commonly used in fiction or nonfiction writing because it directly addresses the reader using the pronouns *you, your*, and *yourself*. Second-person perspective is more appropriate in direct communication, such as business letters or emails.

Point of View	Pronouns used
First person	I, me, we, us, our, my, myself
Second person	You, your, yourself
Third person	He, she, it, they

77

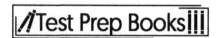
Word Choice

Precision

People often think of precision in terms of math, but precise word choice is another key to successful writing. Since language itself is imprecise, it's important for the writer to find the exact word or words to convey the full, intended meaning of a given situation. For example:

> The number of deaths has gone down since seat belt laws started.

There are several problems with this sentence. First, the word *deaths* is too general. From the context, it's assumed that the writer is referring only to deaths caused by car accidents. However, without clarification, the sentence lacks impact and is probably untrue. The phrase "gone down" might be accurate, but a more precise word could provide more information and greater accuracy. Did the numbers show a slow and steady decrease of highway fatalities or a sudden drop? If the latter is true, the writer is missing a chance to make their point more dramatically. Instead of "gone down" they could substitute *plummeted*, *fallen drastically*, or *rapidly diminished* to bring the information to life. Also, the phrase "seat belt laws" is unclear. Does it refer to laws requiring cars to include seat belts or to laws requiring drivers and passengers to use them? Finally, *started* is not a strong verb. Words like *enacted* or *adopted* are more direct and make the content more real. When put together, these changes create a far more powerful sentence:

> The number of highway fatalities has plummeted since laws requiring seat belt usage were enacted.

However, it's important to note that precise word choice can sometimes be taken too far. If the writer of the sentence above takes precision to an extreme, it might result in the following:

> The incidence of high-speed, automobile accident related fatalities has decreased 75% and continued to remain at historical lows since the initial set of federal legislations requiring seat belt use were enacted in 1992.

This sentence is extremely precise, but it takes so long to achieve that precision that it suffers from a lack of clarity. Precise writing is about finding the right balance between information and flow. This is also an issue of conciseness.

The last thing to consider with precision is a word choice that's not only unclear or uninteresting, but also confusing or misleading. For example:

> The number of highway fatalities has become hugely lower since laws requiring seat belt use were enacted.

In this case, the reader might be confused by the word *hugely*. Huge means large, but here the writer uses *hugely* to describe something small. Though most readers can decipher this, doing so disconnects them from the flow of the writing and makes the writer's point less effective.

Strong Words and Phrases

If a writer feels strongly about a subject, or has a passion for it, strong words and phrases can be chosen. Think of the types of rhetoric (or language) our politicians use. Each word, phrase, and idea is carefully crafted to elicit a response. Hopefully, that response is one of agreement to a certain point of view, especially among voters. Writers use the same types of language to achieve the same results. For example, the word "bad" has a

certain connotation, but the words "horrid," "repugnant," and "abhorrent" paint a far better picture for the reader. They're more precise. They're interesting to read and they should all illicit stronger feelings in the reader than the word "bad." Writers should look for words and phrases that capture one's attention. Consider words that make the reader feel sounds and envision imagery. Pay attention to the rhythm of fluid sentences and to the use of words that evoke emotion.

Clear and Coherent Writing

Coherent writing uses a logical order and consists of information that is both relevant to the topic and reliable. Coherent writing ensures that the language usage appropriately activates the audience's background knowledge and keeps the audience interested. For writing to be considered coherent, the author must also consider the structure and its relevance to the writing goal.

Although separate and distinct in definition, both coherent writing and writing clarity are interrelated and impact each other. For writing to be fully coherent, it must also be written clearly and for writing to be written clearly, it needs to be coherent. **Writing clarity** refers to the conventions of the English language. Has the author paid considerable attention to the spelling, grammar, and punctuation? For example, the misspelling of a word can confuse a reader and negatively impact writing clarity. The use of visual aids in the form of graphs, diagrams, maps, and charts can also greatly strengthen the writing clarity by allowing students to see examples of what they are reading.

Concise Writing

"Less is more" is a good rule to follow when writing. Unfortunately, writers often include extra words and phrases that seem necessary at the time but add nothing to the main idea. This confuses the reader and creates unnecessary repetition. Writing that lacks conciseness is usually guilty of excessive wordiness and redundant phrases. Here's an example containing both of these issues:

> When legislators decided to begin creating legislation making it mandatory for automobile drivers and passengers to make use of seat belts while in cars, a large number of them made those laws for reasons that were political reasons.

There are several empty or "fluff" words here that take up too much space. These can be eliminated while still maintaining the writer's meaning. For example:

- "Decided to begin" could be shortened to "began"
- "Making it mandatory for" could be shortened to "requiring"
- "Make use of" could be shortened to "use"
- "A large number" could be shortened to "many"

In addition, there are several examples of redundancy that can be eliminated:

- "Legislators decided to begin creating legislation" and "made those laws"
- "Automobile drivers and passengers" and "while in cars"
- "Reasons that were political reasons"

These changes are incorporated as follows:

> When legislators began requiring drivers and passengers to use seat belts, many of them did so for political reasons.

79

There are many general examples of redundant phrases, such as "add an additional," "complete and total," "time schedule," and "transportation vehicle." If asked to identify a redundant phrase on the test, look for words that are close together with the same (or similar) meanings.

Mode and Purpose of Writing

To distinguish between the common modes of writing, it is important to identify the primary purpose for the work. The writer can determine this by deciding what they want to say to the reader. Although there are countless different styles of writing, all written works tend to fall under four primary categories: argumentative/persuasive, informative expository, descriptive, and narrative.

The table below highlights the purpose, distinct characteristics, and examples of each rhetorical mode:

Writing Mode	Purpose	Distinct Characteristics	Examples
Argumentative	To persuade	Opinions, loaded or subjective language, evidence, suggestions of what the reader should do, calls to action	Critical reviews Political journals Letters of recommendation Cover letters Advertising
Informative	To teach or inform	Objective language, definitions, instructions, factual information	Business and scientific reports Textbooks Instruction manuals News articles Personal letters Wills Informative essays Travel guides Study guides
Descriptive	To deliver sensory details to the reader	Heavy use of adjectives and imagery, language that appeals to any of the five senses	Poetry Journal entries Often used in narrative mode
Narrative	To tell a story, share an experience, entertain	Series of events, plot, characters, dialogue, conflict	Novels Short stories Novellas Anecdotes Biographies Epic poems Autobiographies

The author's *primary purpose* is defined as the reason an author chooses to write a selection, and it is often dependent on their *audience*. A biologist writing a textbook, for example, does so to communicate scientific knowledge to an audience of people who want to study biology. An audience can be as broad as the entire global population or as specific as women fighting for equal rights in the bicycle repair industry. Whatever the

80

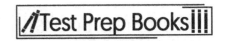
audience, it is important that the author considers its demographics—age, gender, culture, language, education level, etc.

If the author's purpose is to persuade or inform, he or she will consider how much the intended audience knows about the subject. For example, if an author is writing on the importance of recycling to anyone who will listen, he or she will use the informative mode—including background information on recycling—and the argumentative mode—evidence for why it works, while also using simple diction so that it is easy for everyone to understand. If, on the other hand, the writer is proposing new methods for recycling using solar energy, the audience is probably already familiar with standard recycling processes and will require less background information, as well as more technical language inherent to the scientific community.

If the author's purpose is to entertain through a story or a poem, he or she will need to consider whom he/she is trying to entertain. If an author is writing a script for a children's cartoon, the plot, language, conflict, characters, and humor would align with the interests of the age demographic of that audience. On the other hand, if an author is trying to entertain adults, he or she may write content not suitable for children. The author's purpose and audience are generally interdependent.

Style, Tone, and Audience

An author's *writing style*—the way in which words, grammar, punctuation, and sentence fluidity are used—is the most influential element in a piece of writing, and it is dependent on the purpose and the audience for whom it is intended. Together, a writing style and mode of writing form the foundation of a written work, and a good writer will choose the most effective mode and style to convey a message to readers.

Writers should first determine what they are trying to say and then choose the most effective mode of writing to communicate that message. Different writing modes and *word choices* will affect the tone of a piece—that is, its underlying attitude, emotion, or character. The argumentative mode may utilize words that are earnest, angry, passionate, or excited whereas an informative piece may have a sterile, germane, or enthusiastic tone. The tones found in narratives vary greatly, depending on the purpose of the writing. *Tone* will also be affected by the audience—teaching science to children or those who may be uninterested would be most effective with enthusiastic language and exclamation points whereas teaching science to college students may take on a more serious and professional tone, with fewer charged words and punctuation choices that are inherent to academia.

Sentence fluidity—whether sentences are long and rhythmic or short and succinct—also affects a piece of writing as it determines the way in which a piece is read. Children or audiences unfamiliar with a subject do better with short, succinct sentence structures as these break difficult concepts up into shorter points. A period, question mark, or exclamation point is literally a signal for the reader to stop and takes more time to process. Thus, longer, more complex sentences are more appropriate for adults or educated audiences as they can fit more information in between processing time.

The amount of *supporting detail* provided is also tailored to the audience. A text that introduces a new subject to its readers will focus more on broad ideas without going into greater detail whereas a text that focuses on a more specific subject is likely to provide greater detail about the ideas discussed.

Writing styles, like modes, are most effective when tailored to their audiences. Having awareness of an audience's demographic is one of the most crucial aspects of properly communicating an argument, a story, or a set of information.

Choosing the Most Appropriate Type of Writing

Before beginning any writing, it is imperative that a writer have a firm grasp on the message he or she wishes to convey and how he or she wants readers to be affected by the writing. For example, does the author want readers to be more informed about the subject? Does the writer want readers to agree with their opinion? Does the writer want readers to get caught up in an exciting narrative? The following steps are a guide to determining the appropriate type of writing for a task, purpose, and audience:

- Step 1: Identifying the purpose for writing the piece
- Step 2: Determining the audience
- Step 3: Adapting the writing mode, word choices, tone, and style to fit the audience and the purpose

It is important to distinguish between a work's purpose and its main idea. The essential difference between the two is that the *main idea* is what the author wants to communicate about the topic at hand whereas the *primary purpose* is why the author is writing in the first place. The primary purpose is what will determine the type of writing an author will choose to utilize, not the main idea, though the two are related. For example, if an author writes an article on the mistreatment of animals in factory farms and, at the end, suggests that people should convert to vegetarianism, the main idea is that vegetarianism would reduce the poor treatment of animals. The primary purpose is to convince the reader to stop eating animals. Since the primary purpose is to galvanize an audience into action, the author would choose the argumentative writing mode.

The next step is to consider to whom the author is appealing as this will determine the type of details to be included, the diction to be used, the tone to be employed, and the sentence structure to be used. An audience can be identified by considering the following questions:

- What is the purpose for writing the piece?

- To whom is it being written?

- What is their age range?

- Are they familiar with the material being presented, or are they just being newly introduced to it?

- Where are they from?

- Is the task at hand in a professional or casual setting?

- Is the task at hand for monetary gain?

These are just a few of the numerous considerations to keep in mind, but the main idea is to become as familiar with the audience as possible. Once the audience has been understood, the author can then adapt the writing style to align with the readers' education and interests. The audience is what determines the *rhetorical appeal* the author will use—ethos, pathos, or logos. *Ethos* is a rhetorical appeal to an audience's ethics and/or morals. Ethos is most often used in argumentative and informative writing modes. *Pathos* is an appeal to the audience's emotions and sympathies, and it is found in argumentative, descriptive, and narrative writing modes. *Logos* is an appeal to the audience's logic and reason and is used primarily in informative texts as well as in supporting details for argumentative pieces. Rhetorical appeals are discussed in depth in the informational texts and rhetoric section of the test.

If the author is trying to encourage global conversion to vegetarianism, he or she may choose to use all three rhetorical appeals to reach varying personality types. Those who are less interested in the welfare of animals but are interested in facts and science would relate more to logos. Animal lovers would relate better to an emotional appeal. In general, the most effective works utilize all three appeals.

Finally, after determining the writing mode and rhetorical appeal, the author will consider word choice, sentence structure, and tone, depending on the purpose and audience. The author may choose words that convey sadness or anger when speaking about animal welfare if writing to persuade, or he or she will stick to dispassionate and matter-of-fact tones, if informing the public on the treatment of animals in factory farms. If the author is writing to a younger or less-educated audience, he or she may choose to shorten and simplify sentence structures and word choice. If appealing to an audience with more expert knowledge on a particular subject, writers will more likely employ a style of longer sentences and more complex vocabulary.

Depending on the task, the author may choose to use a first person, second person, or third person point of view. First person and second person perspectives are inherently more casual in tone, including the author and the reader in the rhetoric, while third person perspectives are often seen in more professional settings.

Evaluating the Effectiveness of a Piece of Writing

An effective and engaging piece of writing will cause the reader to forget about the author entirely. Readers will become so engrossed in the subject, argument, or story at hand that they will almost identify with it, readily adopting beliefs proposed by the author or accepting all elements of the story as believable. On the contrary, poorly written works will cause the reader to be hyperaware of the author, doubting the writer's knowledge of a subject or questioning the validity of a narrative. Persuasive or expository works that are poorly researched will have this effect, as well as poorly planned stories with significant plot holes. An author must consider the task, purpose, and audience to sculpt a piece of writing effectively.

When evaluating the effectiveness of a piece, the most important thing to consider is how well the purpose is conveyed to the audience through the mode, use of rhetoric, and writing style.

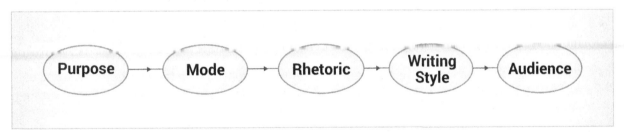

The purpose must pass through these three aspects for effective delivery to the audience. If any elements are not properly considered, the reader will be overly aware of the author, and the message will be lost.

The following is a checklist for evaluating the effectiveness of a piece:

- Does the writer choose the appropriate writing mode—argumentative, narrative, descriptive, informative—for their purpose?

- Does the writing mode employed contain characteristics inherent to that mode?

- Does the writer consider the personalities/interests/demographics of the intended audience when choosing rhetorical appeals?

- Does the writer use appropriate vocabulary, sentence structure, voice, and tone for the audience demographic?

- Does the author properly establish himself/herself as having authority on the subject, if applicable?

- Does the piece make sense?

Another thing to consider is the medium in which the piece was written. If the medium is a blog, diary, or personal letter, the author may adopt a more casual stance towards the audience. If the piece of writing is a story in a book, a business letter or report, or a published article in a journal or if the task is to gain money or support or to get published, the author may adopt a more formal stance. Ultimately, the writer will want to be very careful in how he or she addresses the reader.

Style, Tone, and Mood

Style, tone, and mood are often thought to be the same thing. Though they're closely related, there are important differences to keep in mind. The easiest way to do this is to remember that style "creates and affects" tone and mood. More specifically, style is *how the writer uses words* to create the desired tone and mood for their writing.

Style
Style can include any number of technical writing choices. A few examples of style choices include:

- Sentence Construction: When presenting facts, does the writer use shorter sentences to create a quicker sense of the supporting evidence, or do they use longer sentences to elaborate and explain the information?

- Technical Language: Does the writer use jargon to demonstrate their expertise in the subject, or do they use ordinary language to help the reader understand things in simple terms?

- Formal Language: Does the writer refrain from using contractions such as *won't* or *can't* to create a more formal tone, or do they use a colloquial, conversational style to connect to the reader?

- Formatting: Does the writer use a series of shorter paragraphs to help the reader follow a line of argument, or do they use longer paragraphs to examine an issue in great detail and demonstrate their knowledge of the topic?

Tone
Tone refers to the writer's attitude toward the subject matter. Tone conveys how the writer feels about characters, situations, events, ideas, etc. Nonfiction writing is sometimes thought to have no tone at all, but this is incorrect.

A lot of nonfiction writing has a neutral tone, which is an extremely important tone for the writer to take. A neutral tone demonstrates that the writer is presenting a topic impartially and letting the information speak for itself. On the other hand, nonfiction writing can be just as effective and appropriate if the tone isn't neutral. For instance, take the previous examples involving seat belt use. In them, the writer mostly chooses to retain a neutral tone when presenting information. If the writer would instead include their own personal experience of losing a friend or family member in a car accident, the tone would change dramatically. The tone would no longer be neutral. Now it would show that the writer has a personal stake in the content, allowing

84

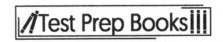

them to interpret the information in a different way. When analyzing tone, consider what the writer is trying to achieve in the passage, and how they *create* the tone using style.

Mood

Mood refers to the feelings and atmosphere that the writer's words create for the reader. Like tone, many nonfiction pieces can have a neutral mood. To return to the previous example, if the writer would choose to include information about a person they know being killed in a car accident, the passage would suddenly carry an emotional component that is absent in the previous examples. Depending on how they present the information, the writer can create a sad, angry, or even hopeful mood. When analyzing the mood, consider what the writer wants to accomplish and whether the best choice was made to achieve that end.

Consistency

Whatever style, tone, and mood the writer uses, good writing should remain consistent throughout. If the writer chooses to include the tragic, personal experience above, it would affect the style, tone, and mood of the entire piece. It would seem out of place for such an example to be used in the middle of a neutral, measured, and analytical piece. To adjust the rest of the piece, the writer needs to make additional choices to remain consistent. For example, the writer might decide to use the word *tragedy* in place of the more neutral *fatality*, or they could describe a series of car-related deaths as an *epidemic*. Adverbs and adjectives such as *devastating* or *horribly* could be included to maintain this consistent attitude toward the content. When analyzing writing, look for sudden shifts in style, tone, and mood, and consider whether the writer would be wiser to maintain the prevailing strategy.

Composing Writing of Different Genres

No matter the genre or format, all authors are writing to persuade, inform, entertain, or express feelings. Often, these purposes are blended, with one dominating the rest. It's useful to learn to recognize the author's intent.

Persuasive writing is used to persuade or convince readers of something. It often contains two elements: the argument and the counterargument. The argument takes a stance on an issue, while the counterargument pokes holes in the opposition's stance. Authors rely on logic, emotion, and writer credibility to persuade readers to agree with them. If readers are opposed to the stance before reading, they are unlikely to adopt that stance. However, those who are undecided or committed to the same stance are more likely to agree with the author.

Informative writing tries to teach or inform. Workplace manuals, instructor lessons, statistical reports, and cookbooks are examples of informative texts. Informative writing is usually based on facts and is often void of emotion and persuasion. Informative texts generally contain statistics, charts, and graphs. Though most informative texts lack a persuasive agenda, readers still must examine the text carefully to determine whether one exists within a given passage.

Stories or narratives are designed to entertain. When you go to the movies, you often want to escape for a few hours, not necessarily to think critically. Entertaining writing is designed to delight and engage the reader. However, sometimes this type of writing can be woven into more serious materials, such as persuasive or informative writing to hook the reader before transitioning into a more scholarly discussion.

Emotional writing works to evoke the reader's feelings, such as anger, euphoria, or sadness. The connection between reader and author is an attempt to cause the reader to share the author's intended emotion or tone.

85

Sometimes in order to make a piece more poignant, the author simply wants readers to feel the same emotions that the author has felt. Other times, the author attempts to persuade or manipulate the reader into adopting his stance. While it's okay to sympathize with the author, be aware of the individual's underlying intent.

Letters

Composition

When composing letters, it is important for the writer to think about their audience and how they will receive the motive of the letter. For example, if the letter is written to express the author's feelings about student loan debt, it may be effective to gear the letter toward college-aged adults. Regardless of the subject, the writing should be presented in a way that suits the people reading it.

Although letters are less formal than research reports, there should still be a focus on clarity and logic within the writing. Stay focused on the purpose of the letter and use factual information to support it. Use a strong voice within the writing with which the reader can connect. This could be done through including compassionate or motivational language. It is effective to use *we* and *us* as inclusive pronouns. This kind of tone in the writing will keep readers engaged and willing to listen.

Analysis

When analyzing letters, the main objective is to understand what the author is trying to convey. Every letter has a purpose or message that the author wants the reader to take away. It is helpful to understand who the author is, what their background is like, and why they might have written the letter. The same goes for the recipient of the letter. Knowing the relationship between the writer and the audience will help with understanding the purpose and tone of the letter.

Letters are primary sources of information and are not generally polished like a scholarly article. An understanding of the author may reveal biases that exist in their writing. This context may help readers analyze the soundness of the letter's argument within the context it was written. Take notes on the topic, evidence, tone, and structure of the letter.

To demonstrate, the following passage has been marked to illustrate *the addressee*, the author's purpose, and word choices:

> *To Whom It May Concern*:
>
> I am <u>extraordinarily excited</u> to be applying to the Master of Environmental Science program at Australian National University. I believe the richness in biological and cultural diversity, as well as Australia's close proximity to the Great Barrier Reef, would provide a <u>deeply fulfilling</u> educational experience. *I am writing to express why I believe I would be an <u>excellent</u> addition to the program.*
>
> While in college, I participated in a three-month public health internship in Ecuador, where I spent time both learning about medicine in a third world country and also about the Ecuadorian environment, including the Amazon Jungle and the Galápagos Islands. <u>My favorite experience</u> through the internship, besides swimming with sea lions in San Cristóbal, was helping to neutralize parasitic potable water and collect samples for analysis in Puyo.

Though my undergraduate studies related primarily to the human body, I took several courses in natural science, including a year of chemistry, biology, and physics as well as a course in a calculus. <u>I am confident</u> that my fundamental knowledge in these fields will prepare me for the science courses integral to the Masters of Environmental Science.

Having identified the *addressee*, it is evident that this selection is a letter of some kind. Further inspection into the author's purpose shows that the author is trying to explain why he or she should be accepted into the environmental science program, which automatically places it into the argumentative mode as the writer is trying to persuade the reader to agree and to incite the reader into action by encouraging the program to accept the writer as a candidate. In addition to revealing the purpose, the use of emotional language—extraordinarily, excellent, deeply fulfilling, favorite experience, confident—illustrates that this is a persuasive piece. It also provides evidence for why this person would be an excellent addition to the program—their experience in Ecuador and with scientific curriculum.

Arguments

Composition

Strong arguments tend to follow a fairly defined format. In the introduction, background information regarding the problem is shared, the implications of the issue, and the writer's thesis or claims. Supporting evidence is then presented in the body paragraphs, along with the counterargument, which then gets refuted with specific evidence. Lastly, in the conclusion, the writer summarizes the points and claims again.

Arguments use evidence and reasoning to support a position or prove a point. Claims are typically controversial and may be faced with some degree of contention. Thus, writers support claims with evidence. Two arguments might present different types of evidence that readers will need to evaluate for merit, worthiness, accuracy, relevance, and impact. Evidence can take on many forms such as numbers (statistics, measurements, numerical data, etc.), expert opinions or quotes, testimonies, anecdotal evidence or stories from individuals, and textual evidence, such as that obtained from documents like diaries, newspapers, and laws.

Premises and Conclusions

Premises are the why, and **conclusions** are the what. Stated differently, premises are the evidence or facts supporting why the conclusion is logical and valid. Logically-sound arguments do not require evaluation of the factual accuracy; instead, an argument's logical strength is assessed. For example:

John eats all red food. Apples are red. Therefore, John eats apples.

This argument is logically sound, despite having no factual basis in reality. Below is an example of a practice argument:

Julie is an American track athlete. She's the star of the number one collegiate team in the country. Her times are consistently at the top of national rankings. Julie is extremely likely to represent the United States at the upcoming Olympics.

In this example, the conclusion, or the *what*, is that she will likely be on the American Olympic team. The author supports this conclusion with two premises. First, Julie is the star of an elite track team. Second, she runs some of the best times of the country. This is the *why* behind the conclusion. The following builds off this basic argument:

Julie is an American track athlete. She's the star of the number one collegiate team in the country. Her times are consistently at the top of national rankings. Julie is extremely likely to represent the United States at the upcoming Olympics. Julie will continue to develop after the Olympic trials. She will be a frontrunner for the gold. Julie is likely to become a world-famous track star.

These additions to the argument make the conclusion different. Now, the conclusion is that Julie is likely to become a world-famous track star. The previous conclusion, Julie will likely be on the Olympic team, functions as a **sub-conclusion** in this argument. Like conclusions, premises must adequately support sub-conclusions. However, sub-conclusions function like premises, since sub-conclusions also support the overall conclusion.

Analysis

A reader must be able to evaluate the argument or point the author is trying to make and determine if it is adequately supported. The first step is to determine the main idea. The main idea is what the author wants to say about a specific topic. The next step is to locate the supporting details. An author uses supporting details to illustrate the main idea. These are the details that provide evidence or examples to help make a point. Supporting details often appear in the form of quotations, paraphrasing, or analysis. Readers should then examine the text to make sure the author connects details and analysis to the main point. These steps are crucial to understanding the text and evaluating how well the author presents their argument and evidence. The following graphic demonstrates the connection between the main idea and the supporting details.

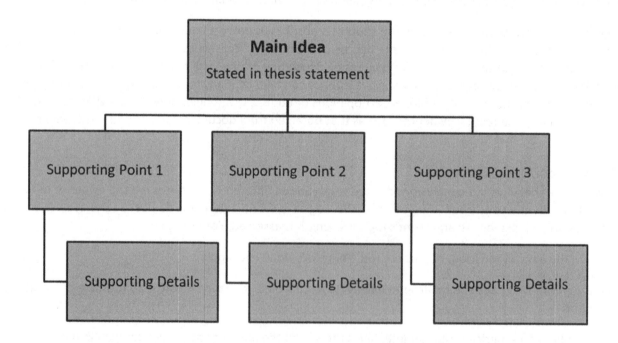

A reader must also be able to identify any **logical fallacies**—logically-flawed statements—that an author may make as those fallacies impact the validity and veracity of the author's claims.

88

Some of the more common fallacies are shown in the following chart:

Fallacy	Definition
Slippery Slope	A fallacy that is built on the idea that a particular action will lead to a series of events with negative results
Red Herring	The use of an observation or distraction to remove attention from the actual issue
Straw Man	An exaggeration or misrepresentation of an argument so that it is easier to refute
Post Hoc Ergo Propter Hoc	A fallacy that assumes an event to be the consequence of an earlier event merely because it came after it
Bandwagon	A fallacy that assumes because the majority of people feel or believe a certain way then it must be the right way
Ad Hominem	The use of a personal attack on the person or persons associated with a certain argument rather than focusing on the actual argument itself

Readers who are aware of the types of fallacious reasoning are able to weigh the credibility of the author's statements in terms of effective argument. Rhetorical text that contains a myriad of fallacious statements should be considered ineffectual and suspect.

Composing Informative/Explanatory Text

Writing informative and explanatory texts such as career development documents is a useful skill to have. This may include business letters, job applications, or project proposals. These are documents that serve a specific purpose and need to reflect a certain level of professionalism. They often need to capture the interests of the readers and convey the abilities of the writer.

In general, informative texts should be organized and logical. They often will require evidence that is well researched and scholarly. The amount of time spent on research will depend largely on the document being written. A job application will not need the research that a project proposal does.

To begin, it is necessary to identify the subject of the writing. The context of the writing will depend on its explanatory purpose. After the subject is nailed down, decide what related points should be covered. For example, if tasked with writing a project proposal related to environmental conservation for work, multiple subjects, such as agriculture and fracking, could be included. Narrowing down the purpose of the writing will make it easier to research scholarly articles within library databases and online.

Some informative texts require in-depth explanations, whereas others should remain as concise as possible. The structure of the writing will depend on the context. A business letter should remain brief, and a research report may be lengthier. Regardless of the length, the writing should be structured in a way that clearly presents the topic at the beginning, necessary information in the body, and a conclusion that reminds the reader what they should be taking away from the writing.

The content of the writing should be well developed. Define terms that may be unfamiliar to the audience. Reference data and facts through quotations from studies or the inclusion of visual features. Give examples that break down difficult concepts for ease of understanding. Connect these ideas with topics that may be more relevant to the audience.

An important part of explanatory writing is knowing what information to include and what to leave out. Although it may be tempting to include every detail about a subject, it is typically unnecessary and can overwhelm readers. To discern what information is worth including, pick out main concepts and the most relevant details. What details are vital for the audience to know? From there, analyze which points support the argument being made. It is a good idea to offer a counterpoint or two in some situations. In an argumentative report, address an opposing viewpoint and give a specific rebuttal against it. For example, if writing a report that is against fracking, it may be useful to address why some people are supportive of fracking. Other than situations like this, the information should purely strengthen the writing.

In the case of career development documents, the writing should not be overly exaggerated. For example, a job application or cover letter should be truthful and straightforward. It should emphasize all of a person's skills and experience. However, stretching the truth or sounding arrogant will not work in the person's favor. Let the writing have a genuine tone.

Composing Narratives

When composing a narrative, it is important to find a writing technique that allows for well-structured event sequences and descriptive details. This is true for both real and imagined events. A strong technique will not only make the writing itself better but will also make for a more streamlined process.

One technique that will help in composing narratives is to outline what needs to be written. This could include making a timeline of the events that will be featured. It may also be helpful to map out what the writing will include. A good narrative has a plot, characters, setting, conflict, and theme. Planning these out beforehand will help keep the narrative organized and easy for readers to understand. There are various ways to organize a narrative that can add a stylistic element to the text.

Descriptive details that are both relevant and interesting will keep readers entertained. These may include descriptions of the settings, characters, and events taking place. Including too many details may make the writing seem overly verbose and difficult to follow. Rather than using too many descriptive words, choose specific words that are vivid and convey a lot of meaning without adding excessive length to the narrative. Carefully chosen diction will create imagery for the readers so that they can easily imagine the events they are reading.

Figurative language is another way to strengthen a narrative. Metaphors and similes enrich the writing. Similar to strong diction, figurative language helps create a sensory experience for readers. Using the line, "Her cheeks were as red as roses," adds more depth to the story than simply saying, "Her cheeks were red." This type of writing can make the narrative unique and more entertaining.

90

Summaries

While summarizing information from a text seems like an easy concept at first, it is more complex than one thinks. **Summarizing** involves the ability to extract the most important elements in writing, to eliminate elements of lesser importance, to reorganize the information, to rewrite information in one's own words, and, finally, to condense the writing into a significantly smaller text than that of the original. Thus, learning to summarize consists of many individual skills that all converge and overlap. There are two forms of summary: (1) summaries that aid the reader in understanding the text and (2) summaries that aid others in their understanding of the text.

Summarizing should be explicitly taught beginning in the primary school years with continual reinforcement and gradual introduction to more complex texts as students progress. In order to summarize effectively, children need to demonstrate the following abilities:

- Text comprehension
- Identification of main idea
- Elimination of inconsequential information
- Ability to condense
- Ability to paraphrase
- Ability to organize writing in a logical order

Educators are encouraged to first assist children in summarizing texts as a means to strengthen personal comprehension. For instance, when children are able to identify a text's main idea, state that idea in their own words, and back up that main idea with supporting evidence, they are learning to summarize, and their comprehension undoubtedly strengthens.

Summarizing for oneself is also an invaluable tool for studying and memorizing, which children will use throughout their academic careers. When students summarize for themselves, the goal is to strengthen overall comprehension of the text, arrive at the author's point of view, and isolate the main idea. Since the summary is intended to be only for the student, there is no need to pay particular attention to spelling, grammar, or sentence structure. Students are learning to make personal notes for the purpose of comprehension strengthening and, possibly, memorization for upcoming tests.

Once children have demonstrated a clear ability to summarize a variety of texts for their own understanding, educators may begin to introduce them to the skill of **summarizing for others**. This involves a more complex approach to summarization. Now that students have ownership of the given text, they inherit the challenge of explaining the text's meaning to an audience. In addition to extracting the main idea, eliminating unimportant text elements, reorganizing and condensing the text, and paraphrasing, students must now pay close attention to the summary's length, the mechanics of writing, and the audience. For example, are students writing to classmates to help them better understand the text? Are they writing the summary for their teacher, in an effort to demonstrate their ability to summarize? Since this type of summarization involves a polished finish, children must also employ proofreading and revision skills.

Educators who are introducing summarization for the first time should focus on less complex texts that involve familiar subject matter, and the texts should be well organized, with titles, possible subtitles, and easily identifiable main ideas. Allowing children to refer to the text as often as possible while learning to summarize is also an important teaching strategy. Children at the early stages of summarizing should not be expected to have memorized and clearly understood what they have read. Sometimes children need to reread the same

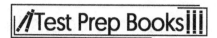

text several times before beginning a summarization. By explicitly teaching children how to recognize signaling devices, educators help them summarize and isolate a text's main idea. Some signaling devices may be found in an introductory or summary statement or specific words or phrases that have been placed in italics, bold print, or are underlined.

The more advanced students become with summarizing texts, the greater their comprehension and ability to apply what they learn will be.

The following checklist lists items that writers should include in a summary:

- Title of the story
- Someone: Who is or are the main character(s)?
- Wanted: What did the character(s) want?
- But: What was the problem?
- So: How did the character(s) solve the problem?
- Then: How did the story end? What was the resolution?

Composing and Analyzing Research Reports

Composition

When composing research reports, there is a methodology that will help with presenting information in a logical and digestible manner. This will help readers understand what they should be taking away from the report for their own use. A strong structure will also allow readers to locate the information they need.

A report should have a strong thesis that is made clear in the beginning. This lets readers know what to expect in the entirety of the report. The majority of the report should be dedicated to going into depth about the thesis using evidence to support any points related to the thesis. The end of the report should summarize the findings.

In addition, a report should have strong references. Information should come from original research or sources that are scholarly and peer-reviewed. This information should be synthesized to relate back to the relevant thesis.

Analysis

It is important to analyze research reports to ensure that they are a factual and reliable source of information. Before even reading the report, the author(s) should be vetted for scholarly merit. Their credibility will help add to the reliability of the report. The same should be done for the publisher of the report.

After checking that the research report is coming from an academic source, there are a few key factors to analyze. First, the report should contain relevant and current information. This information should be backed by evidence and references. The report should be unbiased and cover all angles of the subject. It should present the information in a way that clearly shows the line of logic. At the end, the results of the research report should be clear.

Integrating Technology, Multimedia, and Visual Displays

Teachers are learning to adapt their writing instruction to integrate today's technology standards and to enhance engagement in the writing process. The key is to still build a strong foundation of the fundamentals of

writing while using current technology. Gone are the days when writing relied solely on handwritten pieces and when the tools of the trade were pencils, paper, hardback dictionaries, and encyclopedias. Online resources are now the backbone of the writing experience. It is now possible to integrate photo, video, and other interactive components into a completed project to provide a well-rounded engagement with media. In order to have an education conducive to college and career readiness and success, students need online research and digital media writing skills.

There are many compelling reasons to teach students to be digitally aware and prudent users of technology when it comes to their writing. With current digital technology, the writing process has become a much more collaborative experience. In higher education and in career settings, collaborative skills are essential. Publishing and presenting are now simplified such that completed work is often read by a wide variety of audiences. Writing can be instantly shared with parents, peers, educators, and the general public, including experts in the field. Students are more apt to take an interest in the writing process when they know that others are reading their writing. Feedback is also simplified because so many platforms allow comments from readers. Teachers can be interactive with the students throughout the process, allowing formative assessment and integration of personalized instruction. Technology is simply a new vehicle for human connection and interactivity.

A student may be exposed to a plethora of technology, but this does not mean that she or he necessarily knows how to use it for learning. The teacher is still responsible for guiding, monitoring, and scaffolding the students toward learning objectives. It is critical that educators teach students how to locate credible information and to reliably cite their sources using bibliographies. Platforms and apps for online learning are varied and plentiful.

Here are some ideas for how to use technology for writing instruction in the classroom:

- Use a projector with a tablet to display notes and classwork for the group to see. This increases instructional time because notes are already available rather than having to be written in real-time. This also provides the ability to save, email, and post classwork and notes for students and parents to access on their own time. A student can work at their own pace and still keep up with instruction. Student screens can be displayed for peer-led teaching and sharing of class work.

- More technology in class means less paperwork. Digital drop-boxes can be used for students to turn in assignments. Teachers can save paper, keep track of student revisions of work, and give feedback electronically.

- Digital media can be used to differentiate instruction for multiple learning styles and multiple skill levels. Instead of using standardized textbook learning for everyone, teachers can create and collect resources for individualizing course content.

- Inquiry- and problem-based learning is easier with increased collaborative capabilities provided by digital tools.

- Digital textbooks and e-readers can replace hardback versions of text that are prone to damage and loss. Students can instantly access definitions for new words, as well as annotate and highlight useful information without ruining a hardbound book.

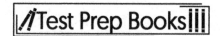

- Library databases can be used to locate reliable research information and resources. There are digital tools for tracking citation information, allowing annotations for internet content, and for storing internet content.

- Mobile devices may be used in the classroom to encourage reading and writing when students use them to text, post, blog, and tweet.

- PowerPoint and other presentation software can be used to model writing for students and to provide a platform for presenting their work.

- Students can create a classroom blog, review various blog sites, and use blogs as they would diaries or journals. They can even write from the perspective of the character in a book or a famous historical person.

- Web quests can be used to help guide students on research projects. They can get relevant information on specific topics and decide what pieces to include in their writing.

- Students can write about technology as a topic. They can "teach" someone how to use various forms of technology, specific learning platforms, or apps.

- Students can create webpages, make a class webpage, and then use it to help with home-school communication.

- Online feedback and grading systems can be used. There are many to choose from. This may allow students to see the grading rubric and ask questions or receive suggestions from the teacher.

- Students and teachers can use email to exchange ideas with other schools or experts on certain topics that are being studied in the classroom.

- Game show-style reviews can be created for units of study to use on computers or on an overhead projector.

- A wiki website can be created that allows students to collaborate, expand on each other's work, and do peer editing and revision.

- Publishing tools can be used to publish student work on the web or in class newspapers or social media sites.

Non-Written and Written Communication: Non-Written Communication

Non-Written Genres and Traditions

Before language was ever put down on paper, poets had been reciting verses in front of audiences for thousands of years. Epic poems, especially, were popular forms of entertainment in Greek culture for their oral storytelling appeal. The storyteller was known as a "rhapsode" and sometimes played a lyre while reciting verse or song. The content of epic poetry was mixed with the myth and folklore of Greek culture. The two most popular epic poems we know of today are *The Iliad* and *The Odyssey*. Another oral poetry tradition that began

in Greece is known as the lyric, made famous by the Greek poet Sappho. Lyrics are close in content and form to modern music: they reflect confessional or personal events or emotions and they are shorter in length than an epic poem.

Characteristics of Non-Written Presentations

A non-written narrative features unique characteristics that differentiate the experience from the written word. It can be expressed orally or through performance. It often has a level of spontaneity that is not found in literature. The organization is often more varied and can change based on the audience. The audience may even be involved in storytelling. It has factors that rely on the storyteller, such as volume, pitch, gestures, and facial expressions. These are unique to non-written narratives and are generally not a part of written communication.

Persuasive pieces rely on capturing the listener's attention and convincing them of something. This could be anything from buying a product to voting for a certain politician. This form of non-written communication relies on ethos, logos, and pathos. Ethos is the credibility of the persuasive speaker and the sources they are using. Logos refers to the logic of their argument. Pathos refers to the emotion they put into their argument. A persuasive piece will combine all three of these for a powerful effect. The speaker may change the balance of ethos, logos, and pathos based on the response of the audience and what they respond to best.

Research presentations should have a clear objective. The thesis for the research should be presented at the beginning and end of the presentation. Research presentations are typically rehearsed and do not have the spontaneity that other forms of non-written communication have. They typically include visual features, such as graphs or maps, that help illustrate the points being made. Research presentations should have references to scholarly information to add credibility.

Poetry recitations vary greatly in their characteristics. This is generally due to the context of the recitation and the contents of the poetry. Poetry is often deeply personal, and the interpretation of the poem will affect its recitation. A poem that is somber will generally have a slower, melancholy tone to its presentation. A poem meant to evoke anger may be louder and more forceful. This is meant to emphasize the poem's meaning and the audience's response to it. Poems often feature rhyme schemes or stylistic organization. The speaker should pay attention to this when reciting the poem aloud.

Non-written responses to literature may range from informal, casual conversation to rehearsed, organized discussion. In the classroom, a group of students may organize photos based on the events, characters, and/or plot in the literature. Everyone in the classroom may share their opinion on the events of the story. These are two examples of non-written responses to literature.

Interpreting Media and Non-Print Text

In the 21st century, rhetoric is evident in a variety of formats. Blogs, vlogs, videos, news footage, advertisements, and live video fill informational feeds, and readers see many shortened images and snapshot texts a day. It's important to note that the majority of these formats use images to appeal to emotion over factual information. Online visuals spread more quickly and are more easily adopted by consumers as fact than printed formats.

Critical readers should be aware that media and non-print text carries some societal weight to the population. In being inundated with pictures and live footage, readers often feel compelled to skip the task of critical

reading analysis and accept truth at literal face value. Authors of non-print media are aware of this fact and frequently capitalize on it.

To critically address non-print media requires that the consumer address additional sources and not exclude printed text in order to reach sound conclusions. While it's tempting for consumers to get swept away in the latest viral media, it's important to remember that creators of such have an agenda, and unless the non-print media in question is backed up with sound supporting evidence, any thesis or message cannot be considered valid or factual. Memes, gifs, and looped video cannot tell the whole, truthful story although they may appeal to opinions with which readers already agree. Sharing such non-print media online can precipitate widespread misunderstanding.

When presented with non-print media, critical readers should consider these bits of information as teasers to be investigated for accuracy and veracity. Of course, certain non-print media exists solely for entertainment, but the critical reader should be able to separate out what's generalized for entertainment's sake and what's presented for further verification, before blindly accepting the message. Increasingly, this has become more difficult for readers to do, only because of the onslaught of information to which they are exposed.

If a reader is not to fall prey to strong imagery and non-print media, he or she will need to fact-check. This, of course, requires time and attention on the reader's part, and in current culture, taking the time to fact-check seems counterproductive. However, in order to maintain credibility themselves, readers must be able to evaluate multiple sources of information across media formats and be able to identify the emotional appeal used in the smaller sound bites of non-print media. Readers must view with a discerning eye, listen with a questioning ear, and think with a critical mind.

Evaluating Motives and Arguments of Presentations

Diverse media presentations generally have a specific motive behind them that contributes to the choice of medium. It is up to the audience to discern whether this motive is social, commercial, or political in nature. Listeners should evaluate the purpose behind a speaker's argument and determine if their claims are logically sound.

Understanding the motive behind a speaker's argument will help listeners gauge the validity of the evidence being presented. For example, if the presentation is being given by a spokesperson for a large company that sells directly to consumers, it is probably motivated by the commercial need for sales. The evidence being presented will most likely support the claims about their product. Pay attention to not only what is being said but what has not been mentioned.

Evidence provided to support an argument should be unbiased and generally performed by a party unrelated to the speaker and their organization. For example, a political candidate may only present evidence gathered by a group that aligns with their policies, even if another study covers both sides of the argument more effectively. Listeners may find it helpful to take notes on the speaker's evidence and fact-check it after the presentation.

Planning Developmentally Appropriate Instruction

Language is a vital part of a child's development. As a child goes through the various stages of language development, instruction must adapt and become appropriate for the child's level. The stages for language development include pre-production, early production, speech emergent, intermediate fluency, and advanced fluency.

Pre-production instruction happens when the child is not yet speaking. This is typically younger than 6 months of age. Although the child may understand certain aspects of language, they are not able to put it to use during this stage. A child may be able to communicate through gestures or drawings at this point. Instructors should focus on prompting the child with simple questions. For example, the prompt "Show me your nose" allows the child to prove their understanding through gesturing rather than vocalization.

Early production instruction takes place as the child first begins to speak. This is typically around age 1. They are beginning to recognize language more and can verbalize what they are learning. This is usually limited to only a few words and the present tense. Instructors should prompt children with simple questions that require a one- or two-word response. For example, asking the child how they are feeling should prompt a response of "Good" or Bad," which are both vocabulary words appropriate for this level.

The speech emergent stage generally occurs from ages 1 to 3. The child should be speaking with more complexity and in short sentences. This is an exploratory stage that will have many mistakes. Instructors should begin to read books with more complexity and encourage the child to look at the words. It is useful to prompt the child with questions that require more depth in their answers. A good example is asking the child why they want to do something or how something happened. This requires them to create a sentence with multiple words that logically explain their answer.

The intermediate fluency stage generally occurs from ages 3 to 5. The child should understand most of what is being said and be able to reply easily. As a result, instructors should ask more difficult questions that require the child to speak in multiple sentences. This could include asking them to explain what they did during the day. Errors will still be common during this stage.

The advanced fluency stage generally occurs from ages 5 to 7. This is the stage in which the child should have a strong grasp of the language. Their vocabulary has advanced, and they can speak at length about multiple topics. Speech becomes an automatic process, and there are fewer grammatical errors. Instructors should have the child come up with original stories or give detailed accounts of an event.

Engaging Oral Presentations

Oral presentations can cause panic in a classroom as children scramble to figure out how, when, where, why, and what to speak about. However, if given proper guidance, appropriate time, and constructive feedback, the panic will soon fade, and in turn, students will learn how to give powerful oral presentations.

In order to be effective, educators should follow best practices, including sharing a well-designed rubric with the class, discussing the importance of each skill listed, answering any questions the children might have, and providing ongoing and constructive feedback while children develop their presentations.

Verbal and Non-Verbal Components of Speech

Vocal characteristics, fluency, and pronunciation are all vital parts of creating strong speech. Nonverbal components such as eye contact and gestures are also important for communication purposes. Verbal and nonverbal elements of speech should be analyzed to ensure strong development. Struggling with one or more of these characteristics of speech may indicate that extra time needs to be spent developing in that area.

Vocal characteristics such as volume, tone, and pitch should be contextually appropriate. In normal speaking scenarios, this means keeping a volume that is not too loud to be jarring and not too quiet that it is hard to hear. Tone should be metered and reasonable. Pitch should align with the natural speaking voice and change

naturally throughout the conversation. Inflection should be placed on words that are contextually significant. Speech should not be too fast or slow but follow a natural flow that makes listening easy.

Fluency and pronunciation show a firm grasp of the language and strengthen speech overall. This means saying words with ease and using vocabulary without excessive pause. As speech develops, fluency and pronunciation of more complex language should as well. Using words or pronunciations that are not a part of standard English may be a sign of an accent or dialect. These are not indicators of speech development and are normal deviations.

Nonverbal components are an important part of communicative speech. It is helpful to make eye contact when speaking. It is also normal, and even encouraged, to use gestures while speaking. This signifies engagement in communication. They can also be used to emphasize parts of speech that are especially important. Eye contact and gestures should not be excessive, because they can become distracting to communication.

Dialects, Idiolects, and Changes in Standard Usage

Dialects, idiolects, and changes in standard oral English usage may affect an audience's perception of a speaker's performance. It is important to recognize that these variations in the spoken language are often stereotyped and unfairly judged despite not being an actual reflection on the strength of a presentation. Stereotyping and biases against unconventional speech should be avoided.

Dialects are unique forms of language that are specific to a region or group of people. An example of a dialect is African American Vernacular English. Idiolects refer to the unique speech patterns of one person. An example of this could be phrases or words that are used within a family household but are not recognized in society. These changes in speech may not align with the presentation performance that has become typical in academia. However, variations in speech do not represent the quality of the research that has gone into a presentation. The focus of the audience should be on the content of the presentation and the strength of the research or narrative. The organization of information, audience engagement, and other features of speech, such as pacing and volume, should be considered rather than unconventional speech.

Developing Skills Necessary for Speaking and Presenting

Developing Speaking Skills
Similar to listening skills, students also need to be taught speaking and presenting skills. Students need to learn such skills as:

- How to introduce themselves effectively
- How to make appropriate eye contact with listeners
- How to begin a conversation and keep it going
- How to interact with various types of audiences
- How to answer questions in an interview
- How to stand and deliver a speech with confidence
- How to ask for and answer questions during a presentation

The following strategies can help teach conversational and speaking skills:

- Students can be taught to use "conversation enhancers" when working with others. Some examples are: "Really?" "Wow!" "That's interesting" "Tell me more about …" "Can you say that in another way?" "Tell me what you are thinking …" and "Can you add to my idea?"

- Good conversational skills can be modeled as frequently as possible in one- to two-minute one-on-one dialogues with students. This is especially important for the introverted and shy students.

- A safe speaking environment can be fostered by teaching good manners to listeners, and by challenging students who are disrespectful listeners to act in a different way.

- Students should be asked open-ended questions that have no right or wrong answer and that invite lengthy answers instead of just "yes" or "no" responses.

- "I don't know" should not be accepted for an answer. Students should be taught that their thinking is valued rather than whether they *know* something.

- Students should be taught how to take turns in the classroom fairly and to not interrupt one another.

- Students should be instructed not to read their presentations word for word, and to speak toward the audience instead of toward the project or PowerPoint slide.

- Videos of good and poor presentations can be shown as models for students to critique.

- Students should be taught to build in humor and good non-verbal communication into their presentations.

- Students should be shown how to curb involuntary habits such as repeating themselves or saying "um" or "like" too much.

Task, Purpose, and Audience

Teaching students to present and speak to an audience involves teaching them how to structure a presentation so that it is appropriate for the task, purpose, and audience. **Task** is what the students are required to do with their presentation. **Purpose** is the reason for the presentation and how it will achieve the outcome of the task. **Audience** is whom the presentation is for, the population it is trying to reach, and why it is specifically for that group. Some presentation tips that teachers should impart to students are as follows:

- During student preparation, students should ask themselves: "Why am I giving this presentation?" "What do I want people to take away from the presentation?" and "How much does my audience already know about the topic?"

- Presentations should be structured with an effective introduction, covering each item on their agenda succinctly, and wrapping up with a memorable conclusion.

- Presentations should be given with clarity and impact. The audience won't remember everything a student presents, so he or she needs to highlight the key points clearly and concisely and then expand and illustrate as needed.

99

- Visual aids should be used to enhance the presentation without causing distractions—such as useless images and animated transitions between slides—from the information.

- Presentations should be given without memorization. Students should be charged with becoming more familiar with their content and to "test drive" the presentation beforehand.

- Appropriate pauses should be used during presentations to help the audience better absorb the information.

- Various techniques can be employed if there is a "stumbling point" or a piece of information is forgotten during the presentation.

Collaborative Discussions with Diverse Partners

Once an appropriate topic has been chosen, discussions should be monitored to facilitate appropriate behavior. It is very important to stress that all perspectives will be welcome and respected and to make sure that student inquiries and responses are in alignment with that principle. The following are suggestions for facilitating appropriate discussion behavior in a group setting:

- Cultivating an environment of inclusion and mutual respect

- Students should introduce themselves and be encouraged to address each other by name. "Icebreaker" games are an effective way to get students to know each other before engaging in any discussions.

- Allowing enough time for students to think about the topic and thoughtfully contribute to the discussion will encourage inclusion.

- The use of insulting or disrespectful language, tone, or body language should not be permitted.

- Students should be made aware of differences in cultural and social perspectives.

- Students should be encouraged to be mindful of the language they are using.

- Teachers should not make assumptions on how students will respond or behave based on their cultural, racial, or religious backgrounds.

- Everyone should have a chance to speak—e.g., teachers should not show favoritism towards a particular student or set of students or allow more tenacious students to dominate the discussion.

- Particular perspectives or ideas should not be verbally or nonverbally discouraged. Instead, students should be encouraged to think critically about what is being discussed and what they are saying.

- It's important not to rush students or make any student feel as though their comments and ideas are not important.

- Facilitators should not display a sense of superiority.

- Keeping discussions productive

- Teachers should be explicit about the expectations or goals of the discussion and guide students back towards the topic if they get off track.

- Demonstrating what disrespectful behavior looks like at the start of the discussion can help establish clear expectations. Students should be reminded not to take things personally or to identify with any emotions they may experience from the discussion and, instead, approach the topics with logic.

- Ideas or counterarguments should be related to personal experiences or backed with evidence. Students should validate each other's ideas first before arguing in a respectful way, such as "I respect what you are saying," or "I understand where you are coming from."

- Stereotyping and sweeping generalizations should be identified when used and subsequently avoided.

- If a student goes off on a tangent, he or she should be guided back to the primary topic or purpose by asking him/her to summarize what he/she is saying.

- If the discussion becomes heated or emotional, students should be encouraged to explore the real issue that is causing the emotions. The teacher might say, "I think there is a greater issue here that we should discuss openly and respectfully." Alternatively, students can be asked if they would like to take break and resume the discussion later. A teacher may also wish to bring up the differing values that are being displayed in the conference in an unbiased way so that students can recognize what they're truly arguing about.

- It's important that teachers avoid arguing with a student if the student attacks them. Acknowledging this kind of behavior only validates it.

- Encouraging participants/guiding the flow of discussion

- For shy students, it's helpful to call on them by name and ask if they have any thoughts/feedback, while being nonjudgmental if they admit they don't know or don't have anything to say.

- Asking questions and requesting examples when students make a comment or present an idea helps guide the discussion flow.

- Writing student comments down and asking for other participants to elaborate on them will encourage more participation.

- Depending on the exercise, giving the students a topic or asking a student to present one will elicit participation.

- For students who have trouble participating in large groups, breaking up discussion into smaller groups will help them feel more comfortable.

Evaluating Effectiveness of Strategies for Initiating and Participating Effectively in Discussions

To increase student participation in discussion, teachers should consider the following strategies:

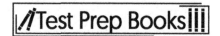

- Asking students what they know about the topic and writing their responses on the white or blackboard, which creates an outline of what the students do and don't know as well as increases their self-esteem.

- Having an anonymous question box where students can write down questions that can be read before or during the discussion, being careful not to react negatively to any questions, verbally or non-verbally, so as not to damage self-esteem

- Allowing students to teach each other, proven as the most effective way to learn something is to teach someone else what has been learned—e.g., writing their own tests or homework, conducting one-on-one conferences

- Dividing the class into smaller groups if students seem non-responsive, which helps shy students feel less intimidated and more comfortable in smaller settings

- Allowing students to work together, which encourages them to interact with others and allows them to feel more comfortable with doing so when it comes time for group discussion

- Asking students to create a topic to get them to initiate the conversation

- Using games to make the discussion fun and motivate students to participate

The effectiveness of these strategies will depend entirely on the class. Teachers should use assessment tools to determine whether the techniques have been effective and adjust the teaching style accordingly.

Many of the above strategies can be used for one-on-one discussions as well. The most important things to keep in mind in keeping a student engaged and comfortable during a one-on-one discussion are as follows:

- Asking follow-up questions

- Clarifying any unclear or obscure questions or statements

- Never making the student feel unintelligent or inadequate

- Being as reassuring as possible, particularly if a student expresses insecurity in their abilities

- Being patient and allowing time for the student to sort out thoughts and ask necessary questions

Non-Written and Written Communication: Research to Build and Present Knowledge

Research Process

The following list depicts the steps relevant to the research process. Each step should be performed in chronological order, as they depend on each other for optimal work. For example, without the "Revise and edit" step, step 8 would be a poorly written first draft:

- Step 1: Decide on a topic to research
- Step 2: Set the purpose of the research

- Step 3: Locate sources of information—print, digital, experts
- Step 4: Evaluate the sources
- Step 5: Summarize information and cite sources
- Step 6: Write draft
- Step 7: Revise and edit
- Step 8: Publish writing

Identifying Effective Research Practices

The purpose of all research is to provide an answer to an unknown question. Therefore, all good research papers pose the topic in the form of a question, which they will then seek to answer with clear ideas, arguments, and supporting evidence.

A **research question** is the primary focus of the research piece, and it should be formulated on a unique topic. To formulate a research question, writers begin by choosing a general topic of interest and then research the literature to determine what sort of research has already been done—the **literature review**. This helps them narrow the topic into something original and determine what still needs to be asked and researched about the topic. A solid question is very specific and avoids generalizations. The following question is offered for evaluation:

What is most people's favorite kind of animal?

This research question is extremely broad without giving the paper any particular focus—it could go any direction and is not an exceptionally unique focus. To narrow it down, the question could consider a specific population:

What is the favorite animal of people in Ecuador?

While this question is better, it does not address exactly why this research is being conducted or why anyone would care about the answer. Here's another possibility:

What does the animal considered as the most favorite of people in different regions throughout Ecuador reveal about their socioeconomic status?

This question is extremely specific and gives a very clear direction of where the paper or project is going to go. However, sometimes the question can be too limited, where very little research has been conducted to create a solid paper, and the researcher most likely does not have the means to travel to Ecuador and travel door-to-door conducting a census on people's favorite animals. In this case, the research question would need to be broadened. Broadening a topic can mean introducing a wider range of criteria. Instead of people in Ecuador, the topic could be opened to include the population of South America or expanded to include more issues or considerations.

Gathering Relevant Information from Credible Sources

Relevant information is that which is pertinent to the topic at hand. Particularly when doing research online, it is easy to get overwhelmed with the wealth of information available. Before conducting research, the researcher needs begin with a clear idea of the question they want to answer.

103

For example, the researcher may be interested in learning more about marriage practices in Jane Austen's England. If that researcher types "marriage" into a search engine, they will have to sift through thousands of unrelated sites before finding anything related to that topic. Narrowing down search parameters can aid in locating relevant information.

When using a book, the researcher can consult the table of contents, glossary, or index to discover whether the book contains relevant information before using it as a resource. If the researcher finds a hefty volume on Jane Austen, they can flip to the index in the back, look for the word marriage, and find out how many page references are listed in the book. If there are few or no references to the subject, it is probably not a relevant or useful source.

In evaluating research articles, one may also consult the title, abstract, and keywords before reading the article in its entirety. Referring to the date of publication will also determine whether the research contains up-to-date discoveries, theories, and ideas about the subject, or whether it is outdated.

Learning how to locate key information within sources requires a basic understanding of written structure. If the source of information is written well, there should be titles, subtitles, headings, and subheadings that researchers can use to zero in on key information. Additionally, informational texts often employ the use of an index and table of contents, which helps them locate specific information. Similarly, digital sources often employ titles, subtitles, headings, and subheadings, and they will generally offer a search box to look for specific information or key terms within the website.

Primary sources refer to first-hand accounts of events, a subject matter, an individual, or a time period. Primary sources also include original works of art. They can also be non-interpretive, factual pieces of information. Some examples include diaries, journals, letters, government records, maps, plays, novels, and songs.

Secondary sources refer to the analysis or interpretation of primary sources and are, therefore, usually considered more subjective than objective. In other words, researchers may discover contradictory information on the same subject from different secondary sources. Some examples include literary and film reviews, newspaper articles, and biographies.

Both primary and secondary sources of information are useful. They both offer invaluable insight that helps the writer learn more about the subject matter. However, researchers are cautioned to examine the information closely and to consider the time period as well as the cultural, political, and social climate in which accounts were given. Learning to distinguish between reliable sources of information and questionable accounts is paramount to a quality research report.

Credibility and Accuracy of Sources

When conducting research, one must be able to distinguish between reliable and unreliable sources in order to develop a well-written research report. Credible print sources are those that have been edited and published, reveal the author or authors, and clearly identify their expertise on the subject matter. Scholarly reviews are typically very reliable sources as they are written by experts in the field and, more often than not, have been evaluated by their respective peers. Credible digital sources may sometimes prove a little more difficult to discern, and researchers must employ due diligence to ensure the sources are reliable. Distinguishing between biased and unbiased websites, objective versus subjective information, as well as informative versus persuasive writing can prove confusing at times. By paying attention to a website's URL and carefully considering the language and tone applied to the writing, researchers should be able to evaluate the website's

reliability. Generally speaking, websites with.edu, .gov, or .org as the Top Level Domain are considered reliable, but the researcher must still question any possible political or social bias. Personal blogs, tweets, personal websites, online forums, and any site that clearly demonstrates bias, strong opinions, or persuasive language are considered unreliable sources.

The following questions will help determine whether a source is credible:

- Author
- Who is he or she?
- Does he or she have the appropriate credentials—e.g., M.D, PhD?
- Is this person authorized to write on the matter through their job or personal experiences?
- Is he or she affiliated with any known credible individuals or organizations?
- Has he or she written anything else?
- Publisher
- Who published/produced the work? Is it a well-known journal, like National Geographic, or a tabloid, like The National Enquirer?
- Is the publisher from a scholarly, commercial, or government association?
- Do they publish works related to specific fields?
- Have they published other works?
- If a digital source, what kind of website hosts the text? Does it end in .edu, .org, or .com?
- Bias
- Is the writing objective? Does it contain any loaded or emotional language?
- Does the publisher/producer have a known bias, such as Fox News or CNN?
- Does the work include diverse opinions or perspectives?
- Does the author have any known bias—e.g., Michael Moore, Bill O'Reilly, or the Pope? Is he or she affiliated with any organizations or individuals that may have a known bias—e.g., Citizens United or the National Rifle Association?
- Does the magazine, book, journal, or website contain any advertising?
- References
- Are there any references?
- Are the references credible? Do they follow the same criteria as stated above?
- Are the references from a related field?
- Accuracy/reliability
- Has the article, book, or digital source been peer reviewed?
- Are all of the conclusions, supporting details, or ideas backed with published evidence?
- If a digital source, is it free of grammatical errors, poor spelling, and improper English?
- Do other published individuals have similar findings?
- Coverage
- Are the topic and related material both successfully addressed?
- Does the work add new information or theories to those of their sources?
- Is the target audience appropriate for the intended purpose?

Constructing Interpretations of Claims and Research Findings

When constructing reports and narratives, it is important to first conduct research and interpret the information that is worth including. Claims should be backed up by firm evidence and with a direct citation to

105

where the information was found. It should be relevant to the new work. For example, a response to literature should cite literature reviews, and a scientific argument should cite research data. There are methods of interpreting research to help this process.

When reading through research documents, it is helpful to take notes on what information is relevant to the report or narrative that will be written. Categorization of important points will also help illuminate what the author'(s') purpose was in their original research. This information can then be pared down to what fits best within the new work. This includes identifying the locations within the report or narrative where the research findings work well and support the nature of the writing.

Use of Quotations

It can be daunting to integrate so many sources into a research paper while still maintaining fluency and coherency. Most source material is incorporated in the form of quotations or paraphrases, while citing the source at the end of their respective references. There are several guidelines to consider when integrating a source into writing:

- The piece should be written in the author's voice. Quotations, especially long ones, should be limited and spaced evenly throughout the paper.

- All paragraphs should begin with the author's own words and end with their own words; quotations should never start or end a paragraph.

- Quotations and paraphrases should be used to emphasize a point, give weight to an idea, and validate a claim.

- Supporting evidence should be introduced in a sentence or paragraph, and then explained afterwards: According to Waters (1979) [signal phrase], "All in all, we're just another brick in the wall" (p.24). The wall suggests that people are becoming more alienated, and the bricks symbolize a paradoxical connection to that alienation [Explanation].

- When introducing a source for the first time, the author's name and a smooth transition should be included: In Pink Floyd's groundbreaking album The Wall, Roger Waters argues that society is causing people to become more alienated.

- There should be an even balance between quotations and paraphrases.

- Quotations or paraphrases should never be taken out of context in a way that alters the original author's intent.

- Quotations should be syntactically and grammatically integrated.

- Quotations should not simply be copied and pasted in the paper, rather, they should be introduced into a paper with natural transitions

- As argued in Johnson's article...
- Evidence of this point can be found in Johnson's article, where she asserts that...
- The central argument of John's article is...

106

Focused and Coherent Emphasis of Relevant Evidence, Reasoning, and Details

All information should be presented with a clear beginning, middle, and end. Distinct organization always makes any work more clear, concise, and logical. For a presentation, this should involve choosing a primary topic and then discussing it in the following format:

- Introducing the speaker and the main topic
- Providing evidence, supporting details, further explanation of the topic in the main body
- Concluding it with a firm resolution and repetition of the main point

The beginning, middle, and end should also be linked with effective transitions that make the presentation flow well. For example, a presentation should always begin with an introduction by the speaker, including what he/she does and what he/she is there to present. Good transitional introductions may begin with statements such as *For those who do not know me, my name is...*, *As many of you know, I am...* or *Good morning everyone, my name is ___, and I am the new project manager*. A good introduction grabs the attention and interest of the audience.

After an introduction has been made, the speaker will then want to state the purpose of the presentation with a natural transition, such as *I am here to discuss the latest editions to our standard of procedure...* or *This afternoon, I would like to present the results of our latest findings*. Once the purpose has been identified, the speaker will want to adhere to the main idea announced. The presenter should be certain to keep the main idea to one sentence as too much information can confuse an audience; an introduction should be succinct and to the point.

Supporting information should always be presented in concise, easy-to-read formats such as bullet points or lists—if visual aids are presented during the presentation. Good transitions such as *Let's begin with...* or *Now to look at...* make the presentation flow smoothly and logically, helping listeners to keep ideas organized as they are presented. Keeping the material concise is extremely important in a presentation, and visual aids should be used only to emphasize points or explain ideas. All the supporting information should relate back to the main idea, avoiding unnecessary tangents.

Finally, a firm conclusion involves repeating the main point of the presentation by either inspiring listeners to act or by reiterating the most important points made in the speech. It should also include an expression of gratitude to the audience as well as transition to opening the floor for questions.

Paraphrasing and Plagiarizing

Paraphrasing is restating one's own words, text, passage, or any information that has already been heard, read, or researched. A tip for paraphrasing is to read a passage over three times. Once you read the passage and understand what the author is saying, cover the original passage and begin to write everything you remember from that passage into your own words. Usually, if you understand the content well enough, you will have translated the main idea of the author into your own words with your own writing style. An effective paraphrase will be as long as the original passage but will have a different writing structure. When readers and writers paraphrase, they need to avoid copying the text—that is plagiarism. Plagiarizing is the copying of a text, passage, or any other information in print or digital format, and claiming the work as one's own.

It is also important to include as many details as possible when restating the facts. Not only will this help readers and writers recall information, but by putting the information into their own words, they demonstrate

that they fully comprehend the text or passage. The example below shows an original text and how to paraphrase it.

Original Text: *Fenway Park is home to the beloved Boston Red Sox. The stadium opened on April 20, 1912. The stadium currently seats over 37,000 fans, many of whom travel from all over the country to experience the iconic team and nostalgia of Fenway Park.*

Paraphrased: *On April 20, 1912, Fenway Park opened. Home to the Boston Red Sox, the stadium now seats over 37,000 fans. Many spectators travel to watch the Red Sox and experience the spirit of Fenway Park.*

Paraphrasing, summarizing, and quoting can often cross paths with one another. The chart below shows the similarities and differences between the three strategies:

Paraphrasing	Summarizing	Quoting
Uses own words	Puts main ideas into own words	Uses words that are identical to text
References original source	References original source	Requires quotation marks
Uses own sentences	Shows important ideas of source	Uses author's words and ideas

Citation

Citing sources at the end of a research paper is critical to the overall quality of work. If sources are not cited or poorly cited, a researcher's work risks losing credibility. There are various accepted methods to use when citing information. The method used often depends on the preferences of the authority that has assigned the research. The most generally accepted methods for citing sources are MLA, APA, and Chicago/Turabian style. Although each citation format is distinct in structure, order, and requirements, they all identify key information. Citation formats also ensure that published authors of given works receive full credit.

MLA Style

For an MLA style citation, components must be included or excluded depending on the source, so writers should determine which components are applicable to the source being cited. Here are the basic components:

- Author—last name, first name
- Title of source
- Title of container—e.g., a journal title or website
- Other contributors—e.g., editor or translator
- Version
- Number
- Publisher
- Publication date
- Location—e.g., the URL or DOI
- Date of Access—optional

APA Style

The following components can be found in APA style citations. Components must be included or excluded depending on the source, so writers should determine which components are applicable to the source being cited. The basic components are as follows:

- Author—last name, first initial, middle initial
- Publication date
- Title of chapter, article, or text
- Editor— last name, first initial, middle initial
- Version/volume
- Number/issue
- Page numbers
- DOI or URL
- Database—if article is difficult to locate
- City of publication
- State of publication, abbreviated
- Publisher

Chicago/Turabian Style

Chicago/Turabian style citations are also referred to as note systems and are used most frequently in the humanities and the arts. Components must be included or excluded depending on the source, so writers should determine which components are applicable to the source being cited. They contain the following elements:

- Author—last name, first name, middle initial
- Title of chapter or article—in quotation marks
- Title of source
- Editor—first name, last name
- Page numbers
- Version/volume
- Number/issue
- Page numbers
- Date of access
- DOI
- Publication location—city and state abbreviation/country
- Publisher
- Publication Date

Examples

The following information contains examples of the common types of sources used in research as well as the formats for each citation style. First lines of citation entries are presented flush to the left margin, and second/subsequent details are presented with a hanging indent. Some examples of bibliography entries are presented below:

- Book
- MLA

  - *Format*: Last name, First name, Middle initial. *Title of Source*. Publisher, Publication Date.

  - *Example*: Sampson, Maximus R. *Diaries from an Alien Invasion*. Campbell Press, 1989.

- APA

  - *Format*: Last name, First initial, Middle initial. (Year Published) *Book Title*. City, State: Publisher.

  - *Example*: Sampson, M. R. (1989). *Diaries from an Alien Invasion. Springfield, IL*: Campbell Press.

- Chicago/Turabian

  - *Format*: Last name, First name, Middle initial. *Book Title*. City, State: Publisher, Year of publication.

  - *Example*: Sampson, Maximus R. *Diaries from an Alien Invasion. Springfield, IL*: Campbell Press, 1989.

- A Chapter in an Edited Book
- MLA

  - *Format*: Last name, First name, Middle initial. "Title of Source." *Title of Container*, Other Contributors, Publisher, Publication Date, Location.

  - *Example*: Sampson, Maximus R. "The Spaceship." *Diaries from an Alien Invasion*, edited by Allegra M. Brewer, Campbell Press, 1989, pp. 45-62.

- APA

  - *Format*: Last name, First Initial, Middle initial. (Year Published) Chapter title. In First initial, Middle initial, Last Name (Ed.), *Book title* (pp. page numbers). City, State: Publisher.

  - *Example*: Sampson, M. R. (1989). The Spaceship. In A. M. Brewer (Ed.), *Diaries from an Alien Invasion* (pp. 45-62). Springfield, IL: Campbell Press.

- Chicago/Turabian

  - *Format*: Last name, First name, Middle initial. "Chapter Title." In Book Title, edited by Editor's Name (First, Middle In. Last), Page(s). City: Publisher, Year Published.

  - *Example*: Sampson, Maximus R. "The Spaceship," in *Diaries from an Alien Invasion*, edited by Allegra M. Brewer, 45-62. Springfield: Campbell Press, 1989.

110

- Article in a Journal
- MLA

  - *Format*: Last name, First name, Middle initial. "Title of Source." *Title of Journal, Number, Publication* Date, Location.

  - *Example*: Rowe, Jason R. "The Grief Monster." *Strong Living*, vol. 9, no. 9, 2016, pp 25-31.

- APA

  - *Format*: Last name, First initial, Middle initial. (Year Published). Title of article. *Name of Journal*, *volume*(issue), page(s).

  - *Example*: Rowe, J. R. (2016). The grief monster. *Strong Living, 9*(9), 25-31.

- Chicago/Turabian:

  - *Format*: Last name, First name, Middle initial. "Title of Article." *Name of Journal* volume, issue (Year Published): Page(s).

  - *Example*: Rowe, Jason, R. "The Grief Monster." *Strong Living* 9, no. 9 (2016): 25-31.

- Page on a Website
- MLA

  - *Format*: Last name, First name, Middle initial. "Title of Article." *Name of Website*, date published (Day Month Year), URL. Date accessed (Day Month Year).

  - *Example*: Rowe, Jason. "The Grief Monster." *Strong Living Online*, 9 Sept. 2016. http://www.somanylosses.com/the-grief-monster/html. Accessed 13 Sept. 2016.

- APA

  - *Format*: Last name, First initial. Middle initial. (Date Published—Year, Month Day). Page or article title. Retrieved from URL

  - *Example*: Rowe, J. W. (2016, Sept. 9). The grief monster. Retrieved from http://www.somanylosses.com/ the-grief-monster/html

- Chicago/Turabian

  - *Format*: Last Name, First Name, Middle initial. "Page Title." *Website Title*. Last modified Month day, year. Accessed month, day, year. URL.

  - *Example*: Rowe, Jason. "The Grief Monster." Strong Living Online. Last modified September 9, 2016. Accessed September 13, 2016. http://www.somanylosses.com/the-grief-monster/html.

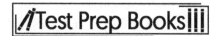

In-Text Citations

Most of the content found in a research paper will be supporting evidence that must be cited in-text, i.e., directly after the sentence that makes the statement. In-text citations contain details that correspond to the first detail in the bibliography entry—usually the author.

- MLA style - In-text citations will contain the author and the page number (if the source has page numbers) for direct quotations. Paraphrased source material may have just the author.

- According to Johnson, liver cancer treatment is "just beyond our reach" (976).

- The treatment of liver cancer is not within our reach, currently (Johnson).

- The narrator opens the story with a paradoxical description: "It was the best of times, it was the worst of times" (Dickens 1).

- APA Style - In text citations will contain the author, the year of publication, and a page marker—if the source is paginated—for direct quotations. Paraphrased source material will include the author and year of publication.

- According to Johnson (1986), liver cancer treatment is "just beyond our reach" (p. 976).

- The treatment of liver cancer is not within our reach, currently (Johnson, 1986).

- Chicago Style - Chicago style has two approaches to in-text citation: notes and bibliography or author-date.

- Notes – There are two options for notes: endnotes—provided in a sequential list at the end of the paper and separate from bibliography—or footnotes provided at the bottom of a page. In either case, the use of superscript indicates the citation number.

  - Johnson states that treatment of liver cancer is "just beyond our reach."[1]

  - 1. Robert W. Johnson, Oncology in the Twenty-first Century (Kentville, Nova Scotia: Kentville Publishing, 1986), 159.

- Author-Date – The author-date system includes the author's name, publication year, and page number.

  - Johnson states that treatment of liver cancer is "just beyond our reach" (1986, 159).

Integrating Technology, Multimedia, and Visual Displays into Presentations

Each visual aid has its advantages and disadvantages and should be used sparingly to avoid distracting the audience. Visual aids should be used to emphasize a presentation's message, not overwhelm it.

Microsoft PowerPoint is currently the most commonly used visual aid. It allows for pictures, words, videos, and music to be presented on the same screen and is essentially just a projection of a computer screen, allowing easy and quick access to all forms of media as well as the Internet. However, a PowerPoint presentation should not be overwhelmed with information, such as text-heavy slides, as audience members will spend more time reading the slides than listening to the speaker. Conversely, they may avoid reading it entirely, and the

112

presentation will serve no purpose. A PowerPoint presentation that uses too many animations and visual elements may also detract from the presence of the speaker.

Handouts are a great way for the audience to feel more involved in a presentation. They can present lots of information that may be too much for a PowerPoint, and they can also be taken home and reviewed later. The primary disadvantage of handouts is that the audience may choose to read rather than to listen, thus missing the main points the speaker is trying to make, or they may decide not to read it at all. The best handouts are those that do not contain all the information of a presentation, but allow for the audience to take notes and complete the handout by listening or asking questions.

Whiteboards and **blackboards** are excellent for explaining difficult concepts by allowing the audience to follow along with a process and copy down their own version of what is being written on the board. This visual aid is best used to explain concepts in mathematics and science. The main problem with the board, however, is that there can be limited space, and if the presenter runs out of room, he or she will have to erase the content written on the board and will be unable to refer back to it later. He or she may also have to wait for the entire audience to write the information down, which slows down the presentation.

Overhead projectors are wonderful in that a speaker can use a prepared transparency and draw images or add words to emphasize or explain concepts. They can also erase these additions but still keep the original content if they wish to alter their method to fit the audience or provide further explanations. Similar to PowerPoint presentations, overhead projections should limit the amount of text to keep the audience focused on listening.

Physical objects are a useful way to connect with the audience and allow them to feel more involved. Because people interact with the physical world, physical objects can help solidify understanding of difficult concepts. However, they can be distracting if not properly introduced. If they are presented too early or are visible during the presentation, the audience will focus on the objects, wondering what purpose they may serve instead of listening to the speaker. Objects should instead be hidden until it is time to show them and then collected when they are no longer useful.

Videos are a great way to enliven a presentation by giving it sound, music, flow, and images. They are excellent for emphasizing points, providing evidence for ideas, giving context, or setting tone. The major issue with videos is that the presenter is unable to speak at this point, so this form of media should be used sparingly and purposefully. Also, overly-long videos may lose the audience's attention.

Effective public speakers are aware of the advantages and disadvantages of all forms of media and often choose to utilize a combination of several different types to keep the presentations lively and the audience engaged.

Effective Speech and Presentation Delivery

When giving a speech or presentation, it is important to deliver the information in an effective manner. This means presenting salient information in a way that is digestible and interesting to the audience. Knowing how to give a strong presentation can increase confidence for the future and have a positive effect on all future public-speaking endeavors.

Eye contact is a vital part of giving a strong presentation. Eye contact makes the listeners feel connected to the speaker and what they are saying. Keeping a friendly and open expression will make the audience feel more connected to the presenter as well. Avoid gesturing too much and potentially distracting the audience.

It is also important to find an appropriate and consistent volume for the space and number of people within it. Maintaining a comfortable rate of speaking will help listeners to steadily follow along. In addition, pay attention to tone and pitch while speaking because it can change how the audience perceives the information that is being shared.

Reading Comprehension and Analysis: Reading Literature

Characteristics and Elements of Literary Genres

Genre is a method of categorizing literature by form, content, style, and technique. When selections of literature share enough characteristics and literary elements, they are classified into the same genre. Genre is more than just a categorization system, though; genre identifies literature by its communicative purpose. Authors write to accomplish any of a variety of social purposes: to inform, to explain, to entertain, to persuade, to maintain relationships, and so on. All types of texts fall into one of the following five genres: fiction, nonfiction, poetry, drama, and folklore. Each of these has a variety of subgenres. A particular piece of writing may fall into more than one genre or subgenre.

A variety of texts must be used to teach literature and reading. Folklore and poetry both have aspects to enhance comprehension. Poetry teaches lyrical reading and emphasis; it is written with specific structure and rhythm. There are many types of poetry, such as ballads, lyrics, couplets, epics, and sonnets. Poetry teaches students about adhering to punctuation while reading and allows students to read with pauses. A great teaching strategy to employ with poetry lessons is the use of blank poetry books that students can use to take notes and create their own specific poems. Poetry contains similes, personification, and onomatopoeia; therefore, poems are a great way to teach imagery and figurative language.

Drama, or plays, can emphasize voice, and gives students the option to take on a role of a character. One way to teach drama is to divide students into groups and host a reader's theater. Students and teachers have a lot of fun preparing to present a play in front of the class. Prose text covers a wide range of literature from novels, to folklore, to biographies. Developing a unit dedicated to the various types of folklore (short stories, tall tales, myth, legend, and fantasy) can be creative and fun for students. Autobiographies, biographies, and historical fiction can help teach facts. Providing students with the opportunity to research a person in history and present the findings to the class develops comprehension, presentation, speaking, writing, and research skills.

Fiction
Fiction is imaginative text that is invented by the author—e.g., *Mark Twain's Adventures of Huckleberry Finn*. Fiction is characterized by the following literary elements:

- **Characters:** the people, animals, aliens, or other living figures the story is about
- **Setting:** the location, surroundings, and time the story takes place in
- **Conflict:** a dilemma the characters face either internally or externally
- **Plot:** the sequence and the rise and fall of excitement in the action of a story
- **Resolution:** the solution to the conflict that is discovered as a result of the story
- **Point of View:** the lens through which the reader experiences the story
- **Theme:** the moral to the story or the message the author is sending to the reader

Historical Fiction

Historical fiction is a story that occurs in the past and uses a realistic setting and authentic time period characters. Historical fiction usually has some historically accurate events mixed and balanced with invented plot and characters.

Science Fiction

Science fiction is an invented story that occurs in the future or an alternate universe. It often deals with space, time travel, robots or aliens, and highly-advanced technology.

Fantasy

Fantasy is a subgenre of fiction that involves magic or supernatural elements and/or takes place in an imaginary world. Examples include talking animals, superheroes rescuing the day, or characters taking on a mythical journey or quest—e.g., J.R.R. Tolkien's *The Hobbit* and J.K. Rowling's *Harry Potter and the Sorcerer's Stone*.

Mystery and Adventure

Mystery fiction is a story that involves a puzzle or crime to be solved by the main characters. The mystery is driven by suspense and foreshadowing. The reader must sift through clues and distractions to solve the puzzle with the protagonist. **Adventure stories** are driven by the risky or exciting action that happens in the plot.

Realistic and Contemporary Fiction

Realistic fiction depends on the author portraying the world without speculation. The characters are ordinary, and the action could happen in real life. The conflict often involves growing up, family life, or learning to cope with some significant emotion or challenge.

Nonfiction Literature

Nonfiction literature is true and accurate in detail. Nonfiction can cover virtually any topic in the natural world. Nonfiction writers conduct research and carefully organize facts before writing. Nonfiction has the following subgenres:

- **Informational Text.** This is text written to impart information to the reader. It may have literary elements such as charts, graphs, indexes, glossaries, or bibliographies.

- **Persuasive Text:** This is text that is meant to sway the reader to have a particular opinion or take a particular action.

- **Biographies and Autobiographies:** This is text that tells intimate details of someone's life. If an author writes the text about someone else, it is a **biography**. If the author writes it about himself or herself, it is an **autobiography.**

- **Communicative text:** This is text used to communicate with another person. It includes such texts as emails, formal and informal letters, and social media posts. This content often consists of two-sided dialogue between people.

Drama

Drama is any writing that is intended to be performed in front of an audience, such as scripts for plays, TV, and movies. Dialogue and action are central to convey the author's theme. **Comedy** is any drama designed to be funny or lighthearted. **Tragedy** is any drama designed to be serious or sad.

115

A drama, or a play, is almost exclusively delivered as a dialogue and performed live on a stage. The audience observes the story unfolding as opposed to reading it in a book. The actors or actresses in a drama follow written scripts, which are divided into acts and further divided into scenes. The only written material generally given to the audience is the cast of characters, which lists all the character names with an accompanying brief description of their role in the play. This is the only written assistance the audience will receive, so it is imperative that they read through the cast of characters and then carefully follow each scene in the play to understand the story.

Stage directions in a drama refer to the directions or descriptions given to the actors in each scene. They are often presented in italics or in parentheses to differentiate the directions from the dialogue. Stage directions may tell actors where to stand, what direction to face, how to deliver lines, and whom to address.

Poetry

Poetry is fiction in verse that has a unique focus on the rhythm of language and focuses on intensity of feeling. It is not an entire story, though it may tell one; it is compact in form and in function. Poetry can be considered as a poet's brief word picture for a reader. Poetic structure is primarily composed of lines and stanzas. Together, poetic structure and devices are the methods that poets use to lead readers to feeling an effect and, ultimately, to the interpretive message. Different poetic structures and devices are used to create the various major forms of poetry. Some of the most common forms are discussed in the following chart.

Type	Poetic Structure	Example
Ballad	A poem or song passed down orally which tells a story and in English tradition usually uses an ABAB or ABCB rhyme scheme	William Butler Yeats' "The Ballad Of Father O'Hart"
Epic	A long poem from ancient oral tradition which narrates the story of a legendary or heroic protagonist	Homer's The Odyssey Virgil's The Aeneid
Haiku	A Japanese poem of three unrhymed lines with five, seven, and five syllables (in English) with nature as a common subject matter	Matsuo Bashō An old silent pond... A frog jumps into the pond, splash! Silence again.
Limerick	A five-line poem written in an AABBA rhyme scheme, with a witty focus	From Edward Lear's Book of Nonsense— "There was a Young Person of Smyrna Whose grandmother threatened to burn her..."
Ode	A formal lyric poem that addresses and praises a person, place, thing, or idea	Edna St. Vincent Millay's "Ode To Silence"
Sonnet	A fourteen-line poem written in iambic pentameter	Shakespeare's Sonnets 18 and 130
Lyric	A lyric poem expresses the personal and emotional feelings of the author	Emily Dickinson "I Felt a Funeral in my Brain"
Narrative	A narrative poem tells a story	Edgar Allan Poe "The Raven"
Dramatic Monologue	A dramatic monologue is a poem where a character speaks to an auditor for the entire poem	Robert Browning "My Last Duchess"

Poetry often involves descriptive imagery and beautiful mastery of language. It is often personal, emotional, and introspective. Poetry is often considered a work of art.

Generally speaking, **rhyme** goes hand and hand with the study of poetry and involves the repetition of similar sounds. Sounds may rhyme at the end of every two or more lines, referred to as **end rhyme**, or may even rhyme in the middle of a line, referred to as **internal rhyme**.

The following offers examples of both:

> I went to school *today*,
>
> Not wanting to leave the *house*,
>
> And as I passed the *day*,
>
> I remained as quiet as a *mouse*.
>
> In rain or *shine*, your house or *mine*,
>
> We'll meet *again*, my dear *friend*.

The first poem demonstrates the example of end rhyme. The second example demonstrates internal rhyme.

Meter is the rhythm of the syllables within a poem. Each type of meter equates to the specific number of syllables and, possibly, the way the syllables are stressed. There are five basic meters: *iambic, trochaic, spondaic, anapestic,* and *dactylic*. Recognizing the meter within poetry helps readers understand the poem's rhythm and guides the reader in how to read the poem with the poet's intended emphasis. Meter also helps poets develop and maintain the structural elements within the poem.

Folklore

Folklore is literature that has been handed down from generation to generation by word of mouth. Folklore is not based in fact but in unsubstantiated beliefs. It is often very important to a culture or custom. The following are some common types of folklore:

- **Fairy Tales:** These are usually written for children and often carry a moral or universal truth. They are stories written about fairies or other magical creatures—e.g., Hans Christian Anderson's *The Little Mermaid, Cinderella* by the Brothers Grimm.

- **Fables:** Similar to fairy tales, fables are written for children and include tales of supernatural people or animals that speak like people—e.g., *Aesop's Fables*. They often are built around a moral lesson.

- **Myths:** These tales often tell about pagan gods and use symbolism to speak about historical events or reveal human behavior—e.g., Greek myths, Genesis I and II in the Bible, Arthurian legends. Sometimes they provide far-fetched explanations of historical events or natural phenomena.

- **Legends:** Exaggerated and only partially truthful, these are tales of heroes and significant events.

- **Tall Tales:** Often funny stories and sometimes set in the Wild West, these are tales that contain extreme exaggeration and were never true.

Literary Response and Analysis Skills

When it comes to the study of stories or literary texts, it is important for children to gain an understanding and awareness of text structures and organization. All literary texts involve various story elements, including characters, setting, and plot. Being able to identify these elements and show their relationship to one another is key to understanding the story.

Characters

A story may have both main characters and minor characters, but all characters, regardless of their level of importance, work to provide the story's framework. The more children identify with various characters in a story, the stronger their overall comprehension will be. Therefore, it is important for students to be able to list and describe all characters that appear throughout a story.

The following questions aid students in this endeavor:

- What do the characters look like?
- How old are they?
- What language or languages do they speak?
- What is their personality like?
- How do they relate to one another?
- Do you know of anyone like this in your life?
- Have you come across a similar character in another story?
- How are they the same?
- How are they different?

Characters can assume primary, secondary, or minor roles. **Central** or **major** characters are those who are integral to the story—the plot cannot be resolved without them. A central character can be a **protagonist** or hero. There may be more than one protagonist, and they don't always have to possess good characteristics. A character can also be an **antagonist**—the force against a protagonist.

Character development is when the author takes the time to create dynamic characters that add uniqueness and depth to the story. **Dynamic** characters are characters that change over the course of the plot's timeline. **Static** characters do not change. A **symbolic** character is one that represents an author's idea about society in general—for example, Peter Pan from *Peter Pan* by J.M. Barrie. **Stock** characters are those that appear across genres and embrace stereotypes—for example, the cowboy of the Wild West or the evil villain in a fairy tale. A **flat** character is one that does not present a lot of complexity or depth, whereas a **rounded** character does. Sometimes, the **narrator** of a story or the **speaker** in a poem can be a character—for example, the wolf in Jon Scieszka's *The True Story of the Three Little Pigs* or the speaker in *Green Eggs and Ham* by Dr. Seuss. The narrator might also function as a character in prose, although not be part of the story—for example, the reader in *Don't Let the Pigeon Drive the Bus!* by Mo Willems.

When readers compare and contrast characters, it is important that they ask themselves three questions:

- Why compare/contrast characters?
- What is compared/contrast between characters?
- How are they the same/different?

Setting

The **setting** is the time, place, or set of surroundings in which the story occurs. It includes time or time span, place(s), climates, cultural environments geography—man-made or natural. Evaluating the relevance of the setting impacts a text's direction. For example, how is the storyline affected by the time and location of the story's events? The setting is very important to a story's framework and may even change periodically as the story unfolds. Understanding when and where a story takes place helps children visualize the various scenes and relate the story's setting to a time and place in their own lives or to a similar setting in another story. Questions that aid in the understanding of setting include the following:

- What country are the characters in?
- What year or era is it?
- Does the story take place in a suburban, urban, or rural location?
- Is the setting similar or different to where you live?
- How is it similar?
- How is it different?
- Does this setting remind you of a setting in another story?
- How are the settings similar? How are they different?
- Would you like to visit this setting? Give clear reasons why or why not.

A story's setting is critical to helping children make sense of a character's language, dress, attitude, relationships with others, and character traits. Building a stronger understanding of each character within a story will assist young readers in their overall text comprehension.

Plot

The **plot** is what happens in the story. Generally speaking, the **plot** of a literary text involves the introduction of a key problem at the beginning of a story, which is usually resolved by the story's end. Educators build a bridge that strengthens students' story comprehension by helping children connect the story's plot to a familiar scenario in another story or by helping children connect the problem in the text with a problem they have encountered in their own lives. For instance, the plot can involve dealing with a bully, battling the elements of nature, or learning to overcome personal obstacles. The more children are able to relate to a story's plot, the greater their comprehension and appreciation of the story will be.

When teaching children about the various elements in literary texts, the use of visual aids, such as story maps, can provide invaluable assistance to a child's overall understanding:

Plots may be singular, containing one problem, or they may be very complex, with many sub-plots. The **conflict** drives the plot and is something that the reader expects to be resolved. The plot carries those events along until there is a resolution to the conflict. All plots have an exposition, a conflict, a climax, and a resolution:

- **Exposition:** This is where the author introduces characters and establishes the setting.
- **Rising Action:** This is where the conflict starts to develop and complications may form.
- **Climax:** This is when the conflict is at its highest moment.
- **Falling Action:** This is where characters make choices that will determine the end result.
- **Resolution:** This is how the story ends and, over all, the outcome.

Analysis of Explicit and Implicit Meaning

A literary text can be especially difficult to write effective research for because much of it is open to interpretation. Textual evidence takes information from the work or other sources to support these interpretations. This evidence must be cited. Citations are an important part of strong analysis and can help support arguments about the explicit and implicit meanings behind literary texts. Explicit meaning is what is directly stated and is clearly identifiable as the meaning. Implicit meaning is implied, and the reader may have to make inferences.

Citations can be done in several different ways. First, the citation should be checked for scholarly merit and a peer-reviewed status if it is not from the original literary text. Read through the cited work and highlight portions that are most relevant to the analysis of the explicit and implicit meanings. These sections can be incorporated through direct quotations or paraphrasing. Never copy the work directly without proper citation etiquette for the style of the analysis.

Identifying Central Ideas or Themes of a Text

The **theme** is the central message of a fictional work, whether that work is structured as prose, drama, or poetry. It is the heart of what an author is trying to say to readers through the writing, and theme is largely conveyed through literary elements and techniques. The theme can often be determined by considering the overarching narrative conflict within the work.

Authors employ a variety of techniques to present a theme. They may compare or contrast characters, events, places, ideas, or historical or invented settings to speak thematically. They may use analogies, metaphors, similes, allusions, or other literary devices to convey the theme. An author's use of diction, syntax, and tone can also help convey the theme. Authors will often develop themes through the development of characters, use of the setting, repetition of ideas, use of symbols, and through contrasting value systems. Authors of both fiction and nonfiction genres will use a variety of these techniques to develop one or more themes.

Texts may carry recurring themes like acceptance, courage, loyalty, man versus nature, and life. There are many themes that may overlap in a variety of texts. It is important for teachers to remember to coordinate texts with recurring themes in order for students to clearly understand the intent or message. Other common themes in children's literature are family, friendship, growing up, self-esteem, and morality.

Family

Family tends to be a common theme in children's literature. Authors provide readers with examples of relationships such as father/son, mother/daughter, grandparent/grandchild, and cousin/cousin. These relationships may display positive or negative feelings of love, joy, pain, or sadness. They can also find strengths or weaknesses in family communication or togetherness. One popular children's book centered on family is *A Chair for My Mother* by Vera B. Williams. In this story, a family works hard to save money to buy their mother a special chair after all of her furniture is lost in a fire. The tale of hard work, sacrifice, and love teaches many lessons to students of all ages.

Friendship

Another common theme in children's literature is friendship. Children are greatly influenced by friends. Texts may portray positive or negative choices among friends leading to a great or poor outcome. Throughout friendship-themed literature, children learn all sorts of valuable lessons like compromise, coping skills, togetherness, caring for others, inclusion, and adversity. One popular children's book centered on friendship is *Charlotte's Web* by E.B. White. In this story, unlikely friendships occur in many forms. A young girl and a pig, a pig and a spider, and a goose and a horse all celebrate one another's differences and support each other's decisions through this children's tale.

Growing Up

Growing up is another common theme in children's literature. Children's literature has countless texts of kids going through different scenarios as they get older. Overlapping themes include friendship, puberty, judgment calls, overcoming challenges, and accepting responsibilities. For example, the children's book, *Alice in Wonderland,* by Lewis Carroll, demonstrates concepts such as the challenges of being big and small, as well as decision-making.

Self-Esteem

Self-esteem is the emotional feelings one has about himself or herself. Self-esteem–themed children's literature tries to demonstrate positive feelings and emotions to build self-esteem. Acceptance, love, learning opportunities, goal setting, pride, and trying new things are common subjects in self-esteem–themed texts.

122

For example, the children's book, *I Like Myself,* by Karen Beaumont, discusses how to be proud and confident regardless of physical appearances.

Morality

Morality is the judgment of right from wrong. Children always have choices. Morality-themed children's books share the principles and outcomes of good and poor choices. Themes such as honesty, friend choices, respect, and sharing are common in morality-themed children's texts. For example, the children's book series, *The Berenstain Bears,* by Stan and Jan Berenstain, always reveals a predicament where the kids or adults need to use problem-solving skills to solve the issue. One of the books in the series, *The Berenstain Bears and the Truth,* discusses how to feel proud of telling the truth and how important truth telling is.

Themes or Central Ideas Derived from Cultural Patterns and Symbols

Culturally significant literature is impactful and enhances the classroom learning experience. Many themes in literature are derived from cultural patterns and symbols found in rituals, mythologies, and traditions. It is important to recognize the origin behind these central ideas because it can empower readers and inspire cultural awareness. Interdisciplinary research can help explain where these themes come from and why they are culturally significant.

A focus on the pretext information that is provided with a piece of literature should show the literature's culture. Culturally relevant literature can then be researched further through library databases. This background information should be provided before, during, and after instruction. Awareness of the rituals, mythologies, and traditions of that culture will deepen the instruction and allow greater critical thinking.

During instruction, with the interdisciplinary knowledge obtained prior to reading students can draw connections between central themes and cultural patterns. These connections will then span across multiple works and various cultures. This encourages cultural consciousness and community understanding. One example of a culturally relevant book is *Day of the Dead* by Tony Johnston. It describes a town in Mexico that prepares for the Day of the Dead celebration. It covers themes of death and community while presenting a culture that may be unfamiliar to some.

Dialogue and Story Events

Action and dialogue are the tools used in drama and fiction to tell the story. **Dialogue** refers to the conversations that occur within a story. Dialogue can help to move the plot along and also to give insight into characters, setting, mood, and other aspects of the story. **Story events** are the different elements of a story that are ordered to create the plot or action. In order to understand characters in a text, readers should keep the following questions in mind:

- What does the character say? Does their dialogue seem to be straightforward, or are they hiding some thoughts or emotions?

- What actions can be observed from this character? How do their actions reflect their feelings?

123

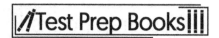

Literary Devices

<u>Poetry</u>
Poetic Devices
Rhyme is the poet's use of corresponding word sounds in order to create an effect. Most rhyme occurs at the ends of a poem's lines, which is how readers arrive at the **rhyme scheme**. Each line that has a corresponding rhyming sound is assigned a letter—A, B, C, and so on. When using a rhyme scheme, poets will often follow lettered patterns.

Robert Frost's *"The Road Not Taken"* uses the ABAAB rhyme scheme:

Two roads diverged in a yellow wood,	A
And sorry I could not travel both	B
And be one traveler, long I stood	A
And looked down one as far as I could	A
To where it bent in the undergrowth;	B

Another important poetic device is **rhythm**—metered patterns within poetry verses. When a poet develops rhythm through **meter**, he or she is using a combination of stressed and unstressed syllables to create a sound effect for the reader.

Rhythm is created by the use of **poetic feet**—individual rhythmic units made up of the combination of stressed and unstressed syllables. A line of poetry is made up of one or more poetic feet. There are five standard types in English poetry, as depicted in the chart below.

Foot Type	Rhythm	Pattern
Iamb	buh Buh	Unstressed/stressed
Trochee	Buh buh	Stressed/unstressed
Spondee	Buh Buh	Stressed/stressed
Anapest	buh buh Buh	Unstressed/unstressed/stressed
Dactyl	Buh buh buh	Stressed/unstressed/unstressed

Structure
Poetry is most easily recognized by its structure, which varies greatly. For example, a structure may be strict in the number of lines it uses. It may use rhyming patterns or may not rhyme at all. There are three main types of poetic structures:

- **Verse**—poetry with a consistent meter and rhyme scheme
- **Blank verse**—poetry with consistent meter but an inconsistent rhyme scheme
- **Free verse**—poetry with inconsistent meter or rhyme

Verse poetry is most often developed in the form of **stanzas**—groups of word lines. Stanzas can also be considered **verses**. The structure is usually formulaic and adheres to the protocols for the form. For example, the English **sonnet** form uses a structure of fourteen lines and a variety of different rhyming patterns. The English **ode** typically uses three ten-line stanzas and has a particular rhyming pattern.

Poets choose poetic structure based on the effect they want to create. Some structures—such as the ballad and haiku—developed out of cultural influences and common artistic practice in history, but in more modern poetry, authors choose their structure to best fit their intended effect.

Figurative Language
Figurative language can be used to give additional insight into the theme or message of a text by moving beyond the usual and literal meaning of words and phrases. It can also be used to appeal to the senses of readers and create a more in-depth story.

Similes and Metaphors
Similes and **metaphors** are types of figurative language that are used as rhetorical devices. Both are comparisons between two things, but their formats differ slightly. A simile says that two things are similar and makes a comparison using "like" or "as"—*A* is like *B,* or *A* is as [some characteristic] as *B*—whereas a metaphor states that two things are exactly the same—*A* is *B*. In both cases, similes and metaphors invite the reader to think more deeply about the characteristics of the two subjects and consider where they overlap. Sometimes the poet develops a complex metaphor throughout the entire poem; this is known as an extended metaphor. An example of metaphor can be found in the sentence: "His pillow was a fluffy cloud." An example of simile can be found in the first line of Robert Burns' famous poem:

> My love is like a red, red rose

This is comparison using "like," and the two things being compared are love and a rose. Some characteristics of a rose are that it is fragrant, beautiful, blossoming, colorful, vibrant—by comparing his love to a red, red rose, Burns asks the reader to apply these qualities of a rose to his love. In this way, he implies that his love is also fresh, blossoming, and brilliant.

Sound Repetition
In addition to rhetorical devices that play on the meanings of words, there are also rhetorical devices that use the sounds of words. These devices are most often found in poetry but may also be found in other types of literature and in nonfiction writing like texts for speeches.

Alliteration and assonance are both varieties of sound repetition. Other types of sound repetition include: **anaphora**—repetition that occurs at the beginning of the sentences; **epiphora**—repetition occurring at the end of phrases; and **antimetabole**—repetition of words in a succession.

Alliteration refers to the repetition of the first sound of each word. Recall Robert Burns' opening line:

> My love is like a red, red rose

This line includes two instances of alliteration: "love" and "like" (repeated *L* sound), as well as "red" and "rose" (repeated *R* sound). Next, **assonance** refers to the repetition of vowel sounds, and can occur anywhere within a word (not just the opening sound). Here is the opening of a poem by John Keats:

> When I have fears that I may cease to be

> Before my pen has glean'd my teeming brain

Assonance can be found in the words "fears," "cease," "be," "glean'd," and "teeming," all of which stress the long *E* sound. Both alliteration and assonance create a harmony that unifies the writer's language.

125

Onomatopoeia

Another sound device is **onomatopoeia**—words whose spelling mimics the sound they describe. Words like "crash," "bang," and "sizzle" are all examples of onomatopoeia. Use of onomatopoetic language adds auditory imagery to the text.

Puns

Readers are probably most familiar with the technique of using a **pun**. A pun is a play on words, taking advantage of two words that have the same or similar pronunciation. Puns can be found throughout Shakespeare's plays, for instance:

> Now is the winter of our discontent

> Made glorious summer by this son of York

These lines from *Richard III* contain a play on words. Richard III refers to his brother—the newly crowned King Edward IV—as the "son of York," referencing their family heritage from the house of York. However, while drawing a comparison between the political climate and the weather (times of political trouble were the "winter," but now the new king brings "glorious summer"), Richard's use of the word "son" also implies another word with the same pronunciation, "sun"—so Edward IV is also like the sun, bringing light, warmth, and hope to England. Puns are a clever way for writers to suggest two meanings at once.

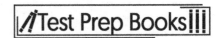

Table of Literary Devices		
Device	**Definition**	**Example**
Alliteration	Repeating the same beginning sound or letter in a phrase for emphasis	The busy baby babbled.
Allusion	A reference to a famous person, event, or significant literary text as a form of significant comparison	"We are apt to shut our eyes against a painful truth, and listen to the song of that siren till she transforms us into beasts." Patrick Henry
Anaphora	The repetition of the same words at the beginning of successive words, phrases, or clauses, designed to emphasize an idea	"We shall not flag or fail. We shall go on to the end. We shall fight in France, we shall fight on the seas and oceans, we shall fight with growing confidence ... we shall fight in the fields and in the streets, we shall fight in the hills. We shall never surrender." Winston Churchill
Antithesis	A part of speech where a contrast of ideas is expressed by a pair of words that are opposite of each other.	"That's one small step for man, one giant leap for mankind." Neil Armstrong
Foreshadowing	Giving an indication that something is going to happen later in the story	I wasn't aware at the time, but I would come to regret those words.
Hyperbole	Using exaggeration not meant to be taken literally	The girl weighed less than a feather.
Idiom	Using words with predictable meanings to create a phrase with a different meaning	The world is your oyster.
Imagery	Appealing to the senses by using descriptive language	The sky was painted with red and pink and streaked with orange.
Metaphor	Compares two things as if they are the same	He was a giant teddy bear.
Onomatopoeia	Using words that imitate sound	The tire went off with a bang and a crunch.
Parallelism	A syntactical similarity in a structure or series of structures used for impact of an idea, making it memorable	"A penny saved is a penny earned." Ben Franklin
Personification	Attributing human characteristics to an object or an animal	The house glowered menacingly with a dark smile.
Rhetorical question	A question posed that is not answered by the writer though there is a desired response, most often designed to emphasize a point	"Can anyone look at our reduced standing in the world today and say, 'Let's have four more years of this?'" Ronald Reagan

Simile	Compares two things using "like" or "as"	Her hair was like gold.
Device	**Definition**	**Example**
Symbolism	Using symbols to represent ideas and provide a different meaning	The ring represented the bond between us.
Understatement	A statement meant to portray a situation as less important than it actually is to create an ironic effect	"The war in the Pacific has not necessarily developed in Japan's favor." Emperor Hirohito, surrendering Japan in World War II

Meaning of Words and Phrases

By now, it should be apparent that language is not as simple as one word directly correlated to one meaning. Rather, one word can express a vast array of diverse meanings, and similar meanings can be expressed through different words. However, there are very few words that express exactly the same meaning. For this reason, it is important to be able to pick up on the nuances of word meaning.

Many words contain two levels of meaning: connotation and denotation. A word's **denotation** is its most literal meaning—the definition that can readily be found in the dictionary. A word's **connotation** includes all of its emotional and cultural associations.

In literary writing, authors rely heavily on connotative meaning to create mood and characterization. The following are two descriptions of a rainstorm:

> The rain slammed against the windowpane and the wind howled through the fireplace. A pair of hulking oaks next to the house cast eerie shadows as their branches trembled in the wind.

> The rain pattered against the windowpane and the wind whistled through the fireplace. A pair of stately oaks next to the house cast curious shadows as their branches swayed in the wind.

Description A paints a creepy picture for readers with strongly emotional words like *slammed*, connoting force and violence. *Howled* connotes pain or wildness, and *eerie* and *trembled* connote fear. Overall, the connotative language in this description serves to inspire fear and anxiety.

However, as can be seen in description B, swapping out a few key words for those with different connotations completely changes the feeling of the passage. *Slammed* is replaced with the more cheerful *pattered*, and *hulking* has been swapped out for *stately*. Both words imply something large, but *hulking* is more intimidating whereas *stately* is more respectable. *Curious* and *swayed* seem more playful than the language used in the earlier description. Although both descriptions represent roughly the same situation, the nuances of the emotional language used throughout the passages create a very different sense for readers.

Selective choice of connotative language can also be extremely impactful in other forms of writing, such as editorials or persuasive texts. Through connotative language, writers reveal their biases and opinions while trying to inspire feelings and actions in readers:

> Parents won't stop complaining about standardized tests.

> Parents continue to raise concerns about standardized tests.

128

Readers should be able to identify the nuance in meaning between these two sentences. The first one carries a more negative feeling, implying that parents are being bothersome or whiny. Readers of the second sentence, though, might come away with the feeling that parents are concerned and involved in their children's education. Again, the aggregate of even subtle cues can combine to give a specific emotional impression to readers, so from an early age, students should be aware of how language can be used to influence readers' opinions.

Another form of non-literal expression can be found in **figures of speech**. As with connotative language, figures of speech tend to be shared within a cultural group and may be difficult to pick up on for learners outside of that group. In some cases, a figure of speech may be based on the literal denotation of the words it contains, but in other cases, a figure of speech is far removed from its literal meaning. A case in point is **irony**, where what is said is the exact opposite of what is meant:

The new tax plan is poorly planned, based on faulty economic data, and unable to address the financial struggles of middle-class families. Yet legislators remain committed to passing this brilliant proposal.

When the writer refers to the proposal as brilliant, the opposite is implied—the plan is "faulty" and "poorly planned." By using irony, the writer means that the proposal is anything but brilliant by using the word in a non-literal sense.

Another figure of speech is **hyperbole**—extreme exaggeration or overstatement. Statements like "I love you to the moon and back" or "Let's be friends for a million years" utilize hyperbole to convey a greater depth of emotion, without literally committing oneself to space travel or a life of immortality.

Figures of speech may sometimes use one word in place of another. **Synecdoche**, for example, uses a part of something to refer to its whole. The expression "Don't hurt a hair on her head!" implies protecting more than just an individual hair, but rather her entire body. "The art teacher is training a class of Picassos" uses Picasso, one individual notable artist, to stand in for the entire category of talented artists. Another figure of speech using word replacement is **metonymy**, where a word is replaced with something closely associated to it. For example, news reports may use the word *Washington* to refer to the American government or *the crown* to refer to the British monarch.

Impact of Word Choice on Meaning, Style, and Tone

Authors choose their words carefully in order to artfully depict meaning, style, and tone, which is most commonly inferred through the use of adjectives and verbs. The **tone** of a story reflects the attitude or feelings that an author has towards the subject matter of the story or text, a character, or an event. Tone can be expressed through word choice, imagery, figurative language, syntax, and other details. The emotion or mood the reader experiences relates back to the tone of the story. Some examples of possible tones are humorous, somber, sentimental, and ironic. The style of a text is where the speaker's creative expression comes in. The style of writing is the speaker/writer's lack or presence of creative expression and personality. Different ways to use style in speaking include tone, diction, figurative language, and word choice.

An author's word choice can have a dramatic effect on the meaning and tone of a text. This is most often a purposeful decision that the author makes for a specific effect. Analogies and allusions to other texts can also impact how a reader perceives the writing. An analogy is a comparison between two things. An allusion is a reference to something without outright mentioning what it is.

Diction can be connotative or denotative in nature. Connotative words are based on their implied meaning. Denotative is the literal definition of the word. There is a nuance to certain words that lends a new meaning to the text. For example, using the word *cocky* to describe a person will create a different image than using the word *confident,* despite having very similar literal meanings. This is due to the connotative or implied meaning. Connotation can be either positive or negative, and it changes the tone of the text.

Analogies and allusions add depth to the text and change the meaning, depending on the context of the reference. They may also help readers understand the underlying meaning of a text where it is otherwise not obvious. For example, comparing a character's personality to a historical figure such as Abraham Lincoln would allow the readers to make several connections. Abraham Lincoln was known to be honest and humble, so it can be assumed that the character is as well. A lot of meaning can be conveyed in just one analogy or allusion.

To review, an **adjective** is a word used to describe something, and usually precedes the **noun**, a person, place, or object. A **verb** is a word describing an action. For example, the sentence "The scary woodpecker ate the spider" includes the adjective "scary," the noun "woodpecker," and the verb "ate." Reading this sentence may rouse some negative feelings, as the word "scary" carries a negative charge. The **charge** is the emotional connotation that can be derived from the adjectives and verbs and is either positive or negative. Recognizing the charge of a particular sentence or passage is an effective way to understand the meaning and tone the author is trying to convey.

Many authors have conflicting charges within the same text, but a definitive tone can be inferred by understanding the meaning of the charges relative to each other. It's important to recognize key **conjunctions**, or words that link sentences or clauses together. There are several types and subtypes of conjunctions. Three are most important for reading comprehension:

- **Cumulative conjunctions** add one statement to another.
  - Examples: *and, both, also, as well as, not only*
  - e.g. The juice is sweet *and* sour.
- **Adversative conjunctions** are used to contrast two clauses.
  - Examples: *but, while, still, yet, nevertheless*
  - e.g. She was tired, *but* she was happy.
- **Alternative conjunctions** express two alternatives.
  - Examples: *or, either, neither, nor, else, otherwise*
  - e.g. He must eat, *or* he will die.

Identifying the meaning and tone of a text can be accomplished with the following steps:

- Identify the adjectives and verbs.
- Recognize any important conjunctions.
- Label the adjectives and verbs as positive or negative.
- Understand what the charge means about the text.

To demonstrate these steps, examine the following passage from the classic children's poem, "The Sheep":

Lazy sheep, pray tell me why

In the pleasant fields you lie,

Eating grass, and daisies white,

130

From the morning till the night?

Everything can something do,

But what kind of use are you?

–Taylor, Jane and Ann. "The Sheep."

This selection is a good example of conflicting charges that work together to express an overall tone. Following the first two steps, identify the adjectives, verbs, and conjunctions within the passage. For this example, the adjectives are <u>underlined</u>, the verbs are in **bold**, and the conjunctions *italicized*:

<u>Lazy</u> sheep, pray **tell** me why

In the <u>pleasant</u> fields you **lie**,

Eating grass, and daisies <u>white,</u>

From the morning till the night?

Everything can something do,

But what kind of use are you?

For step three, read the passage and judge whether feelings of positivity or negativity arose. Then assign a charge to each of the words that were outlined. This can be done in a table format, or simply by writing a + or − next to the word.

The word <u>lazy</u> carries a negative connotation; it usually denotes somebody unwilling to work. To **tell** someone something has an exclusively neutral connotation, as it depends on what's being told, which has not yet been revealed at this point, so a charge can be assigned later. The word <u>pleasant</u> is an inherently positive word. To **lie** could be positive or negative depending on the context, but as the subject (the sheep) is lying in a pleasant field, then this is a positive experience. **Eating** is also generally positive.

After labeling the charges for each word, it might be inferred that the tone of this poem is happy and maybe even admiring or innocuously envious. However, notice the adversative conjunction, "but" and what follows. The author has listed all the pleasant things this sheep gets to do all day, but the tone changes when the author asks, "What kind of use are you?" Asking someone to prove their value is a rather hurtful thing to do, as it implies that the person asking the question doesn't believe the subject has any value, so this could be listed under negative charges. Referring back to the verb **tell**, after reading the whole passage, it can be deduced that the author is asking the sheep to tell what use the sheep is, so this has a negative charge.

+	−
Pleasant	Lazy
Lie in fields	Tell me
From morning to night	What kind of use are you

Upon examining the charges, it might seem like there's an even amount of positive and negative emotion in this selection, and that's where the conjunction "but" becomes crucial to identifying the tone. The conjunction

131

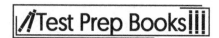
"but" indicates there's a contrasting view to the pleasantness of the sheep's daily life, and this view is that the sheep is lazy and useless, which is also indicated by the first line, "lazy sheep, pray tell me why."

It might be helpful to look at questions pertaining to tone. For this selection, consider the following question:

The author of the poem regards the sheep with a feeling of what?
    a. Respect
    b. Disgust
    c. Apprehension
    d. Intrigue

Considering the author views the sheep as lazy with nothing to offer, Choice *A* appears to reflect the opposite of what the author is feeling.

Choice *B* seems to mirror the author's feelings towards the sheep, as laziness is considered a disreputable trait, and people (or personified animals, in this case) with unfavorable traits might be viewed with disgust.

Choice *C* doesn't make sense within context, as laziness isn't usually feared.

Choice *D* is tricky, as it may be tempting to argue that the author is intrigued with the sheep because they ask, "pray tell me why." This is another out-of-scope answer choice as it doesn't *quite* describe the feelings the author experiences and there's also a much better fit in Choice *B*.

An author's choice of words—also referred to as **diction**—helps to convey meaning in a particular way. Through diction, an author can convey a particular tone—e.g., a humorous tone, a serious tone—in order to support the thesis in a meaningful way to the reader.

Effect of Structure on Meaning and Style

The structure of a work changes how readers interpret the style and meaning of the text. An author will carefully construct their work to convey something specific. For example, the author may choose to not include certain information until later in their work in order to create mystery and suspense. A poem may use a unique structure to put emphasis on certain words on which the reader should focus.

A few well-known structures are prominent in literature. For example, the Fichtean Curve is a common structure style that goes in the order of rising action, climax, and falling action. Another example is the Hero's Journey structure where a hero goes on an adventure with multiple points of action, experiences a major crisis, and then returns home victorious. These examples of story structures create a genre-specific style that readers come to expect, and they affect how readers interpret the text.

Point of View

The **point of view** is the position the narrator takes when telling the story in prose. If a narrator is incorporated in a drama, the point of view may vary; in poetry, point of view refers to the position the speaker in a poem takes.

First Person

The first person point-of-view is when the writer uses the word *I* in the text. Poetry often uses first person, e.g., William Wordsworth's "I Wandered Lonely as a Cloud." Two examples of prose written in first person are Suzanne Collins's *The Hunger Games* and Anthony Burgess's *A Clockwork Orange*.

Second Person

The second person point-of-view is when the writer uses the pronoun *you*. It is not widely used in prose fiction, but as a technique, it has been used by writers such as William Faulkner in *Absalom, Absalom!* And Albert Camus in *The Fall*. It is more common in poetry—e.g., Pablo Neruda's "If You Forget Me."

Third Person

Third person point-of-view is when the writer utilizes pronouns such as *him*, *her*, or *them*. It may be the most utilized point of view in prose as it provides flexibility to an author and is the one with which readers are most familiar. There are two main types of third person used in fiction. **Third person omniscient** uses a narrator that is all-knowing, relating the story by conveying and interpreting thoughts/feelings of all characters. In **third person limited,** the narrator relates the story through the perspective of one character's thoughts/feelings, usually the main character.

Voice

Voice is the way in which the narrator conveys their message of a given text. The voice in a text grabs a reader's attention. It makes the text relatable and expressive. There are two main types of voices: author's voice and character's voice. When using an author's voice, the author uses their own language style and flow to influence how the text is interpreted. When the author uses a character's voice, he or she uses the main character of the text to portray a message. First- and third-person perspectives are commonly used in a character's voice.

Impact of Point of View

The points of view of a story's characters can change the effect of textual effects such as suspense or humor. First-, second-, and third-person points of view all provide a different insight into the story and characters. Information is either withheld or freely given, depending on the point of view.

First-person point of view is driven by being in the mind of the main character, and therefore the reader's interpretation of events and characters will be skewed by their thoughts. This may prohibit a level of suspense that would be present without inner thoughts being revealed. The reader may also have access to humor within the person's thoughts because they are privy to information other characters are not. For example, the main character may think humorous thoughts about their friend who does not know they have a funny sign stuck to the back of their shirt.

Second-person point of view can be more difficult to create suspense and humor for, but it is still entirely possible. This is because the writing is directed at the reader. The writing can make humorous callouts and assumptions about the reader. The writing could also be framed as if something scary is coming after the reader. Second-person point of view can be exciting to read because the reader feels more involved in what is happening. However, the suspension of disbelief may not work for all readers.

Third-person point of view is very common and easily creates suspense and humor. An omniscient narrator means that the audience can have information about the characters that nobody else knows. For example, the audience may know that something terrible is about to happen and can then read the events leading up to that with suspense. Humor can be created through insight into the thoughts of all characters.

Reading Comprehension and Analysis: Reading Informational Text

Informational Texts

Informational texts are a category of texts within the genre of nonfiction. Their intent is to inform, and while they do convey a point of view and may include literary devices, they do not utilize other literary elements, such as characters or plot. An informational text also reflects a **thesis**—an implicit or explicit statement of the text's intent and/or a **main idea**—the overarching focus and/or purpose of the text, generally implied. Some examples of informational texts are informative articles, instructional/how-to texts, factual reports, reference texts, and self-help texts.

Organizational Structure Within Informational Text

When reading informational text, it is important that readers are able to understand its organizational structure as the structure often directly relates to an author's intent to inform and/or persuade the reader. Informational text is specifically designed to relate factual information, and although it is open to a reader's interpretation and application of the facts, the structure of the presentation is carefully designed to lead the reader to a particular conclusion.

The first step in identifying the text's structure is to determine the thesis or main idea. The thesis statement and organization of a work are closely intertwined. **A thesis statement** indicates the writer's purpose and may include the scope and direction of the text. It may be presented at the beginning of a text or at the end, and it may be explicit or implicit.

Once a reader has a grasp of the thesis or main idea of the text, he or she can better determine its organizational structure. It may be necessary to read informational text passages more than once in order to comprehend the material fully. It is also helpful to examine any text features present in the text including the table of contents, index, glossary, headings, footnotes, and visuals. The analysis of these features and the information presented within them can offer additional clues about the central idea and structure of a text. The following questions should be considered when considering structure:

- How does the author assemble the parts to make an effective whole argument?

- Is the passage linear in nature and if so, what is the timeline or thread of logic?

- What is the presented order of events, facts, or arguments? Are these effective in contributing to the author's thesis?

- How can the passage be divided into sections? How are they related to each other and to the main idea or thesis?

- What key terms are used to indicate the organization?

The first line or two of each body paragraph should contain the **topic sentences**. Key **transitional terms**, such as *on the other hand, also, because, however, therefore, most importantly,* and *first*, within the text can also

134

signal organizational structure. Based on these clues, readers should then be able to identify what type of organizational structure is being used. The following organizational structures are most common:

- **Problem/solution**—organized by an analysis/overview of a problem, followed by potential solution(s)

- **Cause/effect**—organized by the effects resulting from a cause or the cause(s) of a particular effect

- **Spatial order**—organized by points that suggest location or direction—e.g., top to bottom, right to left, outside to inside

- **Chronological/sequence order**—organized by points presented to indicate a passage of time or through purposeful steps/stages

- **Comparison/Contrast**—organized by points that indicate similarities and/or differences between two things or concepts

- **Order of importance**—organized by priority of points, often most significant to least significant or vice versa

Analyzing Informational Text

Once a reader has determined an author's thesis or main idea, he or she will need to understand how textual evidence supports interpretation of that thesis or main idea. Readers should be able to comprehend literal and figurative meanings within the text passage, be able to draw inferences from provided information, and be able to separate important evidence from minor supporting detail.

After identifying an author's thesis or main idea, a reader should look at the supporting details that the author provides to back up their assertions, identifying those additional pieces of information that help expand the thesis. From there, readers should examine the additional information and related details for credibility, the author's use of outside sources, and be able to point to direct evidence that supports the author's claims. It's also imperative that readers be able to identify what is strong support and what is merely additional information that is nice to know but not necessary.

Summarizing Information

A helpful tool is the ability to summarize the information that you have read in a paragraph or passage format. This process is similar to creating an effective outline. First, a summary should accurately define the main idea of the passage though the summary does not need to explain this main idea in exhaustive detail. The summary should continue by laying out the most important supporting details or arguments from the passage. All of the significant supporting details should be included, and none of the details included should be irrelevant or insignificant. Also, the summary should accurately report all of these details. Too often, the desire for brevity in a summary leads to the sacrifice of clarity or accuracy. Summaries are often difficult to read because they omit all of the graceful language, digressions, and asides that distinguish great writing. However, an effective summary should contain much the same message as the original text.

135

Interpreting Words and Phrases

It is important when evaluating informational texts to consider the use of both literal and figurative meanings. The words and phrases an author chooses to include in a text must be evaluated. How does the word choice affect the meaning and tone? By recognizing the use of literal and figurative language, a reader can more readily ascertain the message or purpose of a text. Literal word choice is the easiest to analyze as it represents the usual and intended way a word or phrase is used. It is also more common in informational texts because it is used to state facts and definitions. While figurative language is typically associated with fiction and poetry, it can be found in informational texts as well. The reader must determine not only what is meant by the figurative language in context, but also how the author intended it to shape the overall text.

Connotation is when an author chooses words or phrases that invoke ideas or feelings other than their literal meaning. An example of the use of connotation is the word *cheap*, which suggests something is poor in value or negatively describes a person is reluctant to spend money. When something or someone is described this way, the reader is more inclined to have a particular image or feeling about it or him/her. Thus, connotation can be a very effective language tool in creating emotion and swaying opinion.

Denotation refers to An author's use of words or phrases to mean exactly what they say. It is helpful when a writer wants to present hard facts or vocabulary terms with which readers may be unfamiliar. Some examples of denotation are the words *inexpensive* and *frugal*. *Inexpensive* refers to the cost of something, not its value, and *frugal* indicates that a person is conscientiously watching their spending. These terms do not elicit the same emotions that *cheap* does.

Authors sometimes choose to use both, but what they choose and when they use it is what critical readers need to differentiate. One method isn't inherently better than the other; however, one may create a better effect, depending upon an author's intent. If, for example, an author's purpose is to inform, to instruct, and to familiarize readers with a difficult subject, their use of connotation may be helpful. However, it may also undermine credibility and confuse readers. An author who wants to create a credible, scholarly effect in their text would most likely use denotation, which emphasizes literal, factual meaning and examples.

An author's use of less literal words and phrases requires readers to make more inference when they read. **Inference** refers to the reader's ability to understand the unwritten text, i.e., "read between the lines" in terms of an author's intent or message. The strategy asks that a reader not take everything he or she reads at face value but instead, add their own interpretation of what the author seems to be trying to convey. A reader's ability to make inferences relies on their ability to think clearly and logically about the text. It does not ask that the reader make wild speculation or guess about the material but demands that he or she be able to come to a sound conclusion about the material. Since inference involves **deduction**—deriving conclusions from ideas assumed to be true—there's more room for interpretation. Still, critical readers who employ inference, if careful in their thinking, can still arrive at the logical, sound conclusions the author intends.

Test takers and critical readers alike should be very aware of technical language used within informational text. **Technical language** refers to terminology that is specific to a particular industry and is best understood by those specializing in that industry. This language is fairly easy to differentiate, since it will most likely be unfamiliar to readers. It's critical to be able to define technical language either by the author's written definition, through the use of an included glossary—if offered—or through context clues that help readers clarify word meaning.

Text Features

In informational texts, certain features function to organize the information and also act as guides, which in turn supports the reader's overall comprehension. Features, such as graphics, illustrations, captions, and maps, are used to support the text. They are meant to show evidence or claims in a way that allows a different perspective than simply reading text.

There are a few steps to evaluate these text features. First, read the title or caption that accompanies the feature. This will generally provide information about what the feature contains. It may also reference a part of the text that will need to be read for context.

The next step is to determine what the text feature is adding to the text. Some features may be showing new data that elaborate on a thesis. Other features may be adding an artistic illustration to provide imagery for a story. Viewing and analyzing these features in conjunction with the text will create additional depth.

Headings include titles and subtitles that identify the topic of study. They also help a reader to arrive at a clearer understanding with regard to the text's main idea. Headings can help readers make connections between background knowledge and the information in the text, which helps them make predictions before reading begins. Headings also strategically organize a text into sections so that one section at a time can be studied.

Sidebars are found in the right or left margins of informational texts. Sidebars often provide the reader with helpful, additional information about a topic that appears on that particular page. By providing examples, interesting facts, definitions of key terms, and more, sidebars emphasize important information that the author wishes to convey.

Hyperlinks are in-text links to specific website addresses that a reader may wish to visit to further their understanding of a specific topic. When authors insert hyperlinks into modern informational texts, they create a text that is more interactive, providing further resources for children to strengthen their comprehension of a given topic.

Bias and Stereotyping

Informational texts should ideally be as free from bias and stereotyping as possible. Although it is normal for an author to take a stance in their writing, whether subtly or outright, it should never cross the line into having strong bias or stereotyping. It is difficult for humans to think about things without some level of bias, so it is important to be diligent in identifying and analyzing instances where it occurs.

Informational texts should generally look at all sides of a topic. If an author is heavily covering one side of a topic but not another that is equally important, they may be showing a bias. If an author making an argument does not look at the opposing side with the same level of analysis, this may also show a bias. If an informational text discusses various types of people (race, gender, sexuality, socioeconomic status, etc.) yet treats them differently in a way that is not relevant to the research, stereotyping could be at play.

Pay attention to the type of language used to describe the information being provided. Biased language may be assumptive and not backed by verifiable research. Rather than just reading the informational text and taking it at face value, do an analysis of the text to ensure that it is unbiased.

Reading Comprehension and Analysis: Text Complexity

Measuring Text Complexity

When selecting texts for classroom reading, it is imperative that educators consider the three main factors that measure complexity, which will best predict a child's reading success:

- Quantitative
- Qualitative
- Reader and Task

Quantitative Measures

When selecting appropriate texts for the classroom, educators must consider the type of words used throughout the text, the number of syllables in each word, and the spelling complexity of the words. Educators should also ask themselves if the text mostly contains decodable words or a significant number of sight word vocabulary. Finally, educators must consider the sentence lengths and the level of sentence complexity, since sentences vary from simple sentences to compound-complex sentences that may be too advanced for the students.

Qualitative Measures

Educators must also take into account the age of their students and whether or not certain subject matter is developmentally appropriate. Do children tend to have background knowledge in the subject, or will they likely be introduced to this new concept for the first time? Does the author employ the use of explicit language or figurative language that may be too complicated for younger students?

Reader and Task Measures

When educators go a step further in their planning by considering the needs of their individual students, reading instruction will be more effective. Educators should consider the various reader variables, such as level of reading fluency, the number of reluctant and motivated readers in the classroom, and the degree of home support for reading.

All of these factors combined significantly impact the type of text, level of complexity, and the tasks children are given to accomplish based on the reading material. Considering these factors that measure text complexity will also assist educators in choosing instruction and evaluation techniques.

Text Leveling

For educators to apply quantitative, qualitative, and reader and task considerations effectively prior to introducing a reading assignment, they must first understand and consider the unique features of text-leveling systems:

Quantitative Measures	Qualitative Measures	Student and Task Measures
Total word count	Text predictability	Reluctant readers
Number of different words	Text structure and organization	Motivated readers
Number of high-frequency words	Visual aid, illustration, and info graphics support	Struggling readers
Number of low-frequency words	Background knowledge of topic	Interest in topic
Sentence length	Single theme vs. multi-themes	
Sentence complexity		

Text leveling means assigning levels to different texts. For example, a teacher might label books to denote their level and then arrange them on a bookshelf from simplest to most complex. This system would allow the teacher to always know the level of difficulty of the text they are assigning, and it would also help the teacher show students how to find books at the correct level during independent reading.

Leveling takes many factors into account. Although the next section will provide a more detailed analysis of these factors, they fall into three broad categories: qualitative factors, quantitative factors, and reader and task. **Qualitative factors** are subjective features of the text, such as whether the illustrations help guide readers toward comprehension and the level of background information required to understand the text. **Quantitative factors**, on the other hand, are objective facts about the text that can typically be expressed in numbers, such as the word count and average sentence length of the text. **Reader and reading task** refers to the connection between the student and the text. For example, a student who is passionate about chemistry will have an easier time reading a chemistry text than a student who hates the subject. Reader and task is a factor teachers must consider on a case-by-case basis because leveling systems cannot take students' interest and background knowledge into account. Therefore, teachers may sometimes need to mentally adjust the level of a text for individual students.

One common method of leveling is the **Learning A-Z Text Leveling System**, which rates books from aa (simple texts for kindergartners and raw beginners), through all the letters of the alphabet, to z^2 (complicated texts suitable for everyone from fifth graders to university students). Because the twenty-nine levels of this system divide texts into such specific difficulty levels, teachers can use this method to closely measure small improvements within a grade level. Another leveling system is the **Lexile Text Measure**, which keeps a database of prose ranked from 200L (beginner) to 1200L (advanced). Lexile offers a test, the **Lexile Reading Measure**, that ranks students' abilities on the same scale so teachers can easily find appropriate books for them to read.

Selecting Appropriate Texts

Student Learning Goals

Each student will have different learning goals that match their educational journey. It is important to match the text complexity of their assignments to their learning goals. Text complexity is the level of difficulty of a reading task. Assigning students texts with complexity that is too low will not challenge them to advance their reading skills. It will be difficult for them to stay engaged. Assigning students with text complexity far above their abilities will leave them confused and even demotivated. Picking an appropriate text can be a challenge, but when done correctly it will help students reach their learning goals.

Student learning goals will be different for every student. There are many factors that go into deciding a student's learning goals. Goals may be specific or broad, depending on the needs of the student. They should be attainable in a reasonable amount of time. In order to determine if the goals have been met, the students should be given assessments based on what they should have learned during that time.

Reader Variables

Language, culture, motivation, background knowledge, experiences, and skill levels are all reader variables that go into picking appropriate texts for student learning goals. The text complexity should match the student's language level. English language learners may need different considerations than native speakers. Cultural relevancy should also be considered. The goal is to always have the reader engaged with the text. Assigning texts that feature various cultures, including their own, will help the reader connect with the text.

Motivation is a big part of effective learning goals. Students may become unmotivated with goals that seem too large to overcome. For these students, it may be helpful to increase text complexity at a steady rate rather than making large jumps. Assign specific goals that can be easily focused on, rather than broad subjects that may be overwhelming. The background knowledge and experiences of a student may help with assigning texts that grab their attention and keep motivation high. For example, if a student enjoys having knowledge about various bugs, assigning texts related to that subject may help keep them interested.

Perhaps the most important consideration for choosing appropriate texts is skill level. Students, regardless of grade level, will have various reading skills. Students should be assigned texts that challenge them in an engaging way. They should be learning new skills from the text without the difficulty becoming too much. This may require adjustments as the students vocalize how they feel about the text. Assessments will also show how their skill level is progressing.

Task Variables

Task variables should be accounted for when selecting appropriate texts for student learning goals. The two major variables are complexity and purpose. The complexity of a text should match the student's skill level. A low-complexity text will generally have a simple structure and explicit meaning. A high-complexity text will take on a varied structure that is unconventional. It may also contain layers of meaning that are difficult for some readers to understand. Texts that use conventional language will be easier to read. Texts that use historical forms of the language or layer the work in figurative language will be difficult to read.

There are tasks that will have a specific purpose. Informational or nonfiction texts will have an explicit purpose. It is important to pick texts with a purpose that aligns with the student's learning goals. For example, a text that has a purpose of teaching particle physics may not be appropriate for a young student. Subjects that the student is learning outside of reading development are appropriate choices.

World History: Ancient Civilizations

Mesopotamia

Mesopotamia was a region around modern-day Iraq where many early civilizations developed and flourished. The most defining geographical feature of Mesopotamia—and the greatest contributor to the success of early civilizations there—are its two rivers, the Euphrates and the Tigris. The area around these rivers largely consisted of deserts in the north and marshes in the south. This region was extremely fertile, which led to the early development of farming and agricultural technologies. Unpredictable annual floods often wiped out crops, so farmers developed methods of irrigation to bring water from the rivers and built dams to mitigate flood damage. Mesopotamia is sometimes known as the Fertile Crescent thanks to the advancements in agriculture during this era.

Despite early innovations, the climate and terrain still proved challenging. The arid climate meant wood was a relatively scarce resource, so structures were instead made from clay or stone. In addition, early farming was largely supplemented by nomadic or fishing lifestyles. Nomads herded sheep and goats from the rivers to the desert edges. In the far south where the Euphrates and Tigris met, fishing cultures developed instead in the dense marshlands. Early civilizations like Babylon and Sumer developed, and humanity thrived in Mesopotamia.

Mesopotamian religion was polytheistic, and the people believed in many major and minor gods. Every city had its own patron god or goddess, so every culture had its own gods whom the people valued most. Priests held the second-highest power position in society, below only kings. Kings were believed to be chosen by the gods and therefore ruled with a form of divine authority. Even though they were viewed as all-powerful, Mesopotamian gods were still portrayed as being mostly human, capable of eating, drinking, enjoying themselves, and even being injured.

Ancient Mesopotamian art was detailed and intricate, rivaled only by Egyptian art of the time. The artworks that have survived the passage of time reveal a lot of technical secrets in their creation. Sculptures were made of stone and clay for durability, and while many were painted, very few have had their paint last to today. Stone stelae (singular: stele) were also constructed as small monuments to honor battles or feasts. These stelae were simple slabs of stone that either depicted art or inscriptions of their purpose. Perhaps the most innovative art form of the time was the Mesopotamian cylinder seal. These were small stone cylinders, only about an inch or two long, that were engraved with various scenes all around the outside of the cylinder. These seals could then be pressed into softer clay and rolled across it to create an impression on the clay of the scene on the seal. While these did display artistic scenes, cylinder seals were often used as an ancient form of signature or branding and were carried by officials or artisans. This means cylinder seals served a similar ancient purpose to the medieval wax seals that would be used thousands of years later.

Mesopotamian civilizations also relied on trade with each other and neighboring civilizations. For all the natural bounty that Mesopotamia had, it lacked many metals. Therefore, its people had to trade with Egypt and the Indus River Valley civilizations for metals like copper, gold, and silver. In exchange, they exported ceramics, grain, and textiles like reeds—all materials they could easily find and shape or grow. Mesopotamian trade is what inspired the adoption of the wheel to create vehicles and roads for transporting goods.

Egypt

Ancient Egypt was a relatively isolated region surrounded by natural barriers: the Mediterranean Sea to the north, the Red Sea and desert to the east, more desert to the west, and mountains to the south. Thanks to this protective isolation, Egypt was initially able to focus on growing agriculturally and did not have to worry about needing a military force. Inside this area was the Nile River, which flowed from the southern mountains to the north, exiting at the Mediterranean Sea. As it reached the Mediterranean Sea, it began to split into many smaller rivers, forming a great river delta of fertile land. The Nile River was the lifeblood of ancient Egypt thanks to its annual flooding. While this pattern was not uncommon for similar civilizations like Mesopotamia or China, the Nile's annual flooding was unique in how predictable it was. The sheer size and length of the river allowed for regular precautions to be taken and for the creation of a solid cycle of agriculture. It flooded during the summer months (June through September) before receding heavily in the winter months (November through January). Crops could then be planted, and the floodplains were so fertile that they could be harvested by March or April, well before the next annual flood began.

Egyptian agriculture thrived with a large variety of crops. Grains and barley were staple food crops, but many vegetables like beans, onions, garlic, and radishes were grown too. Fruit was also grown, like palm dates and eventually figs and grapes, but these required significantly more irrigation and complex agriculture. Because Egypt was so agriculturally advanced, it was even able to produce many industrial crops like papyrus and flax. Papyrus could be turned into paper and used to construct Egyptian boats, and flax was made into rope or linen for clothes. In addition to making advanced agriculture possible, the Nile provided plenty of marshland for animals to graze and thrive, so pastures and hunting game were equally plentiful. The dry climate made wood a rare material for building houses, so early houses were constructed from a combination of mud and reeds. However, these houses were easily washed away by flooding, so people began to create mud bricks mixed with straw and clay to make their houses sturdier. Since all of Egypt developed along or very near the Nile, transportation was also easy—Egyptians could simply sail upstream or ride currents downstream. The many bounties provided by the Nile gave Egyptians a comfortable lifestyle to prosper and grow.

The ease of transportation along the Nile was also a boon for Egyptian trade. Traders sailed up and down the Nile as a major route, then stopped and delivered goods by camel or cart. The mouth of the Nile that exited into the Mediterranean served as an effective center for external trade, where Egyptians traded gold and other precious metals for wood, copper, iron, and ivory. Egyptian trade with other cultures like Mesopotamia and Greece also influenced the style of Egyptian artists. Some Egyptian artists began putting a greater focus on detail in sculpture and emphasizing imagery in a more Grecian style. Egyptian trade was carried out through barter, where goods of equal value were exchanged instead of currency.

Egyptian religion was polytheistic with a large pantheon of gods that each served different purposes. Many religious rituals centered around the Egyptian pharaohs, people who acted as rulers of Egypt and were believed to have divine powers. Pharaohs performed rituals or took action to maintain balance and order, though everyone was free to pray or appeal to any of the gods. These rituals and prayers were conducted at massive stone temples filled with sculptures and statues. One aspect of Egyptian religion that stands out was a reverence for the afterlife. Pharaohs had elaborate tombs constructed long before their death, massive stone pyramids that housed little more than their burial chamber and some rooms for offerings. Upon their death, the pharaohs were buried with many offerings and goods. Ancient Egyptians believed these offerings would be directly used by the pharaoh's soul in the afterlife.

Ancient Egyptian art was only rivaled by ancient Mesopotamian art for its detail and beauty. Soft stone like limestone was carved to make reliefs and tall statues were carved into the walls of temples. Much of their art

142

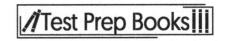

focused on the bounty of the Nile River or their reverence for death, and the two beliefs were seen as interconnected. The artistic influence didn't stop at statues, ceramics, or reliefs; wood and jewelry were used to create elaborate sarcophagi for the burial of pharaohs and other important figures.

Kush

South of ancient Egypt and further upstream along the Nile River was a region called the Nubian Desert. Between the first cataract of the Nile and the merging point of the Blue and White Nile Rivers, a small civilization called the Kush grew. (These people were also sometimes called the Nubians because of the Nubian Desert.) This civilization shared many of the benefits of being located near the Nile along with Egypt—predictable flooding, fertile farmland, and even the Nile's cultural significance. Kush used the Nile for trade and communication like Egypt, needing only to sail up or down the river. Kushites grew wheat and barley for food as well as cotton for clothes.

While a period is known to exist between 2500 BC and 1500 BC during which Kush's culture was a collection of beliefs from smaller kingdoms, many of the early Kushite beliefs were lost around 1600 BC, when Egypt, at the height of its power, raided and conquered Kush. Afterward, Egypt imposed its beliefs upon the Kush, and the Kushite religion became focused on Egyptian gods and beliefs. Kush gained its independence from Egypt around 1070 BC but kept many Egyptian beliefs including the importance of priests and kings and a respect for the cycle of life and death. They even built pyramids used as tombs for their kings and queens. The Kush also constructed tombs carved into rock faces called speoi (singular: speos), and this influence spread back to Egypt.

The major geographical difference between Kush and Egypt was that Kush had access to gold and iron. Iron was used to make some of the strongest weapons and tools at the time. These iron weapons, along with Kushite's skilled archers, made Kush a powerful military force. Gold was a rare metal used to trade for other valuables, along with exotic trade goods like ivory and animal hides obtained from further south and west in Africa. Initially, Kush traded with Egypt or other small kingdoms, but around 728 BC Kush began to leverage its military power and invade a fragmented Egypt. Kush successfully conquered Egypt, but only ruled for less than 100 years before the Assyrians invaded and conquered Egypt themselves, pushing Kush back into the Nubian Desert. It was around this time that Kush moved its capital from Napata to the city of Meroe, further up the Nile, to distance itself from the invading Assyrians.

Hebrew

The ancient Hebrews developed in the region known today as Israel. The eastern mountains and western coastline with the Mediterranean Sea meant there was a diverse range of land that included fertile farmland, dry deserts, and rocky mountains. However, farming was not as widely successful in the region, so pasturing animals was more common. This led to an early nomadic lifestyle, mostly around the one river that passed through the area—the Jordan River. This river travels from north to south, splitting the region down the middle and ending at the Dead Sea, a large salt lake. Gradually two main kingdoms began to form—the Kingdom of Israel and the Kingdom of Judah.

Early Hebrew religion was a variation of polytheism called henotheism, the recognition of multiple deities but with primary worship of only one or two gods. Both Israel and Judah believed in Yahweh as their primary god and frequently worshipped Yahweh in temples or through festivals and rituals like Yom Kippur. Both cultures also focused on ethical behavior as a form of devotion to Yahweh. They respected and helped each other and believed that otherwise Yahweh would abandon the temple. A collection of Hebrew texts containing details of

events with great religious significance dating back to around 300 BC have been discovered in various caves all around the Dead Sea. These are known as the Dead Sea Scrolls and are some of the oldest surviving Hebrew religious texts.

Both kingdoms traded with each other and with other civilizations across the Mediterranean Sea. They were also close enough by land to other civilizations like Egypt, Phoenicia, and Mesopotamia that they served as a land bridge to connect trade between these civilizations. Initially, agricultural goods were all the Hebrews could offer. Farmers grew olives and grapes and traded them for cheese and milk from the herders or for wood and raw materials from other civilizations. Later, ores and metals were discovered in the mountains, and artisans were able to trade silver and bronze goods as well as wine and medicinal plant products. The efforts of these artisans were crucial for the kingdoms' economies, and through trade both kingdoms were able to secure a comfortable lifestyle.

Greek

Ancient Greece formed along the coastline and islands of the eastern Mediterranean Sea. The mainland was extremely mountainous, which made land travel difficult and formed natural barriers to protect early city-states. Many settlements formed around the Aegean Sea, a specific region of the Mediterranean Sea. Travel was easier across the Aegean Sea than through the mountains, so the Greeks were much more dependent on the ocean to sustain themselves, such as through fishing for food. Since it was difficult to travel on land or establish a singular rule, most of Greece consisted of individual city-states instead of a single empire. These city-states, such as Athens and Sparta, all spoke the same language and held similar beliefs but developed and operated independently of each other.

Ancient Greek religion is perhaps the most well-known ancient polytheistic religion. The Greek pantheon had twelve major gods that were worshipped at various shrines and temples, including Zeus, Athena, Poseidon, Ares, Artemis, and many others. Similar to the way there was no central Greek empire and governments operated at the city-state level, Greek religious beliefs were also carried out individually by each city-state. Different cities might focus their worship on different gods or have individual variations on stories and myths. Some gods were associated with certain cities, but different cities might have different perceptions of the same god. Whether it was despite all these differences in beliefs or because of them, the Greeks valued the actions someone took more than what they believed in.

Temples and shrines were not the only highlights of ancient Greek architecture. The Greeks also constructed large open-air theatres, public squares, monuments, and stadiums. Many Greek structures were constructed to emphasize the sheer size and spectacle of their design. This was demonstrated through elaborate columns and decorative art, but also in more nuanced ways, like placing important buildings on higher ground where they could be seen from all angles. Some famous Greek structures include the Parthenon (a famous temple to Athena) and the Temple of Olympian Zeus, both located in Athens.

Ancient Greek art could be an entire subject in itself, considering how detailed it was and the development it underwent. To highlight just some of this history, the Greeks made art in many forms: pottery, metalworks, sculptures, mosaics, figurines, and even in architectural design. Early art focused on geometric shapes and motifs, but over time it evolved into naturalistic and representational styles, with the intent of trying to depict the human form accurately. Some Greek art was made to represent the gods, such as the *Venus de Milo*, an impressively detailed sculpture believed to represent the goddess of love, Aphrodite. Others represented average Greeks such as the *Discobolus*, a bronze sculpture of a Greek athlete preparing to throw a discus. As

Greek art evolved, so too did the art in other areas of the world, as Greek art was often traded to other civilizations and influenced their art styles.

In terms of trade, few early civilizations were in as beneficial a position as the Greeks were. Their position in the Mediterranean Sea, as well as their established reliance on travel by boat, made them able to easily trade both locally and abroad. The Greeks exported wine and high-quality pottery, spreading their beliefs and culture all over the Mediterranean while trading with Egypt and Phoenicia for gold, copper, and ivory. They also traded for wood, papyrus, and luxuries like spices.

India

Ancient Indian civilizations formed in a region called the Indus River Valley around modern-day Pakistan and northwestern India. The Indus River Valley was a rich, bountiful region. There was plenty of farmland for growing a variety of crops like rice, wheat, fruits, and cotton. Animals thrived, fresh water was easily available, and wood and precious metals were plentiful. Early civilization boomed in the region, creating many large cities. The two largest of these cities that served as huge hubs for trade in the region were Harappa and Mohenjo-Daro. They even had advanced amenities for the time like organized houses, a sewer system, and storage warehouses. However, not everything was perfect. Frequent disastrous monsoons were a major challenge to living in the region. From June to October, wet monsoons blew in from the ocean to the southwest, causing flooding and ruining crops. From October to February, dry monsoons came down from the mountains to the northeast, causing huge storms and damage. These storms were unpredictable and could cause lasting damage. So as bountiful as the Indus River Valley was, the danger of monsoons was always present and made life difficult.

Two major religious beliefs had their beginnings in the Indus River Valley civilizations: Hinduism and Buddhism. Hinduism is a set of philosophical beliefs that focus on the goals of human life as well as virtues such as honesty, patience, and compassion. While Hinduism does have some gods like Vishnu, Brahma, and Shiva, they are not considered superior or inferior to many of the religion's other beliefs. There are too many important beliefs of Hinduism to concisely describe here, but two of the most important and well-known ones are karma (actions and consequences) and samsara (the cycle of death and rebirth). Buddhism is an offshoot of Hinduism and does not believe in any god. Instead, it focuses intensely on the belief that "our life is shaped by our mind; we become what we think." Buddhist beliefs state that by finding beauty in the transience of life and avoiding becoming too attached to impermanent things, one can find true inner peace and escape suffering. Both religions are still prominent in the region and around the world today.

Surprisingly, not much art of the Indus River Valley civilizations has survived. There was little public large-scale art, and what few pieces have survived the collapse of these civilizations are simple. Figurines made of gold or stone were made depicting people in the forms of dance or representing animals like cows, monkeys, and dogs. Some carved seals depicting animals or human-like figures have also been found. Beyond these figurines and seals, however, very little art has survived from this period.

On the other hand, the architecture of the Indus River Valley civilizations is well documented. Many buildings were built with bricks, at first with mud, but later with fired clay instead. Buildings from Harappa were the first in the world to use a combination of bricks and mortar, bonding the bricks together during construction for even stronger buildings. The people of the Indus River Valley even made drainage systems in their cities, and the additional presence of streets with buildings parallel to them suggests that Harappan cities conducted urban planning, a very advanced idea for the time period.

Ancient Indian trade was very lucrative. Harappans became known as accomplished sea traders, traveling to Mesopotamia to trade gold, textiles, and spices. This exchange persisted for many years and made Indus River Valley civilizations wealthy and cultured. Sea trade was the primary method of trade for a long time, but China eventually constructed the Silk Road to connect to India and other civilizations by land, which expanded India's trade even further. This led to further growth through trade for Indian civilizations, especially by trading silks, spices, and incense.

China

Like the Tigris and Euphrates of Mesopotamia, two major rivers formed the basis of Ancient China: the Yellow River and the Yangtze River. Both rivers were extremely fertile, so between fishing and farming, early Chinese civilizations quickly prospered. However, floods were common, so irrigation canals and protective dikes were developed to protect against floods destroying farmland and crops. Around these two river valleys, China experienced strong natural isolation. The tallest mountains in the world—the Himalayas—blocked off the south and west, while the Gobi Desert and Pacific Ocean blocked the north and east respectively. This isolation effectively protected early Chinese dynasties from outside invasion, giving Chinese civilization time and safety to grow.

Ancient Chinese art mostly took the form of pottery, jade, and bronze items. When dynasties began to form later on, calligraphy (a form of writing where the art is the writing itself) also became common. Pottery used simple geometric patterns or human face-like decorations. Jade items were mostly created using jade found around the Yangtze River and included large ritual items like cylinders, pendants, and plaques. Many bronze artifacts were made primarily for rituals and ceremonies, such as cauldrons or vessels for holding liquids and solids during various ceremonies. Chinese architecture focused on concepts that carried artistic significance such as bilateral symmetry, where buildings were designed to be symmetrical across certain lines. Larger properties had a hierarchy system where the orientation of the door for a room signified the room's function or role. The wealthy built large properties horizontally, using the width and scale to inspire respect rather than height.

Ancient Chinese trade is most famous for the Silk Road, a massive collection of land routes through the western mountains of China that extended both south into India as well as further west to Europe and the Mediterranean Sea. While silk was the route's namesake trade good, China also traded spices, porcelain, and tea for cotton, ivory, gold, and silver. The routes were so long that few merchants traveled the whole length of the Silk Road and instead often stopped to trade with other merchants or settlements along the way. Religions like Buddhism also "traveled" the Silk Road and helped expand Chinese culture with new beliefs. The Silk Road—and future additions to the routes over the ocean—was China's primary method of trade for centuries.

Roman

The Roman Empire is one of history's most famous and powerful civilizations, but it had humble beginnings. It began as a village along the Tiber River in what is now modern-day Italy. Fresh water, a large fertile river valley, and easy transportation along the river provided ideal conditions for the early Romans to flourish. They also benefitted from a naturally defensible position. The Tiber River was about halfway down the peninsula and came down from the Apennine Mountains, a mountain range that ran down the middle of the peninsula. These mountains, along with the Alps further to the north and the many forested hills surrounding Rome, made it extremely difficult for invaders to approach and gave the Romans plenty of time to prepare for the attack.

Ancient Roman religion was culturally important, as Roman leaders even attributed their global successes to being devout and respectful of their gods. Their polytheistic pantheon was extremely similar to that of the Greeks, to the point that Romans adapted Greek myths to fit within their own gods. Religion was primarily focused on proper observance and practice rather than a specific belief or faith. This meant that religious ceremony and daily practice or prayer was extremely important. The Roman calendar was even structured to fit the observance of religious days as public events. This focus on observance over beliefs meant it was irrelevant whether a central pantheon or a local deity was being worshipped as long as they were respected and worshipped correctly.

Because the early Romans had access to the Mediterranean Sea coastline, they were able to trade with other Mediterranean cities and civilizations of the time. They traded olives, grain, gold, spices, and silks with Egypt and other civilizations, as well as among themselves as the Roman Empire grew. They were even able to trade goods with China thanks to the Silk Road. Rome eventually fought against another major Mediterranean trade power—Carthage—over trade routes and expansion in a series of wars called the Punic Wars.

Roman art took a variety of forms, including pottery, metalworks, ivory carvings, and engraved gems. However, the two most important artistic forms to the Romans were sculptures and architecture. Despite the importance Romans placed on their art and architecture, their style was rarely original and often heavily influenced by Greek, Etruscan, and even Egyptian art. Roman sculptures emphasized naturalism and the human form of both leaders and gods such as in the *Equestrian Statue of Marcus Aurelius*, a detailed bronze statue of Roman emperor Marcus Aurelius riding a horse and posed as if he is issuing commands to an army. Roman architecture was reminiscent of Greek styles with tall columns and large, prominent buildings. Where Roman architecture diverged was in the development of new materials like Roman concrete, as well as building techniques like the arch and the dome, all of which helped create incredibly durable structures. Examples of these durable structures include the famous Colosseum in Rome (where gladiatorial combat took place) and the Arena of Nimes in modern-day southern France (which was used for similar gladiator combat and general public events).

World History: Medieval and Early Modern Times

China

As China developed through the Middle Ages, several events were shaped by China's geography. During the Sui dynasty in the year 609, the Grand Canal project was completed. This canal, also called the Jing-Hang Grand Canal, connected the Yangtze and Yellow Rivers and also provided extended canal access to other farmland areas. Parts of the canal date back to ancient China, but the sections weren't all connected and routed to the capital city until the Middle Ages. This project let China connect farmers of grain and other crops directly to the political and military hubs, which helped centralize power. The Grand Canal's waterways were also sometimes intentionally destroyed during wars as a way of washing away enemy troops, which occasionally caused additional economic damage to the region.

China was bordered on the north by the Gobi Desert and by mountains beyond them, but in that region lived wandering nomads that frequently raided northern Chinese settlements. China spent many years constructing a massive wall to block off the northern raiders, known today as the Great Wall of China. While the wall was reasonably successful at first, in the early 1200s the nomads to the north, known as the Mongols, began to centralize power. Led by Genghis Khan, the Mongols became a powerful empire. Eventually, Genghis's

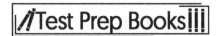

successor Kublai Khan led a successful invasion of all of China. This invasion ended the Song Dynasty and marked the beginning of the Yuan Dynasty.

Years later in 1405, a Chinese explorer named Zheng He began a series of expeditions to the rest of the world. The Silk Road trade routes brought many goods into China, but not many Chinese people knew much about the world outside their isolated land. He left on seven different diplomatic missions, sent by the Ming emperor Yongle to trade and meet with foreign powers. Zheng He sailed trade fleets along known ocean trade routes to India and eastern Africa, meeting with regional leaders and returning to China with new goods and ideas. Ultimately, Zheng He's missions were only mildly successful to the emperor, but for many other Chinese people, he established an interest in foreign culture, ideas, and luxuries. The next emperor, Xuande, canceled Zheng He's missions and returned China to an isolationist nation, but the seeds had been scattered among the Chinese populace. Interest in foreign culture, ideas, and luxuries was growing. Future Chinese explorers followed in Zheng He's footsteps and expanded China's role as a trade power many years later.

Japan

Medieval Japan (1185 to 1590), also called feudal Japan, saw many internal wars for power. Shoguns and their subordinates grappled for power, trying to become the next ruler of Japan. However, there were two attempts by outside forces to invade Japan. Kublai Khan attempted to invade Japan amid his campaign to conquer China. Initially, he successfully took a couple of smaller islands, but before he could take the mainland, his forces were pushed back by an overnight storm. Having already suffered leadership losses, Kublai Khan's forces retreated and prepared for a second invasion a few years later. Once his conquest of China was complete, he turned his full attention to Japan, only for almost the exact same thing to happen again. Kublai's forces took the same islands and began to push into the mainland, only for a massive storm to approach from the west. Unable to escape, the Mongolian forces were devastated, and only a few survivors got away. Many more were killed, either by the storm or by the Japanese afterward.

A few centuries and several shogunate changes later, another outside empire arrived in Japan, this time seeking trade instead of war. Several Portuguese explorers arrived in 1543 and opened trade with Japan. Portuguese trade began to expand, especially as they acted as intermediaries in trade with China, which Japanese merchants were forbidden to engage in normally. These Portuguese explorers also introduced Japan to firearms, and within a year Japanese smiths could reproduce the firearms themselves. This was a short period of rapid change for Japan. More traders from Europe arrived, including the Spanish, English, and Dutch, bringing new goods and beliefs like Christianity into Japan. Meanwhile, a powerful daimyo (warlord) named Oda Nobunaga used firearms to quickly equip and enhance the strength of his armies. Nobunaga was a brilliant military leader but also a shrewd negotiator, keeping a close eye on all of his rivals and exploiting every weakness he saw to gradually conquer all of Japan's shoguns and daimyos. However, he was suddenly betrayed by one of his generals for unknown reasons late into his conquest and committed seppuku (honorable suicide), ordering the castle he was in burned down so nobody could get his head. One of his retainers, Toyotomi Hideyoshi, went on to use firearm-equipped armies to avenge Nobunaga and successfully unify all of Japan under one rule.

However, Hideyoshi became disgusted at Portuguese traders engaging in the slave trade with Japanese people, purchasing Japanese slaves and selling them elsewhere in the world. He demanded Portugal immediately stop this trade and return as many Japanese slaves as they could. When Portugal refused to comply, Hideyoshi banned Christianity from Japan and ordered the nation into isolation. Christian priests were forced to leave, and most foreign traders were forbidden from trading with Japan. Only a select few Dutch and Chinese traders were allowed to continue trading, and only at specific cities like Hirado and later Dejima.

Africa

Africa in the Middle Ages was full of emerging empires and kingdoms. The Mali Empire established itself in western Africa in 1235 and was famous for being a source of gold for many other civilizations in the world. Mansa Musa, leader of Mali in 1324, went on a famous pilgrimage to Mecca to show off his extravagant wealth to other nations. Another kingdom, the Kingdom of Kongo in central Africa, rose to power around 1390 and became a central trade hub in the region, specializing in natural resources and ivory. It started as a small collection of smaller kingdoms that formed alliances to help each other maintain power and eventually centralized that power to one kingdom by granting the subordinate kingdoms electors. In the mid-1400s, the Songhai Empire also rose to power in western Africa, seizing control of lands from the Mali Empire and gradually exceeding Mali in wealth and luxury. The tribes that formed the Songhai were experienced with living in and around the massive and punishing Sahara Desert and were able to establish control over trans-Saharan land trade routes to help expand their wealth. Another central-African power, the Kingdom of Luba, appeared in the modern-day Congo region in 1585. Many of these empires were small and only focused on ruling their own lands or establishing trade with other world empires.

However, the largest trade of the African empires was the slave trade. Around the 1500s, the slave trade began, and African empires with access to the western coast sold slaves to European nations like the Spanish, Portuguese, English, and Dutch. These European nations took the slaves elsewhere, usually to the Americas, and used slave labor for the mass production of crops or goods. African slave labor became commonplace from the North American colonies to the Caribbean and South America. Meanwhile, the African empires became increasingly destabilized, and the disparities between the empires grew bigger. Some states grew wealthy by conquering others and selling the entire population as slaves. African societies became depopulated and unable to develop further, with most populations living in fear of captivity. While nations abandoned the practice over time, it was hundreds of years before the practice was completely ended, and in that time an estimated 12 million slaves were sold as part of the slave trade.

Arabia

The Arabian Peninsula was a battleground between two major empires during the early Middle Ages: the Byzantines and the Persians. As one of the only two land connections between Europe and Asia, the peninsula was a major trade pathway, and both empires vied for power over key cities in upper Mesopotamia to be able to control that trade. In the early 600s, however, both empires were at a low, weak point and were caught off guard by the arrival of Islam. The religion of Islam began to spread rapidly, with leaders called caliphs serving as political and religious successors to the Islamic prophet Muhammad. The Arab Caliphates swiftly took control of not just the southern Arabian Peninsula, but also the upper Mesopotamian battleground, pushing back both the Byzantines and the Persians. The sudden spread of Islam reinvigorated culture in the region. Rapid advancements in architecture, science, technology, and more began the Islamic Golden Age, which lasted for most of the Middle Ages.

In the mid-1000s, the Seljuk Turks suddenly and rapidly expanded from Central Asia and quickly conquered most of the Arab Caliphate, only stopped by the Byzantine Empire. The Byzantines were essentially the wall holding back invaders from moving on to Europe, and they kept trade between Europe and Asia flowing. Concerned with the rapid Seljuk expansion, the Byzantines asked the Christian Pope to intervene and get other European empires to help. This led to the beginning of the Crusades, a series of holy wars during which Christian knights and armies tried to push Islamic-believing cultures out of the Holy Land. This Holy Land was the region between the Mediterranean and the Jordan River, where both Christianity and Judaism originated. The First Crusade began in 1095, and over the next 200 years many crusades were conducted. While the First

149

Crusade did capture Jerusalem in 1099, most crusades either did not get very far or were entirely unsuccessful, as most of the Christian knights were unprepared for battle in the Middle East.

The Mongol Empire also controlled land in the Middle East for a time, but when Mongke Khan died in 1259, chaos ensued, as nobody could decide who to elect as their new Great Khan. As the Mongols retreated, they were replaced by the Ottoman Turks, who conquered most of the region and beyond. The Ottomans were also finally able to break the Byzantine Empire and conquered its capital, Constantinople, in 1453.

Mesoamerica

The Middle Ages in Mesoamerica was a period of flourishing arts, sciences, and urbanism. Many cities in the region began to concentrate their population within urban developments such as Teotihuacan. While it's still unclear today if Teotihuacan was part of an empire in the region, it was undoubtedly the largest city in the region for many years, located within the Valley of Mexico. The Valley of Mexico itself was a hub for many populous cities centered around the large Lake Texcoco.

However, in 536, three simultaneous volcanic eruptions devastated the region. The exact three volcanoes responsible are unknown and could have been located anywhere in the world, with most known documentation of their eruptions coming from Constantinople in Eastern Europe. The effects included a massive volcanic winter that led to cooler temperatures and crop failures across the Northern Hemisphere. Mesoamerica was one of the regions hit the hardest by this volcanic winter, leading to the fall of many of the region's cities including Teotihuacan. Evidence suggests the city was intentionally destroyed, with fires concentrated around buildings related to the upper or ruling classes, as well as signs of drought and famine. The most popular theory is that environmental factors caused a drought, leading to a famine, leading to an uprising from lower classes targeted at the upper classes. Eventually, the entire city was abandoned.

The region bounced back relatively quickly, with new city-states appearing like Cacaxtla, Xochicalco, Teotenango, and El Tajin. With the disappearance of Teotihuacan, however, the Mayans were able to assert more control over the region. The Mayan Empire had existed previously, but Teotihuacan's influence prevented it from expanding more until the city's collapse. The Mayan society was advanced, creating a dominant calendar system and even an early form of astronomical study. However, sometime in the 800s, Mayan society experienced widespread political collapse, and most cities were abandoned. Following the collapse of the Mayans, several other civilizations centering around lakes and rivers rose and fell, like the Toltecs, Mixtecs, and Aztecs. The Aztecs, in particular, asserted dominance over all other cultures and were poised to attain a level of power over the Valley of Mexico on par with Teotihuacan. This ended around 1520 when the Spanish arrived to conquer and colonize Mesoamerica.

Andean Highland

Many different Andean Highland civilizations rose and fell during the Middle Ages. Not all are noteworthy, but a few are worth discussing. The Nazca culture arose in 100 BC in southwestern Peru along the coast and lasted until about 800. The southern and western coastlines of the Andean Highlands are extremely arid, making it difficult for most civilizations to find suitable land for agriculture without significant irrigation. People couldn't usually go inland for farming either, as there were tall mountains almost immediately next to the arid coastlines, with very few valleys suitable for farming and not enough fertile soil available higher up. The Nazca are known for their extensive aqueducts built to solve the irrigation problem, as well as massive geoglyphs called Nazca Lines. The Tiwanaku Empire lasted from around 600 to 1000 and was notable for having one of

the most populous capitals of its time in the city of Tiwanaku. It was also not strictly an empire and more closely resembled a collection of cities.

In 1230, Manco Capac founded the Kingdom of Cusco, a small city-state higher up in the Andean Highlands that became the foundation for the Inca. It lasted for about 200 years, and in 1438 the Sapa Inca (supreme leader) Pachacuti formed the Incan Empire and quickly expanded across the whole Andean Highlands. The Inca assimilated most other civilizations in the area, whether through conquest or peace. They built extensive roads and massive stoneworks, all constructed without wheels, draft animals, or knowledge of iron. One of their most famous stonework creations was the city of Machu Picchu, an elaborate stone citadel constructed so perfectly by Incan engineers that not even a thin knife blade could fit between the stones. This is especially interesting considering there was no mortar to hold the buildings together. The stones fitting together so tightly made the buildings surprisingly stable against the environmental dangers of earthquakes and volcanic eruptions. The Incan Empire itself, however, was not quite as stable. After the last Sapa Inca, Huayna Capac, died of smallpox in 1527, a civil war of succession in combination with more smallpox cases significantly weakened the Incan Empire. When the Spanish arrived around this time, the Incans were easily conquered by Francisco Pizarro in 1533.

Europe

When Rome fell in 476, Europe became divided by geography with no single government to unite it. Kingdoms grew around rivers and coastlines and were divided by mountain ranges or river borders. The Mediterranean Sea, English Channel, and Atlantic Ocean were ocean barriers on the south, north, and west sides respectively. Rivers became focal points for civilization to rebuild, such as the Rhine, Danube, Volga, Vistula, and Seine Rivers. Many of these rivers were significantly wide enough to act as natural borders. Mountain borders included the Alps that separated Italy from central Europe, the Pyrenees Mountains in the southwest that separated modern-day Spain and Portugal from mainland Europe, and the Carpathian Mountains in the east that separated modern-day Ukraine and Russia from southeastern Europe. These divisions incentivized people to develop their own cultures and trade with each other to survive, and several kingdoms began to grow out of these changes.

The Gaul tribes were united into the Franks by King Clovis I around 481. Initially, the Franks were located primarily around the Rhine and Meuse Rivers, but they expanded west and then south, and by 800 theirs was the largest post-Roman European empire. Pope Leo III even crowned the then-leader of the Franks, Charlemagne, as the new Roman Emperor. Charlemagne did not like being bestowed this title, however, and it only triggered disputes with the Byzantine Empire that had formed from the division of the Western and Eastern Roman Empires. The Frankish Empire eventually divided into three parts in 840. West Francia eventually became modern-day France, while East Francia eventually became the Holy Roman Empire and later the territories of Germany, Austria, and Switzerland. Middle Francia was further divided into three provinces: Lotharingia, Burgundy, and Italy Lombardy. These three provinces eventually dissolved their kingdoms and either merged with neighboring countries or formed new ones like Belgium, the Netherlands, and Luxembourg.

The region that became Spain, then known as Hispania, was a battleground between Islamic and Christian factions. Initially, it was settled by several Germanic tribes, but they ultimately united under the Visigoths in 410. This unity did not last long, as invading refugees forced the Visigoths back out into Gaul, but they gradually expanded back out into Hispania and eventually reclaimed their rule. During these times, the tribes in the region were gradually undergoing "Romanization," adopting a belief in Christianity and shifting from raiding to general settlements. In 710, the Umayyad Caliphate that controlled North Africa sent a conquering

party and quickly invaded, ending the Visigoths and taking control of the entire Iberian Peninsula. Only the Franks stopped them from invading Central Europe. These conquerors—known as Moors—converted the population to Islam and then brought the region under heavier Arabic influence. However, Christian rebels from the northern mountains succeeded in raising support and pushed out some of the Caliphate control. From this point on until around the 1400s, raids and small wars occasionally broke out between a number of small kingdoms vying for control of the whole region. They finally settled down in the late 1400s when Isabella I of Castille married King Ferdinand II of Aragon. The union of these two states was enough to set the stage for modern-day Spain to eventually arise. Isabella and Ferdinand oversaw the end of the Reconquista period of Spanish history, where non-Christians were forced to convert or else face slaughter or expulsion, and the famous Spanish Inquisition ensured the populace complied.

Decline of the Western Roman Empire

Rome's decline began well before its eventual fall. There are many aspects to Rome's demise, including social, political, moral, religious, and economic. Each took their toll on the strength of the empire, and by 400 A.D., Rome collapsed under public unrest and religious discord, along with the invasion of the Huns of Mongolia and Germanic tribes. Although ultimately defeated, Rome's legacy extends all the way through to the present day. The Roman Republic's democratic elements and robust civil service would be the model for much of the West, especially the United States. That is to say nothing of the advancements in literature, technology, architecture, urban planning, and hygiene across the empire that influenced every future Western civilization.

Feudalism

The European socioeconomic order revolved around agriculture from 1200 to 1450 due to the prevalence of feudalism. The powerful landed class of feudal nobles typically organized their land under the manorial system. The vast majority of European nobles served as the Lord of the Manor, and their extensive landholdings were known as **fiefs**. Peasants who lived on the fief were allowed to farm the land, but they were obligated to pay the Lord of the Manor taxes either in the form of free labor or percentage of crops. Furthermore, the Lord of the Manor held all political power, and even more importantly, created and oversaw the legal system that applied to the fief. Nobles' legal and economic dominance over the peasants is why they held such power under feudalism. Although trade and urban centers generally increased from 1200 to 1450, Europe was still an overwhelmingly agriculture society due to the number and size of fiefs across the continent.

Japanese Feudalism

Feudal Japan was a period from 1185 to 1603 when the military shoguns had more control over the country and society than the emperor and his court did. The shoguns assigned land to stewards (jito) and military leaders (shugo) as rewards for their military service and loyalty. These jito and shugo were not technically landowners but eventually accrued enough power to rival the shoguns themselves. Japanese feudalism was slightly different from European feudalism; instead of being essentially a contract between a lord and vassals, the bond was more personal and formed from an almost familial respect from the vassal to the lord. While the system benefited the shoguns initially, allowing them to control vast amounts of land, Japanese feudalism eventually crumbled due to a combination of a lack of any formal government structure and the jito and shugo gaining enough power to rival the shoguns themselves.

Art, Architecture, and Science of Pre-Columbian America

Pre-Columbian Mesoamerica had three distinct periods of art, mostly defined by the dominant civilization of the era. In the Pre-classic period, the Olmecs built large ceremonial structures and massive stone heads

thought to be representations of Olmec rulers. They also made many items out of jade, such as figurines and face masks used by the nobility.

The Classic period was dominated by the Maya, a very agricultural civilization. They mostly made art focused on rain and crops in the form of reliefs or simple surface paintings. These decorations and glyphs were often used to decorate their architecture, such as the large pyramid temple in Chichen Itza. Mayan royalty commissioned art to commemorate their rule, requesting scenes of rituals with hieroglyphics that depicted the events. The Maya were also one of the first civilizations to work out a system of astronomy, which allowed them to study the stars.

The Post-classic period had three major civilizations: the Toltecs, the Mixtecs, and the Aztecs. Not much art, culture, or architecture of the Toltecs or Mixtecs has survived that can be properly credited to their cultures, unfortunately. The Toltecs were known for massive block-like sculptures used as columns in architecture, and the Mixtecs developed a style of painting that involved covering all available space with figures or geometric shapes. The Aztecs are more well-known, though some Aztec works suggest they saw the Toltecs and Mixtecs as their cultural predecessors. Aztecs made many kinds of art, including stone sculptures, decorated skulls, and headdresses. Much of their art focused on religious worship, but some also focused on the concept of naturalism, making their art more life-like so it would be more understandable.

Expansion of Christianity

Belief systems were at the forefront of the cultural diffusion that occurred through interregional contact. As belief systems interacted with each other, syncretism often occurred. **Syncretism** is the merging of different belief systems, resulting in changes to one of the belief systems or the creation of a new belief system. Less orthodox Christian denominations, such as Nestorian and Arian Christianity, merged with local religious beliefs and practices. On the Indian subcontinent, syncretism between Buddhism and Hinduism merged the doctrines closer together. Similar to Christianity, Buddhist doctrine was altered after spreading into new regions, especially in China.

Early Christians were a persecuted religious minority in the Roman Empire, and they struggled to gain new followers. Therefore, Christianity heavily emphasized proselytism to convert more followers and gain widespread acceptance. Following the Roman Empire's conversion to Christianity, Christian proselytizing began to spread as increasing numbers of missionaries traveled on the Silk Road and ventured deeper into Roman territories. When preaching to local populations that were entirely unfamiliar with Christianity, missionaries often discussed Christianity in the context of local religion and culture. This merging of Christianity and local religion naturally led to the development of novel belief systems.

Nestorian Christianity differed from Nicene Christianity, the form of Christianity that was ultimately adopted by the Roman Empire as the state religion. Like Arians, Nestorian Christians did not believe in the Holy Trinity—the notion that God, Jesus, and the Holy Spirit were all coequal and indivisibly divine. **Nestorian Christians** primarily believed that Jesus Christ had both human and divine elements. Due to their rejection of religious orthodoxy, Nestorian Christian missionaries' flexibility facilitated their success in converting new followers on the Silk Road and beyond. Specifically, Central Asians understood Nestorian Christianity as a form of shamanism and Jesus Christ as a shaman with the most powerful connection to higher powers. Thus, Central Asians altered Nestorian Christianity through the adoption of more rituals and superstitious beliefs. For example, many Central Asian Christians believed the cross was a powerful relic that could be used to fight evil spirits. Similar to the merging of Christianity and shamanism in Central Asia, Christianity merged with religious

practices in China. For example, Chinese Christian artists often combined traditional Christian symbolism with the yin and yang.

Similar syncretism between Christianity and local religion occurred during the conversion of the Germanic and Celtic tribes. Rather than adopting Nicene Christianity's orthodox doctrine, many of these tribes adopted Arianism, including the influential Goths and Vandals. Like Nestorian Christianity, **Arian Christianity** was more flexible when it came to religious doctrine. However, some syncretism occurred even when Germanic tribes adopted the more orthodox doctrine of Nicene Christianity. For example, the King of the Franks, Clovis I, famously converted to Roman Catholicism, and he claimed to fight wars against the pagan and Arian Germanic tribes.

However, Clovis I believed that Jesus Christ provided him with the military strength required to subjugate his enemies—a belief very similar to Germanic pagan beliefs. Despite the mass conversion of Germanic tribes to Christianity, syncretism frustrated attempts at spreading orthodox Christian beliefs. Consequently, Christian missionaries began cutting down sacred trees that continued to be revered by Germanic tribes even after their conversion. Following the collapse of the Western Roman Empire, disputes over the true meaning of Christianity continued across Europe for centuries due to the uneven merging of paganism, Arianism, and Catholicism.

Predominant Religions in Europe

From 1200 to 1450, the predominant religions in Europe were Christianity, Judaism, and Islam. During this period, nearly all European countries had a majority Christian population, and the overwhelming majority of European governments were closely associated with Christianity. Large Jewish communities existed in most European states, especially in urban areas, but they were a distinct minority in comparison to the majority Christian population. Islam spread into Europe through the Ottoman Empire's conquest of the Byzantine Empire in 1453, and large Muslim populations lived in the independent Islamic states established on the Iberian Peninsula.

Christianity, Judaism, and Islam in Europe

Prior to the fall of Constantinople in 1453, most Eastern Europeans followed the Eastern Orthodox Church, whereas Western Europeans predominantly belonged to the Roman Catholic Church. This divide dates back to the East-West Schism of 1054, and the major difference between the two Christian groups is that the Eastern Orthodox Church disputes the pope's authority as the foremost Christian leader.

The Roman Catholic popes enjoyed considerable power during much of this period, even rivaling monarchs of large European states in terms of power and influence in Europe. However, the papacy hit a low point during the **Western Schism** (1378–1416) when Pope Clement V moved to Avignon, France, in 1309 over political differences with Rome, which was the papacy's historic home. After sixty-nine years of Roman Catholic popes ruling from France, the Roman Catholic Church elected an Italian, Pope Urban VI, and he vowed to return the papacy to Rome. In response, French cardinals elected a Frenchman, Pope Clement VII, so there were two Roman Catholic popes serving simultaneous terms. These dual papacies continued for forty years, and both groups petitioned European governments for support. In 1409, a council attempted to resolve the issue by declaring a compromise pope, Alexander V, but neither faction conceded. As a result, there were three active papacies. The situation worsened until July 1417 when all three active popes were deposed, and the council in Constance elected Pope Martin V as the new undisputed pope.

Over the next century, the papacy mostly recovered its religious authority, particularly in reaffirming the Roman Catholic Church's strong ties with Western European monarchs during the Renaissance Papacy (1417–1517). The Renaissance popes functioned as the secular rulers of the Italian city-states, particularly in the patronizing of artists and intellectuals. Furthermore, the Renaissance Papacy is widely associated with popes intervening in worldly affairs and advising European governments in matters of diplomacy and exploration.

The Jewish experience in Europe was marred by widespread persecution in nearly all European states. Christians often scapegoated these communities during times of trouble. For example, in response to an outbreak of a bubonic plague known as the **Black Death** (1346–1353), Christians accused Jewish people of poisoning wells and bewitching the sick. In response, several European states, including England, France, Spain, Germany, and Italy, expelled their Jewish communities.

Islam spread into Eastern Europe through the Ottoman Empire's conquest of the Byzantine Empire in 1453. Although the Ottoman Empire formally permitted the Eastern Orthodox Church to continue its operations, Islamic law constituted the highest law of the land in the Ottoman Empire's Eastern European territories. Consequently, Christians often lacked the freedom to express their religion and faced persecution to various degrees. Aside from Eastern Europe, there were large populations of Muslims living in present-day Spain and Portugal. These Muslim states reached their apex in the tenth century, but the Emirate of Granada (1212–1492) persisted until the Christian Crown of Castile conquered it in 1492, completing the **Reconquista**.

Rise of Islamic States

Numerous Islamic states either developed or expanded between 1200 and 1450. **Sunni Islam** was the most popular and powerful sect between 1200 and 1450 because the most powerful Islamic states promoted it. The Delhi Sultanate, Mamluk Caliphate, Ottoman Empire, and Ajuran Sultanate all adopted Sunni Islam as their state religion during this period, and these states incorporated Sharia law, which is based on Sunni ideology, into their legal system. The Delhi Sultanate (1206–1526) conquered most of the Indian subcontinent in the thirteenth century. Following the Abbasid Caliphate's (750–1258) collapse, its rulers established a new state, the Mamluk Sultanate (1261–1517), in present-day Egypt. The Ajuran Sultanate (1200–1700) was one of the most powerful Islamic states in Africa, and it controlled maritime trade on the Indian Ocean for centuries. The **Ottoman Empire** (1299–1922) consolidated power in present-day Turkey and launched a successful invasion of Eastern Europe. With its powerful navy and superior military, the Ottoman Empire controlled Mediterranean trade routes and supported Muslim states, including those established in present-day Spain and Portugal.

Despite the widespread popularity of Sunni Islam in this period, there were some differences in practice within each state. The Ottoman Empire adopted the **Maturdi creed**, which is an orthodox Sunni Islam belief system. The Maturdi creed was also popular in present-day Iran prior to the region's conversion to Shi'a Islam in the sixteenth century. The **Mamluk Caliphate** considered itself to be the leader of the Muslim world during the fourteenth and fifteenth centuries, largely to legitimize their rule. As such, the Mamluk Caliphate generally supported any large Muslim group that supported the sultan. Along with supporting several **madhhabs** (schools) of Sunni Islam, the Mamluk sultans also promoted Sufi madhhabs. **Sufism** is characterized by its emphasis on mysticism, asceticism, and strict adherence to Islamic law. Sufi schools are called **tariqas**, and they could be found all over the Muslim world from 1200 to 1450.

This history is a major reason why Sunni has continued to be practiced at much higher rates than **Shi'a Islam** in the present day. The major difference between Sunni and Shi'a Islam is a dispute over the Islamic prophet Muhammad's successor and interpretations of the *Hadith* (historical accounts of Muhammad).

Intellectual Innovation in Dar al-Islam

Dar al-Islam represented a major innovation in that it protected and promoted Islamic culture. The term roughly translates to "house of Islam," and it refers to parts of the world governed under Islamic law. The Ottoman Empire, Delhi Sultanate, Ajuran Sultanate, and Mamluk Caliphate were considered to be the leaders of Dar al-Islam from 1200 to 1450 because they were the most powerful states during this period. Within these Islamic cultures, intellectual pursuits thrived, especially in the translation and preservation of important historical texts.

Encouragement of Intellectual Innovations by Muslim States

Muslim states heavily sponsored intellectual innovations during what's known as the **Islamic Golden Age** (700–1300). Some historians believe Muslim states' patronage budget was equal to present-day Western countries' investment in medical research, and top scholars were paid like present-day elite athletes. These Muslim states believed the *Quran* and *Hadith* rewarded intellectual achievements and scientific advancements. As such, Muslim states sponsored the Translation Movement to acquire knowledge from foreign civilizations. This patronage resulted in the translation of Chinese, Egyptian, Greek, Indian, and Phoenician texts into Arabic and Persian, depending on the sponsoring state. Many of these ancient texts would've been lost if not for the Translation Movement.

In addition, Islamic scholars conducted original research and made numerous groundbreaking discoveries, especially in mathematics and medicine. Islamic states often sent their scholars to the Abbasid Caliphate's House of Wisdom in Baghdad, which housed libraries full of ancient texts on astronomy, mathematics, medicine, and philosophy. Mongol forces destroyed the House of Wisdom in 1258, but Islamic states continued their heavy sponsorship of intellectual innovations for more than another century.

Renaissance

While most medieval scholars focused their studies on Latin translations of scholarly works, **Renaissance scholars** focused their studies on Greek translations of works written by Plato, Ptolemy, Archimedes, and pre-Socratic philosophers. These new translations undermined the authority of medieval scholarship, which had relied heavily on Latin translations of Aristotle and Galen. New debates over truth emerged as a result of this shift in scholarship. In particular, these debates focused on scientific truth, which challenged the classical philosophical translations of the Middle Ages. The result, in some instances, was an outright rejection of medieval philosophies, which launched Europe into a new era of Enlightenment that reinforced a broader Scientific Revolution in the early modern period.

Renaissance artists also promoted new ideas based on close observation and experimentation. Their artistic perspectives, in turn, influenced scientific inquiry. These artists challenged classical views of the cosmos, nature, and the human body by using observation to accurately depict the world around them. In their artwork, they tried to accurately imitate plants, animals, and humans, and they established new standards for depicting natural phenomena. Specifically, they changed the ways in which people understood perspective and accurate anatomical proportions. As a result, they created greater interest in scientific observation and human anatomy. Many Renaissances artists, such as Leonardo da Vinci and Albrecht Dürer, were also mathematicians and engineers. While traditional conceptions of knowledge and the universe persisted, especially in the Roman Catholic ecclesiastical hierarchy, new ideas in science based on observation, experimentation, and mathematics began slowly chipping away at these old belief systems.

Humanist teachings during the Italian Renaissance stressed the importance of human free will and contribution to society, called "virtú." Teachings from Plato were popular, with a strong emphasis placed on living a life of reason and having a nature for happiness. By the end of the 1400s, most of the classic Roman and Greek writings had been translated and distributed, becoming a bedrock of knowledge for humanist thinkers of the time. The new teachings valued a liberal arts education of grammar, poetry, philosophy, and history. Humanists also taught the importance of serving in government or being active in civic affairs, called "civic humanism." An adequate education was thought to be one that prepared young people to be political leaders, and humanist thinkers often served in government.

Renaissance educators taught the importance of civic duty and contribution to society, leading to an increased sense of duty and creation of a stronger political entity. Latin made a comeback as a language by the end of the 1400s, and Italian states began to resemble that of the early Roman Empire. While Italy became increasingly more secular, this by no means meant that the government became nonreligious. Rather, Italian thinkers promoted that God valued human beings above all else, particularly their free will to choose. This new style of individualism brought about vast changes in Italian culture.

Ideas and advancements from the Italian Renaissance began to spread into Northern Europe, albeit much later than the Italian Renaissance. The Italian Renaissance lasted from the late 1300s through roughly 1550. The **Northern Renaissance** began to gain traction around 1650. Humanist teachings in particular became more widely known as more people gained access to Italian writing and translations. Human-centered naturalism flourished during the Northern Renaissance, which built upon humanism, and encouraged the idea that human beings and everyday life were appropriate figures for artistic expression, focusing on raw emotion and unique mannerisms.

The German humanist **Rudolf Agricola** studied in Italy and returned with a breadth of humanist teachings to spread to the rest of Germany. His teachings inspired the work of a poet named Conrad Celtis and a knight named Ulrich von Hutten. Celtis and Hutten led a humanist revolution in Germany that blended Agricola's teachings with that of an increasing tinge of nationalism.

The military conquests that extended into Italy brought humanism back to France. **Guillaume Bude**, a French thinker and humanist, as well as **Jacques Lefevre**, a French biblical scholar, brought humanist thought to the forefront of French life. Lefevre in particular was very aggressive in teaching humanism to young French students, leading to many publications of his work and inspiring future thinkers such as Martin Luther and John Calvin. These men played significant roles in the coming Reformation period.

Thomas More, an English philosopher, lawyer, and author, was a very influential humanist of the time. More served in high office, reaching Lord Chancellor in King Henry VIII's government. He wrote the influential book *Utopia* published in 1516, which described a seemingly perfect society. This perfect society, he argued, could not be achieved because of disputes over rights to land. For those problems to truly be solved, More believed, people must be willing to sacrifice individual gains for the common good.

Arguably the most famous influence during this time period, however, was the English writer, poet, and playwright, **William Shakespeare**. Shakespeare dominated the English Renaissance, with most of his works remaining famous today. His work drew from Greek and Roman culture, as well as using themes of humanism and individualism. His tragedies include *Romeo and Juliet, Hamlet, Othello*, and *Macbeth*. His other plays include *The Taming of the Shrew, A Midsummer Night's Dream, Much Ado About Nothing*, and *As You Like It*.

Spain reacted differently from its English and French counterparts. While humanism seemed to be weakening religious influence in other countries, humanist teachings actually helped to strengthen the Catholic Church in Spain. Queen Isabella even appointed a "Grand Inquisitor," a humanist thinker named **Francisco Jimenez de Cisneros**. Cisneros pushed for reforming the Catholic Church for a multitude of abuses.

The **Christian humanist movement** used early writings of Christianity to try to improve society and the Catholic Church. While still drawing influence from Greek and Roman teachings, the Christian humanists used religious ideals to shape their thinking and interpretations of societal standards. They used very early Greek and Hebrew texts of the Bible to set new guidelines for Christian behavior, and they placed an emphasis on education. These new teachings contained stark criticisms of the Catholic Church.

Perhaps the most famous of these Christian humanists was **Erasmus**, who sought to revolutionize the Catholic Church. He was a master of Greek, and he used Greek teachings to support his criticism of the Church. He retranslated the New Testament into Greek and Latin. Erasmus also wrote *In Praise of Folly*, which was the second-highest selling book for its time, after the bible. This work heavily criticized the Catholic Church and pushed for religious reforms.

Scientific Revolution

Prior to the 1500s, most scientific thinkers believed in a geocentric universe. Most scholars followed the abstract theories of Aristotle, and most medical practitioners believed that human bodies worked in the same ways as pig bodies. The **Scientific Revolution** dispelled all these archaic frameworks for thinking, which had been heralded as truths by the Roman Catholic Church. Indeed, the Scientific Revolution replaced all these abstract old assumptions by emphasizing mathematical logic and scientific reason. The **Enlightenment** simultaneously exposed the world to classical philosophers that had previously been forgotten in the archives and storehouses of Muslim universities and private collections. New political, social, and ethical theories emerged that honored the past—through neoclassical frameworks—but also challenged the present by paving the path to a previously unimagined future.

What was once considered reason in the Middle Ages proved to be entirely unreasonable by the time the Scientific Revolution was in full swing. Aristotle and Galen's influence on medieval thinking crumbled in the wake of new discoveries and ideas. The concepts and practices of the Scientific Revolution were applied to political, social, and ethical issues to create entirely new conceptions of reason in the early modern era. The Scientific Revolution's emphasis on systematic observation challenged the abstract notions of reason set forth by medieval scholars. As new discoveries, such as Galileo's telescopic validation of Copernicus's heliocentric theory, challenged the ecclesiastic canon of Roman Catholic Church, inevitably these discoveries challenged the Church itself. The Church, in turn, resisted. The result was a new wave of inquisition and censorship by the Roman Catholic Church that affected the scientists of the era. Galileo's theories were seen as a threat to the religious and political order of the time.

Both sides of the "heliocentric vs. geocentric" debate claimed to be inspired by reason. Nonetheless, the new emphasis on scientific—rather than theological—reason eventually won the favor of the masses. This paradigm shift created skeptics out of former believers, and the consequence of this new, widespread skepticism was revolutionary foment. By challenging theological ethics, scientists also challenged the Church. By challenging the Church, they ultimately challenged the political order of the time. These developments laid the foundation for future revolutions.

Put simply, the Scientific Revolution and the Enlightenment attacked the irrational nature of medieval science and philosophy. Reason, backed by new scientific tools and methods, became the new truth; it gradually displaced abstract theology as the primary way to understand the world. European culture underwent a distinct *rational* turn, one that was publicly challenged by the inquisitions of the Roman Catholic Church. The early modern world subsequently became a battleground between rationalism and traditionalism. Some historians, noting the wave of Enlightenment revolutions that followed, would say that rationalism won this battle (though tradition continued to exist, in open resistance and in isolation).

Capitalism and Global Consequences

The development of **capitalism** represented a major breakthrough in the rise of global markets. During the mid-eighteenth century, British economists challenged mercantilist policies and their underlying assumptions about economic competition between states, namely, that economic growth could be achieved without harming rival states. In general, capitalism prioritized freedom in economic activities, and states implemented free trade policies to support the growth of international commerce. Rather than treating other states as economic competitors, states began specializing in economic sectors where they were the most efficient and trading their surplus for the goods they no longer produced. Free trade agreements also allowed states to trade with their rival's colonies, which further expanded the global marketplace. For indigenous populations in the colonies, capitalism strongly mirrored mercantilism in continuing to oppress them. The primary difference between the two systems was that under capitalism most state-owned enterprises were replaced with private industries.

Capitalism promoted the private accumulation of wealth and free markets. Economic freedom triggered a period of rapid industrialization with numerous social, political, and cultural effects. The most dramatic consequence was the creation of a middle class. As more merchants and industrialists joined the middle class, this social group challenged traditional political authorities such as monarchies. The middle class also had sufficient disposable income to purchase significant amounts of domestic and foreign consumer goods. A greater diversity of consumer goods had a deep cultural impact, especially in allowing individuals to be more selective about what they consumed. In effect, capitalism's emphasis on the individual placed further pressure on political and social systems to be more responsive and flexible.

Commercial Rivalries

European rivalries directly led to the growth of a global market during the late seventeenth century. To gain an advantage over rivals, European states sought to conquer and exploit colonial territories. Consequently, the Netherlands, Portugal, Spain, France, and Britain engaged in a fierce maritime competition to establish colonies and increase access to foreign markets.

European states especially valued Atlantic trade routes because they connected Europe with the Americas and West Africa. Britain and France had previously established West African colonies largely for the purpose of securing a steady supply of slaves, but a handful of European states had other economic interests in this region. In the Americas, several powers, including the Netherlands, Portugal, Spain, France, and Britain, controlled vast colonies. Therefore, these European states maintained large naval forces to protect and strengthen their overseas economic interests.

European Sea Powers

During the eighteenth century, Britain emerged as the preeminent naval power after its Royal Navy defeated Dutch forces in the Caribbean and thwarted French expansion in North America. Along with warfare, commercial rivalries had a heavy influence on diplomacy. Military conflicts often ended with states agreeing to

expand or limit foreign access to its colonies. Given its disproportionate power and influence, Britain steadfastly refused to loosen its colonial monopoly and aggressively deployed diplomatic means to expand British merchants' access to foreign markets. Most infamously, Britain implemented a series of Navigation Acts, which prohibited foreign ships from entering British colonial ports or transporting British goods. By the end of the eighteenth century, Britain had emerged as the leading commercial power on the Atlantic Ocean.

Rivalries in Asia

European rivals similarly vied for control over lucrative territory in Southeast Asia and on the Indian subcontinent. In Southeast Asia, European states established colonies to consolidate control over the spice trade and gain access to the lucrative Chinese market. Spain, Portugal, and the Netherlands held numerous islands and archipelagos located in the present-day countries of Indonesia and the Philippines. French Indochina consisted of territory in present-day Cambodia, Laos, and Vietnam, while Britain controlled territory in present-day Borneo, Brunei, Myanmar, Malaysia, and Thailand. Of particular importance, the Netherlands' control of the East Indies funded its empire. Britain, in addition to holding vast territories in Southeast Asia, forced Danish, Dutch, French, and Portuguese merchants to abandon their trading posts on the Indian subcontinent.

Evolution of the Idea of Representative Democracy

Magna Carta to the Enlightenment

The Magna Carta was a document first created in June of 1215, though it was not fully enacted until 1217. Its purpose was to create protections for the church and lower-nobility barons against abusive policies from the king, to be implemented by a council of barons. This represented the beginnings of the Parliament of England: a regular meeting of the king, his ministers, council members, bishops, and lesser lords like barons and earls. While the king and his council still created laws, the Parliament was needed to ratify them and to consent to any taxation requested by the king. Over time, the Parliament of England expanded to include more and more democratic elements. English citizens were allowed to elect their representatives and petition Parliament to address complaints. The monarchy's power was increasingly limited, eventually only able to influence Parliament through its supporters.

These changes all began to take place during the Enlightenment period. The Age of Enlightenment was a period between the seventeenth and eighteenth centuries that saw a resurgence of intellectual ideas centered around the value of human happiness. In regard to representative democracy, the Enlightenment peaked with the passage of the Bill of Rights 1689 in the Parliament of England, which established many basic rights for English citizens and rules regarding the rights and powers of the monarchy and Parliament. This bill was influenced by many of the political thinkers of the time like John Locke, Montesquieu, and Jean-Jacques Rousseau.

Over the span of decades in the 1700s, Enlightenment philosophers created a paradigm shift in thinking, one that upheld reason, nature, happiness, progress, liberty, and inalienable rights as the penultimate objectives of the human experience. Philosophers like Voltaire, Baron de Montesquieu, Jean Jacques Rousseau, and John Locke established a new precedent for human philosophy. Reexamining the role of religion, they encouraged humanist ideals that placed human rights and sentiments at the fore of existence. They believed reason should empirically challenge old notions of faith, encouraging scientific discovery as a new lens for understanding the world around them.

The Enlightenment laid the foundation for a series of revolutions that altered political systems in the Americas and Europe between 1750 and 1950. New political ideas, particular those established by John Locke,

demanded new social contracts be created between governments and citizens. The people legitimized the government by sacrificing some freedom to their authority, and in exchange, the government was obligated to protect the people's legal rights. Accordingly, the government's failure to fulfill this obligation would violate the social contract, effectively opening the door to a revolution. Philosophers like Locke and his followers believed citizens had the right to rebel. This new reason-based belief system consequently helped motivate many of the revolutionary efforts of the eighteenth and nineteenth centuries, moving humanity further from monarchy and closer to reimagined classical philosophies such as democracy, liberalism, and republicanism.

When combined with nationalism, social contract theory functioned as an effective justification for revolution. During the late eighteenth and nineteenth centuries, the Enlightenment influenced revolutions across the Atlantic world, including the American Revolution, French Revolution, and the Latin American wars of independence.

By the 1700s, the New World, disrupted by Enlightenment ideals, was hit with a wave of revolutionary sentiment. American colonists, fueled by new ideological notions of liberty, equality, and human rights, began challenging centralized imperial governments in the region. The colonial powers of the previous century – Britain, France, Spain, and Portugal – were challenged by new colonial-based identities that became culturally distinct from their mother country. **Monarchy**, in particular, was attacked vehemently by Enlightenment thinkers and revolutionary soldiers. Monarchy was seen as a threat because it consolidated political and economic power under the rule of one figurehead. **Republicanism** and **democracy**—classical Roman and Greek political structures—were heralded as the political solutions for the coming age of revolt against monarchy. As colonists gained more independence and power through geographic separation, they sought to decentralize the power of democracy. And, in many cases, they were successful—the American, Haitian, and Latin American independence movements of the era were effective in their efforts to decentralize colonial power.

United States History: Early Exploration, Colonial Era, and the War for Independence

European Explorations

When examining how Europeans explored what would become the United States of America, one must first examine why Europeans came to explore the New World as a whole. In the fifteenth century, tensions increased between the Eastern and Mediterranean nations of Europe and the expanding Ottoman Empire to the east. As war and piracy spread across the Mediterranean, the once-prosperous trade routes across Asia's Silk Road began to decline, and nations across Europe began to explore alternative routes for trade. Italian explorer Christopher Columbus proposed a westward route. Contrary to popular lore, proving that the world was round was not the main challenge that Columbus faced in finding backers. In fact, much of Europe's educated elite knew that the world was round; the real issue was that they rightly believed that a westward route to Asia, even assuming a lack of obstacles, would be too long to be practical. Nevertheless, Columbus set sail in 1492 after obtaining support from Spain, and arrived in the West Indies three months later.

Spain launched further expeditions to the new continents and established **New Spain**. The colony consisted not only of Central America and Mexico, but also the American Southwest and Florida. France claimed much of what would become Canada, along with the Mississippi River region and the Midwest. In addition, the Dutch established colonies that covered New Jersey, New York, and Connecticut. Each nation managed its colonies differently, and thus influenced how they would assimilate into the United States. For instance, Spain strove to

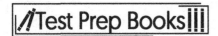
establish a system of Christian missions throughout its territory, while France focused on trading networks and had limited infrastructure in regions such as the Midwest.

Even in cases of limited colonial growth, the land of America was hardly vacant because a diverse array of Native American nations and groups were already present. Throughout much of colonial history, European settlers commonly misperceived native peoples as a singular, static entity. In reality, Native Americans had a variety of traditions depending on their history and environment. Additionally, their culture continued to change throughout the course of their interactions with European settlers; for instance, tribes such as the Cheyenne and Comanche used horses, which were introduced by white settlers, to become powerful warrior nations. However, a few generalizations can be made: many, but not all, tribes were matrilineal, which gave women a fair degree of power, and land was commonly seen as belonging to everyone. These differences, particularly European settlers' continual focus on land ownership, contributed to increasing prejudice and violence.

News of success sparked a number of other expeditions and the British, French, Dutch, Spanish, and Portuguese all eventually laid claim to lands in the New World. Columbus himself made three more voyages to the Americas. The French and Dutch focused mostly on the lucrative fur trade in North America. The Spanish and Portuguese sought gold in Central and South America but also tried to convert Native Americans to Christianity. British settlers also sought economic opportunity and created the first British colony at Jamestown, Virginia, in 1607. However, the Puritans, who landed at Plymouth Rock in 1620, left for the New World in order to establish their ideal religious community.

European Colonization

Spanish Colonization Efforts

Spain largely pursued colonization to maintain its status as a European and global power. As a result, once Spain discovered large deposits of precious metals in the Americas, it implemented policies to maximize the extraction of wealth from its colonies. The pursuit of profit necessitated the seizure of strategic and valuable territory and the acquisition of a cheap labor source. So, Spain pressed its military advantages, took advantage of the devastation caused by deadly diseases, and encouraged political infighting to conquer powerful indigenous confederations such as the Inca Empire and Aztec Empire.

The Spanish crown initially allowed **conquistadores** to fully enslave the Native Americans, but over time they sought to better incorporate indigenous populations into colonial society. Religion played a major role in this transformation, including both missionary work and forced large-scale conversions after Spanish conquests. Additionally, reforms introduced through the *repartimiento* system protected some aspects of indigenous societies as well, assuming they fulfilled Spanish demands for labor or tribute. Within territories directly under the colonial system, Spain enforced a strict racial caste system which granted freedoms and opportunities based on blood purity. In a practical sense, the racialization of the caste system served to maintain Spanish superiority in the colonies by formalizing the limitations on mixed-race individuals, Native Americans, and African slaves.

Caste System

To increase socioeconomic stability, Spain instituted a highly unique and complex racial caste system in its American colonies. The **caste system** classified the colonial population based on residents' ancestry and purity of blood. These racial classifications functioned as the foundation of a rigid social system that determined residents' legal status, rights, and obligations within the Spanish Empire.

The highest classes had the closest connections to Spain and the most Spanish blood. As such, Spaniards born in Spain (**peninsulares**) occupied the highest tier in the caste system. Slightly below the **peninsulares** were the American-born Spaniards (**criollos**). Mixed-race classes were significantly below these two European classes, but they occupied the middle tiers of the caste system. Examples of mixed-race classes included: Spanish and indigenous (**mestizo**), Spanish and mestizo (**castizos**), Spanish and African (**mulatto**), and Spanish and mulatto (**moriscos**). Despite the severe restrictions Spain placed on mixed-race residents' property and legal rights, they were still above two classes—African slaves (**negros**) and indigenous peoples (**indios**). African slaves effectively had no rights, while indigenous societies enjoyed some very limited protections under the **repartimiento system**. Given the dramatic disparities in class status, people in the Spanish Empire often attempted to forge ancestral histories and pass as a member of a different class.

French and Dutch Colonization Efforts

French and Dutch colonization efforts were unique because they relied on maintaining economic relationships with indigenous societies to a far greater degree than Spanish and English colonies. During the sixteenth century, Dutch colonies were generally limited to the northeastern United States, and France mostly colonized eastern Canada. Because these regions couldn't support large-scale mining or agriculture, they mostly extracted wealth through fur trapping and trade with the Native Americans. Oftentimes, a colonial government would control a city or central region, and then joint-stock companies would establish trading posts in the outlying wilderness. Because geographic separation restricted the extent to which French and Dutch colonial governments could protect remote trading posts, they were often motivated to maintain peaceful diplomatic relations with indigenous confederations.

French settlements later developed more permanent structures to support the booming fur trapping trade, which ratcheted up tensions with the Iroquois Confederacy (originally known as the Iroquois League or the Six Nations). The French and Iroquois fought a prolonged series of conflicts, collectively known as the **Beaver Wars**, from 1640 to 1701. The wars began in 1629 when the Iroquois started conquering neighboring tribes as a result of declining beaver populations, but they did not come into conflict with the French until several decades later. The conflict ended in a stalemate with the French consolidating control over present-day eastern Canada and the Iroquois Confederacy establishing itself as the hegemonic power in the Great Lakes region and the wilderness surrounding New England.

English Colonization Efforts

English colonies attracted relatively more European migrants than their competitors for several reasons. England's thirteen colonies in the present-day United States featured a wide array of different climates and ecosystems. As a result, the colonies offered many different types of prosperous economic opportunities such as plantation agriculture, family farming, fur trapping, manufacturing, fishing, and shipping. More broadly, the sheer amount of cheap land offered migrants hope of socioeconomic mobility. Several major groups of Christian dissidents migrated to British North America to establish their own religious communities, which further increased British colonial diversity.

Economies also attracted different European immigrant groups based on different labor demands. For most of the seventeenth century, the southern Atlantic colonies' plantations mostly relied on African slaves, as did the British West Indies. So, the overwhelming bulk of European immigrants, lacking the resources to invest in a plantation, sought to settle further north on the Atlantic Coast where there were more economic opportunities. Northern colonies also attracted more indentured servants compared to other colonial systems. **Indentured servitude** involved colonists paying a European man or woman's immigration and living costs in

163

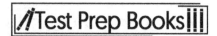

exchange for a designated future period of free labor. The practice was most cost effective for small-scale farming.

Overall, the English colonies were characterized by their agricultural focus on the lands they had taken from Native Americans.

Cooperation and Conflict Between Europeans and Native Americans

Cooperation

Indigenous peoples adopted a variety of diplomatic and military strategies to resist European colonization between 1491 and 1607. Some indigenous tribes, like those encountered by **Hernando de Soto** during his expedition across the present-day southeastern United States, provided European explorers with gifts and guides as a sign of friendship. Other tribes, like the **Powhatan** in present-day Virginia, initially accepted European colonies' boundaries and graciously traded maize to prevent the newly arrived colonists from starving. However, by 1609 the English and the Powhatan were at war. **Squanto** was an Algonquian Indian who helped English settlers in Massachusetts survive by teaching them how to plant native crops. However, the arrival of Europeans in the Americas quickly posed an existential challenge to indigenous people's way of life.

Indigenous groups regularly sought and secured military alliances with European groups to gain an advantage in regional conflicts with other indigenous nations. Naturally, Native Americans adjusted to the initial stages of colonization by incorporating European groups into their traditional diplomatic and military systems, treating them like ascendant and powerful indigenous nations. Europeans routinely exploited this opportunity to carry out a divide-and-conquer strategy. Overall, European powers and indigenous groups acted in their self-interest, resulting in a fluid system of shifting military alliances.

Given the deep and complex regional rivalries within indigenous communities, it was common for colonial conflicts to have alliances of Native American groups aligned on both sides. The rise of the Iroquois Confederacy during the seventeenth century is indicative of European and indigenous alliances. During the **Beaver Wars**, the French established alliances with numerous Algonquian societies including the Erie, Huron, and Mohican (also spelled Mahican). The Algonquians believed they would be rewarded for their support of the rising French power and that any losses suffered by the Iroquois would automatically be their gain. On the other side, the Dutch and English supported the Iroquois to undermine the French. However, once the Iroquois emerged as the clear-cut indigenous power, they began to threaten the British North American frontier.

Although the early years of their interactions were often marked by mutual misunderstandings, over time, Europeans and Native Americans did adopt some aspects of one another's culture that proved useful. For example, European technology, such as hatchets, weapons, and kettles, were adopted by some Native American tribes. A Native American agricultural technique, known as **companion planting**, for crops such as the **Three Sisters** (maize, winter squash, and climbing beans), was adopted by Europeans who had settled in New England and the Chesapeake areas. Because these three crops, when planted together, benefited one another, Europeans were able to have a reliable food source and stay alive.

Conflict

Native Americans and Europeans often came into conflict, frequently over land use, power, land ownership, religion, and family dynamics. Native Americans did not understand the concept of landownership or sale. While Native Americans did occupy territories, they viewed land as a common resource of the tribe that could, at most, be leased for its use. Europeans, on the other hand, believed strongly in owning land and, after its purchase, enjoying the exclusive use of that land. When they entered into agreements with the colonists,

Native Americans thought they were allowing the settlers to farm the land temporarily, rather than retain it in perpetuity. However, colonists were frustrated when Native Americans continued to hunt and fish on lands they had "sold."

Compared to Native Americans, Europeans were far less likely to consider the long-term sustainability of land use practices. North America is Native Americans' ancestral homeland, but colonization was a for-profit venture for Europeans. Likewise, although Native Americans regularly consolidated power at the expense of their rivals, their conquests were far more regionally based and limited in scope. Europeans held a much more global attitude. European powers were already fighting all over the globe before they arrived in North America. As such, they didn't just want to make a tidy profit, they wanted to monopolize power and conquer as much territory as they possibly could.

Europeans seized vast swathes of indigenous territory and violated indigenous peoples' **political sovereignty**, meaning the ability to self-govern without external interference. Similarly, Europeans enslaved indigenous people and disrupted ancient patterns of trade, effectively stunting indigenous economic development. Indigenous cultural values also came under attack through forced conversions to Christianity and limitations placed on the role of women in tribal leadership.

Europeans were almost universally Christian, and many leaders believed non-Christians were condemned to eternal damnation. So, European colonizers often believed it was their moral duty to convert Native Americans by any means necessary. In contrast, Native American groups rarely proselytized and practiced a diverse array of traditional religions, ranging from nature-based monotheism to polytheistic animism. Furthermore, Native American family dynamics were relatively egalitarian, with women and elders assuming key leadership roles in many groups. Europeans were far more hierarchical, with men serving as the head of the household and holding undisputed authority. Native Americans also valued kinship and revered elders, whereas aggressive young men with few family ties dominated European colonial expeditions and early settlements.

Military Conflicts Between the British and American Indians

British colonies' aggressive territorial expansion, broad consolidation of resources, and wanton violation of treaties naturally resulted in near-constant conflicts with many Native American nations. By the late seventeenth century, most British colonies had survived starvation-like conditions, established a consistent agricultural food supply, and commanded well-armed and robust military units featuring a strong mix of imperial troops and more informal citizen militia-type forces. At this point, most indigenous leaders viewed Europeans as rising regional competitors, not as an existential threat to indigenous societies. Although Britain was generally less successful than its European rivals at decimating local indigenous power centers, the British fiercely protected their territory and engaged in incremental expansion.

King Philip's War (1675–1678, also called Metacom's War) was one of the most influential conflicts with an indigenous confederation in British colonial history. **King Philip, or Metacom,** was a Wampanoag chief who formed an alliance with New England-based indigenous tribes such as the Narragansetts and Podunks. The New England colonies barely survived King Philip's War. Approximately half of New England colonial villages were attacked during the conflict, and more than a dozen towns totally collapsed. Despite the heavy losses, King Philip's War forged an American identity because it marked the first time the colonists fought without any imperial support.

Governing in the Colonies

The thirteen colonies formed when royal charters were granted, either to individuals or corporations, and the colonies were allowed limited **self-rule**. A governor for the colonies was appointed by England, but each colony could rule by its own laws enacted by colonial assemblies. The method in which these men were appointed, and the laws of each colony, differed based on the type of charter each had, if any. In **royal colonies** — Virginia, Massachusetts, New Hampshire, New York, New Jersey, North Carolina, South Carolina, and Georgia — the king of England was the direct authority of the colony and chose the governor, among other things. **Proprietary colonies**, which included Pennsylvania, Delaware, and Maryland, were under the authority of the owner of the colony, while Rhode Island and Connecticut were self-governing and had no direct authority. They elected members to their legislatures.

Development and Institutionalization of African Slavery

Slavery is believed to be as old as civilization itself, likely beginning during the First Agricultural Revolution nearly ten thousand years ago. The enslavement of human beings was integral to such early civilizations as Egypt, China, the Mayan Empire, Greece, and Rome. Nevertheless, race did not become the primary driving force behind human captivity and forced labor until the so-called Age of Exploration. Once the Europeans made contact with the New World, they developed a new system of slavery in the Atlantic World that categorized black and indigenous persons as naturally inferior.

The Transatlantic Slave Trade was built upon the foundations of the need for cheap labor. The **transatlantic slave trade** involved European merchants acquiring slaves from West Africa and transporting them to the Americas. During the early sixteenth century, Portugal and Spain were the dominant powers in West Africa, and as a result, they played an outsized role in shaping the transatlantic slave trade in its early stages. However, by the beginning of the seventeenth century, Dutch, English, and French merchants had become significantly more involved in the slave trade. Slavery in the Americas became a hereditary phenomenon during the peak centuries of the Transatlantic Slave Trade.

The competition was fierce due to the immense value of African slaves because they were the most profitable source of labor for plantation-based agriculture and mining in the Americas. The sugar and tobacco plantations of the Americas demanded an excess of cheap or free labor. Initially, European Americans looked to Native Americans as their enslaved labor supply. Quickly, however, millions of Native Americans died because of the spread of unfamiliar diseases. By the 18th century, the slave trade industry grew because of the higher labor demands. This slave trade lasted from the 1400s well into the late nineteenth century.

Slavery had been practiced in West Africa for many centuries prior to the arrival of Europeans, and most slaves were prisoners of war. European merchants originally worked within this traditional framework; however, when demand for labor increased in the Americas, European merchants sought to increase the supply of slaves. Consequently, the merchants allied themselves with individual tribes and financed military expeditions for the explicit purpose of enslaving the conquered people. These tribal conflicts also benefited the Europeans by sowing chaos and preventing the consolidation of political power under a united African kingdom.

Causes of the War for Independence

Competition among several imperial powers in eastern areas of North America led to conflicts that would later bring about the independence of the United States. The **French and Indian War** from 1754 to 1763, which was a subsidiary war of the **Seven Years' War**, ended with Great Britain claiming France's Canadian territories as

well as the Ohio Valley. The war was costly for all the powers involved, which led to increased taxes on the Thirteen Colonies. In addition, the new lands to the west of the colonies attracted new settlers, and they came into conflict with Native Americans and British troops that were trying to maintain the boundaries laid out by treaties between Great Britain and the Native American tribes. These growing tensions with Great Britain, as well as other issues, eventually led to the American Revolution, which ended with Britain relinquishing its control of the colonies.

As the colonies grew in population, they began to develop local institutions and a separate sense of identity. For example, it became common for ministers to receive their education at seminaries in North America rather than Britain. Newspapers began to focus on printing more local news as well. Perhaps most importantly, the colonies began to exercise more control over their own political affairs. The British government retained control over international issues, such as war and trade, but the colonists controlled their own domestic affairs. Colonies began to form their own political assemblies and elect landowners who represented local districts. In addition, communications between the colonies and Britain were very slow because it took months for a ship to cross the Atlantic and return with a response.

Taxes were imposed in an effort to help reduce the debt Britain amassed during the French and Indian War. In 1764, Parliament passed the **Sugar Act**, which reduced the tax on molasses but also provided for greater enforcement powers. Some colonists protested by organizing boycotts on British goods. One year later, in 1765, Parliament passed the **Quartering Act**, which required colonists to provide housing and food to British troops. This law was also very unpopular and led to protests in the North American colonies.

The **Stamp Act** of 1765 required the colonists to pay a tax on legal documents, newspapers, magazines, and other printed materials. Colonial assemblies protested the tax and petitioned the British government in order to have it repealed. Merchants also organized boycotts and established correspondence committees in order to share information. Eventually, Parliament repealed the Stamp Act but simultaneously reaffirmed the Crown's right to tax the colonies.

In 1767, Parliament introduced the **Townshend Acts**, which imposed a tax on goods the colonies imported from Britain, such as tea, lead, paint, glass, and paper. The colonies protested again and British imperial officials were assaulted in some cases. The British government sent additional troops to North America to restore order. The arrival of troops in Boston only led to more tension that eventually culminated in the **Boston Massacre** in 1770, where five colonists were killed and eight were wounded. Except for the duty on tea, all of the Townshend Act taxes were repealed after the Boston Massacre.

Parliament passed the **Tea Act** in 1773 and, although it actually reduced the price of tea, it was another unpopular piece of legislation. The Tea Act made the British East India Company the sole legal seller of tea in the colonies in North America and allowed the Company to ship its products directly to the colonies without stopping in England and paying import taxes, effectively cutting out colonial merchants and stirring more Anglo-American anger and resentment. This resulted in the **Boston Tea Party** in 1773, an incident in which colonial tea merchants disguised themselves as Indians before storming several British ships that were anchored in Boston harbor. Once aboard, the disguised colonists dumped more than 300 chests of tea into the water.

Because the British government was unable to identify the perpetrators, Parliament passed a series of laws that punished the entire colony of Massachusetts. These acts were known as the **Coercive** or **Intolerable Acts**. The first law closed the port of Boston until the tea had been paid for (an estimated $1.7 million in today's currency). The second act curtailed the authority of Massachusetts' colonial government. Instead of being

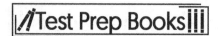

elected by colonists, most government officials were now appointed by the king. In addition, the act restricted town meetings, the basic form of government in Massachusetts, and limited most villages to one meeting per year. This act angered colonists throughout the thirteen colonies because they feared their rights could be stripped away as well. A third act allowed for British soldiers to be tried in Britain if they were accused of a crime. The fourth act once again required colonists to provide food and shelter to British soldiers.

Colonists responded by forming the **First Continental Congress** in 1774, and all the colonies except for Georgia sent delegates. The delegates sought a compromise with the British government instead of launching an armed revolt. The First Continental Congress sent a petition to King George III affirming their loyalty but demanding the repeal of the Intolerable Acts. The delegates organized a boycott of imports from and exports to Britain until their demands were met. The colonists began to form militias and gather weapons and ammunition.

The War for Independence

The first battle of the revolution began at Lexington and Concord in April 1775 when British troops tried to seize a supply of gunpowder and were confronted by about eighty Minutemen. A brief skirmish left eight colonists dead and ten wounded. Colonial reinforcements poured in and harassed the British force as they retreated to Boston. Although the battle did not result in many casualties, it marked the beginning of war.

A month later, the Second Continental Congress convened in Philadelphia. The delegates formed an army and appointed George Washington as commander in chief. Delegates were still reluctant to repudiate their allegiance to King George III and did not do so until they issued the **Declaration of Independence** on July 4, 1776. The Declaration drew on the ideas of the Enlightenment and declared that the colonists had the right to life, liberty, and the pursuit of happiness. The Declaration stated that the colonists had to break away from Britain because King George III had violated their rights.

After the Battle of Lexington and Concord, British troops retreated to Boston and the colonial militias laid siege to the city. Colonists built fortifications on Bunker Hill outside the city and British troops attacked the position in June 1775. The colonists inflicted heavy casualties on the British and killed a number of officers. However, the defenders ran out of ammunition and British troops captured Bunker Hill on the third assault. Although it was a defeat for the colonists, the Battle of Bunker Hill demonstrated that they could stand and fight against the disciplined and professional British army.

The British army initially had the upper hand and defeated colonial forces in a number of engagements. The Americans did not achieve a victory until the **Battle of Trenton** in December 1776. Washington famously crossed the Delaware River on Christmas Day and launched a surprise attack against Hessian mercenaries. They captured more than 1,000 soldiers and suffered minimal casualties. The victory at Trenton bolstered American morale and showed that they could defeat professional European soldiers.

The **Battle of Saratoga** in New York in the fall of 1777 was an important turning point in the American War for Independence. American troops surrounded and captured more than 6,000 British soldiers. This victory convinced the French king to support the revolutionaries by sending troops, money, weapons, and ships to the American continent. French officers who fought alongside the Patriots brought back many ideas with them that eventually sparked a revolution in France in 1789.

In 1781, the primary British army under **General Cornwallis** was defeated by an American and French coalition at Yorktown, Virginia, which paved the way for peace negotiations. The **Treaty of Paris** (1783) ended the war, recognized the former colonies' independence from Great Britain, and gave America control over territory

between the Appalachian Mountains and Mississippi River. However, the state of the new nation was still uncertain.

Support During the Revolutionary War

The American Independence movement suffered several glaring and large-scale disadvantages at the outset of the **American Revolutionary War** (1775–1783). Britain was the undisputed European superpower due to its hegemonic naval superiority and influence over global trade. Furthermore, Britain enjoyed a significant amount of loyalist support within the colonies. While the rebel forces worked to present the struggle as a united, patriotic effort, the colonies remained divided throughout the war. Thousands of colonists, known as **Loyalists** or **Tories**, supported Britain. Even the revolutionaries proved to be significantly fragmented, and many militias only served in their home states. The **Continental Congress** was also divided over whether to reconcile with Britain or push for full separation. These issues hindered the ability of the revolutionary armies to resist the British, who had superior training and resources at their disposal. Despite these difficulties, the Americans stunned the world and won the war with their ideological strength, asymmetric warfare, brilliant military leadership, and foreign assistance.

The ideological emphasis on liberty helped generate a steady supply of volunteers and popular support for the American war effort. American militias terrorized British supply lines and defense positions throughout the conflict. The militias refused to wear uniforms and violated traditional norms of warfare, like conducting surprise attacks on lightly defended targets and targeting British officers in battle. This asymmetric warfare stretched the British military's resources to the breaking point, and the **Continental Army**, under General **George Washington**, gradually built up a force that utilized Prussian military training and backwoods guerrilla tactics to make up for their limited resources. Although the British forces continued to win significant battles, the Continental Army gradually reduced Britain's will to fight as the years passed. Furthermore, Americans appealed to the rivalry that other European nations had with the British Empire. The support was initially limited to indirect assistance, but aid gradually increased. For example, French loans and training also helped transform the Continental Army into a modern military, and Dutch and Spanish merchants broke the British blockade to provide the Americans with supplies and weapons. After the American victory at the **Battle of Saratoga** in 1777, France and other nations began to actively support the American cause by providing much-needed troops and equipment.

Political and Military Leadership During the Revolutionary War

George Washington was the most significant leader of the Revolutionary War, both in politics and in the war. He acted as commander-in-chief of the Continental Army and led the entire war effort against the British. He answered to the Second Continental Congress, the acting government of the United States of America during this time. When the war ended, he went on to become the first president of the United States and established many political traditions, such as the inaugural address and the cabinet system of political advisors.

Many other founding fathers and political figures contributed to bringing the new nation to life. Thomas Jefferson was responsible for writing the Declaration of Independence and went on to serve as a diplomat and eventually as president. John Adams was a skilled orator who played a critical role in getting all the colonies to agree to vote for independence. Patrick Henry was a strong advocate for independence and gave a speech in 1775 that became famous for the line, "Give me liberty, or give me death!" Benjamin Franklin was a diplomat who spent the Revolutionary War in France, working to secure an alliance between France and the fledgling nation. Alexander Hamilton was key to establishing the nation's new treasury and banking systems. Many others served equally essential roles to create the United States of America.

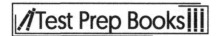

On the military front, there were several standout leaders. Nathanael Greene served as the Continental Army's Quartermaster General, and quickly developed a reputation as one of the army's best strategists. Benedict Arnold was a strong leader in the early stages of the war and won several battles, but later defected to the British after a plot was uncovered that he planned to intentionally surrender West Point. Marquis de Lafayette served under Washington while in Philadelphia and held the line in Virginia while waiting for Washington's army to arrive. Henry Knox served as the Continental Army's chief artillery officer, eventually creating an artillery training center that later evolved into the United States Military Academy.

On the other side of the Atlantic Ocean, King George III stood in charge of the British Empire. His attempts to restrict the freedoms of the colonies sparked the Revolutionary War, and he was described as a tyrant in the Declaration of Independence. Thomas Gage was a British military governor in Massachusetts whose actions led to the Battles of Lexington and Concord. He later suffered a Pyrrhic victory at the Battle of Bunker Hill and was subsequently replaced by William Howe. In turn, Howe initially succeeded but eventually resigned after poor planning during the Saratoga campaign brought the French into the war as allies of America. Charles Cornwallis was a British general who was famous for his role in the final British defeat; his surrender in Yorktown led to the end of the Revolutionary War.

Impact of the Revolutionary War on Americans

New American life was very different in some ways after the war but not so different in others. More political participation was encouraged as more men gained the right to vote and society shifted toward meritocracy over aristocracy. The British Empire's restrictions on trade and expansion were now null and void, so new markets and trade opportunities could be found everywhere. American industries began to boom, seeking complete freedom from British manufacturing.

However, there were still colonists who supported Britain during the war. These Loyalist colonists found themselves ostracized by Americans but felt out of place returning to Britain. Many eventually left to settle in new lands like Nova Scotia and Quebec. The rhetoric of "freedom" that was touted as the rallying cry during the war was turned inside out and examined closely after the war. Some Americans highlighted all the inequalities still present to continue pushing for further civil rights and freedoms.

United States History: Development of the Constitution and the Early Republic

The Articles of Confederation

The thirteen States ratified the **Articles of Confederation, adopted by the Continental Congress on November 15, 1777,** on March 1, 1781. The Articles broadly sought to maintain some degree of unity between the former British colonies and avoid destructive European-like regional rivalries.

The Articles of Confederation established a formal agreement or confederation between the original thirteen states. The Articles of Confederation established a central government composed of a unicameral legislative assembly, called the **Confederation Congress**, in which each state had a single representative. Passing a bill required votes from nine of the thirteen representatives. Under the Articles of Confederation, the Confederation Congress was granted very limited powers, rendering it largely ineffective.

Those powers included:

- Borrowing money from states or foreign governments
- Creating post offices
- Appointing military offices
- Declaring war
- Signing treaties with foreign states

Due to the colonial experience with a centralized constitutional monarchy, the central government under the Articles of Confederation was comically weak. Right from the outset, the **Confederation Congress** was severely undermined by states' reservation of robust powers. For example, states held the power to print currency, assume debt, and pursue independent foreign trade deals; the central government couldn't implement a uniform economic agenda under this power-sharing scheme. In addition, states enjoyed veto power over the central government, effectively allowing minority opinions to override the entire confederation. The central government also lacked an executive branch because political leaders believed it would lead to tyrannical rule. As a result, even when the Confederation Congress passed laws, enforcement was close to impossible.

The early American political system deteriorated rapidly. Domestic unrest and border conflicts sapped the central government of its legitimacy and forced American political leaders to realize they needed to revamp the entire system.

The Constitutional Convention

The **Constitutional Convention** met in Philadelphia in May 1787 after the new country was rocked by economic troubles and Shays' Rebellion, an uprising in Massachusetts due to the debt crisis from the Revolutionary War, with the goal of creating a stronger federal government. However, delegates disagreed over how to structure the new system. The **Virginia Plan** was one proposal that included a bicameral legislature where states were awarded representation based on their population size. This would benefit more populous states at the expense of smaller states.

The other main proposal was the **New Jersey Plan**, which retained many elements of the Articles of Confederation including a unicameral legislature with one vote per state. This plan would put states on an equal footing regardless of population. Eventually, delegates agreed to support the **Connecticut Compromise** (also known as the **Great Compromise**), which incorporated elements from both the Virginia and New Jersey Plans and embodied federalism. Under the new Constitution, Congress would be a bicameral body. In the House of Representatives, states would be allocated seats based on population, but in the Senate each state would have two votes. The Constitution also included a president and judiciary that would each serve to check the power of other branches of government. In addition, Congress had the power to tax and had more enforcement powers.

Slavery

Even more than political representation and separation of powers, disputes over slavery threatened the Constitutional Convention. From the very beginning, overt limitations on chattel slavery were a political nonstarter, carrying the risk of a complete withdrawal of the southern Atlantic state delegations from the Constitutional Convention. With the continuation of slavery being a foregone conclusion, the founding fathers eventually reached two pivotal compromises over slavery.

The first compromise was the **Three-Fifths Compromise**, which determined that three-fifths of the slave population of each state would be counted for both taxes and representation. This was an effort to appease both the Southern states, who wanted slaves to be counted as part of the population for the purpose of representation but not counted for the purpose of taxes, and the Northern states, who demanded slaves be counted for taxes but not representation. This generally worked to the benefit of large slave-holding states because it inflated their populations by counting nonvoters while still giving a massive tax cut to slave owners who treated Africans purely as a commodity.

Second, the southern states agreed to a future federal prohibition on the international slave trade. The prohibition, called the **Commerce and Slave Trade Compromise**, would take effect in 1808, so southern states knew they had thirty years to safeguard slavery. This eased Southerners' fears that the Northern states would control the federal government and enforce antislavery policies. Shortly after ratification, the importation of African slaves increased exponentially, partially due to the booming cotton industry. So, by 1808, domestic slave populations had become self-sustainable, and the domestic slave trade easily kept pace with demand. The southern states also accepted the future prohibition because they, correctly, assumed it would be impossible to enforce.

Debates Over Ratifying the Constitution

Once the Constitution had been drafted, nine of the thirteen states had to ratify it for it to take effect. Vigorous debate erupted over whether or not the Constitution should be approved. Two different political factions emerged. The **Federalists** supported the Constitution because they felt a stronger central government was necessary in order to promote economic growth and improve national security. Several leading federalists, including Alexander Hamilton, John Jay, and James Madison, published a series of articles collectively called the Federalist Papers urging voters to support the Constitution. However, the **Anti-Federalists**, including Thomas Jefferson and Patrick Henry, felt that the Constitution took too much power away from the states and gave it to the national government. They also thought there weren't enough protections for individual rights and lobbied for the addition of a **Bill of Rights** that guaranteed basic liberties.

The debates between these two parties continued for two years and inspired two series of essays known as the **Federalist Papers** and the **Anti-Federalist Papers** that debated various topics surrounding the ratification of the Constitution. The essays were authored anonymously by leaders of the respective parties. Scholars are fairly confident of the authorship of the Federalist Papers, but the authorship of many of the Anti-Federalist Papers is still uncertain.

Notable Federalists include:

- **Alexander Hamilton**: founder of the Federalist Party, advocate for a centralized financial system, and author of 51 of the Federalist Papers

- **James Madison**: one of the primary drafters of the Constitution, the future fourth president of the United States, and author of 29 of the Federalist Papers

- **John Jay**: president of the Continental Congress, future first chief justice of the United States, and author of 5 of the Federalist Papers

- **John Adams**: future second president of the United States

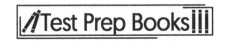

- **George Washington**: commander-in-chief of the Continental Army and future first president of the United States (Washington never officially joined the Federalist party, but he was a strong supporter of ratifying the Constitution)

Notable anti-Federalists include:

- **Thomas Jefferson**: primary author of the Declaration of Independence and future third president of the United States

- **Patrick Henry**: governor of Virginia (1776–1779, 1784–1786) and author of works frequently included in the Anti-Federalist Papers

- **Samuel Adams**: governor of Massachusetts (1794–1797), lieutenant governor of Massachusetts (1789–1794), and president of the Massachusetts Senate (1782–1785, 1787–1788)

- **George Mason**: one of only three delegates who did not sign the Constitution at the Constitutional Convention and author of Objections to This Constitution of Government (1787) and the Virginia Declaration of Rights of 1776, which served as the basis for the Bill of Rights

- Possible authors of the Anti-Federalist Papers include **Robert Yates, George Clinton, Samuel Bryan, Melancton Smith, Richard Henry Lee**, and **Patrick Henry**

The first state to ratify the Constitution was Delaware in a unanimous vote on December 7, 1787. Pennsylvania, New Jersey, Georgia, Connecticut, Massachusetts, Maryland, and South Carolina followed and, after six months, New Hampshire became the ninth state to ratify the Constitution in June 1788. However, some states still remained divided between Federalist and anti-Federalist sentiments and had yet to approve the document, including the two most populous states, Virginia and New York. To reconcile their differing views, the Federalists agreed to include a bill of rights if anti-Federalists supported the new Constitution. Federalist sentiment prevailed, and the remaining states approved the document. On May 29, 1790, the last holdout, Rhode Island, ratified the Constitution by two votes. As promised, the **Bill of Rights**—the first 10 amendments to the Constitution—was added in 1791, providing expanded civil liberty protection and due process of law.

The Constitution

Separation of Powers

To strengthen the central government, while still appeasing the individual states who preferred to remain sovereign over their territories, the framers of the Constitution based the new government upon the principle of **Federalism**—a compound government system that divides powers between a central government and various regional governments. The Constitution clearly defined the roles of both the state governments and the new federal government, specifying the limited power of the federal government and reserving all other powers not specifically granted by the Constitution to the federal government to the states in the Tenth Amendment to the Constitution, commonly referred to as the **Reservation Clause**.

The Constitution establishes the specific powers granted to the federal and state governments:

- **Delegated powers**: the specific powers granted to the federal government by the Constitution

- **Implied powers**: the unstated powers of the federal government that can be reasonably inferred from the Constitution

- **Inherent powers**: the reasonable powers required by the federal government to manage the nation's affairs and maintain sovereignty

- **Reserved powers**: the unspecified powers belonging to the states that are not expressly granted to the federal government or denied to the state governments by the Constitution

- **Concurrent powers**: the powers shared between the federal and state governments

The Constitution delegated the following expanded powers to the federal government:

- Coin money
- Declare war
- Establish federal courts
- Sign foreign treaties
- Expand the territories of the United States and admit new states into the union
- Regulate immigration
- Regulate interstate commerce

The following powers were reserved for the states:

- Establish local governments
- Hold elections
- Implement welfare and benefit programs
- Create public school systems
- Establish licensing standards and requirements
- Regulate state corporations
- Regulate commerce within the state

The **concurrent powers** granted to both the federal and state governments in the Constitution include:

- The power to levy taxes
- The power to borrow money
- The power to charter corporations

The Constitution established a federal government divided into three branches: legislative, executive, and judicial.

The Three Branches of the U.S. Government

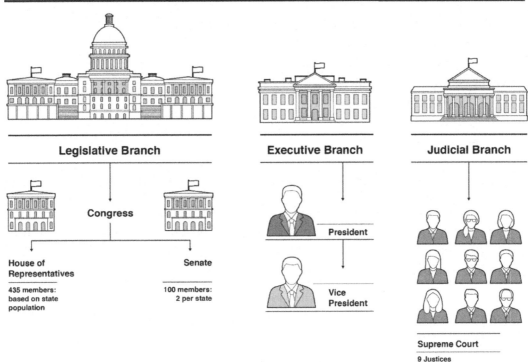

Executive Branch

The **executive branch** is responsible for enforcing the laws. The executive branch consists of the president, the vice president, the president's cabinet, and federal agencies created by Congress to execute some delegated task or authority.

The **president** of the United States:

- serves a four-year term and is limited to two terms in office.

- is the chief executive officer of the United States and commander-in-chief of the armed forces.

- is elected by the Electoral College.

- appoints cabinet members, federal judges, and the heads of federal agencies.

- vetoes or signs bills into law.

175

- handles foreign affairs, including appointing diplomats and negotiating treaties.

- must be at least thirty-five years old, a natural-born US citizen, and have lived in the United States for at least fourteen years.

The **vice president**:

- serves four-year terms alongside and at the will of the president.
- acts as president of the Senate.
- assumes the presidency if the president is incapacitated.
- assumes any additional duties assigned by the president.

The **cabinet members**:

- are appointed by the president.
- act as heads for the fifteen executive departments.
- advise the president in matters relating to their departments and carry out delegated power.

Note that the president can only sign and veto laws and cannot initiate them himself. As head of the executive branch, it is the responsibility of the president to execute and enforce the laws passed by the legislative branch.

Although Congress delegates their legislative authority to agencies in an enabling statute, they are located in the executive branch because they are tasked with executing their delegated authority. The president enjoys the power of appointment and removal over all federal agency workers, except those tasked with quasi-legislative or quasi-judicial powers.

Legislative Branch

The **legislative branch** is responsible for enacting federal laws. This branch possesses the power to declare war, regulate interstate commerce, approve or reject presidential appointments, and investigate the other branches. The legislative branch is **bicameral**, meaning it consists of two houses: the lower house, called the **House of Representatives**, and the upper house, known as the **Senate**. Both houses are elected by popular vote.

Members of both houses are intended to represent the interests of the constituents in their home states and to bring their concerns to a national level while also being consistent with the interests of the nation as a whole. Drafts of laws, called **bills**, are proposed in one chamber and then are voted upon according to that chamber's rules; should the bill pass the vote in the first house of Congress, the other legislative chamber must approve it before it can be sent to the president.

The two houses (or **chambers**) are similar though they differ on some procedures such as how debates on bills take place.

House of Representatives

The **House of Representatives** is responsible for enacting bills relating to revenue; impeaching federal officers, including the president and Supreme Court justices; and electing the president in the case of no candidate reaching a majority in the Electoral College.

In the House of Representatives:

- each state's representation in the House of Representatives is determined proportionally by population, with the total number of voting seats limited to 435.

- there are six nonvoting members in the House, one each from Washington, D.C.; Puerto Rico; American Samoa; Guam; the Northern Mariana Islands; and the US Virgin Islands.

- the Speaker of the House is elected by the other representatives and is responsible for presiding over the House. In the event that the president and vice president are unable to fulfill their duties, the Speaker of the House will succeed to the presidency.

- the representatives of the House serve two-year terms.

- the requirements for eligibility in the House include:

- Must be twenty-five years of age
- Must have been a US citizen for at least seven years
- Must be a resident of the state they are representing by the time of the election

Senate

The **Senate** has the exclusive powers to confirm or reject all presidential appointments, ratify treaties, and try impeachment cases initiated by the House of Representatives.

In the Senate:

- the number of representatives is one hundred, with two representatives from each state.
- the vice president presides over the Senate and breaks a tied vote, if necessary.
- the representatives serve six-year terms.
- the requirements for eligibility in the Senate include:

- Must be thirty years of age
- Must have been a US citizen for the past nine years
- Must be a resident of the state they are representing at the time of their election

Legislative Process

Although all members of the houses vote on whether or not bills should become laws, the senators and representatives also serve on committees and subcommittees dedicated to specific areas of policy. These committees are responsible for debating the merit of bills, revising bills, and passing or killing bills that are assigned to their committee. If it passes, they then present the bill to the entire Senate or House of Representatives (depending on which they are a part of). In most cases, a bill can be introduced in either the Senate or the House, but a majority vote of both houses is required to approve a new bill before the President may sign the bill into law.

Judicial Branch

The **judicial branch**, though it cannot pass laws itself, is tasked with interpreting the law and ensuring citizens receive due process under the law. The judicial branch consists of the **Supreme Court**, the highest court in the country, overseeing all federal and state courts. Lower federal courts are the district courts and the courts of appeals.

In the Supreme Court:

- judges are appointed by the president and confirmed by the Senate.
- judges serve until retirement, death, or impeachment.
- judges possess sole power to judge the constitutionality of a law.
- judges set precedents for lower courts based on their decisions.
- judges try appeals that have proceeded from the lower courts.

Checks and Balances

A system of deliberate **checks and balances** between the branches exists to ensure that no branch oversteps its authority. They include:

- Checks on the Legislative Branch:

- The president can veto bills passed by Congress.
- The president can call special sessions of Congress.
- The judicial branch can rule legislation unconstitutional.

- Checks on the Executive Branch:

- Congress has the power to override presidential vetoes by a two-thirds majority vote.
- Congress can impeach or remove a president, and the chief justice of the Supreme Court presides over impeachment proceedings.
- Congress can refuse to approve presidential appointments or ratify treaties.
- Congress, particularly the House of Representatives, has the power of the purse (the ability to tax and spend money for the federal government). All bills concerning revenue must be introduced in the House of Representatives.

- Checks on the Judicial Branch:

- The president appoints justices to the Supreme Court, as well as district courts and courts of appeals.
- The president can pardon federal prisoners.
- The executive branch can refuse to enforce court decisions.
- Congress can create federal courts below the Supreme Court.
- Congress can determine the number of Supreme Court justices.
- Congress can set the salaries of federal judges.
- Congress can refuse to approve presidential appointments of judges.
- Congress can impeach and convict federal judges.

The three branches of government operate separately, but they must rely on each other to create, enforce, and interpret the laws of the United States.

Checks and Balances

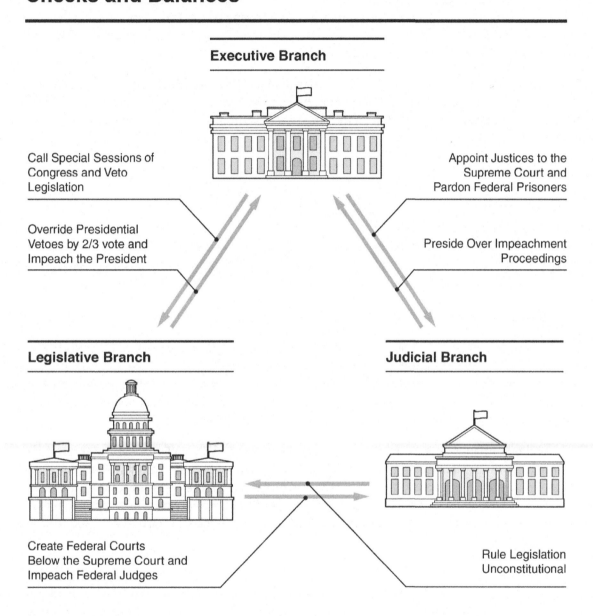

Executive Branch

Call Special Sessions of Congress and Veto Legislation

Override Presidential Vetoes by 2/3 vote and Impeach the President

Appoint Justices to the Supreme Court and Pardon Federal Prisoners

Preside Over Impeachment Proceedings

Legislative Branch

Judicial Branch

Create Federal Courts Below the Supreme Court and Impeach Federal Judges

Rule Legislation Unconstitutional

Formation of Political Parties

American political leaders held conflicting views on numerous critical issues. Following the ratification of the Constitution, **Federalists** dominated the Washington administration and enacted policies designed to centralize political power. Washington's Treasury Secretary Alexander Hamilton was an especially fierce advocate for free trade, central banking, federal taxes, and economic interventions. More broadly, the

Federalists valued an organized and efficient government more than maximizing the protection of personal freedoms.

Organized opposition to the Federalists increased during Washington's second term through the formation of the **Democratic Republican Party** during the late 1790s. The Democratic Republicans favored limited government, civil liberty protections, and decentralized banking. In addition, the Democratic Republicans were less committed to free trade and an isolationist foreign policy. Many Democratic Republican leaders, including Thomas Jefferson and James Madison, viewed the **Jay Treaty** as a betrayal of Republican values for its concessions to Britain in exchange for reduced tensions on the frontier.

The Democratic Republicans nominated a presidential candidate, **Thomas Jefferson**, for the first time in 1796. Although Jefferson lost to the Federalist John Adams, he was victorious in the presidential election of 1800. Democratic Republicans then proceeded to control the executive branch until Andrew Jackson won the presidential election of 1828.

Distinct Regional Identities

Historical, Cultural, Economic, and Geographic Factors
Chesapeake and North Carolina Colonies
Colonial economies in the **mid-Atlantic** (present-day North Carolina and southern Virginia) and **Chesapeake Bay** (present-day Maryland, Delaware, and northern Virginia) regions primarily engaged in tobacco and family farming. Compared to New England, there was less centralization, smaller urban centers, and minimal industrial production. In contrast, North Carolina and Virginia disproportionately relied on producing a single cash crop, **tobacco**, with family farming accounting for the region's only other vibrant economic sector.

Despite their common reliance on agricultural and similar rural settlement patterns, colonial North Carolina and Virginia were strikingly different than the **southern Atlantic colonies** (South Carolina and Georgia). Unlike the southern Atlantic colonies' plantation-based agriculture, farming in North Carolina and Virginia occurred on smaller plots of land. Tobacco was less compatible with large-scale production, and environmental conditions prevented the near-continual production that occurred deeper south.

Chesapeake and mid-Atlantic agriculture also uniquely relied more heavily on European indentured servitude than African slavery for its labor demands from the outset. Consequently, colonies in present-day North Carolina and Virginia had much more ethnic and religious diversity than the more universally British southern Atlantic colonies. However, African slaves gradually overtook indentured servitude as the dominant labor system, largely because the ever-increasing supply of African slaves in the southern Atlantic led to major cost reductions.

New England Colonies
Connecticut, New Hampshire, Massachusetts, and Rhode Island were considered the **New England colonies**. The settlements in New England were based around an economy focused on fishing and lumber. These colonies maintained puritanical and Congregationalist religious beliefs, and developed around family farms situated near small towns.

Middle Colonies
While English Puritans mostly settled in New England, a wide variety of colonists settled in the mid-Atlantic region. English, Scottish, Dutch, and Swedish settlers came to Delaware, New York, New Jersey, and Pennsylvania. As a result, the mid-Atlantic colonies were more religiously diverse and tolerant than the

settlements in New England. Because the land in the region was so fertile, agriculture was the foundation of the economy in mid-Atlantic colonies. The primary output was **cereal crops** such as wheat, rye, and corn. For this reason, the Middle Colonies were also known as the **Bread Basket colonies**. Shipbuilding and lumbering were also common because of the abundant forests. Settlements were more dispersed, and government and administration were based on counties instead of towns.

Southern Atlantic Coast and the British West Indies Colonies
The Southern Atlantic (South Carolina and Georgia) and British West Indies' tropical climate, long growing seasons, and rich soil supported the development of plantation-based economies. Agricultural production had a sizable effect on these colonies' economic development and demographic makeup. Because land was divided into plantations under the control of societal elites, there was minimal commercial growth and few employment options. As such, the European population of plantation-based economies often consisted only of an elite cadre of ultra-wealthy landlords and a small managerial class to support operational logistics.

Unlike most other English colonies, plantation agriculture primarily relied upon African slaves as a labor force. In many instances, African slaves accounted for the majority of the population in England's plantation-based colonies. Fearing a slave insurrection, plantation owners attempted to enforce slave codes that were designed to be as draconian, dehumanizing, and profitable as possible. To keep the races more firmly separated by skin color, Southern Atlantic and British West Indian slave codes emphasized and sought to preserve the purity of race. The codes enforced prohibitions on interracial relationships and enslaved all descendants of African mothers. Eventually the plantation-based colonies transitioned into using "**one drop**" racial policies, meaning that anyone with any African ancestry was subject to enslavement.

New Forms of National and Regional Culture
The development of a national culture transformed the United States over the latter half of the eighteenth century. A cohesive national culture first formed in the aftermath of the French and Indian War (1754–1763) as American colonists increasingly established militias and self-governing political institutions to defend their land. During the 1770s and 1780s, Enlightenment philosophies popularized the concepts of civil liberties, private property rights, and limited government. A robust publishing industry helped disseminate these ideas across the country, which led to the inclusion of **Enlightenment ideas** in the US Constitution (1789) and Bill of Rights (1791). These ideas laid the foundation for a capitalist economic system and shaped government policies, especially in terms of promoting individual liberties.

The new national culture was relatively diverse for its time. A new national culture developed in the United States combining European identities, Christian beliefs, and regional diversity. Once the United States began expanding westward and industrializing, European immigration diversified considerably with large groups coming from Germany, Ireland, and Scandinavia during the first half of the nineteenth century. Immigration rates also skyrocketed in this period. For example, compared to the rates between 1790 and 1820, immigration increased tenfold by the 1840s. As a result, American culture developed as a melting pot where cultural values and traditions fused together.

Likewise, the promise of religious freedom resulted in more Christian sects taking root in the United States than anywhere else in the world. Christian revivalist movements also contributed to the growth of uniquely American religious beliefs, such as the importance of personal spiritual connections to the divine.

Unlike other countries, an American national culture was heavily influenced by regional economic development. Northern economies featured large-scale industrialization, urbanization, and immigration, which resulted in a greater emphasis on commerce and more frequent interactions among people of different

181

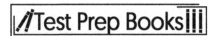

cultures. Wealthy owners of plantations and slaves dominated the Southern economy, resulting in a hierarchical society and culture. In the Western territories, the regional culture was optimistic and adventurous as frontiersmen sought prosperity in the wilderness.

Southern Agricultural Economy

The Southern regional identity was steeped in agriculture. To maximize the profit potential of large-scale production, plantations primarily grew cash crops such as sugar, tobacco, and, most importantly, cotton. However, less wealthy family farms continued to produce traditional agricultural staple foods such as rice, citrus fruits, wheat, and legumes. Southern plantation owners regularly struggled with the decision of where to export crops. While Northern markets were closer and had less onerous shipping costs, European markets generally offered higher prices.

Aside from protecting slavery, Southern politicians were most adamant about protecting their agricultural exports. For example, during the **Nullification Crisis** (1832–1833), South Carolina passed legislation to nullify the so-called **Tariff of Abominations**, a high protective tariff from 1828 designed to protect Northern industry, and the **Tariff of 1832**, which lowered the protectionist measures but still did not satisfy Southern concerns. South Carolina attempted to nullify the tariffs because of their negative effect on the Southern economy. The crisis only ended in 1833 when Congress passed the **Force Bill**, which authorized President Andrew Jackson to use the army to enforce federal law in South Carolina, and also passed the Compromise Tariff, which satisfied South Carolina's concerns. South Carolina nullified the **Force Bill three days later** as a symbolic gesture.

The impact of agriculture on the Southern regional identity cannot be overstated. Southern lands were almost exclusively devoted to agricultural production, which curbed the development of major urban centers. Without alternatives, Southerners either worked in agriculture or migrated outside the region. People lived and died with each successive harvest, and they were united in opposition to anything that threatened their way of life.

Northwest Ordinance and Westward Expansion

Northwest Ordinance

A driving force behind the American Revolution was overwhelming opposition to British restrictions on westward expansion. Once Americans gained independence, settlers streamed across the Appalachian Mountains and settled in land between the Ohio River and Great Lakes.

The Confederation Congress passed a series of land ordinances to disentangle states' claims to the land and directly oversee its development during the transition to statehood. The **Northwest Ordinance** of 1787 was arguably the Confederation Congress's most impactful piece of legislation passed, marking one of the few times they successfully centralized political power. This legislation established federal conservatorship over territories as public domain until they qualified for statehood, effectively denying states the power to expand their individual boundaries. As such, the federal government enjoyed the power to enforce property rights and direct the development of civic institutions, such as a public education system, in the territories. Additionally, the Northwest Ordinance enacted one of the few federal prohibitions on slavery, and the area between the Appalachian Mountains and Mississippi River became an extension of the **Mason-Dixon Line**, which later divided free and slave states. During the nineteenth century, the Northwest Territories became the states of Ohio (1803), Indiana (1816), Illinois (1818), Michigan (1837), Wisconsin (1848), and Minnesota (1858).

Louisiana Purchase

The United States greatly benefited from the tumultuous conditions of the **Napoleonic Era** (1799–1815). With incessant warfare drowning French finances, Napoleon decided to abandon much of his North American colonial project and sell France's vast Louisiana Territory to the United States. The Louisiana Purchase (1803) nearly doubled American territory, and over the next several decades, the United States subsidized exploratory missions, commercial enterprises, and pioneer settlements to populate its new territory. As the United States expanded, Americans increasingly claimed Manifest Destiny to justify further conquests as a divine right.

Migrants

Westward expansion across the Appalachian Mountains attracted a diverse group of migrants. The British colonies had rapidly increased in population density over the late seventeenth century and into the eighteenth century, and migrants hoped to settle what they viewed as unclaimed lands. British colonists accounted for the vast majority of migrants, but there was considerable religious diversity as minority Christian sects sought even greater levels of independence. French, Spanish, and Dutch merchants also joined westward expeditions in the hopes of establishing a commercial presence in the early development of frontier settlements. Indigenous populations also had significantly more commercial and cultural interactions with frontier settlements, and it wasn't uncommon for indigenous people to live alongside frontier groups. Similarly, people of color often fled to the frontier due to the Northwest Territory's prohibitions on slavery, economic opportunities, and less traditional social institutions.

The clashing of cultures on the frontier often resulted in seething tensions and chilling violence. The diverse groups were interacting in a mostly lawless geographic area, and they often held conflicting values, beliefs, and economic interests. So, when political, social, and economic disputes arose, groups were quick to violence because they knew there was little hope of a central authority providing assistance or enforcing consequences.

Immigration

Immigration to the United States grew exponentially during the early nineteenth century. Diverse ethnic and religious groups set sail for American shores to obtain civil liberties, economic opportunities, and religious freedom. Soaring immigration rates led to the development of ethnic communities across the United States. Between 1844 and 1877, German and Irish migrants were the largest migrant group, marking the first time Britain didn't account for the overwhelming majority of immigrants. German immigrants primarily came to the United States due to the economic and political turmoil in Germany prior to its unification in 1871. The **Great Famine** (1845–1849) prompted millions of Irish people to emigrate to the United States during the latter half of the nineteenth century and the early twentieth century.

German and Irish immigrants typically arrived in port cities on the Atlantic seaboard. Most of these immigrants initially settled in cities due to the superior economic opportunities offered in urban and industrial centers like New York City and Boston. Urban ethnic communities helped assimilate newly arrived immigrants. In addition, the communities successfully preserved cultural traditions including language, religious practices, and food. For example, German immigrants are widely credited with introducing kindergartens, Christmas trees, hamburgers, and hot dogs to the United States. When Northeastern urban environments became more crowded and expensive, immigrant communities often ventured westward, settling in the developing cities and often establishing exclusive settlements that protected their culture and history. Germans constituted one of the largest immigrant groups that settled outside of the original British colonies on the western frontier, located in the present-day Midwestern United States.

Diversity

Frontier communities located near the Appalachian Mountains, the Ohio River Valley, and the Mississippi River were amongst the most diverse in the world. Given the British colonial history in the formally recognized states, the federal territories attracted international migrants at elevated rates. Appalachian communities especially experienced tremendous growth in the early nineteenth century due to their proximity to the states. Irish and German immigrants arrived en masse and established rural settlements, which strongly resembled urban immigrant communities except on a far wider territorial scale. American Indian and African cultural beliefs were also more likely to be incorporated within the Western frontier due to the general lack of manpower and resources. This desire for sustained growth is also why the frontier generally supported unification plans, such as the infrastructure promised under the American System.

Governmental Efforts to Control North America

Constant immigration meant that land prices in the eastern United States rose and people sought new economic opportunities on the frontier where land was cheaper. The United States government tried purchasing land from Native Americans, but most refused to relinquish their territories. Native Americans continued to defend their land until the Shawnee chief Tecumseh, who had formed a confederacy of Native American tribes to establish a self-governing Indian nation and oppose US expansion into the Northwest Territory, was defeated and killed in the **War of 1812**. This defeat helped secure the **Northwest Territory**, and more settlers began pouring in. After the Louisiana Purchase, Lewis and Clark paved the way for expansion into the Great Plains and further west.

By the mid-1800s, the revolutions of Latin America ceased and only a few areas remained under European rule. The US President James Monroe issued the **Monroe Doctrine (1823)**, which stated that the Americas could no longer be colonized. It was an attempt to stop European nations, especially Spain, from colonizing areas or attempting to recapture areas they had previously colonized. England's navy contributed to the success of the doctrine, as they were eager to increase trade with the Americas and establish an alliance with the United States.

The concept of **Manifest Destiny** emerged during the 1800s and introduced the idea that God wanted Americans to civilize and control the entire North American continent. This led to conflict when the province of Texas declared its independence from Mexico and asked to be annexed by the United States. President James K. Polk tried to buy Texas, but when Mexico refused, he sent troops into the disputed territory. Mexican troops responding by attacking an American unit, which led to the **Mexican-American War** (1846–1848). Manifest Destiny also sparked a desire to expand American influence into Central and South America. Adventurers launched several unsuccessful attempts to invade Nicaragua and Cuba.

Struggles Between Federal Government and American Indian Tribes

The United States had a contentious and, in some cases, ambiguous relationship with Native American tribes. Frontier groups actively pressed into tribal lands, so westward expansion was a continual source of conflict due to the resulting displacement of indigenous populations. In many instances, the federal government was forced into the role of mediator between tribes, states, and settlers.

The federal government signed dozens of agreements with Native American tribes during the late eighteenth century, but the **Treaty of Harmar** (1789) illustrates what ultimately occurred under almost all the agreements. The Americans had agreed to limit settlers and reduce violence in the Great Lakes territories, but even if it desperately wanted to, the federal government lacked the authority and power to enforce the treaty on

184

frontier communities. In response, indigenous regional powers, including the Huron and Delaware tribes, formed the **Western Confederation**. The West Confederation inflicted some of the worst defeats in American military history, but the Americans ultimately recovered and achieved a decisive victory at the **Battle of Fallen Timbers** (1794). Capitalizing on this victory, the federal government agreed to split the Northwest Territories with the Western Confederation under the **Treaty of Greenville** (1795), which was similarly violated in short order.

Indian Removal Act and the Trail of Tears

Despite multiple treaties guaranteeing the land rights of Native American tribes in the Eastern United States, tensions continued to grow between the tribes and white settlers. Andrew Jackson was the first President to initiate a policy of Indian Removal – relocating tribes from the Eastern United States to lands beyond the Mississippi. In 1830 Congress passed the **Indian Removal Act**, which gave the President the authority to negotiate removal with the Native American tribes. While the removal was supposed to be voluntary, threats, bribes, and outright war were all used to convince the tribes to move. In 1833 President Martin van Buren, Jackson's successor, ordered the US Army to force the removal of the remaining Cherokee people. Out of approximately sixteen thousand Cherokee, an estimated four thousand died on what became known as the **Trail of Tears**.

United States' Efforts to Create an Independent Global Presence

The United States encountered significant difficulties in competing with European powers on the world stage during the first half of the nineteenth century. As a result, the United States sharpened its focus on increasing foreign trade and expanding its North American territories, which were far more achievable goals.

The United States relied on foreign trade to stimulate economic growth and gain global influence. During the early nineteenth century, the United States primarily traded with Europe, and cotton represented its most valuable export. In particular, the United States leveraged its commercial power to navigate the Anglo-French rivalry. After fighting Great Britain to a stalemate in the War of 1812, the United States quickly established itself as an important ally and trade partner with its former colonizer. Furthermore, the United States sought and gained export markets for its manufactured goods in Latin America and China.

Governmental Efforts to Gain Control over Western Hemisphere

The United States combined skillful diplomacy and military might to dominate the Western hemisphere during the first half of the nineteenth century. Several presidential administrations skillfully deployed diplomacy to mitigate the threat posed by European powers operating in the Western hemisphere. President Thomas Jefferson exploited Napoleon's precarious financial and military situation when negotiating the Louisiana Purchase, and France's departure from continental North America shored up the United States' western border. President James Monroe similarly acquired Florida for cash in the **Adams-Onis Treaty** of 1819 and also issued the highly influential Monroe Doctrine (1823) to threaten retaliation against European interventions in the newly independent Latin American states. The United States likely couldn't have prevented such an intervention, but this public declaration resulted in the United States developing a near-exclusive sphere of influence in Central and South America. The United States also signed a multitude of border treaties with Great Britain. For example, the **Oregon Treaty** (1846) established the 49th parallel of north latitude as the American-Canadian border from present-day Minnesota to Washington.

African American Communities in the Early Republic

Enslaved African Americans collectively struggled to preserve their humanity against the horrors of slavery. Although slaves were descended from different and culturally diverse West African tribes, they crafted unique Afro-American languages to foster and strengthen interpersonal relationships. Likewise, slaves maintained cultural traditions and family structures even when slave owners prohibited such activities. When faced with separation, slaves often escaped to reunite with loved ones, and former slaves established independently governed communities.

Free African Americans similarly established tight-knit communities in the North to collectively thwart kidnappers, and these communities often strongly supported the abolitionist movement. **Frederick Douglass** pushed for equality of all people regardless of race and gender, and his *Narrative of the Life of Frederick Douglass, an American Slave* (1845) was an international bestseller. The brothers Charles Henry Langston and John Mercer Langston formed the **Ohio Anti-Slave Society** to protest the westward expansion of slavery. African Americans' personal anecdotes had the most remarkable impact in terms of persuading the public. For example, former slaves injected the deplorable conditions and sexual abuse of enslaved women into the public consciousness when such topics were flatly denied and widely considered taboo.

New Roles in a New Country

Many Americans freed their slaves after the war, in keeping with the new beliefs in liberty. However, not everyone agreed, and while many northern states gradually passed emancipation laws, southern states revoked offers of freedom in exchange for service in the war, forcing slaves back into slavery. This led to a generation split between free and enslaved Black Americans. Even freed Black Americans still found themselves at a disadvantage and pushed for the antislavery movement.

Women served in all manner of critical positions during the Revolutionary War but did not see their service paid back in kind after the war. No new civic rights were extended to them, so married women were still unable to own property or vote. Some opportunities as educators opened up, but these positions were still seen as "motherly" roles to raise new citizens of the country. Dissatisfied, many women continued to involve themselves in politics and became more educated. They earned respect as mothers while still fighting to seek more respect in the nation, a gradual process that took a long time to accomplish any significant changes.

Many Native Americans participated in the war on the British side, as British restrictions were what kept settlers from pushing further and further west into their lands. An American victory, however, meant that Americans were now free to continue expanding west. And because Native Americans had supported the British, Americans had an easy excuse to expand into Native lands and brutally force them out, culminating in horrible expansionist events like the Trail of Tears in the early to mid-1800s.

Many immigrants, however, found new opportunities in the new nation. Anyone fleeing famine, job shortages, or rising taxes saw the fledgling country as a land of opportunity, and many immigrants took a chance with America. Irish immigrants, in particular, flocked to the nation in the sixty years following the war. Many were artisans or professionals of some kind and were quickly welcomed into the nation. Conditions were typically challenging, but the growth America experienced thanks to early immigration led to a thriving new nation.

United States History: Civil War and Reconstruction

Sectionalism

In the early 1800s, political and economic differences between the North and South became more apparent. Politically, a small but vocal group of abolitionists emerged in the North who demanded a complete end to slavery throughout the United States. William Lloyd Garrison edited the abolitionist newspaper *The Liberator* and vehemently denounced the brutality of slavery. His criticism was so vicious that the legislature of Georgia offered a $5,000 bounty to anyone who could capture Garrison and deliver him to state authorities. Other activists participated in the Underground Railroad—a network that helped fugitive slaves escape to the Northern United States or Canada.

Economic differences emerged as the North began to industrialize, especially in the textile industry where factories increased productivity. However, the Southern economy remained largely agricultural and focused on labor-intensive crops such as tobacco and cotton. This meant that slavery remained an essential part of the Southern economy. In addition, the North built more roads, railroads, and canals, while the Southern transportation system lagged behind. The Northern economy was also based on cash, while many Southerners still bartered for goods and services. This led to growing sectional tension between the North and South as their economies began to diverge.

These economic differences led to political tension as well, especially over the debate about the expansion of slavery. This debate became more important as the United States expanded westward into the Louisiana Purchase and acquired more land after the Mexican-American War. Most Northerners were not abolitionists. However, many opposed the expansion of slavery into the western territories because it would limit their economic opportunities. If a territory was open to slavery, it would be more attractive to wealthy slave owners who could afford to buy up the best land. In addition, the presence of slave labor would make it hard for independent farmers, artisans, and craftsman to make a living because they would have to compete against slaves who did not earn any wages. For their part, Southerners felt it was essential to continue expanding in order to strengthen the southern economy and ensure that the Southern way of life survived. As intensive farming depleted the soil of nutrients, Southern slave owners sought more fertile land in the west.

Both the North and South also feared losing political power as more states were admitted to the nation. For example, neither side wanted to lose influence in the United States senate if the careful balance of free and slave state representation was disrupted. Several compromises were negotiated in Congress, but they only temporarily quieted the debate. The first such effort, called the Missouri Compromise, was passed in 1820, and it maintained political parity in the US Senate by admitting Missouri as a slave state and Maine as a free state. The Missouri Compromise banned slavery in the portion of the Louisiana Purchase that was north of the 36°30' parallel and permitted slavery in the portion south of that line as well as Missouri.

However, the slavery debate erupted again after the acquisition of new territory during the Mexican-American War. The Compromise of 1850 admitted California as a free state and ended the slave trade in Washington, D.C., but not slavery itself, in order to please Northern politicians. In return, Southern politicians were able to pass a stronger fugitive slave law and demanded that New Mexico and Utah be allowed to vote on whether or not slavery would be permitted in their state constitutions. This introduced the idea of popular sovereignty where the residents of each new territory, and not the federal government, could decide whether or not states entering the union would become a slave state or a free state. This essentially negated the Missouri Compromise of 1820. The enhanced fugitive slave law also angered many Northerners because it empowered

187

federal marshals to deputize anyone, even residents of a free state, and force them to help recapture escaped slaves. Anyone who refused would be subject to a $1,000 fine (equivalent to more than $28,000 in 2015).

The debate over slavery erupted again only a few years later when the territories of Kansas and Nebraska were created by the Kansas-Nebraska Act in 1854. The application of popular sovereignty meant that pro- and anti-slavery settlers flooded into these two territories to ensure that their faction would have a majority when it came time to vote on the state constitution. Tension between pro- and anti-slavery forces in Kansas led to an armed conflict known as Bleeding Kansas.

John Brown was a militant abolitionist who fought in Bleeding Kansas and murdered five pro-slavery settlers there in 1856 in response to a pro-slavery attack on Lawrence, Kansas, that resulted in widespread looting and destruction. He returned to the eastern United States and attacked the federal arsenal at Harper's Ferry, Virginia, in 1859. He hoped to seize the weapons there and launch a slave rebellion, but federal troops killed or captured most of Brown's accomplices and Brown himself was executed. The attack terrified Southerners and reflected the increasing hostility between North and South.

Anti-Slavery Efforts by African Americans and White Abolitionists

African Americans and abolitionists resisted slavery in a variety of ways. Frederick Douglass and William Lloyd Garrison led the charge in building anti-slavery coalitions and spreading awareness about slavery's deep-rooted immorality. Anti-slavery activists often leveraged the extensive influence and reach of the American publishing industry. For example, Harriet Beecher Stowe's *Uncle Tom's Cabin* was the bestselling novel in the nineteenth century, only trailing the Bible in terms of total publication. While these moral arguments carried the Republican Party into national prominence, many anti-slavery activists pursued more direct action.

Abolitionists tirelessly worked to expand the **Underground Railroad**—a series of secretive networks across the United States that helped slaves escape to the northern US and Canada—in defiance of federal Fugitive Slave Acts. Escaped slave Harriet Tubman was its most famous "conductor." Estimates vary but it's likely as many as 100,000 slaves escaped to Canada during the nineteenth century.

Slavery Supporters

Slavery's supporters raised racial, moral, and legal arguments to defend its continuation. Racial arguments justified the enslavement of Africans based on beliefs about white supremacy. Generally speaking, slave owners believed might made right and characterized the enslavement of Africans as an expression of the natural order. White supremacy was also closely tied to moral arguments claiming that slavery actually benefited Africans. Devout Christians were the most likely to adopt moral arguments because they genuinely believed the gift of eternal salvation outweighed the burden of enslavement. Furthermore, many plantation owners portrayed slavery as a social good since the institution boosted economic output and stabilized societal power structures.

While racial and moral arguments were commonly asserted to gain public support for slavery, legal arguments ensured that slavery would be protected from government interference. According to slave owners, the United States Constitution's references to slavery without expressing any reservations or limitations, except for a nominal compromise over the international slave trade, were conclusive proof of slavery's legality. In addition, slave owners relentlessly cited the Tenth Amendment to classify slavery as one of the rights reserved to the states. Although many Southerners sincerely believed in federalism, arguments about states' rights were almost always connected to slavery.

Societal Mobilization and Opposition to the Civil War

The sectional differences that emerged in the last several decades culminated in the presidential election of 1860. Abraham Lincoln led the new Republican Party, which opposed slavery on moral and economic grounds. The question of how best to expand slavery into new territories split the Democratic Party into two different factions that each nominated a presidential candidate. A fourth candidate also ran on a platform of preserving the union by trying to ignore the slavery controversy.

Lincoln found little support outside of the North but managed to win the White House since the Democratic Party was divided. Southern states felt threatened by Lincoln's anti-slavery stance and feared he would abolish slavery throughout the country. South Carolina was the first Southern state to secede from the Union and ten more eventually followed. By February 1861, they had formed the new nation of the Confederate States of America, electing Jefferson Davis as their president in November of that year. Lincoln declared that the Union could not be dissolved and swore to defend federal installations. The Civil War began when Confederate troops fired on Fort Sumter in Charleston in 1861.

The Union and the Confederacy both quickly adopted a total war military strategy during the American **Civil War** (1861–1865). Total war involved mass mobilization of economic and societal resources for military purposes. The Union and the Confederacy both instituted military drafts after a year of fighting discouraged volunteerism. Along with a draft, the Union granted immigrants citizenship if they joined the military. As in the world wars, women achieved significant socioeconomic gains due to the wartime reduction in the workforce.

Mounting military costs eventually forced the Union and the Confederacy to alter economic policies. Both sides issued paper money backed by government credit rather than precious metals. Governments also regularly explicitly ordered or tacitly permitted the seizure of food, manufactured goods, and railway systems to support the war effort.

The Union and the Confederacy each faced considerable domestic resistance to the war. In the early stages of the conflict, President Lincoln suspended some civil liberties in Baltimore to quell rioting that threatened the capital. Many Northern cities also experienced violent draft riots. For example, President Lincoln diverted forces from the **Battle of Gettysburg** (1863) to suppress draft riots in New York City. Confederate leaders similarly moved to suppress slave insurrections that would have undermined agricultural production.

The Civil War

The **First Battle of Bull Run** (also known as the **First Battle of Manassas**) in 1861 was the first major infantry engagement of the Civil War. Both the Northern and Southern troops were inexperienced and, although they had equal numbers, the Confederates emerged victorious. Many had thought the war would be short, but it continued for another four years.

The Union navy imposed a blockade on the Confederacy and captured the port of New Orleans in 1862. The Union navy was much stronger than the Confederate fleet and prevented the Southern states from selling cotton to foreign countries or buying weapons.

In 1862, Union forces thwarted a Confederate invasion of Maryland at the **Battle of Antietam**. This engagement was the single bloodiest day of the war and more than 23,000 men on both sides were killed or wounded. Union troops forced the Confederates to retreat, and that gave Lincoln the political capital he needed to issue the **Emancipation Proclamation** in 1863. This declaration did not abolish slavery, but it did free slaves in the Southern states that were in rebellion against the Union. It also allowed African Americans to

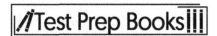

join the Union Army and Navy and about 200,000 did so. The 54th Massachusetts Infantry was a famous unit of African American soldiers who led an assault on Fort Wagner in South Carolina in 1863. Although the attack failed, the 54th Massachusetts demonstrated African American troops fighting bravely under fire.

The **Siege of Vicksburg** in 1863 was a major Union victory because the Union gained control of the Mississippi River and cut the Confederacy in half. This made it difficult the Confederacy to move troops around and communicate with their forces. General **Ulysses S. Grant** commanded the Northern forces in the siege and eventually became the Union army's top general.

The **Battle of Gettysburg** in 1863 marked the turning point of the Civil War. General **Robert E. Lee** led Confederate troops into Pennsylvania, but in three days of heavy fighting, the Union army forced them to retreat. The victory bolstered Northern morale and weakened Southern resolve. Never again would Confederate forces threaten Northern territory.

In 1864, Union general **William T. Sherman** captured Atlanta, Georgia, and then marched more than 200 miles to Savannah. Along the way, he destroyed anything that could support the Southern war effort, such as railroads and cotton mills. At this point, the Southern economy was beginning to collapse. The North had more manpower than the South and could afford to sustain more casualties. The North also had more industrial capacity to produce weapons and supplies and more railroads to transport men and equipment.

Eventually, Robert E. Lee surrendered to Ulysses S. Grant at Appomattox, Virginia, on April 9, 1865. Five days later, **John Wilkes Booth** assassinated Lincoln in Washington, D.C. Vice President **Andrew Johnson**, a Democrat, succeeded him and soon came into conflict with Republicans in Congress about how to reintegrate Southern states into the nation. This process was known as **Reconstruction** and lasted from 1865 to 1877.

Reconstruction

The **Reconstruction Era** (1865–1877) transformed the relationship between the federal government, states, and citizens. Despite the moderating forces within President Andrew Johnson's administration, the more radical branch of the Republican Party successfully forced the federal government to take some unprecedented action.

Federal forces conducted a large-scale occupation of states' territories for the first time in American history. This occupation was not strictly a punitive measure; the goal was to enforce the Reconstruction amendments in the former Confederate states. Consequently, African Americans gained new commercial opportunities and were elected to myriad public offices for the first time. However, white Southerners deeply resented this occupation and intervention, decrying it as yet another act of Northern aggression. Northern support for Reconstruction faded in the mid-1870s as white Southerners mounted more violent resistance, and President Rutherford B. Hayes officially withdrew federal forces in 1877. Immediately afterward, Southern states passed Jim Crow laws to legalize racial segregation and disenfranchisement, which obstructed the Reconstruction Amendments' enforcement for nearly a century.

Radical Republicans
Johnson opposed equal rights for African Americans and pardoned many Confederate leaders. However, many Congressional Republicans wanted to harshly punish Southerners for their attempts to secede from the Union. They were known as **Radical Republicans** because they also wanted to give former slaves equal rights.

Johnson vetoed bills that were designed to protect the rights of freed slaves, but Congress overrode his vetoes. This led to increasing conflict between Johnson and Congress, which eventually caused Radical Republicans to

impeach him. Although Johnson was acquitted in 1868, he had very little power, and Radical Republicans took control of the Reconstruction process.

Radical Republicans won the debate over citizenship for former slaves and people of color. After ratifying the Thirteenth Amendment to abolish slavery, they spearheaded the passage of the Fourteenth and Fifteenth Amendments to guarantee due process under the law and universal male suffrage regardless of "race, color, or previous condition of servitude." Other minority groups, such as Chinese and Mexican immigrants, celebrated the Reconstruction amendments for the progress they made toward racial equality; however, the women's rights movement was much more divided. The Fourteenth Amendment added "male" to the US Constitution for the first time, and many suffragettes believed the use of gendered terminology would impede the fight for women's rights. The Fifteenth Amendment proved even more controversial because it only applied to men.

Thirteenth, Fourteenth, and Fifteenth Amendments

The **Thirteenth Amendment** abolished slavery and involuntary servitude, except as punishment for a crime. The issue of slavery was no longer in the states' hands. Although the Emancipation Proclamation freed slaves in the Confederacy, the status of former slaves remained uncertain as the war neared its conclusion. Many Northerners did not hold strong views on slavery, but most wanted to punish the South and resolve the primary cause of the bloody Civil War. The Northern states all immediately ratified the amendment, and in December, 1865, enough reconstructed Southern states ratified the amendment for it to be adopted into law.

The **Fourteenth Amendment** (1868) granted citizenship to all persons born or naturalized in the United States; prohibited states from depriving any citizen of life, liberty, or property without due process of law; and prevented the states from violating equal protection based on race, color, or previous condition of servitude. Although revolutionary for the theoretical rights of all American citizens, newly freed or otherwise, the Fourteenth Amendment was not federally enforced until the Civil Rights Act of 1964.s were considered legal citizens. Although revolutionary for the theoretical rights of all American citizens, newly freed or otherwise, the Fourteenth Amendment did not provide actual federally enforced equal protection until the **Civil Rights Act** of 1964.

The **Fifteenth Amendment** prohibits the government from denying a citizen the right to vote for reasons of race, color, or previous condition of servitude. Adopted in 1870, the last of the **Reconstruction Amendments**, the Fifteenth Amendment sought to protect newly freed slaves' right to vote. As discussed below, most states interpreted the amendment to only apply to male suffrage. In addition, Southern states passed a series of laws to systematically disenfranchise African Americans including poll taxes, literacy tests, and residency rules. The use of violence and intimidation for political purposes was also common. Meaningful change did not occur until the Civil Rights Movement, nearly one hundred years later. In 1964, the **Twenty-Fourth Amendment** prohibited the states and federal government from charging a poll tax or fee to vote. Later, the **Voting Rights Act** of 1965 empowered the federal government to enforce the Fifteenth Amendment in the states for the first time.

Women's Rights

Debate over the Fourteenth and Fifteenth Amendments sharply divided the women's rights movement. Suffragettes had strongly supported abolitionism to generate intersectional solidarity among oppressed Americans, and many women's rights leaders felt abandoned by the Reconstruction Amendments' failure to address gender inequality.

Tensions within the women's rights movement reached a boiling point at the **American Equal Rights Association** (AERA) annual meeting in 1869, which was held during the run-up to the ratification of the

191

Fifteenth Amendment. Two of the movement's preeminent leaders, Susan B. Anthony and Elizabeth Cady Stanton, stridently opposed the amendment, and Anthony went so far as to tell Frederick Douglass that white women were currently more oppressed than African Americans. In contrast, the majority of attendees and some important leaders, such as Lucy Stone and Julia Ward Howe, viewed the enfranchisement of African Americans as a positive step toward universal suffrage.

The AERA collapsed shortly after this meeting, and two competing organizations took its place. Anthony and Stanton formed the National Woman Suffrage Association, and Stone and Howe established the American Woman Suffrage Association. The organizations' relationship remained contentious until the formation of the National American Woman Suffrage Association in 1890.

Sharecropping

Policies enacted and implemented during the Reconstruction era failed to achieve long-term, meaningful land reform. While the Radical Republicans did greatly expand newly freed slaves' political rights and protections through the Reconstruction Amendments, economic measures missed the mark. At the tail end of the American Civil War, Union General **Tecumseh Sherman** had implemented orders to seize plantations and provide every former slave with "forty acres and a mule." However, President Andrew Johnson reversed Sherman's orders. This reversal allowed wealthy plantation owners to retain the vast majority of their land despite the material support they had provided to the traitorous Confederacy.

Once Reconstruction drew to a close, Southern state legislatures immediately passed legislation to obstruct African Americans and other people of color from exercising political rights as granted under federal law. The federal government refused to intervene, and disenfranchisement only compounded the already minimal economic opportunities available to African Americans.

Given the lack of open land and economic opportunity, poor whites and African Americans were forced into **sharecropping**, meaning they farmed small plots of land in exchange for a small portion of the harvest while the rest went to the landowner. Some sharecroppers lived on what little they could raise in subsistence farming, and some went into debt to their landlords so they could buy food and other goods. Sharecropping was incredibly exploitative, a problem which only increased as time went on since agricultural outputs steadily declined due to rapid soil degradation.

Abandonment of Reconstruction

Reconstruction officially ended with the Compromise of 1877. After the intensely disputed election of 1876, the Democrats offered to let the Republicans have the White House if they agreed to end Reconstruction. After the Republicans agreed, federal troops were withdrawn and African Americans in the South were subjected to discrimination until the Civil Rights movement of the 1960s. Southern states circumvented the Fourteenth Amendment and imposed what were referred to as Jim Crow laws, which established racial segregation of public facilities. These "separate but equal" facilities included the military, workplaces, public schools, restaurants, restrooms, transportation, and recreational facilities. Despite the label of "separate but equal," most facilities reserved for African Americans were considerably inferior. Scholars often consider the Reconstruction era the beginning of **Jim Crow** and a transition into a new form of "institutionalized racism."

United States History: The Rise of Industrial America

Rapid Economic Development and Business Consolidation

During the **Second Industrial Revolution** (1870–1914), the American economy underwent a radical transformation due to the rise of large-scale industrial systems, technological advancements, and modern business organizations.

Innovations in assembly lines, the mass production of interchangeable parts, and electrification spurred rapid growth in American industrial production. As a result, the supply of consumer goods exponentially increased across nearly all economic sectors, which led to steep price reductions for consumer goods. Consumerism also increased due to the creation of new industrial employment opportunities, especially in terms of middle-class management positions, which boosted households' discretionary spending. In addition, businesses applied management principles known as **Taylorism** to reorganize departments, enhance supervision, and provide more detailed instructions to employees. Increased efficiency and profits led to more business consolidation, including the establishment of corporate trusts with widespread investments. For example, John D. Rockefeller's Standard Oil Company established a monopoly over the oil industry through the vertical integration of smaller companies it acquired.

Myriad technological breakthroughs drove this economic expansion, particularly in terms of advancements in steel, chemicals, fertilizers, electrical power, and mechanical engines. Several additional breakthroughs revolutionized international commercial networks. Intercontinental railways expedited the shipment of goods across North America, and modernized ships cut down travel times abroad. In addition, the invention of the telegraph facilitated communication with international business partners, which increased business investments and the dissemination of technical knowledge.

Democrats and Republicans both supported pro-growth economic policies such as low taxes, limited regulations, and minimal oversight mechanisms. For much of this era, trade policy was the most divisive economic issue. Republicans favored maintaining high tariffs to protect domestic industries, and Democrats advocated for free trade to help businesses access foreign markets.

Industrial Revolution

The **Industrial Revolution** transformed the relationship between producers and consumers in the marketplace. Prior to the development of large-scale industrial manufacturing, economies depended on specialized tradesmen to produce goods for trade. Following the creation of interchangeable parts and mechanized tools, industrial production output soared. American entrepreneurs were early adopters of these British innovations, and they spearheaded the establishment of novel forms of economic organization such as company mills and factories.

Samuel Slater is generally recognized as the father of the American Industrial Revolution. During the late eighteenth century, Slater toured British textile mills, memorized their designs, and then emigrated to the United States, where he adapted British innovations to American conditions. Slater built the first textile mills and factory towns in the United States, with most of his commercial empire located in Massachusetts and Rhode Island. Like Slater, **Francis Cabot Lowell** famously financed an innovative company town in the present-day city of Lowell, Massachusetts. Lowell pioneered new methods of corporate financing to raise capital investments, and his Boston Manufacturing Company was one of the first to employ women as factory

193

workers. Lowell had a lasting impact on American manufacturing due to the Waltham-Lowell system's application of textile machinery to boost production.

Innovations and Inventions

The American Industrial Revolution was powered and accelerated by technological innovations. Of all the innovations, the concept of using interchangeable parts was arguably the most influential in its impact on myriad industries. With interchangeable parts, workers could be assigned specific and isolated tasks, rather than bearing responsibility for an entire finished product. This more efficient model of production both reduced the skill requirements for workers and increased total industrial output as factories implemented increasingly complex assembly lines.

Similar groundbreaking innovations occurred in agriculture, such as advancements to Eli Whitney's cotton gin and the invention of mechanized farming equipment. The resulting increase in cotton production directly supported the deployment of textile machinery, such as the spinning jenny and the water frame, in order to mass produce garments.

Other inventions increased the efficiency of transportation and communication, which contributed to more economic integration and unification. The steam engine increased the reliability and speed of maritime travel on the Atlantic Ocean as well as critical domestic waterways like the Mississippi River. Likewise, the telegraph provided an unprecedented form of expedited communication across vast distances. As a result, interrelated networks of commercial relationships between consumers, producers, and investors sprang up all across the United States and even extended overseas.

Impact of Immigration

Immigration played an important part in the economic and social changes that occurred during the late nineteenth century. Immigration patterns changed during this time and immigrants from Southern and Eastern Europe, such as Italy and Poland, began to surpass the number of arrivals from Northern and Western Europe. An increasing number of immigrants also came from Asia. The immigrants sought economic opportunity in the United States because wages for unskilled workers were higher than in their home countries. Immigrants and internal migrants also moved to escape religious persecution and either poverty or the inability to readily improve their socioeconomic status.

As the industrial workforce expanded, business owners had to diversify the employee pool. Rural migrants generally moved to urban cities for economic opportunities, and since this group had previously worked in the agricultural sector, they were mostly placed in entry-level jobs on factory assembly lines. Likewise, immigrants frequently remained in port cities, working in factories to secure basic needs and potentially save enough to travel west. Consequently, factories became the most diverse workplaces in America. Along with immigration from Britain, Ireland, and Germany, immigration from Central and Eastern Europe increased markedly after 1880. In the West, railroads and factories hired Chinese immigrants, but a racist backlash led to the passage of the Chinese Exclusion Act (1882), which prohibited Chinese laborers from immigrating into the United States. Some Americans resented the influx of immigrants because they spoke different languages and many practiced Catholicism. In 1924, Congress passed a law that restricted immigration from Southern and Eastern Europe.

Increase of Women and Children in the Workforce

Business magnates sought to enlist rural migrants, immigrants, children, and women into their workforces between 1865 and 1898. This trend had begun in northern cities in the run-up to the American Civil War, but the pace quickened afterward due to a massive spike in the demand for industrial labor. Women and children joined the workforce in record numbers during this period. Both groups primarily worked for textile manufacturers, and they were often the least compensated. Some industries especially valued orphaned children because they were viewed as expendable assets capable of working in tight spaces such as coal shafts.

Urban Neighborhoods

Increased urbanization was the last factor that contributed to the rapid changes of the Gilded Age. Factories were located near cities in order to draw upon a large pool of potential employees. Immigrants flooded into cities in search of work, and new arrivals often settled in the same neighborhoods where their compatriots lived. Between 1860 and 1890, the urbanization rate increased from about 20 percent to 35 percent. Urban neighborhoods often formed from city dwellers with similar races, ethnicities, or socioeconomic classes. However, cities struggled to keep up with growing populations, and services such as sanitation and water often lagged behind demand. Immigrants often lived in crowded conditions that facilitated the spread of diseases.

Impact of Industrialization on Standard of Living

Americans' standard of living changed dramatically over the latter half of the nineteenth century. Prior to the Industrial Revolution, the overwhelming majority of Americans were employed in the agricultural sector. As industrial production expanded throughout the nineteenth century, Americans became increasingly more likely to live in cities and work in factories. These changes had a mixed effect on Americans' standard of living.

On the one hand, industrialization triggered a steep decline in the price of goods, a greater diversification of goods and services, and the growth of a middle class. Consequently, a consumer culture swept across the United States as retail outlets attained the status of cultural centers. Cities also attracted diverse migrants from outlying rural areas as well as foreign countries, resulting in dynamic and syncretic cultural exchanges. Furthermore, literacy rates, life expectancy, and childhood survival rates generally increased, especially at the end of the nineteenth century.

Conversely, capital consolidation wildly outstripped real wage growth, which is why this period is known as the **Gilded Age** (1870–1900). As business elites achieved unprecedented levels of wealth, the working poor struggled to make ends meet. Conditions were the worst in working class neighborhoods due to the prevalence of overcrowding, dilapidated buildings, and untreated sewage.

Labor and Management Battles

The writer Mark Twain called the late nineteenth century the Gilded Age because the era was one of extreme social inequality where the top "gilded" levels of society covered a rotten underbelly. Some corporations expanded and began to control entire industries. For example, by 1890, the Standard Oil Company produced 88 percent of all the refined oil in the nation. This made a few individuals, such as **John D. Rockefeller,** who owned Standard Oil, extremely wealthy. On the other hand, many workers earned low wages and began to form labor unions, such as the American Federation of Labor in 1886, to demand better working conditions and higher pay. Strikes were one of the most common ways workers could express their dissatisfaction, and the **Pullman Strike** of 1894 was one of the largest such incidents in the nineteenth century. Workers went on

195

strike after the Pullman Company, which manufactured railroad cars, cut wages by about 25 percent. More than 125,000 workers around the country walked off the job and attacked workers hired to replace them. Federal troops were sent in to end the strike, and more than eighty workers were killed or wounded during confrontations. The strike was unsuccessful, but Congress passed a law making Labor Day a federal holiday in order to placate union members.

California History: The Pre-Columbian Period Through the Gold Rush

Impact of California's Physical Geography on History

California is not only one of the most diverse states in terms of demographics; it is one of the most diverse with regard to physical geography and climate. In fact, it may be argued that the physical and climatic diversity of California has paved the way to its cultural and demographic diversity. As one of the largest states, California offers a breadth of unique geological and ecological features. It is home to the lowest point in the United States (Death Valley) and the highest peak in the contiguous states (Mount Whitney), making it home to both snowy peaks and arid deserts. It is also home to foggy redwood forests and sunny southern coastlands.

As one of the westernmost states in the Union, California has benefited, historically speaking, from its remote position which, for the most part, helped it avoid the revolutionary upheavals, international battles, and civil wars of the nineteenth century. Its remoteness has also helped create an escapist aura that surrounds California history. Its remote geography has helped make it a home for outlaws, gold miners, bandits, religious outcasts, Dust Bowl refugees, wanderlust-struck travelers, Hollywood hopefuls, down-and-out homeless citizens, documented and undocumented immigrants, civically engaged hipsters, and drug-induced hippies. The character of California's geographic landscape has helped make it a frontier of the American dream, its ideas, and its downfalls.

California's American Indian Peoples

Isolated in their own right by the geographic remoteness of California, and specifically the geographic remoteness caused by separation from the rest of the American continent by the Sierra Nevada mountains, the earliest American Indians in California remained alienated for several centuries before European colonization. Tribes scattered along the coasts and Central Valley of California "lived close to the soil," meaning they were primarily hunters and gatherers rather than traditional agriculturalists. These various tribes—which included the Hupa and Yurok—fed their families with acorns, snails, caterpillars, crickets, grubs, seafood, shellfish, cacti, roots, and game.

Their economy was mostly self-sustaining and built upon the backbone of bartering systems. They were governed by family structures and loose bonds with neighbors and were generally nomadic, wandering from place to place in search of food and shelter. Thus, their roving bands never reached the socio-governmental complexity of other early American Indian civilizations. In terms of religion and folklore, they believed the world was created by a flood, one that wiped out many creatures, and a supreme being only allowed the chosen ones to survive.

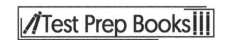

Spanish Colonization in California

Spanish colonization in California expanded throughout the eighteenth century. Franciscan friars migrated from Spanish colonies further south in present-day Mexico and western South America, founding **mission settlements** in coastal California. Mission settlements often began with a group of friars backed by a small retinue of laborers and/or soldiers, and the friars led a theocratic colonial system.

The mission settlements implemented the same policies toward indigenous populations as other Spanish colonies. The friars used forced conversions and persuasive proselytizing to gain some degree of cultural and societal control over the local population and actively pursued alliances with influential groups and leaders. Once they were in a position to carry out enforcement, the friars instituted the **repartimiento labor system**, which required indigenous populations to provide free labor in exchange for some limited legal rights and protections.

Combined with a massive amount of undeveloped land and an abundance of natural resources, the region's relatively small population of Spanish soldiers and migrants enjoyed more social mobility than nearly anywhere else in the world. Greater accommodation of indigenous culture and Europeans led to considerable cross-cultural interactions, including the development of syncretic religious beliefs and interracial family blending.

Mexican Rule in California

California transferred hands from the Spanish Crown to the Mexican Republic in 1821 when revolutionary leader Augustine Iturbide successfully led a revolt. Iturbide declared himself the emperor of the new Mexican government on May 19, 1822. Following this declaration, he began using the California region of North America as a dumping ground for those who went against the new revolutionary government. During this transition, the Mexican government disbanded the Spanish-Catholic missionary system in favor of a new secular system of governance. All officers from the presidios and all padres from the mission houses were obligated to pledge an oath of allegiance to the new Mexican Republic. California avoided the vortex of the revolutionary struggle for the most part but absorbed much of the tumult and uncertainty of its aftermath.

The era of Mexican control in California was consequently wrought with aggravated local tensions. During this era, residents witnessed periodic challenges to gubernatorial leadership. The era even created a cultural rift between Northern and Southern California that continues—to a certain degree—to this day. The era was also ripe with American infiltration, as settlers from the east flocked to the fruits of the Wild West. The tumult and rifts of this era thus paved the way to the eventual cessation of the California territory following the Mexican-American War.

War Between Mexico and the United States

The war between the Mexican Republic and the United States was catalyzed by the American desire to carry forth its so-called Manifest Destiny to conquer all lands between the Atlantic Ocean and Pacific Ocean. The Mexican-American War was, first and foremost, a war of expansion—the US government and its citizens honed in on Texas and California as possible lands for American annexation and/or Mexican cessation. Both territories had already witnessed an impressive infiltration of Anglo-American settlers that stirred US sympathies. The Mexican-American War was also a war over resources—the US government had its sights set on the cotton plantations of Texas and the gold, timber, crops, and minerals of California. Lastly, the Mexican-American War was a war that displaced domestic sectional tensions—the United States, on the eve of its own

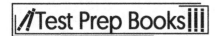

civil war, looked westward and southwestward in an attempt to solve the sectionalism ingrained in the American fiber. The new territories that were sought after became key players in the battle over slavery and abolition.

In terms of consequences, the Mexican-American War opened up California for a brief Bear Flag Revolt that witnessed the declaration of an independent California Republic. The Bear Flag Republic was more romanticism than reality, however, and William Ide, the leader of the incipient skirmish, remains just a footnote in US and California history. With the signing of the Treaty of Guadalupe-Hidalgo on February 2, 1848, the Mexican-American War officially ended, and the California region officially became a part of the United States. The California territory remained unsettled following the war, as government power slipped from the hands of Latinos into the hands of Anglo-Americans. As a result, Hispanic culture slowly slipped into isolated shadows, only to be revealed in more vibrant colors in later decades. The ensuing gold rush brought even more white settlers to cities like Los Angeles and San Francisco, paving the way to a new era of US occupation.

Discovery of Gold in California

Native Americans discovered gold in California years before the Anglo-American discovery of gold there. Nevertheless, the American historical mythos traditionally points to January 24, 1848, as the paradigm-shifting date of gold discovery on the North American continent. On this date, Scotsman James Wilson Marshall gathered up and inspected gold nuggets and flakes for the first time at Johann Sutter's infamous sawmill. This "discovery" set into motion decades of movement west from the urban corridors of the Northeast and Midwest to the gold mines of the Sierra Nevada mountains. The discovery was even applauded by President James K. Polk in a presidential address on December 5, 1848, creating more of a romantic allure about the California gold rush. By 1849, hundreds of thousands of settlers and immigrants flocked to the Golden Gate of San Francisco, California, to try their luck in mining and/or entrepreneurship.

Culturally speaking, states like California quickly became hubs of diversity, serving as the homes of thousands of Chinese, Mexican, black, and American Indian laborers. Socially, however, these diversities created racial tensions, leading to the persecution of "racial others" by white settlers. Wars ensued between US citizens and American Indians in the West, paving the way to the creation of more reservations. These racialized others were also exploited for railroad construction. Chinese immigrants eventually became demonized by white US politicians, leading to the passage of the xenophobic exclusion acts in the late nineteenth century. The Chinese Exclusion Act of 1882 is famous, for example, for embedding xenophobic sentiments into US law. Mexican nationals also struggled to find their place as Anglicized politics and economics pushed them further to the sociocultural margins. All residents—white or nonwhite—were affected by the boom-and-bust atmosphere of the gold rush. Very few residents became rich; many became broke in this staunchly capitalist tycoon environment.

California History: Economic, Political, and Cultural Development Since the 1850s

California Constitution

The California Constitution was first ratified on November 13, 1849, after convention members toiled for nearly a month to create and edit the document. One of the earliest debates of the first California constitutional convention was over the state line of demarcation—some convention members wanted the state of California to extend into the deserts surrounding the Salt Lake Basin; others wanted the state to use

the crest of the Sierra Nevada mountain range as a boundary. Eventually, convention members decided to place the line of demarcation just east of the Sierra Crest. Another crucial debate was over whether or not California would be admitted into the Union as a free or slave state. Following the infamous Compromise of 1850, convention members, influenced by the lobbying miners and gold rushers who were staunchly abolitionist, chose to make California a free state.

On September 9, 1850, its statehood became official. The California Constitution of 1849, which pushed the region into statehood, was considered fundamental law in the region for nearly thirty years. It was finally revised on September 28, 1878. The second constitutional convention included 152 convention delegates. Most delegates were either lawyers or farmers. Many felt the pressure of labor demands in this era, focusing their efforts on the rise of violence and the exploitation of railroad companies. The Constitution of 1879 was also riddled with xenophobic sentiments, offering many anti-Asian clauses and condemning the act of Asiatic "coolieism" (i.e., contracted labor) as slavery. On the flip side, the Constitution of 1879 paved the way to the foundation of the University of California public university system. After 157 days of deliberation, it was ratified as a cataloged code of laws.

Since 1879, the California Constitution has been amended over four hundred times. A lot of these amendments came during the Progressive Era of the early twentieth century. Women did not receive suffrage, for example, until 1911, and many of the restraints on corporations did not fully come into effect until this Progressive Era. These Progressive politicians, however, still fueled Californians' xenophobia by reinforcing Asian exclusionary laws. These laws were not repealed until later decades.

The California Constitution is built upon the same principles of liberty, justice, and equality as the US Constitution. However, the two constitutions differ in three major ways. First, the California Constitution limits state Supreme Court terms to just twelve years; the US Constitution appoints judges who serve for life. Second, the California Constitution does not allow the state to ratify treaties like the US Constitution allows the federal government to ratify treaties. Third, the California Constitution requires a term limit for its congressional delegates, while the US Constitution does not. They are similar, however, in that they both restrict their executive leadership to two terms.

Patterns of Immigration to California

Immigration has always been a key factor in the demographic growth and cultural diversity in California. This historical trend began in the mid-to-late nineteenth century with the gold rush years that brought hundreds of thousands of new immigrants to the Pacific coast. Cultural hubs like San Francisco and Los Angeles played host to Irish, German, and Italian immigrants, leading to an impressive urban growth that reached well into the Progressive Era.

Thousands of Chinese and Southeast Asian immigrants flocked to the railroad industry through the Golden Gate of California, but this led to changes in immigration policy. California witnessed even more growth during the era of the Dust Bowl and the Great Depression in the 1930s, as hundreds of thousands of migrants from the Midwest and Great Plains made their way to the "Land of Milk and Honey." These new migrants added to the diversity of California. World War II and the postwar era witnessed yet another immigrant surge, as thousands of Mexican farmers and laborers flocked to Southern California to escape Depression economics in favor of the rising prospects of the military industrial complex and agribusiness.

The end of Asian exclusion and the opening of immigration channels via the Immigration Act of 1965 helped bring hundreds of thousands of Vietnamese, Korean, Japanese, Chinese, Filipino, and Pacific Islander

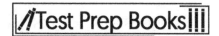
immigrants to Los Angeles and San Francisco. Latinos continue to add to the diverse fiber of the Golden State. As of 2010, Latinos make up nearly 40 percent of the state population. Today, many undocumented Latino immigrants flock to California for the refuge and protection of sanctuary cities such as San Francisco. This trend has catalyzed an era of divisive politics concerning undocumented immigration.

Effects of Federal and State Law on Immigrants' Legal Status

California has a long history of immigrants contributing to the state, but their legal status has fluctuated over time. In 1870, a revision to the 1802 Naturalization Law allowed Black people to become proper American citizens—before this, only those of White descent could do so. In 1882, the Chinese Exclusion Act banned all Chinese laborer immigration for ten years; in 1892 this was extended by the Geary Act for another ten years. Immigration Acts passed in both 1917 and 1924 continued to heavily restrict immigration from Asian areas. Throughout the first half of the 1900s, many actions were taken to continue to heavily restrict immigration or outright change the legal status of immigrant Americans. For example, the Japanese Internment Camps during World War II forced Japanese Americans into camps with poor living conditions for "national security." It wasn't until 1965 that the Immigration and Nationality Act finally passed and removed many of these restrictions. To this day, while naturalization is open to all, there are many undocumented immigrants in California whose legal status is in limbo until they can become true citizens.

Historical and Contemporary Perspectives on Cultural Diversity

The United States, ever since its early days, has been a culturally diverse nation. The state of California has an intimate history with cultural diversity. Indigenous tribes first settled in the area thousands of years ago with diversity among the tribes even then. Europe first colonized California when Spain sent explorers to claim the land and spread the Christian religion to the natives. America sent settlers to California in the early 1800s, though the area was still loosely under Mexican control. It wasn't until the Mexican-American War in 1846 that America gained full control over the California region, with Mexico ceding control after the war.

America's diversity is often seen as a boon; exposing people to others of different races and beliefs allows for fresh perspectives. Learning about each other helps people avoid stereotypes and negative biases. However, in times of fear, war, or economic turmoil, America's diversity has experienced its greatest difficulties. When people are afraid, they often look to anyone who is "different" to find someone to blame. America's diversity—and by extension California's diversity—means that people often lash out at their neighbors or make assumptions about their behaviors. Its strengths are still present, however, and by coming together people can overcome both their troubles and their prejudices.

Major Economic Activities in California

Since the initial years of the California gold rush in the late 1840s, mining has long been a cornerstone of the California economy. California's mining industry has annually called the Sierra Nevadas and the surrounding deserts its home. Large-scale agriculture has blessed California's Central Valley, Southern California, and coastal California since the Dust Bowl migrations of the 1930s and the wartime boom of the 1940s. California's Mediterranean climate has made it an ideal location for fruit farms, vineyards, and the olive oil and tree nut industries. Recreation, as an economic industry, is scattered throughout the state, though Los Angeles, and particularly Hollywood and Disneyland, have always been beacons of American film and leisure. Throughout the Cold War 1980s, and even in contemporary times, Silicon Valley has blossomed to become the epicenter of the global aerospace, electronics, and international trade industries. The entire Bay Area has skyrocketed its

real estate prices due to this tech boom. Places like San Francisco have now become major players in the Asian-Pacific trade economy that spans from Tokyo to the California coast.

California's Water Delivery System

Migration and civilization in California would not be possible without the complex California water delivery system that has been built throughout the twentieth and twenty-first centuries. After a series of bills and multistate compacts were passed by the federal government and the western states of the United States in the early twentieth century, California began an impressive, multidecade initiative with dam and canal construction. One of the crown jewels of this initiative was the creation of the Hoover Dam, located in Boulder Canyon of the Colorado River system. The result was the creation of Lake Mead, a 242-mile-long artificial lake that serves as an aquatic hub for the corridor between modern Las Vegas and Los Angeles. Other dams, canals, and aqueducts followed, especially as a result of the California agricultural boom brought on by the Dust Bowl era of American history.

Even today, California's farmers continue to soak up about 80 percent of the state's water delivery system. The system continues to sustain arid and semi-arid regions, as well as lush valleys. The delivery system has placed a strain not only on California's water resources, but also its entire geographic environment. Urban sprawl has contributed to droughts and subsequent wild fires. The system has carved the natural environment with concrete and metal, ingraining an artificial character onto the land. Today, conservationists are trying to stave off the destruction wrought by society and its insatiable thirst for water and resources in California.

Constructed-Response Questions

Constructed-response questions allow CSET test takers to break free from the monotonous, restrictive limitations multiple-choice questions place on one's knowledge. They provide a platform for writers of any skill level to openly display their content knowledge and test-prep capabilities. Fortunately, test takers are assessed solely on subject matter knowledge and not writing skills, though it never hurts to brush up on writing techniques (i.e. grammar, style, syntax). These constructed-response questions demand, at the very least, a 100-to 200-word short essay.

The key to a successful response is to meticulously read each assignment and its directions. If time permits, test takers should outline their responses on scratch paper. CSET scorers will assess test-taker responses with rubrics that examine the following three categories: 1) Purpose, 2) Subject Matter Knowledge, and 3) Support. In assessing purpose, CSET scorers look for test takers to make connections between content knowledge and the specific parameters of the question. In assessing subject matter knowledge, CSET scorers will, quite literally, be comparing the subject matter applied in the essay to a checklist of necessary and expected CSET content specifications. In assessing support, CSET scorers will rate the quality of the supporting evidence. All three of these categories should be evidenced through the quality of a writer's organization (rather than the quality of grammar, style, and syntax). Nonetheless, most CSET test-prep experts will agree that streamlined and organized grammar, style, and syntax will assist test takers in appropriately communicating their points.

The following sections provide advice and helpful tips to consider when planning, organizing, and writing essay-type responses, such as the constructed-response assignments on the CSET: Multiple Subjects exam:

Brainstorming

One of the most important steps in writing an essay is prewriting. Before drafting an essay, it's helpful to think about the topic for a moment or two, in order to gain a more solid understanding of the task. Then, spending about five minutes jotting down the immediate ideas that could work for the essay is recommended. It is a way to get some words on the page and offer a reference for ideas when drafting. Scratch paper is provided for writers to use any prewriting techniques such as webbing, free writing, or listing. The goal is to get ideas out of the mind and onto the page.

Considering Opposing Viewpoints

In the planning stage, it's important to consider all aspects of the topic, including different viewpoints on the subject. There are more than two ways to look at a topic, and a strong argument considers those opposing viewpoints. Considering opposing viewpoints can help writers present a fair, balanced, and informed essay that shows consideration for all readers. This approach can also strengthen an argument by recognizing and potentially refuting opposing viewpoint(s).

Drawing from personal experience may help to support ideas. For example, if the goal for writing is a personal narrative, then the story should come from the writer's own life. Many writers find it helpful to draw from personal experience, even in an essay that is not strictly narrative. Personal anecdotes or short stories can help to illustrate a point in other types of essays as well.

Moving from Brainstorming to Planning

Once the ideas are on the page, it's time to turn them into a solid plan for the essay. The best ideas from the brainstorming results can then be developed into a more formal outline. An outline typically has one main point (the thesis) and at least three sub-points that support the main point. Here's an example:

Main Idea

- Point #1
- Point #2
- Point #3

Of course, there will be details under each point, but this approach is the best for dealing with timed writing.

Staying on Track

Basing the essay on the outline aids in both organization and coherence. The goal is to ensure that there is enough time to develop each sub-point in the essay, roughly spending an equal amount of time on each idea. Keeping an eye on the time will help. If there are fifteen minutes left to draft the essay, then it makes sense to spend about 5 minutes on each of the ideas. Staying on task is critical to success, and timing out the parts of the essay can help writers avoid feeling overwhelmed.

Parts of the Essay

The introduction has to do a few important things:

- Establish the topic of the essay in original wording (i.e., not just repeating the prompt)

- Clarify the significance/importance of the topic or purpose for writing (not too many details, a brief overview)

- Offer a thesis statement that identifies the writer's own viewpoint on the topic (typically one-two brief sentences as a clear, concise explanation of the main point on the topic)

Body paragraphs reflect the ideas developed in the outline. Three-four points is probably sufficient for a short essay, and they should include the following:

- A topic sentence that identifies the sub-point (e.g., a reason why, a way how, a cause or effect)

- A detailed explanation of the point, explaining why the writer thinks this point is valid

- Illustrative examples, such as personal examples or real-world examples, that support and validate the point (i.e., "prove" the point)

- A concluding sentence that connects the examples, reasoning, and analysis to the point being made

The conclusion, or final paragraph, should be brief and should reiterate the focus, clarifying why the discussion is significant or important. It is important to avoid adding specific details or new ideas to this paragraph. The purpose of the conclusion is to sum up what has been said to bring the discussion to a close.

Don't Panic!

Writing an essay can be overwhelming, and performance panic is a natural response. The outline serves as a basis for the writing and helps writers keep focused. Getting stuck can also happen, and it's helpful to remember that brainstorming can be done at any time during the writing process. Following the steps of the writing process is the best defense against writer's block.

Timed essays can be particularly stressful, but assessors are trained to recognize the necessary planning and thinking for these timed efforts. Using the plan above and sticking to it helps with time management. Timing each part of the process helps writers stay on track. Sometimes writers try to cover too much in their essays. If time seems to be running out, this is an opportunity to determine whether all of the ideas in the outline are necessary. Three body paragraphs are sufficient, and more than that is probably too much to cover in a short essay.

More isn't always better in writing. A strong essay will be clear and concise. It will avoid unnecessary or repetitive details. It is better to have a concise, five-paragraph essay that makes a clear point, than a ten-paragraph essay that doesn't. The goal is to write one to two pages of quality writing. Paragraphs should also reflect balance; if the introduction goes to the bottom of the first page, the writing may be going off-track or be repetitive. It's best to fall into the one-two page range, but a complete, well-developed essay is the ultimate goal.

The Final Steps

Leaving a few minutes at the end to revise and proofread offers an opportunity for writers to polish things up. Putting one's self in the reader's shoes and focusing on what the essay actually says helps writers identify problems—it's a movement from the mindset of writer to the mindset of editor. The goal is to have a clean, clear copy of the essay. The following areas should be considered when proofreading:

- Sentence fragments
- Awkward sentence structure
- Run-on sentences
- Incorrect word choice
- Grammatical agreement errors
- Spelling errors
- Punctuation errors
- Capitalization errors

The Short Overview

The essay may seem challenging, but following these steps can help writers focus:

- Take one or two minutes to think about the topic.
- Generate some ideas through brainstorming (three-four minutes).
- Organize ideas into a brief outline, selecting just three-four main points to cover in the essay (eventually the body paragraphs).

Develop essay in parts:

- Introduction paragraph, with intro to topic and main points
- Viewpoint on the subject at the end of the introduction
- Body paragraphs, based on outline
- Each paragraph: makes a main point, explains the viewpoint, uses examples to support the point
- Brief conclusion highlighting the main points and closing
- Read over the essay (last five minutes).
- Look for any obvious errors, making sure that the writing makes sense.

Mathematics

Number Sense: Numbers, Relationships Among Numbers, and Number Systems

Place Value of Digits

The number system that is used consists of only ten different digits or characters. However, this system is used to represent an infinite number of values. The place value system makes this infinite number of values possible. The position in which a digit is written corresponds to a given value. Starting from the decimal point (which is implied, if not physically present), each subsequent place value to the left represents a value greater than the one before it. Conversely, starting from the decimal point, each subsequent place value to the right represents a value less than the one before it.

The names for the place values to the left of the decimal point are as follows:

...	Billions	Hundred- Millions	Ten- Millions	Millions	Hundred- Thousands	Ten- Thousands	Thousands	Hundreds	Tens	Ones

*Note that this table can be extended infinitely further to the left.

The names for the place values to the right of the decimal point are as follows:

Decimal Point (.)	Tenths	Hundredths	Thousandths	Ten- Thousandths	...

*Note that this table can be extended infinitely further to the right.

When given a multi-digit number, the value of each digit depends on its place value. Consider the number 682,174.953. Referring to the chart above, it can be determined that the digit 8 is in the ten-thousands place. It is in the fifth place to the left of the decimal point. Its value is 8 ten-thousands or 80,000. The digit 5 is two places to the right of the decimal point. Therefore, the digit 5 is in the hundredths place. Its value is 5 hundredths or $\frac{5}{100}$ (equivalent to .05).

Base-10 System

Value of Digits

In accordance with the base-10 system, the value of a digit increases by a factor of ten each place it moves to the left. For example, consider the number 7. Moving the digit one place to the left (70), increases its value by a factor of 10 ($7 \times 10 = 70$). Moving the digit two places to the left (700) increases its value by a factor of 10 twice ($7 \times 10 \times 10 = 700$). Moving the digit three places to the left (7,000) increases its value by a factor of 10 three times ($7 \times 10 \times 10 \times 10 = 7,000$), and so on.

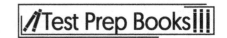

Conversely, the value of a digit decreases by a factor of ten each place it moves to the right. (Note that multiplying by $\frac{1}{10}$ is equivalent to dividing by 10). For example, consider the number 40. Moving the digit one place to the right (4) decreases its value by a factor of 10 ($40 \div 10 = 4$). Moving the digit two places to the right (0.4), decreases its value by a factor of 10 twice ($40 \div 10 \div 10 = 0.4$) or ($40 \times \frac{1}{10} \times \frac{1}{10} = 0.4$). Moving the digit three places to the right (0.04) decreases its value by a factor of 10 three times ($40 \div 10 \div 10 \div 10 = 0.04$) or ($40 \times \frac{1}{10} \times \frac{1}{10} \times \frac{1}{10} = 0.04$), and so on.

Exponents to Denote Powers of 10

The value of a given digit of a number in the base-10 system can be expressed utilizing powers of 10. A power of 10 refers to 10 raised to a given exponent such as 10^0, 10^1, 10^2, 10^3, etc. For the number 10^3, 10 is the base and 3 is the exponent. A base raised by an exponent represents how many times the base is multiplied by itself. Therefore:

$$10^1 = 10$$

$$10^2 = 10 \times 10 = 100$$

$$10^3 = 10 \times 10 \times 10 = 1,000$$

$$10^4 = 10 \times 10 \times 10 \times 10 = 10,000 \text{ etc.}$$

Any base with a zero exponent equals one.

Powers of 10 are utilized to decompose a multi-digit number without writing all the zeroes. Consider the number 872,349. This number is decomposed to:

$$800,000 + 70,000 + 2,000 + 300 + 40 + 9$$

When utilizing powers of 10, the number 872,349 is decomposed to:

$$(8 \times 10^5) + (7 \times 10^4) + (2 \times 10^3) + (3 \times 10^2) + (4 \times 10^1) + (9 \times 10^0)$$

The power of 10 by which the digit is multiplied corresponds to the number of zeroes following the digit when expressing its value in standard form. For example, 7×10^4 is equivalent to 70,000 or 7 followed by four zeros.

Structure of the Number System

The mathematical number system is made up of two general types of numbers: real and complex. **Real numbers** are both irrational and rational numbers. **Complex numbers** are those composed of both a real number and an imaginary one. Imaginary numbers are the result of taking the square root of -1, and $\sqrt{-1} = i$.

The real number system is often explained using a Venn diagram similar to the one below. After a number has been labeled as a real number, further classification occurs when considering the other groups in this diagram. If a number is a never-ending, non-repeating decimal, it falls in the irrational category. Otherwise, it is rational. More information on these types of numbers is provided in the previous section. Furthermore, if a number does not have a fractional part, it is classified as an integer, such as -2, 75, or zero. Whole numbers are an even smaller group that only includes positive integers and zero. The last group of natural numbers is made up of only positive integers, such as 2, 56, or 12.

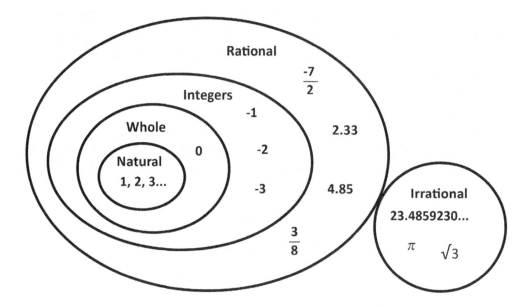

Real numbers can be compared and ordered using the number line. If a number falls to the left on the real number line, it is less than a number on the right. For example, $-2 < 5$ because -2 falls to the left of zero, and 5 falls to the right. Numbers to the left of zero are negative while those to the right are positive.

Complex numbers are made up of the sum of a real number and an imaginary number. Some examples of complex numbers include $6 + 2i$, $5 - 7i$, and $-3 + 12i$. Adding and subtracting complex numbers is similar to collecting like terms. The real numbers are added together, and the imaginary numbers are added together.

For example, if the problem asks to simplify the expression $6 + 2i - 3 + 7i$, the 6 and -3 are combined to make 3, and the $2i$ and $7i$ combine to make $9i$. Multiplying and dividing complex numbers is similar to working with exponents. One rule to remember when multiplying is that $i * i = -1$. For example, if a problem asks to simplify the expression $4i(3 + 7i)$, the $4i$ should be distributed throughout the 3 and the $7i$. This leaves the final expression $12i - 28$. The 28 is negative because $i * i$ results in a negative number. The last type of operation to consider with complex numbers is the conjugate. The **conjugate** of a complex number is a technique used to change the complex number into a real number. For example, the conjugate of $4 - 3i$ is $4 + 3i$. Multiplying $(4 - 3i)(4 + 3i)$ results in $16 + 12i - 12i + 9$, which has a final answer of $16 + 9 = 25$.

The order of operations—PEMDAS—simplifies longer expressions with real or imaginary numbers. Each operation is listed in the order of how they should be completed in a problem containing more than one operation. Parentheses can also mean grouping symbols, such as brackets and absolute value. Then, exponents are calculated. Multiplication and division should be completed from left to right, and addition and subtraction should be completed from left to right.

Simplification of another type of expression occurs when radicals are involved. As explained previously, root is another word for radical. For example, the following expression is a radical that can be simplified: $\sqrt{24x^2}$.

First, the number must be factored out to the highest perfect square. Any perfect square can be taken out of a radical. Twenty-four can be factored into 4 and 6, and 4 can be taken out of the radical. $\sqrt{4} = 2$ can be taken out, and 6 stays underneath. If $x > 0$, x can be taken out of the radical because it is a perfect square. The simplified radical is $2x\sqrt{6}$. An approximation can be found using a calculator.

There are also properties of numbers that are true for certain operations. The **commutative** property allows the order of the terms in an expression to change while keeping the same final answer. Both addition and multiplication can be completed in any order and still obtain the same result. However, order does matter in subtraction and division. The **associative** property allows any terms to be "associated" by parentheses and retain the same final answer.

For example, $(4 + 3) + 5 = 4 + (3 + 5)$. Both addition and multiplication are associative; however, subtraction and division do not hold this property. The **distributive** property states that $a(b + c) = ab + ac$. It is a property that involves both addition and multiplication, and the a is distributed onto each term inside the parentheses.

Integers can be factored into prime numbers. To **factor** is to express as a product. For example, $6 = 3 \cdot 2$, and $6 = 6 \cdot 1$. Both are factorizations, but the expression involving the factors of 3 and 2 is known as a **prime factorization** because it is factored into a product of two **prime numbers**—integers which do not have any factors other than themselves and 1. A **composite number** is a positive integer that can be divided into at least one other integer other than itself and 1, such as 6. Integers that have a factor of 2 are even, and if they are not divisible by 2, they are odd. Finally, a **multiple** of a number is the product of that number and a counting number—also known as a **natural number**. For example, some multiples of 4 are 4, 8, 12, 16, etc.

Positive and Negative Numbers

Signs
Aside from 0, numbers can be either positive or negative. The sign for a positive number is the plus sign or the + symbol, while the sign for a negative number is the minus sign or the − symbol. If a number has no designation, then it's assumed to be positive.

Absolute Values
Both positive and negative numbers are valued according to their distance from 0. Look at this number line for +3 and -3:

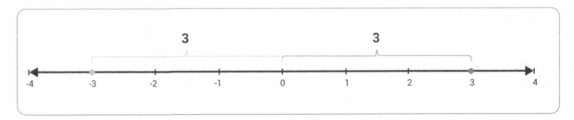

Both 3 and -3 are three spaces from 0. The distance from 0 is called its absolute value. Thus, both -3 and 3 have an absolute value of 3 since they're both three spaces away from 0.

An absolute number is written by placing | | around the number. So, |3| and |−3| both equal 3, as that's their common absolute value.

Rational Numbers on a Number Line

A number line typically consists of integers (...3, 2, 1, 0, -1, -2, -3...), and is used to visually represent the value of a rational number. Each rational number has a distinct position on the line determined by comparing its value with the displayed values on the line. For example, if plotting -1.5 on the number line below, it is necessary to recognize that the value of -1.5 is .5 less than -1 and .5 greater than -2. Therefore, -1.5 is plotted halfway between -1 and -2.

Number lines can also be useful for visualizing sums and differences of rational numbers. Adding a value indicates moving to the right (values increase to the right), and subtracting a value indicates moving to the left (numbers decrease to the left). For example, $5 - 7$ is displayed by starting at 5 and moving to the left 7 spaces, if the number line is in increments of 1. This will result in an answer of -2.

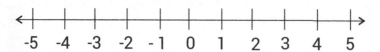

Comparing, Classifying, and Ordering Rational Numbers

A **rational number** is any number that can be written as a fraction or ratio. Within the set of rational numbers, several subsets exist that are referenced throughout the mathematics topics. Counting numbers are the first numbers learned as a child. Counting numbers consist of 1,2,3,4, and so on.

Whole numbers include all counting numbers and zero (0,1,2,3,4,...). Integers include counting numbers, their opposites, and zero (..., -3, -2, -1, 0, 1, 2, 3, ...). Rational numbers are inclusive of integers, fractions, and decimals that terminate, or end (1.7, 0.04213) or repeat (0.136$\underline{5}$).

When comparing or ordering numbers, the numbers should be written in the same format (decimal or fraction), if possible. For example, $\sqrt{49}$, 7.3, and $\frac{15}{2}$ are easier to order if each one is converted to a decimal, such as 7, 7.3, and 7.5. A number line is used to order and compare the numbers. Any number that is to the right of another number is greater than that number. Conversely, a number positioned to the left of a given number is less than that number.

Basic Concepts of Number Theory

Prime and Composite Numbers

Whole numbers are classified as either prime or composite. A prime number can only be divided evenly by itself and one. For example, the number 11 can only be divided evenly by 11 and one; therefore, 11 is a prime number. A helpful way to visualize a prime number is to use concrete objects and try to divide them into equal piles. If dividing 11 coins, the only way to divide them into equal piles is to create 1 pile of 11 coins or to create 11 piles of 1 coin each. Other examples of prime numbers include 2, 3, 5, 7, 13, 17, and 19.

A composite number is any whole number that is not a prime number. A composite number is a number that can be divided evenly by one or more numbers other than itself and one. For example, the number 6 can be divided evenly by 2 and 3. Therefore, 6 is a composite number. If dividing 6 coins into equal piles, the possibilities are 1 pile of 6 coins, 2 piles of 3 coins, 3 piles of 2 coins, or 6 piles of 1 coin. Other examples of composite numbers include 4, 8, 9, 10, 12, 14, 15, 16, 18, and 20.

To determine if a number is a prime or composite number, the number is divided by every whole number greater than one and less than its own value. If it divides evenly by any of these numbers, then the number is composite. If it does not divide evenly by any of these numbers, then the number is prime. For example, when attempting to divide the number 5 by 2, 3, and 4, none of these numbers divide evenly. Therefore, 5 must be a prime number.

Factors and Multiples of Numbers

The factors of a number are all integers that can be multiplied by another integer to produce the given number. For example, 2 is multiplied by 3 to produce 6. Therefore, 2 and 3 are both factors of 6. Similarly, $1 \times 6 = 6$ and $2 \times 3 = 6$, so 1, 2, 3, and 6 are all factors of 6. Another way to explain a factor is to say that a given number divides evenly by each of its factors to produce an integer. For example, 6 does not divide evenly by 5. Therefore, 5 is not a factor of 6.

Multiples of a given number are found by taking that number and multiplying it by any other whole number. For example, 3 is a factor of 6, 9, and 12. Therefore, 6, 9, and 12 are multiples of 3. The multiples of any number are an infinite list. For example, the multiples of 5 are 5, 10, 15, 20, and so on. This list continues without end. A list of multiples is used in finding the least common multiple, or LCM, for fractions when a common denominator is needed. The denominators are written down and their multiples listed until a common number is found in both lists. This common number is the LCM.

Prime factorization breaks down each factor of a whole number until only prime numbers remain. All composite numbers can be factored into prime numbers. For example, the prime factors of 12 are 2, 2, and 3 $(2 \times 2 \times 3 = 12)$. To produce the prime factors of a number, the number is factored, and any composite numbers are continuously factored until the result is the product of prime factors only. A factor tree, such as the one below, is helpful when exploring this concept.

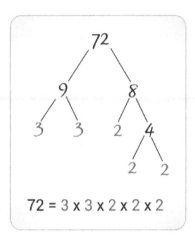

72 = 3 x 3 x 2 x 2 x 2

Number Relationships

The set of natural numbers can be separated into a variety of different types such as odds, evens, perfect squares, cubes, primes, composite, Fibonacci, etc. Number theory concepts can be used to prove relationships between these subsets of natural numbers. One of the main goals of number theory is to discover relationships between different subsets and prove that they are true. For example, some number theory proofs involve showing that the sum of two odd numbers is even and the sum of two even numbers is even.

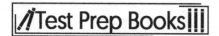

Properties of Exponents

Exponents are used in mathematics to express a number or variable multiplied by itself a certain number of times. For example, x^3 means x is multiplied by itself three times. In this expression, x is called the **base**, and 3 is the **exponent**. Exponents can be used in more complex problems when they contain fractions and negative numbers.

Fractional exponents can be explained by looking first at the inverse of exponents, which are **roots**. Given the expression x^2, the square root can be taken, $\sqrt{x^2}$, cancelling out the 2 and leaving x by itself, if x is positive. Cancellation occurs because $\sqrt{x}$ can be written with exponents, instead of roots, as $x^{\frac{1}{2}}$. The numerator of 1 is the exponent, and the denominator of 2 is called the root (which is why it's referred to as **square root**). Taking the square root of x^2 is the same as raising it to the $\frac{1}{2}$ power.

Written out in mathematical form, it takes the following progression:

$$\sqrt{x^2} = (x^2)^{\frac{1}{2}} = x$$

From properties of exponents, $2 \cdot \frac{1}{2} = 1$ is the actual exponent of x. Another example can be seen with $x^{\frac{4}{7}}$. The variable x, raised to four-sevenths, is equal to the seventh root of x to the fourth power: $\sqrt[7]{x^4}$. In general, $x^{\frac{1}{n}} = \sqrt[n]{x}$ and $x^{\frac{m}{n}} = \sqrt[n]{x^m}$.

Negative exponents also involve fractions. Whereas y^3 can also be rewritten as $\frac{y^3}{1}$, y^{-3} can be rewritten as $\frac{1}{y^3}$. A negative exponent means the exponential expression must be moved to the opposite spot in a fraction to make the exponent positive. If the negative appears in the numerator, it moves to the denominator. If the negative appears in the denominator, it is moved to the numerator. In general, $a^{-n} = \frac{1}{a^n}$, and a^{-n} and a^n are reciprocals.

Take, for example, the following expression: $\frac{a^{-4}b^2}{c^{-5}}$. Since a is raised to the negative fourth power, it can be moved to the denominator. Since c is raised to the negative fifth power, it can be moved to the numerator. The b variable is raised to the positive second power, so it does not move. The simplified expression is as follows: $\frac{b^2c^5}{a^4}$.

In mathematical expressions containing exponents and other operations, the order of operations must be followed. *PEMDAS* states that exponents are calculated after any parentheses and grouping symbols but before any multiplication, division, addition, and subtraction.

Scientific Notation

Scientific Notation is used to represent numbers that are either very small or very large. For example, the distance to the sun is approximately 150,000,000,000 meters. Instead of writing this number with so many zeros, it can be written in scientific notation as $1.5 * 10^{11}$ meters.

The same is true for very small numbers, but the exponent becomes negative. If the mass of a human cell is 0.000000000001 kilograms, that measurement can be easily represented by $1.0 * 10^{-12}$ kilograms. In both

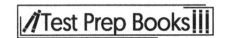
situations, scientific notation makes the measurement easier to read and understand. Each number is translated to an expression with one digit in the tens place times an expression corresponding to the zeros.

When two measurements are given and both involve scientific notation, it is important to know how these interact with each other:

- In addition and subtraction, the exponent on the ten must be the same before any operations are performed on the numbers. For example, $(1.3 * 10^4) + (3.0 * 10^3)$cannot be added until one of the exponents on the ten is changed. The $3.0 * 10^3$ can be changed to $0.3 * 10^4$, then the 1.3 and 0.3 can be added. The answer comes out to be $1.6 * 10^4$.

- For multiplication, the first numbers can be multiplied and then the exponents on the tens can be added. Once an answer is formed, it may have to be converted into scientific notation again depending on the change that occurred.

  o The following is an example of multiplication with scientific notation: $(4.5 * 10^3) * (3.0 * 10^{-5}) = 13.5 * 10^{-2}$. Since this answer is not in scientific notation, the decimal is moved over to the left one unit, and 1 is added to the ten's exponent. This results in the final answer: $1.35 * 10^{-1}$.

- For division, the first numbers are divided, and the exponents on the tens are subtracted. Again, the answer may need to be converted into scientific notation form, depending on the type of changes that occurred during the problem.

- **Order of magnitude** relates to scientific notation and is the total count of powers of 10 in a number. For example, there are 6 orders of magnitude in 1,000,000. If a number is raised by an order of magnitude, it is multiplied times 10. Order of magnitude can be helpful in estimating results using very large or small numbers. An answer should make sense in terms of its order of magnitude.

  o For example, if area is calculated using two dimensions with 6 orders of magnitude, because area involves multiplication, the answer should have around 12 orders of magnitude. Also, answers can be estimated by rounding to the largest place value in each number. For example, 5,493,302 * 2,523,100 can be estimated by 5 * 3 = 15 with 12 orders of magnitude.

Implications for Addition and Subtraction

For addition, if all numbers are either positive or negative, simply add them together. For example, 4 + 4 = 8 and -4 + -4 = -8. However, things get tricky when some of the numbers are negative, and some are positive.

Take 6 + (-4) as an example. First, take the absolute values of the numbers, which are 6 and 4. Second, subtract the smaller value from the larger. The equation becomes $6 - 4 = 2$. Third, place the sign of the original larger number on the sum. Here, 6 is the larger number, and it's positive, so the sum is 2.

Here's an example where the negative number has a larger absolute value: (-6) + 4. The first two steps are the same as the example above. However, on the third step, the negative sign must be placed on the sum, as the absolute value of (-6) is greater than 4. Thus, -6 + 4 = -2.

The absolute value of numbers implies that subtraction can be thought of as flipping the sign of the number following the subtraction sign and simply adding the two numbers. This means that subtracting a negative number will in fact be adding the positive absolute value of the negative number. Here are some examples:

$$-6 - 4 = -6 + -4 = -10$$

$$3 - -6 = 3 + 6 = 9$$

$$-3 - 2 = -3 + -2 = -5$$

Implications for Multiplication and Division

For multiplication and division, if both numbers are positive, then the product or quotient is always positive. If both numbers are negative, then the product or quotient is also positive. However, if the numbers have opposite signs, the product or quotient is always negative.

Simply put, the product in multiplication and quotient in division is always positive, unless the numbers have opposing signs, in which case it's negative. Here are some examples:

$$(-6) \times (-5) = 30$$

$$(-50) \div 10 = -5$$

$$8 \times |-7| = 56$$

$$(-48) \div (-6) = 8$$

If there are more than two numbers in a multiplication or division problem, then whether the product or quotient is positive or negative depends on the number of negative numbers in the problem. If there is an odd number of negatives, then the product or quotient is negative. If there is an even number of negative numbers, then the result is positive.

Here are some examples:

$$(-6) \times 5 \times (-2) \times (-4) = -240$$

$$(-6) \times 5 \times 2 \times (-4) = 240$$

Number Sense: Computational Tools, Procedures, and Strategies

Order of Operations

When solving equations with multiple operations, special rules apply. These rules are known as the Order of Operations. The order is as follows: Parentheses, Exponents, Multiplication and Division from left to right, and Addition and Subtraction from left to right. A popular mnemonic device to help remember the order is Please Excuse My Dear Aunt Sally (PEMDAS). Evaluate the following two problems to understand the Order of Operations:

1) $4 + (3 \times 2)^2 \div 4$

First, solve the operation within the parentheses: $4 + 6^2 \div 4$.

Second, solve the exponent: $4 + 36 \div 4$.

Third, solve the division operation: $4 + 9$.

Fourth, finish the operation with addition for the answer, 13.

2) $2 \times (6 + 3) \div (2 + 1)^2$

$2 \times 9 \div (3)^2$

$2 \times 9 \div 9$

$18 \div 9$

2

Strategies and Algorithms to Perform Operations on Rational Numbers

A rational number is any number that can be written in the form of a ratio or fraction. Integers can be written as fractions with a denominator of 1 ($5 = \frac{5}{1}$; $-342 = \frac{-342}{1}$; etc.). Decimals that terminate and/or repeat can also be written as fractions ($47 = \frac{47}{100}$; $.33 = \frac{1}{3}$). For more on converting decimals to fractions, see the section *Converting Between Fractions, Decimals,* and *Percent.*

When adding or subtracting fractions, the numbers must have the same denominators. In these cases, numerators are added or subtracted, and denominators are kept the same.

For example, $\frac{2}{7} + \frac{3}{7} = \frac{5}{7}$ and $\frac{4}{5} - \frac{3}{5} = \frac{1}{5}$. If the fractions to be added or subtracted do not have the same denominator, a common denominator must be found. This is accomplished by changing one or both fractions to a different but equivalent fraction.

Consider the example $\frac{1}{6} + \frac{4}{9}$. First, a common denominator must be found. One method is to find the least common multiple (LCM) of the denominators 6 and 9. This is the lowest number that both 6 and 9 will divide into evenly. In this case the LCM is 18. Both fractions should be changed to equivalent fractions with a denominator of 18. To obtain the numerator of the new fraction, the old numerator is multiplied by the same number by which the old denominator is multiplied. For the fraction $\frac{1}{6}$, 6 multiplied by 3 will produce a denominator of 18.

Therefore, the numerator is multiplied by 3 to produce the new numerator $\left(\frac{1 \times 3}{6 \times 3} = \frac{3}{18}\right)$.

For the fraction $\frac{4}{9}$, multiplying both the numerator and denominator by 2 produces $\frac{8}{18}$. Since the two new fractions have common denominators, they can be added $\left(\frac{3}{18} + \frac{8}{18} = \frac{11}{18}\right)$.

When multiplying or dividing rational numbers, these numbers may be converted to fractions and multiplied or divided accordingly. When multiplying fractions, all numerators are multiplied by each other and all denominators are multiplied by each other. For example:

$$\frac{1}{3} \times \frac{6}{5} = \frac{1 \times 6}{3 \times 5} = \frac{6}{15}$$

and

$$\frac{-1}{2} \times \frac{3}{1} \times \frac{11}{100} = \frac{-1 \times 3 \times 11}{2 \times 1 \times 100} = \frac{-33}{200}$$

When dividing fractions, the problem is converted by multiplying by the reciprocal of the divisor. This is done by changing division to multiplication and "flipping" the second fraction, or divisor. For example:

$$\frac{1}{2} \div \frac{3}{5} \rightarrow \frac{1}{2} \times \frac{5}{3}$$

and

$$\frac{5}{1} \div \frac{1}{3} \rightarrow \frac{5}{1} \times \frac{3}{1}$$

To complete the problem, the rules for multiplying fractions should be followed.

Note that when adding, subtracting, multiplying, and dividing mixed numbers (ex. $4\frac{1}{2}$), it is easiest to convert these to improper fractions (larger numerator than denominator). To do so, the denominator is kept the same. To obtain the numerator, the whole number is multiplied by the denominator and added to the numerator. For example:

$$4\frac{1}{2} = \frac{9}{2}$$

and

$$7\frac{2}{3} = \frac{23}{3}$$

Also, note that answers involving fractions should be converted to the simplest form.

Converting Between Fractions, Decimals, and Percent

To convert a fraction to a decimal, the numerator is divided by the denominator. For example, $\frac{3}{8}$ can be converted to a decimal by dividing 3 by 8 ($\frac{3}{8} = 0.375$).

To convert a decimal to a fraction, the decimal point is dropped, and the value is written as the numerator. The denominator is the place value farthest to the right with a digit other than zero. For example, to convert .48 to a fraction, the numerator is 48, and the denominator is 100 (the digit 8 is in the hundredths place).

216

Therefore, $.48 = \frac{48}{100}$. Fractions should be written in the simplest form, or reduced. To reduce a fraction, the numerator and denominator are divided by the largest common factor. In the previous example, 48 and 100 are both divisible by 4. Dividing the numerator and denominator by 4 results in a reduced fraction of $\frac{12}{25}$.

To convert a decimal to a percent, the number is multiplied by 100. To convert .13 to a percent, .13 is multiplied by 100 to get 13 percent. To convert a fraction to a percent, the fraction is converted to a decimal and then multiplied by 100. For example, $\frac{1}{5} = .20$ and .20 multiplied by 100 produces 20 percent.

To convert a percent to a decimal, the value is divided by 100. For example, 125 percent is equal to 1.25 ($\frac{125}{100}$). To convert a percent to a fraction, the percent sign is dropped, and the value is written as the numerator with a denominator of 100. For example, $80\% = \frac{80}{100}$. This fraction can be reduced ($\frac{80}{100} = \frac{4}{5}$).

Representing Rational Numbers and Their Operations

Concrete Models

Concrete objects are used to develop a tangible understanding of operations of rational numbers. Tools such as tiles, blocks, beads, and hundred charts are used to model problems. For example, a hundred chart (10×10) and beads can be used to model multiplication. If multiplying 5 by 4, beads are placed across 5 rows and down 4 columns producing a product of 20. Similarly, tiles can be used to model division by splitting the total into equal groups. If dividing 12 by 4, 12 tiles are placed one at a time into 4 groups. The result is 4 groups of 3. This is also an effective method for visualizing the concept of remainders.

Representations of objects can be used to expand on the concrete models of operations. Pictures, dots, and tallies can help model these concepts. Utilizing concrete models and representations creates a foundation upon which to build an abstract understanding of the operations.

Multiplication and Division Problems

Multiplication and division are inverse operations that can be represented by using rectangular arrays, area models, and equations. Rectangular arrays include an arrangement of rows and columns that correspond to the factors and display product totals.

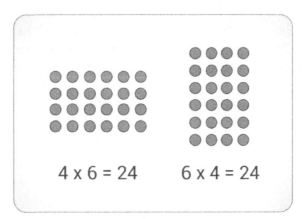

Another method of multiplication can be done with the use of an *area model*. An area model is a rectangle that is divided into rows and columns that match up to the number of place values within each number. Take the

217

example 29×65. These two numbers can be split into simpler numbers: $29 = 25 + 4$ and $65 = 60 + 5$. The products of those 4 numbers are found within the rectangle and then summed up to get the answer. The entire process is:

$$(60 \times 25) + (5 \times 25) + (60 \times 4) + (5 \times 4)$$

$$1,500 + 240 + 125 + 20 = 1,885$$

Here is the actual area model:

	25	4
60	60x25 1,500	60x4 240
5	5x25 125	5x4 20

$$\begin{array}{r} 1,500 \\ 240 \\ 125 \\ +\quad 20 \\ \hline 1,885 \end{array}$$

Dividing a number by a single digit or two digits can be turned into repeated subtraction problems. An area model can be used throughout the problem that represents multiples of the divisor. For example, the answer to $8580 \div 55$ can be found by subtracting 55 from 8580 one at a time and counting the total number of subtractions necessary.

However, a simpler process involves using larger multiples of 55. First, $100 \times 55 = 5,500$ is subtracted from 8,580, and 3,080 is leftover. Next, $50 \times 55 = 2,750$ is subtracted from 3,080 to obtain 380. $5 \times 55 = 275$ is subtracted from 330 to obtain 55, and finally, $1 \times 55 = 55$ is subtracted from 55 to obtain zero. Therefore, there is no remainder, and the answer is $100 + 50 + 5 + 1 = 156$.

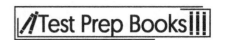

Here is a picture of the area model and the repeated subtraction process:

$$8580 \div 55$$

	55
100	5500
50	2750
5	275
1	55

```
55 | 8580
    -5500   (100 x 55)
     3080
    -2750   (50 x 55)
      330
     -275   (5 x 55)
       55
      -55   (1 x 55)
        0
```

Determining Reasonableness of Results

When solving math word problems, the solution obtained should make sense within the given scenario. The step of checking the solution will reduce the possibility of a calculation error or a solution that may be **mathematically** correct but not applicable in the real world. Consider the following scenarios:

A problem states that Lisa got 24 out of 32 questions correct on a test and asks to find the percentage of correct answers. To solve the problem, a student divided 32 by 24 to get 1.33, and then multiplied by 100 to get 133 percent. By examining the solution within the context of the problem, the student should recognize that getting all 32 questions correct will produce a perfect score of 100 percent. Therefore, a score of 133 percent with 8 incorrect answers does not make sense, and the calculations should be checked.

A problem states that the maximum weight on a bridge cannot exceed 22,000 pounds. The problem asks to find the maximum number of cars that can be on the bridge at one time if each car weighs 4,000 pounds. To solve this problem, a student divided 22,000 by 4,000 to get an answer of 5.5. By examining the solution within the context of the problem, the student should recognize that although the calculations are mathematically correct, the solution does not make sense. Half of a car on a bridge is not possible, so the student should determine that a maximum of 5 cars can be on the bridge at the same time.

Mental Math Estimation

Once a result is determined to be logical within the context of a given problem, the result should be evaluated by its nearness to the expected answer. This is performed by approximating given values to perform mental math. Numbers should be rounded to the nearest value possible to check the initial results.

Consider the following example: A problem states that a customer is buying a new sound system for their home. The customer purchases a stereo for $435, 2 speakers for $67 each, and the necessary cables for $12. The customer chooses an option that allows him to spread the costs over equal payments for 4 months. How much will the monthly payments be?

After making calculations for the problem, a student determines that the monthly payment will be $145.25. To check the accuracy of the results, the student rounds each cost to the nearest ten $(440 + 70 + 70 + 10)$ and determines that the total is approximately $590. Dividing by 4 months gives an approximate monthly payment of $147.50. Therefore, the student can conclude that the solution of $145.25 is very close to what should be expected.

When rounding, the place-value that is used in rounding can make a difference. Suppose the student had rounded to the nearest hundred for the estimation. The result:

$$(400 + 100 + 100 + 0 = 600; \; 600 \div 4 = 150)$$

will show that the answer is reasonable but not as close to the actual value as rounding to the nearest ten.

Algebra and Functions: Patterns and Functional Relationships

Number Patterns

Given a sequence of numbers, a mathematical rule can be defined that represents the numbers if a pattern exists within the set. For example, consider the sequence of numbers 1, 4, 9, 16, 25, etc. This set of numbers represents the positive integers squared, and an explicitly defined sequence that represents this set is $f_n = n^2$. An important mathematical concept is recognizing patterns in sequences and translating the patterns into an explicit formula. Once the pattern is recognized and the formula is defined, the sequence can be extended easily. For example, the next three numbers in the sequence are 36, 49, and 64.

Predicting Values

In a similar sense, patterns can be used to make conjectures, predictions, and generalizations. If a pattern is recognized in a set of numbers, values can be predicted that aren't originally provided. For example, if an experiment results in the sequence of numbers 1, 4, 9, 16, and 25, where 1 represents the first trial, 2 represents the second trial, etc., one expects the tenth trial to result in a value of 100 because that value is equal to the square of the trial number.

Recursively Defined Functions

Similar to recursively defined sequences, recursively defined functions are not explicitly defined in terms of a variable. A recursive function builds on itself and consists of a smaller argument, such as $f(0)$ or $f(1)$ and the actual definition of the function. For example, a recursively defined function is the following:

$$f(0) = 3$$

$$f(n) = f(n - 1) + 2n$$

Contrasting an explicitly defined function, a recursively defined function must be evaluated in order. The first five terms of this function are:

$$f(0) = 3, f(1) = 5, f(2) = 9, f(3) = 15, and \; f(4) = 23$$

Some recursively defined functions have an explicit counterpart and, like sequences, they can be used to model real-life applications. The Fibonacci numbers can also be thought of as a recursively defined function if $f(n) = f_n$.

Closed-Form Functions

A **closed-form function** can be evaluated using a finite number of operations such as addition, subtraction, multiplication, and division. An example of a function that's not a closed-form function is one involving an infinite sum.

For example, $y = \sum_{n=1}^{\infty} x$ isn't a closed-form function because it consists of a sum of infinitely many terms. Many recursively defined functions can be expressed as a closed-form expression. To convert to a closed-form expression, a formula must be found for the nth term. This means that the recursively defined sequence must be converted to its explicit formula.

Translating Between Verbal and Symbolic Forms

Being able to translate verbal scenarios into symbolic forms is a critical skill in mathematics. This idea is seen mostly when solving word problems. First, the problem needs to be read carefully several times until one can state clearly what is being sought. Then, variables that represent the unknown quantities need to be defined. Equations can be defined using those variables that model the verbal conditions of the given problem. The equations then need to be solved to answer the problem's questions. The problem-solving skills learned in these types of problems is an invaluable skill, and is ultimately more important than finding the answer to each individual problem.

Ratios and Proportions

*Ratio*s are used to show the relationship between two quantities. The ratio of oranges to apples in the grocery store may be 3 to 2. That means that for every 3 oranges, there are 2 apples. This comparison can be expanded to represent the actual number of oranges and apples. Another example may be the number of boys to girls in a math class. If the ratio of boys to girls is given as 2 to 5, that means there are 2 boys to every 5 girls in the class. Ratios can also be compared if the units in each ratio are the same. The ratio of boys to girls in the math class can be compared to the ratio of boys to girls in a science class by stating which ratio is higher and which is lower.

Rates are used to compare two quantities with different units. **Unit rates** are the simplest form of rate. With unit rates, the denominator in the comparison of two units is one. For example, if someone can type at a rate of 1000 words in 5 minutes, then their unit rate for typing is $\frac{1000}{5} = 200$ words in one minute or 200 words per minute. Any rate can be converted into a unit rate by dividing to make the denominator one. 1000 words in 5 minutes has been converted into the unit rate of 200 words per minute.

Ratios and rates can be used together to convert rates into different units. For example, if someone is driving 50 kilometers per hour, that rate can be converted into miles per hour by using a ratio known as the **conversion factor**. Since the given value contains kilometers and the final answer needs to be in miles, the ratio relating miles to kilometers needs to be used. There are 0.62 miles in 1 kilometer. This, written as a ratio and in fraction form, is $\frac{0.62\ miles}{1\ km}$.

To convert 50km/hour into miles per hour, the following conversion needs to be set up:

$$\frac{50\ km}{hour} * \frac{0.62\ miles}{1\ km} = 31\ miles\ per\ hour$$

221

The ratio between two similar geometric figures is called the **scale factor**. For example, a problem may depict two similar triangles, A and B. The scale factor from the smaller triangle A to the larger triangle B is given as 2 because the length of the corresponding side of the larger triangle, 16, is twice the corresponding side on the smaller triangle, 8. This scale factor can also be used to find the value of a missing side, x, in triangle A. Since the scale factor from the smaller triangle (A) to larger one (B) is 2, the larger corresponding side in triangle B (given as 25) can be divided by 2 to find the missing side in A (x= 12.5). The scale factor can also be represented in the equation $2A = B$ because two times the lengths of A gives the corresponding lengths of B. This is the idea behind similar triangles.

Much like a scale factor can be written using an equation like $2A = B$, a **relationship** is represented by the equation $Y = kX$. X and Y are proportional because as values of X increase, the values of Y also increase. A relationship that is inversely proportional can be represented by the equation $Y = \frac{k}{X}$, where the value of Y decreases as the value of x increases and vice versa.

Proportional reasoning can be used to solve problems involving ratios, percentages, and averages. Ratios can be used in setting up proportions and solving them to find unknowns. For example, if a student completes an average of 10 pages of math homework in 3 nights, how long would it take the student to complete 22 pages? Both ratios can be written as fractions. The second ratio would contain the unknown. The following proportion represents this problem, where x is the unknown number of nights:

$$\frac{10 \; pages}{3 \; nights} = \frac{22 \; pages}{x \; nights}$$

Solving this proportion entails cross-multiplying and results in the following equation: $10x = 22 * 3$. Simplifying and solving for x results in the exact solution: $x = 6.6 \; nights$. The result would be rounded up to 7 because the homework would actually be completed on the 7th night.

The following problem uses ratios involving percentages:

If 20% of the class is girls and 30 students are in the class, how many girls are in the class?

To set up this problem, it is helpful to use the common proportion: $\frac{\%}{100} = \frac{is}{of}$. Within the proportion, % is the percentage of girls, 100 is the total percentage of the class, *is* is the number of girls, and *of* is the total number of students in the class.

Most percentage problems can be written using this language. To solve this problem, the proportion should be set up as $\frac{20}{100} = \frac{x}{30}$, and then solved for x. Cross-multiplying results in the equation $20 * 30 = 100x$, which results in the solution $x = 6$. There are 6 girls in the class.

Ratios can be used to solve problems that concern length, volume, and other units. For example, a problem may ask for the volume of a cone to be found that has a radius, $r = 7m$ and a height, $h = 16m$. Referring to the formulas provided on the test, the volume of a cone is given as: $V = \pi r^2 \frac{h}{3}$, where r is the radius, and h is the height.

Plugging $r = 7$ and $h = 16$ into the formula, the following is obtained:

$$V = \pi (7^2)\frac{16}{3}$$

222

Therefore, the volume of the cone is found to be approximately 821m³. Sometimes, answers in different units are sought. If this problem wanted the answer in liters, 821m³ would need to be converted. Using the equivalence statement 1m³ = 1000L, the following ratio would be used to solve for liters:

$$821m^3 * \frac{1000L}{1m^3}$$

Cubic meters in the numerator and denominator cancel each other out, and the answer is converted to 821,000 liters, or $8.21 * 10^5$ L.

Other conversions can also be made between different given and final units. If the temperature in a pool is 30°C, what is the temperature of the pool in degrees Fahrenheit? To convert these units, an equation is used relating Celsius to Fahrenheit. The following equation is used:

$$T_{°F} = 1.8T_{°C} + 32$$

Plugging in the given temperature and solving the equation for T yields the result:

$$T_{°F} = 1.8(30) + 32 = 86°F$$

Units in both the metric system and US customary system are widely used.

Solving Problems by Quantitative Reasoning

Dimensional analysis is the process of converting between different units using equivalent measurement statements. For instance, running 5 kilometers is approximately the same as running 3.1 miles. This conversion can be found by knowing that 1 kilometer is equal to approximately 0.62 miles.

When setting up the dimensional analysis calculations, the original units need to be opposite one another in each of the two fractions: one in the original amount (essentially in the numerator) and one in the denominator of the conversion factor. This enables them to cancel after multiplying, leaving the converted result.

Calculations involving formulas, such as determining volume and area, are a common situation in which units need to be interpreted and used. However, graphs can also carry meaning through units. The graph below is an example. It represents a graph of the position of an object over time. The y-axis represents the position or the number of meters the object is from the starting point at time s, in seconds. Interpreting this graph, the origin shows that at time zero seconds, the object is zero meters away from the starting point. As the time increases to one second, the position increases to five meters away. This trend continues until 6 seconds, where the object is 30 meters away from the starting position. After this point in time—since the graph remains horizontal from 6 to 10 seconds—the object must have stopped moving.

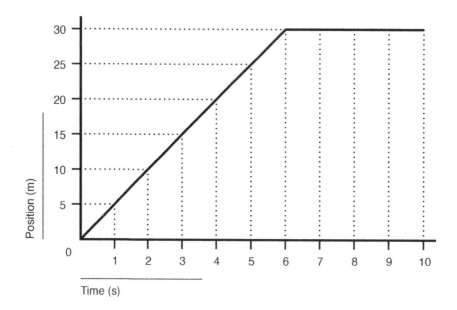

Time (s)

When solving problems with units, it's important to consider the reasonableness of the answer. If conversions are used, it's helpful to have an estimated value to compare the final answer to. This way, if the final answer is too distant from the estimate, it will be obvious that a mistake was made.

Functions

A **function** is defined as a relationship between inputs and outputs where there is only one output value for a given input. As an example, the following function is in function notation:

$$f(x) = 3x - 4$$

The $f(x)$ represents the output value for an input of x. If $x = 2$, the equation becomes:

$$f(2) = 3(2) - 4 = 6 - 4 = 2$$

The input of 2 yields an output of 2, forming the ordered pair $(2, 2)$.

The following set of ordered pairs corresponds to the given function: $(2, 2), (0, -4), (-2, -10)$. The set of all possible inputs of a function is its **domain**, and all possible outputs is called the **range**. By definition, each member of the domain is paired with only one member of the range.

Functions can also be defined recursively. In this form, they are not defined explicitly in terms of variables. Instead, they are defined using previously-evaluated function outputs, starting with either $f(0)$ or $f(1)$. An example of a recursively-defined function is:

$$f(1) = 2, f(n) = 2f(n - 1) + 2n, n > 1$$

The domain of this function is the set of all integers.

224

Domain and Range

The domain and range of a function can be found visually by its plot on the coordinate plane. In the function $f(x) = x^2 - 3$, for example, the domain is all real numbers because the parabola stretches as far left and as far right as it can go, with no restrictions. This means that any input value from the real number system will yield an answer in the real number system. For the range, the inequality $y \geq -3$ would be used to describe the possible output values because the parabola has a minimum at $y = -3$. This means there will not be any real output values less than -3 because -3 is the lowest value it reaches on the y-axis.

These same answers for domain and range can be found by observing a table. The table below shows that from input values $x = -1$ to $x = 1$, the output results in a minimum of -3. On each side of $x = 0$, the numbers increase, showing that the range is all real numbers greater than or equal to -3.

x (domain/input)	y (range/output)
-2	1
-1	-2
0	-3
-1	-2
2	1

Finding Zeros of Functions

The zeros of a function are the points where its graph crosses the x-axis. At these points, $y = 0$. One way to find the zeros is to analyze the graph. If given the graph, the x-coordinates can be found where the line crosses the x-axis. Another way to find the zeros is to set $y = 0$ in the equation and solve for x. Depending on the type of equation, this could be done by using opposite operations, by factoring the equation, by completing the square, or by using the quadratic formula. If a graph does not cross the x-axis, then the function may have complex roots.

Translating Functions

A function can be translated in many ways. Typical translations involve shifting, reflecting, and scaling graphs. A shift is a translation that does not change the original shape of the function. A vertical shift adds or subtracts a constant from every y-coordinate, and is represented as $y = f(x) \pm c$. A horizontal shift adds or subtracts a constant from every x-coordinate, and is represented as $y = f(x \pm c)$.

A reflection involves flipping a function over an axis. To reflect about the y-axis, every x-coordinate needs to be multiplied times -1. This reflection is represented as $y = f(-x)$. To reflect about the x-axis, every y-coordinate needs to be multiplied times -1. This reflection is represented as $y = -f(x)$.

Finally, a scale involves changing the shape of the graph through either a shrink or stretch. A scale either multiplies or divides each coordinate by a constant. A vertical scale involves multiplying or dividing every y-coordinate by a constant. This scaling is represented by $y = kf(x)$ and is a vertical stretch if $k > 1$ and vertical shrink if $0 < k < 1$. A horizontal scale involves multiplying or dividing every x-coordinate by a constant. This scaling is represented by $y = f(kx)$ and is a horizontal stretch if $0 < k < 1$ and horizontal shrink if $k > 1$.

Graphing Functions

Typically, a function can be graphed using a graphing calculator. However, some characteristics can be found that allow for enough information to be compounded to graph a very good sketch without technology. Such information includes significant points such as zeros, local extrema, and points where a function is not continuous and not differentiable. Zeros are points in which a function crosses the y-axis. These points are found by plugging 0 into the independent variable x and solving for the dependent variable y.

Local extrema are points in which a function is either a local maxima or minima. These points occur where the derivative of the function is either equal to zero or undefined, and those points are known as critical values. The first derivative test can be used to decide whether a critical value is a maximum or minimum. If a function increases to a point, showing that the first derivative is positive over that interval, and if a function decreases after that same point, showing that the derivative is negative over that interval, then the point is a local maximum. The opposite occurs at a local minimum. Finally, points in which a function is not continuous or not differentiable are also important points. A function is continuous over its domain. A function is not differentiable at a point if there exists a vertical tangent at that point, if there is a corner or a cusp at that point, or if the function is not defined at that point.

Asymptotes

An **asymptote** is a line that approaches the graph of a given function, but never meets it. Vertical asymptotes correspond to denominators of zero for a rational function. They also exist in logarithmic functions and trigonometric functions, such as tangent and cotangent. In rational functions and trigonometric functions, the asymptotes exist at x-values that cause a denominator equal to zero. For example, vertical asymptotes exist at $x = \pm 2$ for the function:

$$f(x) = \frac{x + 1}{(x - 2)(x + 2)}$$

Horizontal and oblique asymptotes correspond to the behavior of a curve as the x-values approach either positive or negative infinity. For example, the graph of $f(x) = e^x$ has a horizontal asymptote of $y = 0$ as x approaches negative infinity. In regards to rational functions, there is a rule to follow. Consider the following rational function:

$$f(x) = \frac{ax^n + \cdots}{bx^m + \cdots}$$

The numerator is an nth degree polynomial and the denominator is an mth degree polynomial. If $m < n$, the line $y = 0$ is a horizontal asymptote. If $n = m$, the line $y = \frac{a}{b}$ is a horizontal asymptote. If $m > n$, then there is an oblique asymptote. In order to find the equation of the oblique asymptote, the denominator is divided into the numerator using long division. The result, minus the remainder, gives the equation of the oblique asymptote.

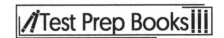

Here is a graph that shows an example of both a slant and a vertical asymptote:

Graphed Asymptotes

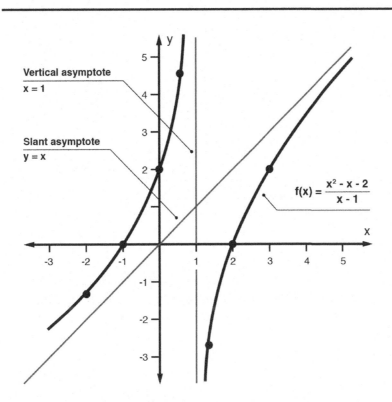

Inverse Variation and Rational Functions

The variable y varies inversely with respect to x if $y = \frac{k}{x}$, where k is the constant of variation. This means that as x decreases, y increases, and y is said to be inversely proportional to x. Also, this can be written as $k = xy$, and this specific example is known as inverse linear variation. The function $f(x) = \frac{k}{x}$ is a rational function because it is a rational fraction in which both the numerator and denominator are polynomials. Other types of inverse variation exist with nonlinear factors. The variable y can vary inversely with respect to x^2, and in this case: $y = \frac{k}{x^2}$. The exponent on the variable x can be any positive real number. In any case, the function will always be a rational function.

Rate of Change

Rate of change for any line calculates the steepness of the line over a given interval. Rate of change is also known as the slope or rise/run. The rates of change for nonlinear functions vary depending on the interval being used for the function. The rate of change over one interval may be zero, while the next interval may have a positive rate of change. The equation plotted on the graph below, $y = x^2$, is a quadratic function and non-linear.

The average rate of change from points $(0, 0)$ to $(1, 1)$ is 1 because the vertical change is 1 over the horizontal change of 1. For the next interval, $(1, 1)$ to $(2, 4)$, the average rate of change is 3 because the slope is $\frac{3}{1}$.

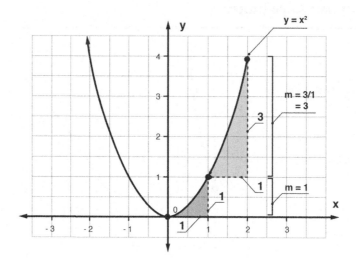

The rate of change for a linear function is constant and can be determined based on a few representations. One method is to place the equation in slope-intercept form: $y = mx + b$. Thus, m is the slope, and b is the y-intercept. In the graph below, the equation is $y = x + 1$, where the slope is 1 and the y-intercept is 1. For every vertical change of 1 unit, there is a horizontal change of 1 unit. The x-intercept is -1, which is the point where the line crosses the x-axis.

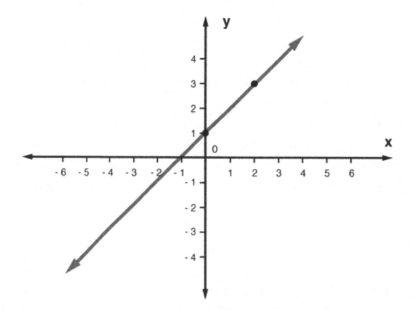

Solving Line Problems

Two lines are parallel if they have the same slope and a different intercept. Two lines are perpendicular if the product of their slope equals -1. Parallel lines never intersect unless they are the same line, and perpendicular lines intersect at a right angle. If two lines aren't parallel, they must intersect at one point. Determining

equations of lines based on properties of parallel and perpendicular lines appears in word problems. To find an equation of a line, both the slope and a point the line goes through are necessary. Therefore, if an equation of a line is needed that's parallel to a given line and runs through a specified point, the slope of the given line and the point are plugged into the point-slope form of an equation of a line. Secondly, if an equation of a line is needed that's perpendicular to a given line running through a specified point, the negative reciprocal of the slope of the given line and the point are plugged into the point-slope form. Also, if the point of intersection of two lines is known, that point will be used to solve the set of equations. Therefore, to solve a system of equations, the point of intersection must be found. If a set of two equations with two unknown variables has no solution, the lines are parallel.

Modeling Functions

Mathematical functions such as polynomials, rational functions, radical functions, absolute value functions, and piecewise-defined functions can be utilized to approximate, or model, real-life phenomena. For example, a function can be built that approximates the average amount of snowfall on a given day of the year in Chicago. This example could be as simple as a polynomial. Modeling situations using such functions has limitations; the most significant issue is the error that exists between the exact amount and the approximate amount. Typically, the model will not give exact values as outputs. However, choosing the type of function that provides the best fit of the data will reduce this error. Technology can be used to model situations. For example, given a set of data, the data can be inputted into tools such as graphing calculators or spreadsheet software that output a function with a good fit. Some examples of polynomial modeling are linear, quadratic, and cubic regression.

Representing Exponential and Logarithmic Functions

The logarithmic function with base b is denoted $y = x$. Its base must be greater than 0 and not equal to 1, and the domain is all $x > 0$. The exponential function with base b is denoted $y = b^x$. Exponential and logarithmic functions with base b are inverses. By definition, if $y = x$, $x = b^y$. Because exponential and logarithmic functions are inverses, the graph of one is obtained by reflecting the other over the line $y = x$. A common base used is e, and in this case $y = e^x$ and its inverse $y = x$ is commonly written as the natural logarithmic function $y = \ln \ln x$.

Here is the graph of both functions:

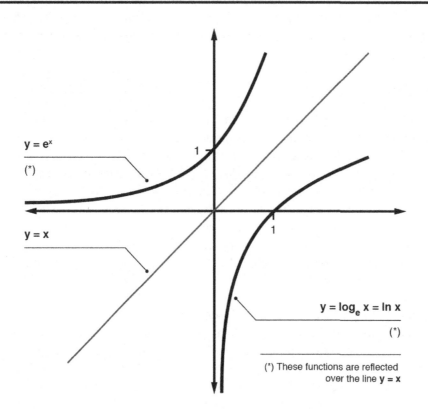

The Graphs of Exponential and Logarithmic Functions are Inverses

Graphing Functions

The x-intercept of the logarithmic function $y = x$ with any base is always the ordered pair $(1, 0)$. By the definition of inverse, the point $(0, 1)$ always lies on the exponential function $y = b^x$. This is true because any real number raised to the power of 0 equals 1. Therefore, the exponential function only has a y-intercept. The exponential function also has a horizontal asymptote of the x-axis as x approaches negative infinity. Because the graph is reflected over the line $y = x$, to obtain the graph of the logarithmic function, the asymptote is also reflected. Therefore, the logarithmic function has a one-sided vertical asymptote at $y = 0$. These asymptotes can be seen in the above graphs of $y = e^x$ and $y = ln \, ln \, x$.

Solving Logarithmic and Exponential Functions

To solve an equation involving exponential expressions, the goal is to isolate the exponential expression. Once this process is completed, the logarithm—with the base equaling the base of the exponent of both sides— needs to be taken to get an expression for the variable. If the base is e, the natural log of both sides needs to be taken.

To solve an equation with logarithms, the given equation needs to be written in exponential form, using the fact that $y = x$ means $b^x = y$, and then solved for the given variable. Lastly, properties of logarithms can be used to simplify more than one logarithmic expression into one.

Some equations involving exponential and logarithmic functions can be solved algebraically, or analytically. To solve an equation involving exponential functions, the goal is to isolate the exponential expression. Then, the logarithm of both sides is found in order to yield an expression for the variable. Laws of Logarithms will be helpful at this point.

To solve an equation with logarithms, the equation needs to be rewritten in exponential form. The definition that $x = y$ means $b^y = x$ needs to be used. Then, one needs to solve for the given variable. Properties of logarithms can be used to simplify multiple logarithmic expressions into one.

Other methods can be used to solve equations containing logarithmic and exponential functions. Graphs and graphing calculators can be used to see points of intersection. In a similar manner, tables can be used to find points of intersection. Also, numerical methods can be utilized to find approximate solutions.

Exponential Growth and Decay
Exponential growth and decay are important concepts in modeling real-world phenomena. The growth and decay formula is $A(t) = Pe^{rt}$, where the independent variable t represents temperature, P represents an initial quantity, r represents the rate of increase or decrease, and $A(t)$ represents the amount of the quantity at time t. If $r > 0$, the equation models exponential growth and a common application is population growth. If $r < 0$, the equation models exponential decay and a common application is radioactive decay. Exponential and logarithmic solving techniques are necessary to work with the growth and decay formula.

Logarithmic Scales
A logarithmic scale is a scale of measurement that uses the logarithm of the given units instead of the actual given units. Each tick mark on such a scale is the product of the previous tick mark multiplied by a number. The advantage of using such a scale is that if one is working with large measurements, this technique reduces the scale into manageable quantities that are easier to read. The Richter magnitude scale is the famous logarithmic scale used to measure the intensity of earthquakes, and the decibel scale is commonly used to measure sound level in electronics.

Using Exponential and Logarithmic Functions in Finance Problems
Modeling within finance also involves exponential and logarithmic functions. Compound interest results when the bank pays interest on the original amount of money – the principal – and the interest that has accrued. The compound interest equation is:

$$A(t) = P\left(1 + \frac{r}{n}\right)^{nt}$$

where P is the principal, r is the interest rate, n is the number of times per year the interest is compounded, and t is the time in years. The result, $A(t)$, is the final amount after t years. Mathematical problems of this type that are frequently encountered involve receiving all but one of these quantities and solving for the missing quantity. The solving process then involves employing properties of logarithmic and exponential functions. Interest can also be compounded continuously. This formula is given as $A(t) = Pe^{rt}$.

If \$1,000 was compounded continuously at a rate of 2% for 4 years, the result would be $A(4) = 1000e^{0.02 \cdot 4} = $ \$1,083.

Rate of Change Proportional to Current Quantity

Many quantities grow or decay as fast as exponential functions. Specifically, if such a quantity grows or decays at a rate proportional to the quantity itself, it shows exponential behavior. If a data set is given with such specific characteristics, the initial amount and an amount at a specific time, t, can be plugged into the exponential function $A(t) = Pe^{rt}$ for A and P. Using properties of exponents and logarithms, one can then solve for the rate, r. This solution yields enough information to have the entire model, which can allow for an estimation of the quantity at any time, t, and the ability to solve various problems using that model.

Mathematical Models to Represent Real-World Situations

A mathematical model is a representation in mathematical terms of a real-world situation, and is widely used in science and engineering. Formulas are derived that model phenomena such as population growth and decay. In any model, simplifications must be made to create such formulas, and parameters within the model usually do not represent the physical world exactly. Once the model is formulated, its output can be compared to real-world scenarios to judge how valid the model is. If a model is deemed to be inaccurate, original assumptions and restrictions can be lifted that initially simplified the model.

Using Multiple Representations of Mathematical Concepts

There are many different areas of mathematics, and a single mathematical concept can have meaning in more than one area. Some of the main divisions of math include arithmetic, algebra, calculus, geometry, and statistics. A concept that spans across those divisions is *area*. Many different formulas in geometry involve calculating the area of different shapes. For example, area of a circle $A = \pi r^2$ is a quadratic function in r, the radius of the circle. In calculus, an area problem can involve calculating the area under a curve from two points on the x-axis, which is known as the definite integral. Also, the area between two curves is discussed. Finally, in statistics, the area under a density curve is defined to be probability.

Communicating Mathematical Ideas

Many different types of representations are useful in mathematics, and the most widely-used are written symbols, pictures or diagrams, models, spoken words, and real-world experiences. Real-world experiences and spoken words are both representations that can be expressed by written symbols that impart mathematical meaning to the situation being discussed. Pictures or diagrams, including graphs and geometric figures, allow for visual representations of mathematical concepts. These external representations are widely used and have been developed for centuries. Similarly, written representations, such as symbolic methods like equations and functions, are also widely used and are used the most in math classes.

Using Visual Media

Students benefit from the use of visual media that represents mathematical information, and teachers should be able to go back and forth between each type. They should know which type of representation is useful in

given a scenario. For example, a function can be represented by a diagram, a table, a graph, and a set of numbers simultaneously. Here is such an example:

Multiple Representations of a Function

Mapping

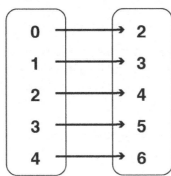

Table

x	y
0	2
1	3
2	4
3	5
4	6

Graph

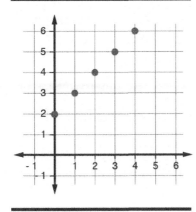

Ordered Pairs

{(0,2),(1,3),(2,4),(3,5),(4,6)}

Using Math Terminology

Using appropriate vocabulary that represents mathematical ideas is a critical skill in both being able to teach mathematics and use mathematical techniques to solve real-world situations. Each area in mathematics has its own set of definitions, and the translation of ideas onto paper requires a deep understanding of all the terminology. An important application of this idea is being able to translate word problems into equations that can be solved.

Algebra and Functions: Linear and Quadratic Equations and Inequalities

Rewriting Expressions

Algebraic expressions are made up of numbers, variables, and combinations of the two, using mathematical operations. Expressions can be rewritten based on their factors.

For example, the expression $6x + 4$ can be rewritten as $2(3x + 2)$ because 2 is a factor of both $6x$ and 4. More complex expressions can also be rewritten based on their factors. The expression $x^4 - 16$ can be rewritten as:

$$(x^2 - 4)(x^2 + 4)$$

This is a different type of factoring, where a difference of squares is factored into a sum and difference of the same two terms. With some expressions, the factoring process is simple and only leads to a different way to represent the expression. With others, factoring and rewriting the expression leads to more information about the given problem.

In the following quadratic equation, factoring the binomial leads to finding the zeros of the function:

$$x^2 - 5x + 6 = y$$

This equation factors into $(x - 3)(x - 2) = y$, where 2 and 3 are found to be the zeros of the function when y is set equal to zero. The zeros of any function are the x-values where the graph of the function on the coordinate plane crosses the x-axis.

Factoring an equation is a simple way to rewrite the equation and find the zeros, but factoring is not possible for every quadratic. Completing the square is one way to find zeros when factoring is not an option. The following equation cannot be factored:

$$x^2 + 10x - 9 = 0$$

The first step in this method is to move the constant to the right side of the equation, making it $x^2 + 10x = 9$.

Then, the coefficient of x is divided by 2 and squared. This number is then added to both sides of the equation, to make the equation still true. For this example, $\left(\frac{10}{2}\right)^2 = 25$ is added to both sides of the equation to obtain:

$$x^2 + 10x + 25 = 9 + 25$$

This expression simplifies to:

$$x^2 + 10x + 25 = 34$$

which can then be factored into:

$$(x + 5)^2 = 34$$

Solving for x then involves taking the square root of both sides and subtracting 5.

234

This leads to two zeros of the function:

$$x = \pm\sqrt{34} - 5$$

Depending on the type of answer the question seeks, a calculator may be used to find exact numbers.

Given a quadratic equation in standard form:

$$ax^2 + bx + c = 0$$

The sign of a tells whether the function has a minimum value or a maximum value. If $a > 0$, the graph opens up and has a minimum value. If $a < 0$, the graph opens down and has a maximum value. Depending on the way the quadratic equation is written, multiplication may need to occur before a max/min value is determined.

Exponential expressions can also be rewritten, just as quadratic equations. Properties of exponents must be understood. Multiplying two exponential expressions with the same base involves adding the exponents:

$$a^m a^n = a^{m+n}$$

Dividing two exponential expressions with the same base involves subtracting the exponents:

$$\frac{a^m}{a^n} = a^{m-n}$$

Raising an exponential expression to another exponent includes multiplying the exponents:

$$(a^m)^n = a^{mn}$$

The zero power always gives a value of 1: $a^0 = 1$. Raising either a product or a fraction to a power involves distributing that power:

$$(ab)^m = a^m b^m \text{ and } \left(\frac{a}{b}\right)^m = \frac{a^m}{b^m}$$

Finally, raising a number to a negative exponent is equivalent to the reciprocal including the positive exponent:

$$a^{-m} = \frac{1}{a^m}$$

Polynomial Identities

Difference of squares refers to a binomial composed of the difference of two squares. For example, $a^2 - b^2$ is a difference of squares. It can be written $(a)^2 - (b)^2$, and it can be factored into $(a - b)(a + b)$. Recognizing the difference of squares allows the expression to be rewritten easily because of the form it takes. For some expressions, factoring consists of more than one step. When factoring, it's important to always check to make sure that the result cannot be factored further. If it can, then the expression should be split further. If it cannot be, the factoring step is complete, and the expression is completely factored.

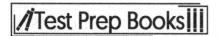
A sum and difference of cubes is another way to factor a polynomial expression. When the polynomial takes the form of addition or subtraction of two terms that can be written as a cube, a formula is given. The following graphic shows the factorization of a difference of cubes:

$$a^3 - b^3 = (a - b)(a^2 + ab + b^2)$$

same sign

opposite sign

always +

This form of factoring can be useful in finding the zeros of a function of degree 3. For example, when solving $x^3 - 27 = 0$, this rule needs to be used.

$x^3 - 27$ is first written as the difference two cubes, $(x)^3 - (3)^3$ and then factored into:

$$(x - 3)(x^2 + 3x + 9)$$

This expression may not be factored any further. Each factor is then set equal to zero. Therefore, one solution is found to be $x = 3$, and the other two solutions must be found using the quadratic formula. A sum of squares would have a similar process. The formula for factoring a sum of squares is:

$$a^3 + b^3 = (a + b)(a^2 - ab + b^2)$$

The opposite of factoring is multiplying. Multiplying a square of a binomial involves the following rules:

$$(a + b)^2 = a^2 + 2ab + b^2$$

and

$$(a - b)^2 = a^2 - 2ab + b^2$$

The binomial theorem for expansion can be used when the exponent on a binomial is larger than 2, and the multiplication would take a long time. The binomial theorem is given as:

$$(a + b)^n = \sum_{k=0}^{n} \binom{n}{k} a^{n-k} b^k$$

$$\text{where} \quad \binom{n}{k} = \frac{n!}{k!(n-k)!}$$

The **Remainder Theorem** can be helpful when evaluating polynomial functions $P(x)$ for a given value of x. A polynomial can be divided by $(x - a)$, if there is a remainder of 0.

This also means that $P(a) = 0$ and $(x - a)$ is a factor of $P(x)$.

In a similar sense, if P is evaluated at any other number b, $P(b)$ is equal to the remainder of dividing $P(x)$ by $(x - b)$.

236

Zeros of Polynomials

Finding the zeros of polynomial functions is the same process as finding the solutions of polynomial equations. These are the points at which the graph of the function crosses the x-axis. As stated previously, factors can be used to find the zeros of a polynomial function. The degree of the function shows the number of possible zeros. If the highest exponent on the independent variable is 4, then the degree is 4, and the number of possible zeros is 4. If there are complex solutions, the number of roots is less than the degree.

Given the function:

$$y = x^2 + 7x + 6$$

y can be set equal to zero, and the polynomial can be factored. The equation turns into:

$$0 = (x + 1)(x + 6)$$

where $x = -1$ and $x = -6$ are the zeros. Since this is a quadratic equation, the shape of the graph will be a parabola. Knowing that zeros represent the points where the parabola crosses the x-axis, the maximum or minimum point is the only other piece needed to sketch a rough graph of the function. By looking at the function in standard form, the coefficient of x is positive; therefore, the parabola opens *up*. Using the zeros and the minimum, the following rough sketch of the graph can be constructed:

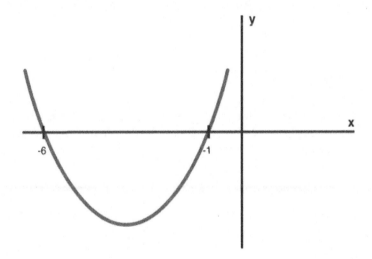

Operations with Polynomials

Addition and subtraction operations can be performed on polynomials with like terms. **Like terms refers to terms** that have the same variable and exponent. The two following polynomials can be added together by collecting like terms:

$$(x^2 + 3x - 4) + (4x^2 - 7x + 8)$$

The x^2 terms can be added as:

$$x^2 + 4x^2 = 5x^2$$

237

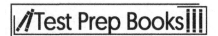

The x terms can be added as:

$$3x + -7x = -4x$$

and the constants can be added as:

$$-4 + 8 = 4$$

The following expression is the result of the addition:

$$5x^2 - 4x + 4$$

When subtracting polynomials, the same steps are followed, only subtracting like terms together.

Multiplication of polynomials can also be performed. Given the two polynomials, $(y^3 - 4)$ and $(x^2 + 8x - 7)$, each term in the first polynomial must be multiplied by each term in the second polynomial. The steps to multiply each term in the given example are as follows:

$$(y^3 * x^2) + (y^3 * 8x) + (y^3 * -7) + (-4 * x^2) + (-4 * 8x) + (-4 * -7)$$

Simplifying each multiplied part, yields:

$$x^2y^3 + 8xy^3 - 7y^3 - 4x^2 - 32x + 28$$

None of the terms can be combined because there are no like terms in the final expression. Any polynomials can be multiplied by each other by following the same set of steps, then collecting like terms at the end.

Equations and Inequalities

The sum of a number and 5 is equal to -8 times the number. To find this unknown number, a simple equation can be written to represent the problem. Key words such as difference, equal, and times are used to form the following equation with one variable:

$$n + 5 = -8n$$

When solving for n, opposite operations are used. First, n is subtracted from $-8n$ across the equals sign, resulting in $5 = -9n$. Then, -9 is divided on both sides, leaving $n = -\frac{5}{9}$. This solution can be graphed on the number line with a dot as shown below:

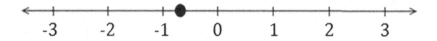

If the problem were changed to say, "The sum of a number and 5 is greater than -8 times the number," then an inequality would be used instead of an equation. Using key words again, *greater than* is represented by the symbol >. The inequality $n + 5 > -8n$ can be solved using the same techniques, resulting in $n < -\frac{5}{9}$. The only time solving an inequality differs from solving an equation is when a negative number is either multiplied times or divided by each side of the inequality. The sign must be switched in this case. For this example, the graph of

the solution changes to the following graph because the solution represents all real numbers less than $-\frac{5}{9}$. Not included in this solution is $-\frac{5}{9}$ because it is a *less than* symbol, not *equal to*.

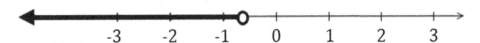

Equations and inequalities in two variables represent a relationship. Jim owns a car wash and charges $40 per car. The rent for the facility is $350 per month. An equation can be written to relate the number of cars Jim cleans to the money he makes per month. Let x represent the number of cars and y represent the profit Jim makes each month from the car wash. The equation

$$y = 40x - 350$$

can be used to show Jim's profit or loss. Since this equation has two variables, the coordinate plane can be used to show the relationship and predict profit or loss for Jim.

The following graph shows that Jim must wash at least nine cars to pay the rent, where $x = 9$. Anything nine cars and above yield a profit shown in the value on the y-axis.

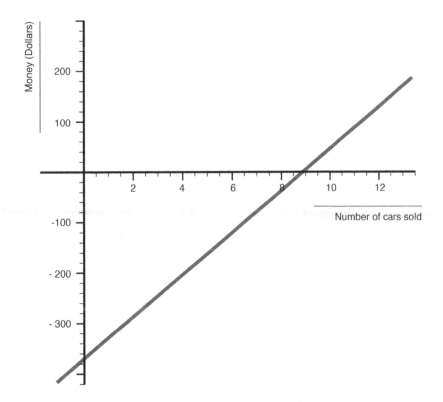

With a single equation in two variables, the solutions are limited only by the situation the equation represents. When two equations or inequalities are used, more constraints are added. For example, in a system of linear equations, there is often—although not always—only one answer. The point of intersection of two lines is the solution. For a system of inequalities, there are infinitely many answers.

The intersection of two solution sets gives the solution set of the system of inequalities. In the following graph, the darker shaded region is where two inequalities overlap. Any set of x and y found in that region satisfies both inequalities. The line with the positive slope is solid, meaning the values on that line are included in the solution. The line with the negative slope is dotted, so the coordinates on that line are not included.

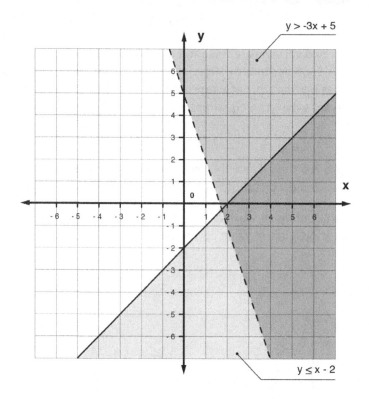

Formulas with two variables are equations used to represent a specific relationship. For example, the formula $d = rt$ represents the relationship between distance, rate, and time. If Bob travels at a rate of 35 miles per hour on his road trip from Westminster to Seneca, the formula $d = 35t$ can be used to represent his distance traveled in a specific length of time. Formulas can also be used to show different roles of the variables, transformed without any given numbers. Solving for r, the formula becomes $\frac{d}{t} = r$. The t is moved over by division so that *rate* is a function of distance and time.

Solving Equations

Solving equations with one variable is the process of isolating a variable on one side of the equation. For example:

$$3x - 7 = 20$$

The variable x needs to be isolated. Using opposite operations, the -7 is moved to the right side of the equation by adding seven to both sides:

$$3x - 7 + 7 = 20 + 7$$

This results in $3x = 27$.

Dividing by three on each side, $\frac{3x}{3} = \frac{27}{3}$, results in isolation of the variable. It is important to note that if an operation is performed on one side of the equals sign, it has to be performed on the other side to maintain equality. The solution is found to be $x = 9$.

This solution can be checked for accuracy by plugging $x=7$ in the original equation. After simplifying the equation, $20 = 20$ is found, which is a true statement.

When solving radical and rational equations, extraneous solutions must be accounted for when finding the answers. For example, the equation:

$$\frac{x}{x-5} = \frac{3x}{x+3}$$

has two values that create a 0 denominator: $x \neq 5, -3$.

When solving for x, these values must be considered because they cannot be solutions. In the given equation, solving for x can be done using cross-multiplication, yielding the equation:

$$x(x+3) = 3x(x-5)$$

Distributing results in the quadratic equation yields:

$$x^2 + 3x = 3x^2 - 15x$$

therefore, all terms must be moved to one side of the equals sign.

This results in $2x^2 - 18x = 0$, which in factored form is $2x(x-9) = 0$.

Setting each factor equal to zero, the apparent solutions are $x = 0$ and $x = 9$. These two solutions are neither 5 nor -3, so they are viable solutions. Neither 0 nor 9 create a 0 denominator in the original equation.

A similar process exists when solving radical equations. One must check to make sure the solutions are defined in the original equations. Solving an equation containing a square root involves isolating the root and then squaring both sides of the equals sign. Solving a cube root equation involves isolating the radical and then cubing both sides. In either case, the variable can then be solved for because there are no longer radicals in the equation.

Methods for Solving Equations

Equations with one variable can be solved using the addition principle and multiplication principle. If $a = b$, then $a + c = b + c$, and $ac = bc$. Given the equation:

$$2x - 3 = 5x + 7$$

the first step is to combine the variable terms and the constant terms. Using the principles, expressions can be added and subtracted onto and off both sides of the equals sign, so the equation turns into

$$-10 = 3x$$

Dividing by 3 on both sides through the multiplication principle with $c = \frac{1}{3}$ results in the final answer of:

$$x = \frac{-10}{3}$$

Some equations have a higher degree and are not solved by simply using opposite operations. When an equation has a degree of 2, completing the square is an option. For example, the quadratic equation:

$$x^2 - 6x + 2 = 0$$

can be rewritten by completing the square. The goal of completing the square is to get the equation into the form:

$$(x - p)^2 = q$$

Using the example, the constant term 2 first needs to be moved over to the opposite side by subtracting. Then, the square can be completed by adding 9 to both sides, which is the square of half of the coefficient of the middle term $-6x$.

The current equation is:

$$x^2 - 6x + 9 = 7$$

The left side can be factored into a square of a binomial, resulting in:

$$(x - 3)^2 = 7$$

To solve for x, the square root of both sides should be taken, resulting in:

$(x - 3) = \pm\sqrt{7}$, and $x = 3 \pm \sqrt{7}$

Other ways of solving quadratic equations include graphing, factoring, and using the quadratic formula. The equation $y = x^2 - 4x + 3$ can be graphed on the coordinate plane, and the solutions can be observed where it crosses the x-axis. The graph will be a parabola that opens up with two solutions at 1 and 3.

The equation can also be factored to find the solutions. The original equation:

$$y = x^2 - 4x + 3$$

can be factored into:

$$y = (x - 1)(x - 3)$$

Setting this equal to zero, the x-values are found to be 1 and 3, just as on the graph. Solving by factoring and graphing are not always possible. The quadratic formula is a method of solving quadratic equations that always results in exact solutions.

The formula is:

$$x = \frac{-b \pm \sqrt{b^2 - 4ac}}{2a}$$

242

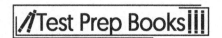

where a, b, and c are the coefficients in the original equation in standard form $y = ax^2 + bx + c$. For this example:

$$x = \frac{4 \pm \sqrt{(-4)^2 - 4(1)(3)}}{2(1)}$$

$$\frac{4 \pm \sqrt{16 - 12}}{2} = \frac{4 \pm 2}{2} = 1, 3$$

The expression underneath the radical is called the **discriminant**. Without working out the entire formula, the value of the discriminant can reveal the nature of the solutions. If the value of the discriminant $b^2 - 4ac$ is positive, then there will be two real solutions. If the value is zero, there will be one real solution. If the value is negative, the two solutions will be imaginary or complex. If the solutions are complex, it means that the parabola never touches the x-axis. An example of a complex solution can be found by solving the following quadratic:

$$y = x^2 - 4x + 8$$

By using the quadratic formula, the solutions are found to be:

$$x = \frac{4 \pm \sqrt{(-4)^2 - 4(1)(8)}}{2(1)} = \frac{4 \pm \sqrt{16 - 32}}{2}$$

$$\frac{4 \pm \sqrt{-16}}{2} = 2 \pm 2i$$

The solutions both have a real part, 2, and an imaginary part, $2i$.

Systems of Equations

A **system of equations** is a group of equations that have the same variables or unknowns. These equations can be linear, but they are not always so. Finding a solution to a system of equations means finding the values of the variables that satisfy each equation. For a linear system of two equations and two variables, there could be a single solution, no solution, or infinitely many solutions.

A single solution occurs when there is one value for x and y that satisfies the system. This would be shown on the graph where the lines cross at exactly one point. When there is no solution, the lines are parallel and do not ever cross. With infinitely many solutions, the equations may look different, but they are the same line. One equation will be a multiple of the other, and on the graph, they lie on top of each other.

The process of elimination can be used to solve a system of equations. The word "elmination" should be un-bolded, and one variable cancels out. For example, the following equations make up a system:

$$x + 3y = 10$$

and

$$2x - 5y = 9$$

243

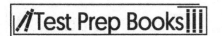
Immediately adding these equations does not eliminate a variable, but it is possible to change the first equation by multiplying the whole equation by -2.

This changes the first equation to:

$$-2x - 6y = -20$$

The equations can be then added to obtain $-11y = -11$.

Solving for y yields $y = 1$. To find the rest of the solution, 1 can be substituted in for y in either original equation to find the value of $x = 7$. The solution to the system is (7, 1) because it makes both equations true, and it is the point in which the lines intersect. If the system is *dependent*—having infinitely many solutions— then both variables will cancel out when the elimination method is used, resulting in an equation that is true for many values of x and y. Since the system is dependent, both equations can be simplified to the same equation or line.

A system can also be solved using **substitution**. This involves solving one equation for a variable and then plugging that solved equation into the other equation in the system. For example:

$$x - y = -2$$

and

$$3x + 2y = 9$$

can be solved using substitution. The first equation can be solved for x, where $x = -2 + y$. Then it can be plugged into the other equation:

$$3(-2 + y) + 2y = 9$$

Solving for y yields $-6 + 3y + 2y = 9$, where $y = 3$. If $y = 3$, then $x = 1$.

This solution can be checked by plugging in these values for the variables in each equation to see if it makes a true statement.

Finally, a solution to a system of equations can be found graphically. The solution to a linear system is the point or points where the lines cross. The values of x and y represent the coordinates (x, y) where the lines intersect. Using the same system of equations as above, they can be solved for y to put them in slope-intercept form, $y = mx + b$.

These equations become $y = x + 2$ and:

$$y = -\frac{3}{2}x + 4.5$$

244

The slope is the coefficient of x, and the y-intercept is the constant value. This system with the solution is shown below:

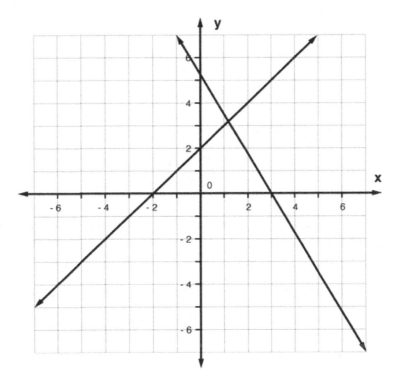

A system of equations may also be made up of a linear and a quadratic equation. These systems may have one solution, two solutions, or no solutions. The graph of these systems involves one straight line and one parabola. Algebraically, these systems can be solved by solving the linear equation for one variable and plugging that answer in to the quadratic equation. If possible, the equation can then be solved to find part of the answer. The graphing method is commonly used for these types of systems. On a graph, these two lines can be found to intersect at one point, at two points across the parabola, or at no points.

Matrices can also be used to solve systems of linear equations. Specifically, for systems, the coefficients of the linear equations in standard form are the entries in the matrix. Using the same system of linear equations as above, $x - y = -2$ and $3x + 2y = 9$, the matrix to represent the system is:

$$[1 \ -1 \ 3 \ 2][x \ y] = [-2 \ 9]$$

To solve this system using matrices, the inverse matrix must be found. For a general 2x2 matrix, $[a \ b \ c \ d]$, the inverse matrix is found by the expression:

$$\frac{1}{ad - bc}[d \ -b \ -c \ a]$$

The inverse matrix for the system given is:

$$\frac{1}{2 - -3}[2 \ 1 \ -3 \ 1] = \frac{1}{5}[2 \ 1 \ -3 \ 1]$$

The next step in solving is to multiply this identity matrix by the system matrix.

245

This is given by the following equation:

$$\frac{1}{5}[2\ 1\ -3\ 1\ ][1\ -1\ 3\ 2\ ][x\ y\ ] = [-2\ 9\ ][2\ 1\ -3\ 1\ ]\frac{1}{5}$$

This simplifies to:

$$\frac{1}{5}[5\ 0\ 0\ 5\ ][x\ y\ ] = \frac{1}{5}[5\ 15\ ]$$

Solving for the solution matrix, the answer is:

$$[1\ 0\ 0\ 1\ ][x\ y\ ] = [1\ 3\ ]$$

Since the first matrix is the identity matrix, the solution is $x = 1$ and $y = 3$.

Finding solutions to systems of equations is essentially finding what values of the variables make both equations true. It is finding the input value that yields the same output value in both equations. For functions $g(x)$ and $f(x)$, the equation $g(x) = f(x)$ means the output values are being set equal to each other.

Solving for the value of x means finding the x-coordinate that gives the same output in both functions.

For example, $f(x) = x + 2$ and $g(x) = -3x + 10$ is a system of equations.

Setting $f(x) = g(x)$ yields the equation $x + 2 = -3x + 10$.

Solving for x, gives the x-coordinate $x = 2$ where the two lines cross. This value can also be found by using a table or a graph. On a table, both equations can be given the same inputs, and the outputs can be recorded to find the point(s) where the lines cross. Any method of solving finds the same solution, but some methods are more appropriate for some systems of equations than others.

Systems of Linear Inequalities

Systems of **linear inequalities** are like systems of equations, but the solutions are different. Since inequalities have infinitely many solutions, their systems also have infinitely many solutions. Finding the solutions of inequalities involves graphs. A system of two equations and two inequalities is linear; thus, the lines can be graphed using slope-intercept form. If the inequality has an equals sign, the line is solid. If the inequality only has a greater than or less than symbol, the line on the graph is dotted. Dashed lines indicate that points lying on the line are not included in the solution. After the lines are graphed, a region is shaded on one side of the line. This side is found by determining if a point—known as a **test point**—lying on one side of the line produces a true inequality. If it does, that side of the graph is shaded. If the point produces a false inequality, the line is shaded on the opposite side from the point. The graph of a system of inequalities involves shading the intersection of the two shaded regions.

Measurement and Geometry: Two- and Three-Dimensional Geometric Objects

Points, Lines, Planes, and Angles

A point is a place, not a thing, and therefore has no dimensions or size. A set of points that lies on the same line is called collinear. A set of points that lies on the same plane is called coplanar.

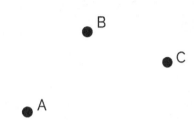

The image above displays point *A*, point *B*, and point *C*.

A line is as series of points that extends in both directions without ending. It consists of an infinite number of points and is drawn with arrows on both ends to indicate it extends infinitely. Lines can be named by two points on the line or with a single, cursive, lower case letter. The lines below are named: line *AB* or line *BA* or $\overleftrightarrow{AB}$ or $\overleftrightarrow{BA}$; and line *m*.

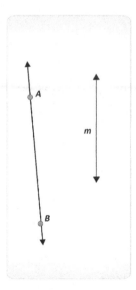

Two lines are considered parallel to each other if, while extending infinitely, they will never intersect (or meet). Parallel lines point in the same direction and are always the same distance apart. Two lines are considered

perpendicular if they intersect to form right angles. Right angles are 90°. Typically, a small box is drawn at the intersection point to indicate the right angle.

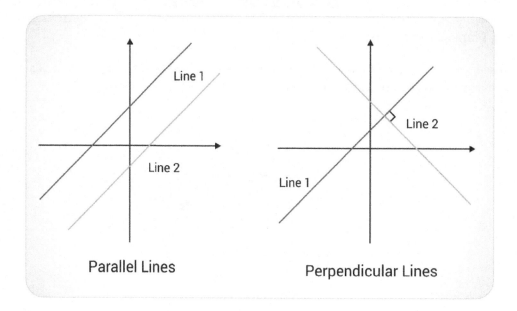

Line 1 is parallel to line 2 in the left image and is written as line 1 || line 2. Line 1 is perpendicular to line 2 in the right image and is written as line 1 ⊥ line 2.

A ray has a specific starting point and extends in one direction without ending. The endpoint of a ray is its starting point. Rays are named using the endpoint first, and any other point on the ray. The following ray can be named ray *AB* and written $\overrightarrow{AB}$.

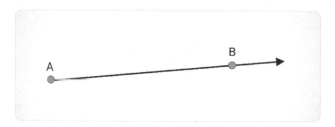

A line segment has specific starting and ending points. A line segment consists of two endpoints and all the points in between. Line segments are named by the two endpoints. The example below is named segment *GH* or segment *HG*, written $\underline{GH}$ or $\underline{HG}$.

Two- and Three-Dimensional Shapes

A polygon is a closed geometric figure in a plane (flat surface) consisting of at least 3 sides formed by line segments. These are often defined as two-dimensional shapes. Common two-dimensional shapes include

circles, triangles, squares, rectangles, pentagons, and hexagons. Note that a circle is a two-dimensional shape without sides.

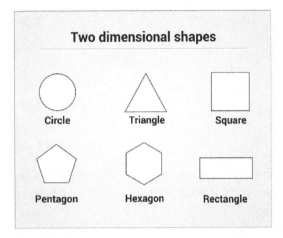

A solid figure, or simple solid, is a figure that encloses a part of space. Some solids consist of flat surfaces only while others include curved surfaces. Solid figures are often defined as three-dimensional shapes. Common three-dimensional shapes include spheres, prisms, cubes, pyramids, cylinders, and cones.

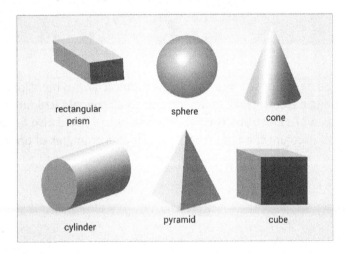

Composing two- or three-dimensional shapes involves putting together two or more shapes to create a new larger figure. For example, a semi-circle (half circle), rectangle, and two triangles can be used to compose the figure of the sailboat shown below.

Similarly, solid figures can be placed together to compose an endless number of three-dimensional objects.

Decomposing two- and three-dimensional figures involves breaking the shapes apart into smaller, simpler shapes. Consider the following two-dimensional representations of a house:

This complex figure can be decomposed into the following basic two-dimensional shapes: large rectangle (body of house); large triangle (roof); small rectangle and small triangle (chimney). Decomposing figures is often done more than one way. To illustrate, the figure of the house could also be decomposed into: two large triangles (body); two medium triangles (roof); two smaller triangles of unequal size (chimney).

Polygons and Solids

A polygon is a closed two-dimensional figure consisting of three or more sides. Polygons can be either convex or concave. A polygon that has interior angles all measuring less than 180° is convex. A concave polygon has one or more interior angles measuring greater than 180°. Examples are shown below:

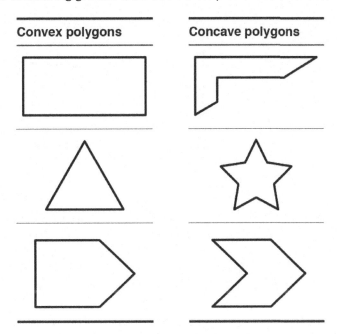

Polygons can be classified by the number of sides (also equal to the number of angles) they have. The following are the names of polygons with a given number of sides or angles:

# of Sides	Name of Polygon
3	Triangle
4	Quadrilateral
5	Pentagon
6	Hexagon
7	Septagon (or heptagon)
8	Octagon
9	Nonagon
10	Decagon

Equiangular polygons are polygons in which the measure of every interior angle is the same. The sides of equilateral polygons are always the same length. If a polygon is both equiangular and equilateral, the polygon is defined as a regular polygon. Examples are shown below:

251

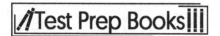
Triangles can be further classified by their sides and angles. A triangle with its largest angle measuring 90° is a right triangle. A triangle with the largest angle less than 90° is an acute triangle. A triangle with the largest angle greater than 90° is an obtuse triangle.

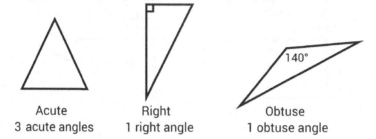

A triangle consisting of two equal sides and two equal angles is an isosceles triangle. A triangle with three equal sides and three equal angles is an equilateral triangle. A triangle with no equal sides or angles is a scalene triangle.

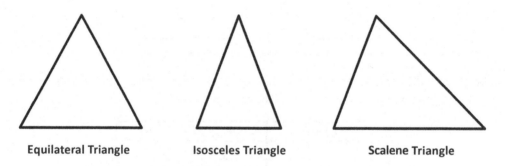

Quadrilaterals can be further classified according to their sides and angles. A quadrilateral with exactly one pair of parallel sides is called a trapezoid. A quadrilateral that shows both pairs of opposite sides parallel is a parallelogram. Parallelograms include rhombuses, rectangles, and squares. A rhombus has four equal sides. A

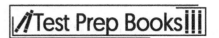

rectangle has four equal angles (90° each). A square has four 90° angles and four equal sides. Therefore, a square is both a rhombus and a rectangle.

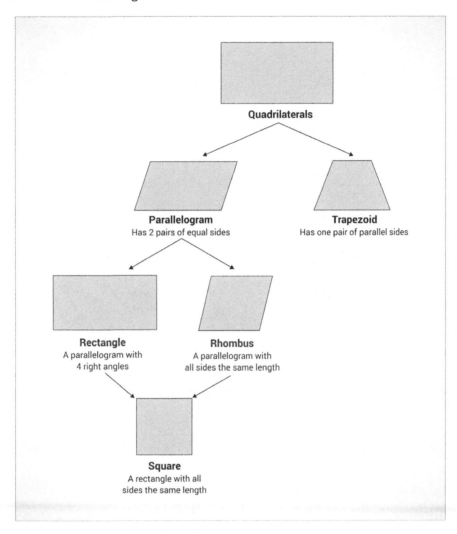

A solid is a three-dimensional figure that encloses a part of space. Solids consisting of all flat surfaces that are polygons are called polyhedrons. The two-dimensional surfaces that make up a polyhedron are called faces. Types of polyhedrons include prisms and pyramids. A prism consists of two parallel faces that are congruent (or the same shape and same size), and lateral faces going around (which are parallelograms).

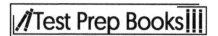
A prism is further classified by the shape of its base, as shown below:

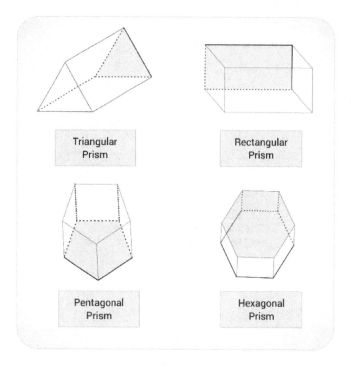

A pyramid consists of lateral faces (triangles) that meet at a common point called the vertex and one other face that is a polygon, called the base. A pyramid can be further classified by the shape of its base, as shown below:

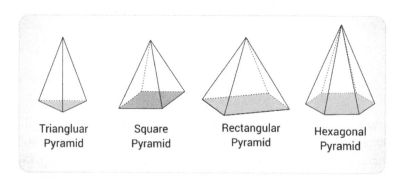

A tetrahedron is another name for a triangular pyramid. All the faces of a tetrahedron are triangles.

Solids that are not polyhedrons include spheres, cylinders, and cones. A sphere is the set of all points a given distance from a given center point. A sphere is commonly thought of as a three-dimensional circle. A cylinder consists of two parallel, congruent (same size) circles and a lateral curved surface. A cone consists of a circle as its base and a lateral curved surface that narrows to a point called the vertex.

Similar polygons are the same shape but different sizes. More specifically, their corresponding angle measures are congruent (or equal) and the length of their sides is proportional. For example, all sides of one polygon may be double the length of the sides of another. Likewise, similar solids are the same shape but different

sizes. Any corresponding faces or bases of similar solids are the same polygons that are proportional by a consistent value.

Properties of certain polygons allow that the perimeter may be obtained by using formulas. A rectangle consists of two sides called the length (*l*), which have equal measures, and two sides called the width (*w*), which have equal measures. Therefore, the perimeter (*P*) of a rectangle can be expressed as *P* = *l* + *l* + *w* + *w*. This can be simplified to produce the following formula to find the perimeter of a rectangle:

$$P = 2l + 2w \; or \; P = 2(l + w)$$

A regular polygon is one in which all sides have equal length and all interior angles have equal measures, such as a square and an equilateral triangle. To find the perimeter of a regular polygon, the length of one side is multiplied by the number of sides. For example, to find the perimeter of an equilateral triangle with a side of length of 4 feet, 4 feet is multiplied by 3 (number of sides of a triangle). The perimeter of a regular octagon (8 sides) with a side of length of $\frac{1}{2}$cm is $\frac{1}{2}cm \times 8 = 4cm$.

Classification of Angles

An angle consists of two rays that have a common endpoint. This common endpoint is called the vertex of the angle. The two rays can be called sides of the angle. The angle below has a vertex at point *B* and the sides consist of ray *BA* and ray *BC*. An angle can be named in three ways:

- 1. Using the vertex and a point from each side, with the vertex letter in the middle.
- 2. Using only the vertex. This can only be used if it is the only angle with that vertex.
- 3. Using a number that is written inside the angle.

The angle below can be written ∠*ABC* (read angle *ABC*), ∠*CBA*, ∠*B*, or ∠1:

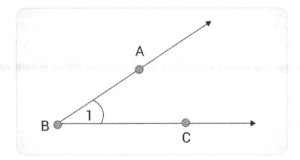

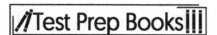

An angle divides a plane, or flat surface, into three parts: the angle itself, the interior (inside) of the angle, and the exterior (outside) of the angle. The figure below shows point *M* on the interior of the angle and point *N* on the exterior of the angle:

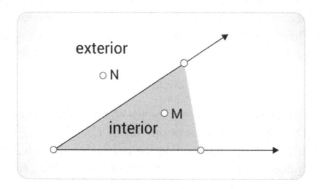

Angles can be measured in units called degrees, with the symbol °. The degree measure of an angle is between 0° and 180° and can be obtained by using a protractor:

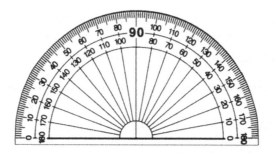

A straight angle (or simply a line) measures exactly 180°. A right angle's sides meet at the vertex to create a square corner. A right-angle measures exactly 90° and is typically indicated by a box drawn in the interior of the angle. An acute angle has an interior that is narrower than a right angle. The measure of an acute angle is any value less than 90° and greater than 0°. For example, 89.9°, 47°, 12°, and 1°. An obtuse angle has an interior that is wider than a right angle. The measure of an obtuse angle is any value greater than 90° but less than 180°. For example, 90.1°, 110°, 150°, and 179.9°.

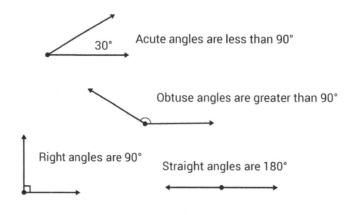

Effects of Changes to Dimensions on Area and Volume

Similar polygons are figures that are the same shape but different sizes. Likewise, similar solids are different sizes but are the same shape. In both cases, corresponding angles in the same positions for both figures are congruent (equal), and corresponding sides are proportional in length. For example, the triangles below are similar. The following pairs of corresponding angles are congruent: ∠A and ∠D; ∠B and ∠E; ∠C and ∠F. The corresponding sides are proportional:

$$\frac{AB}{DE} = \frac{6}{3} = 2$$

$$\frac{BC}{EF} = \frac{9}{4.5} = 2$$

$$\frac{CA}{FD} = \frac{10}{5} = 2$$

In other words, triangle ABC is the same shape but twice as large as triangle DEF.

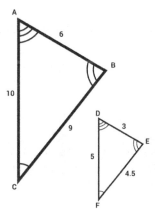

An example of similar triangular pyramids is shown below:

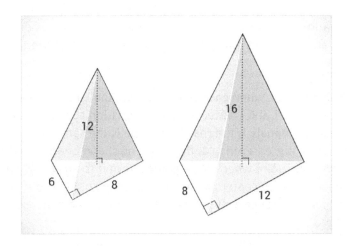

Given the nature of two- and three-dimensional measurements, changing dimensions by a given scale (multiplier) does not change the area of volume by the same scale. Consider a rectangle with a length of 5 centimeters and a width of 4 centimeters. The area of the rectangle is $20cm^2$. Doubling the dimensions of the rectangle (multiplying by a scale factor of 2) to 10 centimeters and 8 centimeters *does not* double the area to $40cm^2$. Area is a two-dimensional measurement (measured in square units). Therefore, the dimensions are multiplied by a scale that is squared (raised to the second power) to determine the scale of the corresponding areas.

For the previous example, the length and width are multiplied by 2. Therefore, the area is multiplied by 2^2, or 4. The area of a 5cm × 4cm rectangle is $20cm^2$. The area of a 10cm × 8cm rectangle is $80cm^2$.

Volume is a three-dimensional measurement, which is measured in cubic units. Therefore, the scale between dimensions of similar solids is cubed (raised to the third power) to determine the scale between their volumes. Consider similar right rectangular prisms: one with a length of 8 inches, a width of 24 inches, and a height of 16 inches; the second with a length of 4 inches, a width of 12 inches, and a height of 8 inches.

The first prism, multiplied by a scalar of $\frac{1}{2}$, produces the measurement of the second prism. The volume of the first prism, multiplied by $(\frac{1}{2})^3$, which equals $\frac{1}{8}$, produces the volume of the second prism.

The volume of the first prism is 8in × 24in × 16in which equals $3,072in^3$. The volume of the second prism is 4in × 12in × 8in which equals:

$$384in^3 \ (3,072in^3 \times \frac{1}{8} = 384in^3)$$

The rules for squaring the scalar for area and cubing the scalar for volume only hold true for similar figures. In other words, if only one dimension is changed (changing the width of a rectangle but not the length) or dimensions are changed at different rates (the length of a prism is doubled and its height is tripled) the figures are not similar (same shape). Therefore, the rules above do not apply.

Congruence and Similarity in Terms of Transformations

Rigid Motion

A **rigid motion** is a transformation that preserves distance and length. Every line segment in the resulting image is congruent to the corresponding line segment in the pre-image. Congruence between two figures means a series of transformations (or a rigid motion) can be defined that maps one of the figures onto the other. Basically, two figures are congruent if they have the same shape and size.

Dilation

A shape is dilated, or a **dilation** occurs, when each side of the original image is multiplied by a given scale factor. If the scale factor is less than 1 and greater than 0, the dilation contracts the shape, and the resulting shape is smaller. If the scale factor equals 1, the resulting shape is the same size, and the dilation is a rigid motion. Finally, if the scale factor is greater than 1, the resulting shape is larger and the dilation expands the shape. The **center of dilation** is the point where the distance from it to any point on the new shape equals the scale factor times the distance from the center to the corresponding point in the pre-image. Dilation isn't an isometric transformation because distance isn't preserved. However, angle measure, parallel lines, and points on a line all remain unchanged.

The following figure is an example of translation, rotation, dilation, and reflection:

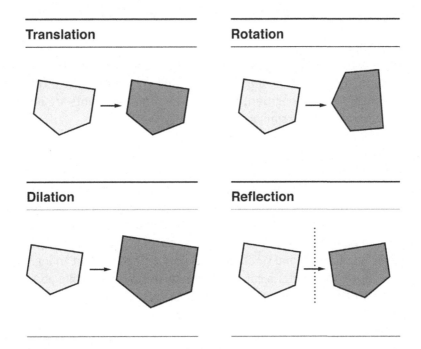

Determining Congruence

Two figures are congruent if there is a rigid motion that can map one figure onto the other. Therefore, all pairs of sides and angles within the image and pre-image must be congruent. For example, in triangles, each pair of the three sides and three angles must be congruent. Similarly, in two four-sided figures, each pair of the four sides and four angles must be congruent.

Similarity

Two figures are **similar** if there is a combination of translations, reflections, rotations, and dilations, which maps one figure onto the other. The difference between congruence and similarity is that dilation can be used in similarity. Therefore, side lengths between each shape can differ. However, angle measure must be preserved within this definition. If two polygons differ in size so that the lengths of corresponding line segments differ by the same factor, but corresponding angles have the same measurement, they are similar.

Triangle Congruence

There are five theorems to show that triangles are congruent when it's unknown whether each pair of angles and sides are congruent. Each theorem is a shortcut that involves different combinations of sides and angles that must be true for the two triangles to be congruent. For example, **side-side-side (SSS)** states that if all sides are equal, the triangles are congruent.

Side-angle-side (SAS) states that if two pairs of sides are equal and the included angles are congruent, then the triangles are congruent. Similarly, **angle-side-angle (ASA)** states that if two pairs of angles are congruent and the included side lengths are equal, the triangles are similar. **Angle-angle-side (AAS)** states that two triangles are congruent if they have two pairs of congruent angles and a pair of corresponding equal side lengths that aren't included. Finally, **hypotenuse-leg (HL)** states that if two right triangles have equal hypotenuses and an equal pair of shorter sides, then the triangles are congruent. An important item to note is that angle-angle-

259

angle **(AAA)** is not enough information to have congruence. It's important to understand why these rules work by using rigid motions to show congruence between the triangles with the given properties. For example, three reflections are needed to show why **SAS** follows from the definition of congruence.

Similarity for Two Triangles
If two angles of one triangle are congruent with two angles of a second triangle, the triangles are similar. This is because, within any triangle, the sum of the angle measurements is 180 degrees. Therefore, if two are congruent, the third angle must also be congruent because their measurements are equal. Three congruent pairs of angles mean that the triangles are similar.

Proving Congruence and Similarity
The criteria needed to prove triangles are congruent involves both angle and side congruence. Both pairs of related angles and sides need to be of the same measurement to use congruence in a proof. The criteria to prove similarity in triangles involves proportionality of side lengths. Angles must be congruent in similar triangles; however, corresponding side lengths only need to be a constant multiple of each other. Once similarity is established, it can be used in proofs as well. Relationships in geometric figures other than triangles can be proven using triangle congruence and similarity. If a similar or congruent triangle can be found within another type of geometric figure, their criteria can be used to prove a relationship about a given formula. For instance, a rectangle can be broken up into two congruent triangles.

Relationships Between Angles
Supplementary angles add up to 180 degrees. **Vertical angles** are two nonadjacent angles formed by two intersecting lines. **Corresponding angles** are two angles in the same position whenever a straight line (known as a **transversal**) crosses two others. If the two lines are parallel, the corresponding angles are equal. In the following diagram, angles 1 and 3 are corresponding angles but aren't equal to each other:

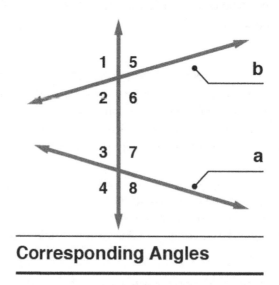

Corresponding Angles

 Alternate interior angles are also a pair of angles formed when two lines are crossed by a transversal. They are opposite angles that exist inside of the two lines. In the corresponding angles diagram above, angles 2 and 7 are alternate interior angles, as well as angles 6 and 3. **Alternate exterior angles** are opposite angles formed by a transversal but, in contrast to interior angles, exterior angles exist outside the two original lines.

Therefore, angles 1 and 8 are alternate exterior angles and so are angles 5 and 4. Finally, **consecutive interior angles** are pairs of angles formed by a transversal. These angles are located on the same side of the transversal and inside the two original lines. Therefore, angles 2 and 3 are a pair of consecutive interior angles, and so are angles 6 and 7. These definitions are instrumental in solving many problems that involve determining relationships between angles.

Medians, Midpoints, and Altitudes

A **median** of a triangle is a line segment that connects a vertex to the midpoint on the other side of the triangle. A triangle has three medians, and their point of intersection is known as the **centroid**. An **altitude** is a line drawn from a vertex perpendicular to the opposite side. A triangle has three altitudes, and their point of intersection is known as the **orthocenter**. An altitude can actually exist outside, inside, or on the triangle depending on the placement of the vertex. Many problems involve these definitions. For example, given one endpoint of a line segment and the midpoint, the other endpoint can be determined by using the midpoint formula. In addition, area problems heavily depend on these definitions. For example, it can be proven that the median of a triangle divides it into two regions of equal areas. The actual formula for the area of a triangle depends on its altitude.

Special Triangles

An **isosceles triangle** contains at least two equal sides. Therefore, it must also contain two equal angles and, subsequently, contain two medians of the same length. An isosceles triangle can also be labelled as an **equilateral triangle** (which contains three equal sides and three equal angles) when it meets these conditions. In an equilateral triangle, the measure of each angle is always 60 degrees. Also within an equilateral triangle, the medians are of the same length. A **scalene triangle** can never be an equilateral or an isosceles triangle because it contains no equal sides and no equal angles. Also, medians in a scalene triangle can't have the same length. However, a **right triangle**, which is a triangle containing a 90-degree angle, can be a scalene triangle. There are two types of special right triangles. The **30-60-90 right triangle** has angle measurements of 30 degrees, 60 degrees, and 90 degrees. Because of the nature of this triangle, and through the use of the Pythagorean theorem, the side lengths have a special relationship. If x is the length opposite the 30-degree angle, the length opposite the 60-degree angle is $\sqrt{3}x$, and the hypotenuse has length $2x$. The *45-45-90 right triangle* is also special as it contains two angle measurements of 45 degrees. It can be proven that, if x is the length of the two equal sides, the hypotenuse is $x\sqrt{2}$. The properties of all of these special triangles are extremely useful in determining both side lengths and angle measurements in problems where some of these quantities are given and some are not.

Special Quadrilaterals

A special quadrilateral is one in which both pairs of opposite sides are parallel. This type of quadrilateral is known as a **parallelogram.** A parallelogram has six important properties:

- Opposite sides are congruent.

- Opposite angles are congruent.

- Within a parallelogram, consecutive angles are supplementary, so their measurements total 180 degrees.

- If one angle is a right angle, all of them have to be right angles.

- The diagonals of the angles bisect each other.

- These diagonals form two congruent triangles.

A parallelogram with four congruent sides is a **rhombus.** A quadrilateral containing only one set of parallel sides is known as a **trapezoid.** The parallel sides are known as bases, and the other two sides are known as legs. If the legs are congruent, the trapezoid can be labelled an **isosceles trapezoid.** An important property of a trapezoid is that their diagonals are congruent. Also, the median of a trapezoid is parallel to the bases, and its length is equal to half of the sum of the base lengths.

Quadrilateral Relationships

Rectangles, squares, and rhombuses are **polygons** with four sides. By definition, all rectangles are parallelograms, but only some rectangles are squares. However, some parallelograms are rectangles. Also, it's true that all squares are rectangles, and some rhombuses are squares. There are no rectangles, squares, or rhombuses that are trapezoids though, because they have more than one set of parallel sides.

Diagonals and Angles

Diagonals are lines (excluding sides) that connect two vertices within a polygon. **Mutually bisecting diagonals** intersect at their midpoints. Parallelograms, rectangles, squares, and rhombuses have mutually bisecting diagonals. However, trapezoids don't have such lines. **Perpendicular diagonals** occur when they form four right triangles at their point of intersection. Squares and rhombuses have perpendicular diagonals, but trapezoids, rectangles, and parallelograms do not. Finally, **perpendicular bisecting** diagonals (also known as **perpendicular bisectors**) form four right triangles at their point of intersection, but this intersection is also the midpoint of the two lines. Both rhombuses and squares have perpendicular bisecting angles, but trapezoids, rectangles, and parallelograms do not. Knowing these definitions can help tremendously in problems that involve both angles and diagonals.

Polygons with More Than Four Sides

A **pentagon** is a five-sided figure. A six-sided shape is a **hexagon.** A seven-sided figure is classified as a **heptagon,** and an eight-sided figure is called an **octagon.** An important characteristic is whether a polygon is regular or irregular. If it's **regular**, the side lengths and angle measurements are all equal. An **irregular** polygon has unequal side lengths and angle measurements. Mathematical problems involving polygons with more than four sides usually involve side length and angle measurements. The sum of all internal angles in a polygon equals $180(n - 2)$ degrees, where n is the number of sides. Therefore, the total of all internal angles in a pentagon is 540 degrees because there are five sides so $180(5 - 2)$ = 540 degrees. Unfortunately, area formulas don't exist for polygons with more than four sides. However, their shapes can be split up into triangles, and the formula for area of a triangle can be applied and totaled to obtain the area for the entire figure.

Congruency

Two figures are congruent if they have the same shape and same size. The two figures could have been rotated, reflected, or translated. Two figures are similar if they have been rotated, reflected, translated, and resized. Angle measure is preserved in similar figures. Both angle and side length are preserved in congruent figures.

Trigonometric Ratios in Right Triangles

Trigonometric Functions

Within similar triangles, corresponding sides are proportional, and angles are congruent. In addition, within similar triangles, the ratio of the side lengths is the same. This property is true even if side lengths are different. Within right triangles, trigonometric ratios can be defined for the acute angle within the triangle. The functions are defined through ratios in a right triangle. Sine of acute angle, A, is opposite over hypotenuse, cosine is adjacent over hypotenuse, and tangent is opposite over adjacent. Note that expanding or shrinking the triangle won't change the ratios. However, changing the angle measurements will alter the calculations.

Complementary Angles

Angles that add up to 90 degrees are *complementary*. Within a right triangle, two complementary angles exist because the third angle is always 90 degrees. In this scenario, the *sine* of one of the complementary angles is equal to the *cosine* of the other angle. The opposite is also true. This relationship exists because sine and cosine will be calculated as the ratios of the same side lengths.

Pythagorean Theorem

The *Pythagorean theorem* is an important relationship between the three sides of a right triangle. It states that the square of the side opposite the right triangle, known as the *hypotenuse* (denoted as c^2), is equal to the sum of the squares of the other two sides ($a^2 + b^2$). Thus, $a^2 + b^2 = c^2$.

Both the trigonometric functions and the Pythagorean theorem can be used in problems that involve finding either a missing side or a missing angle of a right triangle. To do so, one must look to see what sides and angles are given and select the correct relationship that will help find the missing value. These relationships can also be used to solve application problems involving right triangles. Often, it's helpful to draw a figure to represent the problem to see what's missing.

Solving Line Problems

Two lines are parallel if they have the same slope and a different intercept. Two lines are perpendicular if the product of their slope equals -1. Parallel lines never intersect unless they are the same line, and perpendicular lines intersect at a right angle. If two lines aren't parallel, they must intersect at one point. Determining equations of lines based on properties of parallel and perpendicular lines appears in word problems. To find an equation of a line, both the slope and a point the line goes through are necessary. Therefore, if an equation of a line is needed that's parallel to a given line and runs through a specified point, the slope of the given line and the point are plugged into the point-slope form of an equation of a line. Secondly, if an equation of a line is needed that's perpendicular to a given line running through a specified point, the negative reciprocal of the slope of the given line and the point are plugged into the point-slope form. Also, if the point of intersection of two lines is known, that point will be used to solve the set of equations. Therefore, to solve a system of equations, the point of intersection must be found. If a set of two equations with two unknown variables has no solution, the lines are parallel.

Solving Problems with Parallel and Perpendicular Lines

Two lines can be parallel, perpendicular, or neither. If two lines are parallel, they have the same slope. This is proven using the idea of similar triangles. Consider the following diagram with two parallel lines, L1 and L2:

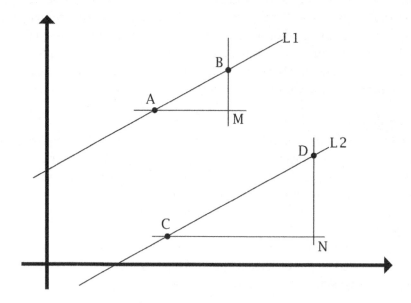

A and B are points on L1, and C and D are points on L2. Right triangles are formed with vertex M and N where lines BM and DN are parallel to the y-axis and AM and CN are parallel to the x-axis. Because all three sets of lines are parallel, the triangles are similar. Therefore, $\frac{BM}{DN} = \frac{MA}{NC}$. This shows that the rise/run is equal for lines L1 and L2. Hence, their slopes are equal.

Secondly, if two lines are perpendicular, the product of their slopes equals -1. This means that their slopes are negative reciprocals of each other. Consider two perpendicular lines, l and n:

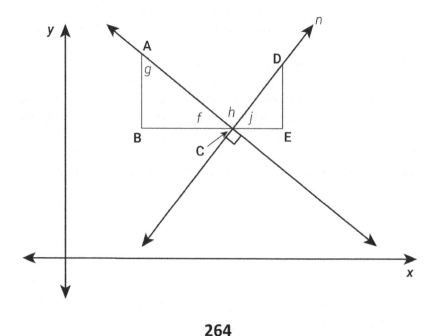

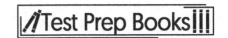

Right triangles ABC and CDE are formed so that lines BC and CE are parallel to the x-axis, and AB and DE are parallel to the y-axis. Because line BE is a straight line, angles:

$$f + h + i = 180 \ degrees$$

However, angle h is a right angle, so $f + j = 90 \ degrees$.

By construction, $f + g = 90$, which means that $g = j$.

Therefore, because angles $B = E$ and $g = j$, the triangles are similar and $\frac{AB}{BC} = \frac{CE}{DE}$.

Because slope is equal to rise/run, the slope of line l is $-\frac{AB}{BC}$ and the slope of line n is $\frac{DE}{CE}$. Multiplying the slopes together gives:

$$-\frac{AB}{BC} \cdot \frac{DE}{CE} = -\frac{CE}{DE} \cdot \frac{DE}{CE} = -1$$

This proves that the product of the slopes of two perpendicular lines equals -1. Both parallel and perpendicular lines can be integral in many geometric proofs, so knowing and understanding their properties is crucial for problem-solving.

Measurement and Geometry: Representational Systems

Three-Dimensional Figures with Nets

A net is a construction of two-dimensional figures that can be folded to form a given three-dimensional figure. More than one net may exist to fold and produce the same solid, or three-dimensional figure. The bases and faces of the solid figure are analyzed to determine the polygons (two-dimensional figures) needed to form the net.

Consider the following triangular prism:

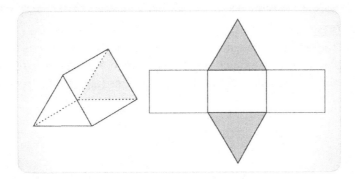

The surface of the prism consists of two triangular bases and three rectangular faces. The net beside it can be used to construct the triangular prism by first folding the triangles up to be parallel to each other, and then folding the two outside rectangles up and to the center with the outer edges touching.

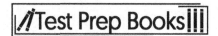
Consider the following cylinder:

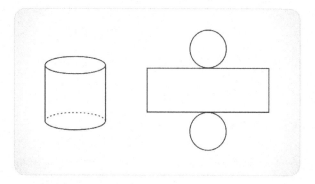

The surface consists of two circular bases and a curved lateral surface that can be opened and flattened into a rectangle. The net beside it can be used to construct the cylinder by first folding the circles up to be parallel to each other, and then curving the sides of the rectangle up to touch each other. The top and bottom of the folded rectangle should be touching the outside of both circles.

Consider the following square pyramid below on the left. The surface consists of one square base and four triangular faces. The net below on the right can be used to construct the square pyramid by folding each triangle towards the center of the square. The top points of the triangle meet at the vertex.

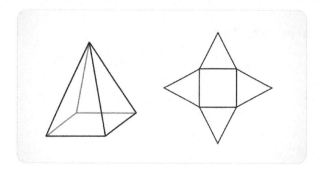

Simplifying Three-Dimensional Objects

Three-dimensional objects can be simplified into related two-dimensional shapes to solve problems. This simplification can make problem-solving a much easier experience. An isometric representation of a three-dimensional object can be completed so that important properties (e.g., shape, relationships of faces and

surfaces) are noted. Edges and vertices can be translated into two-dimensional objects as well. For example, below is a three-dimensional object that's been partitioned into two-dimensional representations of its faces:

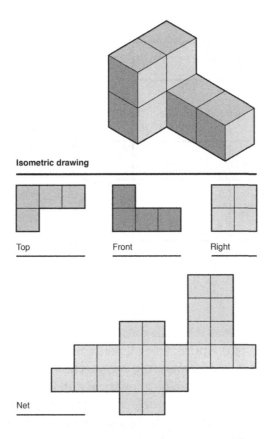

The net represents the sum of the three different faces. Depending on the problem, using a smaller portion of the given shape may be helpful, by simplifying the steps necessary to solve.

Visualizing Relationships Between Two-Dimensional and Three-Dimensional Objects

Cross-Sections and Nets of Three-Dimensional Shapes

One way to analyze a three-dimensional shape is to view its cross-sections in a two-dimensional plane. A cross-section is an intersection of the shape with a plane. Also, a three-dimensional shape can be represented in a two-dimensional plane by its net, which is an unfolded, flat representation of the all sides of the shape. For

example, a rectangular prism has cross sections that are squares and rectangles and the following figure shows its net:

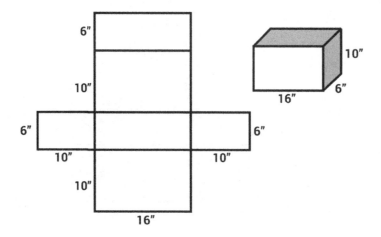

Cross Sections and Rotations

Two-dimensional objects are formed when three-dimensional objects are "sliced" in various ways. For example, any cross section of a sphere is a circle. Some three-dimensional objects have different cross sections depending on how the object is sliced. For example, the cross section of a cylinder can be a circle or a rectangle, and the cross section of a pyramid can be a square or a triangle. In addition, three-dimensional objects can be formed by rotating two-dimensional objects. Certain rotations can relate the two-dimensional cross sections back to the original three-dimensional objects. The objects must be rotated around an imaginary line known as the **rotation axis.** For example, a right triangle can be rotated around one of its legs to form a cone. A sphere can be formed by rotating a semicircle around a line segment formed from its diameter. Finally, rotating a square around one of its sides forms a cylinder.

Solving Problems in the Coordinate Plane

The location of a point on a coordinate grid is identified by writing it as an ordered pair. An ordered pair is a set of numbers indicating the x-and y-coordinates of the point. Ordered pairs are written in the form (x, y) where x and y are values which indicate their respective coordinates. For example, the point (3, -2) has an x-coordinate of 3 and a y-coordinate of -2.

Plotting a point on the coordinate plane with a given coordinate means starting from the origin $(0, 0)$. To determine the value of the x-coordinate, move right (positive number) or left (negative number) along the x-axis. Next, move up (positive number) or down (negative number) to the value of the y-coordinate. Finally, plot and label the point. For example, plotting the point $(1, -2)$ requires starting from the origin and moving right along the x-axis to positive one, then moving down until straight across from negative 2 on the y-axis. The

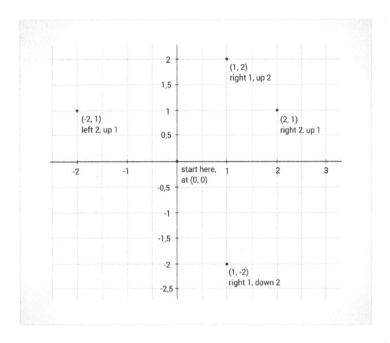

To write the coordinates of a point on the coordinate grid, a line should be traced directly above or below the point until reaching the x-axis (noting the value on the x-axis). Then, returning to the point, a line should be traced directly to the right or left of the point until reaching the y-axis (noting the value on the y-axis). The ordered pair (x, y) should be written with the values determined for the x- and y-coordinates.

Polygons can be drawn in the coordinate plane given the coordinates of their vertices. These coordinates can be used to determine the perimeter and area of the figure. Suppose triangle RQP has vertices located at the points: $R(-2, 0)$, $Q(2, 2)$, and $P(2, 0)$. By plotting the points for the three vertices, the triangle can be constructed as follows:

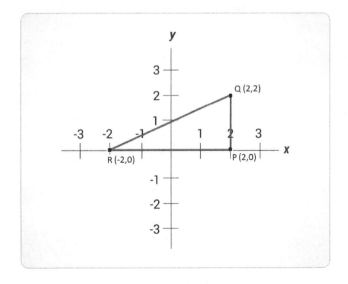

269

Because points R and P have the same y-coordinates (they are directly across from each other), the distance between them is determined by subtracting their x-coordinates (or simply counting units from one point to the other): $2 - (-2) = 4$. Therefore, the length of side RP is 4 units. Because points Q and P have the same x-coordinate (they are directly above and below each other), the distance between them is determined by subtracting their y-coordinates (or counting units between them): $2 - 0 = 2$. Therefore, the length of side PQ is 2 units. Knowing the length of side RP, which is the base of the triangle, and the length of side PQ, which is the height of the triangle, the area of the figure can be determined by using the formula:

$$A = \frac{1}{2}bh$$

To determine the perimeter of the triangle, the lengths of all three sides are needed. Points R and Q are neither directly across nor directly above and below each other. Therefore, the distance formula must be used to find the length of side RQ. The distance formula is as follows:

$$d = \sqrt{(x_2 - x_1)^2 + (y_2 - y_1)^2}$$

$$d = \sqrt{(2 - (-2))^2 + (2 - 0)^2}$$

$$d = \sqrt{(4)^2 + (2)^2}$$

$$d = \sqrt{16 + 4} \rightarrow d = \sqrt{20}$$

The perimeter is determined by adding the lengths of the three sides of the triangle.

Measurement and Geometry: Techniques, Tools, and Formulas for Determining Measurements

Perimeter and Area

Perimeter is the measurement of a distance around something. Think of perimeter as the length of the boundary, like a fence. In contrast, area is the space occupied by a defined enclosure, like a field enclosed by a fence.

The perimeter of a polygon is the distance around the outside of the two-dimensional figure. Perimeter is a one-dimensional measurement and is therefore expressed in linear units such as centimeters (*cm*), feet (*ft.*), and miles (*mi*). The perimeter (*P*) of the figure below is calculated by:

$$P = 9m + 5m + 4m + 6m + 8m \rightarrow P = 32\,m$$

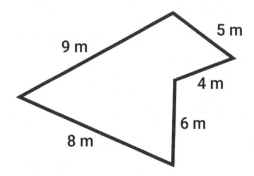

The perimeter of a square is measured by adding together all of the sides. Since a square has four equal sides, its perimeter can be calculated by multiplying the length of one side by 4. Thus, the formula is $P = 4 \times s$, where *s* equals one side. The area of a square is calculated by squaring the length of one side, which is expressed as the formula $A = s^2$.

Like a square, a rectangle's perimeter is measured by adding together all of the sides. But as the sides are unequal, the formula is different. A rectangle has equal values for its lengths (long sides) and equal values for its widths (short sides), so the perimeter formula for a rectangle is:

$$P = l + l + w + w = 2l + 2w$$

where *l* equals length and *w* equals width. The area is found by multiplying the length by the width, so the formula is $A = l \times w$.

A triangle's perimeter is measured by adding together the three sides, so the formula is $P = a + b + c$, where a, b, and *c* are the values of the three sides. The area is calculated by multiplying the length of the base times the height times ½, so the formula is:

$$A = \frac{1}{2} \times b \times h = \frac{bh}{2}$$

The base is the bottom of the triangle, and the height is the distance from the base to the peak. If a problem asks to calculate the area of a triangle, it will provide the base and height.

A circle's perimeter—also known as its circumference—is measured by multiplying the diameter (the straight line measured from one end to the direct opposite end of the circle) by π, so the formula is $\pi \times d$. This is sometimes expressed by the formula:

$$C = 2 \times \pi \times r$$

where *r* is the radius of the circle. These formulas are equivalent, as the radius equals half of the diameter. The area of a circle is calculated through the formula $A = \pi \times r^2$.

271

The test will indicate either to leave the answer with π attached or to calculate to the nearest decimal place, which means multiplying by 3.14 for π.

The perimeter of a parallelogram is measured by adding the lengths and widths together. Thus, the formula is the same as for a rectangle:

$$P = l + l + w + w = 2l + 2w$$

However, the area formula differs from the rectangle. For a parallelogram, the area is calculated by multiplying the length by the height: $A = h \times l$

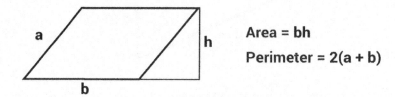

Area = bh

Perimeter = 2(a + b)

The perimeter of a trapezoid is calculated by adding the two unequal bases and two equal sides, so the formula is

$$P = a + b_1 + c + b_2$$

Although unlikely to be a test question, the formula for the area of a trapezoid is $A = \frac{b_1 + b_2}{2} \times h$, where h equals height, and b_1 and b_2 equal the bases.

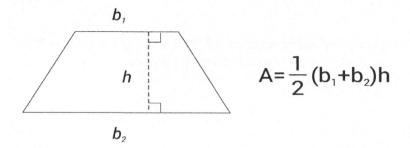

$$A = \frac{1}{2}(b_1 + b_2)h$$

Irregular Shapes

The perimeter of an irregular polygon is found by adding the lengths of all of the sides. In cases where all of the sides are given, this will be very straightforward, as it will simply involve finding the sum of the provided

lengths. Other times, a side length may be missing and must be determined before the perimeter can be calculated. Consider the example below:

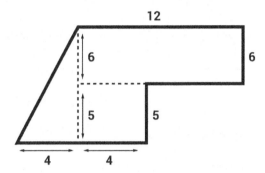

All of the side lengths are provided except for the angled side on the left. Test takers should notice that this is the hypotenuse of a right triangle. The other two sides of the triangle are provided (the base is 4 and the height is 6 + 5 = 11). The Pythagorean Theorem can be used to find the length of the hypotenuse, remembering that $a^2 + b^2 = c^2$.

Substituting the side values provided yields $(4)^2 + (11)^2 = c^2$.

Therefore, $c = \sqrt{16 + 121} = 11.7$

Finally, the perimeter can be found by adding this new side length with the other provided lengths to get the total length around the figure: 4+4+5+8+6+12+11.7=50.7.

Although units are not provided in this figure, remember that reporting units with a measurement is important.

The area of an irregular polygon is found by decomposing, or breaking apart, the figure into smaller shapes. When the area of the smaller shapes is determined, these areas are added together to produce the total area of the area of the original figure. Consider the same example provided before:

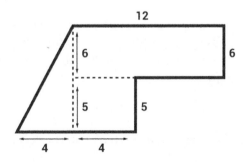

The irregular polygon is decomposed into two rectangles and a triangle. The area of the large rectangles

$$(A = l \times w \to A = 12 \times 6)$$

is 72 square units. The area of the small rectangle is 20 square units ($A = 4 \times 5$).

The area of the triangle ($A = \frac{1}{2} \times b \times h \to A = \frac{1}{2} \times 4 \times 11$) is 22 square units.

The sum of the areas of these figures produces the total area of the original polygon:

$$A = 72 + 20 + 22 \to A = 114 \text{ square units}$$

Surface Area of Three-Dimensional Figures

The area of a two-dimensional figure refers to the number of square units needed to cover the interior region of the figure. This concept is similar to wallpaper covering the flat surface of a wall. For example, if a rectangle has an area of 21 square centimeters (written $21cm^2$), it will take 21 squares, each with sides one centimeter in length, to cover the interior region of the rectangle. Note that area is measured in square units such as: square feet or ft^2; square yards or yd^2; square miles or mi^2.

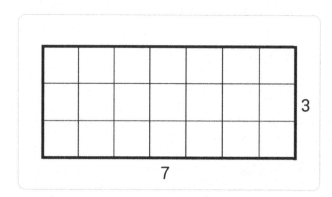

The surface area of a three-dimensional figure refers to the number of square units needed to cover the entire surface of the figure. This concept is similar to using wrapping paper to completely cover the outside of a box. For example, if a triangular pyramid has a surface area of 17 square inches (written $17in^2$), it will take 17 squares, each with sides one inch in length, to cover the entire surface of the pyramid. Surface area is also measured in square units.

Many three-dimensional figures (solid figures) can be represented by nets consisting of rectangles and triangles. The surface area of such solids can be determined by adding the areas of each of its faces and bases. Finding the surface area using this method requires calculating the areas of rectangles and triangles. To find the area (A) of a rectangle, the length (l) is multiplied by the width:

$$(w) \to A = l \times w$$

The area of a rectangle with a length of 8cm and a width of 4cm is calculated:

$$A = (8cm) \times (4cm) \to A = 32cm^2$$

To calculate the area (A) of a triangle, the product of $\frac{1}{2}$, the base (b), and the height (h) is found → $A = \frac{1}{2} \times b \times h$. Note that the height of a triangle is measured from the base to the vertex opposite of it forming a right angle with the base. The area of a triangle with a base of 11cm and a height of 6cm is calculated:

$$A = \frac{1}{2} \times (11cm) \times (6cm) \rightarrow A = 33cm^2$$

Consider the following triangular prism, which is represented by a net consisting of two triangles and three rectangles:

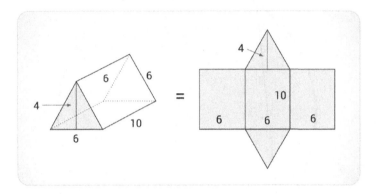

The surface area of the prism can be determined by adding the areas of each of its faces and bases. The surface area (SA) = area of triangle + area of triangle + area of rectangle + area of rectangle + area of rectangle.

$$SA = \left(\frac{1}{2} \times b \times h\right) + \left(\frac{1}{2} \times b \times h\right) + (l \times w) + (l \times w) + (l \times w)$$

$$SA = \left(\frac{1}{2} \times 6 \times 4\right) + \left(\frac{1}{2} \times 6 \times 4\right) + (6 \times 10) + (6 \times 10) + (6 \times 10)$$

$$SA = (12) + (12) + (60) + (60) + (60)$$

$$SA = 204 \; square \; units$$

Circles

Circle Angles

The distance from the middle of a circle to any other point on the circle is known as the **radius**. A **chord** of a circle is a straight line formed when its endpoints are allowed to be any two points on the circle. Many angles exist within a circle. A **central angle** is formed by using two radii as its rays and the center of the circle as its vertex. An inscribed angle is formed by using two chords as its rays, and its vertex is a point on the circle itself.

Finally, a **circumscribed angle** has a vertex that is a point outside the circle and rays that intersect with the circle. Some relationships exist between these types of angles, and, in order to define these relationships, arc measure must be understood. An **arc** of a circle is a portion of the circumference. Finding the **arc measure** is the same as finding the degree measure of the central angle that intersects the circle to form the arc. The measure of an inscribed angle is half the measure of its intercepted arc. It's also true that the measure of a

circumscribed angle is equal to 180 degrees minus the measure of the central angle that forms the arc in the angle.

Quadrilateral Angles

If a quadrilateral is inscribed in a circle, the sum of its opposite angles is 180 degrees. Consider the quadrilateral ABCD centered at the point O:

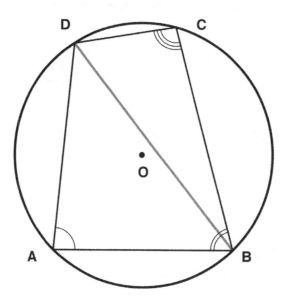

Each of the four line segments within the quadrilateral is a chord of the circle. Consider the diagonal DB. Angle DAB is an inscribed angle leaning on the arc DCB. Therefore, angle DAB is half the measure of the arc DCB. Conversely, angle DCB is an inscribed angle leaning on the arc DAB. Therefore, angle DCB is half the measure of the arc DAB. The sum of arcs DCB and DAB is 360 degrees because they make up the entire circle. Therefore, the sum of angles DAB and DCB equals half of 360 degrees, which is 180 degrees.

Circle Lines

A **tangent line** is a line that touches a curve at a single point without going through it. A **compass** and a **straightedge** are the tools necessary to construct a tangent line from a point P outside the circle to the circle. A tangent line is constructed by drawing a line segment from the center of the circle O to the point P, and then finding its midpoint M by bisecting the line segment. By using M as the center, a compass is used to draw a circle through points O and P. N is defined as the intersection of the two circles. Finally, a line segment is drawn through P and N. This is the tangent line. Each point on a circle has only one tangent line, which is perpendicular to the radius at that point. A line similar to a tangent line is a **secant line.** Instead of intersecting

276

the circle at one point, a secant line intersects the circle at two points. A **chord** is a smaller portion of a secant line.

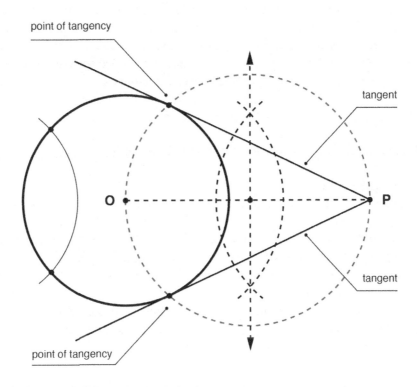

Applying Geometric Concepts to Real-World Situations

Real-World Geometry

Many real-world objects can be compared to geometric shapes. Describing certain objects using the measurements and properties of two- and three-dimensional shapes is an important part of geometry. For example, basic ideas such as angles and line segments can be seen in real-world objects. The corner of any room is an angle, and the intersection of a wall with the floor is like a line segment. Building upon this idea, entire objects can be related to both two- and three-dimensional shapes. An entire room can be thought of as square, rectangle, or a sum of a few three-dimensional shapes. Knowing what properties and measures are needed to make decisions in real life is why geometry is such a useful branch of mathematics. One obvious relationship between a real-life situation and geometry exists in construction. For example, to build an addition onto a house, several geometric measurements will be used.

Density

The **density** of a substance is the ratio of mass to area or volume. It's a relationship between the mass and how much space the object actually takes up. Knowing which units to use in each situation is crucial. Population density is an example of a real-life situation that's modeled by using density concepts. It involves calculating the ratio of the number of people to the number of square miles. The amount of material needed per a specific unit of area or volume is another application. For example, estimating the number of BTUs per cubic foot of a home is a measurement that relates to heating or cooling the house based on the desired temperature and the house's size.

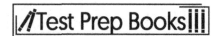

Solving Design Problems

Design problems are an important application of geometry (e.g., building structures that satisfy physical constraints and/or minimize costs). These problems involve optimizing a situation based on what's given and required. For example, determining what size barn to build, given certain dimensions and a specific budget, uses both geometric properties and other mathematical concepts. Equations are formed using geometric definitions and the given constraints. In the end, such problems involve solving a system of equations and rely heavily on a strong background in algebra. **Typographic grid systems** also help with such design problems. A grid made up of intersecting straight or curved lines can be used as a visual representation of the structure being designed. This concept is seen in the blueprints used throughout the graphic design process.

Converting Within and Between Standard and Metric Systems

American Measuring System

The measuring system used today in the United States developed from the British units of measurement during colonial times. The most typically used units in this customary system are those used to measure weight, liquid volume, and length, whose common units are found below. In the customary system, the basic unit for measuring weight is the ounce (oz); there are 16 ounces (oz) in 1 pound (lb) and 2000 pounds in 1 ton. The basic unit for measuring liquid volume is the ounce (oz); 1 ounce is equal to 2 tablespoons (tbsp) or 6 teaspoons (tsp), and there are 8 ounces in 1 cup, 2 cups in 1 pint (pt), 2 pints in 1 quart (qt), and 4 quarts in 1 gallon (gal). For measurements of length, the inch (in) is the base unit; 12 inches make up 1 foot (ft), 3 feet make up 1 yard (yd), and 5280 feet make up 1 mile (mi). However, as there are only a set number of units in the customary system, with extremely large or extremely small amounts of material, the numbers can become awkward and difficult to compare.

Common Customary Measurements		
Length	**Weight**	**Capacity**
1 foot = 12 inches	1 pound = 16 ounces	1 cup = 8 fluid ounces
1 yard = 3 feet	1 ton = 2,000 pounds	1 pint = 2 cups
1 yard = 36 inches		1 quart = 2 pints
1 mile = 1,760 yards		1 quart = 4 cups
1 mile = 5,280 feet		1 gallon = 4 quarts
		1 gallon = 16 cups

Metric System

Aside from the United States, most countries in the world have adopted the metric system embodied in the International System of Units (SI). The three main SI base units used in the metric system are the meter (m), the kilogram (kg), and the liter (L); meters measure length, kilograms measure mass, and liters measure volume.

These three units can use different prefixes, which indicate larger or smaller versions of the unit by powers of ten. This can be thought of as making a new unit, which is sized by multiplying the original unit in size by a factor.

Metric Prefixes			
Prefix	Symbol	Multiplier	Exponential
kilo	k	1,000	10^3
hecto	h	100	10^2
deca	da	10	10^1
no prefix		1	10^0
deci	d	0.1	10^{-1}
centi	c	0.01	10^{-2}
milli	m	0.001	10^{-3}

The correct prefix is then attached to the base. Some examples include:

- 1 milliliter equals .001 liters.
- 1 kilogram equals 1,000 grams.

Choosing the Appropriate Measuring Unit

Some units of measure are represented as square or cubic units depending on the solution. For example, perimeter is measured in linear units, area is measured in square units, and volume is measured in cubic units.

Also be sure to use the most appropriate unit for the thing being measured. A building's height might be measured in feet or meters while the length of a nail might be measured in inches or centimeters. Additionally, for SI units, the prefix should be chosen to provide the most succinct available value. For example, the mass of a bag of fruit would likely be measured in kilograms rather than grams or milligrams, and the length of a bacteria cell would likely be measured in micrometers rather than centimeters or kilometers.

Conversion

Converting measurements in different units between the two systems can be difficult because they follow different rules. The best method is to look up an English to Metric system conversion factor and then use a series of equivalent fractions to set up an equation to convert the units of one of the measurements into those of the other. The table below lists some common conversion values that are useful for problems involving measurements with units in both systems:

English System	Metric System
1 inch	2.54 cm
1 foot	0.3048 m
1 yard	0.914 m
1 mile	1.609 km
1 ounce	28.35 g
1 pound	0.454 kg
1 fluid ounce	29.574 mL
1 quart	0.946 L
1 gallon	3.785 L

Consider the example where a scientist wants to convert 6.8 inches to centimeters. The table above is used to find that there are 2.54 centimeters in every inch, so the following equation should be set up and solved:

$$6.8 \ in \ \times \ \frac{2.54 \ cm}{1 \ in} = 17.272 \ cm$$

Notice how the inches in the numerator of the initial figure and the denominator of the conversion factor cancel out. (This equation could have been written simply as $6.8 \ in \ \times \ 2.54 \ cm = 17.272 \ cm$, but it was shown in detail to illustrate the steps). The goal in any conversion equation is to set up the fractions so that the units you are trying to convert from cancel out and the units you desire remain.

For a more complicated example, consider converting 2.15 kilograms into ounces. The first step is to convert kilograms into grams and then grams into ounces:

$$2.15 \ kg \ \times \frac{1000g}{kg} = 2150 \ g$$

Then, use the conversion factor from the table to convert grams to ounces:

$$2150g \ \times \frac{1 \ oz}{28.35g} = 75.8 \ oz$$

Precision and Accuracy

Precision and accuracy are used to describe groups of measurements. **Precision** describes a group of measures that are very close together, regardless of whether the measures are close to the true value. **Accuracy** describes how close the measures are to the true value.

Since accuracy refers to the closeness of a value to the true measurement, the level of accuracy depends on the object measured and the instrument used to measure it. This will vary depending on the situation. If measuring the mass of a set of dictionaries, kilograms may be used as the units. In this case, it is not vitally important to have a high level of accuracy. If the measurement is a few grams away from the true value, the discrepancy might not make a big difference in the problem.

In a different situation, the level of accuracy may be more significant. Pharmacists need to be sure they are very accurate in their measurements of medicines that they give to patients. In this case, the level of accuracy is vitally important and not something to be estimated. In the dictionary situation, the measurements were given as whole numbers in kilograms. In the pharmacist's situation, the measurements for medicine must be taken to the milligram and sometimes further, depending on the type of medicine.

When considering the accuracy of measurements, the error in each measurement can be shown as absolute and relative. **Absolute error** tells the actual difference between the measured value and the true value. The **relative error** tells how large the error is in relation to the true value. There may be two problems where the absolute error of the measurements is 10 grams. For one problem, this may mean the relative error is very small because the measured value is 14,990 grams, and the true value is 15,000 grams. Ten grams in relation to the true value of 15,000 is small: 0.06%. For the other problem, the measured value is 290 grams, and the true value is 300 grams. In this case, the 10-gram absolute error means a high relative error because the true value is smaller. The relative error is 10/300=0.03, or 3%.

Statistics, Data Analysis, and Probability: Collection, Organization, and Representation of Data

Interpreting Displays of Data

A set of data can be visually displayed in various forms allowing for quick identification of characteristics of the set. Histograms, such as the one shown below, display the number of data points (vertical axis) that fall into given intervals (horizontal axis) across the range of the set. The histogram below displays the heights of black cherry trees in a certain city park. Each rectangle represents the number of trees with heights between a given five-point span. For example, the furthest bar to the right indicates that two trees are between 85 and 90 feet. Histograms can describe the center, spread, shape, and any unusual characteristics of a data set.

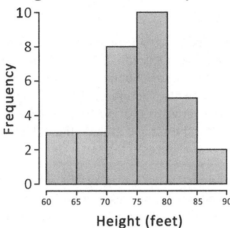

A box plot, also called a box-and-whisker plot, divides the data points into four groups and displays the five-number summary for the set as well as any outliers. The five-number summary consists of:

- The lower extreme: the lowest value that is not an outlier
- The higher extreme: the highest value that is not an outlier
- The median of the set: also referred to as the second quartile or Q_2
- The first quartile or Q_1: the median of values below Q_2
- The third quartile or Q_3: the median of values above Q_2

To construct a box (or box-and-whisker) plot, the five-number summary for the data set is calculated as follows: the second quartile (Q_2) is the median of the set. The first quartile (Q_1) is the median of the values below Q_2. The third quartile (Q_3) is the median of the values above Q_2. The upper extreme is the highest value in the data set if it is not an outlier (greater than 1.5 times the interquartile range Q_3- Q_1). The lower extreme is the least value in the data set if it is not an outlier (more than 1.5 times lower than the interquartile range). To construct the box-and-whisker plot, each value is plotted on a number line, along with any outliers. The box

consists of Q_1 and Q_3 as its top and bottom and Q_2 as the dividing line inside the box. The whiskers extend from the lower extreme to Q_1 and from Q_3 to the upper extreme.

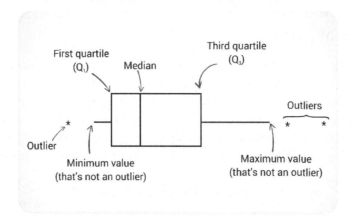

Suppose the box plot displays IQ scores for 12th grade students at a given school. The five-number summary of the data consists of: lower extreme (67); upper extreme (127); Q_2 or median (100); Q_1 (91); Q_3 (108); and outliers (135 and 140). Although all data points are not known from the plot, the points are divided into four quartiles each, including 25% of the data points. Therefore, 25% of students scored between 67 and 91, 25% scored between 91 and 100, 25% scored between 100 and 108, and 25% scored between 108 and 127. These percentages include the normal values for the set and exclude the outliers. This information is useful when comparing a given score with the rest of the scores in the set.

A scatter plot is a mathematical diagram that visually displays the relationship or connection between two variables. The independent variable is placed on the *x*-axis, or horizontal axis, and the dependent variable is placed on the *y*-axis, or vertical axis. When visually examining the points on the graph, if the points model a linear relationship, or if a line of best-fit can be drawn through the points with the points relatively close on either side, then a correlation exists. If the line of best-fit has a positive slope (rises from left to right), then the variables have a positive correlation. If the line of best-fit has a negative slope (falls from left to right), then the variables have a negative correlation. If a line of best-fit cannot be drawn, then no correlation exists. A positive or negative correlation can be categorized as strong or weak, depending on how closely the points are graphed around the line of best-fit.

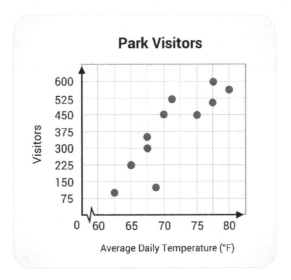

Graphical Representation of Data

Like a scatter plot, a line graph compares variables that change continuously, typically over time. Paired data values (ordered pairs) are plotted on a coordinate grid with the x- and y-axis representing the variables. A line is drawn from each point to the next, going from left to right. The line graph below displays cell phone use for given years (two variables) for men, women, and both sexes (three data sets).

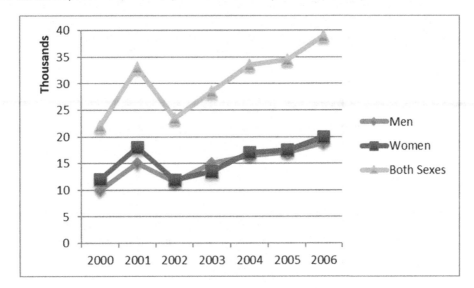

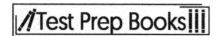

A line plot, also called dot plot, displays the frequency of data (numerical values) on a number line. To construct a line plot, a number line is used that includes all unique data values. It is marked with x's or dots above the value the number of times that the value occurs in the data set.

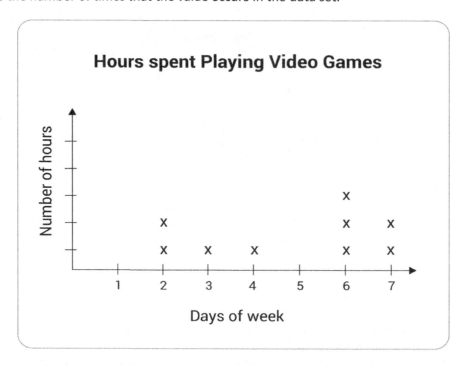

A *bar graph* is a diagram in which the quantity of items within a specific classification is represented by the height of a rectangle. Each type of classification is represented by a rectangle of equal width. Here is an example of a bar graph:

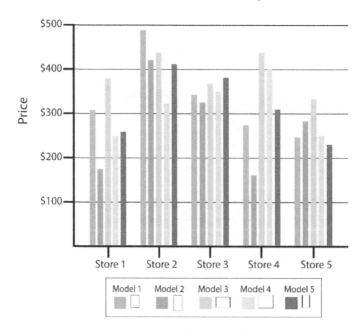

A circle graph, also called a pie chart, shows categorical data with each category representing a percentage of the whole data set. To make a circle graph, the percent of the data set for each category must be determined. To do so, the frequency of the category is divided by the total number of data points and converted to a percent. For example, if 80 people were asked what their favorite sport is and 20 responded basketball, basketball makes up 25% of the data ($\frac{20}{80} = 0.25 = 25\%$). Each category in a data set is represented by a *slice* of the circle proportionate to its percentage of the whole:

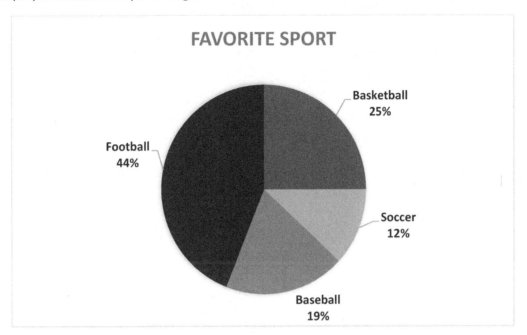

Choice of Graphs to Display Data

Choosing the appropriate graph to display a data set depends on what type of data is included in the set and what information must be displayed. Histograms and box plots can be used for data sets consisting of individual values across a wide range. Examples include test scores and incomes. Histograms and box plots will indicate the center, spread, range, and outliers of a data set. A histogram will show the shape of the data set, while a box plot will divide the set into quartiles (25% increments), allowing for comparison between a given value and the entire set.

Scatter plots and line graphs can be used to display data consisting of two variables. Examples include height and weight, or distance and time. A correlation between the variables is determined by examining the points on the graph. Line graphs are used if each value for one variable pairs with a distinct value for the other variable. Line graphs show relationships between variables.

Line plots, bar graphs, and circle graphs are all used to display categorical data, such as surveys. Line plots and bar graphs both indicate the frequency of each category within the data set. A line plot is used when the categories consist of numerical values. For example, the number of hours of TV watched by individuals is displayed on a line plot. A bar graph is used when the categories consists of words. For example, the favorite ice cream of individuals is displayed with a bar graph. A circle graph can be used to display either type of categorical data. However, unlike line plots and bar graphs, a circle graph does not indicate the frequency of each category. Instead, the circle graph represents each category as its percentage of the whole data set.

285

Describing a Set of Data

A set of data can be described in terms of its center, spread, shape and any unusual features. The center of a data set can be measured by its mean, median, or mode. The spread of a data set refers to how far the data points are from the center (mean or median). The spread can be measured by the range or by the quartiles and interquartile range. A data set with all its data points clustered around the center will have a small spread. A data set covering a wide range of values will have a large spread.

When a data set is displayed as a histogram or frequency distribution plot, the shape indicates if a sample is normally distributed, symmetrical, or has measures of skewness or kurtosis. When graphed, a data set with a normal distribution will resemble a bell curve:

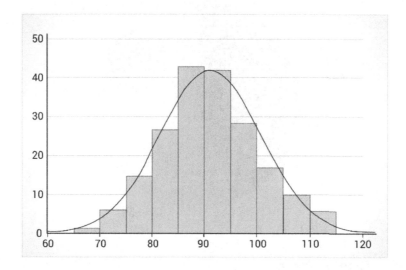

If the data set is symmetrical, each half of the graph when divided at the center is a mirror image of the other. If the graph has fewer data points to the right, the data is skewed right. If it has fewer data points to the left, the data is skewed left:

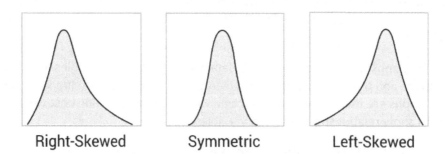

Right-Skewed   Symmetric   Left-Skewed

Kurtosis is a measure of whether the data is heavy-tailed with a high number of outliers, or light-tailed with a low number of outliers.

A description of a data set should include any unusual features such as gaps or outliers. A gap is a span within the range of the data set containing no data points. An outlier is a data point with a value either extremely large or extremely small when compared to the other values in the set.

286

Normal Distribution

A **normal distribution** of data follows the shape of a bell curve. In a normal distribution, the data set's median, mean, and mode are equal. Therefore, 50 percent of its values are less than the mean and 50 percent are greater than the mean. Data sets that follow this shape can be generalized using normal distributions. Normal distributions are described as **frequency distributions** in which the data set is plotted as percentages rather than true data points. A **relative frequency distribution** is one where the y-axis is between zero and 1, which is the same as 0% to 100%. Within a standard deviation, 68 percent of the values are within 1 standard deviation of the mean, 95 percent of the values are within 2 standard deviations of the mean, and 99.7 percent of the values are within 3 standard deviations of the mean. The number of standard deviations that a data point falls from the mean is called the **z-score.** The formula for the z-score is $Z = \frac{x-\mu}{\sigma}$, where μ is the mean, σ is the standard deviation, and x is the data point.

This formula is used to fit any data set that resembles a normal distribution to a standard normal distribution in a process known as **standardizing**. Here is a normal distribution with labeled z-scores:

Normal Distribution with Labelled Z-Scores

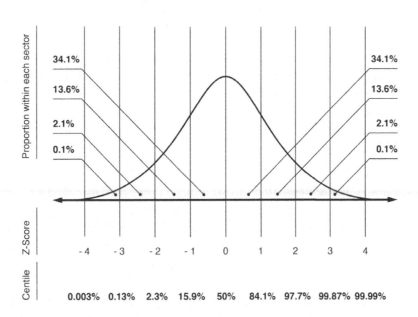

Population percentages can be estimated using normal distributions. For example, the probability that a data point will be less than the mean, or that the z-score will be less than 0, is 50%. Similarly, the probability that a data point will be within 1 standard deviation of the mean, or that the z-score will be between -1 and 1, is about 68.2%. When using a z-table, the left column states how many standard deviations (to one decimal place) away from the mean the point is, and the row heading states the second decimal place. The entries in the table corresponding to each column and row give the probability, which is equal to the area.

Measures of Center and Range

The center of a set of data (statistical values) can be represented by its mean, median, or mode. These are sometimes referred to as measures of central tendency. The mean is the average of the data set. The mean can be calculated by adding the data values and dividing by the sample size (the number of data points). Suppose a student has test scores of 93, 84, 88, 72, 91, and 77. To find the mean, or average, the scores are added and the sum is divided by 6 because there are 6 test scores:

$$\frac{93 + 84 + 88 + 72 + 91 + 77}{6} = \frac{505}{6} = 84.17$$

Given the mean of a data set and the sum of the data points, the sample size can be determined by dividing the sum by the mean. Suppose you are told that Kate averaged 12 points per game and scored a total of 156 points for the season. The number of games that she played (the sample size or the number of data points) can be determined by dividing the total points (sum of data points) by her average (mean of data points): $\frac{156}{12} = 13$. Therefore, Kate played in 13 games this season.

If given the mean of a data set and the sample size, the sum of the data points can be determined by multiplying the mean and sample size. Suppose you are told that Tom worked 6 days last week for an average of 5.5 hours per day. The total number of hours worked for the week (sum of data points) can be determined by multiplying his daily average (mean of data points) by the number of days worked (sample size): $5.5 \times 6 = 33$. Therefore, Tom worked a total of 33 hours last week.

The median of a data set is the value of the data point in the middle when the sample is arranged in numerical order. To find the median of a data set, the values are written in order from least to greatest. The lowest and highest values are simultaneously eliminated, repeating until the value in the middle remains. Suppose the salaries of math teachers are:

$35,000; $38,500; $41,000; $42,000; $42,000; $44,500; $49,000

The values are listed from least to greatest to find the median. The lowest and highest values are eliminated until only the middle value remains. Repeating this step three times reveals a median salary of $42,000. If the sample set has an even number of data points, two values will remain after all others are eliminated. In this case, the mean of the two middle values is the median. Consider the following data set: 7, 9, 10, 13, 14, 14. Eliminating the lowest and highest values twice leaves two values, 10 and 13, in the middle. The mean of these values $\left(\frac{10+13}{2}\right)$ is the median. Therefore, the set has a median of 11.5.

The mode of a data set is the value that appears most often. A data set may have a single mode, multiple modes, or no mode. If different values repeat equally as often, multiple modes exist. If no value repeats, no mode exists. Consider the following data sets:

- A: 7, 9, 10, 13, 14, 14
- B: 37, 44, 33, 37, 49, 44, 51, 34, 37, 33, 44
- C: 173, 154, 151, 168, 155

Set A has a mode of 14. Set B has modes of 37 and 44. Set C has no mode.

The range of a data set is the difference between the highest and the lowest values in the set. The range can be considered the span of the data set. To determine the range, the smallest value in the set is subtracted from the largest value. The ranges for the data sets A, B, and C above are calculated as follows:

- A: $14 - 7 = 7$
- B: $51 - 33 = 18$
- C: $173 - 151 = 22$.

Best Description of a Set of Data

Measures of central tendency, namely mean, median, and mode, describe characteristics of a set of data. Specifically, they are intended to represent a **typical** value in the set by identifying a central position of the set. Depending on the characteristics of a specific set of data, different measures of central tendency are more indicative of a typical value in the set.

When a data set is grouped closely together with a relatively small range and the data is spread out somewhat evenly, the mean is an effective indicator of a typical value in the set. Consider the following data set representing the height of sixth grade boys in inches: 61 inches, 54 inches, 58 inches, 63 inches, 58 inches. The mean of the set is 58.8 inches. The data set is grouped closely (the range is only 9 inches) and the values are spread relatively evenly (three values below the mean and two values above the mean). Therefore, the mean value of 58.8 inches is an effective measure of central tendency in this case.

When a data set contains a small number of values either extremely large or extremely small when compared to the other values, the mean is not an effective measure of central tendency. Consider the following data set representing annual incomes of homeowners on a given street: $71,000; $74,000; $75,000; $77,000; $340,000. The mean of this set is $127,400. This figure does not indicate a typical value in the set, which contains four out of five values between $71,000 and $77,000. The median is a much more effective measure of central tendency for data sets such as these. Finding the middle value diminishes the influence of outliers, or numbers that may appear out of place, like the $340,000 annual income. The median for this set is $75,000 which is much more typical of a value in the set.

The mode of a data set is a useful measure of central tendency for categorical data when each piece of data is an option from a category. Consider a survey of 31 commuters asking how they get to work with results summarized below.

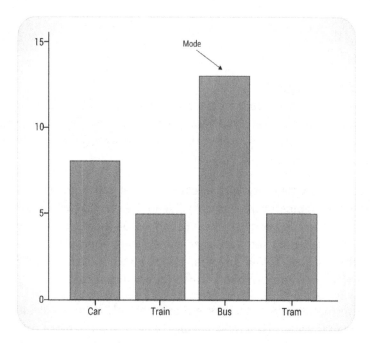

The mode for this set represents the value, or option, of the data that repeats most often. This indicates that the bus is the most popular method of transportation for the commuters.

Effects of Changes in Data

Changing all values of a data set in a consistent way produces predictable changes in the measures of the center and range of the set. A linear transformation changes the original value into the new value by either adding a given number to each value, multiplying each value by a given number, or both. Adding (or subtracting) a given value to each data point will increase (or decrease) the mean, median, and any modes by the same value. However, the range will remain the same due to the way that range is calculated. Multiplying (or dividing) a given value by each data point will increase (or decrease) the mean, median, and any modes, and the range by the same factor.

Consider the following data set, call it set P, representing the price of different cases of soda at a grocery store: $4.25, $4.40, $4.75, $4.95, $4.95, $5.15. The mean of set P is $4.74.

The median is $4.85.

The mode of the set is $4.95.

The range is $0.90.

Suppose the state passes a new tax of $0.25 on every case of soda sold. The new data set, set T, is calculated by adding $0.25 to each data point from set P.

Therefore, set T consists of the following values: $4.50, $4.65, $5.00, $5.20, $5.20, $5.40.

290

The mean of set *T* is $4.99. The median is $5.10.

The mode of the set is $5.20.

The range is $.90.

The mean, median and mode of set *T* is equal to $0.25 added to the mean, median, and mode of set *P*. The range stays the same.

Now suppose, due to inflation, the store raises the cost of every item by 10 percent. Raising costs by 10 percent is calculated by multiplying each value by 1.1. The new data set, set *I*, is calculated by multiplying each data point from set *T* by 1.1.

Therefore, set *I* consists of the following values: $4.95, $5.12, $5.50, $5.72, $5.72, $5.94.

The mean of set *I* is $5.49.

The median is $5.61.

The mode of the set is $5.72.

The range is $0.99.

The mean, median, mode, and range of set *I* is equal to 1.1 multiplied by the mean, median, mode, and range of set *T* because each increased by a factor of 10 percent.

Comparing Data

Data sets can be compared by looking at the center and spread of each set. Measures of central tendency involve median, mean, midrange, and mode. The **mode** of a data set is the data value or values that appears the most frequently. The **midrange** is equal to the maximum value plus the minimum value divided by two. The **median** is the value that is halfway into each data set; it splits the data into two intervals. The **mean** is the sum of all data values divided by the number of data points. Two completely different sets of data can have the same mean. For example, a data set having values ranging from 0 to 100 and a data set having values ranging from 44 to 46 could both have means equal to 50. The first data set would have a much wider range, which is known as the **spread** of the data. It measures how varied the data is within each set. Spread can be defined further as either interquartile range or standard deviation. The **interquartile range (IQR)** is the range of the middle fifty percent of the data set. The **standard deviation, s,** quantifies the amount of variation with respect to the mean. A lower standard deviation shows that the data set does not differ much from the mean. A larger standard deviation shows that the data set is spread out farther away from the mean. The formula used for standard deviation depends on whether it's being used for a population or a sample (a subset of a population). The formula for sample standard deviation is:

$$s = \sqrt{\dfrac{\sum (x - \underline{x})^2}{n - 1}}$$

In this formula, *s* represents the standard deviation value, *x* is each value in the data set, $\underline{x}$ is the sample mean, and *n* is the total number of data points in the set. Note that sample standard deviations use *one less than the total* in the denominator. The population standard deviation formula is similar:

$$\sigma = \sqrt{\sum \frac{(x - \mu)^2}{N}}$$

For population standard deviations, sigma (σ) represents the standard deviation, x represents each value in the data set, mu (μ) is the population mean, and N is the total number of data points for the population. The square of the standard deviation is known as the **variance** of the data set. A data set can have outliers, and measures of central tendency that are not affected by outliers are the mode and median. Those measures are labeled as resistant measures of center.

Statistics, Data Analysis, and Probability: Inferences, Predictions, and Arguments Based on Data

Making Inferences and Justifying Conclusions from Samples, Experiments, and Observational Studies

Data Gathering Techniques

Statistics involves making decisions and predictions about larger sets of data based on smaller data sets. The information from a small subset can help predict what happens in the entire set. The smaller data set is called a **sample** and the larger data set for which the decision is being made is called a **population.** The three most common types of data gathering techniques are sample surveys, experiments, and observational studies. **Sample surveys** involve collecting data from a random sample of people from a desired population. The measurement of the variable is only performed on this set of people. To have accurate data, the sampling must be unbiased and random. For example, surveying students in an advanced calculus class on how much they enjoy math classes is not a useful sample if the population should be all college students based on the research question. There are many methods to form a random sample, and all adhere to the fact that every sample that could be chosen has a predetermined probability of being chosen. Once the sample is chosen, statistical experiments can then be carried out to investigate real-world problems.

An **experiment** is the method by which a hypothesis is tested using a controlled process called the scientific method. A cause and the effect of that cause are measured, and the hypothesis is accepted or rejected. Experiments are usually completed in a controlled environment where the results of a control population are compared to the results of a test population. The groups are selected using a randomization process in which each group has a representative mix of the population being tested. Finally, an **observational study** is similar to an experiment. However, this design is used when circumstances prevent or do not allow for a designated control group and experimental group (e.g., lack of funding or unrealistic expectations). Instead, existing control and test populations must be used, so this method has a lack of randomization.

Interpreting Statistical Information

To make decisions concerning populations, data must be collected from a sample. The sample must be large enough to be able to make conclusions. A common way to collect data is via surveys and polls. Every survey and poll must be designed so that there is no bias. An example of a biased survey is one with loaded questions, which are either intentionally worded or ordered to obtain a desired response. Once the data is obtained, conclusions should not be made that are not justified by statistical analysis. One must make sure the difference between correlation and causation is understood. Correlation implies there is an association between two variables, and correlation does not imply causation.

Population Mean and Proportion

Both the population mean and proportion can be calculated using data from a sample. The **population mean** (μ)is the average value of the parameter for the entire population. Due to size constraints, finding the exact value of μ is impossible, so the mean of the sample population is used as an estimate instead. The larger the sample size, the closer the sample mean gets to the population mean. An alternative to finding μ is to find the **proportion** of the population, which is the part of the population with the given characteristic. The proportion can be expressed as a decimal, a fraction, or a percentage, and can be given as a single value or a range of values. Because the population mean and proportion are both estimates, there's a **margin of error**, which is the difference between the actual value and the expected value.

T-Tests

A **randomized experiment** is used to compare two treatments by using statistics involving a **t-test,** which tests whether two data sets are significantly different from one another. To use a t-test, the test statistic must follow a normal distribution. The first step of the test involves calculating the t value, which is given as:

$$t = \frac{x_1 - x_2}{s_{\underline{x}_1 - \underline{x}_2}}$$

where $\underline{x}_1$ and $\underline{x}_2$ are the averages of the two samples. Also:

$$s_{\underline{x}_1 - \underline{x}_2} = \sqrt{\frac{s_1^2}{n_1} + \frac{s_2^2}{n_2}}$$

where s_1 and s_2 are the standard deviations of each sample and n_1 and n_2 are their respective sample sizes. The **degrees of freedom** for two samples are calculated as:

$$df = \frac{(n_1 - 1) + (n_2 - 1)}{2}$$

rounded to the lowest whole number. Also, a significance level α must be chosen, where a typical value is $\alpha = 0.05$.Once everything is compiled, the decision is made to use either a **one-tailed test** or a **two-tailed test**. If there's an assumed difference between the two treatments, a one-tailed test is used. If no difference is assumed, a two-tailed test is used.

Analyzing Test Results

Once the type of test is determined, the t-value, significance level, and degrees of freedom are applied to the published table showing the t distribution. The row is associated with degrees of freedom and each column corresponds to the probability. The t-value can be exactly equal to one entry or lie between two entries in a row. For example, consider a t-value of 1.7 with degrees of freedom equal to 30. This **test statistic** falls between the p values of 0.05 and 0.025.

For a one-tailed test, the corresponding p value lies between 0.05 and 0.025.

For a two-tailed test, the p values need to be doubled so the corresponding p value falls between 0.1 and 0.05.

Once the probability is known, this range is compared to α.If $p < \alpha$, the hypothesis is rejected. If $p > \alpha$, the hypothesis isn't rejected. In a two-tailed test, this scenario means the hypothesis is accepted that there's no

difference in the two treatments. In a one-tailed test, the hypothesis is accepted, indicating that there's a difference in the two treatments.

Evaluating Completed Tests

In addition to applying statistical techniques to actual testing, evaluating completed tests is another important aspect of statistics. Reports can be read that already have conclusions, and the process can be evaluated using learned concepts. For example, deciding if a sample being used is appropriate. Other things that can be evaluated include determining if the samples are randomized or the results are significant. Once statistical concepts are understood, the knowledge can be applied to many applications.

Sample Statistics

A **point estimate** is a single point used to estimate a population parameter. The sample proportion is the best point estimate of the population proportion. It is used because it is an **unbiased estimator,** meaning that it is a statistic that targets the value of the population parameter by assuming the mean of the sampling distribution is equal to the mean of the population distribution. Other unbiased estimators include the mean and variance. **Biased estimators** do not target the value of the population parameter, and such values include median, range, and standard deviation. A **confidence interval** consists of a range of values that is utilized to approximate the true value of a population parameter. The **confidence level** is the probability that the confidence interval does contain the population parameter, assuming the estimation process is repeated many times.

Population Inferences Using Distributions

Samples are used to make inferences about a population. The sampling distribution of a sample mean is a distribution of all sample means for a fixed sample size, n, which is part of a population. Depending on different criteria, either a binomial, normal, or geometric distribution can be used to determine probabilities. A normal distribution uses a continuous random variable, and is bell-shaped and symmetric. A binomial distribution uses a discrete random variable, has a finite number of trials, and only has two possible outcomes: a success and a failure. A geometric distribution is very similar to a binomial distribution; however, the number of trials does not have to be finite.

Creating and Interpreting Linear Regression Models

Linear Regression

Regression lines are a way to calculate a relationship between the independent variable and the dependent variable. A straight line means that there's a linear trend in the data. Technology can be used to find the equation of this line (e.g., a graphing calculator or Microsoft Excel®). In either case, all of the data points are entered, and a line is "fit" that best represents the shape of the data. Other functions used to model data sets include quadratic and exponential models.

Estimating Data Points

Regression lines can be used to estimate data points not already given. For example, if an equation of a line is found that fit the temperature and beach visitor data set, its input is the average daily temperature and its output is the projected number of visitors. Thus, the number of beach visitors on a 100-degree day can be estimated. The output is a data point on the regression line, and the number of daily visitors is expected to be greater than on a 96-degree day because the regression line has a positive slope.

Plotting and Analyzing Residuals

Once the function is found that fits the data, its accuracy can be calculated. Therefore, how well the line fits the data can be determined. The difference between the actual dependent variable from the data set and the estimated value located on the regression line is known as a **residual.** Therefore, the residual is known as the predicted value $\hat{y}$ minus the actual value y. A residual is calculated for each data point and can be plotted on the scatterplot. If all the residuals appear to be approximately the same distance from the regression line, the line is a good fit. If the residuals seem to differ greatly across the board, the line isn't a good fit.

Interpreting the Regression Line

The formula for a regression line is $y = mx + b$, where m is the slope and b is the y-intercept. Both the slope and y-intercept are found in the **Method of Least Squares**, which is the process of finding the equation of the line through minimizing residuals. The slope represents the rate of change in y as x gets larger. Therefore, because y is the dependent variable, the slope actually provides the predicted values given the independent variable. The y-intercept is the predicted value for when the independent variable equals zero. In the temperature example, the y-intercept is the expected number of beach visitors for a very cold average daily temperature of zero degrees.

Correlation Coefficient

The **correlation coefficient (r)** measures the association between two variables. Its value is between -1 and 1, where -1 represents a perfect negative linear relationship, 0 represents no relationship, and 1 represents a perfect positive linear relationship. A **negative linear relationship** means that as x values increase, y values decrease. A **positive linear relationship** means that as x values increase, y values increase. The formula for computing the correlation coefficient is:

$$r = \frac{n(\sum xy) - (\sum x)(\sum y)}{\sqrt{n(\sum x^2) - (\sum x)^2}\sqrt{n(\sum y^2) - (\sum y)^2}}$$

n is the number of data points.

Both Microsoft Excel® and a graphing calculator can evaluate this easily once the data points are entered. A correlation greater than 0.8 or less than -0.8 is classified as "strong" while a correlation between -0.5 and 0.5 is classified as "weak."

Correlation Versus Causation

Correlation and causation have two different meanings. If two values are correlated, there is an association between them. However, correlation doesn't necessarily mean that one variable causes the other. **Causation** (or "cause and effect") occurs when one variable causes the other. Average daily temperature and number of beachgoers are correlated and have causation. If the temperature increases, the change in weather causes more people to go to the beach. However, alcoholism and smoking are correlated but don't have causation. The more someone drinks the more likely they are to smoke, but drinking alcohol doesn't cause someone to smoke.

Regression Models

Regression lines are straight lines that calculate a relationship between nonlinear data involving an independent variable and a dependent variable. A regression line is of the form $y = mx + b$, where m is the slope and b is the y-intercept. Both the slope and y-intercept are found using the **Method of Least Squares**,

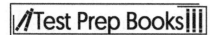
which involves minimizing residuals – the difference between the dependent variable from the data set and the estimated value located on the regression line. The slope represents the rate of change in y as x increases. The y-intercept is the predicted value when the independent variable is equal to 0. Technology, such as a graphing calculator or Microsoft Excel®, can also be utilized to find the equation of this line. In either case, the data points are entered, and a line is "fit" that best represents the shape of the data.

Here is an example of a data set and its regression line:

The Regression Line is the Line of Best Fit

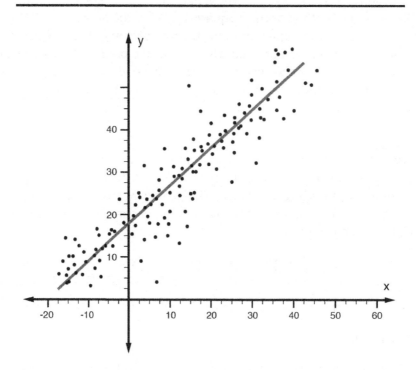

Regression models are highly used for forecasting, and linear regression techniques are the simplest models. If the nonlinear data follows the shape of exponential, logarithmic, or power functions, those types of functions can be used to more accurately model the data rather than lines.

Here is an example of both an exponential regression and a logarithmic regression model:

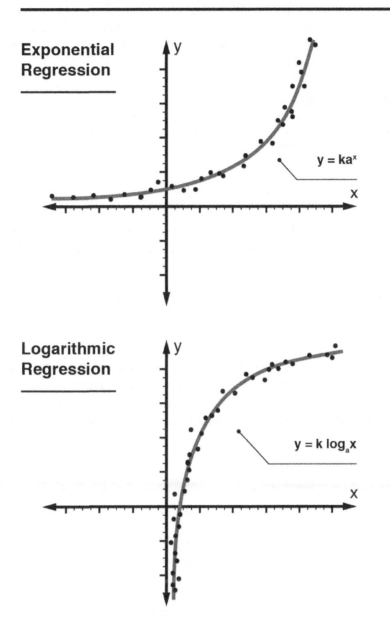

Nonlinear Regression

Exponential Regression

$y = ka^x$

Logarithmic Regression

$y = k \log_a x$

The Law of Large Numbers and the Central Limit Theorem

The *Law of Large Numbers* states that as the number of experiments increase, the actual ratio of outcomes will approach the theoretical probability. The **Central Limit Theorem** states that through using a sufficiently large sample size N, meaning over 30, the sampling distribution of the mean approaches a normal distribution with a mean of μ and variance of σ^2/N. The variance of the actual population is σ^2 and its mean is μ. In other words, as the sample size increases, the distribution will behave normally.

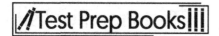

Estimating Parameters

A point estimate of a population parameter is a single statistic. For example, the sample mean is a point estimate of the population mean. Once all calculations are made, a confidence interval is used to express the accuracy of the sampling method used. The confidence interval consists of a confidence level, the statistic, and a margin of error. A 95% confidence level indicates that 95% of all confidence intervals will contain the population parameter. Also, the margin of error gives a range of values above and below the sample statistic, which helps to form a confidence interval.

Principles of Hypotheses Testing

The *P*-value approach to hypothesis testing involves assuming a null hypothesis is true and then determining the probability of a test statistic in the direction of the alternative hypothesis. The test statistic is defined as the *t*-statistic:

$$t^* = \frac{x - \mu}{s/\sqrt{n}}$$

which follows a *t*-distribution with *n*-1 degrees of freedom. The *P*-value is then calculated as the probability that if the null hypothesis is true, a more extreme test statistic in the direction of the alternative hypothesis would be observed. A significance level, α, is set (usually at 0.05 or 0.001) and the *P*-value is compared to α.

If $P \leq \alpha$, one rejects the null hypothesis and accepts the alternative hypothesis. If $P > \alpha$, one accepts the null hypothesis.

Measuring Probabilities with Two-Way Frequency Tables

When measuring event probabilities, two-way frequency tables can be used to report the raw data and then used to calculate probabilities. If the frequency tables are translated into relative frequency tables, the probabilities presented in the table can be plugged directly into the formulas for conditional probabilities. By plugging in the correct frequencies, the data from the table can be used to determine if events are independent or dependent.

Differing Probabilities

The probability that event A occurs differs from the probability that event A occurs given B. When working within a given model, it's important to note the difference. $P(A|B)$ is determined using the formula:

$$P(B) = \frac{P(A \text{ and } B)}{P(B)}$$

and represents the total number of A's outcomes left that could occur after B occurs. $P(A)$ can be calculated without any regard for B. For example, the probability of a student finding a parking spot on a busy campus is different once class is in session.

Uniform and Non-Uniform Probability Models

A **uniform probability model** is one where each outcome has an equal chance of occurring, such as the probabilities of rolling each side of a die. A **non-uniform probability** model is one where each result has a different chance of taking place. In a uniform probability model, the conditional probability formulas for $P(B|A)$ and $P(A|B)$ can be multiplied by their respective denominators to obtain two formulas for $P(A \text{ and } B)$.

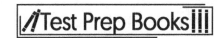

Therefore, the multiplication rule is derived as:

$$P(A \text{ and } B) = P(A)P(A) = P(B)P(B)$$

In a model, if the probability of either individual event is known and the corresponding conditional probability is known, the multiplication rule allows the probability of the joint occurrence of A and B to be calculated.

Binomial Experiments

In statistics, a **binomial experiment** is an experiment that has the following properties. The experiment consists of n repeated trial that can each have only one of two outcomes. It can be either a success or a failure. The probability of success, p, is the same in every trial. Each trial is also independent of all other trials. An example of a binomial experiment is rolling a die 10 times with the goal of rolling a 5. Rolling a 5 is a success while any other value is a failure. In this experiment, the probability of rolling a 5 is $\frac{1}{6}$. In any binomial experiment, x is the number of resulting successes, n is the number of trials, p is the probability of success in each trial, and $q = 1 - p$ is the probability of failure within each trial. The probability of obtaining x successes within n trials is:

$$P(X = x) = \frac{n!}{x! \, (n - x)!} p^x (1 - p)^{n-x}$$

With the following being the **binomial coefficient**:

$$(n \; x \,) = \frac{n!}{x! \, (n - x)!}$$

Within this calculation, $n!$ is n factorial that's defined as:

$$n \cdot (n - 1) \cdot (n - 2) \dots 1$$

Let's look at the probability of obtaining 2 rolls of a 5 out of the 10 rolls.

Start with $P(X = 2)$, where 2 is the number of successes. Then fill in the rest of the formula with what is known, $n=10$, $x=2$, $p=1/6$, $q=5/6$:

$$P(X = 2) = \left(\frac{10!}{2! \, (10 - 2)!}\right) \left(\frac{1}{6}\right)^2 \left(1 - \frac{1}{6}\right)^{10-2}$$

Which simplifies to:

$$P(X = 2) = \left(\frac{10!}{2! \, 8!}\right) \left(\frac{1}{6}\right)^2 \left(\frac{5}{6}\right)^8$$

Then solve to get:

$$P(X = 2) = \left(\frac{3628800}{80640}\right) (.0277)(.2325) = .2898$$

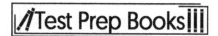

Statistical Questions

A statistical question is answered by collecting data with variability. Data consists of facts and/or statistics (numbers), and variability refers to a tendency to shift or change. Data is a broad term, inclusive of things like height, favorite color, name, salary, temperature, gas mileage, and language. Questions requiring data as an answer are not necessarily statistical questions. If there is no variability in the data, then the question is not statistical in nature. Consider the following examples: what is Mary's favorite color? How much money does your mother make? What was the highest temperature last week? How many miles did your car get on its last tank of gas? How much taller than Bob is Ed?

None of the above are statistical questions because each case lacks variability in the data needed to answer the question. The questions on favorite color, salary, and gas mileage each require a single piece of data, whether a fact or statistic. Therefore, variability is absent. Although the temperature question requires multiple pieces of data (the high temperature for each day), a single, distinct number is the answer. The height question requires two pieces of data, Bob's height and Ed's height, but no difference in variability exists between those two values. Therefore, this is not a statistical question. Statistical questions typically require calculations with data.

Consider the following statistical questions:

How many miles per gallon of gas does the 2016 Honda Civic get?

To answer this question, data must be collected. This data should include miles driven and gallons used. Different cars, different drivers, and different driving conditions will produce different results. Therefore, variability exists in the data. To answer the question, the mean (average) value could be determined.

Are American men taller than German men? To answer this question, data must be collected. This data should include the heights of American men and the heights of German men. All American men are not the same height and all German men are not the same height. Some American men are taller than some German men and some German men are taller than some American men. Therefore, variability exists in the data. To answer the question, the median values for each group could be determined and compared.

The following are more examples of statistical questions:

What proportion of 4th graders have a favorite color of blue?

How much money do teachers make?

Is it colder in Boston or Chicago?

Statistical Processes

Samples and Populations

Statistics involves making decisions and predictions about larger data sets based on smaller data sets. Basically, the information from one part or subset can help predict what happens in the entire data set or population at large. The entire process involves guessing, and the predictions and decisions may not be 100 percent correct all of the time; however, there is some truth to these predictions, and the decisions do have mathematical support. The smaller data set is called a **sample** and the larger data set (in which the decision is being made) is called a **population.** A **random sample** is used as the sample, which is an unbiased collection of data points

300

that represents the population as well as it can. There are many methods of forming a random sample, and all adhere to the fact that every potential data point has a predetermined probability of being chosen.

Goodness of Fit

Goodness of fit tests show how well a statistical model fits a given data set. They allow the differences between the observed and expected quantities to be summarized to determine if the model is consistent with the results. The **Chi-Squared Goodness of Fit Test** (or *Chi-Squared Test* for short) is used with one categorical variable from one population, and it concludes whether or not the sample data is consistent with a hypothesized distribution. Chi-Squared is evaluated using the following formula:

$$\chi^2 = \sum \frac{(O - E)^2}{E}$$

where O is the observed frequency value and E is the expected frequency value. Also, the **degree of freedom** must be calculated, which is the number of categories in the data set minus one. Then a Chi-Squared table is used to test the data. The **degree of freedom value** and a **significance value,** such as 0.05, are located on the table. The corresponding entry represents a critical value.

If the calculated χ^2 is greater than the critical value, the data set does not work with the statistical model. If the calculated χ^2 is less than the critical value, the statistical model can be used.

Statistics, Data Analysis, and Probability: Basic Notions of Chance and Probability

Counting Techniques

There are many counting techniques that can help solve problems involving counting possibilities. For example, the **Addition Principle** states that if there are m choices from Group 1 and n choices from Group 2, then $n + m$ is the total number of choices possible from Groups 1 and 2. For this to be true, the groups can't have any choices in common. The **Multiplication Principle** states that if Process 1 can be completed n ways and Process 2 can be completed m ways, the total number of ways to complete both Process 1 and Process 2 is $n \times m$. For this rule to be used, both processes must be independent of each other. Counting techniques also involve permutations. A **permutation** is an arrangement of elements in a set for which order must be considered. For example, if three letters from the alphabet are chosen, ABC and BAC are two different permutations. The multiplication rule can be used to determine the total number of possibilities. If each letter can't be selected twice, the total number of possibilities is:

$$26 \times 25 \times 24 = 15,600$$

A formula can also be used to calculate this total. In general, the notation $P(n, r)$ represents the number of ways to arrange r objects from a set of n and, the formula is:

$$P(n,r) = \frac{n!}{(n - r)!}$$

In the previous example:

$$P(26,3) = \frac{26!}{23!} = 15,600$$

Contrasting permutations, a **combination** is an arrangement of elements in which order doesn't matter. In this case, ABC and BAC are the same combination. In the previous scenario, there are six permutations that represent each single combination. Therefore, the total number of possible combinations is $15,600 \div 6 = 2,600$. In general, $C(n,r)$ represents the total number of combinations of n items selected r at a time where order doesn't matter. Another way to represent the combinations of r items selected out of a set of n items is $\binom{n}{r}$. The formula for select combinations of items is:

$$\binom{n}{r} = C(n,r) = \frac{n!}{(n-r)!\,r!}$$

Therefore, the following relationship exists between permutations and combinations:

$$C(n,r) = \frac{P(n,r)}{r!} = \frac{P(n,r)}{P(r,r)}$$

Probabilities Involving Finite Sample Spaces and Independent Trials

Fundamental Counting Principle

The **fundamental counting principle** states that if there are m potential ways an event can occur, and n potential ways a second event can occur, then there are $m \times n$ potential ways both events can occur. For example, there are two events that can occur after flipping a coin and six events that can occur after rolling a die, so there are $2 \cdot 6 = 12$ total possible event scenarios if both are done simultaneously. This principle can be used to find probabilities involving finite sample spaces and independent trials because it calculates the total number of possible outcomes. For this principle to work, the events must be independent of each other.

Computing Probabilities of Simple Events, Probabilities of Compound Events, and Conditional Probabilities

Simple and Compound Events

A **simple event** consists of only one outcome. The most popular simple event is flipping a coin, which results in either heads or tails. A **compound event** results in more than one outcome and consists of more than one simple event. An example of a compound event is flipping a coin while tossing a die. The result is either heads or tails on the coin and a number from one to six on the die. The probability of a simple event is calculated by dividing the number of possible outcomes by the total number of outcomes. Therefore, the probability of obtaining heads on a coin is $\frac{1}{2}$, and the probability of rolling a 6 on a die is $\frac{1}{6}$. The probability of compound events is calculated using the basic idea of the probability of simple events. If the two events are independent, the probability of one outcome is equal to the product of the probabilities of each simple event. For example, the probability of obtaining heads on a coin and rolling a 6 is equal to:

$$\frac{1}{2} \times \frac{1}{6} = \frac{1}{12}$$

302

The probability of either A or B occurring is equal to the sum of the probabilities minus the probability that both A and B will occur. Therefore, the probability of obtaining either heads on a coin or rolling a 6 on a die is:

$$\frac{1}{2} + \frac{1}{6} - \frac{1}{12} = \frac{7}{12}$$

The two events aren't mutually exclusive because they can happen at the same time. If two events are mutually exclusive, and the probability of both events occurring at the same time is zero, the probability of event A or B occurring equals the sum of both probabilities. An example of calculating the probability of two mutually exclusive events is determining the probability of pulling a king or a queen from a deck of cards. The two events cannot occur at the same time.

Sample Spaces

Probabilities are based on observations of events. The probability of an event occurring is equal to the ratio of the number of favorable outcomes over the total number of possible outcomes. The total number of possible outcomes is found by constructing the sample space. The sum of probabilities of all possible distinct outcomes is equal to 1. A simple example of a sample space involves a deck of cards. They contain 52 distinct cards, and therefore the sample space contains each individual card. To find the probability of selecting a queen on one draw from the deck, the ratio would be equal to $\frac{4}{52} = \frac{1}{13}$, which equals 4 possible queens over the total number of possibilities in the sample space.

Solving Probability Problems Using Geometric Ratios

The ratio between two similar geometric figures is called the **scale factor**. In the following example, there are two similar triangles. The scale factor from figure A to figure B is 2 because the length of the corresponding side of the larger triangle, 14, is twice the corresponding side on the smaller triangle, 7.

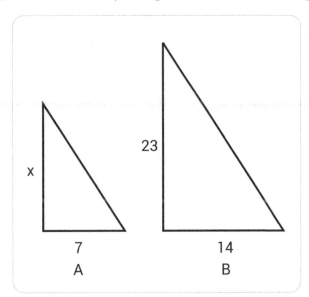

This scale factor can also be used to find the value of X. Since the scale factor from small to large is 2, the larger number, 23, can be divided by 2 to find the missing side: X = 11.5. The scale factor can also be represented in the equation $2A = B$ because two times the lengths of A gives the corresponding lengths of B. This is the idea behind similar triangles.

Problems involving volume, length, and other units can also be solved using ratios. If the following graphic of a cone is given, the problem may ask for the volume to be found.

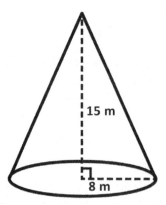

Referring to the formulas provided on the test, the volume of a cone is given as: $V = \pi r^2 \frac{h}{3}$, where r is the radius, and h is the height.

Plugging $r = 7$ and $h = 16$ from the graphic in to the formula, the following is obtained:

$$V = \pi(7^2)\frac{16}{3}$$

Therefore, the volume of the cone is found to be approximately 821m³. Sometimes, answers in different units are sought. If this problem wanted the answer in liters, 821m³ would need to be converted. Using the equivalence statement 1m³ = 1000L, the following ratio would be used to solve for liters: $821m^3 * \frac{1000L}{1m^3}$.

Cubic meters in the numerator and denominator cancel each other out, and the answer is converted to 821,000 liters, or $8.21 * 10^5$ L.

Other conversions can also be made between different given and final units. If the temperature in a pool is 30°C, what is the temperature of the pool in degrees Fahrenheit? To convert these units, an equation is used relating Celsius to Fahrenheit. The following equation is used: $T_{°F} = 1.8T_{°C} + 32$.

Plugging in the given temperature and solving the equation for T yields the result:

$$T_{°F} = 1.8(30) + 32 = 86°F$$

Units in both the metric system and US customary system are widely used.

Probability Axioms

The **addition rule** is necessary to find the probability of event A or event B occurring, or both occurring at the same time. If events A and B are mutually exclusive, which means they cannot occur at the same time, $P(A \text{ or } B) = P(A) + P(B)$. If events A and B are not mutually exclusive,

$$P(A \text{ or } B) = P(A) + P(B) - P(A \text{ and } B)$$

where $P(A \text{ and } B)$ represents the probability of event A and B both occurring at the same time. The **multiplication rule** is necessary to find the probability that both A and B occur in two separate trials. This rule

differs if the events are independent or dependent. Two events, A and B, are labeled as **independent** if the occurrence of one event does not affect the probability that the other event will occur.

If A and be are not independent, they are **dependent.**

If events A and B are independent, $P(A\ and\ B) = P(A)P(B)$, and if events A and B are dependent, $P(A\ and\ B) = P(A)P(A)$ where $P(A)$ represents the probability event B occurs given that event A has already occurred.

$P(A)$ represents **conditional probability.** $P(B|A)$ can be found using the formula $P(A) = \frac{P\ (A\ and\ B)}{P\ (A)}$, and represents the total number of outcomes remaining for B to occur after A occurs.

Probability Distributions

Probability is a measure of the likelihood of something happening or being the case. The probability of an event A is written P(A) and is assigned a value between zero (can't happen) and one (is certain to happen): $0 \leq$ P(A) $\leq$ 1.

Probabilities can be objectively assigned by sampling or reviewing historical data to determine how frequently the outcome has occurred in the past.

If the probability of a parameter's value is calculated and plotted along its entire possible range, a probability distribution function (PDF) can be determined. The normal probability distribution is a continuous PDF.

The binomial probability distribution is an important discrete PDF giving the probability of getting exactly k successes in n trials of a "yes-no," or **binomial**, test:

$$P(k) = (n\ k\ )p^k(1 - p)^{n-k}$$

where p is the probability of success for each trial. The binomial coefficient $(n\ k\ )$ is the number of possible ways k values can be selected from a group of n items and is calculated as n!/(k!(n − k)!, where:

$$k! = k \times (k - 1) \times (k - 2) \times \ldots \times 2 \times 1$$

The value of 0! is defined as 1 to allow calculation of the probability of zero occurrences of the event in a time interval.

For example, to determine the probability of getting exactly 4 heads in 10 tosses of a fair coin:

$$p(H) = p(T) = 0.5$$

and

$$P(4) = (10\ 4\ )0.5^4(1 - 0.5)^6 = 0.2051$$

The Poisson discrete PDF is used for modeling the number of times a discrete event occurs in an interval of time. It is valid for events occurring with a known average rate, λ, and probability independent of the time since the last event:

$$P(k\ events) = \frac{\lambda^k e^{-\lambda}}{k!}$$

305

where λ is the average number of events per interval, e is the base of natural logarithms (2.7182…), and k! is calculated as discussed above.

Discrete and Continuous Random Variables

A **discrete random variable** consists of a collection of values that is either finite or countable. If there are infinitely many values, being countable means that each individual value can be counted. For example, the number of coin tosses before getting heads could potentially be infinite, but the total number of tosses is countable. A continuous random variable has infinitely many values and is not countable. The individual items cannot be counted, and an example is a measurement. Because of the use of decimals, there are infinitely many heights of human beings. Each type of variable has its own **probability distribution**, which is a description that shows the probability for each potential value of the random variable. They are usually seen in tables, formulas, or graphs. The **expected value** of a random variable represents what the mean value should be in either a large sample size or after many trials. According to the Law of Large Numbers, after many trials, the actual mean and that of the probability distribution should be approximately equal to the expected value. The expected value is a weighted average that is calculated as:

$$E(X) = \sum x_i p_i$$

where x_i represent the value of each outcome and p_i represent the probability of each outcome. The expected value if all probabilities are equal is:

$$E(X) = \frac{x_1 + x_2 + \cdots + x_n}{n}$$

Expected value is often called the mean of the random variable and is also a measure of central tendency. A **binomial probability distribution** is a probability distribution in which there is a fixed number of trials, all trials are independent, each trial has an outcome classified as either a success or a failure, and the probability of a success is the same in each trial. Within any binomial experiment, x is the number of resulting successes, n is the number of trials, P is the probability of success within each trial, and $Q = 1 - P$ is the probability of failure within each trial. The probability of obtaining x successes within n trials is:

$$(n\ x\ )P^x(1 - P)^{n-x}$$

The combination $(n\ x\ ) = \frac{n!}{x!(n-x)!}$ is called the **binomial coefficient** and represents the number of possible outcomes where exactly x many successes occur out of n trials.

A **geometric probability distribution** is a binomial probability distribution where the number of trials is not fixed. A **uniform probability distribution** exists when there is constant probability. Each random variable has equal probability and its graph is a rectangle. Finally, a **uniform probability distribution** has a graph that is symmetric and bell-shaped.

Population percentages can be estimated using normal distributions. For example, the probability that a data point will be less than the mean is 50%. Similarly, the probability that a data point will be within one standard deviation of the mean, or that the z-score will be between -1 and 1, is about 68.2%. When using a z-table, the left column states how many standard deviations (to one decimal place) away from the mean the point lies, and the row heading states the second decimal place. The entries in the table corresponding to each column

306

and each row gives the probability, which is equal to the area under the curve. The area under the entire curve of a standard normal distribution is equal to 1.

Independence and Conditional Probability

Sample Subsets

A sample can be broken up into subsets that are smaller parts of the whole. For example, consider a sample population of females. The sample can be divided into smaller subsets based on the characteristics of each female. There can be a group of females with brown hair and a group of females that wear glasses. There also can be a group of females that have brown hair *and* wear glasses. This "and" relates to the **intersection** of the two separate groups of brunettes and those with glasses. Every female in that intersection group has both characteristics. Similarly, there also can be a group of females that either have brown hair *or* wear glasses. The "or" relates to the union of the two separate groups of brunettes and glasses. Every female in this group has at least one of the characteristics. Finally, the group of females who do not wear glasses can be discussed. This "not" relates to the **complement** of the glass-wearing group. No one in the complement has glasses. **Venn diagrams** are useful in highlighting these ideas. When discussing statistical experiments, this idea can also relate to events instead of characteristics.

Verifying Independent Events

Two events aren't always independent. For example, having glasses and having brown hair aren't independent characteristics. There definitely can be overlap because people with brown hair can wear glasses. Also, two events that exist at the same time don't have to have a relationship. For example, even if everyone in a given sample is wearing glasses, the characteristics aren't related. In this case, the probability of a brunette wearing glasses is equal to the probability of a person being a brunette multiplied by the probability of a person wearing glasses. This mathematical test of

$P(A \cap B) = P(A)P(B)$ verifies that two events are independent.

Conditional Probability

Conditional probability is the probability that event A will happen given that event B has already occurred. An example of this is calculating the probability that a person will eat dessert once they have eaten dinner. This is different than calculating the probability of a person just eating dessert. The formula for the conditional probability of event A occurring given B is:

$$P(B) = \frac{P(A \text{ and } B)}{P(B)}$$

and it's defined to be the probability of both A and B occurring divided by the probability of event B occurring. If A and B are independent, then the probability of both A and B occurring is equal to $P(A)P(B)$, so $P(B)$ reduces to just $P(A)$. This means that A and B have no relationship, and the probability of A occurring is the same as the conditional probability of A occurring given B. Similarly:

$$P(A) = \frac{P(B \text{ and } A)}{P(A)} = P(B)$$

if A and B are independent.

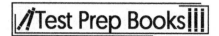

Independent Versus Related Events

To summarize, conditional probability is the probability that an event occurs given that another event has happened. If the two events are related, the probability that the second event will occur changes if the other event has happened. However, if the two events aren't related and are therefore independent, the first event to occur won't impact the probability of the second event occurring.

Science

Physical Sciences: Structure and Properties of Matter

Physical and Chemical Properties

In the physical sciences, it is important to break things down to their simplest components in order to truly understand why they act and react the way they do. It may seem burdensome to separate out each part of an object or to diagram each movement made by an object, but these methods provide a solid basis for understanding how to accurately depict the motion of objects and then correctly predict their future movements.

Everything around us is composed of different materials. To properly understand and sort objects, we must classify what types of materials they comprise. This includes identifying the foundational properties of each object such as its reaction to chemicals, heat, water, or other materials. Some objects might not react at all and this is an important property to note. Other properties include the physical appearance of the object or whether it has any magnetic properties. The importance of being able to sort and classify objects is the first step to understanding them.

- **Matter**: anything that has mass and takes up space

- **Substance**: a type of matter that cannot be separated out into new material through a physical reaction

- **Elements**: substances that cannot be broken down by either physical or chemical reactions. Elements are in the most basic form and are grouped by identified properties using the Periodic Table. The periodic table groups elements based on similar properties. Metallic elements, inert elements, and transition elements are a few categories used to organize elements on the periodic table. New elements are added as they are discovered or created, and these newer elements tend to be heavier, fall into the metal section of the periodic table, and are often unstable. Examples of elements include carbon, gold, and helium.

- **Atoms**: the building blocks of all elements. Atoms are the smallest particles of matter that retain their identities during chemical reactions. Atoms have a central nucleus that includes positively charged protons, and neutrons, which carry no charge. Atoms are also surrounded by electrons that carry a negative charge. The amount of each component determines what type of atom is formed when the components come together. For example, two hydrogen atoms and one oxygen atom can bond together to form water, but the hydrogen and oxygen atoms still remain true to their original identities.

- **Mass**: the measure of how much of a substance exists in an object. The measure of mass is not the same as weight, area, or volume.

309

Both physical and chemical properties are used to sort and classify objects:

- **Physical properties**: refers to the appearance, mass, temperature, state, size, or color of an object or fluid; a physical change indicates a change in the appearance, mass, temperature, state, size or color of an object or fluid.

- **Chemical properties**: refers to the chemical makeup of an object or fluid; a chemical change refers to an alteration in the makeup of an object or fluid and forms a new solution or compound.

Basic Properties of Solids, Liquids, and Gases

States of matter refers to the form substances take such as solid, liquid, gas, or plasma. **Solid** refers to a rigid form of matter with a flexed shape and a fixed volume. Solids generally maintain their shape when exposed to outside forces. **Liquid** refers to the fluid form of matter with no fixed shape and a fixed volume. Liquids can be transferred from one container to another, but cannot be forced to fill containers of different volumes via compression without causing damage to the container. For example, if one attempts to force a given volume or number of particles of a liquid, such as water, into a fixed container, such as a small water bottle, the container would likely explode from the extra water.

Gas refers to an easily compressible fluid form of matter with no fixed shape that expands to fill any space available. A gas can easily be compressed into a confined space, such as a tire or an air mattress. Gases have no fixed shape or volume. They can also be subjected to outside forces, and the number of gas molecules that can fill a certain volume vary with changes in temperature and pressure.

Liquids and gases are considered fluids, which have no set shape. Liquids are fluid, yet are distinguished from gases by their incompressibility (incapable of being compressed) and set volume

Finally, **plasma** refers to an ionized gas where electrons flow freely from atom to atom.

Examples

A rock is a solid because it has a fixed shape and volume. Water is considered to be a liquid because it has a set volume, but not a set shape; therefore, you could pour it into different containers of different shapes, as long as they were large enough to contain the existing volume of the water. Oxygen is considered to be a gas. Oxygen does not have a set volume or a set shape; therefore, it could expand or contract to fill a container or even a room. Gases in fluorescent lamps become plasma when electric current is applied to them.

Chemical and Physical Changes

Physical change is the changing of the size or shape of an object without altering its chemical makeup. An example of a physical change is tearing a piece of paper in half. This changes the shape of the matter, but it is still paper. Other examples include the heating or cooling of water, change of state (solid, liquid, gas), the freezing of water into ice, or cutting a piece of wood in half.

Conversely, a **chemical change** alters the chemical composition or identity of matter. An example of a chemical change is burning a piece of paper. The heat necessary to burn the paper alters the chemical composition of the paper. This chemical change cannot be easily undone, since it has created at least one form of matter different than the original matter.

When two or more materials are combined, it is called a **mixture**. Generally, a mixture can be separated out into the original components. When one type of matter is dissolved into another type of matter (a solid into a liquid or a liquid into another liquid), and cannot easily be separated back into its original components, it is called a **solution**.

Matter can change from one state to another in many ways, including through heating, cooling, or a change in pressure. Changes of state are identified as:

- **Melting**: solid to liquid

- **Sublimation**: solid to gas

- **Evaporation**: liquid to gas

- **Freezing**: liquid to solid

- **Condensation**: gas to liquid

- **Non-reversible change** (chemical change): When one or more types of matter change and it results in the production of new materials. Examples include burning, rusting, and combining solutions. If a piece of paper is burned it cannot be turned back into its original state. It has forever been altered by a chemical change.

States of Matter and Factors that Affect Phase Changes

A solid has a distinct shape and a defined volume. A liquid has a more loosely defined shape and a definite volume, while a gas has no definite shape or volume. The **Kinetic Theory of Matter** states that matter is composed of a large number of small particles (specifically, atoms and molecules) that are in constant motion. The distance between the separations in these particles determines the state of the matter: solid, liquid, or gas. In gases, the particles have a large separation and no attractive forces. In liquids, there is moderate separation between particles and some attractive forces to form a loose shape. Solids have almost no separation between their particles, causing a defined and set shape. The constant movement of particles causes them to bump into each other, thus allowing the particles to transfer energy between each other. This bumping and transferring of energy helps explain the transfer of heat and the relationship between pressure, volume, and temperature.

The **Ideal Gas Law** states that pressure, volume, and temperature are all related through the equation: $PV = nRT$, where P is pressure, V is volume, n is the amount of the substance in moles, R is the gas constant, and T is temperature.

When pressure, temperature, or volume change in matter, a change in state can occur. Changes in state include solid to liquid (melting), liquid to gas (evaporation), solid to gas (sublimation), gas to solid (deposition), gas to liquid (condensation), and liquid to solid (freezing). There is one other state of matter called **plasma**, which is seen in lightning, television screens, and neon lights. Plasma is most commonly converted from the gas state at extremely high temperatures.

The amount of energy needed to change matter from one state to another is labeled by the terms for phase changes. For example, the temperature needed to supply enough energy for matter to change from a liquid to a gas is called the **heat of vaporization**. When heat is added to matter in order to cause a change in state, there will be an increase in temperature until the matter is about to change its state. During its transition, all of

311

the added heat is used by the matter to change its state, so there is no increase in temperature. Once the transition is complete, then the added heat will again yield an increase in temperature.

Each state of matter is considered to be a phase, and changes between phases are represented by phase diagrams. These diagrams show the effects of changes in pressure and temperature on matter. The states of matter fall into areas on these charts called **heating curves**.

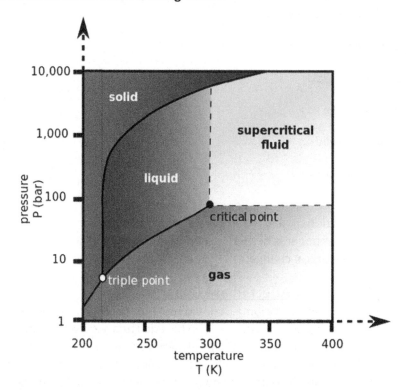

Conservation of Energy

The first law of thermodynamics is also known as the **conservation of energy**. This law states that energy cannot be created or destroyed, but is just transferred or converted into another form through a thermodynamic process. For example, if a liquid is boiled and then removed from the heat source, the liquid will eventually cool. This change in temperature is not because of a loss of energy or heat, but from a transfer of energy or heat to the surroundings. This can include the heating of nearby air molecules, or the transfer of heat from the liquid to the container or to the surface where the container is resting.

This law also applies to the idea of perpetual motion. A self-powered perpetual motion machine cannot exist. This is because the motion of the machine would inevitably lose some heat or energy to friction, whether from materials or from the air.

The conservation of energy is seen in the conservation of matter in chemical systems. This is helpful when attempting to understand chemical processes, since these processes must balance out. This means that extra matter cannot be created or destroyed, it must all be accounted for through a chemical process.

Atoms, Molecules, and Ions

The basic building blocks of matter are **atoms,** which are extremely small particles that retain their identity during chemical reactions. Atoms can be singular or grouped to form elements. Elements are composed of one type of atom with the same properties.

Molecules are a group of atoms—either the same or different types—that are chemically bonded together by attractive forces. For example, hydrogen and oxygen are both atoms but, when bonded together, form water.

Ions are electrically-charged particles that are formed from an atom or a group of atoms via the loss or gain of electrons.

Atomic Models

Theories of the atomic model have developed over the centuries. The most commonly referenced model of an atom was proposed by Niels Bohr. Bohr studied the models of J.J. Thomson and Ernest Rutherford and adapted his own theories from these existing models. Bohr compared the structure of the atom to that of the Solar System, where there is a center, or nucleus, with various sized orbitals circulating around this nucleus. This is a simplified version of what scientists have discovered about atoms, including the structures and placements of any orbitals. Modern science has made further adaptations to the model, including the fact that orbitals are actually made of electron "clouds."

Atomic Structure: Nucleus, Electrons, Protons, and Neutrons

Following the Bohr model of the atom, the nucleus, or core, is made up of positively charged **protons** and neutrally charged **neutrons.** The neutrons are theorized to be in the nucleus with the protons to provide greater "balance" at the center of the atom. The nucleus of the atom makes up the majority (more than 99%) of the mass of an atom, while the orbitals surrounding the nucleus contain negatively charged **electrons.** The entire structure of an atom is incredibly small.

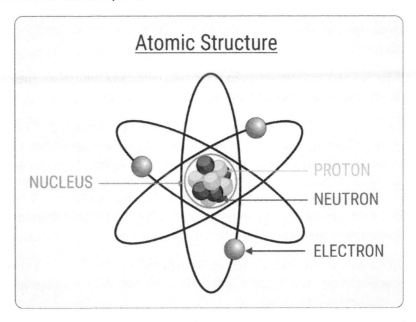

Atomic Number, Atomic Mass, and Isotopes

The **atomic number** of an atom is determined by the number of protons within the nucleus. When a substance is composed of atoms that all have the same atomic number, it is called an **element**. Elements are arranged by atomic number and grouped by properties in the **periodic table**.

An atom's **mass number** is determined by the sum of the total number of protons and neutrons in the atom. Most nuclei have a net neutral charge, and all atoms of one type have the same atomic number. However, there are some atoms of the same type that have a different mass number, due to an imbalance of neutrons. These are called **isotopes**. In isotopes, the atomic number, which is determined by the number of protons, is the same, but the mass number, which is determined by adding the protons and neutrons, is different due to the irregular number of neutrons.

Electron Arrangements

Electrons are most easily organized into distributions of subshells called **electron configurations**. Subshells fill from the inside (closest to the nucleus) to the outside. Therefore, once a subshell is filled, the next shell farther from the nucleus begins to fill, and so on. Atoms with electrons on the outside of a noble gas core (an atom with an electron inner shell that corresponds to the configuration of one of the noble gases, such as Neon) and pseudo-noble gas core (an atom with an electron inner shell that is similar to that of a noble gas core along with $(n-1)\,d^{10}$ electrons), are called **valence** electrons. Valence electrons are primarily the electrons involved in chemical reactions. The similarities in their configurations account for similarities in properties of groups of elements. Essentially, the groups (vertical columns) on the periodic table all have similar characteristics, such as solubility and reactivity, due to their similar electron configurations.

Elements, Compounds, and Mixtures

Everything that takes up space and has mass is composed of **matter**. Understanding the basic characteristics and properties of matter helps with classification and identification.

An **element** is a substance that cannot be chemically decomposed to a simpler substance, while still retaining the properties of the element.

Compounds are composed of two or more elements that are chemically combined. The constituent elements in the compound are in constant proportions by mass.

When a material can be separated by physicals means (such as sifting it through a colander), it is called a **mixture**. Mixtures are categorized into two types: **heterogeneous** and **homogeneous**. Heterogeneous mixtures have physically distinct parts, which retain their different properties. A mix of salt and sugar is an example of a heterogeneous mixture. With heterogenous mixtures, it is possible that different samples from the same parent mixture may have different proportions of each component in the mixture. For example, in the sugar and salt mixture, there may be uneven mixing of the two, causing one random tablespoon sample to be mostly salt, while a different tablespoon sample may be mostly sugar.

A homogeneous mixture, also called a **solution,** has uniform properties throughout a given sample. An example of a homogeneous solution is salt fully dissolved in warm water. In this case, any number of samples taken from the parent solution would be identical.

Periodicity and States of Matter

Periodic Table of Elements

Using the periodic table, elements are arranged by atomic number, similar characteristics, and electron configurations in a tabular format. The columns, called **groups**, are sorted by similar chemical properties and characteristics such as appearance and reactivity. This can be seen in the shiny texture of metals, the high melting points of alkali Earth metals, and the softness of post-transition metals. The rows are arranged by electron valance configurations and are called **periods**.

Periodic Table of the Elements

1A																	8A
1 H hydrogen 1.008	2A											3A	4A	5A	6A	7A	2 He helium 4.003
3 Li lithium 6.94	4 Be beryllium 9.012											5 B boron 10.81	6 C carbon 12.01	7 N nitrogen 14.01	8 O oxygen 16.00	9 F fluorine 19.00	10 Ne neon 20.18
11 Na sodium 22.99	12 Mg magnesium 24.31	3B	4B	5B	6B	7B		8B		1B	2B	13 Al aluminum 26.98	14 Si silicon 28.09	15 P phosphorus 30.97	16 S sulfur 32.06	17 Cl chlorine 35.45	18 Ar argon 39.95
19 K potassium 39.10	20 Ca calcium 40.08	21 Sc scandium 44.96	22 Ti titanium 47.88	23 V vanadium 50.94	24 Cr chromium 52.00	25 Mn manganese 54.94	26 Fe iron 55.85	27 Co cobalt 58.93	28 Ni nickel 58.69	29 Cu copper 63.55	30 Zn zinc 65.39	31 Ga gallium 69.72	32 Ge germanium 72.64	33 As arsenic 74.92	34 Se selenium 78.96	35 Br bromine 79.90	36 Kr krypton 83.79
37 Rb rubidium 85.47	38 Sr strontium 87.62	39 Y yttrium 88.91	40 Zr zirconium 91.22	41 Nb niobium 92.91	42 Mo molybdenum 95.96	43 Tc technetium (98)	44 Ru ruthenium 101.1	45 Rh rhodium 102.9	46 Pd palladium 106.4	47 Ag silver 107.9	48 Cd cadmium 112.4	49 In indium 114.8	50 Sn tin 118.7	51 Sb antimony 121.8	52 Te tellurium 127.6	53 I iodine 126.9	54 Xe xenon 131.3
55 Cs cesium 132.9	56 Ba barium 137.3	57-71	72 Hf hafnium 178.5	73 Ta tantalum 180.9	74 W tungsten 183.9	75 Re rhenium 186.2	76 Os osmium 190.2	77 Ir iridium 192.2	78 Pt platinum 195.1	79 Au gold 197.0	80 Hg mercury 200.5	81 Tl thallium 204.4	82 Pb lead 207.2	83 Bi bismuth 209.0	84 Po polonium (209)	85 At astatine (210)	86 Rn radon (222)
87 Fr francium (223)	88 Ra radium (226)	89-103	104 Rf rutherfordium (265)	105 Db dubnium (268)	106 Sg seaborgium (271)	107 Bh bohrium (270)	108 Hs hassium (277)	109 Mt meitnerium (276)	110 Ds darmstadtium (281)	111 Rg roentgenium (280)	112 Cn copernicium (285)	113 Uut ununtrium (284)	114 Fl flerovium (289)	115 Uup ununpentium (288)	116 Lv livermorium (293)	117 Uus ununseptium (294)	118 Uuo ununoctium (294)

Lanthanide Series

57 La lanthanum 138.9	58 Ce cerium 140.1	59 Pr praseodymium 140.9	60 Nd neodymium 144.2	61 Pm promethium (145)	62 Sm samarium 150.4	63 Eu europium 152.0	64 Gd gadolinium 157.2	65 Tb terbium 158.9	66 Dy dysprosium 162.5	67 Ho holmium 164.9	68 Er erbium 167.3	69 Tm thulium 168.9	70 Yb ytterbium 173.0	71 Lu lutetium 175.0

Actinide Series

89 Ac actinium (227)	90 Th thorium 232	91 Pa protactinium 231	92 U uranium 238	93 Np neptunium (237)	94 Pu plutonium (244)	95 Am americium (243)	96 Cm curium (247)	97 Bk berkelium (247)	98 Cf californium (251)	99 Es einsteinium (252)	100 Fm fermium (257)	101 Md mendelevium (258)	102 No nobelium (259)	103 Lr lawrencium (262)

Legend:
- Alkaline Metal
- Alkaline Earth
- Transition Metal
- Basic Metal
- Semimetal
- Nonmetal
- Halogen
- Noble Gas
- Lanthanide
- Actinide

316

The elements are set in ascending order from left to right by atomic number. As mentioned, the atomic number is the number of protons contained within the nucleus of the atom. For example, the element helium has an atomic number of 2 because it has two protons in its nucleus.

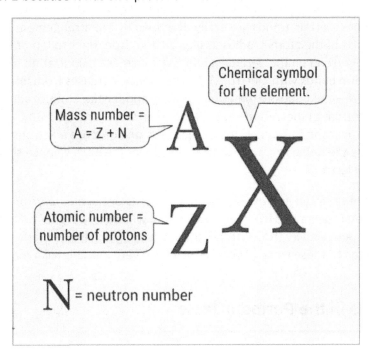

An element's mass number is calculated by adding the number of protons and neutrons of an atom together, while the atomic mass of an element is the weighted average of the naturally occurring atoms of a given element, or the relative abundance of isotopes that might be used in chemistry. For example, the atomic (mass) number of chlorine is 35; however, the atomic mass of chlorine is 35.5 amu (atomic mass unit). This discrepancy exists because there are many isotopes (meaning the nucleus could have 36 instead of 35 protons) occurring in nature. Given the prevalence of the various isotopes, the average of all of the atomic masses turns out to be 35.5 amu, which is slightly higher than chlorine's number on the periodic table. As another example, carbon has an atomic number of 12, but its atomic mass is 12.01 amu because, unlike chlorine, there are few naturally occurring isotopes to raise the average number.

Elements are arranged according to their valance electron configurations, which also contribute to trends in chemical properties. These properties help to further categorize the elements into blocks, including metals, non-metals, transition metals, alkali metals, alkali earth metals, metalloids, lanthanides, actinides, diatomics, post-transition metals, polyatomic non-metals, and noble gases. Noble gases (the far-right column) have a full outer electron valence shell. The elements in this block possess similar characteristics such as being colorless, odorless, and having low chemical reactivity. Another block, the metals, tend to be shiny, highly conductive, and easily form alloys with each other, non-metals, and noble gases.

The symbols of the elements on the periodic table are a single letter or a two-letter combination that is usually derived from the element's name. Many of the elements have Latin origins for their names, and their atomic symbols do not match their modern names. For example, iron is derived from the word **ferrum**, so its symbol is Fe, even though it is now called iron. The naming of the elements began with those of natural origin and their ancient names, which included the use of the ending "ium." This naming practice has been continued for all

Science

elements that have been named since the 1940s. Now, the names of new elements must be approved by the International Union of Pure and Applied Chemistry.

The elements on the periodic table are arranged by number and grouped by trends in their physical properties and electron configurations. Certain trends are easily described by the arrangement of the periodic table, which includes the increase of the atomic radius as elements go from right to left and from top to bottom on the periodic table. Another trend on the periodic table is the increase in ionization energy (or the tendency of an atom to attract and form bonds with electrons). This tendency increases from left to right and from bottom to top of the periodic table—the opposite directions of the trend for the atomic radius. The elements on the right side and near the bottom of the periodic table tend to attract electrons with the intent to gain, while the elements on the left and near the top usually lose, or give up, one or more electrons in order to bond. The only exceptions to this rule are the noble gases. Since the noble gases have full valence shells, they do not have a tendency to lose or gain electrons.

Chemical reactivity is another trend identifiable by the groupings of the elements on the periodic table. The chemical reactivity of metals decreases from left to right and while going higher on the table. Conversely, non-metals increase in chemical reactivity from left to right and while going lower on the table. Again, the noble gases present an exception to these trends because they have very low chemical reactivity.

Trends in the Periodic Table

Nonmetalic character

Ionization energy

Metallic character

Electron affinity

Atomic Radius

318

Acid-Base Chemistry

If something has a sour taste, it is acidic, and if something has a bitter taste, it is basic. Unfortunately, it can be extremely dangerous to ingest chemicals in an attempt to classify them as an acid or a base. Therefore, acids and bases are generally identified by the reactions they have when combined with water. An acid will increase the concentration of the hydrogen ion (H^+), while a base will increase the concentration of the hydroxide ion (OH^-).

To better categorize the varying strengths of acids and bases, the pH scale is used. The pH scale provides a logarithmic (base 10) grading to acids and bases based on their strength. The pH scale contains values from 0 through 14, with 7 being neutral. If a solution registers below 7 on the pH scale, it is considered an acid. If it registers higher than 7, it is considered a base. To perform a quick test on a solution, litmus paper can be used. A base will turn red litmus paper blue, whereas an acid will turn blue litmus paper red. To gauge the strength of an acid or base, a test of phenolphthalein can be used. An acid will turn red phenolphthalein colorless, and a base will turn colorless phenolphthalein pink. As demonstrated with these types of tests, acids and bases neutralize each other. When acids and bases react with one another, they produce salts (also called ionic substances).

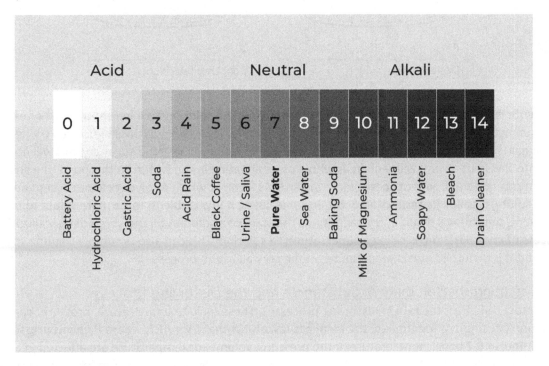

Solutions and Solubility

Types of Solutions

A **solution** is a homogenous mixture of more than one substance. A **solute** is another substance that can be dissolved into a substance called a **solvent**. If only a small amount of solute is dissolved in a solvent, the solution formed is said to be **diluted**. A solution is considered **concentrated** if a large amount of solute is

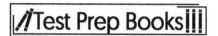

dissolved into the solvent. For example, water from a typical, unfiltered household tap is diluted because it contains other minerals in very small amounts.

Solution Concentration

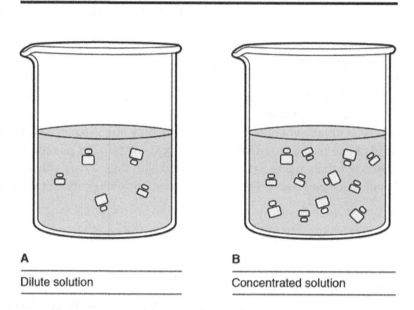

A
Dilute solution

B
Concentrated solution

If more solute is being added to a solvent, but not dissolving, the solution is called **saturated**. For example, when hummingbirds eat sugar-water from feeders, they prefer it as sweet as possible. When trying to dissolve enough sugar (solute) into the water (solvent), there will be a point where the sugar crystals will no longer dissolve into the solution and will remain as whole pieces floating in the water. At this point, the solution is considered saturated and cannot accept more sugar. This level, at which a solvent cannot accept and dissolve any more solute, is called its **saturation point**. In some cases, it is possible to force more solute to be dissolved into a solvent, but this will result in crystallization. The state of a solution on the verge of crystallization, or in the process of crystallization, is called a **supersaturated** solution. This can also occur in a solution that seems stable, but if it is disturbed, the change can begin the crystallization process.

Factors Affecting the Solubility of Substances and the Dissolving Process

Certain factors can affect the rate in dissolving processes. These include temperature, pressure, particle size, and agitation (stirring). As mentioned, the **ideal gas law** states that $PV = nRT$, where P equals pressure, V equals volume, and T equals temperature. If the pressure, volume, or temperature are affected in a system, it will affect the entire system. Specifically, if there is an increase in temperature, there will be an increase in the dissolving rate. An increase in the pressure can also increase the dissolving rate. Particle size and agitation can also influence the dissolving rate, since all of these factors contribute to the breaking of intermolecular forces that hold solute particles together. Once these forces are broken, the solute particles can link to particles in the solvent, thus dissolving the solute.

Physical Sciences: Principles of Motion and Energy

Forces and Motion

People have been studying the movement of objects since ancient times, sometimes prompted by curiosity, and sometimes by necessity. On earth, items move according to specific guidelines and have motion that is fairly predictable. In order to understand why an object moves along its path, it is important to understand what role forces have on influencing an object's movements. The term **force** describes an outside influence on an object. Force does not have to refer to something imparted by another object. Forces can act upon objects by touching them with a push or a pull, by friction, or without touch like a magnetic force or even gravity. Forces can affect the motion of an object.

In order to study an object's motion, the object must be locatable and describable. When locating an object's position, it can help to locate it relative to another known object, or put it into a frame of reference. This phrase means that if the placement of one object is known, it is easier to locate another object with respect to the position of the original object.

The measurement of an object's movement or change in position (x), over a change in time (t) is an object's speed. The measurement of speed with direction is **velocity**. A "change in position" refers to the difference in location of an object's starting point and an object's ending point. In science, the Greek letter **Delta**, Δ, represents a change.

Equation:
$$velocity \ (v) = \frac{\Delta x}{\Delta t}$$

Position is measured in meters, and time is measured in seconds. The standard measurement for velocity is meters/second (m/s).

$$\frac{\text{meters}}{\text{second}} = \frac{\text{m}}{\text{s}}$$

The measurement of an object's change in velocity over time is an object's **acceleration**. **Gravity** is considered to be a form of acceleration.

Equation:
$$acceleration \ (a) = \frac{\Delta v}{\Delta t}$$

Velocity is measured in meters/second and time is measured in seconds. The standard measurement for acceleration is meters/second² (m/s²).

$$\frac{\text{meters}}{\text{second}} \div \text{second} = \frac{\text{meters}}{\text{second}^2} = \frac{\text{m}}{\text{s}^2}$$

For example, consider a car traveling down the road. The speed can be measured by calculating how far the car is traveling over a certain period of time. However, since the car is traveling in a direction (north, east, south, west), the distance over time is actually the car's velocity. It can be confusing, as many people will often interchange the words speed and velocity. But if something is traveling a certain distance, during a certain time period, in a direction, this is the object's velocity. Velocity is speed with direction.

The change in an object's velocity over a certain amount of time is the object's acceleration. If the driver of that car keeps pressing on the gas pedal and increasing the velocity, the car would have a change in velocity

321

over the change in time and would be accelerating. The reverse could be said if the driver were depressing the brake and the car was slowing down; it would have a negative acceleration, or be decelerating. Since acceleration also has a direction component, it is possible for a car to accelerate without changing speed. If an object changes direction, it is accelerating.

Motion creates something called **momentum**. This is a calculation of an object's mass multiplied by its velocity. Momentum can be described as the amount an object wants to continue moving along its current course. Momentum in a straight line is called **linear momentum**. Just as energy can be transferred and conserved, so can momentum.

For example, a car and a truck moving at the same velocity down a highway will not have the same momentum, because they do not have the same mass. The mass of the truck is greater than that of the car, therefore the truck will have more momentum. In a head-on collision, the vehicles would be expected to slide in the same direction of the truck's original motion because the truck has a greater momentum.

The amount of force during a length of time creates an **impulse**. This means that if a force acts on an object during a given amount of time, it will have a determined impulse. However, if the length of time can be extended, the force will be less, due to the conservation of momentum.

Consider another example: when catching a fast baseball, it helps soften the blow of the ball to follow through, or cradle the catch. This technique is simply extending the time of the application of the force of the ball, so the impact of the ball does not hurt the hand. As a final example, if a martial arts expert wants to break a board by executing a chop from their hand, they need to exert a force on a small point on the boards, extremely quickly. If they slow down the time of the impact from the force of their hand, they will probably injure their hand and not break the board.

Displacement

Displacement refers to an object's complete change in position and is considered a vector. Quantities that are completely described by direction and magnitude are vector quantities. Displacement is represented by an arrow, which points from an initial to a final position. Displacement (Δx) can be represented mathematically as:

$$\Delta x = x_f - x_i$$

The final position is given by x_f and the initial position by x_i. To find the displacement of an object, consider a car that moves along a path through points A, B, C, and D. The magnitude of the displacement will be equal to the distance of AD, which can be determined by the Pythagorean theorem.

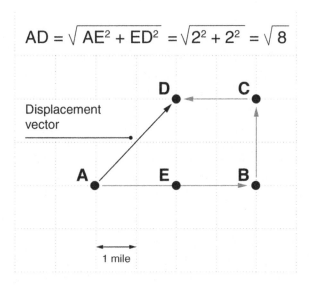

$$AD = \sqrt{AE^2 + ED^2} = \sqrt{2^2 + 2^2} = \sqrt{8}$$

The magnitude of the displacement will be equal to the distance of AD, which represents the difference between the initial and final positions.

Friction

Friction is a force that opposes motion. It can be caused by a number of materials; there is even friction caused by air. Whenever two differing materials touch, rub, or pass by each other, it will create friction, or an oppositional force, unless the interaction occurs in a true vacuum. To move an object across a floor, the force exerted on the object must overcome the frictional force keeping the object in place. Friction is also why people can walk on surfaces. Without the oppositional force of friction to a shoe pressing on the floor, a person would not be able to grip the floor to walk—similar to the challenge of walking on ice. Without friction, shoes slip and are unable to help people propel forward and walk.

Newton's Three Laws of Motion

Sir Isaac Newton spent a great deal of time studying objects, forces, and how an object's motion responds to forces. Newton made great advancements by using mathematics to describe the motion of objects and to predict future motions of objects by applying his mathematical models to situations. Through his extensive research, Newton is credited for summarizing the basic laws of motion for objects here on Earth. These laws are as follows:

First Law

The first law is the **law of inertia**. An object in motion remains in motion, unless acted upon by an outside force. An object at rest remains at rest, unless acted upon by an outside force. Simply put, inertia is the natural tendency of an object to continue along with what it is already doing; an outside force would have to act upon the object to make it change its course. This includes an object that is sitting still. The inertia of an object is relative to its momentum.

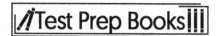

Example: If a car is driving at a constant speed in a constant direction (also called a constant velocity), it would take a force in a different direction to change the path of the car. Conversely, if the car is sitting still, it would take a force greater than that of friction from any direction to make that stationary car move.

Second Law

The force (F) on an object is equal to the mass (m) multiplied by the acceleration (a) on that object. **Mass** (m) refers to the amount of a substance and **acceleration** (a) refers to a rate of velocity over time. In the case of an object falling on Earth, the value of gravity will be placed in for acceleration (a). In the case of an object at rest on Earth, gravity is placed in for acceleration (a), and the force calculated by $F = ma$ is called **Weight** (W). It is important to discern that an object's mass (measured in kilograms, kg) is not the same as an object's weight (measured in Newtons, N). Weight is the mass times the gravity.

Example: The gravity on the earth's moon is considerably less than the gravity on earth. Therefore, the weight of an object on the earth's moon would be considerably less than the weight of the object on earth. In each case, a different value for acceleration/gravity would be used in the equation $F = ma$. Mass is used to calculate weight, and they are not the same.

Example: If a raisin is dropped into a bowl of pudding, it would make a small indentation and stick in the pudding a bit, but if a grapefruit is dropped into the same bowl of pudding, it would splatter the pudding out of the bowl and most likely hit the bottom of the bowl. Even though both items are accelerating at the same rate (gravity), the mass of the grapefruit is larger than that of the raisin; therefore, the force with which the grapefruit hits the bowl of pudding is considerably larger than the force from the raisin hitting the bowl of pudding.

Third Law

The third law of motion states that for every action there is an equal and opposite reaction. If someone pounds a fist on a table, the reactionary force from the table causes the person to feel a sharp force on the fist. The magnitude of the force felt on the fist increases the harder that they pound on the table. It should be noted that action/reaction pairs occur simultaneously. As the fist applies a force on the table, the table instantaneously applies an equal and opposite force on the fist.

Example: Imagine a person is wearing ice skates on ice and attempts to push on a heavy sled sitting in front of them. They will be pushed in the direction opposite of their push on the sled; the push the skater is experiencing is equal and opposite to the force they are exerting on the sled. This is a good example of how the icy surface helps to lessen the effects of friction and allows the reactionary force to be more easily observed.

Forces are anything acting upon an object either in motion or at rest; this includes friction and gravity. These forces are often depicted by using a force diagram or free body diagram. A **force diagram** shows an object as the focal point, with arrows denoting all the forces acting upon the object. The direction of the head of the

324

arrow indicates the direction of the force. The object at the center can also be exerting forces on things in its surroundings.

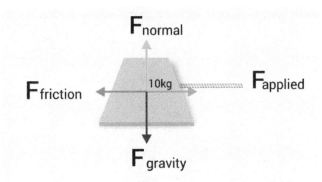

Equilibrium

If an object is in constant motion or at rest (its acceleration equals zero), the object is said to be in **equilibrium**. It does not imply that there are no forces acting upon the object, but that all of the forces are balanced in order for the situation to continue in its current state. This can be thought of as a "balanced" situation.

Note that if an object is resting on top of a mountain peak or traveling at a constant velocity down the side of that mountain, both situations describe a state of equilibrium.

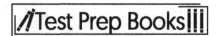

Simple Machines

A simple machine is a mechanical device that changes the direction or magnitude of a force. There are six basic types of simple machines: lever, wedge, screw, inclined plane, wheel and axle, and pulley.

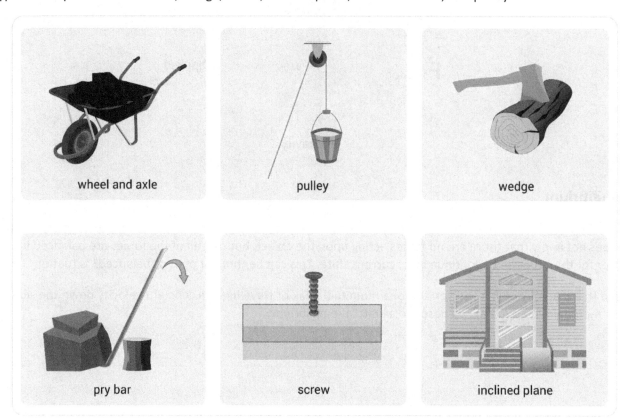

Here is how each type works and an example:

- A lever helps lift heavy items higher with less force, such as a crowbar lifting a large cast iron lid.

- A wedge helps apply force to a specific area by focusing the pressure, such as an axe splitting a tree.

- An inclined plane, such as a loading dock ramp, helps move heavy items up vertical distances with less force.

- A screw is an inclined plane wrapped around an axis and allows more force to be applied by extending the distance of the plane. For example, a screw being turned into a piece of wood provides greater securing strength than hitting a nail into the wood.

- A wheel and axle allows the use of rotational force around an axis to assist with applying force. For example, a wheelbarrow makes it easier to haul large loads by employing a wheel and axle at the front.

- A pulley is an application of a wheel and axle with the addition of cords or ropes and it helps move objects vertically. For example, pulling a bucket out of a well is easier with a pulley and ropes.

Using a simple machine employs an advantage to the user. This is referred to as the mechanical advantage. It can be calculated by comparing the force input by the user to the simple machine with the force output from the use of the machine (also displayed as a ratio).

$$Mechanical Advantage = \frac{output force}{input force}$$

$$MA = \frac{F_{out}}{F_{in}}$$

In the following instance of using a lever, it can be helpful to calculate the torque, or circular force, necessary to move something. This is also employed when using a wrench to loosen a bolt.

$$Torque = F \times distance of lever arm from the axis of rotation \ (called \ the \ moment \ arm)$$

$$T = F \times d$$

Forms of Energy

The entire universe is composed of matter and energy. Matter refers to a substance that occupies space; it can be detected by touch, smell, or vision. Energy is generally defined as a property of a specific system that can perform work. Energy can be observed when energy is transformed or transferred from one substance to another.

Nuclear energy is a pollution-free energy that utilizes uranium and plutonium elements as nuclear fuel and contains the most concentrated form of usable energy. For a given mass of nuclear fuel, nuclear reactions release a million times more energy compared to chemical reactions.

Solar energy is energy that is created from the Sun and may be converted to electrical or thermal energy. Solar energy is created by a nuclear fusion process whereby protons of hydrogen atoms collide and fuse to form a helium atom. The radiant energy emitted by the Sun consists of a spectrum of electromagnetic energy. Solar energy in the form of ultraviolet radiation is primarily absorbed by the Earth's atmosphere but felt as thermal energy, causing sunburn when UV rays contact the surface of the skin.

The Sun acts as a source of wind and hydroelectric energy. Most of the heat arriving from the Sun comes as infrared radiation. The uneven heating of the Earth's surfaces, in addition to the Earth's rotation, results in wind formation, which is the movement of gaseous molecules (nitrogen, oxygen, etc.) called air. Large wind turbines that are stationed across the country harness the wind to produce electrical or mechanical energy. The kinetic energy created by the wind is converted into mechanical power, which can be transformed into electricity using a generator.

Chemical energy is stored energy found in atoms and molecules. Fuels like coal, natural gas, wood, and petroleum are sources of chemical energy. As fuel is burned, chemical energy is converted to thermal energy— e.g., the combustion of gasoline in a car. The combustion or chemical reaction of octane with oxygen gas produces carbon dioxide, water, and heat.

Electrical energy is possible with sunlight. When sunlight evaporates water, gaseous water collects in the air. The water later falls to the Earth as rain and collects into rivers, which can flow against a water dam. As water is directed to the turbines of a dam, it generates electricity.

327

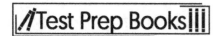

Magnetic energy is derived from the motion of negatively charged electrons around the protons found in atoms and molecules. An electrical current has an associated magnetic field; the movement of electrons creates a magnetic field. Based on Maxwell's equations, magnetic and electrical energy are considered one force and are known as electromagnetic energy.

Electromagnetic energy is a type of energy that consists of magnetic and electrical components. Light energy consists of a spectrum of electromagnetic radiation or energy that differs by wavelength and frequency. Light emitted by the Sun is described as discrete packets of energy called photons. Gamma rays have the highest frequency and shortest wavelengths. On the opposite end of the spectrum, radio waves have the lowest frequencies and longest wavelengths.

Sound energy involves the physical vibration of matter and refers to the movement of energy in the form of waves through substances such as air or water. Sound energy is created when a substance vibrates, which involves compression and expansion of matter through air or water.

Electricity and Magnetism

Electrical Nature of Common Materials

Generally, an atom carries no net charge because the positive charges of the protons in the nucleus balance the negative charges of the electrons in the outer shells of the atom. This is considered to be electrically neutral. However, since electrons are the only portion of the atom known to have the freedom to "move," this can cause an object to become electrically charged. This happens either through a gain or a loss of electrons. Electrons have a negative charge, so a gain creates a net negative charge for the object. On the contrary, a loss of electrons creates a positive charge for the object. This charge can also be focused on specific areas of an object, causing a notable interaction between charged objects. For example, if a person rubs a balloon on a carpet, the balloon transfers some of is electrons to the carpet. So, if that person were to hold a balloon near their hair, the electrons in the "neutral" hair would make the hair stand on end. This is due to the electrons wanting to fill the deficit of electrons on the balloon. Unless electrically forced into a charged state, most natural objects in nature tend toward reestablishing and maintaining a neutral charge.

When dealing with charges, it is easiest to remember that **like charges repel** each other and **opposite charges attract** each other. Therefore, negatives and positives attract, while two positives or two negatives will repel each other. Similarly, when two charges come near each other, they exert a force on one another.

When materials readily transfer electricity or electrons, or can easily accept or lose electrons, they are considered to be good conductors. The transferring of electricity is called **conductivity**. If a material does not readily accept the transfer of electrons or readily loses electrons, it is considered to be an **insulator**. For example, plastic is an insulator because it does not transfer electricity. Copper wire, on the other hand, easily transfers electricity; therefore, it is a good conductor.

Basic Properties of Magnetic Fields and Forces

Consider two straight rods that are made from magnetic material. They will naturally have a negative end (pole) and a positive end (pole). These charged poles react just like any charged item: opposite charges attract and like charges repel. They will attract each other when arranged positive pole to negative pole. However, if one rod is turned around, the two rods will now repel each other due to the alignment of negative to negative and positive to positive. These types of forces can also be created and amplified by using an electric current. For example, sending an electric current through a stretch of wire creates an electromagnetic force around the wire from the charge of the current. This force exists as long as the flow of electricity is sustained. This

328

magnetic force can also attract and repel other items with magnetic properties. Depending on the strength of the current in the wire, a greater or smaller magnetic force can be generated around the wire. As soon as the current is stopped, the magnetic force also stops.

Transformations Between Different Forms of Energy

As stated by the conservation of energy, energy cannot be created or destroyed. If a system gains or loses energy, it is transformed within a single system from one type of energy to another or transferred from one system to another. For example, if the roller coaster system has potential energy that transfers to kinetic energy, the kinetic energy can then be transferred into thermal energy or heat released through braking as the coaster descends the hill. Energy can also transform from the chemical energy inside of a battery into the electrical energy that lights a train set. The energy released through nuclear fusion (when atoms are joined together, they release heat) is what supplies power plants with the energy for electricity. All energy is transferred from one form to another through different reactions. It can also be transferred through the simple action of atoms bumping into each other, causing a transfer of heat.

Heat and Temperature

Heat is one type of energy transfer that is due to a difference in temperature. Thermal energy is associated with heat and is the total kinetic energy found within a substance or system of particles. For any phase of a substance (solid, liquid, gas), atoms and molecules are generally moving. A cool cup of water consists of water molecules that are moving relatively slower compared to a hot cup of water. For molecules to move faster, cool water must absorb more heat from its surroundings. The thermal energy of the cool water is increased when warmer water, e.g., boiling water, is transferred to the cup containing cool water. The thermal energy of the cool water system will increase since it absorbs heat from the boiling water, which increases the kinetic energy of the cool water.

Temperature describes the average kinetic energy of a system of particles, is not synonymous with heat, and does not measure heat. Temperature is derived from the use of an instrument, like a thermometer, which uses a relative scale to determine if a substance is hot (high kinetic energy) or cold (low kinetic energy). While heat is concerned with thermal energy, temperature is focused on the kinetic energy of a substance. The Fahrenheit, Celsius, and Kelvin scales are the most common temperature scales.

Temperature Scales

There are three main temperature scales used in science. The scale most often used in the United States is the **Fahrenheit** scale. This scale is based on the measurement of water freezing at 32^0 F and water boiling at 212^0 F. The Celsius scale uses 0^0 C as the temperature for water freezing and 100^0 C for water boiling. The Celsius scale is the most widely used in the scientific community. The accepted measurement by the International System of Units (from the French Système international d'unités), or SI, for temperature is the Kelvin scale. This is the scale employed in thermodynamics, since its zero is the basis for absolute zero, or the unattainable temperature, when matter no longer exhibits degradation.

The conversions between the temperature scales are as follows:

- ^{0}Fahrenheit to ^{0}Celsius: $^0C = \frac{5}{9}(^0F - 32)$
- ^{0}Celsius to ^{0}Fahrenheit: $^0F = \frac{9}{5}(^0C) + 32$
- ^{0}Celsius to Kelvin: $K = {^0C} + 273.15$

329

Transfer and Basic Measurement of Thermal Energy

There are three basic ways in which energy is transferred. The first is through **radiation**. Radiation is transmitted through electromagnetic waves and it does not need a medium to travel (it can travel in a vacuum). This is how the sun warms the Earth, and typically applies to large objects with great amounts of heat or objects with a large difference in their heat measurements.

The second form of heat transfer is **convection**. Convection involves the movement of "fluids" from one place to another. (The term **fluid** does not necessarily apply to a liquid, but any substance in which the molecules can slide past each other, such as gases.) It is this movement that transfers the heat to or from an area. Generally, convective heat transfer occurs through diffusion, which is when heat moves from areas of higher concentrations of particles to those of lower concentrations of particles and less heat. This process of flowing heat can be assisted or amplified through the use of fans and other methods of forcing the molecules to move.

The final process is called **conduction**. Conduction involves transferring heat through the touching of molecules. Molecules can either bump into each other to transfer heat, or they may already be touching each other and transfer the heat through this connection. For example, imagine a circular burner on an electric stove top. The coil begins to glow orange near the base of the burner that is connected to the stove because it heats up first. Since the burner is one continuous piece of metal, the molecules are touching each other. As they pass heat along the coil, it begins to glow all the way to the end.

To determine the amount of heat required to warm the coil in the above example, the type of material from which the coil is made must be known. The quantity of heat required to raise one gram of a substance one degree Celsius (or Kelvin) at a constant pressure is called **specific heat**. This measurement can be calculated for masses of varying substances by using the following equation:

$$Q = C_p \times m \times \Delta T$$

Where Q is the specific heat, C_p is the specific heat capacity of the material being used, m is the mass of the substance being used, and ΔT is the change in temperature.

A calorimeter is used to measure the heat of a reaction (either expelled or absorbed) and the temperature changes in a controlled system. A simple calorimeter can be made by using an insulated coffee cup with a thermometer inside. For this example, a lid of some sort would be preferred to prevent any escaping heat that could be lost by evaporation or convection.

Sources of Light

Photons are particles of light that consist of discrete energy packets (E) of electromagnetic radiation. The energy of light (E) is given by the equation:

$$E = \frac{hc}{\lambda}; \quad c: speed\ of\ light \quad h: Plancks\ constant \quad \lambda: wavelength$$

Incandescent bulbs emit all wavelengths of visible light (red, orange, yellow, green, blue, and purple). These bulbs typically contain tungsten filaments encased in an inert gas to avoid oxidation. As electricity moves through the filament, it heats up due to the metal's resistance to the current. The electrons in a tungsten atom absorb a fixed energy (E) due to heat, causing the electrons in a tungsten atom to move from a less to more excited state. The observed light is due to the emission of a photon, which occurs when the excited electrons

330

move back to a less excited or stable ground state (Figure X). Each atom has a unique emission or colored spectrum. A hot tungsten filament emits every visible frequency and appears white. Neon gas emits frequencies corresponding to orange-red light. Neon signs are made of a sealed glass tube containing metal electrodes filled with rarefied neon gas and other gases at low pressure. When a high electrical voltage is applied to the tube, the electrons separate from the neon atoms, and each particle moves rapidly. When the ionized neon atoms recapture electrons, the electrons move from an excited to less excited (ground) state on the atom and release a photon, which is responsible for the colored glow:

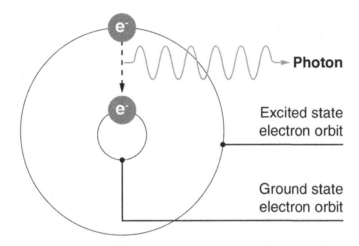

The Sun emits light at different frequencies or wavelengths corresponding to a given energy (E). While the Sun can emit a spectrum of wavelengths ranging from X-rays to radio waves, other light sources on Earth can only emit a specific wavelength.

Interactions of Light with Matter

The wave-particle nature of light constantly interacts with matter. When light passes through the cornea of the eye, the eye lens focuses the light on the retina, located at the back interior of the eye's wall. The retina and other regions such as the fovea consist of millions of light-sensitive cells called photoreceptors, which come in two types: rod and cone cells. Rod cells are long and straight structures that are sensitive to light and assist with seeing in the dark. Cones are oval-shaped cells that are sensitive to color. Both cells contain a disc with a different pigment molecule corresponding to a unique color. For example, cones contain a protein known as photopsin, which comes in red, green, or blue types. Rods consist of the light receptor-photopigment protein called rhodopsin. When the cone or rod absorbs a specific wavelength or color of light, an electrical signal is produced and sent to the brain. In rods, the phototransduction pathway is initiated within the discs. Rhodopsin contains a trans-retinal molecule that absorbs a photon of light, which results in isomerization to the molecule called cis-retinal. Retinal isomerization changes the protein's overall conformational structure of rhodopsin, creating a signal that allows the brain to recognize objects in low light.

Waves

Waves are periodic disturbances in a gas, liquid, or solid that are created as energy is transmitted. Each part of a wave has a different name and is used in different calculations. The four parts of a wave are the crest, the trough, the amplitude, and the wavelength. The **crest** is the highest point, while the **trough** is the lowest. The **amplitude** is the distance between a peak and the average of the wave; it is also the distance between a trough and the average of the wave, but an amplitude is always positive, since it is an absolute value. Finally, the distance between one wave and the exact same place on the next wave is the **wavelength.**

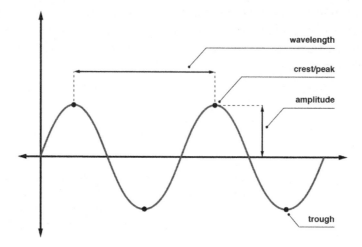

With amplitude and wavelength, it is possible to describe any wave, but an important question still remains unanswered: How fast is the wave traveling? A wave's speed can be shown as either its period or its frequency. A wave's period, T, is how long it takes for the wave to travel one wavelength, while a wave's frequency, f, is how many wavelengths are traveled in one second. These are inversely related, so they are reciprocals of each other, as shown below:

$$f = \frac{1}{T} \text{ and } T = \frac{1}{f}$$

The largest categories of waves are electromagnetic waves and mechanical waves. **Electromagnetic waves** can transmit energy through a vacuum and do not need a medium to travel through, examples of which are light, radio, microwaves, gamma rays, and other forms of electromagnetism. **Mechanical waves** can only transmit energy through another form of matter called a medium. The particles of the medium are shifted as the wave moves through the medium, and can be anything from solids to liquids to gasses. Examples of mechanical waves include auditory sounds heard by human ears in the air as well as percussive shocks like earthquakes.

There are two different forms of waves: transverse and longitudinal waves. **Transverse** waves are waves in which particles of the medium move in a direction perpendicular to the direction waves move, as in most electromagnetic waves. **Compression**, or longitudinal, waves are waves in which the particles of the medium move in a direction parallel to the direction the waves move, as in most mechanical waves. A good example of a longitudinal wave is sound. Waves travel within a medium at a speed that is determined by the wavelength (λ) and frequency (f) of the wave.

$$v = f\lambda$$

There is a proportional relationship between the amplitude of a wave and the potential energy in the wave. This means the taller the wave, the more stored energy it is transmitting.

Basic Wave Phenomena

When a wave crosses a boundary or travels from one medium to another, certain things occur. If the wave can travel through one medium into another medium, it experiences **refraction.** This is the bending of the wave

332

from one medium to another due to a change in density of the mediums, and thus, the speed of the wave changes. For example, when a pencil is sitting in half of a glass of water, a side view of the glass makes the pencil appear to be bent at the water level. What the viewer is seeing is the refraction of light waves traveling from the air into the water. Since the wave speed is slowed in water, the change makes the pencil appear bent.

When a wave hits a medium that it cannot penetrate, it is bounced back in an action called **reflection**. For example, when light waves hit a mirror, they are reflected, or bounced, off the mirror. This can cause it to seem like there is more light in the room, since there is a "doubling back" of the initial wave. This same phenomenon also causes people to be able to see their reflection in a mirror.

When a wave travels through a slit or around an obstacle, it is known as **diffraction**. A light wave will bend around an obstacle or through a slit and cause what is called a **diffraction pattern**. When the waves bend around an obstacle, it causes the addition of waves and the spreading of light on the other side of the opening.

Dispersion is used to describe the splitting of a single wave by refracting its components into separate parts. For example, if a wave of white light is sent through a dispersion prism, the light appears as its separate rainbow-colored components, due to each colored wavelength being refracted in the prism.

When wavelengths hit boundaries, different things occur. Objects will absorb certain wavelengths of light and reflect others, depending on the boundaries. This becomes important when an object appears to be a certain color. The color of an object is not actually within that object, but rather, in the wavelengths being transmitted by that object. For example, if a table appears to be red, that means the table is absorbing all other wavelengths of visible light except those of the red wavelength. The table is reflecting, or transmitting, the wavelengths associated with red back to the human eye, and so it appears red.

Interference describes when an object affects the path of a wave, or another wave interacts with a wave. Waves interacting with each other can result in either **constructive interference** or **destructive interference**, based on their positions. With constructive interference, the waves are in sync with each other and combine to reinforce each other. In the case of deconstructive interference, the waves are out of sync and reduce the effect of each other to some degree. In **scattering**, the boundary can change the direction or energy of a wave, thus altering the entire wave. **Polarization** changes the oscillations of a wave and can alter its appearance in light waves. For example, polarized sunglasses remove the "glare" from sunlight by altering the oscillation pattern observed by the wearer.

When a wave hits a boundary and is completely reflected, or if it cannot escape from one medium to another, it is called **total internal reflection**. This effect can be seen in the diamonds with a brilliant cut. The angle cut on the sides of the diamond causes the light hitting the diamond to be completely reflected back inside the gem, making it appear brighter and more colorful than a diamond with different angles cut into its surface.

The **Doppler effect** applies to situations with both light and sound waves. The premise of the Doppler effect is that, based upon the relative position or movement of a source and an observer, waves can seem shorter or longer than they actually are. When the Doppler effect is noted with sound, it warps the noise being heard by the observer. This makes the pitch or frequency seem shorter or higher as the source is approaching, and then longer or lower as the source is getting farther away. The frequency/pitch of the source never actually changes, but the sound in respect to the observer makes it seem like the sound has changed. This can be observed when a siren passes by an observer on the road. The siren sounds much higher in pitch as it approaches the observer and then lower after it passes and is getting farther away.

The Doppler effect also applies to situations involving light waves. An observer in space would see light approaching as being shorter wavelengths than the light actually is, causing it to look blue. When the light wave gets farther away, the light would appear red because of the apparent elongation of the wavelength. This is called the **red-blue shift**.

Light

The movement of light is described like the movement of waves. Light travels with a wave front, has an amplitude (height from the neutral), a cycle or wavelength, a period, and energy. Light travels at approximately 3.00×10^8 m/s and is faster than anything created by humans thus far.

Light is commonly referred to by its measured wavelengths, or the distance between two successive crests or troughs in a wave. Types of light with the longest wavelengths include radio, TV, and micro, and infrared waves. The next set of wavelengths are detectable by the human eye and create the **visible spectrum**. The visible spectrum has wavelengths of 10^{-7} m, and the colors seen are red, orange, yellow, green, blue, indigo, and violet. Beyond the visible spectrum are shorter wavelengths (also called the **electromagnetic spectrum**) containing ultraviolet light, X-rays, and gamma rays. The wavelengths outside of the visible light range can be harmful to humans if they are directly exposed or are exposed for long periods of time.

Basic Optics

When reflecting light, a mirror can be used to observe a virtual (not real) image. A **plane mirror** is a piece of glass with a coating in the background to create a reflective surface. An image is what the human eye sees when light is reflected off the mirror in an unmagnified manner. If a **curved mirror** is used for reflection, the image seen will not be a true reflection. Instead, the image will either be enlarged or miniaturized compared to its actual size. Curved mirrors can also make the object appear closer or farther away than the actual distance the object is from the mirror.

Lenses can be used to refract or bend light to form images. Examples of lenses are the human eye, microscopes, and telescopes. The human eye interprets the refraction of light into images that humans understand to be actual size. **Microscopes** allow objects that are too small for the unaided human eye to be enlarged enough to be seen. **Telescopes** allow objects to be viewed that are too far away to be seen with the unaided eye. **Prisms** are pieces of glass that can have a wavelength of light enter one side and appear to be divided into its component wavelengths on the other side. This is due to the ability of the prism to slow certain wavelengths more than others.

Sound

Sound travels in waves and is the movement of vibrations through a medium. It can travel through air (gas), land, water, etc. For example, the noise a human hears in the air is the vibration of the waves as they reach the ear. The human brain translates the different frequencies (pitches) and intensities of the vibrations to determine what created the noise.

A tuning fork has a predetermined frequency because of the length and thickness of its tines. When struck, it allows vibrations between the two tines to move the air at a specific rate. This creates a specific tone, or note, for that size of tuning fork. The number of vibrations over time is also steady for that tuning fork and can be matched with a frequency. All pitches heard by the human ear are categorized by using frequency and are measured in Hertz (cycles per second).

The level of sound in the air is measured with sound level meters on a decibel (dB) scale. These meters respond to changes in air pressure caused by sound waves and measure sound intensity. One decibel is 1/10th of a *bel*, named after Alexander Graham Bell, the inventor of the telephone. The decibel scale is logarithmic, so it is measured in factors of 10. This means, for example, that a 10 dB increase on a sound meter equates to a 10-fold increase in sound intensity.

Renewable and Non-Renewable Energy Sources

All presently available energy resources have pros and cons to their utilization. Fossil fuels are a non-renewable resource created from organic sources (such as coal). Two pros for using fossil fuels include the existence of systems that are already in place to use this form of energy, and that a fairly large resource of fossil fuel material still exists. However, burning this resource for energy is a primary contributor to greenhouse gas production and disrupts many ecosystems. Sources are concentrated in certain areas around the globe, which has led to geopolitical conflict and tension. Additionally, the current rate of expenditure is faster than the rate of replenishment. This fact has led to research and development in the alternative energy industry.

Alternative energy sources include any source of energy that protects the environment and can be used as an alternative to fossil fuels. The term usually refers to solar, wind, water, and biomass power, but additional options also exist. In general, alternative energy sources are considered to be sustainable and conserving measures. However, a major con is that the industry is relatively new, and research is ongoing to utilize these sources in the most productive, efficient, and wide-reaching ways. Specific pros and cons of different types of alternative energy sources are listed below.

Nuclear fuel is a renewable resource created by the splitting of uranium atoms. This source greatly limits air pollution, as greenhouse gas emissions are low. Nuclear fuel also enjoys a relatively low production cost. However, upfront costs to build safe facilities are high. Nuclear accidents are also likely to be catastrophic to life, and adequate and safe storage of radioactive waste is another issue yet to resolve.

Hydropower refers to a renewable resource created from fast-flowing water sources that may be natural or man-made. This source is cheap, helps with global irrigation, and can provide drinking water. Disadvantages to hydropower include its inevitable disruption to many ecosystems; facilities are costly and may displace residents; and finally, while the risk of flooding is moderate, the risk of pollution is high.

Wind power refers to a renewable resource created by harnessing air flow. This source is abundant, cheap, clean, and does not require water or large facilities to use. However, wind has to be moving swiftly in order to

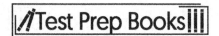

be harnessed, and it cannot be stored. Commercializing a resource that easily crosses man-made borders can become complicated from legal and business standpoints.

Solar power is a renewable resource that uses the sun's rays for energy. This source is abundant, easily accessible, receives capital funding from both government and private sources, and requires minimal maintenance. However, even with subsidizing, initial production can be costly. It requires land or roof space for cell panels, and utilizes large-scale batteries. These can be a major contributor to waste and pollution.

Finally, **geothermal power** is a renewable resource that uses the Earth's core temperature to generate energy. This resource does not involve combustion (therefore no greenhouse gas emission), yet is three-to-five times more efficient than other sources. It can be used to heat or cool any residential or commercial space. However, utilizing this resource has a high upfront cost. It also requires a large amount of water, and can cause underground and well water damage. Additionally, emergency events, such as geyser eruptions and landslides, have a high risk of being catastrophic to life.

Life Sciences: Structure of Living Organisms and Their Function

Levels of Organization

There are two distinct types of cells that make up most living organisms: **prokaryotic** and **eukaryotic**. Both types of cells are enclosed by a cell membrane, which is selectively permeable. Selective permeability essentially means that the membrane is a gatekeeper, allowing certain molecules and ions in and out, and keeping unwanted ones at bay, at least until they are ready for use. Prokaryotes contain ribosomes, DNA, cytoplasm, a cell membrane, a cytoskeleton, and a cell wall. Eukaryotes vary between kingdoms but contain all of these structures except a cell wall because animal cells require so much mobility. One major difference between these types of cells is that in eukaryotic cells, the cell's DNA is enclosed in a membrane-bound nucleus, whereas in prokaryotic cells, the cell's DNA is in a region—called the **nucleoid**—that is not enclosed by a membrane. Another major difference is that eukaryotic cells contain organelles, while prokaryotic cells do not have organelles.

Prokaryotic cells include **bacteria** and archaea. They do not have a nucleus or any membrane-bound organelles, are unicellular organisms, and are generally very small in size. Eukaryotic cells include animal, plant, fungus, and protist cells. Almost all types of protist and some species in fungi kingdom are unicellular, but they still have the complicated organelles of eukaryotes. A few protists, almost all fungi, and all plants and animals are multicellular. Multicellularity leads to development of structures that are perfectly designed for their function. **Fungi** are microorganisms such as yeasts, molds, and mushrooms. Their distinguishing characteristic is the chitin that is in their cell walls. **Protists** are organisms that are not classified as animals, plants, or fungi, and they do not form tissues.

There are about two hundred different types of cells in the human body. Cells group together to form **biological** tissues, and tissues combine to form organs, such as the heart and kidneys. Organs that work together to perform vital functions of the human body form organ systems. There are eleven organ systems in the human body: skeletal, muscular, urinary, nervous, digestive, endocrine, reproductive, respiratory, cardiovascular, integumentary, and lymphatic. Although each system has its own unique function, they all rely on each other, either directly or indirectly, to operate properly. The structures of all of these combinations allow for the maximum functionality of an organism, as demonstrated by the nervous system.

A **neuron** is a cell in the nervous system designed to send and receive electrical impulses. Neurons have dendrites, which are sensors waiting to receive a message. Neurons also have an **axon**, a long arm that sends the message to the neighboring neuron. The axon also has insulation known as **myelin** that speeds the message along. Many neurons combine to form a **nerve**, the tissue of the nervous system, which is like a long wire. The structure of this nerve is perfect—it is a long cable whose function is to send signals to the brain so the brain can process the information and respond. Nerve tissue combines with other tissue to form the **brain**, a complex structure of many parts.

The brain also has glands (epithelial tissue) that release hormones to control processes in our body. The brain and spinal cord together form the central nervous system that controls the stimulus/response signaling in our body. The nervous system coordinates with the circulatory system to make our heart beat, the digestive system to control food digestion, the muscular system to move an arm, the respiratory system to facilitate breathing, and all other body systems to make the entire organism functional. Cells are the basic building block in our bodies, and their structure is critical for their function and the function of the tissues, organs, and systems that they comprise.

The following table lists organ systems in the human body:

Name	Function	Main organs
Nervous	Detect stimuli and direct response	Brain and spinal cord
Circulatory	Pump blood to deliver oxygen to cells so they can perform cellular respiration	Heart
Respiratory	Breathe in oxygen (reactant for cellular respiration) and release carbon dioxide waste	Lungs
Muscular	Movement	Heart and muscles
Digestive	Break down food so that glucose can be delivered to cells for energy	Stomach, small intestine, lots of others
Skeletal	Support and organ protection	All sorts of joints, skull, ribcage

Animal and Plant Cell Organelles

Animal and plant cells contain many of the same or similar **organelles**, which are membrane enclosed structures that each have a specific function; however, there are a few organelles that are unique to either one or the other general cell type. The following cell organelles are found in both animal and plant cells, unless otherwise noted in their description:

- **Nucleus**: The nucleus consists of three parts: the nuclear envelope, the nucleolus, and chromatin. The **nuclear envelope** is the double membrane that surrounds the nucleus and separates its contents from the rest of the cell. The **nucleolus** produces ribosomes. **Chromatin** consists of DNA and protein, which form chromosomes that contain genetic information. Most cells have only one nucleus; however, some cells, such as skeletal muscle cells, have multiple nuclei.

337

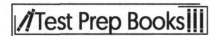

- **Endoplasmic reticulum (ER)**: The ER is a network of membranous sacs and tubes that is responsible for membrane synthesis. It is also responsible for packaging and transporting proteins into vesicles that can move out of the cell. It folds and transports other proteins to the Golgi apparatus. It contains both smooth and rough regions; the rough regions have ribosomes attached, which are the sites of protein synthesis.

- **Flagellum**: Flagella are found only in animal cells. They are made up of a cluster of microtubules projected out of the plasma membrane, and they aid in cell mobility.

- **Centrosome**: The centrosome is the area of the cell where **microtubules**, which are filaments that are responsible for movement in the cell, begin to be formed. Each centrosome contains two centrioles. Each cell contains one centrosome.

- **Cytoskeleton**: The cytoskeleton in animal cells is made up of microfilaments, intermediate filaments, and microtubules. In plant cells, the cytoskeleton is made up of only microfilaments and microtubules. These structures reinforce the cell's shape and aid in cell movement.

- **Microvilli**: Microvilli are found only in animal cells. They are protrusions in the cell membrane that increase the cell's surface area. They have a variety of functions, including absorption, secretion, and cellular adhesion. They are found on the apical surface of epithelial cells, such as in the small intestine. They are also located on the plasma surface of a female's eggs to help anchor sperm that are attempting fertilization.

- **Peroxisome**: A peroxisome contains enzymes that are involved in many of the cell's metabolic functions, one of the most important being the breakdown of very long chain fatty acids. Peroxisomes produces hydrogen peroxide as a byproduct of these processes and then converts the hydrogen peroxide to water. There are many peroxisomes in each cell.

- **Mitochondrion**: The mitochondrion is often called the powerhouse of the cell and is one of the most important structures for maintaining regular cell function. It is where aerobic cellular respiration occurs and where most of the cell's adenosine triphosphate (ATP) is generated. The number of mitochondria in a cell varies greatly from organism to organism, and from cell to cell. In human cells, the number of mitochondria can vary from zero in a red blood cell, to 2000 in a liver cell.

- **Lysosome**: Lysosomes are responsible for digestion and can hydrolyze macromolecules. There are many lysosomes in each cell.

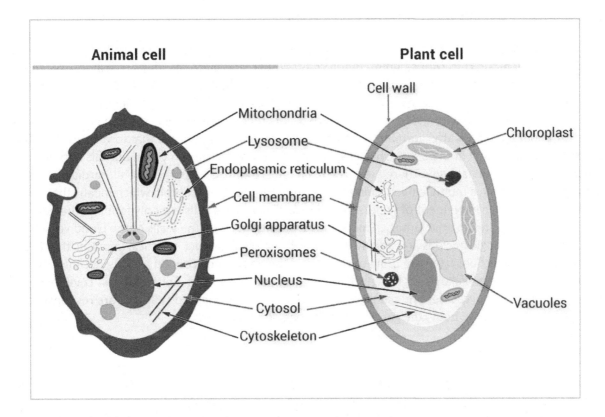

- **Golgi apparatus**: The Golgi apparatus is responsible for the composition, modification, organization, and secretion of cell products. Because of its large size, it was actually one of the first organelles to be studied in detail. There are many Golgi apparatuses in each cell.

- **Ribosomes**: Ribosomes are found either free in the cytosol, bound to the rough ER, or bound to the nuclear envelope. They manufacture proteins within the cell.

- **Plasmodesmata**: The plasmodesmata are found only in plant cells. They are cytoplasmic channels, or tunnels, that go through the cell wall and connect the cytoplasm of adjacent cells.

- **Chloroplast**: Chloroplasts are found only in plant cells. They are responsible for **photosynthesis**, which is the process of converting sunlight to chemical energy that can be stored and used later to drive cellular activities.

- **Central vacuole**: A central vacuole is found only in plant cells. It is responsible for storing material and waste. This is the only vacuole found in a plant cell.

- **Plasma membrane**: The plasma membrane is a phospholipid bilayer that encloses the cell.

- **Cell wall**: Cell walls are only present in plant cells. The cell wall is made up of strong fibrous substances including cellulose and other polysaccharides, and protein. It is a layer outside of the

339

plasma membrane, which protects the cell from mechanical damage and helps maintain the cell's shape.

Major Features of Common Animal Cell Types

The most common animal cell types are blood, muscle, nerve, epithelial, and gamete cells. The three main blood cells are **red blood cells (RBCs), white blood cells (WBCs),** and **platelets.** RBCs transport oxygen and carbon dioxide through the body. They do not have a nucleus and they live for about 120 days in the blood. WBCs defend the body against diseases. They do have a nucleus and live for only three to four days in the human body. Platelets help with the formation of blood clots following an injury. They do not have a nucleus and live for about eight days after formation. **Muscle cells** are long, tubular cells that form muscles, which are responsible for movement in the body. On average, they live for about fifteen years, but this number is highly dependent on the individual body. There are three main types of muscle tissue: skeletal, cardiac, and smooth. **Skeletal muscle cells** have multiple nuclei and are the only voluntary muscle cell, which means that the brain consciously controls the movement of skeletal muscle. **Cardiac muscle cells** are only found in the heart; they have a single nucleus and are involuntary. **Smooth muscle cells** make up the walls of the blood vessels and organs. They have a single nucleus and are involuntary. **Nerve cells** conduct electrical impulses that help send information and instructions from the brain to the rest of the body. They contain a single nucleus and have a specialized membrane that allows for this electrical signaling between cells. **Epithelial** cells cover exposed surfaces, and line internal cavities and passageways. **Gametes** are specialized cells that are responsible for reproduction. In the human body, the gametes are the egg and the sperm.

Integumentary System

Skin consists of three layers: epidermis, dermis, and the hypodermis. There are four types of cells that make up the keratinized stratified squamous epithelium in the epidermis. They are keratinocytes, melanocytes, Merkel cells, and Langerhans cells. Skin is composed of many layers, starting with a basement membrane. On top of that sits the stratum germinativum, the stratum spinosum, the stratum granulosum, the stratum lucidum, and then the stratum corneum at the outer surface. Skin can be classified as thick or thin. These descriptions refer to the epidermis layer. Most of the body is covered with thin skin, but areas such as the palm of the hands are covered with thick skin. The dermis consists of a superficial papillary layer and a deeper reticular layer. The papillary layer is made of loose connective tissue, containing capillaries and the axons of sensory neurons. The reticular layer is a meshwork of tightly packed irregular connective tissue, containing blood vessels, hair follicles, nerves, sweat glands, and sebaceous glands. The hypodermis is a loose layer of fat and connective tissue. Since it is the third layer, if a burn reaches this third degree, it has caused serious damage.

Sweat glands and sebaceous glands are important exocrine glands found in the skin. Sweat glands regulate temperature, and remove bodily waste by secreting water, nitrogenous waste, and sodium salts to the surface of the body. Some sweat glands are classified as apocrine glands. Sebaceous glands are holocrine glands that secrete sebum, which is an oily mixture of lipids and proteins. Sebum protects the skin from water loss, as well as bacterial and fungal infections.

The three major functions of skin are protection, regulation, and sensation. Skin acts as a barrier and protects the body from mechanical impacts, variations in temperature, microorganisms, and chemicals. It regulates body temperature, peripheral circulation, and fluid balance by secreting sweat. It also contains a large network of nerve cells that relay changes in the external environment to the body.

Skeletal System

The skeletal system consists of the 206 bones that make up the skeleton, as well as the cartilage, ligaments, and other connective tissues that stabilize them. Bone is made of collagen fibers and calcium inorganic minerals, mostly in the form of hydroxyapatite, calcium carbonate, and phosphate salts. The inorganic minerals are strong but brittle, and the collagen fibers are weak but flexible, so the combination makes bone resistant to shattering. There are two types of bone: compact and spongy. Compact bone has a basic functional unit, called the Haversian system. Osteocytes, or bone cells, are arranged in concentric circles around a central canal, called the Haversian canal, which contains blood vessels. While Haversian canals run parallel to the surface of the bone, perforating canals, also known as the canals of Volkmann, run perpendicularly between the central canal and the surface of the bone. The concentric circles of bone tissue that surround the central canal within the Haversian system are called lamellae. The spaces that are found between the lamellae are called lacunae. The Haversian system is a reservoir for calcium and phosphorus for blood. Spongy bone, in contrast to compact bone, is lightweight and porous. It has a branching network of parallel lamellae, called trabeculae.

Although spongy bone forms an open framework inside the compact bone, it is still quite strong. Different bones have different ratios of compact-to-spongy bone, depending on their functions. The outside of the bone is covered by a periosteum, which has four major functions. It isolates and protects bones from the surrounding tissue; provides a place for attachment of the circulatory and nervous system structures; participates in growth and repair of the bone; and attaches the bone to the deep fascia. An **endosteum** is found inside the bone; it covers the trabeculae of the spongy bone and lines the inner surfaces of the central canals.

One major function of the skeletal system is to provide structural support for the entire body. It provides a framework for the soft tissues and organs to attach to. The skeletal system also provides a reserve of important nutrients, such as calcium and lipids. Normal concentrations of calcium and phosphate in body fluids are partly maintained by the calcium salts stored in bone. Lipids that are stored in yellow bone marrow can be used as a source of energy. Yellow bone marrow also produces some white blood cells. Red bone marrow produces red blood cells, most white blood cells, and platelets that circulate in the blood. Certain groups of bones form protective barriers around delicate organs. The ribs, for example, protect the heart and lungs, the skull encloses the brain, and the vertebrae cover the spinal cord.

Muscular System

The muscular system of the human body is responsible for all movement that occurs. There are approximately 700 muscles in the body that are attached to the bones of the skeletal system and that make up half of the body's weight. Muscles are attached to the bones through tendons. Tendons are made up of dense bands of connective tissue and have collagen fibers that firmly attach to the bone on one side and the muscle on the other. Their fibers are actually woven into the coverings of the bone and muscle so they can withstand the large forces that are put on them when muscles are moving. There are three types of muscle tissue in the body: Skeletal muscle tissue pulls on the bones of the skeleton and causes body movement; cardiac muscle tissue helps pump blood through veins and arteries; and smooth muscle tissue helps move fluids and solids along the digestive tract and contributes to movement in other body systems. All of these muscle tissues have four important properties in common: They are excitable, meaning they respond to stimuli; contractile, meaning they can shorten and pull on connective tissue; extensible, meaning they can be stretched repeatedly, but maintain the ability to contract; and elastic, meaning they rebound to their original length after a contraction.

Muscles begin at an origin and end at an insertion. Generally, the origin is proximal to the insertion and the origin remains stationary while the insertion moves. For example, when bending the elbow and moving the hand up toward the head, the part of the forearm that is closest to the wrist moves and the part closer to the elbow is stationary. Therefore, the muscle in the forearm has an origin at the elbow and an insertion at the wrist.

Body movements occur by muscle contraction. Each contraction causes a specific action. Muscles can be classified into one of four muscle groups based on the action they perform. Primary movers, or agonists, produce a specific movement, such as flexion of the elbow. Synergists are in charge of helping the primary movers complete their specific movements. They can help stabilize the point of origin or provide extra pull near the insertion. Some synergists can aid an agonist in preventing movement at a joint. Antagonists are muscles whose actions are opposite of the agonist's. If an agonist is contracting during a specific movement, the antagonist is stretched. During flexion of the elbow, the biceps' brachii muscle contracts and acts as an agonist, while the triceps' brachii muscle on the opposite side of the upper arm acts as an antagonist and stretches.

Skeletal muscle tissue has several important functions. It causes movement of the skeleton by pulling on tendons and moving the bones. It maintains body posture through the contraction of specific muscles responsible for the stability of the skeleton. Skeletal muscles help support the weight of internal organs and protect these organs from external injury. They also help to regulate body temperature within a normal range. Muscle contractions require energy and produce heat, which heats the body when cold.

Nervous System

Although the nervous system is one of the smallest organ systems in the human body, it is the most complex. It consists of all of the neural tissue, and is in charge of controlling and adjusting the activities of all of the other systems of the body. Neural responses to stimuli are often fast, but disappear quickly once the neural activity stops. Neural tissue contains two types of cells: neurons and neuroglia. Neurons, or nerve cells, are the main cells responsible for transferring and processing information in the nervous system. Neuroglia support the neurons by providing a framework around them and isolating them from the surrounding environment. They also act as phagocytes and protect neurons from harmful substances.

The nervous system is made of the central nervous system (CNS) and the peripheral nervous system (PNS). The CNS includes the brain and the spinal cord, while the PNS includes the rest of the neural tissue not included in the CNS. The CNS is where intelligence, memory, learning, and emotions are processed. It is responsible for processing and coordinating sensory data and motor commands. The PNS is responsible for relaying sensory information and motor commands between the CNS and peripheral tissues and systems. The PNS has two subdivisions, known as the afferent and efferent divisions. While the afferent division relays sensory information to the CNS, the efferent division transmits motor commands to muscles and glands. The efferent division consists of the somatic nervous system (SNS), which controls skeletal muscle contractions, and the autonomic nervous system (ANS), which regulates activity of smooth muscle, cardiac muscle, and glands.

Two types of pathways are used to communicate information between the brain and the peripheral tissues. Sensory pathways start in a peripheral system and end in the brain. Motor pathways carry information from the brain to peripheral systems. Motor commands often occur in response to the information transmitted through a sensory pathway. Processing in both pathways happens at several points along the way, where neurons pass the information to each other.

The nervous system is responsible for processing both general senses and specialized senses. General senses include temperature, pain, touch, pressure, vibration and proprioception. Specialized senses include olfaction (smell), gustation (taste), equilibrium, hearing, and vision. The information from each sense is processed through a specific receptor for that sense. A receptor that is sensitive to touch may not be responsive to chemical stimuli, for example. The specificity of the receptor is developed either from its individual structure or from accessory cells or structures creating a shield against other senses.

Endocrine System

The endocrine system is made of the ductless tissues and glands that secrete hormones into the interstitial fluids of the body. Interstitial fluid is the solution that surrounds tissue cells within the body. This system works closely with the nervous system to regulate the physiological activities of the other systems of the body to maintain homeostasis. While the nervous system provides quick, short-term responses to stimuli, the endocrine system acts by releasing hormones into the bloodstream that get distributed to the whole body. The response is slow but long-lasting, ranging from a few hours to a few weeks.

Hormones are chemical substances that change the metabolic activity of tissues and organs. While regular metabolic reactions are controlled by enzymes, hormones can change the type, activity, or quantity of the enzymes involved in the reaction. They bind to specific cells and start a biochemical chain of events that changes the enzymatic activity. Hormones can regulate development and growth, digestive metabolism, mood, and body temperature, among other things. Often small amounts of hormone will lead to large changes in the body.

The major endocrine glands are described below:

- **Hypothalamus:** A part of the brain, the hypothalamus connects the nervous system to the endocrine system via the pituitary gland. Although it is considered part of the nervous system, it plays a dual role in regulating endocrine organs.

- **Pituitary Gland:** A pea-sized gland found at the bottom of the hypothalamus. It has two lobes, called the anterior and posterior lobes. It plays an important role in regulating the function of other endocrine glands. The hormones released control growth, blood pressure, certain functions of the sex organs, salt concentration of the kidneys, internal temperature regulation, and pain relief.

- **Thyroid Gland:** This gland releases hormones, such as thyroxine, that are important for metabolism, growth and development, temperature regulation, and brain development during infancy and childhood. Thyroid hormones also monitor the amount of circulating calcium in the body.

- **Parathyroid Glands:** These are four pea-sized glands located on the posterior surface of the thyroid. The main hormone secreted is called parathyroid hormone (PTH) and helps with the thyroid's regulation of calcium in the body.

- **Thymus Gland:** The thymus is located in the chest cavity, embedded in connective tissue. It produces several hormones important for development and maintenance of normal immunological defenses. One hormone promotes the development and maturation of lymphocytes, which strengthens the immune system.

- **Adrenal Gland:** One adrenal gland is attached to the top of each kidney. It produces adrenaline and is responsible for the "fight or flight" reactions in the face of danger or stress. The hormones epinephrine and norepinephrine cooperate to regulate states of arousal.

- **Pancreas:** The pancreas is an organ that has both endocrine and exocrine functions. The endocrine functions are controlled by the pancreatic islets of Langerhans, which are groups of beta cells scattered throughout the gland that secrete insulin to lower blood sugar levels in the body. Neighboring alpha cells secrete glucagon to raise blood sugar.

- **Pineal Gland:** The pineal gland secretes melatonin, a hormone derived from the neurotransmitter serotonin. Melatonin can slow the maturation of sperm, oocytes, and reproductive organs. It also regulates the body's circadian rhythm, which is the natural awake/asleep cycle. It also serves an important role in protecting the CNS tissues from neural toxins.

- **Testes and Ovaries**: These glands secrete testosterone and estrogen, respectively, and are responsible for secondary sex characteristics, as well as reproduction.

Circulatory System

The circulatory system is composed of the heart and blood vessels of the body. The heart is the main organ of the circulatory system. It acts as a pump and works to circulate blood throughout the body. Gases, nutrients, and waste are constantly exchanged between the circulating blood and interstitial fluid, keeping tissues and organs alive and healthy. The circulatory system is divided into the pulmonary and systemic circuits. The pulmonary circuit is responsible for carrying carbon dioxide-rich blood to the lungs and returning oxygen-rich blood to the heart. The systemic circuit transports the oxygen-rich blood to the rest of the body and returns carbon dioxide-rich blood to the heart.

Heart

The heart is located posterior to the sternum, on the left side, in the front of the chest. The heart wall is made of three distinct layers. The outer layer, the epicardium, is a **serous** membrane that is also known as the visceral pericardium. The middle layer is called the myocardium, and contains connective tissue, blood vessels, and nerves within its layers of cardiac muscle tissue. The inner layer is the endocardium, and is made of a simple squamous epithelium. This layer includes the heart valves, and is continuous with the endothelium of the attached blood vessels.

The heart has four chambers: the right atrium, the right ventricle, the left atrium, and the left ventricle. An interatrial septum, or wall, separates the right and left atria, and the right and left ventricles are separated by an interventricular septum. The atrium and ventricle on the same side of the heart have an opening between them that is regulated by a valve. The valve maintains blood flow in only one direction, moving from the atrium to the ventricle, and prevents backflow. The systemic circuit pumps oxygen-poor blood into the right atrium, then pumps it into the right ventricle. From there, the blood enters the pulmonary trunk and then flows into the pulmonary arteries, where it can become re-oxygenated. Oxygen-rich blood from the lungs flows into the left atrium and then passes into the left ventricle. From there, blood enters the aorta and is pumped to the entire systemic circuit.

Blood

Blood circulates throughout the body in a system of vessels that includes arteries, veins, and capillaries. It distributes oxygen, nutrients, and hormones to all the cells in the body. The vessels are muscular tubes that

allow gas exchange to occur. Arteries carry oxygen-rich blood from the heart to the other tissues of the body. The largest artery is the aorta. Veins collect oxygen-depleted blood from tissues and organs, and return it to the heart. The walls of veins are thinner and less elastic than arteries, because the blood pressure in veins is lower than in arteries. Capillaries are the smallest of the blood vessels and do not function individually; instead, they work together in a unit, called a capillary bed. This network of capillaries provides oxygen-rich blood from arterioles to tissues and feeds oxygen-poor blood from tissues back to venules.

Blood comprises plasma and formed elements, which include red blood cells (RBCs), white blood cells (WBCs), and platelets. Plasma is the liquid matrix of the blood and contains dissolved proteins. RBCs transport oxygen and carbon dioxide. WBCs are part of the immune system and help fight diseases. Platelets contain enzymes and other factors that help with blood clotting.

Respiratory System

The respiratory system mediates the exchange of gas between the air and the blood, mainly by the act of breathing. This system is divided into the upper respiratory system and the lower respiratory system. The upper system comprises the nose, the nasal cavity and sinuses, and the pharynx. The lower respiratory system comprises the larynx (voice box), the trachea (windpipe), the small passageways leading to the lungs, and the lungs. The upper respiratory system is responsible for filtering, warming, and humidifying the air that gets passed to the lower respiratory system, protecting the lower respiratory system's more delicate tissue surfaces.

Lungs
The right lung is divided into three lobes: superior, middle, and inferior. The left lung is divided into two lobes: superior and inferior. The left lung is smaller than the right, likely because it shares its space in the chest cavity with the heart. Together, the lungs contain approximately 1500 miles of airway passages. The bronchi, which carry air into the lungs, branch into bronchioles and continue to divide into smaller and smaller passageways, until they become alveoli, which are the smallest passages. Most of the gas exchange in the lungs occurs between the blood-filled pulmonary capillaries and the air-filled alveoli.

Functions of the Respiratory System
The respiratory system has many functions. Most importantly, it provides a large area for gas exchange between the air and the circulating blood. It protects the delicate respiratory surfaces from environmental variations and defends them against pathogens. It is responsible for producing the sounds that the body makes for speaking and singing, as well as for non-verbal communication. It also helps regulate blood volume, blood pressure, and body fluid pH.

Breathing
When a breath of air is inhaled, oxygen enters the nose or mouth, and passes into the sinuses, where the temperature and humidity of the air get regulated. The air then passes into the trachea and is filtered. From there, the air travels into the bronchi and reaches the lungs. Bronchi are tubes that lead from the trachea to each lung and are lined with cilia and mucus that collect dust and germs along the way. Within the lungs, oxygen and carbon dioxide are exchanged between the air in the alveoli and the blood in the pulmonary capillaries. Oxygen-rich blood returns to the heart and is pumped through the systemic circuit. Carbon dioxide-rich air is exhaled from the body.

Breathing is possible due to the muscular diaphragm pulling on the lungs, increasing their volume and decreasing their pressure. Air flows from the external high-pressure system to the low-pressure system inside

345

the lungs. When breathing out, the diaphragm releases its pressure difference, decreases the lung volume, and forces the stale air back out.

Digestive System

The digestive system is a group of organs that work together to transform food and liquids into energy, which can then be used by the body as fuel. Food is ingested and then passes through the alimentary canal, or GI tract, which comprises the mouth, pharynx, esophagus, stomach, small intestine, and large intestine. The digestive system has accessory organs, including the liver, gallbladder, and pancreas, that help with the processing of food and liquids, but do not have food pass directly through them. These accessory organs and the digestive system organs work together in the following functions:

- **Ingestion:** Food and liquids enter the alimentary canal through the mouth.

- **Introductory Mechanical and Chemical Processing:** Teeth grind the food and the tongue swirls it to facilitate swallowing. Enzymes in saliva begin chemical digestion.

- **Advanced Mechanical and Chemical Digestion:** The muscular stomach uses physical force and enzymes, which function at low pH levels, to break down the food and liquid's complex molecules, such as sugars, lipids, and proteins, into smaller molecules that can be absorbed by the small intestine.

- **Secretion:** Most of the acids, buffers, and enzymes that aid in digestion are secreted by the accessory organs, but some are provided by the digestive tract. Bile from the liver facilitates fat digestion.

- **Absorption:** Vitamins, electrolytes, organic molecules, and water are absorbed by the villi and microvilli lining in the small intestine and are moved to the interstitial fluid of the digestive tract.

- **Compaction:** Indigestible materials and organic wastes are dehydrated in the large intestine and compacted before elimination from the body.

- **Excretion:** Waste products are excreted from the digestive tract.

The major organs of the alimentary canal are described below:

- **Stomach:** This organ stores food so the body has time to digest large meals. Its highly acidic environment and enzyme secretions, such as pepsin and trypsin, aid in digestion. It also aids in mechanical processing through muscular contractions.

- **Small Intestine:** This organ is a thin tube that is approximately ten feet long. It secretes enzymes to aid in digestion and has many folds that increase its surface area and allows for maximum absorption of nutrients from the digested food.

- **Large Intestine:** This organ is a long thick tube that is about five feet long. It absorbs water from the digested food and transports waste to be excreted from the body. It also contains symbiotic bacteria that further breaks down the waste products, allowing for any extra nutrients to be absorbed.

The major accessory organs are described below:

346

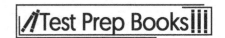

- **Liver:** The liver produces and secretes bile, which is important for the digestion of lipids. It also plays a large role in the regulation of circulating levels of carbohydrates, amino acids, and lipids in the body. Excess nutrients are removed by the liver and deficiencies are corrected with its stored nutrients.

- **Gallbladder:** This organ is responsible for storing and concentrating bile before it gets secreted into the small intestine. While the gallbladder is storing bile, it can regulate the bile's composition by absorbing water, thereby increasing the concentration of bile salts and other components.

- **Pancreas:** The Pancreas has exocrine cells that secrete buffers and digestive enzymes. It contains specific enzymes for each type of food molecule, such as carbohydrases for carbohydrates, lipases for lipids, and proteinases for proteins.

Urinary System

The urinary system is made up of the kidneys, ureters, urinary bladder, and the urethra. It is the main system responsible for getting rid of the organic waste products, excess water, and excess electrolytes. The kidneys are responsible for producing urine, which is a fluid waste product containing water, ions, and small soluble compounds. The urinary system has many important functions related to waste excretion. It regulates the concentrations of sodium, potassium, chloride, calcium, and other ions in the plasma by controlling the amount of each that is excreted in urine. This also contributes to the maintenance of blood pH. It regulates blood volume and pressure by controlling the amount of water lost in the urine, and releasing erythropoietin and renin. It eliminates toxic substances, drugs, and organic waste products, such as urea and uric acid. Kidney cells also synthesize calcitriol, which is a hormone derivative of vitamin D3 that aids in calcium ion absorption by the intestinal epithelium.

Kidneys

Under normal circumstances, humans have two functioning kidneys. They are the main organs are responsible for filtering waste products out of the blood and transferring them to urine. Every day, the kidneys filter approximately 120 to 150 quarts of blood and produce one to two quarts of urine. Kidneys are made of millions of tiny filtering units, called nephrons. Nephrons have two parts: a glomerulus, which is the filter, and a tubule. As blood enters the kidneys, the glomerulus allows fluid and waste products to pass through it and enter the tubule. Blood cells and large molecules, such as proteins, do not pass through and remain in the blood. The filtered fluid and waste then pass through the tubule, where any final essential minerals are sent back to the bloodstream. The final product at the end of the tubule is called urine.

Waste Excretion

Once urine accumulates, it leaves the kidneys. The urine travels through the ureters into the urinary bladder, a muscular organ that is hollow and elastic. As more urine enters the urinary bladder, its walls stretch and become thinner so there is no significant difference in internal pressure. The urinary bladder stores the urine until the body is ready for urination, at which time the muscles contract and force the urine through the urethra and out of the body.

Reproductive System

The reproductive system is responsible for producing, storing, nourishing, and transporting functional reproductive cells, or gametes, in the human body. It includes the reproductive organs, also known as gonads, the reproductive tract, the accessory glands and organs that secrete fluids into the reproductive tract, and the

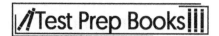

perineal structures, which are the external genitalia. The human male and female reproductive systems are very different from each other.

Male System

The male gonads are called testes. The testes secrete androgens, mainly testosterone, and produce and store 500 million sperms cells, which are the male gametes, each day. An androgen is a steroid hormone that controls the development and maintenance of male characteristics. Once the sperm are mature, they move through a duct system, where they mix with additional fluids secreted by accessory glands, forming a mixture called semen. The sperm cells in semen are responsible for fertilization of the female gametes to produce offspring.

Female System

The female gonads are the ovaries. Ovaries generally produce one immature gamete, or oocyte, per month. They are also responsible for secreting the hormones estrogen and progesterone. When the oocyte is released from the ovary, it travels along the uterine tubes, or Fallopian tubes, and then into the uterus. The uterus opens into the vagina. When sperm cells enter the vagina, they swim through the uterus and may fertilize the oocyte in the Fallopian tubes. The resulting zygote travels down the tube and implants into the uterine wall. The uterus protects and nourishes the developing embryo for nine months until it is ready for the outside environment. If the oocyte is not fertilized, it is released in the uterine, or menstrual, cycle. The menstrual cycle occurs monthly and involves the shedding of the functional part of the uterine lining.

Mammary glands are a specialized accessory organ of the female reproductive system. The mammary glands are located in the breast tissue, and during pregnancy begin to grow, and the cells proliferate in preparation for lactation. After pregnancy, the cells begin to secrete nutrient-filled milk, which is transferred into a duct system and out through the nipple for nourishment of the baby.

Characteristics of Vascular and Nonvascular Plants

Plants that have an extensive vascular transport system are called **vascular plants**. Those plants without a transport system are called **nonvascular plants**. Approximately ninety-three percent of plants that are currently living and reproducing are vascular plants. The cells that comprise the vascular tissue in vascular plants form tubes that transport water and nutrients through the entire plant. Nonvascular plants include mosses, liverworts, and hornworts. They do not retain any water; instead, they transport water using other specialized tissue. They have structures that look like leaves, but are actually just single sheets of cells without a cuticle or stomata.

Structure and Function of Roots, Leaves, and Stems

Roots are responsible for anchoring plants in the ground. They absorb water and nutrients and transport them up through the plant. **Leaves** are the main location of photosynthesis. They contain **stomata**, which are pores used for gas exchange, on their underside to take in carbon dioxide and release oxygen. **Stems** transport materials through the plant and support the plant's body. They contain **xylem**, which conducts water and dissolved nutrients upward through the plant, and **phloem**, which conducts sugars and metabolic products downward through the leaves.

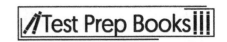

Characteristics of Bacteria, Animals, Plants, Fungi, and Protists

As discussed earlier, there are two distinct types of cells that make up most living organisms: prokaryotic and eukaryotic. Bacteria (and archaea) are classified as prokaryotic cells, whereas animal, plant, fungi, and protist cells are classified as eukaryotic cells.

Although animal cells and plant cells are both eukaryotic, they each have several distinguishing characteristics. **Animal cells** are surrounded by a plasma membrane, while **plant cells** have a cell wall made up of cellulose that provides more structure and an extra layer of protection for the cell. Animals use oxygen to breathe and give off carbon dioxide, while plants do the opposite—they take in carbon dioxide and give off oxygen. Plants also use light as a source of energy. Animals have highly developed sensory and nervous systems and the ability to move freely, while plants lack both abilities. Animals, however, cannot make their own food and must rely on their environment to provide sufficient nutrition, whereas plants do make their own food.

Fungal cells are typical eukaryotes, containing both a nucleus and membrane-bound organelles. They have a cell wall, similar to plant cells; however, they use oxygen as a source of energy and cannot perform photosynthesis. They also depend on outside sources for nutrition and cannot produce their own food. Of note, their cell walls contain **chitin**.

Protists are a group of diverse eukaryotic cells that are often grouped together because they do not fit into the categories of animal, plant, or fungal cells. They can be categorized into three broad categories: protozoa, protophyta, and molds. These three broad categories are essentially "animal-like," "plant-like," and "fungus-like," respectively. All of them are unicellular and do not form tissues. Besides this simple similarity, protists are a diverse group of organisms with different characteristics, life cycles, and cellular structures.

Biological Molecules

Importance of Carbon

Repeating units of monomers (small molecules that bond with identical small molecules) that are linked together are called **polymers**. The most important polymers found in all living things can be divided into five categories: nucleic acids (such as DNA), carbohydrates, proteins, lipids, and enzymes. Carbon (C), hydrogen (H), oxygen (O), nitrogen (N), sulfur (S), and phosphorus (P) are the major elements of most biological molecules. Carbon is the foundation of organic molecules because it has the ability to form four covalent bonds and long polymers. The four organic compounds are lipids, carbohydrates, proteins, and nucleic acids:

- **Lipids** are critical for cell membrane structure, long-term energy storage, and to help form some steroid hormones such as testosterone and cholesterol.

- **Carbohydrates** are important as a medium for energy storage and conversion, but also have structural importance. Cellulose (a monomer of glucose) provides structure for plant cell walls. Chitin provides structure for fungi and animals with exoskeletons (such as crabs and lobsters), and peptidoglycan is a carbohydrate/protein hybrid that forms the cell walls of some prokaryotes.

- **Proteins** are important because enzymes regulate all chemical reactions, but there are also many cell membrane proteins important for structure, transport, and communication.

- **Nucleic acids** include DNA, the genetic instructions of organisms, and RNA, which is the molecule responsible for turning those instructions into products.

All of these organic compounds require the elements carbon (C), hydrogen (H), and oxygen (O), which enter the food chain through the glucose that it produces through photosynthesis. Some compounds contain phosphorus (P), sulfur (S), and nitrogen (N) as well. Elements such as phosphorus and nitrogen diffuse into the roots of plants from the external environment, are incorporated into organic compounds, and are distributed to other organisms through symbiotic relationships or food webs.

DNA and RNA

Nucleotides consist of a five-carbon sugar, a nitrogen-containing base, and one or more phosphate groups. **Deoxyribonucleic acid (DNA)** is made up of two strands of nucleotides coiled together in a double-helix structure. It plays a major role in enabling living organisms to pass their genetic information and complex components on to subsequent generations. There are four nitrogenous bases that make up DNA: adenine, thymine, guanine, and cytosine. Adenine always pairs with thymine, and guanine always pairs with cytosine. **Ribonucleic acid (RNA)** is often made up of only one strand of nucleotides folded in on itself. Like DNA, RNA has four nitrogenous bases; however, in RNA, thymine is replaced by uracil.

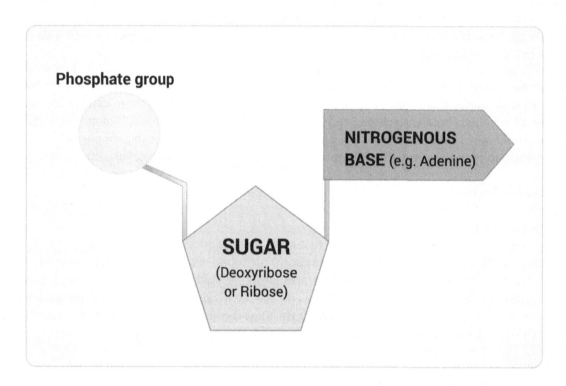

Carbohydrates

Carbohydrates consist of sugars and polymers of sugars, such as starches, which make up the cell walls of plants. The simplest sugar is called a **monosaccharide** and has the molecular formula of CH_2O, or a multiple of that formula. Monosaccharides are important molecules for cellular respiration. Their carbon skeleton can also be used to rebuild new small molecules. **Polysaccharides** are made up of a few hundred to a few thousand monosaccharides linked together.

Proteins

Proteins are essential for almost all functions in living beings. All proteins are made from a set of twenty **amino acids** that are linked in **unbranched polymers**. The amino acids are linked by **peptide bonds**, and polymers of

amino acids are called **polypeptides**. These polypeptides, either individually or in linked combination with each other, fold up and form coils of biologically functional molecules.

There are four levels of protein structure: primary, secondary, tertiary, and quaternary. The **primary structure** is the sequence of amino acids, similar to the letters in a long word. The **secondary structure** comprises the folds and coils that are formed by hydrogen bonding between the slightly charged atoms of the polypeptide backbone. **Tertiary structure** is the overall shape of the molecule that results from the interactions between the side chains that are linked to the polypeptide backbone. **Quaternary structure** is the overall protein structure that occurs when a protein is made up of two or more polypeptide chains.

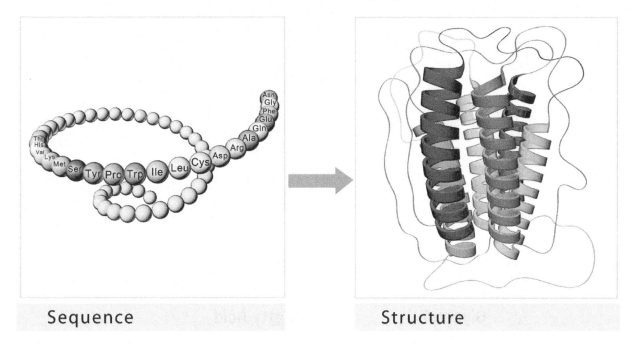

Sequence   Structure

Lipids

Lipids are a class of biological molecules that are **hydrophobic**, which means that they do not mix well with water. They are mostly made up of large chains of carbon and hydrogen atoms, termed **hydrocarbon chains**. The three most important types of lipids are fats, phospholipids, and steroids.

Fats are made up of two types of smaller molecules: three fatty acids and one glycerol molecule. Saturated fats do not have double bonds between the carbons in the fatty acid chain, such as glycerol, pictured below. They are fairly straight molecules and can pack together closely, so they form solids at room temperature. Unsaturated fats have one or more double bonds between carbons in the fatty acid chain. Since they cannot

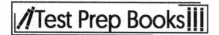
pack together as tightly as saturated fats, they take up more space and are called oils. They remain liquid at room temperature.

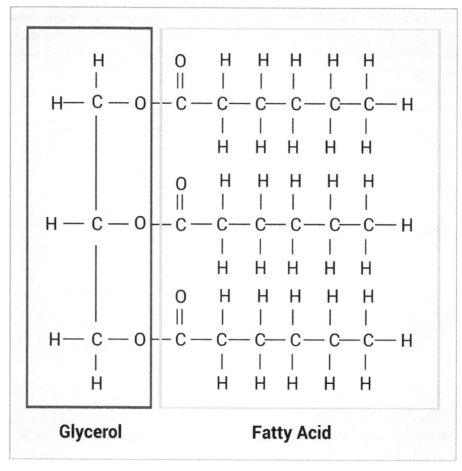

Glycerol   **Fatty Acid**

Phospholipids are made up of two fatty acid molecules linked to one glycerol molecule. When phospholipids are mixed with water, they inherently create double-layered structures, called **bilayers**, which shield their hydrophobic regions from the water molecules.

Steroids are lipids that consist of four fused carbon rings. They can mix in between the phospholipid bilayer cell membrane and help maintain its structure, as well as aid in cell signaling.

Enzymes

Enzymes are biological molecules that accelerate the rate of chemical reactions by lowering the activation energy needed to make the reaction proceed. Although most enzymes can be classified as proteins, some are ribonucleic acid (RNA) molecules. Enzymes function by interacting with a specific substrate in order to create a different molecule, or product. Most reactions in cells need enzymes to make them occur at rates fast enough to sustain life.

Role of Water and Salt in Biological Systems

Water properties, such as cohesion and specific heat capacity, allow for the survival of biological systems. In plants, cohesion in water involves hydrogen bonding and plays a vital role in water transport. Since the specific heat capacity of water (4.184 J/ g °C) is relatively high compared to many materials, it allows for temperature

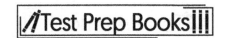

stabilization in water environments and within organisms. For example, water can affect the air temperature by absorbing heat from the Sun's rays and releasing large amounts of heat as the air cools. As a result, ocean temperatures are more stabilized and allow for a favorable marine environment. Organisms made of water can resist changes in temperature more easily since water acts as a buffer by absorbing a lot of heat before the temperature changes drastically. The existence of life under ice is possible due to hydrogen bonding in water. Since solid ice is denser than liquid water, ice will float over water and insulate liquid water below, allowing organisms to survive under the ice.

Living cells require several types of metal ions, such as sodium and calcium, to function properly. Water is vital in transporting metal and nonmetal ions to the cell in biological systems. The polar properties of water allow for the dissolution of salt compounds such as sodium chloride by creating stable hydration shells around the ions.

Photosynthesis

Photosynthesis is the process of converting light energy into chemical energy, which is then stored in sugar and other organic molecules. It can be divided into two stages called the **light reactions** and the **Calvin cycle**. The photosynthetic process takes place in the chloroplast in plants. Inside the chloroplast, there are membranous sacs called **thylakoids. Chlorophyll** is a green pigment that lives in the thylakoid membranes, absorbs photons from light, and starts an electron transport chain in order to produce energy in the form of ATP and NADPH. The ATP and NADPH produced from the light reactions are used as energy to form organic molecules in the Calvin cycle.

The Calvin cycle takes place in the **stroma**, or inner space, of the chloroplasts. The process consumes nine ATP molecules and six NADPH molecules for every one molecule of glyceraldehyde 3-phosphate (G3P) that it produces. The G3P that is produced can be used as the starting material to build larger organic compounds, such as glucose. The complex series of reactions that takes place in photosynthesis can be simplified into the following equation:

$$6\,CO_2 + 12\,H_2O + Light\ Energy \rightarrow C_6H_{12}O_6 + 6\,O_2 + 6\,H_2O$$

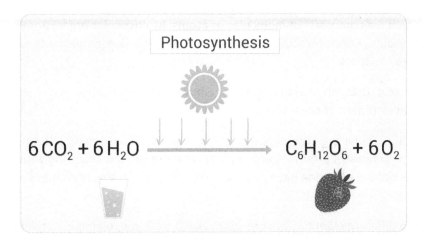

Basically, carbon dioxide and water mix with light energy inside the chloroplast to produce organic molecules, oxygen, and water. It is interesting to note that water is on both sides of the equation. Twelve water molecules are consumed during this process and six water molecules are newly formed as byproducts. Although the

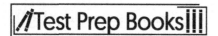

Calvin cycle itself is not dependent on light energy, both steps of photosynthesis usually occur during daylight because the Calvin cycle is dependent upon the ATP and NADPH that is produced by the light reactions.

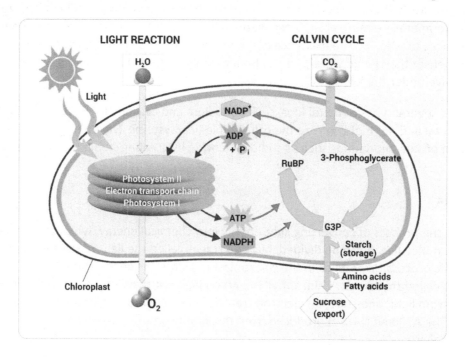

Life Sciences: Living and Nonliving Components in Environments

Characteristics of Living Organisms

All living organisms have similar biological characteristics that include organization, growth, reproduction, environmental response, regulation, homeostasis, and energy processing.

Organisms are highly organized structures that may contain one or several cells. Unicellular organisms consist of cell organelles, which are composed of molecules or atoms. Multicellular organisms consist of cells comprising different tissues, which combine to form organs. Organs have a specific function and work with one another to create organ systems.

The deoxyribonucleic acid (DNA) strands of organisms contain segments called genes with specific instructions for the growth and development of organisms.

During reproduction, unicellular organisms reproduce through DNA duplication, allowing the cell to form two new cells. Multicellular organisms produce germline cells that create new offspring with genes inherited from each parent cell. Genes of the offspring have physical features, such as size or shape, similar to that of the parents.

Organisms respond to different stimuli to ensure survival. For example, plants generally grow toward a light source and even along fences. Bacteria can exhibit a positive response when moving toward a chemical or light source and a negative response when moving away from chemicals or light.

Organisms require regulatory mechanisms to respond to stimuli and environmental stresses. These mechanisms may include internal functions that regulate blood flow and nutrient transport. Organs carry out

354

unique functions that include removing waste, delivering oxygen to cells within the body, and regulating temperature.

Homeostasis, a biological self-regulation process, allows cells to function properly by maintaining proper pH, temperature, and chemical concentration. As the environment changes, organisms maintain cell conditions within a narrow range through a homeostasis or steady state process. The human body continually regulates body temperature, and some organisms, such as polar bears, have body structures that conserve heat to withstand cold temperatures. Insulating structures include fat, feathers, and fur. In warm environments, organisms such as dogs or humans pant to remove excess body heat.

Energy processing differs for various organisms. Animals consume food to extract chemical energy from molecules. Through photosynthesis, plants capture energy from the Sun and convert it to chemical energy.

Basic Needs of Living Organisms

All organisms require nutrients to survive. Through various ecosystems, environmental constraints and resources influence the physiology and structure of organisms. In tropical environments, plants can photosynthesize year-round due to the plentiful solar radiation and warm temperatures. However, in polar regions, photosynthesis may cease due to low temperatures and limited solar radiation. Organisms may equally drive changes in the environment. In antagonistic relationships, organisms compete for resources and even consume or spread diseases to other organisms. In mutualistic associations, organisms may exchange resources with one another or may be codependent. For example, bees consume the pollen and nectar of flowers but also transfer pollen between specific flowers. The pollen transfer leads to fertilization, allowing plants to produce seeds. The development of plants and the creation of rainforest canopies have driven the evolution of apes' forelimb structures, allowing them to swing more efficiently from tree to tree. Photosynthetic organisms have even changed the environment by releasing oxygen into the atmosphere, thereby altering the composition of the Earth's ozone layer. For instance, the creation of the ozone layer has reduced UV radiation and protected organisms that emerged on land.

Response to Stimuli and Homeostasis

A **stimulus** is a change in the environment, either internal or external, around an organism that is received by a sensory receptor and causes the organism to react. **Homeostasis** is the stable state of an organism. When an organism reacts to stimuli, it works to counteract the change in order to reach homeostasis again.

Adaptation

The **theory of adaptation** is defined as an alteration in a species that causes it to become more well-suited to its environment. It increases the probability of survival, thus increasing the rate of successful reproduction. As a result, an adaptation becomes more common within the population of that species.

For examples, bats use reflected sound waves (echolocation) to prey on insects, and chameleons change colors to blend in with their surroundings to evade detection by its prey and predators. These adaptations are believed to be brought about by natural selection.

Adaptive radiation refers to the idea of rapid diversification within a species into an array of unique forms. It's thought to happen as a result of changes in a habitat creating new challenges, ecological niches, or natural resources.

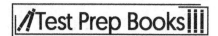
Darwin's finches are often thought of as an example of the theory of adaptive radiation. Charles Darwin documented 13 varieties of finches on the Galapagos Islands. Each island in the chain presented a unique and changing environment, which was believed to cause rapid adaptive radiation among the finches. There was also diversity among finches inhabiting the same island. Darwin believed that as a result of natural selection, each variety of finch developed adaptations to fit into its native environment.

A major difference in Darwin's finches had to do with the size and shapes of beaks. The variation in beaks allowed the finches to access different foods and natural resources, which decreased competition and preserved resources. As a result, various finches of the same species were allowed to coexist, thrive, and diversify. Finches had:

- Short beaks, which were suited for foraging for seeds
- Thin, sharp beaks, which were suited for preying on insects
- Long beaks, which were suited for probing for food inside plants

Darwin believed that the finches on the Galapagos Islands resulted from chance mutations in genes transmitted from generation to generation.

Accommodation

Adaptations are long-term evolutionary changes in response to a new environment. An adaptation results in features created by natural selection for an existing function. In contrast, an accommodation or acclimatization (acclimation) is a short-term adjustment, e.g., phenotypic change, in response to a new environment. The table below shows the differences between adaptation and acclimation.

	Adaptation	Acclimatization
Created through	A new or changing habitat	A new or changing habitat
Timespan	Across several generations	An organism's lifetime
Occurred by evolution	Yes	No
Reversibility of trait	No	Yes

Bird feathers are traits that are not adaptations. Based on fossil records of the earliest known bird called the Archaeopteryx, dinosaurs called theropods appeared to have feathers but were unable to fly. Therefore, feathers were a trait that did not arise when birds began to fly. A feature or adaptation resulting from natural selection must have a trait that:

- Is heritable and genetically encoded.
- Is functional and will perform a specific task.
- Increases the organism's fitness.
- Evolves for a specific function.

The chameleon's ability to camouflage by changing colors to match its surroundings is an adaptation that allows it to evade detection from predators and prey. Snow leopards will acclimate to severe snowstorms by seeking shelter in caves and growing thick coats in the winter; they will leave the cave and shed their coat when the weather becomes warmer. Snow leopards have adapted to cold environments by growing thick coats and large paws to move through the snow.

Community Ecology

An **ecological community** is a group of species that interact and live in the same location. Because of their shared environment, they tend to have a large influence on each other.

Niche

An **ecological niche** is the role that a species plays in its environment, including how it finds its food and shelter. It could be a predator of a different species, or prey for a larger species.

Species Diversity

Species diversity is the number of different species that cohabitate in an ecological community. It has two different facets: **species richness**, which is the general number of species, and **species evenness**, which accounts for the population size of each species.

Interspecific Relationships

Interspecific relationships include the interactions between organisms of different species. The following list defines the common relationships that can occur:

- **Commensalism**: One organism benefits while the other is neither benefited nor harmed

- **Mutualism**: Both organisms benefit

- **Parasitism**: One organism benefits and the other is harmed

- **Competition**: Two or more species compete for limited resources that are necessary for their survival

- **Predation (Predator-Prey)**: One species is a food source for another species

Ecosystems

An **ecosystem** includes all of the living organisms and nonliving components of an environment (each community) and their interactions with each other. All organisms work together so that life can exist. An organism represents one of a species, like the fish below, and all organisms serve a particular function. The fish's niche is to eat aquatic producers and excrete waste that acts as fertilizer.

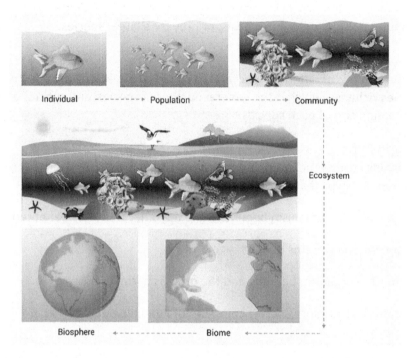

This fish is just one organism within a population. A **population** represents multiple individuals living in the same habitat. The community includes every biotic factor (living organism) within an ecosystem, in this case, the fish, jellyfish, algae, crab, bacteria, etc. An ecosystem includes all the biotic factors as well as the **abiotic**, which includes anything non-living—for the fish, that's a rock, a shipwreck, and a nearby glacier. For biomes, add weather and climate into the mix. The biosphere is all of Earth, which is the combination of all biomes.

Producers (plants, protists, and even some bacteria) photosynthesize and make the food that provides energy required for all chemical reactions to occur and therefore all life to exist. A non-photosynthesizer must find and eat food, and this feeding relationship can be visualized in food chains. Consider this food chain:

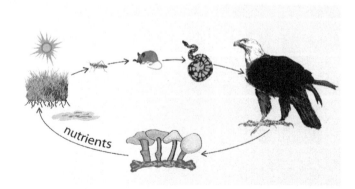

The true source of the energy for every living organism is the sun. Plants absorb the sun's energy to make glucose and are on the **first trophic level** (feeding level). The grasshopper on the **second trophic level** is an example of an herbivore and is a primary consumer, as he is the first eater in the food chain. Unfortunately, he receives only 10 percent of the energy that the plant absorbed (this is known as the 10 percent rule) because the other 90 percent of energy was either used by the plant to grow or will be lost as heat.

The mouse on the **third trophic level** is the secondary consumer, or second eater. Food chains are not as inclusive as **food webs**, which show all feeding relationships in an ecosystem. Looking at this food chain suggests that mice are carnivores (eaters of animals), but mice also eat berries and plants, so they are actually considered omnivores (eaters of both plants and animals). The mouse only gets 10 percent of the energy from the grasshopper, which is actually only 1 percent of the original energy provided by the Sun. The snake on the fourth trophic level is a carnivore, as is the hawk on the highest trophic level.

The arrows in the food chain show the transfer of energy, and fungi as well as bacteria act as decomposers, which break down organic material. Decomposers act at every trophic level because they feed on all organisms; they are non-discriminating omnivores. Decomposers are critical for life, as they recycle the atoms and building blocks of organisms.

Feeding relationships and **predator-prey relationships** (hunter-hunted, like the hawk and the rabbit in the food web shown) are not the only relationships in an ecosystem. There also can be competition within and between species. For example, in the food chain above, the rabbit and snail both eat grass, showing a relationship called **competition**, when two organisms want the same thing. Other relationships include symbiotic relationships, which represent two species living together. Symbiosis comes in three varieties:

- **Mutualism**: an arrangement where both organisms help each other. An example is the relationship between birds and flowers. When birds consume the nectar that the flower produces, pollen rubs on the bird's body so that when it travels to a neighboring plant, it helps with fertilization. The plant helps the bird by providing food, and the bird helps the plant by helping it reproduce. This is a win-win.

- **Parasitism**: when one organism is hurt while the other is helped. Fleas and dogs are a prime example. Fleas suck the dog's blood, and dogs are itchy and lose blood. This is a win-lose.

- **Commensalism**: when one organism is helped and the other is neither harmed nor helped. For example, barnacles are crusty little creatures that attach themselves to whales. They don't feed on the whale like a parasite. Instead, they use the whale to give them a free ride so they have access to food. The whales don't care about the barnacles. This is a win-do not care.

359

Transfer of Energy and Cycling of Matter in Ecosystems

Ecosystems are maintained by cycling the energy and nutrients that they obtain from external sources. The process can be diagramed in a food web, which represents the feeding relationship between species in a community. The different levels of the food web are called trophic levels. The first trophic level generally consists of plants, algae, and bacteria. The second trophic level consists of herbivores. The third trophic level consists of predators that eat herbivores. The trophic levels continue on to larger and larger predators. Decomposers are an important part of the food chain that are not at a specific trophic level. They eat decomposing things on the ground that other animals do not want to eat. This allows them to provide nutrients to their own predators.

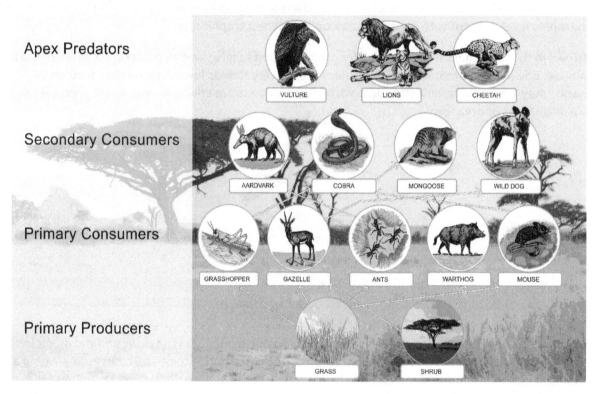

Environmental Factors that Support Ecosystems

Abiotic factors that support the ecosystem include chemical and physical factors. Chemical factors include soil nutrients, water, oxygen content, salinity, and pH. Physical factors include temperature, light, fire, moisture, and soil structure. Stable temperatures allow optimum growing conditions for animals and plants. Organisms generally function within a specific environmental temperature range. If the temperature is below freezing (0 °C), cells will rupture. Temperatures above 45 °C will cause proteins of many organisms to denature.

Water is vital for respiration and photosynthesis and determines how well organisms survive and spread in the environment. Organisms living near the seashore or tidal wetlands are at risk of drying out when the tide recedes. Therefore, organisms such as amphibians—e.g., frogs—are better suited in a humid tropical rainforest environment, which would limit desiccation and gas exchange on the skin of an organism. Water also determines oxygen availability in aquatic environments and flooded soils. For other aquatic organisms, the slow diffusion of oxygen in water can limit cellular respiration. In flooded soils, trees such as mangroves have

360

developed specialized roots that project above the water to help the roots obtain more oxygen. Streams and rivers, unlike flooded wetland soils, are well oxygenated due to rapid gas exchange with the atmosphere.

In many terrestrial environments, the interactions between the soil cycles, water cycles, nutrients, and carbon are vital for sustaining organisms. Soils contain many minerals and organic particles, which contain voids filled with water and air needed for organisms to survive. Common macronutrients include nitrogen, sulfur, phosphorus, potassium, magnesium, and calcium. Examples of micronutrients include metal elements such as iron, boron, and copper. Plants and other organisms have unique life stages in the soil. The egg and larval stages of insect species seek shelter and find food in the soil. The pH of the soil shouldn't be too basic or acidic since it can limit the solubility of toxins or nutrients. For example, minerals such as phosphorus are generally insoluble in basic soils, which will make it more difficult for plants to absorb.

Changes in Ecosystems

While ecosystems are often discussed in their current state, it is important to note that ecosystems are not static; they change over time, which can be a natural process. Weather patterns, geological events, and fires are among the things that can affect an ecosystem. These items can reduce or increase resources, destroy habitats, or even kill individuals. One example of a natural change to an ecosystem is the weather pattern known as El Niño, which is caused by increased water temperatures in the Pacific Ocean and results in weather changes throughout the world. El Niño can have an effect on many ecosystems. In the ocean off the coast of Peru, there are fewer predatory fish because the ocean conditions provide fewer nutrients for the plankton that the fish eat. In areas that experience flooding from El Niño, there can be overflow of salt water into fresh-water systems, which is destructive to those ecosystems. Areas with droughts can see a loss of producers, which is also destructive to ecosystems.

Ecological stability is the ability of an ecosystem to withstand changes that are occurring within it. With **regenerative stability**, an ecosystem may change, but then quickly return to its previous state. **Constant stability** occurs in ecosystems that remain unchanged despite the changes going on around them.

An **ecological disturbance** is a change in the environment that causes a larger change in the ecosystem. Smaller disturbances include fires and floods. Larger disturbances include the **climate change** that is currently occurring. Gas emissions from human activity are causing the atmosphere to warm up, which is changing the Earth's water systems and making weather more extreme. The increase in temperature is causing greater evaporation of the water sources on Earth, creating droughts and depleting natural water sources. This has also caused many of the Earth's glaciers to begin melting, which can change the salinity of the oceans.

Changes in the environment can cause an **ecological succession** to occur, which is the change in structure of the species that coexist in an ecological community. When the environment changes, resources available to the different species also change. For example, the formation of sand dunes or a forest fire would change the environment enough to allow a change in the social hierarchy of the coexisting species.

Climate Change and Greenhouse Gases

Greenhouse gases in the Earth's atmosphere include water vapor, carbon dioxide, methane, nitrous oxide, and **chlorofluorocarbons(CFCs)**, which trap heat between the surface of the Earth and the Earth's lowest atmospheric layer, the troposphere. The increase of these gases leads to warming or cooling trends that cause unpredictable or unprecedented meteorological shifts. These shifts can cause natural disasters, affect plant and animal life, and dramatically impact human health. **Water vapor** is a naturally found gas, but as the Earth's

temperature rises, the presence of water vapor increases; as water vapor increases, the Earth's temperature rises. This creates a somewhat undesirable loop. **Carbon dioxide** is produced through natural causes, such as volcanic eruptions, but also is greatly affected by human activities, such as burning fossil fuels. A significant increase in the presence of atmospheric carbon dioxide has been noted since the Industrial Revolution; this is important as carbon dioxide is considered the most significant influencer of climate change on Earth. **Methane** is produced primarily from animal and agriculture waste and landfill waste. **Nitrous oxide** is primarily produced from the use of fertilizers and fossil fuels. CFCs are completely synthetic and were previously commonly found in aerosol and other high pressure containers; however, after being linked to ozone layer depletion, they have been stringently regulated internationally and are now in limited use. Scientists have stated that the climate shifts recorded since the Industrial Revolution cannot be attributed to natural causes alone, as the patterns do not follow those of climate shifts that took place prior to the Industrial Revolution.

Natural Greenhouse Effect vs. Human Influence

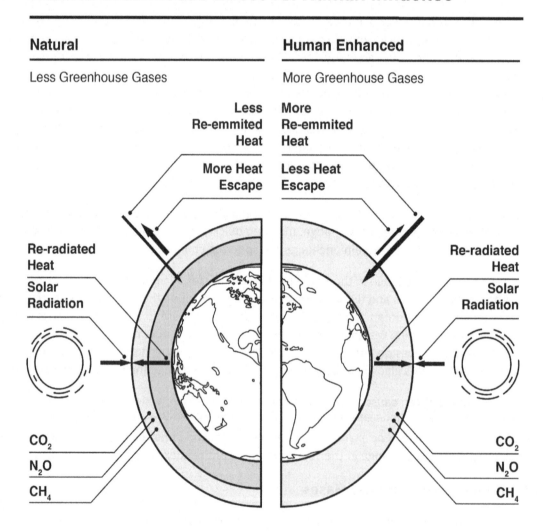

Located in the stratosphere, the **ozone layer** protects the Earth from excessive **ultraviolet B (UVB)** ray exposure. The last century has shown signification depletion of the ozone layer, especially over Antarctica; this region is known as the **ozone hole**, missing almost 70% of its ozone layer. Chlorine molecules are especially

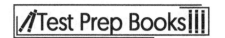

harmful to ozone molecules. CFCs have been a major contributor to the ozone layer's depletion due to their high concentration of chlorine molecules. Almost all CFC production was a result of industrialization and human activity. In 1996, most CFC production was banned; however, it is expected that atmospheric chlorine levels will remain high for the next couple of decades. Additionally, other effects of climate change may prevent the stratosphere from ever reaching the gas composition that existed before CFCs were utilized. While ozone depletion does not contribute to global warming directly, its impact on human health and disease is significant. The consequent increase in UVB exposure is linked to skin cancer in people, and ecosystem and food source disruption in animals. The effect on plants can lead to plant loss, which can indirectly impact the greenhouse effect, global warming, climate change, and human health.

Use and Extraction of Earth's Resources

Extracting resources from the Earth is inherently damaging in its process. **Mining** for minerals and fossil fuels has vast environmental impacts. Surface damage, unnatural erosion, increases in sinkholes, disruption to ecosystems, unnatural animal migration, and pollution are all side effects of mining. **Deforesting** lands to use the land for commercial or residential use or to use the trees for raw materials significantly disrupts ecosystems, contributes to global warming from reduced carbon dioxide consumption, affects water levels, reduces biodiversity, and endangers wildlife. Many rainforests, such as the Amazon rainforest, are believed to have "tipping points" of damage, where the land will be unable to replenish itself and the overall climate will have changed so drastically that it will set off other climate feedback responses. For example, cutting down trees leads to increased atmospheric carbon dioxide in the area, which leads to higher temperatures, which decreases plant water availability, resulting in less vegetation (and the loop continues). **Land reclamation** often focuses on correcting negative impacts to natural resources (i.e., restoring deforested lands by planting indigenous vegetation, replacing sands near beaches that have eroded, and so forth).

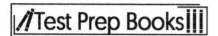

Life Sciences: Life Cycle, Reproduction, and Evolution

Life Cycle

The life cycles of various organisms are described in the following table:

Chicken	Hens are female chickens, and they lay about one egg per day. If there is no rooster (male chicken) around to fertilize the egg, the egg never turns into a chick and instead becomes an egg that we can eat. If a rooster is around, he mates with the female chicken and fertilizes the egg. Once the egg is fertilized, the tiny little embryo (future chicken) will start as a white dot adjacent to the yolk and albumen (egg white) and will develop for 21 days. The mother hen sits on her clutch of eggs (several fertilized eggs) to incubate them and keep them warm. She will turn the eggs to make sure the embryo doesn't stick to one side of the shell. The embryo continues to develop, using the egg white and yolk nutrients, and eventually develops an "egg tooth" on its beak that it uses to crack open the egg and hatch. Before it hatches, it even chirps to let the mom know of its imminent arrival!
Frog	Frogs mate similar to the way chickens do, and then lay eggs in a very wet area. Sometimes, the parents abandon the eggs and let them develop on their own. The eggs, like chickens', will hatch around 21 days later. Just like chickens, a frog develops from a yolk, but when it hatches, it continues to use the yolk for nutrients. A chicken hatches and looks like a cute little chick, but a baby frog is actually a tadpole that is barely developed. It can't even swim around right away, although eventually it will develop gills, a mouth, and a tail. After more time, it will develop teeth and tiny legs and continue to change into a fully grown frog! This type of development is called metamorphosis.
Fish	Most fish also lay eggs in the water, but unlike frogs, their swimming sperm externally fertilize the eggs. Like frogs, when fish hatch, they feed on a yolk sac and are called larvae. Once the larvae no longer feed on their yolk and can find their own nutrients, they are called fry, which are basically baby fish that grow into adulthood.
Butterfly	Like frogs, butterflies go through a process called metamorphosis, where they completely change into a different looking organism. After the process of mating and internal fertilization, the female finds the perfect spot to lay her eggs, usually a spot with lots of leaves. When the babies hatch from the eggs, they are in the larva form, which for butterflies is called a caterpillar. The larvae eat and eat and then go through a process like hibernation and form into a chrysalis, or a chrysalis. When they hatch from the cocoon, the butterflies are in their adult form.
Bugs	After fertilization, other bugs go through incomplete metamorphosis, which involves three states: eggs that hatch, nymphs that look like little adults without wings and molt their exoskeleton over time, and adults.

All of these organisms depend on a proper environment for development, and that environment depends on their form. Frogs need water, caterpillars need leaves, and baby chicks need warmth in order to be born.

Metamorphosis

There are two types of metamorphosis in insects: incomplete metamorphosis, which has three stages, and complete metamorphosis, which has four stages.

Incomplete Metamorphosis: Grasshoppers	Complete Metamorphosis: Butterflies and Beetles
Egg Nymph: a mini-adult with no wings Adult: how the organism will look for the rest of its life	Egg Larva: a wormy, six-legged, massive eater Pupa: a larva encased in a hard shell that dramatically develops and changes in appearance Adult: how the organism will look for the rest of its life

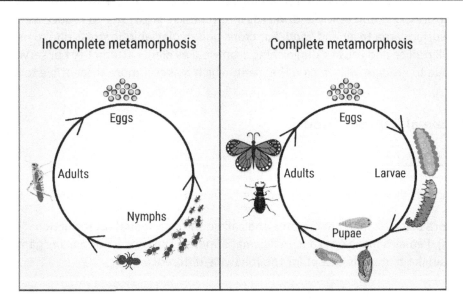

Growth and Development of Plants

The growth and development of plants is affected by the environment. Light, temperature, water/humidity, and nutrition are the main factors controlling growth.

Light varies with each season. Plants have specific photoperiods, which is the amount of time a plant is given light. In general, the more sunlight the plant receives, the greater the plant's capacity to produce food through photosynthesis. Plants generally absorb blue and red light. While blue light is mainly responsible for leaf growth, red light facilitates flowering.

Temperature influences photosynthesis, respiration/transpiration, germination, and flowering. Plant enzymes involved in photosynthesis need an optimum temperature to function. In general, photosynthesis and respiration/transpiration increase when the temperature increases. Cool seasoned crops, such as spinach or lettuce, germinate best between 13°C to 18°C. Warm-season crops, such as petunias or tomatoes, germinate ideally between 18°C to 24°C. If the temperature is too warm, the enzymes involved in photosynthesis will denature, and the plant will not grow.

Gravitropism is a plant's response to gravity and an environmental factor that causes a plant's root to grow downwards (negative gravitropism) and a plant's stem to grow upward (positive gravitropism). Plants contain cytoplasmic components called statoliths, which detect gravity and modify the transportation of plant growth hormones called auxins. In response to gravity, auxins have been observed to redistribute to the lower side of the plant's roots, which helps stimulate plant orientation and growth.

Many plant issues are caused directly or indirectly by environmental stress due to events such as droughts, flooding, extreme temperatures, and mechanical stress. Plants can adapt to harsh environments to ensure continued growth. For instance, trees in windy environments have shorter and stockier trunks. Biotic stress is due to pathogens and herbivores. Abiotic stress tends to be more common and can majorly impact crop yields. For example, if plants receive less water, the plant will wilt since transpiration becomes greater than water absorption. Plants will respond by closing the stomata in the leaf to slow transpiration. The water deficit in the plant will then stimulate the synthesis and release of abscisic acid in the leaves, which helps keep the stomata closed. Some leaves respond differently and will roll into tube-like structures to reduce transpiration by reducing the leaf surface area to air and wind. For crops undergoing abiotic stress due to drought, photosynthesis will reduce and cause a diminishing crop yield as plants attempt to conserve water. In some cases, the stress due to drought will weaken the plant, which makes it more susceptible to attack from insects or disease.

Asexual and Sexual Reproduction

Organism Reproduction

For bacteria, cell reproduction is the same as organism reproduction; **binary fission** is an asexual process that produces two new cells that are clones of each other because they have identical DNA.

Eukaryotes are more complex than prokaryotes and can go through **sexual reproduction**. They produce **gametes** (sex cells). Females make eggs and males make sperm. The process of making gametes is called **meiosis**, which is similar to mitosis except for the following differences:

- There are two cellular divisions instead of one.

- Four genetically different haploid daughter cells (one set of chromosomes instead of two) are produced instead of two genetically identical diploid daughter cells.

- A process called crossing over (**recombination**) occurs, which makes the daughter cells genetically different. If chromosomes didn't cross over and rearrange genes, siblings could be identical clones. There would be no genetic variation, which is a critical factor in the theory of evolution of organisms.

In sexual reproduction, a sperm fertilizes an egg and creates the first cell of a new organism, called the **zygote**. The zygote will go through countless mitotic divisions over time to create the adult organism.

Plant Reproduction

Plants can generate future generations through both asexual and sexual reproduction. Asexually, plants can go through an artificial reproductive technique called **budding**, in which parts from two or more plants of the same species are joined together with the hope that they will begin to grow as a single plant.

Sexual reproduction of flowers can happen in a couple of ways. **Angiosperms** are flowering plants that have seeds. The flowers have male parts that make pollen and female parts that contain ovules. Wind, insects, and

366

other animals carry the pollen from the male part to the female part in a process called **pollination**. Once the ovules are pollinated, or fertilized, they develop into seeds that then develop into new plants. In many angiosperms, the flowers develop into fruit, such as oranges, or even hard nuts, which protect the seeds inside of them.

Nonvascular plants reproduce by sexual reproduction involving **spores**. Parent plants send out spores that contain a set of chromosomes. The spores develop into sperm or eggs, and fertilization is similar to that in humans. Sperm travel to the egg through water in the environment. An embryo forms and then a new plant grows from the embryo. Generally, this happens in damp places.

Cellular Reproduction

Unlike viruses, all living organisms can independently reproduce, but reproduction occurs differently between bacteria and the more complex kingdoms. Bacteria reproduce via **binary fission**, which is a simpler process than eukaryotic division because it doesn't involve splitting a nucleus and doesn't have a web of proteins to pull chromosomes apart. Prokaryotes have simpler DNA compared to cells that have a much larger number of individual chromosomes (humans have two sets of 23 chromosomes—one set from mom and one set from dad, for a total of 46 chromosomes). Think of going from class to class with two identical binders (like bacteria) versus going from class to class with 23 identical pairs of binders (humans); it would be much more difficult to organize the large set of binders than the smaller one.

Binary fission in bacteria is therefore relatively easy. Bacteria copy their DNA in a process called **DNA replication**, grow, and then the replicated DNA moves to either side, and two new cells are made.

Eukaryotic cell division is part of a well-defined cycle. The **cell cycle** is the process by which a cell divides and duplicates itself. There are two processes by which a cell can divide itself: mitosis and meiosis. In **mitosis**, the daughter cells that are produced from parental cell division are identical to each other and the parent. **Meiosis** is a unique process that involves two stages of cell division and produces **haploid cells**, which are cells

367

containing only one set of chromosomes, from **diploid parent cells**, which are cells containing two sets of chromosomes.

The Cell Cycle

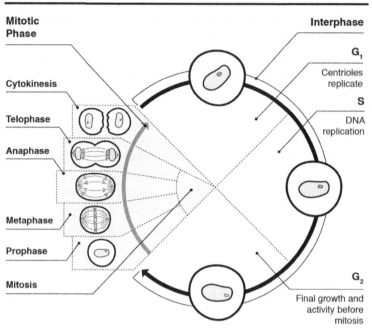

Mitosis

Mitosis can be broken down into five stages: prophase, prometaphase, metaphase, anaphase, and telophase.

- **Prophase**: During this phase, the mitotic spindles begin to form from centrosomes and microtubules. As the microtubules lengthen, the centrosomes move farther away from each other. The nucleolus disappears and the chromatin fibers begin to coil up and form chromosomes. Two sister chromatids, which are two copies of one chromosome, are joined together.

- **Prometaphase**: The nuclear envelope begins to break down and the microtubules enter the nuclear area. Each pair of chromatin fibers develops a **kinetochore**, which is a specialized protein structure in the middle of the adjoined fibers. The chromosomes are further condensed.

- **Metaphase**: In this stage, the microtubules are stretched across the cell and the centrosomes are at opposite ends of the cell. The chromosomes align at the **metaphase plate**, which is a plane that is exactly between the two centrosomes. The kinetochore of each chromosome is attached to the

kinetochore of the microtubules that are stretching from each centrosome to the metaphase plate.

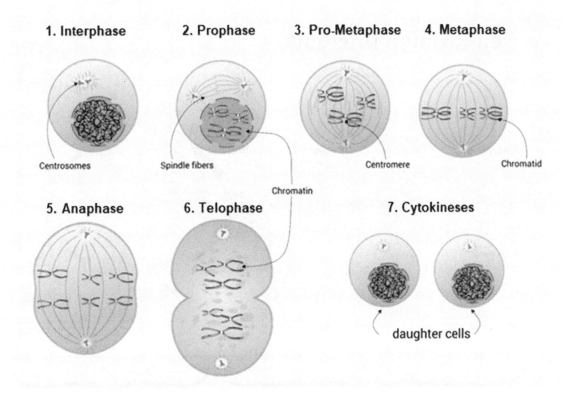

- **Anaphase**: The sister chromatids break apart, forming full-fledged chromosomes. The two daughter chromosomes move to opposite ends of the cell. The microtubules shorten toward opposite ends of the cell as well, and the cell elongates.

- **Telophase**: Two nuclei form at each end of the cell and nuclear envelopes begin to form around each nucleus. The nucleoli reappear and the chromosomes become less condensed. The microtubules are broken down by the cell and mitosis is complete.

Meiosis

Meiosis is a type of cell division in which the daughter cells have half as many sets of chromosomes as the parent cell. In addition, one parent cell produces four daughter cells. Meiosis has the same phases as mitosis, except that they occur twice—once in meiosis I and once in meiosis II. The diploid parent has two sets of chromosomes, set A and set B. During meiosis I, each chromosome set duplicates, producing a second set of A chromosomes and a second set of B chromosomes, and the cell splits into two. Each cell contains two sets of chromosomes. Next, during meiosis II, the two intermediate daughter cells divide again, producing four total haploid cells that each contain one set of chromosomes. Two of the haploid cells each contain one chromosome of set A and the other two cells each contain one chromosome of set B.

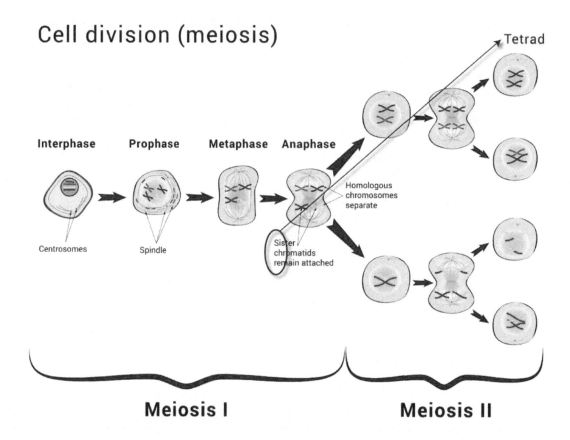

Cytokinesis

Cytokinesis is the division of cytoplasm that occurs immediately following the division of genetic material during cellular reproduction. The process of mitosis or meiosis, followed by cytokinesis, finishes up the cell cycle.

Environmental and Genetics Sources of Variation

Variations are characteristic differences for individuals of the same species. For example, depending on the individual or breed, Canis familiaris, or dogs, have different tail lengths. Inherited variation occurs when genes are passed from the parent to the offspring during reproduction. Environmental variation is due to differences in the surroundings based on what an individual species does. In response to an environmental change, the species will change the phenotype of a specific genotype. For instance, cacti developed thicker stems to keep water and sparse leaves to minimize water evaporation in the heat.

Genetic variation refers to a spontaneous change in genotype between two individuals of a given species. It results from mutations in the DNA base sequence, gene flow, and sexual reproduction.

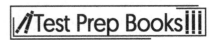

Both environmental and genetic variation can influence the characteristics of an individual species. A dog's weight, for instance, is influenced partly by its genes and partly by how much food it consumes. Similarly, the height of a plant will be determined by its genes and the amount of light and water it obtains.

Principles of Natural and Artificial Selection

Natural selection is a dynamic process during which an individual or species obtains heritable traits that increase its probability of survival. Consequently, those traits allow the species to produce offspring at higher rates than other species with less favorable traits. As time progresses in a given environment, natural selection increases the frequency of adaptation that benefits the species' survival. For instance, the dead-leaf moth *Uropyia meticulodina*, found in the forest floors of eastern Asia, camouflages itself by curling up and using shading to mimic a dead leaf.

Evolution by natural selection will not occur if a species within a population has genetically identical traits. The favorability of a specific trait depends on where the species lives. A new species may arise from environmental changes or when that species settles into a new environment. Through natural selection, species adapt to the new environment. For example, in England, peppered moths were once light gray and black. During the Industrial Revolution of the 1800s, coal burning released smoke and smog into the environment, and trees were darkened with soot. Consequently, the moths were initially more visible on the trees and were more likely to be eaten by birds. Over time, through natural selection, the population of light-peppered moths evolved into dark-colored moths.

Artificial selection refers to the selective breeding of domestic animals and plants so that desirable traits are obtained. A species can be modified over several generations by selecting and breeding a species to obtain a unique trait. For instance, Brassica oleracea is a wild mustard species that was selected and modified over several generations to produce different vegetables with unique traits. The leaves of the wild mustard plant were chosen to produce kale, which has large edible leaves. By selecting different parts of Brassica Oleracea, humans engineered various vegetables over the course of several thousand years.

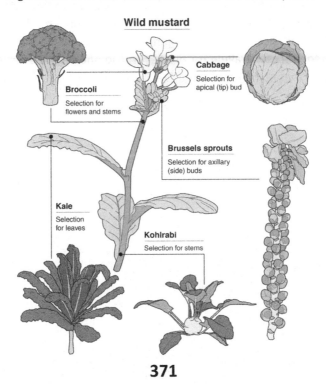

371

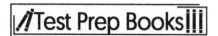

Chromosomes, Genes, and Alleles

Chromosomes are found inside the nucleus of cells and contain the hereditary information of the cell in the form of **genes**. Each gene has a specific sequence of DNA that eventually encodes proteins and results in inherited traits. **Alleles** are variations of a specific gene that occur at the same location on the chromosome. For example, blue and brown are two different alleles of the gene that encodes for eye color.

Dominant and Recessive Traits

In genetics, **dominant alleles** are mostly noted in italic, capital letters (A) and **recessive alleles** are mostly noted in italic, lower case letters (a). There are three possible combinations of alleles among dominant and recessive alleles: AA, Aa (known as a heterozygote), and aa. Dominant traits are phenotypes that appear when at least one dominant allele is present in the gene. Dominant alleles are considered to have stronger phenotypes and, when mixed with recessive alleles, will mask the recessive trait. The recessive trait would only appear as the phenotype when the allele combination is aa because a dominant allele is not present to mask it.

Mendelian Inheritance

A monk named Gregor Mendel is referred to as the father of genetics. He was responsible for coming up with one of the first models of inheritance in the 1860s. His model included two laws to determine which traits are inherited. These laws still apply today, even after genetics has been studied much more in depth.

- **The Law of Segregation**: Each characteristic has two versions that can be inherited. When two parent cells form daughter cells, the two alleles of the gene segregate and each daughter cell can inherit only one of the alleles from each parent.

- **The Law of Independent Assortment**: The alleles for different traits are inherited independent of one another. In other words, the biological selection of one allele by a daughter cell is not linked to the biological selection of an allele for a different trait by the same daughter cell. The genotype that is inherited is the alleles that are encoded on the gene, and the phenotype is the outward appearance of the physical trait for that gene. For example, "A" is the dominant allele for brown eyes and "a" is the recessive allele for blue eyes; the phenotype of brown eyes would occur for two different genotypes: both "AA" and "Aa."

Punnett Squares

For simple genetic combinations, a **Punnett square** can be used to assess the phenotypic ratios of subsequent generations. In a 2 x 2 cell square, one parent's alleles are set up in columns and the other parent's alleles are set up in rows. The resulting allele combinations are shown in the four internal cells.

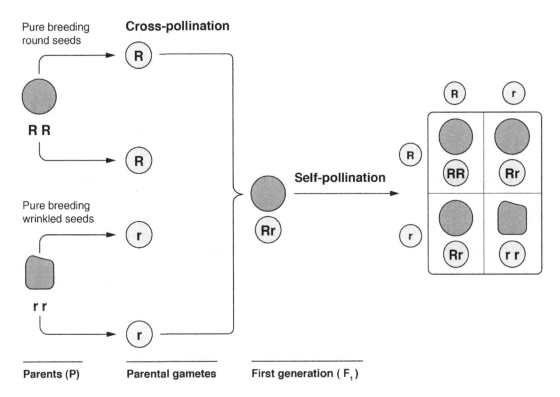

Pedigree

For existing populations where genetic crosses cannot be controlled, phenotype information can be collected over several generations and a **pedigree analysis** can be done to investigate the dominant and recessive characteristics of specific traits. There are several rules to follow when determining the pedigree of a trait. For dominant alleles:

- Affected individuals have at least one affected parent;
- The phenotype appears in every generation; and
- If both parents are unaffected, their offspring will always be unaffected.

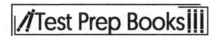
For recessive alleles:

- Unaffected parents can have affected offspring; and
- Affected offspring are male and female.

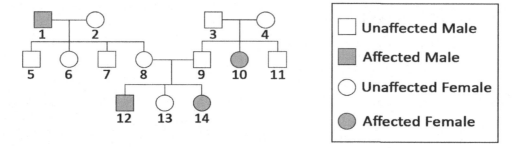

Mutations, Chromosomal Abnormalities, and Common Genetic Disorders

Mutations

Genetic **mutations** occur when there is a permanent alteration in the DNA sequence that codes for a specific gene. They can be small, affecting only one base pair, or large, affecting many genes on a chromosome. Mutations are classified as either hereditary, which means they were also present in the parent gene, or acquired, which means that they occurred after the genes were passed down from the parents. Although mutations are not common, they are an important aspect of genetics and variation in the general population.

Chromosomal Abnormalities and Common Genetic Disorders

Structural chromosomal abnormalities are mutations that affect a large chromosomal segment of more than one gene. This often occurs due to an error in cell division. Acute myelogenous leukemia is caused by a **translocation error**, which is when a segment of one chromosome is moved to another chromosome.

There can also be an abnormal number of chromosomes, which is referred to as **aneuploidy**. Down syndrome is an example of an aneuploidy in which there are three copies of chromosome 21 instead of two copies. Turner syndrome is another example of aneuploidy, in which a female is completely or partially missing an X chromosome. Without the second X chromosome, these females do not develop all of the typical female physical characteristics and are unable to bear children.

Evolution and Natural Selection

Biological evolution is the concept that a population's gene pool changes over generations. According to this concept, populations of organisms evolve, not individuals, and over time, genetic variation and mutations lead to such changes.

Darwin's Theory of Natural Selection

Charles Darwin developed a scientific model of evolution based on the idea of **natural selection**. When some individuals within a population have traits that are better suited to their environment than other individuals, those with the better-suited traits tend to survive longer and have more offspring. The survival and inheritance of these traits through many subsequent generations lead to a change in the population's gene pool. According to natural selection, traits that are more advantageous for survival and reproduction in an environment become more common in subsequent generations.

Evolutionary Fitness

Sexual selection is a type of natural selection in which individuals with certain traits are more likely to find a mate than individuals without those traits. This can occur through direct competition of one sex for a mate of the opposite sex. For example, larger males may prevent smaller males from mating by using their size advantage to keep them away from the females. Sexual selection can also occur through mate choice. This can happen when individuals of one sex are choosy about their mate of the opposite sex, often judging their potential mate based on appearance or behavior. For example, female peacocks often mate with the showiest male with large, beautiful feathers. In both types of sexual selection, individuals with some traits have better reproductive success, and the genes for those traits become more prevalent in subsequent populations.

Adaptations and Natural Selection

Adaptations are inherited characteristics that enhance survival and reproductive capabilities in specific environments. Charles Darwin's idea of natural selection explains *how* populations change—adaption explains *why*. Darwin based his concept of evolution on three observations: the unity of life, the diversity of life, and the suitability of organisms for their environments. There was unity in life based on the idea that all organisms descended from common ancestors. Then, as the descendants of the common ancestors faced changes in their environments, they moved to new environments. There they adapted new features to help them in their new way of life. This concept explains the diversity of life and how organisms are matched to their environments.

An example of natural selection is found in penguins—birds that cannot fly. Over time, populations of penguins lost the ability to fly but became master swimmers. Their habitats are surrounded by water, and their food sources are in the water. Penguins that could dive for food survived better than those that could fly, and the divers produced more offspring. The gene pool changed as a result of natural selection.

Environmental Changes as Selective Mechanisms

The environment constantly changes, which drives selection. Although an individual's traits are determined by their **genotype**, or makeup of genes, natural selection more directly influences **phenotype**, or observable characteristics. The outward appearance or ability of individuals affects their ability to adapt to their environment and survive and reproduce. Phenotypic changes occurring in a population over time are accompanied by changes in the gene pool.

The classic example of this is the peppered moth. It was once a light-colored moth with black spots, though a few members of the species had a genetic variation resulting in a dark color. When the Industrial Revolution hit London, the air became filled with soot and turned the white trees darker in color. Birds were then able to spot and eat the light-colored moths more easily. Within just a few months, the moths with genes for darker color were better able to avoid predation. Subsequent generations had far more dark-colored moths than light ones. Once the Industrial Revolution ended and the air cleared, light-colored moths were better able to survive, and their numbers increased.

Human Impact on Ecosystems

Humans are responsible for many harmful changes to the environment. Deforestation and urbanization cause species to lose the environment to which they are adapted. Overfishing and overhunting greatly decrease the population of many species. Pollution also causes environmental destruction to which species cannot adapt.

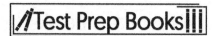
Supporting Evidence for Evolution

Fossil Record

Fossils are the preserved remains of animals and organisms from the past, and they can elucidate the homology of both living and extinct species. Many scientists believe that fossils often provide evidence for evolution. They further propose that looking at the **fossil record** over time can help identify how quickly or slowly evolutionary changes occurred, and can also help match those changes to environmental changes that were occurring concurrently.

Homology

Evolutionists propose that organisms that developed from a common ancestor often have similar characteristics that function differently. This similarity is known as **homology**. For example, humans, cats, whales, and bats all have bones arranged in the same manner from their shoulders to their digits. However, the bones form arms in humans, forelegs in cats, flippers in whales, and wings in bats, and these forelimbs are used for lifting, walking, swimming, and flying, respectively. Evolutionists look to homology, believing that the similarity of the bone structure shows a common ancestry but that the functional differences are the product of evolution.

Homologous Structures

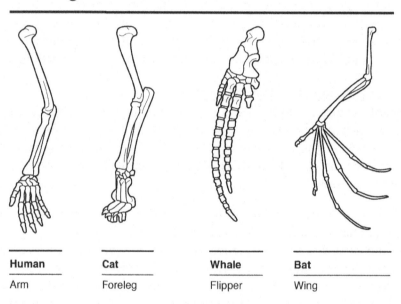

| Human | Cat | Whale | Bat |
| Arm | Foreleg | Flipper | Wing |

Comparative Genetics

In **comparative genetics**, different organisms are compared at a genetic level to look for similarities and differences. DNA sequence, genes, gene order, and other structural features are among the features that may be analyzed in order to look for evolutionary relationships and common ancestors between the organisms.

Earth and Space Sciences: The Solar System and the Universe

Major Features of the Solar System

Structure of the Solar System

The **solar system** is an elliptical planetary system with a large sun in the center that provides gravitational pull on the planets.

Laws of Motion

Planetary motion is governed by three scientific laws called Kepler's laws:

- 1. The orbit of a planet is elliptical in shape, with the Sun as one focus.

- 2. An imaginary line joining the center of a planet and the center of the Sun sweeps out equal areas during equal intervals of time.

- 3. For all planets, the ratio of the square of the orbital period is the same as the cube of the average distance from the Sun.

The most relevant of these laws is the first. Planets move in elliptical paths because of gravity; when a planet is closer to the Sun, it moves faster because it has built up gravitational speed. As illustrated in the diagram below, the second law states that it takes planet 1 the same time to travel along the A1 segment as the A2 segment, even though the A2 segment is shorter.

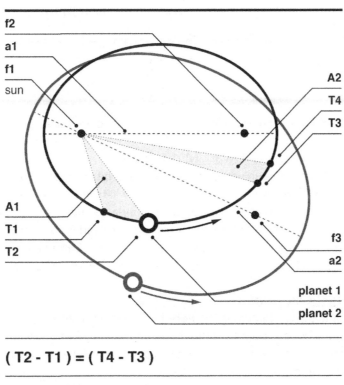

Kepler's Laws of Planetary Motion

(T2 - T1) = (T4 - T3)

Δ TA1 = Δ TA2

377

Characteristics of the Sun, Moon, and Planets

The Sun is comprised mainly of hydrogen and helium. Metals make up only about 2% of its total mass. The Sun is 1.3 million kilometers wide, weighs 1.989×10^{30} kilograms, and has temperatures of 5,800 Kelvin (9980 °F) on the surface and 15,600,000 Kelvin (28 million °F) at the core. The Sun's enormous size and gravity give it the ability to provide sunlight. The gravity of the Sun compresses hydrogen and helium atoms together through nuclear fusion and releases energy and light.

The Moon has a distinct core, mantle, and crust. It has elevations and craters created by impacts with large objects in the solar system. The Moon makes a complete orbit around the Earth every 27.3 days. It's relatively large compared to other moons in the Solar System, with a diameter one-quarter of the Earth and a mass 1/81 of the Earth.

The eight planets of the Solar System are divided into four inner (or terrestrial) planets and four outer (or Jovian) planets. In general, terrestrial planets are small, and Jovian planets are large and gaseous. The planets in the Solar System are listed below from nearest to farthest from the Sun:

- Mercury: the smallest planet in the Solar System; it only takes about 88 days to completely orbit the Sun

- Venus: around the same size, composition, and gravity as Earth and orbits the Sun every 225 days

- Earth: the only known planet with life

- Mars: called the Red Planet due to iron oxide on the surface; takes around 687 days to complete its orbit

- Jupiter: the largest planet in the system; made up of mainly hydrogen and helium

- Saturn: mainly composed of hydrogen and helium along with other trace elements; has 61 moons; has beautiful rings, which may be remnants of destroyed moons

- Uranus: the coldest planet in the system, with temperatures as low as -224.2 °Celsius (-371.56 °F)

- Neptune: the last and third-largest planet; also, the second-coldest planet

Asteroids, Meteoroids, Comets, and Dwarf/Minor Planets

Several other bodies travel through the universe. **Asteroids** are orbiting bodies composed of minerals and rock. They're also known as **minor planets**—a term given to any astronomical object in orbit around the Sun that doesn't resemble a planet or a comet. **Meteoroids** are mini-asteroids with no specific orbiting pattern. **Meteors** are meteoroids that have entered the Earth's atmosphere and started melting from contact with greenhouse gases. **Meteorites** are meteors that have landed on Earth. **Comets** are composed of dust and ice and look like a comma with a tail from the melting ice as they streak across the sky.

Theories of Origin of the Solar System

One theory of the origins of the Solar System is the **nebular hypothesis**, which posits that the Solar System was formed by clouds of extremely hot gas called a **nebula**. As the nebula gases cooled, they became smaller and started rotating. Rings of the nebula left behind during rotation eventually condensed into planets and their satellites. The remaining nebula formed the Sun.

Another theory of the Solar System's development is the **planetesimal hypothesis**. This theory proposes that planets formed from cosmic dust grains that collided and stuck together to form larger and larger bodies. The larger bodies attracted each other, growing into moon-sized protoplanets and eventually planets.

Interactions of the Earth-Moon-Sun System

Earth's Rotation and Orbital Revolution Around the Sun

Besides revolving around the Sun, the Earth also spins like a top. It takes one day for the Earth to complete a full spin, or rotation. The same is true for other planets, except that their "days" may be shorter or longer. One Earth day is about 24 hours, while one Jupiter day is only about nine Earth hours, and a Venus day is about 241 Earth days. Night occurs in areas that face away from the Sun, so one side of the planet experiences daylight and the other experiences night. This phenomenon is the reason that the Earth is divided into time zones.

Time Zones

The concept of time zones was created to provide people around the world with a uniform standard time, so the Sun would rise around 7:00 AM, regardless of location. Longitudinal, or vertical, lines determine how far east or west different regions are from each other. These lines, also known as **meridians,** are the basis for time zones, which allocate different times to regions depending on their position eastward and westward of the prime meridian.

Effect on Seasons

The Earth's tilted axis creates the seasons. When Earth is tilted toward the Sun, the Northern Hemisphere experiences summer while the Southern Hemisphere has winter—and vice versa. As the Earth rotates, the distribution of direct sunlight slowly changes, explaining how the seasons gradually change.

Phases of the Moon

The Moon goes through two phases as it revolves around Earth: waxing and waning. Each phase lasts about two weeks:

- Waxing: the right side of the Moon is illuminated
- New Moon (dark): the Moon rises and sets with the Sun
- Crescent: a tiny sliver of illumination on the right
- First quarter: the right half of the Moon is illuminated
- Gibbous: more than half of the Moon is illuminated
- Full Moon: the Moon rises at sunset and sets at sunrise
- Waning: the left side of the Moon is illuminated
- Gibbous: more than half is illuminated, only here it is the left side that is illuminated
- Last quarter: the left half of the Moon is illuminated
- Crescent: a tiny sliver of illumination on the left
- New Moon (dark): the Moon rises and sets with the Sun

Effect on Tides

Although the Earth is much larger, the Moon still has a significant gravitational force that pulls on Earth's oceans. At its closest to Earth, the Moon's gravitation pull is greatest and creates high tide. The opposite is true when the Moon is farthest from the Earth: less pull creates low tide.

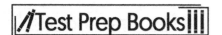
Solar and Lunar Eclipses

Eclipses occur when the Earth, the Sun, and the Moon are all in line. If the three bodies are perfectly aligned, a total eclipse occurs; otherwise, it's only a partial eclipse. A **solar eclipse** occurs when the Moon is between the Earth and the Sun, blocking sunlight from reaching the Earth. A **lunar eclipse** occurs when the Earth interferes with the Sun's light reflecting off the full Moon. The Earth casts a shadow on the Moon, but the particles of the Earth's atmosphere refract the light, so some light reaches the Moon, causing it to look yellow, brown, or red.

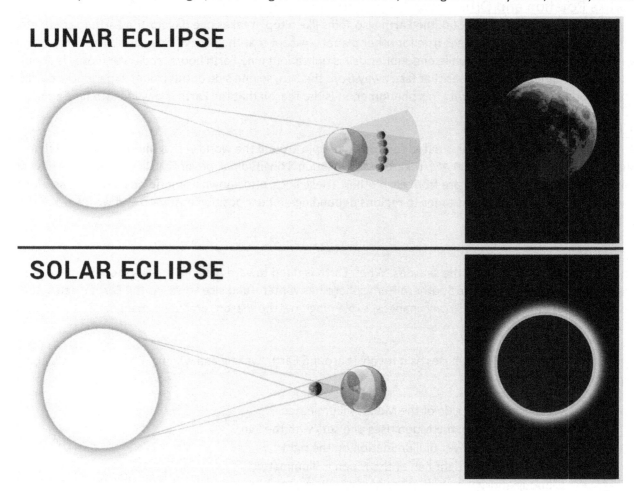

Effect of Solar Wind on the Earth

Solar winds are streams of charged particles emitted by the Sun, consisting of mostly electrons, protons, and alpha particles. The Earth is largely protected from solar winds by its magnetic field. However, the winds can still be observed, as they create phenomena like the beautiful Northern Lights (or Aurora Borealis).

Major Features of the Universe

Galaxies

Galaxies are clusters of stars, rocks, ice, and space dust. Like everything else in space, the exact number of galaxies is unknown, but there could be as many as a hundred billion. There are three types of galaxies: spiral, elliptical, and irregular. Most galaxies are **spiral galaxies**; they have a large, central galactic bulge made up of a cluster of older stars. They look like a disk with spinning arms. **Elliptical galaxies** are groups of stars with no

pattern of rotation. They can be spherical or extremely elongated, and they don't have arms. **Irregular galaxies** vary significantly in size and shape.

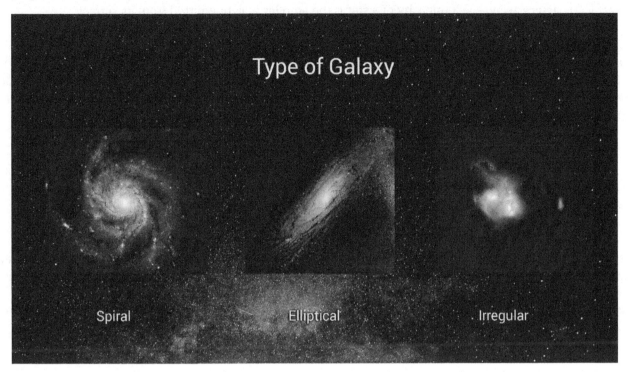

To say that galaxies are large is an understatement. Most galaxies are 1,000 to 100,000 parsecs in diameter, with one **parsec** equal to about 19 trillion miles. The Milky Way is the galaxy that contains Earth's Solar System. It's one of the smaller galaxies that has been studied. The diameter of the Milky Way is estimated to be between 31,000 to 55,000 parsecs.

Characteristics and Life Cycles of Stars

Life Cycle of Stars

All stars are formed from nebulae. Depending on their mass, stars take different pathways during their life. Low- and medium-mass stars start as nebulae and then become red giants and white dwarfs. High-mass stars become red supergiants, supernovas, and then either neutron stars or black holes. Official stars are born as red dwarfs because they have plentiful amounts of gas—mainly hydrogen—to undergo nuclear fusion. Red dwarfs mature into white dwarfs before expending their hydrogen fuel source. When the fuel is spent, it creates a burst of energy that expands the star into a red giant. Red giants eventually condense to form white dwarfs, which is the final stage of a star's life.

Stars that undergo nuclear fusion and energy expenditure extremely quickly can burst in violent explosions called **supernovas**. These bursts can release as much energy in a few seconds as the Sun can release in its entire lifetime. The particles from the explosion then condense into the smallest type of star—a neutron star—and eventually form a **blackhole**, which has such a high amount of gravity that not even light energy can escape. The Sun is currently a red dwarf, early in its life cycle.

Color, Temperature, Apparent Brightness, Absolute Brightness, and Luminosity

The color of a star depends on its surface temperature. Stars with cooler surfaces emit red light, while the hottest stars give off blue light. Stars with temperatures between these extremes, such as the Sun, emit white

381

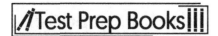

light. The **apparent brightness** of a star is a measure of how bright a star appears to an observer on the Earth. The **absolute brightness** is a measure of the intrinsic brightness of a star and is measured at a distance of exactly 10 parsecs away. The **luminosity** of a star is the amount of light emitted from its surface.

Dark Matter

Dark matter is an unidentified type of matter that comprises approximately 27% of the mass and energy in the observable universe. As the name suggests, dark matter is so dense and small that it doesn't emit or interact with electromagnetic radiation, such as light, making it electromagnetically invisible. Although dark matter has never been directly observed, its existence and properties can be inferred from its gravitational effects on visible objects as well as the cosmic microwave background. Patterns of movement have been observed in visible objects that would only be possible if dark matter exerted a gravitational pull.

Theory About the Origin of the Universe

The **Big Bang theory** is a proposed cosmological model for the origin of the universe. It theorizes that the universe expanded from a high-density and high-temperature state. The theory offers comprehensive explanations for a wide range of astronomical phenomena, such as the cosmic microwave background and Hubble's Law. From detailed measurements of the expansion rate of the universe, Big Bang theorists estimate that the Big Bang occurred approximately 13.8 billion years ago, which is considered the age of the universe. The theory states that after the initial expansion, the universe cooled enough for subatomic particles and atoms to form and aggregate into giant clouds. These clouds coalesced through gravity and formed the stars and galaxies. If this theory holds true, it's predicted that the universe will reach a point where it will stop expanding and start to pull back toward the center due to gravity.

Earth and Space Sciences: The Structure and Composition of the Earth

Types, Basic Characteristics, and Formation Processes of Rocks and Minerals

Rock Cycle

Although it may not always be apparent, rocks are constantly being destroyed while new ones are created in a process called the **rock cycle**. This cycle is driven by plate tectonics and the water cycle, which are discussed in detail later. The rock cycle starts with **magma**, the molten rock found deep within the Earth. As magma moves toward the Earth's surface, it hardens and transforms into igneous rock. Then, over time, igneous rock is broken down into tiny pieces called **sediment** that are eventually deposited all over the surface. As more and more sediment accumulates, the weight of the newer sediment compresses the older sediment underneath and creates sedimentary rock. As sedimentary rock is pushed deeper below the surface, the high pressure and

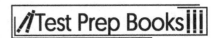

temperature transform it into metamorphic rock. This metamorphic rock can either rise to the surface again or sink even deeper and melt back into magma, thus starting the cycle again.

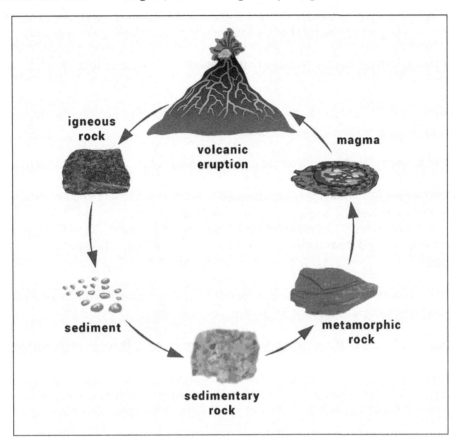

Characteristics and Formation Processes of Rocks

There are three main types of rocks: sedimentary, igneous, and metamorphic. Aside from physical characteristics, one of their main differences is how they are created. **Sedimentary rocks** are formed at the surface, on land and in bodies of water, through processes called deposition and cementation. They can be classified as clastic, biochemical, and chemical. **Clastic rocks**, such as sandstone, are composed of other pieces of inorganic rocks and sediment. **Biochemical rocks** are created from an organic material, such as coal, forming from dead plant life. **Chemical rocks** are created from the deposition of dissolved minerals, such as calcium salts that form stalagmites and stalactites in caves.

Igneous rocks are created when magma solidifies at or near the Earth's surface. When they're formed at the surface, (i.e. from volcanic eruption), they are **extrusive**. When they form below the surface, they're called **intrusive**. Examples of extrusive rocks are obsidian and tuff, while rocks like granite are intrusive.

Metamorphic rocks are the result of a transformation from other rocks. Based on appearance, these rocks are classified as foliated or non-foliated. **Foliated rocks** are created from compression in one direction, making them appear layered or folded like slate. **Non-foliated rocks** are compressed from all directions, giving them a more homogenous appearance, such as marble.

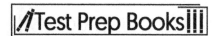

Characteristics and Formation Processes of Minerals

A **mineral**, such as gold, is a naturally occurring inorganic solid composed of one type of molecule or element that's organized into a crystalline structure. Rocks are aggregates of different types of minerals. Depending on their composition, minerals can be mainly classified into one of the following eight groups:

- **Carbonates**: formed from molecules that have either a carbon, nitrogen, or boron atom at the center.

- **Elements**: formed from single elements that occur naturally; includes metals such as gold and nickel, as well as metallic alloys like brass.

- **Halides**: formed from molecules that have halogens; halite, which is table salt, is a classic example.

- **Oxides**: formed from molecules that contain oxygen or hydroxide and are held together with ionic bonds; encompasses the phosphates, silicates, and sulfates.

- **Phosphates**: formed from molecules that contain phosphates; the apatite group minerals are in this class.

- **Silicates**: formed from molecules that contain silicon, silicates are the largest class and usually the most complex minerals; topaz is an example of a silicate.

- **Sulfates**: formed from molecules that contain either sulfur, chromium, tungsten, selenium, tellurium, and/or molybdenum.

- **Sulfides**: formed from molecules that contain sulfide (S^{2-}); includes many of the important metal ores, such as lead and silver.

One important physical characteristic of a mineral is its **hardness**, which is defined as its resistance to scratching. When two crystals are struck together, the harder crystal will scratch the softer crystal. The most common measure of hardness is the Mohs Hardness Scale, which ranges from 1 to 10, with 10 being the hardest. Diamonds are rated 10 on the Mohs Hardness Scale, and talc, which was once used to make baby powder, is rated 1. Other important characteristics of minerals include **luster** or shine, **color,** and **cleavage**, which is the natural plane of weakness at which a specific crystal breaks.

Erosion, Weathering, and Deposition of Earth's Surface Materials and Soil Formation

Erosion and Deposition

Erosion is the process of moving rock and occurs when rock and sediment are picked up and transported. Wind, water, and ice are the primary factors for erosion. **Deposition** occurs when the particles stop moving and settle onto a surface, which can happen through gravity or involve processes such as precipitation or flocculation. **Precipitation** is the solidification or crystallization of dissolved ions that occurs when a solution is oversaturated. **Flocculation** is similar to coagulation and occurs when colloid materials (materials that aren't dissolved but are suspended in the medium) aggregate or clump until they are too heavy to remain suspended.

Chemical and Physical (Mechanical) Weathering

Weathering is the process of breaking down rocks through mechanical or chemical changes. Mechanical forces include animal contact, wind, extreme weather, and the water cycle. These physical forces don't alter the composition of rocks. In contrast, chemical weathering transforms rock composition. When water and

384

minerals interact, they can start chemical reactions and form new or secondary minerals from the original rock. In chemical weathering, the processes of oxidation and hydrolysis are important. When rain falls, it dissolves atmospheric carbon dioxide and becomes acidic. With sulfur dioxide and nitrogen oxide in the atmosphere from volcanic eruptions or burning fossil fuels, the rainfall becomes even more acidic and creates acid rain. Acidic rain can dissolve the rock that it falls upon.

Characteristics of Soil

Soil is a combination of minerals, organic materials, liquids, and gases. There are three main types of soil, as defined by their compositions, going from coarse to fine: sand, silt, and clay. Large particles, such as those found in sand, affect how water moves through the soil, while tiny clay particles can be chemically active and bind with water and nutrients. An important characteristic of soil is its ability to form a crust when dehydrated. In general, the finer the soil, the harder the crust, which is why clay (and not sand) is used to make pottery.

There are many different classes of soil, but the components are always sand, silt, or clay. Below is a chart used by the United States Department of Agriculture (USDA) to define soil types:

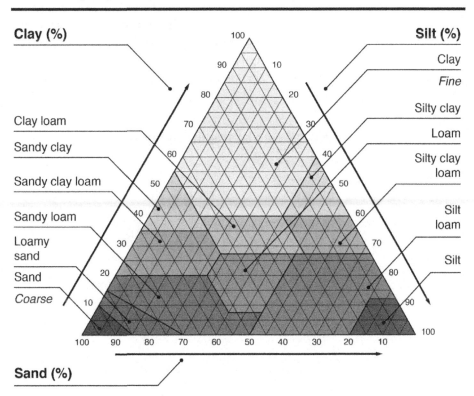

Loam is a term for soil that is a mixture of sand, silt, and clay. It's also the soil most commonly used for agriculture and gardening.

Porosity and Permeability

Porosity and permeability refer to how water moves through rock and soil underground. **Porosity** is a measure of the open space in a rock. This space can be between grains or within cracks and cavities in the rock. **Permeability** is a measure of the ease with which water can move through a porous rock. Therefore, rock that is more porous is also more permeable. When a rock is more permeable, it's less effective as a water purifier because dirty particles in the water can pass through porous rock.

Runoff and Infiltration

An important function of soil is to absorb water to be used by plants or released into groundwater. **Infiltration capacity** is the maximum amount of water that can enter soil at any given time and is regulated by the soil's porosity and composition. For example, sandy soils have larger pores than clays, allowing water to infiltrate them easier and faster. **Runoff** is water that moves across land's surface and may end up in a stream or a rut in the soil. Runoff generally occurs after the soil's infiltration capacity is reached. However, during heavy rainfalls, water may reach the soil's surface at a faster rate than infiltration can occur, causing runoff without soil saturation. In addition, if the ground is frozen and the soil's pores are blocked by ice, runoff may occur without water infiltrating the soil.

Earth's Basic Structure and Internal Processes

Earth's Layers

Earth has three major layers: a thin solid outer surface or **crust**, a dense **core,** and a **mantle** between them that contains most of the Earth's matter. This layout resembles an egg, where the eggshell is the crust, the mantle is the egg white, and the core is the yolk. The outer crust of the Earth consists of igneous or sedimentary rocks over metamorphic rocks. Together with the upper portion of the mantle, it forms the **lithosphere**, which is broken into tectonic plates.

Major plates of the lithosphere

The mantle can be divided into three zones. The **upper mantle** is adjacent to the crust and composed of solid rock. Below the upper mantle is the **transition zone**. The **lower mantle** below the transition zone is a layer of

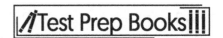

completely solid rock. Underneath the mantle is the molten **outer core** followed by the compact, solid **inner core**. The inner and outer cores contain the densest elements, consisting of mostly iron and nickel.

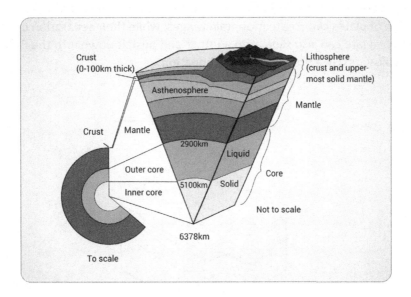

Shape and Size of the Earth

The Earth isn't a perfect sphere; it's slightly elliptical. From center to surface, its radius is almost 4,000 miles, and its circumference around the equator is about 24,902 miles. In comparison, the Sun's radius is 432,288 miles—over 1,000 times larger than the Earth's—and the Moon's radius is about 1,000 miles.

Geographical Features

The Earth's surface is dynamic and consists of various landforms. As tectonic plates are pushed together, **mountains** are formed. **Canyons** are deep trenches that are usually created by plates moving apart, but can also be created by constant weathering and erosion from rivers and runoff. **Deltas** are flat, triangular stretches of land formed by rivers that deposit sediment and water into the ocean. **Sand dunes** are mountains of sand located in desert areas or the bottom of the ocean. They are formed by wind and water movement when there's an absence of plants or other features that would otherwise hold the sand in place.

Plate Tectonics Theory and Evidence

The theory of **plate tectonics** hypothesizes that the continents weren't always separated like they are today, but were once joined and slowly drifted apart. Evidence for this theory is based upon the fossil record. Fossils of one species were found in regions of the world now separated by an ocean. It's unlikely that a single species could have travelled across the ocean.

Folding and Faulting

The exact number of tectonic plates is debatable, but scientists estimate there are around nine to fifteen major plates and almost 40 minor plates. The line where two plates meet is called a **fault**. The San Andreas Fault is where the Pacific and North American plates meet. Faults or boundaries are classified depending on the interaction between plates. Two plates collide at **convergent boundaries. Divergent boundaries** occur when two plates move away from each other. Tectonic plates can move vertically and horizontally.

Continental Drift and Seafloor Spreading

The movement of tectonic plates is similar to pieces of wood floating in a pool of water. They can bob up and down as well as bump, slide, and move away from each other. These different interactions create the Earth's landscape. The collision of plates can create mountain ranges, while their separation can create canyons or underwater chasms. One plate can also slide atop another and push it down into the Earth's hot mantle, creating magma and volcanoes, in a process called **subduction**.

Subduction

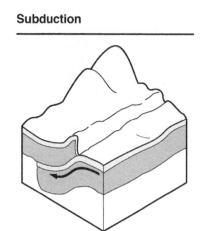

Characteristics of Volcanoes

Volcanoes are mountainous structures that act as vents to release pressure and magma from the Earth's crust. During an **eruption**, the pressure and magma are released, and volcanoes smoke, rumble, and throw ash and **lava**, or molten rock, into the air. **Hot spots** are volcanic regions of the mantle that are hotter than surrounding regions. Chemicals released from volcanic eruptions can fall back to Earth in acid rain.

Characteristics of Earthquakes

Earthquakes occur when tectonic plates slide or collide as a result of the crust suddenly releasing energy. Stress in the Earth's outer layer pushes together two faults. The motion of the planes of the fault continues until something makes them stop. The **epicenter** of an earthquake is the point on the surface directly above where the fault is slipping. If the epicenter is located under a body of water, the earthquake may cause a **tsunami**, a series of large, forceful waves.

Effects of Volcanoes and Earthquakes

Volcanoes are hills or mountains containing an opening or crater whereby hot vapor, gases, and lava (molten rock) erupt from the Earth's crust. Approximately 800 million residents live within 60 miles of the Earth's 1500 most active volcanoes, which have resulted in more than 200,000 fatalities in 500 years. Volcanic ash and gases are hazardous since these substances can lead to the formation of pyroclastic flows, or ardentes, and lahars.

Pyroclastic flows are hot acidic gases mixed with incandescent ash and lava fragments called tephra. These flows may appear as glowing avalanches that race down volcanic slopes at speeds exceeding 100 kilometers per hour. While pyroclastic flows seldom have the force to destroy buildings, these flows are deadly and can cause damage to aircraft. In 1991, pyroclastic flows from Japan's Unzen volcano resulted in homes burning and the displacement of vehicles up to 80 meters. In 2019, an active volcano on Whakaari, or White Island, near

388

New Zealand, erupted and released a superheated pyroclastic flow that caused 22 fatalities; many survivors suffered from third-degree burns.

Lahars are flows that form when volcanic debris and ash combine with water or heavy rain. These flows move down volcanic slopes near stream valleys, forming even when the volcano is not erupting. For example, when the magma is near the surface of a glacial-clad volcano, the ice and snow will melt and combine with volcanic debris. **Lava flows** are streams of hot molten rock or magma that pour from erupting vents. Lava flows are produced by nonexplosive eruptions and move slowly with speeds ranging from 1-30 miles per hour. These flows have temperatures ranging from 800-1000°C and will destroy or ignite anything in their path. Cracks in the Earth's crust allow lava to rise to the surface, which can result in the formation of **volcanic mountains**. For instance, the eruption of magma from the Earth's upper mantle will create a lava flow that deposits ash over the open surface or ocean floor. As the volcano continues erupting, another layer of lava is added to the surface, forming a volcanic mountain. **Volcanic islands** are created by volcanic eruptions that build layers of lava that eventually rise above the water.

While volcanoes are hazardous to property and human health, the impact on the Earth's surface may be positive and negative. The sulfur dioxide produced by volcanoes affects air quality and mixes with rain to form sulfuric acid or acid rain. Ash and acidic rainwater destroy surrounding vegetation and soil. The surface water becomes contaminated when mixed with ash and acidic water, which contaminates groundwater with heavy metals such as arsenic. The contaminants then enter the food chain, a process known as **bioaccumulation**, poisoning livestock and humans.

However, the aftermath of a volcano also has some advantages. For instance, the volcanic rock and ash produced are rich in minerals and offer fertile land for growing coffee and sugar, resulting in high crop yield. Volcanic rocks are often used in building materials, filtration, and infiltration. Volcanoes provide geothermal energy, electricity, and a safe habitat for animals that build nests on the volcano slopes. **Volcanic aerosols** are tiny particles of chemical and ash pushed into the stratosphere. A sufficient amount of aerosols can cool the Earth since the aerosols reflect sunlight away from the Earth's surface.

Tsunamis are destructive sea waves that can be created from powerful volcanic explosions, but they are most commonly caused by earthquakes. An earthquake is an abrupt and rapid movement of blocks of rock slipping against one another along the Earth's faults, resulting in shaking of the ground. The dangers of earthquakes to a population include getting crushed in a collapsed building, drowning due to flooding, getting buried in a landslide, and burning. Seismographs can measure ground motion, which makes it possible to describe the size or magnitude of an earthquake. The **moment magnitude (M_w)** provides an accurate scale of an earthquake and is based on the distance a fault moves and the force required to move that fault. A moment magnitude between 2.5 to 5.4 will cause minor damage, and magnitudes between 5.5 to 6.0 will cause moderate damage to buildings and structures. Magnitudes above 6.1 will cause serious damage. During a strong earthquake, buildings near groundwater or sand may sink due to liquefaction.

Liquefaction is the destabilization of soil or sand when groundwater is forced between grains in the ground. Surface waves may damage buildings, and ground shaking can cause mudslides, avalanches, or landslides on mountains. If a building is located along a fault, ground displacement along the fault will destroy the building. Earthquakes may cause flooding if they break dams along a river. Earthquakes under the ocean can result in tsunamis tens of feet high, which can cause damage to the coastline. An earthquake can cause a fire by severing electrical and gas lines, which was the case for the San Francisco earthquake of 1906. In 2011, *The Great Sendai Earthquake* centered around northeastern Japan had a magnitude of 9.0. The earthquake caused 33-foot tsunami waves, flooding, and widespread structural damage to 400,000 buildings and 56 bridges.

Structural damage at three nuclear power stations in Japan's Fukushima Daiichi complex led to a meltdown, causing a fire and significant radiation leaks. At least 20,000 casualties were reported.

While the earthquake's impact is devastating to human society, earthquakes have benefited life on Earth. Earthquakes recycle the Earth's crust and provide a habitable planet. Specifically, earthquakes have led to the creation of mountains, which are formed when two continental plates of equal thickness and weight collide and buckle. Earthquakes can help regulate the Earth's temperature and even enrich the Earth's soils and oceans with minerals and rare metals.

Factors that Influence Location and Intensity of Earthquakes

Earthquake **intensity** refers to the measured amount of ground vibration at a specified location based on property damage. A modern scale called the modified Mercalli intensity scale uses California buildings as a standard and is a systematic map that uses lines to connect locations of equal damage and ground shaking. The Mercalli scale is a 12-point scale, where a value of **I** indicates an earthquake is not felt, **VII** indicates negligible damage to buildings, and **XII** shows total damage. Approximately 95 percent of the energy earthquakes release originates within a few narrow zones. The **circum-Pacific belt zone** contains the greatest seismic activity and encompasses coastal regions that include the Aleutian Islands, Australia, Indonesia, Japan, Alaska, Central America, and Chile. Earthquakes within the circum-Pacific belt initiate when one plate at a low angle slides against another plate on top. For instance, the **megathrust faults** consist of an overriding plate that sits on top of a subducting plate; the movement of these plates, with respect to one another, have generated Earth's largest earthquakes with magnitudes (Mw) greater than 8. The subduction boundaries span 25,000 miles in the circum-Pacific belt, whereby displacement of the plates is controlled by thrust faulting. The **Alpine-Himalayan belt** is another major concentration of large seismic activity spanning the regions of the Mediterranean and extending past the Himalayan Mountains.

Megathrust Earthquake

Oceanic trench

Subducting plate

Overriding plate

Effects of Tectonic Motion over Time

The development of advanced instruments in the 1960s provided evidence supporting the theory of plate tectonics. Tectonic processes involve the deformation of Earth's crust to create structural features such as ocean basins, continents, and mountains. Over time, Earth's continents gradually moved across the globe, causing blocks of continental material to collide, deforming the Earth's crust and thereby creating mountains. Ocean basins form when a continental block separates.

390

Scientists initially suggested that ice ages occurred when Earth's crustal plates shifted and carried continents from tropical to poleward latitudes. In the book "The Origin of Continents and Oceans," Alfred Wegener outlined the continental drift hypothesis, which challenged the idea that present-day continents and ocean basins had fixed geographic positions. Present-day regions such as Africa, Australia, India, and South America exhibit glacial artifacts and features that suggest the last ice age was 250 million years ago, at the end of the Paleozoic era. During the Paleozoic glaciation, southern continents such as South America, Africa, India, Australia, and Antarctica were one continent located near the South Pole. Present-day regions such as North America and Eurasia did not form glaciers since they lay more toward the equator. After the development of the plate tectonic theory, scientists understood that specific regions of a single supercontinent, called **Pangaea**, contained glacial features, broke into continents, and moved along a different plate to their present-day locations. Over 200 million years, the movement of the plates accounted for many dramatic climate changes. Continents shifted with respect to one another and moved to specific latitudinal positions. The shifting land masses also changed the oceanic circulation, which changed the transportation of moisture and heat; as a result, the climate changed. However, since the movement of plates is gradual (approximately 2 cm per year), climate change is gradual.

Fossilized remains of ancient identical organisms discovered in rocks with a similar age in Antarctica, South America, India, Africa, and Australia supported the existence of Pangaea. Fossil records of a Mesosaurus, a freshwater reptile that lived 260 million years ago, suggested it migrated between present-day Africa and South America. Similarly, fossilized remains of seed ferns, called *Glossopteris*, were dispersed among South America, Africa, India, Australia, and Antarctica. While opponents of continental drift theory suggested transoceanic land bridges were responsible for the distribution of identical organisms, modern seafloor maps do not indicate remnants, thereby supporting the idea of a supercontinent.

Rock types and geological features on different continents provide evidence of continental drift. Igneous rocks in Brazil dating 2.2 billion years are similar to aged rocks in Africa. Other evidence can be identified by the similarity of landforms, such as mountain belts, that end at one coastline but reappear on another continent. For instance, the Appalachian Mountains are found along the northeastern United States and end off the coast of Newfoundland. Likewise, the mountains of Western Africa, the British Isles, and Scandinavia have a similar age and structure. Before Pangaea separated them, the mountain chains in the United States-Newfoundland and Africa-British Isles-Scandinavia formed a continuous belt.

Before

After

Pangaea

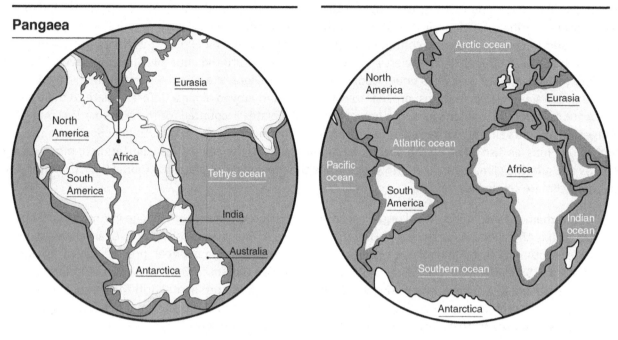

Continental drift of Pangaea began about 200 million years ago.

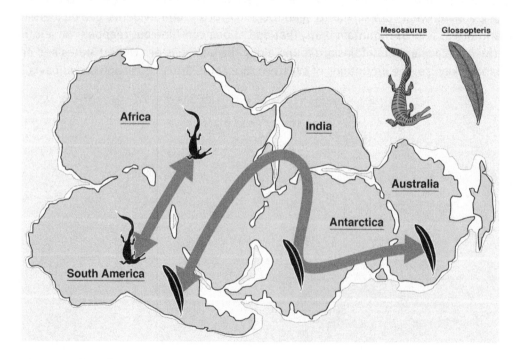

Identical organisms are found in present-day continents due to migration across Pangaea.

Earth and Space Sciences: The Earth's Atmosphere

Basic Structure and Composition of Earth's Atmosphere

Layers

The Earth's atmospheric layers are determined by their temperatures but are reported by their distance above sea level. Listed from closest to sea level on upward, the levels are:

- Troposphere: sea level to 11 miles above sea level
- Stratosphere: 11 miles to 31 miles above sea level
- Mesosphere: 31 miles to 50 miles above sea level
- Ionosphere: 50 miles to 400 miles above sea level
- Exosphere: 400 miles to 800 miles above sea level

The ionosphere and exosphere are together considered the thermosphere. The ozone layer is in the stratosphere and weather experienced on Earth's surface is a product of factors in the troposphere.

Composition of the Atmosphere

The Earth's atmosphere is composed of gas particles: 78% nitrogen, 21% oxygen, 1% other gases such as argon, and 0.039% carbon dioxide. The atmospheric layers are created by the number of particles in the air and gravity's pull upon them.

Atmospheric Pressure and Temperature

The lower atmospheric levels have higher atmospheric pressures due to the mass of the gas particles located above. The air is less dense (it contains fewer particles per given volume) at higher altitudes. The temperature changes from the bottom to top of each atmospheric layer. The tops of the troposphere and mesosphere are colder than their bottoms, but the reverse is true for the stratosphere and thermosphere. Some of the warmest temperatures are actually found in the thermosphere because of a type of radiation that enters that layer.

Basic Concepts of Meteorology

Relative Humidity

Relative humidity is the ratio of the partial pressure of water vapor to water's equilibrium vapor pressure at a given temperature. At low temperatures, less water vapor is required to reach a high relative humidity. More water vapor is needed to reach a high relative humidity in warm air, which has a greater capacity for water vapor. At ground level or other areas of higher pressure, relative humidity increases as temperatures decrease because water vapor condenses as the temperature falls below the dew point. As relative humidity cannot be greater than 100%, the dew point temperature cannot be greater than the air temperature.

Dew Point

The **dewpoint** is the temperature at which the water vapor in air at constant barometric pressure condenses into liquid water due to saturation. At temperatures below the dew point, the rate of condensation will be greater than the rate of evaporation, forming more liquid water. When condensed water forms on a surface, it's called **dew**; when it forms in the air, it's called **fog** or **clouds**, depending on the altitude.

Wind

Wind is the movement of gas particles across the Earth's surface. Winds are generated by differences in atmospheric pressure. Air inherently moves from areas of higher pressure to lower pressure, which is what causes wind to occur. Surface friction from geological features, such as mountains or man-made features can decrease wind speed. In meteorology, winds are classified based on their strength, duration, and direction. **Gusts** are short bursts of high-speed wind, **squalls** are strong winds of intermediate duration (around one minute), and winds with a long duration are given names based on their average strength. **Breezes** are the weakest, followed by **gales**, **storms**, and **hurricanes**.

Cloud Types and Formation

Water in the atmosphere can exist as visible masses called **clouds** composed of water droplets, tiny crystals of ice, and various chemicals. Clouds exist primarily in the troposphere. They can be classified based on the altitude at which they occur:

- **High-clouds**—between 5,000 and 13,000 meters above sea level
- **Cirrus**: thin and wispy "mare's tail" appearance
- **Cirrocumulus**: rows of small puffy pillows
- **Cirrostratus**: thin sheets that cover the sky
- **Middle clouds**—between 2,000 and 7,000 meters above sea level
- **Altocumulus**: gray and white and made up of water droplets
- **Altostratus**: grayish or bluish gray clouds
- *Low clouds*:below 2,000 meters above sea level
- **Stratus**: gray clouds made of water droplets that can cover the sky
- **Stratocumulus**: gray and lumpy low-lying clouds
- **Nimbostratus**: dark gray with uneven bases; typical of rain or snow clouds

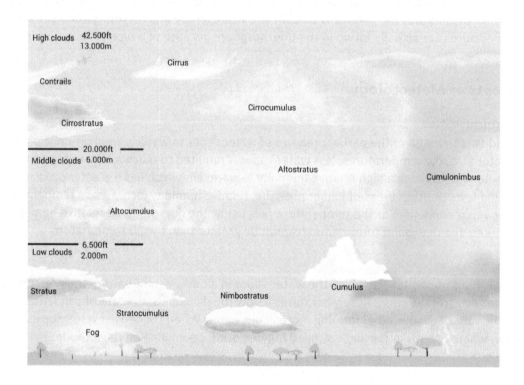

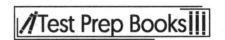

Types of Precipitation

There are three distinct processes by which precipitation occurs. *Convection precipitation* occurs when air rises vertically in a forceful manner, quickly overturning the atmosphere and resulting in heavy precipitation. It's generally more intense and shorter in duration than **stratiform precipitation**, which occurs when large masses of air move over each other. **Orographic precipitation** occurs when moist air is forced upwards over rising terrain, such as a mountain. Most storms are a result of convection precipitation.

Precipitation can fall in liquid or solid phases, as well as any form in between. Liquid precipitation includes rain and drizzle. Frozen precipitation includes snow, sleet, and hail. Intensity is classified by rate of fall or visibility restriction. The forms of precipitation are:

- **Rain**: water vapor that condenses on dust particles in the troposphere until it becomes heavy enough to fall to Earth

- **Sleet**: rain that freezes on its way down; it starts as ice that melts and then freezes again before hitting the ground

- **Hail**: balls of ice thrown up and down several times by turbulent winds, so that more and more water vapor can condense and freeze on the original ice; hail can be as large as golf balls or even baseballs

- **Snow**: loosely packed ice crystals that fall to Earth

Air Masses, Fronts, Storms, and Severe Weather

Airmasses are volumes of air defined by their temperature and the amount of water vapor they contain. A **front** is where two air masses of different temperatures and water vapor content meet. Fronts can be the site of extreme weather, such as thunderstorms, which are caused by water particles rubbing against each other. When they do so, electrons are transferred and energy and electrical currents accumulate. When enough energy accumulates, thunder and lightning occur. **Lightning** is a massive electric spark created by a cloud, and **thunder** is the sound created by an expansion of air caused by the sudden increase in pressure and temperature around lightning.

Extreme weather includes tornadoes and hurricanes. **Tornadoes** are created by changing air pressure and winds that can exceed 300 miles per hour. **Hurricanes** occur when warm ocean water quickly evaporates and rises to a colder, low-pressure portion of the atmosphere. Hurricanes, typhoons, and tropical cyclones are all created by the same phenomena but they occur in different regions. **Blizzards** are similar to hurricanes in that they're created by the clash of warm and cold air, but they only occur when cold Arctic air moves toward warmer air. They usually involve large amounts of snow.

Development and Movement of Weather Patterns

A **weather pattern** is weather that's consistent for a period of time. Weather patterns are created by fronts. A **cold front** is created when two air masses collide in a high-pressure system. A **warm front** is created when a low-pressure system results from the collision of two air masses; they are usually warmer and less dense than high-pressure systems. When a cold front enters an area, the air from the warm front is forced upwards. The temperature of the warm front's air decreases, condenses, and often creates clouds and precipitation. When a warm front moves into an area, the warm air moves slowly upwards at an angle. Clouds and precipitation form, but the precipitation generally lasts longer because of how slowly the air moves.

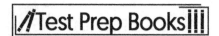
Water Cycle

Evaporation and Condensation
The **water cycle** is the cycling of water between its three physical states: solid, liquid, and gas. The Sun's thermal energy heats surface water so it evaporates. As water vapor collects in the atmosphere from evaporation, it eventually reaches a saturation level where it condenses and forms clouds heavy with water droplets.

Precipitation
When the droplets condense as clouds get heavy, they fall as different forms of precipitation, such as rain, snow, hail, fog, and sleet. **Advection** is the process of evaporated water moving from the ocean and falling over land as precipitation.

Runoff and Infiltration
Runoff and **infiltration** are important parts of the water cycle because they provide water on the surface available for evaporation. Runoff can add water to oceans and aid in the advection process. Infiltration provides water to plants and aids in the transpiration process.

Transpiration
Transpiration is an evaporation-like process that occurs in plants and soil. Water from the stomata of plants and from pores in soil evaporates into water vapor and enters the atmosphere.

Major Factors that Affect Climate and Seasons

Effects of Latitude, Geographical Location, and Elevation
The climate and seasons of different geographical areas are primarily dictated by their sunlight exposure. Because the Earth rotates on a tilted axis while travelling around the Sun, different latitudes get different amounts of direct sunlight throughout the year, creating different climates. Polar regions experience the greatest variation, with long periods of limited or no sunlight in the winter and up to 24 hours of daylight in the summer. Equatorial regions experience the least variance in direct sunlight exposure. Coastal areas experience breezes in the summer as cooler ocean air moves ashore, while areas southeast of the Great Lakes can get "lake effect" snow in the winter, as cold air travels over the warmer water and creates snow on land. Mountains are often seen with snow in the spring and fall. Their high elevation causes mountaintops to stay cold. The air around the mountaintop is also cold and holds less water vapor than air at sea level. As the water vapor condenses, it creates snow.

Effects of Atmospheric Circulation
Global winds are patterns of wind circulation and they have a major influence on global weather and climate. They help influence temperature and precipitation by carrying heat and water vapor around the Earth. These winds are driven by the uneven heating between the polar and equatorial regions created by the Sun. Cold air from the polar regions sinks and moves toward the equator, while the warm air from the equator rises and moves toward the poles. The other factor driving global winds is the **Coriolis Effect**. As air moves from the

396

North Pole to the equator, the Earth's rotation makes it seem as if the wind is also moving to the right, or westbound, and eastbound from South Pole to equator.

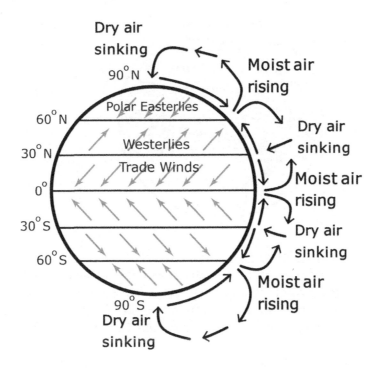

Global wind patterns are given names based on which direction they blow. There are three major wind patterns in each hemisphere. Notice the image above diagramming the movement of warm (dry) air and moist (cold) air.

Tradewinds—easterly surface winds found in the troposphere near the equator—blow predominantly from the northeast in the Northern Hemisphere and from the southeast in the Southern Hemisphere. These winds direct the tropical storms that develop over the Atlantic, Pacific, and Indian Oceans and land in North America, Southeast Asia, and eastern Africa, respectively. **Jet streams** are westerly winds that follow a narrow, meandering path. The two strongest jet streams are the polar jets and the subtropical jets. In the Northern Hemisphere, the polar jet flows over the middle of North America, Europe, and Asia, while in the Southern Hemisphere, it circles Antarctica.

Effects of Ocean Circulation
Ocean currents are similar to global winds because winds influence how the oceans move. Ocean currents are created by warm water moving from the equator towards the poles while cold water travels from the poles to the equator. The warm water can increase precipitation in an area because it evaporates faster than the colder water.

Characteristics and Locations of Climate Zones
Climate zones are created by the Earth's tilt as it travels around the Sun. These zones are delineated by the equator and four other special latitudinal lines: the Tropic of Cancer or Northern Tropic at 23.5° North; the Tropic of Capricorn or Southern Tropic at 23.5° South; the Arctic Circle at 66.5° North; and the Antarctic Circle at 66.5° South. The areas between these lines of latitude represent different climate zones. Tropical climates

are hot and wet, like rainforests, and tend to have abundant plant and animal life, while polar climates are cold and usually have little plant and animal life. Temperate zones can vary and experience the four seasons.

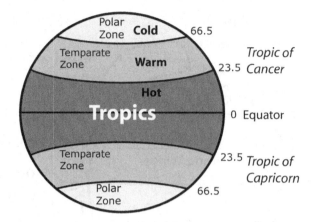

Effect of the Tilt of Earth's Axis on Seasons

In addition to the equator and the prime meridian, other major lines of latitude and longitude divide the world into regions relative to the direct rays of the Sun. These lines correspond with the Earth's 23.5-degree tilt, and are responsible—along with the Earth's revolution around the Sun—for the seasons. For example, the Northern Hemisphere is tilted directly toward the Sun from June 22 to September 23, which creates the summer. Conversely, the Southern Hemisphere is tilted away from the Sun and experiences winter during those months. The area between the Tropic of Cancer and the Tropic of Capricorn tends to be warmer and experiences fewer variations in seasonal temperatures because it's constantly subject to the direct rays of the Sun, no matter which direction the Earth is tilted.

The area between the Tropic of Cancer and the Arctic Circle, which is at 66.5° North, and the Antarctic Circle, which is at 66.5° South, is where most of Earth's population resides and is called the **middle latitudes**. Here, the seasons are more pronounced, and milder temperatures generally prevail. When the Sun's direct rays are over the equator, it's known as an **equinox**, and day and night are almost equal throughout the world. Equinoxes occur twice a year: the fall, or autumnal equinox, occurs on September 22, while the spring equinox occurs on March 20.

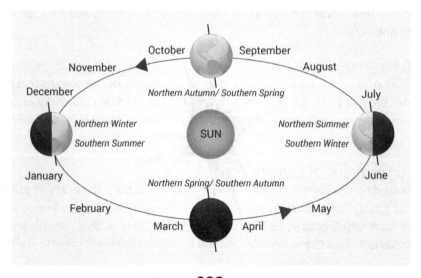

El Niño and La Niña

El Niño and **La Niña** are terms for severe weather anomalies associated with torrential rainfall in the Pacific coastal regions, mainly in North and South America. These events occur irregularly every few years, usually around December, and are caused by a band of warm ocean water that accumulates in the central Pacific Ocean around the equator. The warm water changes the wind patterns over the Pacific and stops cold water from rising toward the American coastlines. The rise in ocean temperature also leads to increased evaporation and rain. These events are split into two phases—a warm, beginning phase called El Niño and a cool end phase called La Niña.

Predicting and Mitigating Impact of Severe Weather and Natural Hazards Using Technology

In 2022, the National Oceanic and Atmospheric Administration (NOAA) estimated that natural disasters in the United States caused $165 billion USD in damage, with most cases due to weather-related disasters. Earthquakes, floods, storms, and heat waves have been the leading cause of fatalities from natural disasters. Scientists have developed many technological tools to improve severe weather forecasting and predict natural disasters to mitigate the loss of life. These tools incorporate **artificial intelligence** (AI), which is a science that involves the design of intelligent computer programs. **Machine learning** is a subcategory of AI that utilizes computer systems to learn and adapt without specific instructions; these systems incorporate statistical models and algorithms to analyze and draw conclusions from data patterns. Machine learning and artificial intelligence have been used to process and interpret large data sets and provide predictive solutions for natural disasters. For instance, researchers at Cornell University have developed machine learning models to forecast slow-slip earthquakes and artificial intelligence to detect earthquake patterns. **DeepShake**, developed at Stanford University, is a neural network computer system that uses machine learning and artificial intelligence to predict earthquake shaking intensity and issue early warnings of strong ground shaking. Artificial intelligence has even been used to create forecasting models that determine where floods will occur and analyze large data sets to make weather prediction more accurate.

Earth and Space Sciences: The Earth's Water

Characteristics and Processes of Oceans and Other Bodies of Water

A **body of water** is any accumulation of water on the Earth's surface. It usually refers to oceans, seas, and lakes, but also includes ponds, wetlands, and puddles. Rivers, streams, and canals are bodies of water that involve the movement of water.

Most bodies of water are naturally occurring geographical features, but they can also be artificially created like lakes created by dams. Saltwater oceans make up 96% of the water on the Earth's surface. Freshwater makes up 2.5% of the remaining water.

Seawater

Seawater is water from a sea or ocean. On average, seawater has a salinity of about 3.5%, meaning every kilogram of seawater has approximately 35 grams of dissolved sodium chloride salt. The average density of saltwater at the surface is 1.025 kg/L, making it denser than pure or freshwater, which has a density of 1.00 kg/L. Because of the dissolved salts, the freezing point of saltwater is also lower than that of pure water; salt water freezes at −2 °C (28 °F). As the concentration of salt increases, the freezing point decreases. Thus, it's

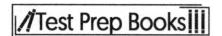

Science

more difficult to freeze water from the Dead Sea—a saltwater lake known to have water with such high salinity that swimmers cannot sink.

Lakes, Ponds, and Wetlands
Lakes and **ponds** are bodies of water that are surrounded by land. They aren't part of the ocean and don't contain flowing water. Lakes are larger than ponds, but otherwise the two bodies don't have a scientific distinction. **Wetlands** are areas of land saturated by water. They have a unique soil composition and provide a nutrient-dense area for vegetation and aquatic plant growth. They also play a role in water purification and flood control.

Streams, Rivers, and River Deltas
A **river** is a natural flowing waterway usually consisting of freshwater that flows toward an ocean, sea, lake, or another river. Some rivers flow into the ground and become dry instead of reaching another body of water. Small rivers are usually called **streams** or **creeks**. River **deltas** are areas of land formed from the sediment carried by a river and deposited before it enters another body of water. As the river reaches its end, the flow of water slows, and the river loses the power to transport the sediment so it falls out of suspension.

Geysers and Springs
A **spring** is a natural occurrence where water flows from an aquifer to the Earth's surface. A **geyser** is a spring that intermittently and turbulently discharges water. Geysers form only in certain hydrogeological conditions. They require proximity to a volcanic area or magma to provide enough heat to boil or vaporize the water. As hot water and steam accumulate, pressure grows and creates the spraying geyser effect.

Estuaries and Barrier Islands
An **estuary** is an area of water located on a coast where a river or stream meets the sea. It's a transitional area that's partially enclosed, has a mix of salty and fresh water, and has calmer water than the open sea. **Barrier islands** are coastal landforms created by waves and tidal action parallel to the mainland coast. They usually occur in chains, and they protect the coastlines and create areas of protected waters where wetlands may flourish.

Islands, Reefs, and Atolls
Islands are land that is completely surrounded by water. **Reefs** are bars of rocky, sandy, or coral material that sit below the surface of water. They may form from sand deposits or erosion of underwater rocks. An **atoll** is a coral reef in the shape of a ring (but not necessarily circular) that encircles a lagoon. In order for an atoll to exist, the rate of its erosion must be slower than the regrowth of the coral that composes the atoll.

Polar Ice, Icebergs, and Glaciers
Polar ice is the term for the sheets of ice that cover the poles of a planet. **Icebergs** are large pieces of freshwater ice that break off from glaciers and float in the water. A **glacier** is a persistent body of dense ice that constantly moves because of its own weight. Glaciers form when snow accumulates at a faster rate than it melts over centuries. They form only on land, in contrast to **icecaps**, which can form from sheets of ice in the ocean. When glaciers deform and move due to stresses created by their own weight, they can create crevasses and other large distinguishing land features.

400

Tides, Waves, and Currents

Tides are caused by the pull of the Moon and the Sun. When the Moon is closer in its orbit to the Earth, its gravity pulls the oceans away from the shore. When the distance between the Moon and the Earth is greater, the pull is weaker, and the water on Earth can spread across more land. This relationship creates low and high tides. Waves are influenced by changes in tides as well as the wind. The energy transferred from wind to the top of large bodies of water creates **crests** on the water's surface and **waves** below. Circular movements in the ocean are called **currents**. They result from the Coriolis Effect, which is caused by the Earth's rotation. Currents spin in a clockwise direction above the equator and counterclockwise below the equator.

Coastline Topography and the Topography of Ocean Floor

Topography is the study of natural and artificial features comprising the surface of an area. **Coastlines** are an intermediate area between dry land and the ocean floor. The ground progressively slopes from the dry coastal area to the deepest depth of the ocean floor. At the continental shelf, there's a steep descent of the ocean floor. Although it's often believed that the ocean floor is flat and sandy like a beach, its topography includes mountains, plateaus, and valleys.

Properties of Water and the Water Cycle

Water is a chemical compound composed of two hydrogen atoms and one oxygen atom (H_2O) and has many unique properties. In its solid state, water is less dense than its liquid form; therefore, ice floats in water. Water also has a very high heat capacity, allowing it to absorb a high amount of the Sun's energy without getting too hot or evaporating. Its chemical structure makes it a polar compound, meaning one side has a negative charge while the other is positive. This characteristic—along with its ability to form strong intermolecular hydrogen bonds with itself and other molecules—make water an effective solvent for other chemicals.

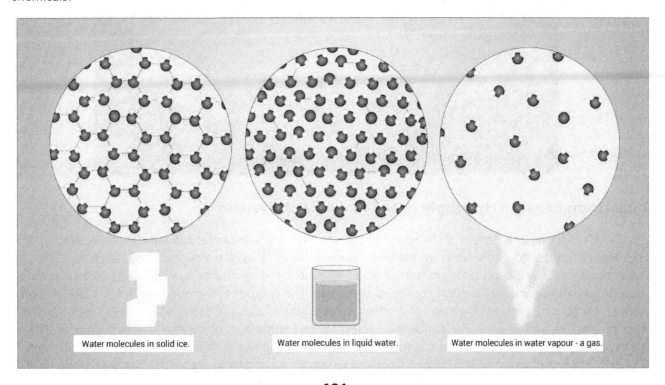

Water molecules in solid ice.   Water molecules in liquid water.   Water molecules in water vapour - a gas.

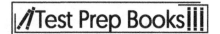

Through advection, water continuously moves through the Earth's atmosphere. The water cycle, or hydrological cycle, is driven by energy from the Sun and gravity. The atmosphere provides an important connection between the continents and the ocean. During evaporation, liquid water from the hydrosphere absorbs energy from the Sun, transforms to water vapor (gas), and moves to the atmosphere. During cloud formation in the atmosphere, water vapor turns into liquid water and condenses to create clouds. When the cloud reaches a saturation point, the liquid water falls from the sky to the Earth, a process called precipitation. During infiltration, water hits the ground, moving downward, until it seeps into streams, lakes, or oceans. In a subsurface flow, water may flow underground in aquifers and return as a spring. Runoff may occur if the snow melts or the ground cannot absorb water, resulting in excess water flow to the lakes or streams. In a percolation process, water flows vertically downward, due to gravity, through the rocks and soil. Transpiration occurs when plants absorb water soaking into the ground. In an interception process, plant foliage allows precipitated water to evaporate into the atmosphere.

The water cycle:

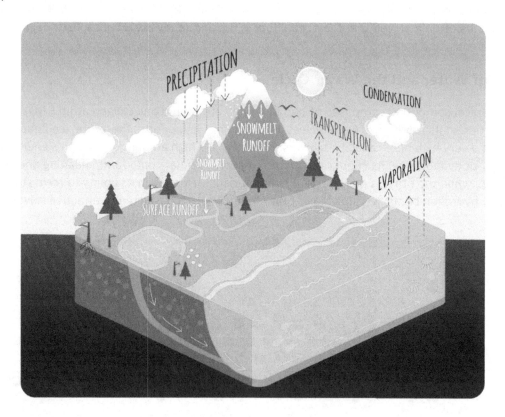

Interaction Between Hydrosphere and Major Earth Systems

The Earth's main spheres consist of the hydrosphere, atmosphere, geosphere, and biosphere. Earth's hydrosphere consists of liquid water in reservoirs, oceans, rivers, lakes, glaciers, and living tissue. Approximately 1.36 billion cubic kilometers of water is found in the hydrosphere, with nearly 96.5 percent stored in the ocean and 1.76 percent contained in glaciers. The atmosphere, groundwater, lakes, and streams account for about 2 percent of water. The cryosphere consists of Earth's surface water in solid forms, such as lake ice, glaciers, and ice caps. The atmosphere refers to the Earth's layer of gas that covers the planet. The gases are denser toward the surface due to gravity. Earth's atmosphere is composed of 78 percent nitrogen gas (N_2), 21 percent oxygen gas (O_2), and 1 percent gases corresponding to argon (Ar), carbon dioxide (CO_2),

402

and other trace gases. The geosphere consists of surface rocks, minerals, and crust soil. The biosphere is the Earth's entire ecosystem and embodies all living things. The Earth's hydrosphere constantly interacts with all other Earth systems and changes the surface of the Earth and its processes.

Spheres	Interaction with the Hydrosphere
Atmosphere	Energy and water are transferred between each sphere through the water cycle via evaporation and precipitation. Water evaporates from the hydrosphere to the atmosphere.
Geosphere	Water is Earth's primary solvent and is the main agent that causes mechanical and chemical erosion of the geosphere. Eroded materials are washed downward to streams, rivers, and back into the ocean.
Biosphere	The hydrosphere provides dissolved nutrients and oxygen needed for species' survival within the biosphere. Animals consume water which may be excreted to the hydrosphere. Plants take water from the surface and move it through its vascular system.
Cryosphere	The melting of snow and ice provides water to rivers and lakes.

Atmospheric Interaction

From the Sun's energy, the evaporation of water in the hydrosphere will constantly add water vapor to the atmosphere. The amount of water cycled through the atmosphere in one year is estimated at 380,000 kilometers, which is enough water to cover the Earth's surface by 1 meter. Since the water cycle is balanced, which keeps the Earth's oceans at a constant level, the amount of water precipitated from the air annually is equivalent to the amount of evaporated water. On land or continents, precipitation will be greater than evaporation. For example, in cold climates and at high latitudes or elevations, water does not evaporate, runoff, or soak into the ground; water becomes a glacier or snowfield. In contrast, the Earth's oceans have an evaporation rate that exceeds precipitation.

Geospheric Interaction

About 36,000 cubic kilometers of water from land will run off to the ocean and cause massive erosion. For example, streams and groundwater are connected to the constant cycling of water on Earth. The movement and distribution of water can shape the Earth's landscape and is responsible for the creation of well-known landmarks such as the Grand Canyon, Mammoth Cave, and Old Faithful. Therefore, water movement from land to the ocean primarily shapes the Earth's land surface.

Fault movement and tectonic activity create depressions on the Earth. As water precipitates, those depressions fill with water to become lakes. Throughout the Earth's history, tectonic activity made mountains with high elevations. Due to water precipitation and gravity, rivers form as the water moves downward from a mountain toward the ocean.

Visual and Performing Arts

Foundations of Art Education

The four general categories of arts are visual arts, dance, music, and theater arts. As children progress through elementary school, they should be exposed to the basic foundations, creative expression and production of each type of art, and the ability to critically analyze a work of art and make connections within a cultural and historical context. Art education should build progressively during childhood so that older children are able to eventually take on these more sophisticated and advanced applications.

There are a wide variety of visual and performing arts that can enhance a child's creativity and learning experience. It is optimal to expose young children to many different types of art – both as a creator and observer – for well-rounded cultural, creative, and comprehensive learning. Depending on the child's age, early childhood educators can tailor art assignments and activities to meet the child's interests, motor skills, attention, and needs.

Each of the four forms of art have a vast list of terminology unique to that art form. Educators should be familiar with such terms to help effectively communicate with and educate students and, more importantly, to empower students to have intelligent and meaningful conversations about artwork with peers, artists, and community members.

Self-Expression and Communication Through Art

One of the fundamental benefits of the arts is their ability to be used as forms of self-expression, creativity, and self-identity, and a means to communicate emotions, culture, and personal and societal narratives. While the youngest students may not fully grasp the ability to express themselves through art, even fairly young children can use art to communicate ideas, stories, and feelings.

Early childhood educators can encourage students to use all forms of art for self-expression and should engage children in active critical thinking and analysis to uncover the meanings and emotions behind artwork generated by others. For example, educators can play a variety of music clips with different tempos, moods, tones, and keys and ask students to explain how the music makes them feel and what they think the composer was trying to express. Compositions in minor keys, at slower largo and adagio tempos, and music with harmonic dissonance may evoke feelings of sadness, trepidation, anxiety, or fear, whereas lively, spirited songs in major keys at faster allegro tempos are likely expressing happier feelings. Students can begin to contrast different moods and types of music and talk about how the moods are conveyed by differences in the music.

Similarly, the students can look at visual artwork and analyze the artist's use of different colors, textures, brushstrokes, etc. to express the feelings behind the artwork. Students can also try to discern the narrative within art, particularly in theater, music, and dance. They can try to understand how stories can be told abstractly and recognize that not every story is told through concrete narrative writing. For example, operatic works and ballets often tell elaborate stories with few or no words. Yet, even when they are presented in foreign languages, operas and ballets can be universally understood by varying audiences due to the emotions and movements present on stage.

While these abstract concepts are likely too complex for young children, as students mature and develop, they will gradually become more aware of the nuances and arts' function as a vehicle of expression. Young children

are able to understand how their pictorial drawings or paintings convey a narrative in their mind; from there, they can begin to understand how artwork generated by another person conveys their storyline. Educators can also encourage students to use art as a cathartic release when they are feeling sad, angry, frustrated, or nervous. Dance, visual arts, and music are constructive, safe, and appropriate ways to temper difficult emotions. Children can use dance choreography and improvisation to express feelings and ideas as well.

Strategies to Promote Critical Analysis and Understanding of the Arts

Early childhood educators should use techniques that foster their students' ability to critically analyze a variety of art forms. Students should develop a toolbox with the appropriate language and terminology to be able to intelligently discuss artwork from a critical standpoint with others. Each form of art has its own unique terms that are important for students to understand, both for their own appreciation and fluency in the arts and for their ability to communicate with others about arts. As students mature and develop their own interests, they will become increasingly able to effectively talk about why they may or may not enjoy a piece of artwork and how it makes them feel. Educators should emphasize that the artistic process is creative and subjective and that each person will have their own opinions about various art forms, but that in every case, the universal principles of respect, diversity, and acceptance apply.

Although generally there is no "right or wrong" in art, the ability to critique creative works is a skill that takes time, maturity, exposure, and intellectual understanding and appreciation of art. Early childhood educators can best help students improve these skills through a broad exposure to many arts, detailed explanations about the intricacies of various types of artwork, and discussions about self-expression through art. For example, a young student may inherently not enjoy a classical piece of music arranged in a quartet, but he or she can learn to critique it from an unbiased position based on that type of music. By understanding the details taking place in the piece (such as how the composer changes the key from major to minor halfway through to invoke sadness or mystery, or how the cello and violin feed off each other as if conversing), students can become more impartial and able to understand art for art's sake.

Educators should instruct students to evaluate questions such as: what was the artist's purpose in creating the work, and is the purpose achieved? Is the style the artist chose appropriate for the expressed purpose of the work? Does the artist have a unique idea in their work? The dialogue underlying these lessons should always focus on showing respect for artwork and creative ideas that are different from the student's own and celebrating diversity of preferences and art forms.

Arts in Various Cultures and Throughout History

It is imperative that early childhood educators focus on the fact that artwork has been used throughout history and in every culture as a means of expression and storytelling. Even seemingly new forms of art were not created out of nowhere, but rather, they have evolved from other previously existing forms of art. One of the best ways to discuss art is actually through embedding it in discussions of history and culture. The evolution of music can easily be discussed through various time periods. For example, the assassination of President John F. Kennedy, the Hippie movement, the Vietnam War, and the Beatles coexisted in the same time period, so students can find similarities and differences among these social and artistic ideals within their historical context.

Students can also study different time periods of art and architecture. In the Classical period, Greek artists focused on physical beauty and the human form, paying particular attention to Olympian gods and their idealized proportions in their works. The Medieval period that occurred in Europe from 500-1400 CE saw a

flourish of Romanesque style art that shifted the emphasis from portraying realism to conveying a message, particularly symbolic Christian ideals.

Students should also learn about the history of art in other countries such as China, with its jade, pottery, bronze, porcelain, and calligraphy. Educators should focus on how various influences over time affected the predominant artwork each period. For example, Buddhism in the early first century BCE increased calligraphy on silks, the Song dynasty created landscape paintings that were popular, and the Ming and Qing dynasties developed color painting and printing with an evolution towards individualism. As China became increasingly influenced by Western society in the nineteenth and early twentieth century's, social realism predominated.

In addition to covering other Asian nations, educators should expose students to traditional African art, which generally demonstrates moral values, focuses on human subjects, and seeks to please the viewer. Educators can also introduce art from the American Indians such as woodcarving, weaving, stitchery, and beading. Art in American Indian populations varies widely from tribe to tribe but tends to beautify everyday objects and create items of spiritual significance. Students should be exposed to music and theater from other cultures and observe the costumes, movements, instruments, and themes in performing arts from places like the Caribbean islands, Japan, Mexico, Australia, Africa, Italy, and Russia.

Dance

Movement

Movement integrates the elements of B.A.S.T.E: body (who), action (what), space (where), time (when), and energy or force (how). The body moves with force through space in time.

- The body may be moved as a whole or as isolated parts; it makes a variety of shapes and patterns.

- Action includes both periods of movement and stillness, as well as movement through space (locomotor) or in one spot (axial).

- The element of space may depend on location, the distance of dancers from each other or other objects, and the direction and pathways of dancers' movement.

- Time comprises speed and rhythm.

- Energy relates to movement flow, power, and weight with characteristics such as sharp or smooth and free or bound.

Stimuli That Inspire Movement
Stimuli serve as the starting point or inspiration for movement. Dancers communicate their response to a stimulus through creative ways of moving. Their interpretations may be literal, inferential/interpretive, or evaluative. The five categories of stimuli include visual, auditory, kinesthetic, tactile, and ideational:

- Visual stimuli include images, sculptures, patterns, and shapes.

- Auditory stimuli include music, human voices, words, and other sounds.

- Kinesthetic stimuli involve movement; examples include animal movements and physical phenomena, such as a tree blowing in the wind or a ticking clock.

- Tactile stimuli are physically touched. Stimuli such as the outdoor environment, objects, and even parts of the human body have different textures and movements.

- Ideational stimuli represent ideas, such as quotes, phrases, poems, books, or other narratives; the dancer's movement aims to tell a story or convey an idea, such as conflict.

Improvisation of Dance Phrases

A dance phrase or movement phrase is a series of movements that convey a complete idea with a beginning, middle, and end, much like a sentence. When introducing phrase improvisation, it is helpful to give students a particular action to focus on or a list of actions to choose from. Incorporating the use of cards or dice with each number linked to a particular action or body part helps randomize the choices. Students may then choose how they will present the movements with different levels, directions, and energy. Provide a chart or graphic organizer to help the students plan how they will vary and perform movement differently in the beginning, middle, and end of the phrase. The sections should be logically connected somehow; movements may flow into one another, be connected by transition movements, or follow a predictable pattern. Encourage students to explore different forms of movement for the same action.

Tools and Techniques in Dance

Dance simultaneously incorporates a variety of elements, including the following:

- *Body:* refers to *who* – the dancer – and may describe the whole body or its parts, the shape of the body (such as angular, twisted, symmetrical), the systems of the body and its anatomy, or inner aspects of the body such as emotions, intention, and identity.

- *Action:* refers to *what* – the movement created in the dance such as the steps, facial changes, or actions with the body – and can occur in short bouts or long, continuous actions.

- *Time:* refers to *when*, and may be metered or free. Time may also refer to clock time or relationships of time such as before, after, in unison with, or faster than something else.

- *Space:* refers to *where* through space, and how the dancer fills the space and interacts with it. For example, it can refer to whether the dancer's body is low to the ground or up high; moving or in place; going forward, backwards, or sideways; in a curved or random pattern; in front or behind others; or in a group or alone.

- *Energy:* refers to *how*. It is with energy that a force or action causes movement. Dancers may play with flow, tension, and weight. Their energy may be powerful or it may be gentle and light.

Technical Skills

Technical skills are those that differentiate dance from movement. They include actions, dynamics, spatial awareness, timing, and rhythmic components, as well as the use of physical skills to create stylistically accurate movements that effectively portray the intended interpretation:

- Physical skills include body alignment, balance, flexibility, and strength.

- Actions include the movement of different body parts, the way the body moves through space and stillness between movements, as well as small gestures and facial expressions.

407

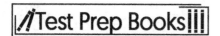
- Dynamics describe movement qualities like the speed (tempo), sharpness, and flow of movement. Flow can be fast, slow, accelerating/decelerating, abrupt/flowing, and sudden or sustained.

- Spatial awareness takes into account pathways, levels, directions, and sizes of movements. Dancers can most effectively use space in their presentation by being aware of other dancers and the surrounding space.

- Timing involves the way dancers move with the beat and rhythm of the music, as well as multiple dancers' ability to dance in unison.

- Rhythm describes how the timing and structure of movements are used to match the music, or the dance beat itself when music isn't used.

Analysis of Dance

A review of dance works considers the artist's intent, meaning, and expression as conveyed through the elements of dance (i.e., body, action, space, time, and energy), technique, production (e.g., costumes, props, lighting), and context (e.g., social, historical, cultural).

Dance interpretation begins with being able to perceive and describe the work: how the dancers move their bodies, as well as their relationship to each other, the music (tempo and rhythm), and the space. Dance elements are analyzed based on how they were used and whether or not they were technically successful.

Beyond describing elements of the work, effective analysis suggests a possible meaning for the movement and production within the context of the work. Consider the choreographer's goal in using the dance elements to entertain, provide commentary, or emotionally stir the audience. What was the choreographer trying to express? Depending on the context and purpose, some research or explanation before a performance can enhance viewers' understanding and ability to analyze the intended meaning.

Based on the above information, evaluate whether or not the dance was technically successful and whether or not it completed its intended goal. Additionally, personal experiences and preferences may be used to form an overall opinion of the work and whether or not it was effective, entertaining, and enjoyable. Finally, a critique may mention specific strengths or weaknesses of the performance, choreography, or production elements and how they could be improved.

Regional, Community, and Cultural Styles and Genres Connected to Historical Contexts

Context Provides A Deeper Understanding Of The Full Implicit Meaning Behind A Style Or Work By explaining influences on different dance genres. Historical events create context, and so can artistic influences, shifts in social norms, innovations, and philosophical ideas.

The origins of dance date back as early as 8000 BCE, as evidenced in cave paintings of dances that appear to be in a religious context. Early dance was commonly ritualistic, though it was also later performed for entertainment. Ballet, one of the earliest performance styles of dancing which dates back to the Italian Renaissance, has been repeatedly deconstructed to create unique forms of dance.

On the other hand, informal, easy-to-learn folk dances at large, casual social gatherings reflected both culture and tradition. The mid-fourteenth century saw an increase in refined aristocratic social gatherings, where demure social dances, either in large-group or couple formations, replaced folk dances in some circles. Dances

408

like the waltz and polka eventually lead to ballroom dances, such as the tango and foxtrot, of the twentieth century.

Changes in music through the voluntary or involuntary migration of people from different cultures was a major force in the formation of dance styles beyond ballroom in America. The advent of jazz music in the 1920s spurred more energetic movements of arms, hips, and torsos while eliminating the requisite synchronized couple form of social dance. From house dance, with its Latin and African influences, to the improvisational roots of breaking and the Black American influence on hip hop, dance forms continue to evolve in the ever-changing context of the cultural landscape.

Dance

Dance incorporates not only music, creativity, and arts, but also physical activity, which is very important to young children. Dance can help improve kinesthetic sense or awareness of one's body in space, rhythm and mathematical thinking, fluidity of motion, and coordination and balance. There are many varieties of dance, and educators should pick age-appropriate music and dances. The youngest children tend to do best with free movement to music or simple choreographed dances such as the hokey pokey, which are accompanied by easy sing-along songs.

Dance Terminology

In dance, a *step* is one isolated movement, and *choreography* refers to the arrangement of a series of steps. Even young students can learn simple choreography that they rehearse with an instructor and perform with classmates as a group. Older students can learn about different styles of dance such as the waltz, tap, jazz, and ballet, as well as more contemporary styles like *lyrical dance* (combining ballet and jazz) or *fusion dance* (a highly rhythmical dance form). Students of ballet should be familiar with terms like *pirouette* (spinning on one foot or on the points of the toes), *arabesque* (standing on one leg while extending one arm in front and the other arm and leg behind), *plié* (bending at the knees while holding the back straight), *elevé* (rising up from flat foot to pointed feet), and *pivot* (turning the body without traveling to a new location; a pirouette is a type of pivot). Students can also learn about folk dances, partner dances, and line dances.

Music

Studies show that learning an instrument, especially at a young age, improves thinking, mathematical skills, attention, and brain activity. Children benefit from being exposed to a variety of instruments and musical genres including woodwinds, strings, brass, piano, vocals, jazz, blues, classical, folk, etc. Older children can learn basic music theory and how to read music, and may be able to take on more advanced instrument lessons and play or sing collaboratively in groups. As children mature, their attention spans, fine motor skills, ability to understand and maintain rhythm and pitch, and musical fluency improve. Activities and expectations should be age-appropriate. Smaller versions of some instruments are also manufactured and available to very young children to fit their small bodies and fingers.

For young children, learning to identify and maintain rhythm and beat is an important early skill and can be practiced by listening to music accompanied by physical movements such as clapping, stomping, dancing, or following the beat with percussive instruments like tambourines or small drums. They can learn to recognize musical notes and the position of the notes on a staff as well as the various characteristics of basic note types such as eighth notes, quarter notes, half notes, and whole notes. Singing and learning basic traditional and folk songs are simple ways to expose children to music as an easy, low-cost group activity. As children get older and

more experienced, the group can be divided into sections to create harmonies and maintain separate singing roles within a varied group, which is a more advanced skill requiring concentration, attention, and group coordination.

Music Terminology

Students should be familiar with terms related to **meter**, which is the repeating pattern of stressed and unstressed sounds in a piece of music. While meter is a somewhat complex concept, students can easily understand the idea of a musical beat, which is the audible result of meter. In written music, meter is noted by a time signature, which looks like a fraction with one number on the top and one number on the bottom, like ¾. The bottom number expresses the beat as a division of a whole note (for example, the number four means that it is a quarter note), while the top number shows how many beats make up a bar (so ¾ means that three quarter note beats make up one bar).

In addition to patterns of stress, music also contains an arrangement of sounds, known as its melody. **Melody** refers to the development of a single tone; when many tones are combined simultaneously in a way that sounds pleasing to the listener, it is referred to as **harmony**. Other sound elements related to tone include **chords** (the combination of musical tones), **keys** (the principal tone in a piece of music), and **scales** (a series of tones at fixed intervals, either ascending or descending, usually beginning at a certain note). These elements can be described as either major or minor.

Words to describe the **tempo**, or the speed of a piece of music, include, from slowest to fastest: *largo, adagio, andante, allegro, vivace,* and *presto*. In terms of the intensity of the sound, *piano* refers to music that is played softly whereas *forte* means played with force. Students should also be familiar with vocabulary terms that describe different instruments, different genres of music, and different musical periods.

Tools and Techniques in Music

Instruments used in the early education classroom typically fall into one of the following categories: melodic instruments (melody bells, xylophones, flutes, and recorders), rhythmic instruments (drums, triangles, tambourines, and blocks), or harmonic instruments (chording instruments such as the autoharp). The key elements of music include rhythm, melody, harmony, form (the structure or design of the music, usually referring to the music's different sections and their repetition, such as binary (AB), ternary (ABA), theme and variation and rondo (ABACA), and the musical phrases), and expression [dynamics (volumes) and timbre].

Musical Ideas and Connections

Musical ideas are the musical creations of composers used to express the concepts of their art. Ideas comprise note choices, changes in rhythm, dynamics, timbre, and emotion connected in a way that tells a story, shapes a commentary, or entertains.

Various thoughts, feelings, and experiences can form the basis of new musical ideas. Visuals, such as photos and other art media, as well as literary stories, historical events, and personal experiences, can serve as inspiration for musical ideas

The context of the idea informs the musical rhythm and the development of the melody, but creating something from nothing can be difficult. Existing music can be used effectively to inspire original arrangements of chords, melodies, drumbeats, and rhythms; mixing such characteristics from different songs can create a unique idea. While people tend to gravitate toward the musical genres they personally prefer, listening to

410

other genres exposes novel characteristics that can be adapted to an idea in a preferred genre. Similarly, improvisation and switching the instruments with which you are working can help inspire new sounds. Finally, creating with another producer can expand the number of options created and increase the likelihood of developing a cohesive idea.

Theater

Theater

Educators can expose young children to theater, both as participants and audience members. Young children may enjoy puppets, and older children can begin to take on roles and learn and memorize short lines. Memorization and recitation skills are transferable to educational activities in other subjects such as spelling words, learning history dates, and memorizing state capitals. Theater activities provide opportunities for imaginative play for children who enjoy dressing up, pretending to be various characters, imagining and acting out scenes, improvising lines, and mimicking jobs, characters, and roles in society. This is healthy and developmentally-appropriate.

Creating a Story

Using Voice and Gestures to Create or Retell Stories

Gestures and facial expressions use the body and face to communicate emotions and personality in a story. For example, a sad face and bouncing shoulders emphasize the sobbing of a distraught character. Storytellers may vary the pace and quality of their gestures to further enhance the story. For example, an athletic character might walk confidently and with strength, while an elderly character moves slowly in a slightly hunched position. Such visuals provide context and add depth to the story, stoking and supplementing the audience's imagination, often without having to say a word. Gestures can be particularly beneficial in highlighting irony or sarcasm—that is, when the character is feeling the opposite of what they are saying.

The tonality, resonance, intonation, and inflection of a storyteller's voice can be altered to emphasize words and phrases, differentiate characters' voices, and create sound effects that add to the story. Additionally, changes in pace, effective use of pauses and silence, and repetition or exaggeration can all add to the audience's engagement with the story.

Design Ideas to Support Stories and Given Circumstances

Given circumstances are the who, when, where, why, and how of a character's environmental, historical, and situational conditions. They challenge the actor to think and act as someone else would by considering how those circumstances would influence the character's actions. The actor is already familiar with these conditions through their knowledge of the story and any additional circumstances they have created for the character. They are tasked with conveying this information to the audience through their performance.

Design elements like costumes, sets, props, and even sounds and lighting, can also help provide context to the audience that implies given circumstances. Sets help stage the location, which gives the audience details such as the time period of the story. Lights of varying brightness and colors can also convey a feeling about the setting, while costumes and props highlight important differences among characters, such as social status. Similarly, sounds and music can emphasize character traits, such as sinister music that plays during a villain's entrance.

Dramatic Play or Guided Drama Experience

Dramatic play (role play), or guided imagery, helps build actors' imaginations and encourages them to place themselves in a role. In guided imagery, actors listen to a story and imagine themselves experiencing the events. By concentrating all of their senses on the experience described in the narrative, they immerse themselves within the role to help them gain knowledge and build emotion as a character within the story. In dramatic play, also known as guided drama, actors assume roles and act out a scenario in the role they have chosen.

Within each type of dramatic play, the actor uses what they know about the role and the given circumstances to create their take on a character. They make decisions about their background, feelings, and reactions to situations within the plot. When engaging in dramatic play or acting out a guided scenario, the actor then makes choices about how to make the character unique, including reacting, incorporating personal feelings into a character, altering the delivery of lines, as well as choosing gestures and facial expressions to enhance both the speaking and non-speaking portions of a story.

Improvisation and Design

Forms of Improvisation

Improvisation is an art form without a predetermined text. It often begins with the informal rule of "Yes, and...." The improviser says "yes" to sharing a word, thought, feeling, or musical expression or, when working with others, to what other improvisers have offered. Then they add something related to build upon the original concept. Joint creators must work together; each taking turns to offer something that helps to define the context and progress the story, song, or idea. Improvisers should accept the offers to keep the idea progressing and then build on it with their own offers.

No matter the medium, artists are encouraged to draw on a mixture of experiences, feelings, memories, and people from their own lives or from existing stories, songs, or histories. They use the starting idea to propel them to another element that comes to them by association and progressively build from there. Associations come in many forms, such as exploring conventions from different periods in time, connecting a place to a person, attributing truthful personal details to fictional situations, describing a related sensation, or even varying words, melodies, or rhythms that sound similar. In addition to pure improvisation, scripted performances may be varied through improvisation in movement, gestures, intonation, accents, rhythm, and timing of delivery, among other things.

Technical Theatre Elements and Non-Representational Materials

Technical elements of theater provide the audience with important information about the setting, time period, and mood of the storyline before the actors say a word. Scenery, lighting, sound, props, and costumes are all important aspects of technical theater. Non-representational materials, or those that don't necessarily closely resemble an object, create many possibilities for students to create technical elements from ordinary materials that are easy and inexpensive to access.

A costume design begins with visualizing the character. Consider details like the season during which the story is set, who the character is, and what styles and colors would suit them. It may be helpful to start with a known character and imagine a costume for a particular experience. A colored drawing or rendering, or alternatively a model, creates a physical representation of the idea that can be modified before starting on the real thing. Non-representational materials, including ordinary clothing, fabric scraps, and recycled resources can be used to create the costume to scale.

Set design involves making decisions that shape the location where the story takes place. The design of the stage affects the position of the audience relative to the action. Stage height may place the actors at the audience's eye level, while a lower stage that shares the floor with the audience draws them closer to the play. Similarly, depth determines how close or far the audience is from all aspects of action on the stage. Set design also includes the nature and type of background or scenery—Will it be three-dimensional? Painted on a backdrop? Will it stay the same for the entire production, or will it change with different scenes? Consider whether a set should include doors, stairs, or other integrated props. Like costume designers, set designers put their ideas into a rendering, or sketch, before they construct models of the set. Sets can be constructed with non-representational materials at hand, including cardboard, desks, chairs, paper, and paint.

While lighting may be reserved for large-scale productions, music and sound effects can easily be integrated into classroom productions. Sounds may be as basic as a knock at the door or more advanced, like a crowd chanting or a weather event. Sounds may be pre-recorded, made live with materials at hand (knocking on a desk to simulate a knock at the door), or through vocalizations (someone offstage making animal sounds).

Contextual Analysis

Contexts or perspectives (e.g., cultural, historical, global, social) impact many aspects of a dramatic work including the language used, the relationships of the characters, and any metaphors implied. The historical context, including the social, religious, and political norms of a time and place, may be explicitly expressed in a drama, such as the story of the 1832 June Rebellion told in *Les Misérables*. Or it may be used to highlight the way history repeats itself through a metaphor. *The Crucible*, for example, is a play ostensibly about the Salem witch hunts of the 1690s but was written in the 1970s as a political commentary on the similar approach American politicians were taking against communists during the Red Scare of the 1950s.

Analyzing the details of a work's context allows the viewer to analyze it not only by current standards but also at a level of understanding intended by the writer. This can allow the viewer to better understand the writer's motives, meaning, and goals for the work. An examination of the circumstances driving a writer helps reveal their motive, whether that's to highlight a specific event, general observations about life, or a commentary on culture or society. Understanding the writer's motive clarifies what they are asking the audience to do; perhaps the work is meant as a call to action or as a means of inspiring reflection.

Theater Arts Terminology

Students can become familiar with a host of terms related to theater productions. In terms of people working in theater, there is the **director** leading the production and **actors** performing it. The **cast** is comprised of a group of actors, and an organization of actors and other theater workers is known as a **company**. During the casting process, actors usually need to **audition** for parts in a play, and they may get a **callback** if their audition goes well! In addition to a main performer, leading roles in a production might also have an **understudy**, an actor who can step into the role when the main performer is unable to appear in the show.

On the technical side, students can learn about *props, sets, costumes* and *wardrobe, effects,* and *staging*. Theater arts education also presents an opportunity to teach students about the literary aspects of a play, such as the **narrator**, *act* and *scene* divisions, and stage directions contained in the script. Students can also become familiar with different dramatic modes like *comedy* and *tragedy.* They can learn about the structure of classic drama as well as more open ended structures like *ad lib* and *improvisation.*

Tools and Techniques in Theater Arts

The main skills of the theatrical arts are literary, technical, and performance elements. For theater, teachers can use a variety of techniques to incorporate dramatic arts into the classroom, including the following:

Theater-in-Education (TIE)

This is performed by teachers and students using curriculum material on social issues. Participants take on roles that enable them to explore and problem-solve in a flexible structure that is also educational. TIE productions are conducted with clear educational objectives, such as teaching facts or communicating a lesson to the audience.

Puppetry

Puppetry can be used for creative drama with either simple puppets and stages made of bags, cardboard, socks, or more elaborate, artistic materials. Using puppets in theater allows students to tell stories about a wide variety of characters and settings without requiring large and complex costumes, props, or sets. Telling stories with puppets also allows children to develop their motor skills.

More formal theater works for children are typically product-oriented and audience-centered, and children can be either participants or audience members. Such forms may include the following:

Traditional Theater

Actors use characters and storylines to communicate and the audience laughs, applauds, or provides other feedback. The performers and audience are separate entities and the acting takes place on a stage, supported by technical workers.

Participation Theater

Students can engage their voices or bodies in the work by contributing ideas, joining the actors, or contributing in other ways. This is more interactive than traditional theater.

Story Theater

Often told with simple sets, story theater can take place easily in the classroom with minimal scenery and costumes. Due to the sparse use of sets, props, and costumes, story theater often incorporates improvisational strategies to communicate character and setting to the audience. The actors function as characters and narrators and play multiple parts, often commenting on their own actions in their roles.

Readers' Theater

Readers perform a dramatic presentation while reading lines (typically from children's literature), enabling performance opportunities in the absence of elaborate staging or script memorization. This allows students to focus on emotional expression and speaking skills while reading their lines. The students can sit or stand but no movement is needed.

Visual Arts

Visual arts include things like drawing, painting, sketching, collage, sculpture, etc. Before the age of three, most artwork is produced less in an artistic way and more in a scientific and sensory way. Children at these youngest ages are more interested in the textures, colors, and shapes of what they create rather than expressing any sort of emotion or symbol. There are a variety of crafting activities that young children enjoy and can benefit from including finger painting, pasting, modeling with Play-Doh and clay, folding paper for origami, tracing and making models, and using a variety of craft supplies in creative ways including pom-poms, googly eyes, glitter, pipe cleaners, felt, and yarn. Craft activities help small children develop fine motor skills as they use instruments such as scissors and try to make precise movements like stringing beads and coloring within boundaries.

As children develop, they can focus for longer periods of time and can handle more precise movements with smaller materials and areas. For example, a three- to four-year-old child may make simple Play-Doh snakes or snowmen, while a six- to eight-year-old child can add spots, a tongue, and facial features to the snowman with smaller bits of material laid in more exact locations. Through arts and crafts, young children can learn about colors and observe colors in the world around them, recognizing things such as green grass and blue sky. Working on arts and crafts projects helps children develop skills in planning, attention and focusing, problem-solving, and originality. It also helps them learn how to observe the world around them, be appreciative of other people's interpretations and ideas, deal with frustrations when things do not go as planned, and develop hand-eye coordination.

Early childhood educators should strive to expose children to a vast array of arts and craft materials and different types of arts. Activities should be age-appropriate. For example, four- to five-year-old children are likely unable to use small beads and fine pencils and markers, and do better with wider drawing utensils and larger beads that are easier to grasp and manipulate. Children who are ten to twelve are able to work with more intricate objects and may be bored with crayons and coloring books. There are a variety of other art

415

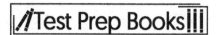

forms that students may view or try to create such as jewelry, pottery, stained glass, wire art, sewing, quilting, knitting, and decoupage.

Techniques, Tools, and Materials

Art has personal (self-expression, gratification, narrative functions), social (collective meaning for a group of people, such as symbolic art honoring a god or political art), and physical (such as a pottery mug for tea) functions that often overlap within a single piece of work. As children go through elementary school, they become familiar with an increasing variety and complexity of visual art forms beginning with things like drawing, painting, and sculpting, then adding printmaking, sponge painting, film animation, and graphics in third and fourth grades, and dabbling in environmental design and art based on personal experience and observation by the fifth grade. They may also try computer-generated art, photography, metalworking, textile arts, and ceramics. Materials include scissors, brushes, papers, glue, beads, clay, film, and computers.

Formal and Conceptual Vocabularies of Art and Design

Though art is inherently subjective, visual artists and designers rely on a loose central vocabulary to identify and describe the means by which they construct their artwork. Some basic formal components are defined and described below:

- A line is defined as a mark or stroke with length and direction. Lines don't need to be thin, straight, or even consistent to be considered lines; they can be thick, wavy, and even broken. Artists and designers employ different types of lines to evoke different emotions or impressions. For example, horizontal lines often create a sense of calm and stability, while diagonal lines can suggest movement or dynamism. The use of line can also imply texture, define boundaries, or lead the viewer's gaze within a composition.

- Shape and form occur when lines meet and enclose an area. Shapes can be geometric—creating squares, circles, and triangles—or they can be organic, irregular, and free flowing. When a shape takes on three dimensions and has volume, it becomes a form. Like shapes, forms can be geometric and create cubes and spheres, or they can be organic like the forms of human figures or most natural objects.

- Color is created by light reflecting off objects. Artists use it to convey emotions and create visual interest. The color wheel is a tool used to understand how hues are made and how they relate to one another. Primary colors (red, blue, and yellow) are the building blocks of all other colors. Secondary colors (orange, green, and purple) are created by mixing primary colors. All hues of the color wheel exist as some combination of primary colors in this way. Artists use warm colors (red, orange, and yellow) to create a sense of energy and vibrancy, and cool colors (blue, green, and purple) to evoke calmness and stillness.

While the above vocabulary focuses on the technical visual elements of art, many aspects of art are not so easily measured. The conceptual vocabulary of art deals with the ideas and meanings behind artwork. Some of the essential terms in an artist's conceptual vocabulary are as follows:

- Composition is a broad term that refers to the arrangement of visual elements in artwork. Artists carefully place shapes, colors, and other elements to create a sense of balance, harmony, and unity. Composition is crucial to advanced art pieces, as it represents the effectiveness with which

artists wield technical components of art, such as lines, shapes, and colors. It can determine the overall impact and message of the art. A well-composed piece achieves visual unity and coherence, capturing the viewer's attention and guiding their perception.

- Balance is a key aspect in a piece's composition and refers to the distribution of visual weight in an artwork. Artists use balance to create a sense of stability or a sense of tension. There are three primary types of balance: symmetrical balance, which has equal weight on both sides; asymmetrical balance, which has unequal but visually balanced weight; and radial balance, which has elements that radiate from a central point. A piece doesn't need to be balanced to be considered good; a sense of visual imbalance can contribute to a piece's quality if done intentionally.

- Movement is another key aspect of composition; it is a more dynamic aspect of visual art that refers to the feeling of motion or visual flow created within a piece. It is achieved through the arrangement of elements such as lines, shapes, and colors to create directional cues that guide the viewer's eye across a piece. Movement can be actual, such as the depiction of physical motion or action, or it can be implied, where the arrangement of elements suggests a sense of movement.

Early learners can focus on the basic vocabulary of visual art like identifying colors and shapes. Older students can be exposed to more nuanced terms in the world of visual art. Some visual art is **representational** and depicts objects as they appear in the real world. One visual tool that heightens the realistic accuracy of visual art is **perspective**, an artistic technique that creates the illusion of depth through the use of line (for example, lines in the foreground converge in the background), size and placement of objects (objects that are supposed to be closer to the viewer appear larger than objects that are further away), or color (for example, a hill that is close to the viewer is depicted in a vibrant green, while a distant mountain appears with a more muted, hazy color).

In contrast to representational art, other visual art is **abstract.** When artists use abstraction, they use line, color, and other elements to communicate the presence of objects and emotions rather than realistically portraying the objects. For example, a swirl of warm colors like red and orange might represent anger or anxiety; cool colors like blue and gray could communicate sadness or passivity. In this way, the artist's **palette**, or range of colors used in their work, can communicate a mood or emotion to the viewer. Some works are **monochromatic**, meaning that they only use one color (although the artist might use different shades of the same color—for example, dark blue and light blue). Different shades of color can also create the illusion of shape or represent different lighting.

Other tools of both abstract and representational visual art include **contrast** (the pairing of dissimilar elements to make each other stand out), **positive** and **negative space** (positive space refers to the areas of the artwork occupied by its subject, whereas negative space includes all the areas that do not contain any subject), balance, and **symmetry**. Some artistic techniques to introduce to students might include caricature, collage, painting, sculpture, portraiture, landscape, and still life.

Somewhat opposite of contrast, **harmony** highlights the similarities in separate but related parts of a composition. Rather than emphasizing their dissimilarities, harmony shows that different things can actually be related to each other and blend together.

Artists often use **emphasis**—make one part of their work stand out from the rest—to guide viewers to pay attention to specific components of their piece. For example, lines and textures in paintings and sculptures

may direct viewers to specific details or target features, and altering the texture of one area may make it stand out in contrast to the rest of the work.

Rhythm involves repeating elements within a work such as colors, shapes, lines, notes, or steps to create a pattern of visual or auditory motion.

If educators are able to take students one museum field trips, students should know museum-related vocabulary terms like **gallery, exhibit,** and **curator.**

Presentation and Preservation of Artwork

Artists and art professionals employ various methods to present and preserve works of art in different contexts. These methods help ensure their longevity, accessibility, and aesthetic impact. Below are a couple of popular ways to present art and increase its public accessibility:

- Exhibitions are the primary means of presenting art and may take place in galleries, museums, art fairs, or public spaces. Curators and artists work together to determine the layout, lighting, and display techniques that enhance the viewer's experience.

- Digital platforms are also increasingly popular for presenting art. Online galleries and portfolios allow artists to showcase their creations to a global audience at zero physical risk to the art itself.

Preservation of artwork is vital to ensuring its longevity. Art conservation specialists employ many techniques for protecting and maintaining art, such as controlling temperature and humidity levels in tailored storage conditions, as well as protective enclosures or display cases to shield delicate artworks from environmental hazards. Below are a couple of popular preservation techniques outside of carefully sequestering a physical piece of art:

- Archiving and cataloging are crucial for preserving and documenting artworks. Institutions maintain extensive collections of physical and digital records, including photographs, descriptions, and provenance details that ensure works of art can be identified and studied.

- Publications and art books serve as a more tangible means to present and preserve art. Exhibition catalogs, monographs, and art magazines all provide comprehensive documentation of artists' works, critical analysis, and historical context with minimal risk to the art itself.

Physical Education

Movement Skills and Movement Knowledge: Basic Movement Skills

Movement Concepts

A person's physical literacy, motor skills, and movement abilities rely on the understanding of one's own body, and basic movement concepts such as body awareness, space awareness, and movement exploration are critical in developing these skills in students. These concepts provide a foundation for understanding and engaging in various physical activities, as well as fostering competence, confidence, and creativity in movement. Some fundamental movement concepts are explained below. Integrating these concepts into physical education programs helps equip students with a holistic understanding of movement that enhances their overall physical competence.

- Body awareness refers to an individual's understanding of their own body and its movements in space. It involves developing a sense of body alignment, posture, balance, and coordination. Through body awareness activities, people learn to recognize and control their body parts, movements, and positions. They become aware of their body's capabilities and limitations, allowing them to execute movements with precision, control, and efficiency. Body awareness activities include exercises focusing on body alignment, balance drills, coordination exercises, and proprioceptive activities that enhance one' kinesthetic awareness, such as balance exercises, kinesthetic games, and yoga.

- Effort and energy are the quality and intensity levels that people employ in their movements. These involve understanding and manipulating factors such as force, speed, flow, and rhythm when moving. When people explore effort and energy, they learn to adapt and modify their movements to achieve different outcomes. They become aware of the effort required for various movements, such as applying force for throwing or kicking, or controlling speed for sprinting or decelerating. Effort and energy activities typically include exercises that focus on varying levels of force, speed, or flow, as well as activities that explore different rhythms or timing patterns.

- Space awareness describes an individual's understanding of the space around them and their ability to navigate and interact within that space. It involves developing spatial perception, directionality, and the ability to judge distances and relationships between objects and people. Space awareness activities help students become aware of personal and general space, as well as different levels, pathways, and directions of movement. They learn to adapt their movements based on the available space and the presence of others. Space awareness activities can include spatial games, obstacle courses, dance routines, and cooperative movement tasks that encourage students to explore, adapt, and interact with the space around them.

- Spatial relationships contribute to space awareness in physical education. Specifically, they denote how individuals interact with objects and other people in their environment while moving. Spatial relationship activities can include partner or group tasks that involve mirroring, leading, and following, sharing weight, or working in coordination with others. By exploring spatial relationships, students can develop skills in collaboration, cooperation, and teamwork. They learn

419

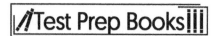

to attentively navigate shared spaces, respond to the movements of others, and interact with objects or equipment responsibly.

- Movement exploration encompasses a range of activities and experiences that encourage students to explore and expand their movement possibilities. It involves creativity, self-expression, and the discovery of new movement patterns and qualities. Movement exploration activities can include improvisation exercises, dance-based activities, creative movement tasks, and guided movement challenges that stimulate students' creativity, problem-solving skills, and satisfaction in movement. These activities allow students to develop their kinesthetic imagination, physical improvisation skills, and personal techniques of movement. This kind of exploration encourages them to take risks, experiment with different movement sequences, and express themselves through movement.

Motor Skills and Movement Patterns in Children

Educators should be familiar with physical and neurological development, especially in terms of motor skills and development, to provide developmentally appropriate motor movement tasks. As young children grow and mature, they develop the ability to handle increasingly complex motor skills. Children learn to move and move to learn and, for this reason, physical activity is especially important in the classroom for young children. As children grow, their physical abilities gradually increase, and educators can begin to modify lessons and activities to continue to challenge and improve new movement patterns and abilities. What looks like "play" actually consists of meaningful movement patterns that help the child move their body and use large muscle groups to develop physical competency. This is known as movement education. Children should learn basic movement patterns and skills for daily life so that they can maneuver safely and appropriately in their environment in relation to other people and objects. After basic skills are mastered, more specific sport-related skills can be achieved. Movement competency is the successful ability of the child to manage their body in both basic and specialized physical tasks despite obstacles in the environment, while perceptual motor competency includes capabilities involving balance, coordination, lateral and backward movements, kinesthetic sense, and knowledge of one's own body and strength.

Educators should be able to assess the level at which students can control specific movements and identify patterns of physical activity that have been mastered. This information can be used to plan developmentally-appropriate movement tasks and activities. In addition, early childhood educators can be helpful in identifying students who seem to be lagging behind in age-appropriate motor abilities. In such cases, early intervention programming and resources may be beneficial.

There are three general categories of basic skills: locomotor, non-locomotor, and manipulative skills; more complex movement patterns combine skills from multiple categories. Locomotor skills – such as walking, running, jumping, and skipping – are the movement skills that children need to travel within a given space or get from one space to another. Non-locomotor skills are typically completed in a stationary position – such as kneeling, pushing, twisting, bouncing, or standing – and help control the body in relation to gravity. Manipulative skills usually involve using the hands and feet, although other body parts may be used. These skills help the child handle, move, or play with an object. Manipulating objects helps advance hand-eye and foot-eye coordination so that the child can more successfully participate in sports activities like throwing, batting, catching, and kicking.

Young children can begin to learn these skills with balls and beanbags at a less challenging level and progress to more difficult levels and activities with practice and development. Early stages usually involve individual

practice first and then progress to involve partners and groups. Throwing and catching are actually quite complex skills that can be as challenging to teach as they are to learn. Early childhood educators should emphasize skill performance and principles such as opposition, following objects with the eyes, weight transfer, follow through, and, eventually, striking targets. Motor planning is the ability of the child to figure out how to complete a new motor task or action and depends on both the sensory motor development of the child as well as their thinking and reasoning skills.

Directions of Body Movement

The following terms describe directions of body movement:

- Inferior: toward the feet
- Superior: toward the head
- Medial: toward the body's midline
- Lateral: away from the body's midline
- Supination: typically used to describe forearm or ankle motion, rotating up and inward
- Pronation: typically used to describe forearm or ankle motion, rotating down and outward
- Flexion: a reduction in joint angle by two body segments around a joint coming closer together
- Extension: an increase in joint angle by two segments of the body around one joint moving apart
- Adduction: movement toward the body's midline
- Abduction: movement away from the body's midline (typically out to the side)
- Hyperextension: movement beyond the normal extension range of a joint
- Rotation: turning to the right or left, often of the head or neck or ankles
- Circumduction: moving in a circular motion, a compound motion involving flexion, extension, abduction, and adduction into one movement
- Agonist: the primary muscle involved in a motion
- Antagonist: the muscle that opposes a given motion
- Stabilizers: provide stability by contracting to hold joints or segments of the body in place while others around it are free to move

Planes of Body Movement

Physical education instructors should understand planes of body movement in order to diversify workouts and focus on all muscles, even smaller, weaker, or assistive muscles. While the body does not necessarily operate in an isolated plane of motion, exercises should focus on combining movements and planes of motion so that the child can more seamlessly flow from movement to movement with more flexibility and to prevent muscle imbalances. Understanding the proper form in which movement should occur in the planes also helps educators notice improper movements and correct them. The planes of movement of the body include the following:

- Frontal/Coronal: splits the body into front and back sections

- Sagittal: splits the body into right and left sections

- Midsagittal: the specific instance of a sagittal plane that divides the body into equal right and left halves

- Transverse: splits the body into top and bottom sections

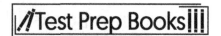

Influence of Gravity, Friction, and Laws of Motion on Body Movement

The body moves the way it does in part due to its own anatomy and in part due to the physics of the world around us. Specific forces and principles in physics play significant roles in determining how our bodies interact with the environment and how we move in many circumstances.

Gravity, the force that attracts objects toward the center of the Earth, has a profound impact on body movement. It acts vertically downward, creating a constant force that affects every movement we make. When we stand, walk, run, or jump, gravity is responsible for keeping us grounded and determining the resistance we encounter. It influences our balance, stability, and the effort required to overcome its pull.

Friction, the resistance encountered when two surfaces rub against each other, affects our ability to initiate, control, and stop movements. It helps us maintain stability and control our speed and direction. When we're walking or running, friction between our feet and the ground provides the necessary traction for propulsion and deceleration.

Sir Isaac Newton's **laws of motion** govern the principles of movement and provide a framework for understanding body motion. Newton's three laws of motion apply to all objects, including the human body, and impact significant body movement factors such as force application, body alignment, and energy distribution. A brief explanation of each law follows:

- The law of inertia states that an object at rest will remain at rest, and an object in motion will continue moving in a straight line at a constant speed unless acted upon by an external force. This law emphasizes the need for external forces to initiate, change, or stop movements.

- The law of acceleration states that the acceleration of an object depends on the object's mass and the net force acting upon it. This law explains how the force we exert influences our acceleration, such as when pushing off the ground to accelerate during running or jumping.

- The law of action-reaction states that for every action, there is an equal and opposite reaction. As a simple example, when walking or running, the force exerted by one's leg on the ground causes the ground to exert an equal and opposite force which pushes the body forward.

Interrelationships Among Center of Gravity, Base of Support, Balance, and Stability

The center of gravity is the location of a theoretical point that represents the total weight of an object. In most humans, the center of gravity is anterior to the second sacral vertebrae.

The base of support refers to the part of an object that serves as the supporting surface, often thought of as feet in contact with the ground. The base of support extends to mean the area between the feet as well, not just the physical structures of the body in contact with the supporting surface. Increasing the base of support makes it easier to be more stable and have an easier time balancing.

Balance is the ability to control the center of mass within the base of support without falling. The wider the base of support and the lower the center of gravity, the easier it is to maintain balance. This concept can be applied to squatting. Teachers can instruct children to widen their base of support, squat back, and bring their hips back (as if they are sitting in a chair) in order to lower their center of mass without disturbing balance. Because younger children have a lower center of mass, they tend to have better balance than older adults.

Stability is the ability to lean or deviate the body in one direction or another without changing base of support (taking a step or replanting the feet). Stability, like balance, is improved with a wider base of support. It can also be improved with core training.

Proper spinal alignment refers to the composition of the spine, which is composed of thirty-three (seven cervical, twelve thoracic, five lumbar, five sacral, and four coccygeal) vertebrae and the discs between them. There are normal curvatures of the spine in the sagittal plane: cervical and lumbar lordosis (convex anteriorly and concave posteriorly) and thoracic and sacral kyphosis (concave anteriorly and convex posteriorly). It is important to utilize good posture during resistance exercises to protect the spine from injury.

Movement Skills and Movement Knowledge: Exercise Physiology: Health and Physical Fitness

Benefits and Risks of a Physically Active Lifestyle

A physically active lifestyle often leads to improved cardiovascular fitness, enhanced strength and flexibility, better mental health, and increased longevity. However, it's important to consider both the bodily safety factors and medical factors that are associated with physical activity, such as asthma and diabetes.

While exercise promotes strength and resilience, certain activities carry inherent risks like minor sprains and strains, as well as more severe **injuries** such as fractures or concussions. Adequate warm-up and cool-down routines, proper technique and form, and the use of appropriate protective gear can help mitigate these risks. It's crucial to engage in activities suitable for one's fitness level, progress gradually, and listen to the body's signals to avoid overexertion and potential injuries.

Medical factors, such as asthma and diabetes, require special considerations when engaging in physical activity. **Asthma**, a chronic respiratory condition, can be managed through proper treatment and monitoring. Regular exercise can improve lung function and overall asthma control, but asthmatic people should be aware of their asthma's triggers, use appropriate medications as prescribed, and exercise in environments with good air quality to minimize the risk of attacks.

Similarly, people with **diabetes** can benefit greatly from regular physical activity. Exercise helps control blood sugar levels, improves insulin sensitivity, and contributes to better management of the condition. However, individuals with diabetes must be mindful of monitoring their blood sugar levels before, during, and after exercise. They may need to make adjustments in medication, diet, and timing of meals to maintain stable blood glucose levels.

Engaging in regular physical activity carries far more benefits than risks. However, it is crucial to approach physical activity mindfully and consider bodily safety factors and medical conditions when doing so.

Importance of Exercise Principles in Selection of Physical Fitness Activities

Exercise principles help individuals establish effective exercise routines that align with their fitness goals and abilities. Below are some examples of standard exercise principles and how they might be used:

- **Frequency** denotes the number of exercise sessions in a given amount of time (usually per week), and how one's exercise time is divided. The optimal frequency of exercise depends on factors such as age, fitness level, goals, and time availability, but it is generally recommended that people

423

spread their exercise frequency across several sessions per week, rather than fitting a week's worth of exercise in a single session.

- **Intensity** refers to the level of effort exerted during exercise and denotes how challenging an activity is for the individual. Moderate-intensity activities should make the individual break a sweat, breathe harder, and elevate their heart rate. Vigorous-intensity activities should increase heart rate significantly and make it difficult to carry on a conversation. Incorporating a variety of intensity levels into an exercise routine helps improve different aspects of fitness, such as cardiovascular endurance and calorie expenditure.

- **Time**, also known as duration, refers to the length of each exercise session. It is the total amount of time spent engaging in physical activity within a period of time, usually a week. The recommended duration of exercise depends on the type and intensity of the activity. For aerobic exercises it is recommended that people aim for at least thirty minutes of moderate-intensity activity per session, or twenty minutes for vigorous-intensity activity. Strength training sessions should last between twenty to thirty minutes and should target multiple major muscle groups with a variety of exercises so as not to overstrain a specific part of the body.

When people understand and apply these exercise principles, they can select activities that safely and effectively serve their physical fitness goals. For example, someone aiming to improve cardiovascular endurance can use the knowledge of these exercise principles to establish a routine of moderate-intensity aerobic activities such as jogging, cycling, or swimming for a duration of thirty minutes at a higher frequency of five days a week.

Components of Physical Fitness

A well-rounded program addresses all five components of health-related physical fitness:

- Cardiovascular fitness: capacity of circulatory and respiratory systems to supply oxygen during continued activity

- Muscular strength: force capability of a muscle

- Muscular endurance: ability to maintain level of muscular work without fatigue

- Body composition: relative amounts of body fat, muscle, bone, and other tissues

- Flexibility: permitted joint range of motion

Body Composition

<u>Major Muscles</u>

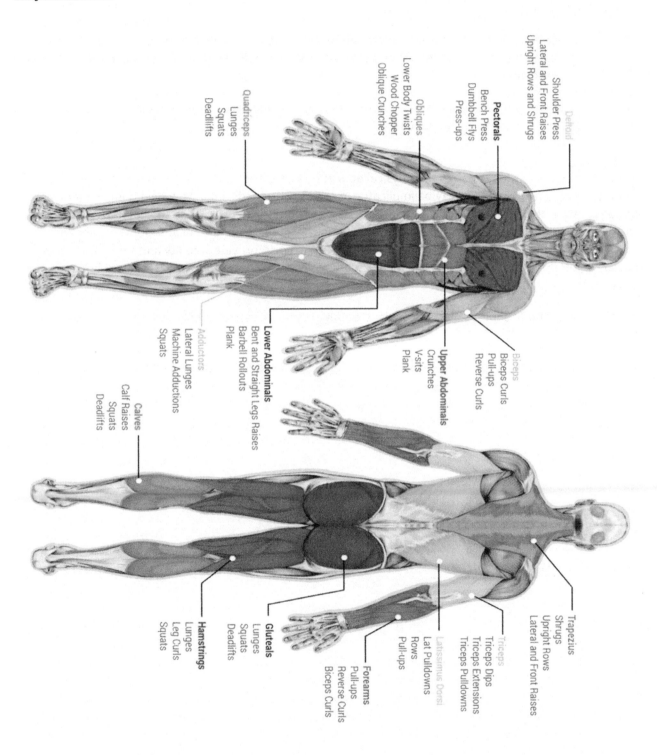

Teachers should not only be aware of muscle names, but also their origins, insertions, primary action, and nerve innervation. An understanding of these criteria can help in identifying injuries. It can also help ensure that exercises are targeting all muscles to maximize strength, strengthen stabilizing muscles, and provide proximal stability for functional distal mobility.

- Upper body muscles: trapezius, pectoralis major, deltoids, serratus anterior, latissimus dorsi, biceps, triceps, rectus abdominis, internal and external obliques, erector spinae, rhomboids, flexor carpi radialis

- Lower body muscles: iliopsoas, gluteus maximus, quadriceps, piriformis, hamstrings, adductors, abductors, soleus, gastrocnemius

Major Bones

Knowledge of bone anatomy enables the physical education instructor to understand the bones involved in joint motions and the bones that may be implicated in certain orthopedic injuries, which is important when communicating with physicians. There are different types of bones. Flat bones, like the cranial bones of the skull and the sternum, protect internal organs. Long bones, like the femur and tibia, support weight and facilitate movement. Short bones, like the carpal bones in the wrist, provide stability and some movement. Irregular bones also protect structures like the vertebrae over the spinal cord. Lastly, sesamoid bones, like the patella, protect tendons from stress.

- Upper body bones: clavicle, scapula, sternum, humerus, carpals, ulna, radius, metacarpals, vertebrae, ribs

- Lower body bones: ilium, ischium, pubis, femur, fibula, tibia, metatarsals, tarsals

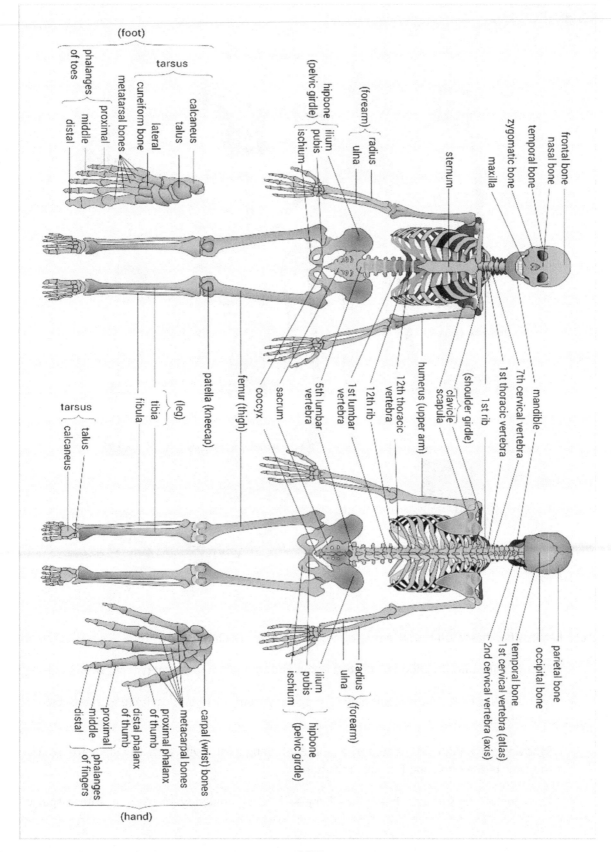

Joint Classifications

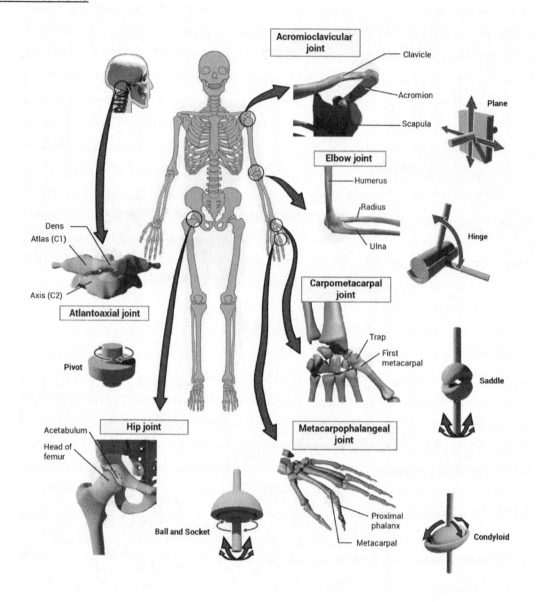

Joints can be classified based on the structure of how the bones are connected:

- Fibrous joints: Bones joined by fibrous tissue and that lack a joint cavity (e.g., sutures of the skull)

- Cartilaginous joints: Bones joined by cartilage and that lack a joint cavity (e.g., the pubic symphysis)

- Synovial joints: Bones separated by a fluid-containing joint cavity with articular cartilage covering the ends of the bone and forming a capsule

- Plane joints: Flat surfaces that allow gliding and transitional movements (e.g., intercarpal joints)

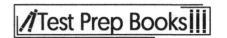

- Hinge joints: Cylindrical projection that nests in a trough-shaped structure, single plane of movement (e.g., the elbow)

- Pivot joints: Rounded structure that sits into a ring-like shape, allowing uniaxial rotation of the bone around the long axis (e.g., radius head on ulna)

- Condyloid joints: Oval articular surface that nests in a complementary depression, allowing all angular movements (e.g., the wrist)

- Saddle joints: Articular surfaces that have both complementary concave and convex areas, allowing more movement than condyloid joints (e.g., the thumb)

- Ball-and-socket joints: Spherical structure that fits in a cuplike structure, allowing multiaxial movements (e.g., the shoulder)

Movement Skills and Movement Knowledge: Movement Forms: Content Areas

Traditional and Nontraditional Movement Forms

In group physical education, students' minds and bodies can be engaged with a wide array of physical activities that promote their movement skills, physical fitness, and overall well-being. Below is a brief collection of examples across multiple activity types:

- Traditional games and sports:

- Basketball is a widely popular team sport that promotes coordination, agility, and teamwork. Through friendly matches and drills, even without establishing formal basketball games, students can learn basic skills such as dribbling, shooting, and passing.

- Soccer is among the most effective sports for full-body exercise in proportion to the amount of equipment it requires. By practicing dribbling, passing, and shooting, either in a game setting or through skill-based drills, students can enhance their fitness, coordination, and spatial awareness through soccer.

- Volleyball focuses on teamwork, hand-eye coordination, and communication. Serving, setting, and spiking all train these skills at any level, and the sport can be modified through court and net size to work at any age and skill level.

- Nontraditional games and activities:

- **Ultimate Frisbee** is a fast-paced team sport that combines elements of soccer and football. It improves cardiovascular fitness, agility, and throwing accuracy.

- Though not as dynamic as competitive sports, yoga is an incredibly valuable physical activity that enhances flexibility, balance, strength, and relaxation for all body types. Students can learn basic yoga poses and breathing techniques at any skill level or physicality. These exercises promote

physical and mental well-being. Yoga can be done as a standalone activity or as part of warm-up and cool-down routines for other, higher-intensity activities.

- Incorporating various dance styles and choreography into exercise is one of the most effective ways to improve coordination, rhythm, and movement creativity. Dance can also be integrated into aerobic activities or as part of standalone thematic units in a curriculum or personal exercise routine.

- Other physical activities:

- **Fitness circuit training** involves designing circuit training stations with different exercises such as jumping jacks, push-ups, lunges, and skipping ropes to provide a well-rounded workout.

- Martial arts disciplines like karate, taekwondo, or judo should only be taught by trained martial arts educators, but they can enhance bodily awareness, critical self-defense skills, mental discipline, balance, and coordination. Students can engage in basic defensive techniques, practice forms, and controlled sparring or self-defense drills with the proper education and safety equipment.

Basic Rules and Social Etiquette for Physical Activities

In a physical education or gym setting, it is important to establish common decency rules to ensure the safety, fairness, and enjoyment of all participants. If you establish and reinforce these rules of conduct in your exercise space, you can cultivate a positive and respectful environment that ensures said safety, fairness, and enjoyment. Below are some essential social etiquette rules for group physical activity:

- Follow instructions. Listen attentively to the instructor or coach and follow their instructions promptly. This promotes safety and allows for organized and efficient group activities.

- Safety first. Prioritize safety by using equipment and facilities as intended. Encourage students to be aware of their surroundings, avoid reckless behavior, and report any potential hazards or injuries to instructors or coaches.

- Respect personal space. Encourage students to respect the personal space of others, give each other enough room to move during activities, and avoid disruptive contact. Most importantly, ensure that they are touching each other only when it is athletically appropriate to do so for an activity, and only in appropriate places.

- Fair play. Emphasize the importance of fairness and good sportsmanship. Students should compete with integrity, respect their opponents, and follow the rules of the game or activity, especially when it is competitive.

- Cleanliness and hygiene. Teach students to keep gym or activity areas sanitary and tidy. Encourage them to follow basic hygiene practices, such as wiping down equipment after use and maintaining personal cleanliness.

Inclusion of all Students in Physical Activities

It is a fundamental truth that different people have different needs and capacities regarding exercise and physical activity, especially when their bodies are still developing. Though there is nothing inherently wrong with smaller, high-intensity exercise sessions, it is also crucial to provide activities that are inclusive and accessible to all students, regardless of their gender, race, culture, body type, or ability level. Below are some examples of engaging and inclusive physical activities:

- Cooperative games such as relay races or obstacle courses can be customized in intensity and often require students to work together, which fosters a sense of unity and cooperation. Engaging students in these games promotes teamwork, collaboration, and inclusivity.

- Setting up fitness stations allows students to engage in individual or small group activities at either their own pace or a controlled and monitored pace from the instructor. Stations can include exercises such as jumping jacks, push-ups, lunges, balancing exercises, jumping rope, and many other activities. Students will rotate through these stations, focusing on their own fitness goals and abilities.

- Unified sports such as basketball, soccer, or track and field generally involve a team made up of different roles that require different strengths. Due to these sports' popularity, they are also more easily understood by a wider array of people who can be brought together on a team to perform activities that require participation from everyone. Such sports promote interaction, encouragement, and friendship among students with different physical abilities.

Modifying Instruction Based on Differences in Growth and Development

To make physical education classes more inclusive, instructors need to modify their lessons based on students' individual physical differences. Teachers need to be aware of students with disabilities and differentiate their instruction so that these students can participate and succeed in physical education class.

Instructors need to get to know their students to determine their strengths and areas that need improvement. They should not make assumptions about students' abilities, especially if those students have disabilities. Over time, teachers will figure out what strategies work best for each student.

One of the first ways to learn how to differentiate instruction is to speak with specialists, such as physical therapists, occupational therapists, or adapted physical education teachers. These professionals can provide instructors with advice for how to assess students and prepare specialized physical education.

Modifying activities is the next step. There are various ways to modify physical education activities for students of all abilities, like the following:

- Eliminating time limits
- Modeling to demonstrate the activity
- Decreasing the number of players on teams
- Allowing students to partner up
- Using lightweight equipment
- Providing balance support
- Slowing down the activity's pace

- Using balls of varying sizes
- Allowing for rest periods

Teachers can adapt rules of certain games so that students can remember them easily. Instructions for all activities should be clear, especially boundaries. Fewer rules can make activities easier to follow, especially for younger students. The instructions can also be written on white boards so that students can refer to them as needed.

Integrating Activities with Other Content Areas

Collaboration with classroom teachers informs the integration of content into the physical education classroom.

Use academics to determine who's "it" in games of tag. For example, use fingers, playing cards, or dice to produce two numbers. The first person to shout out the correct answer using a particular mathematical operation becomes "it." In freeze tag, "frozen" individuals must correctly complete an academic task (e.g., spell a word or identify a chemical element) before returning to the game.

Relay races may be modified so that each team member performs a physical activity and returns to their team with a card. Together, they must solve the problem laid out by the cards, like alphabetizing words, putting events in chronological order, or dividing organisms by kingdom.

"If, then" games involve students completing a different physical activity depending on what the instructor says. If the instructor yells out a prime number, students skip; for a composite number, they run. These games can also be used in language arts (e.g., calling out parts of speech or fiction/nonfiction).

Conversely, physical education activities may be used to provide data for classroom activities. Measurements of jumps, ratios of completed basketball shots, and distance of throws provide data for math or science equations.

Self-Image and Personal Development: Physical Growth and Development

Motor Development

Typical motor development milestones for various age groups are as follows:

- *Ages three to four:* have mastered walking and standing and are now developing gross motor skills such as single foot hopping and balancing, unsupported ascent and descent of stairs, kicking a ball, overhand throwing, catching a ball off of a bounce, moving forward and backward with coordination, and riding a tricycle. Fine motor skills begin to progress including using scissors with one hand, copying capital letters and more complex shapes, and drawing basic shapes from memory.

- *Ages four to five:* tackling increasingly complex gross motor skills that require some coordination and multiple movement patterns combined together such as doing somersaults, swinging, climbing, and skipping. They also can use utensils to eat independently, dress themselves with clothing containing zippers and buttons, and begin to tie shoelaces. Mastery of fine motor

skills begins to progress more rapidly, including cutting and pasting, and drawing shapes, letters, and people with heads, bodies, and arms. They tend to engage in long periods of physical activity followed by a need for a significant amount of rest. Physically, bones are still developing. Girls tend to be more coordinated while boys are stronger, but both sexes lack precise fine motor skills and the ability to focus on small objects for a long time.

Children Enjoy Exercise with Games Like Tag

- *Age six to eight:* skating, biking, skipping with both feet, dribbling a ball. By the end of grade two, children should be able to make smoother transitions between different locomotor skills sequenced together. They can also accomplish more complicated manipulative skills such as dribbling a soccer ball with their feet and can better control their bodies during locomotion, weight-bearing, and balance. Students can begin to use feedback to hone motor skills from a cognitive perspective.

- *Ages nine to eleven:* Children begin to get stronger, leaner, and taller as they enter the pre-adolescent stage and growth accelerates with the beginnings of secondary sex characteristics. Attention span and gross and fine motor skills improve. By the end of grade five, most children can achieve more performance-based outcomes such as hitting targets and can complete specialized sports skills such as fielding baseballs and serving tennis balls. They are also able to combine movements in a more dynamic environment such as moving rhythmically to music. From a cognitive perspective, they can begin to take concepts and feedback learned in other skills or sports and apply them to a new game. An example of this is increasing body stability by bending the knees to lower the center of gravity in basketball during a pick drill; this skill can also be reapplied on the ski slope. Additionally, children begin to observe peers more and can provide feedback to others.

Muscles Involved in Gross Motor Movements

Gross motor skill movement involves using the whole body, especially core stabilizing muscles that involve general functionality, such as those necessary for standing, walking, running, and basic hand-eye coordination. A variety of activities can help improve children's gross motor skills.

433

The following are some suggestions to develop balance:

- Use a balance beam.
- Participate in an obstacle course.
- Jump around on dots on a marked floor.

To develop body control:

- kick balls and balloons.
- jump over objects like lines, boxes, and beanbags.

To prepare children for sports, they can:

- dance to music.
- run, turn, twist, and bend in unique ways.

Muscles Involved in Fine Motor Movements

Fine motor skill movements involve using smaller muscles in the body like those that control the toes, fingers, wrists, and the eyes. Well-developed fine motor skills help a child complete tasks more efficiently and with more autonomy.

A variety of activities can help improve a child's fine motor skills. Opening and closing jars, manipulating beads and small handicrafts, mini golf, ping-pong, and other hand motor skills can augment these skills.

Physical activity helps children develop and refine their motor skills. Physical activity for children can take on many forms, including exercise, martial arts, walking and running, climbing trees, biking, playing tag, and sporting activities.

Additionally, exercise provides a host of benefits to the brain (creating and strengthening neural-pathways), lungs, muscles, the heart, vascular structures, tendons and ligaments, and bones. To maximize the benefits of exercise, children are encouraged to exercise for at least an hour a day.

Influence of Growth Spurts and Body Type on Movement and Coordination

Growth spurts tend to significantly impact movement and coordination for growing bodies. These changes are influenced by factors such as genetics, hormones, and experiential development. During growth spurts, students may experience a temporary lack of coordination as their bodies adjust to rapid changes in height, weight, and limb length. The growth of bones, muscles, and connective tissues can temporarily disrupt the body's sense of balance and spatial awareness. As a result, students may need varying amounts of time to adapt to their changing proportions and develop new motor skills to move efficiently and effectively.

Furthermore, **body type**, which refers to an individual's general body shape and composition, also heavily influences general movement and coordination. The three primary somatotypes of human bodies are ectomorph, mesomorph, and endomorph. **Ectomorphs** are generally characterized as lean and slender, **mesomorphs** tend to have a more athletic build with well-defined musculature, and **endomorphs** are typically described as having a higher proportion of body fat.

Each somatotype has unique strengths and challenges regarding movement and coordination. For example, ectomorphs may excel in activities that require agility and flexibility but might face challenges in developing

434

muscle strength and endurance. Mesomorphs often take more easily to traditional athleticism and may find it easier to build muscle and coordinate movements. Endomorphs are more predisposed to greater physical strength but may need to focus on maintaining flexibility and managing body weight for optimal movement and health.

Factors That Impact Physical Health and Well-Being

Early childhood educators can introduce young children to a wide variety of healthy behaviors that will help improve overall health. An important concept to begin teaching students is that optimal health is brought about through routine practice of daily healthy behaviors and an overall commitment to a healthy lifestyle. For example, educators can discuss the importance of establishing regular physical activity and daily healthy eating habits and that, through these habits, students can control their body weight and help avoid obesity. Obesity is a modifiable risk factor for many diseases including insulin-resistant Type 2 diabetes mellitus and cardiovascular disease.

It is important and empowering for children to start to understand their roles and responsibilities in healthy habits and disease prevention. By giving them the necessary knowledge and tools to put the information into practice in their lives, educators can increase the self-efficacy and behaviors of even young children. In this way, early childhood educators can be instrumental in bringing about a healthier generation of young children who have an awareness of their health and an understanding of their own influence on risk factors for certain diseases.

Nutrition

Children should be taught how to identify foods and the importance of consuming a daily variety of food within each healthy food group. The benefits of trying new foods, especially those from other cultures, can help students understand diversity and challenge their preconceived notions about different cultures and flavors. Older children can learn how to prepare simple foods, recognize the USDA recommended daily allowances of each food group in order to keep the body healthy, and classify foods based on their group and health benefits. Older students can also learn about the role of various nutrients in the body such as fat, fiber, and protein, and how to select nutrient-dense foods from a given list.

Children benefit from understanding what makes a food healthy and knowing options for healthy meals and snacks. By the third grade, students can start learning how to read nutrition labels, how to compare foods based on nutrition labels, and how to modify food choices to improve healthfulness, such as replacing low-fiber foods with higher fiber choices, like opting for apples instead of applesauce. When students are in the fourth grade, educators can start talking about portion sizes and the relationship between food consumption and physical activity on energy balance and weight control. In the context of introducing the basics about calories, prevention of obesity and the ramifications of an unhealthy diet can also be discussed. Children in the fifth and sixth grades can learn about the differences in types of fats, examples of common vitamins and minerals and food sources of these nutrients, the disadvantages of "empty-calories," and how to recognize misleading nutrition information.

Sleep

Early childhood educators should talk about the importance of sleep and why parents set a "bedtime," as well as healthy sleep hygiene and establishing a sleep schedule. Children can learn about how much sleep they need and ways to improve the quality of sleep, such as physical activity and avoiding screen time before bed. Young children who may experience nightmares can benefit from learning relaxation techniques as well as talking about their fears and feelings to trusted adults.

Stress Management

Students should be educated about stress management and exposed to techniques such as mental imagery, relaxation, deep breathing, aerobic exercise, and meditation. Children can be guided through progressive muscle relaxation and should be taught signs of excessive nervousness and stress, how to manage test and performance anxiety, and when and how to get help with excessive stress.

Healthy Relationships

Healthy family and social relationships are important to overall health and happiness. Studies have pointed to a negative impact of parental fighting on a child's wellbeing, including sleep and exercise habits, nutrition choices, stress, and social adjustment. Early childhood educators should talk about aspects of healthy relationships such as communication, emotional support, sharing, and respect. Younger children should learn skills that are helpful in making friends, cultivating relationships, and resolving conflict, especially as they relate to peers and siblings. Cooperation, taking turns, using words rather than physical means to communicate feelings, and exploring feelings are helpful concepts to instill.

Older children should begin to be exposed to dating etiquette and forming healthy romantic relationships. Educators should work to create a classroom environment of inclusion where students have an awareness of peers who may feel left out and work to include everyone. Within discussions of healthy relationships, educators should talk about accepting and appreciating diversity, including differences in cultures, religions, families, physical appearance and abilities, interests, intellect, emotions, lifestyle, and, in older children, sexual orientations. Life skills – such as having self-esteem, making decisions, calming oneself when angry or upset, and using listening skills – should be addressed.

Hydration

Early childhood educators should teach students about the importance of hydration and signs of dehydration as well as healthy choices for fluids, with a special emphasis on water. Children and their parents should be encouraged to send kids to school with a water bottle, and classrooms or hallways should be equipped with water fountains that children can access and use with limited supervision or assistance.

Safety Behaviors

Children should learn basic safety behaviors and the importance of following rules to prevent common injuries. Basic safety behaviors include wearing sunscreen and sunglasses when going outdoors; wearing protective gear in sports such as bicycle helmets, reflective vests, appropriate pads and cups, etc.; and using a car seat and/or always wearing a seat belt. Young children should learn about household safety such as not touching burners and not putting their fingers in electrical sockets nor opening the door to strangers. Educators should have children practice the "no, go, and tell" procedure for unsafe situations. For example, if a stranger offers the child an unknown substance, the child should know how to firmly refuse, carefully leave the situation, and tell a trusted adult. In this lesson, educators should also help children to identify trusted adults in their families and communities.

Educators can also discuss community safety measures such as using sidewalks, contacting city services (police, fire, and ambulance) in emergencies, and crossing the street safely by using crosswalks, holding hands, and looking both ways before crossing. Children should also learn about the health consequences of smoking, how to avoid secondhand smoke, and how to identify and avoid poisonous household substances. Fire safety such as "stop, drop, and roll" and emergency evacuation procedures should be rehearsed. Older children can learn about safety rules for various types of weather and how weather affects their personal safety, what different traffic signs mean, water/swim safety rules, and the importance of weighing consequences before taking risks.

Hygiene

Young children should learn about germs and the spread of infections. Older children can learn about bacteria and viruses. The importance of washing hands (including appropriate demonstration) cannot be overstated in elementary and preschool classrooms.

Other aspects of hygiene such as covering the mouth while coughing and covering the nose while sneezing, not sharing cups, practicing clean bathroom habits, showering and bathing, and, in older children, using deodorants, antiperspirants, and facial cleansers should be included in the curriculum.

Hygiene Stickers Remind Students to Use Healthy Practices

Self-Image and Personal Development: Self-Image

Role of Physical Activity in Development of Positive Self-Image

Engaging in regular physical activity and experiencing its benefits can contribute to improved body image, self-esteem, and overall well-being. Below are a few ways in which physical activity influences self-image positively:

- Physical fitness and competence: Regular physical activity builds one's fitness levels and helps to develop competence in movement skills, both in and out of exercise. As people engage in activities they enjoy or see progress in their abilities, it enhances their confidence and self-perception of their functional physical capabilities. Accomplishing fitness goals, such as running longer distances, lifting heavier weights, or mastering a new sport, fosters a sense of achievement and capability regarding one's physicality.

- Body knowledge and appreciation: Physical activity promotes a positive relationship with the body. Through regular exercise and engagement with one's body, one develops a greater understanding of what one's body needs and what it can do. This results in people beginning to focus less on physical appearance and more on the functional and health-related aspects of their bodies, such as nutrition requirements and endurance levels. In turn, this reduces the likelihood of engaging in negative self-talk or comparing oneself to unrealistic standards.

- Mood enhancement and stress relief: Physical activity releases endorphins, which are known as natural "feel-good" hormones. Through these hormones, regular exercise improves mood, reduces stress, and enhances mental well-being. When people regularly engage in physical activity, they often experience a sense of joy, accomplishment and/or relaxation, which encourages them to continue engaging in physical activity and contributes to good habits for overall positive self-perception.

- Social interaction and support: Participating in physical activities often involves some level of social interaction, whether it's though team sports, group physical education, or workout partners. Engaging in physical activity within a supportive and inclusive community provides a sense of belonging, camaraderie, and encouragement, which bolsters and reinforces one's self-esteem and fosters a positive self-image.

Role of Self-esteem, Self-efficacy, and Locus of Control in Self-concept and Self-identity

Self-esteem is the feeling of personal value or worth, and self-efficacy is an individual's feeling of competence in accomplishing a task. Someone who has strong self-esteem and self-efficacy will be proactive and confident, both socially and vocationally. Having an internal locus of control vs. external locus of control also plays a role in one's identity. An internal locus of control is when someone has the perception that he or she has control over their environment. An external locus of control is when someone believes that their future and life are controlled by factors outside of himself or herself. Those with an internal locus of control have a stronger self-concept and self-identity, leading to superior achievement, greater emotional stability, and more individual responsibility for behaviors.

Engaging in regular physical activity can improve one's self-esteem and self-efficacy. Exercise promotes a sense of physical and psychological wellbeing. Educators should encourage students to adopt a regular practice of physical activity, which enhances positive body image, goal-setting behaviors, and the confidence to achieve such goals.

Psychological Skills That Promote Lifelong Participation in Physical Activity

Introducing students to a variety of activities and encouraging them to find something they enjoy increases the chance they will pursue the activity regularly. Teachers should include activities that are non-competitive, as well as those that are accessible to individuals from all social classes (i.e., ones that do not require expensive equipment or a safe outdoor space to engage).

An activity in goal setting and action planning can support students' ability to integrate physical activity into their routines. Students should set goals that are small, realistic, specific, and achievable within a reasonable amount of time. Give them more frequent opportunities for success to help them maintain the desire to persevere. Introduce them to different means of tracking their progress to assist them in holding themselves accountable and visualizing their progress. Finally, provide a template for an action plan, which specifies the when, where, how, and with whom they will complete their chosen activity.

Promoting Physical Fitness, Responsible Behavior, and Respect in Physical Activity Settings

The youngest students enjoy being physically active for the fun of movement itself, and they particularly enjoy non-structured activities in moderate and high intensities followed by sufficient rest. By the end of second

grade, students will likely voluntarily incorporate activities from physical education class to leisure time activity and, although they are not typically concerned with structured exercise or activity recommendations for health, they do recognize the physical and mental benefits of activity and they self-select game-like play they enjoy. They are able to recognize the physiologic indicators of exercise such as elevated heart rate, sweating, and heavy breathing; they have a general understanding that physical fitness improves health, and they know that there are five components of health-related fitness: cardiovascular endurance, muscular strength, muscular endurance, flexibility, and body composition.

By the end of fifth grade, students should be aware that participation in regular physical activity is a conscious decision, and they should choose activities based on both enjoyment and health benefits. At this age, they begin to develop an awareness of resources and opportunities in the school and community to support activity and may become more interested in healthy food choices, realizing that personal responsibility and their own choices can affect their health. They also become more aware of their body and voice in a complex dynamic environment with others, and have greater focus towards controlling parts of their body and their movements within an environment with others.

Students should also begin to take an interest in improving aspects of fitness for better sports' performance or health indicators, and should apply the results of fitness assessments to gain a deeper understanding of their own personal fitness and health compared with peers and standards. Older students also understand that success comes with practice and effort, and they also enjoy broadening their skills and activities by learning new sports and skills based on prior mastery. They can engage in mutual physical activity with students of differing ability levels.

Social Development: Social Aspects of Physical Education

Physical education classes provide useful opportunities to encourage students' social development. Life skills such as cooperation, competition, goal setting, respecting and understanding differences, and taking risks can all be discussed while participating in sports and physical activity.

It is important that educators continually address the issues of personal and social behavior, especially as it relates to accepting and respecting differences in abilities, ideas, lifestyles, cultures, and choices. By the end of second grade, students should know how to follow the rules and safety procedures in physical education classes and during activities with little to no need for reinforcement. They also understand the social benefits of playing with others and how activities are more fun while interacting with other people. They should be able to effectively communicate during group activities in a respectful way, and enjoy working collaboratively with others to complete motor tasks or goals by combining movements and skills from many people together. By the end of fifth grade, students should be able to work independently or in small or large groups during physical activities in a cohesive and agreeable manner, while understanding that the group can often achieve more than the individual alone. However, individually, the student should understand that he or she is also responsible for personal health behaviors and movements.

Individual Differences in Students

The physical education classroom, by its nature, highlights differences among students. An instructor must not only be aware of these differences but also create a positive classroom culture where all students understand the expectations around inclusion, if not the encouragement of peers. Be aware that exemptions, adaptations, or modifications may be required to maintain accessibility, appropriateness, and equity for all students.

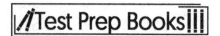

Guidance counselors, equity specialists, or physical and occupational therapists may provide additional considerations to enhance equity and inclusion.

Activities should be diverse in characteristics as well as inclusive of students who are of a variety of sizes, shapes, and abilities to encourage positive, enjoyable experiences for all. Consider using activities to highlight individuals of varied backgrounds (e.g., athletes of various genders, races, and ethnicities; Paralympians; and sports from different cultures). Teachers shouldn't assume that students have been exposed to certain games or activities just because they are considered common knowledge among a particular population.

Developmentally Appropriate Social Behavior in Children

As they progress through school, students' social development can impact their communication, self-esteem, empathy, and ability to resolve conflicts.

For some children, primary grades mark the first time they are spending more time with peers than with adult caregivers. They enjoy cooperative play and are increasingly aware of others' perceptions of them. They may still lack impulse control or the ability to consider consequences before acting. By the age of six or seven and in a stage known as middle childhood, children begin to identify themselves as individuals apart from their parents. This sense of independence makes them more likely to try new things. In addition to building friendships, they may start to compare their failures and successes to those of their peers.

In mid-elementary, students develop a better sense of their individuality while also growing in empathy, which enhances their ability to engage in good sportsmanship and cooperation. They value friendships and are more likely to behave in ways that please or mimic their friends. Sometimes this means challenging parents' preferences in favor of friends' opinions, behaviors, appearance, and interests.

As adolescents refine their sense of self and seek more autonomy, conflicts with non-preferred peers or adults may occur more often. The experiences and cognitive development the student achieves in this stage allow for effective competition to foster communication skills and cooperation with others to achieve a common goal. However, competition at this stage that is too intense for an individual's ability level can cause them to feel self-conscious or give up.

Activities That Provide Enjoyment, Self-Expression, and Communication

Active participation in effective physical education provides students experiences that foster cooperation, respect, good sportsmanship, honesty, turn-taking, goal setting, conflict resolution, and problem-solving.

Plan a variety of activities throughout the school year, including team sports, individual sports, and non-sport activities like dance, yoga, martial arts, weightlifting, and running to increase the likelihood that students will identify physical activities they enjoy. Further, taking activities outdoors in appropriate weather can also increase enjoyment for some students.

Dance activities provide an obvious opportunity for self-expression. Play songs with a variety of tempos and intensities, and encourage students to move their bodies accordingly. Help students understand how other physical activities, like those listed above, can channel their thoughts and emotions into a new, physical form of expression.

Team activities naturally foster interpersonal communication. Focusing on work and cooperation while playing a sport, as opposed to who wins and who loses, can enhance enjoyment and the expression of self through

hard work and tenacity. Other non-sport activities, like relay races and obstacle courses that require cooperation, also strengthen communication and problem-solving skills in a less competitive format that is likely more accessible to a wider population of students.

Social Development: Cultural and Historical Aspects of Movement Forms

Although perhaps less obvious than the arts, some physical activities also have social, cultural, and historical ties. For example, the development of many forms of dance can be traced to particular regions of the world or time periods. For example, ballet began in the Royal Court in Paris, the waltz originated in Venetian ballrooms, tango has its roots in 19th century Buenos Aires, and salsa began in Cuba.

Certain team sports and fitness activities also have cultural significance. For example, soccer, known as football in many countries, is the dominant sport in Brazil and many European nations. Several martial arts disciplines like karate, Judi, and taekwondo have their genesis in Asian nations and remain especially important in the foundations of physical education as well as social sports culture today. Certain East African nations, such as Ethiopia and Kenya produce many of the world's finest distance runners, due to the cultural attitude of prioritizing running as an esteemed pursuit and the natural encouragement of running as a means of transportation and livelihood in the infrastructure of such countries.

Many countries have a designated national sport and the popularity of a sport in a country is also often governed by the climate or environment as well as the social reverence of the activity. For example, curling, which originated in Scotland, is common in Canada along with ice hockey, where the cold climate is conducive to ice sports. Not surprisingly, these sports are far less common in tropical nations where access to indoor ice arenas may be limited. Sports that require water access (like sailing, rowing, kayaking, and swimming) are often less popular in landlocked or otherwise dry environments (with the exception of swimming in areas with designated swimming pools).

Educators can tie physical education activities to their historical or cultural significance to help students develop a more well-rounded understanding and appreciation for the activity. Students of different backgrounds may identify socially or culturally with a particular activity once learning about their personal connection to the activity; such education may thus help motivate them to enjoy a lifelong pursuit of the sport. The historical importance of physical activity throughout several prominent time periods and societies is presented below:

- Primitive Times (up to 10,000 BCE): Nomadic lifestyles were necessary for survival so physical activity was inherent in daily life. Dancing, cultural games, and celebratory walks of up to twenty miles were enjoyed in celebration.

- The Neolithic Agricultural Revolution (10,000-8,000 BCE): Advancements in plant and animal domestication and farming tools and practices transformed the previously physically-demanding hunting and gathering society to a more sedentary one.

- Ancient China (2500-250 BCE): Confucius' ideals encouraged the practice of daily exercise, as it began to be understood that regular physical activity decreased the risk of disease. Cong Fu gymnastics, consisting of different foot positions and animal-inspired movements, was developed. Other forms of exercise, such as badminton, fencing, and dancing, were also practiced.

- Ancient India (2500-250 BCE): In India, exercise outside of various types of Yoga was typically discouraged as the Buddhist and Hindi religions emphasized the spiritual, rather than physical, body.

- The Near East (4000-250 BCE): Rigid fitness training programs starting as early as age six were common in civilizations such as the Persian Empire, Babylonia, and Egypt. Boys were subjected to organized training including marching, javelin throwing, and riding. At the height of the Persian Empire, the goal of such regimented fitness training was to improve strength and stamina to create optimized soldiers, rather than for health benefits.

- Ancient Greece (2500-200 BCE): Ancient Greeks revered the perfection of the human form and encouraged routine exercise for boys and men, especially gymnastics, which took place in supervised arenas. Running, wrestling, throwing, and jumping were also encouraged. Of note, the Spartans also highly valued physical fitness, but mostly for military purposes. Boys, upon reaching the age of six, engaged in military training programs. Females were also encouraged to exercise, with the goal of birthing strong future soldiers.

- The Dark and Middle Ages (476-1400 A.D.): After the fall of the lavish, sedentary Roman Empire, the lifestyle became more physically demanding again (hunting, gathering, farming), so the general fitness of the population improved.

- The Renaissance (1400-1600): The human body was again glorified during this time and organized physical education was implemented in schools to convey the importance of fitness for a healthy body and mind.

- National Period in Europe (1700-1850): Organized gymnastics was particularly popular during this time, especially in countries such as Sweden, Germany, Denmark, and Great Britain. In England, physical educators began recognizing the importance of progressive overload and variation in exercise programs. They also defined elements of purposeful training programs such as the necessary frequency, intensity, and duration of exercise to improve fitness and health.

- United States

- Colonial Period (1700-1776): The agrarian, herding, and hunting lifestyle provided plentiful opportunities for physical activity but no formal exercise programs existed.

- National Period (1776 to 1860): European immigrants often brought fitness practices from their nation of origin with them; gymnastics was popular. The importance of regular exercise was also recognized by early American leaders such as Thomas Jefferson and Benjamin Franklin. Jefferson encouraged a minimum of two hours of daily exercise for a healthy body and mind and Franklin expressed the importance of daily activities like running, swimming, and strength training for health.

- Post-Civil War (1865-1900): Lifestyle physical activity decreased after labor-related advancements developed in the Industrial Revolution. Formal physical education wasn't routinely incorporated into school curriculums until the end of the nineteenth century, also the emphasis was more on sports and game skills rather than fitness for health improvement.

- Early 20th Century Through the Great Depression: President Theodore Roosevelt strongly encouraged Americans to exercise regularly. Statistics from military training programs during and after World War I reveled that one-third of drafted individuals were physically unfit for services. Consequently, legislation was passed mandating improvements in school physical education programs, although this interest was short-lived, and fitness levels declined during the Depression.

- World War II: In addition to the importance placed on fitness for the war, the 1940s also saw formal research applied to fitness, particularly through the work of Dr. Thomas Cureton who investigated how to measure physical fitness and the effectiveness of different modalities. He not only identified exercise intensity guidelines for improving health but he developed fitness tests to evaluate muscular strength, cardiovascular endurance, and flexibility.

- 1950s-1960s: By the 1950s and 1960s, diseases with inactivity as a risk factor (such as cardiovascular disease, Type 2 Diabetes, and certain cancers) emerged. This was due, in large part, to the sedentary lifestyles brought on by advancements in technology, reducing the activity requirements of more jobs and activities for survival. Jack LaLanne encouraged healthy lifestyle habits to prevent disease, and through his television show, he designed aerobics, jumping jacks, water aerobics, and strength programs and developed exercise equipment including several strength training machines. During the Cold War, "Minimum Muscular Fitness Tests in Children" were conducted by Kraus-Hirschland to assess muscular strength and flexibility in the trunk and leg muscles. Results indicated that American children were significantly less fit than European children so President Eisenhower responded by forming the President's Council on Youth Fitness. Several organizations began to promote fitness in the general public such as the American Health Association (AHA) and The American College of Sports Medicine (ACSM). President John F. Kennedy strongly urged Americans to exercise and piloted youth fitness programs. Dr. Ken H. Cooper encouraged aerobics and the necessity if daily exercise to prevent disease.

Human Development

Cognitive Development from Birth Through Adolescence

Typical and Atypical Cognitive Growth and Development

Cognitive development refers to development of a child's capacity for perception, thought, learning, information processing, and other mental processes. The **nature vs. nurture** debate questions whether cognitive development is primarily influenced by genetics or upbringing. Evidence indicates that the interaction between nature and nurture determines the path of development.

Some commonly recognized milestones in early cognitive development are as follows:

- One to three months: focuses on faces and moving objects, differentiates between different types of tastes, sees all colors in the spectrum

- Three to six months: recognizes familiar faces and sounds, imitates expressions

- Six to twelve months: begins to determine how far away something is, understands that things still exist when they are not seen (object permanence)

- One to two years: recognizes similar objects, understands and responds to some words

- Two to three years: sorts objects into appropriate categories, responds to directions, names objects

- Three to four years: Demonstrates increased attention span of five to fifteen minutes, shows curiosity and seeks answers to questions, organizes objects by characteristics

- Four to five years: Draws human shapes, counts to five or higher, uses rhyming words

The **zone of proximal development** is the range of tasks that a child can carry out with assistance, but not independently. Parents and educators can advance a child's learning by providing opportunities within the zone of proximal development, allowing the child to develop the ability to accomplish those actions gradually without assistance.

Piaget's Theory of Cognitive Development

Piaget was the first to study cognitive development systematically. He believed children have a basic cognitive structure and continually restructure cognitive frameworks over time through maturation and experiences.

Key terms are as follows:

- Schema: introduced by Piaget, a concept or a mental framework that allows a person to understand and organize new information

- Assimilation: the way in which an individual understands and incorporates new information into their pre-existing cognitive framework (schema)

- Accommodation: in contrast to assimilation, involves altering one's pre-existing cognitive framework in order to adjust to new information

- Equilibrium: occurs when a child can successfully assimilate new information

- Disequilibrium: occurs when a child cannot successfully assimilate new information

- Equilibration: the mechanism that ensures equilibrium takes place

Stages of Cognitive Development

The stages of cognitive development are sensorimotor, pre-operational, concrete operational, and formal operational. **Sensorimotor** occurs from birth to around approximately age two. The key accomplishment here is developing object permanence—the understanding that objects still exist even when the child cannot see them. **Pre-operational** is from two to seven years. Children become capable of symbolic play and using logic. **Concrete operational** is from seven to eleven years of age. Children are able to make generalizations by drawing conclusions from what they observe (inductive reasoning), yet they are generally unable to come to a conclusion or predict an outcome by using logic pertaining to an abstract idea (deductive reasoning). **Formal operational** occurs from adolescence through early adulthood. People develop abstract thought, metacognition (thinking about thinking), and problem-solving ability.

SENSORIMOTOR STAGE	PREOPERATIONAL STAGE

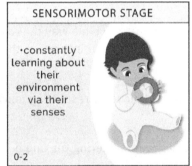
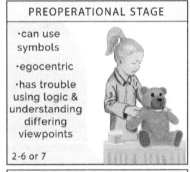

CONCRETE OPERATIONAL STAGE	FORMAL OPERATIONAL STAGE

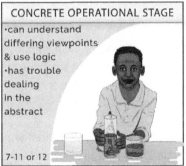

Moral Development

Lawrence Kohlberg

Lawrence Kohlberg (1927–1987), an American psychologist, is known for his work examining how people develop morals. His theory of moral development stated that individuals progress sequentially through three levels, each with two stages. Moral development tends to begin in the preschool to young childhood age range.

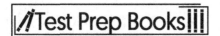

Preconventional Morality

The first level, preconventional morality, is when individuals are influenced by reward and punishment.

- Stage 1: Orientation to obedience and punishment: Children act as prescribed by a figure of authority.

- Stage 2: Individualism and exchange: Children begin to understand that there are gray areas to "right" and "wrong."

Conventional Morality

The second level, conventional morality, occurs when individuals behave morally to win external approval by peers or society and to cultivate positive relationships.

- Stage 3: Good relationships: Individuals seek to gain approval from others.

- Stage 4: Maintaining social order: Moral behavior is determined by social and cultural law, legal obligations, and one's sense of duty.

Postconventional Morality

The third level, postconventional morality, occurs when individuals engage in abstract thinking and development of personal moral principles.

- Stage 5: Social contract and individual rights: Individuals act in a way that considers society and its welfare, rather than maintaining a singular motivation of self-interest as the basis for moral behavior.

- Stage 6: Universal principles: Moral thinking is influenced by respecting universal justice for all people.

Kohlberg believed that one could not progress to a stage without mastering the one before it and that many never reach stages five or six.

Carol Gilligan

Carol Gilligan (1936–) was a student and researcher of Lawrence Kohlberg. Gilligan argued that women underwent completely different personal and social experiences from men to shape their moral standings, and that Kohlberg only considered men's experiences when he developed his theories.

Comparing and Contrasting Models of Moral Development

Psychologists Erik Eriksson, Jean Piaget, and Lawrence Kohlberg provided the most well-known models relating to moral development. Eriksson's and Piaget's models focused more on social and emotional development, but also emphasized how intricately these phases influence a person's concept of morality. Eriksson and Piaget proposed their models in the 1930s. In the late 1950s, Kohlberg built off these ideas (especially Piaget's theories) to develop his widely accepted six stages of moral development.

As previously described, Eriksson proposed an eight-stage theory of emotional development that focused on how people develop emotions based on interactions that occur in their environment. He especially highlighted interactions with parents and caregivers as formative in the development of such as trust and distrust, autonomy and shame, initiative and guilt, industry and inferiority, and secure identity and identity confusion. Based on personal experience and upbringing, people likely develop one or the other of each pairing

throughout their childhoods. More complex emotional pairings, such as intimacy and isolation, generativity and stagnation, and purpose and despair, come through in later years as people find mates, have children, take on careers, and have other experiences that contribute to their sense of self. Through these learned behaviors, people determine subjective moral and ethical ways to behave based on their personal narrative and the situation at hand.

Piaget focused on cognitive development as a determinant of behavior and decision making. His stages of development center on what the brain is capable of logically understanding through different periods of the lifespan, thus driving choice and behavior. Piaget believed that these capabilities are roughly the same across cultures during the same periods of the lifespan (e.g., a two-year-old living in a remote East Asian village will have roughly the same cognitive abilities as a two-year-old living in a Western metropolis) and that people advance through the same stages in order: a **sensorimotor stage**, where the person learns through sensory interactions; a **preoperational stage**, where the person begins to think through symbols and use language to better understand the world; a **concrete operational stage**, where the person becomes more logical and rational but is limited to concrete experiences; and finally, a **formal operational stage** where the person is able to theorize, hypothesize, and come to conclusions without a concrete experience.

Through each of these stages, people make moral and ethical decisions based on what their brain is capable of perceiving, understanding, and rationalizing. For example, a young child in the sensorimotor stage may throw a block at a caregiver simply to see what happens to the block. They do not realize this might cause pain to the caregiver. An adult in the formal operational stage would preemptively realize that throwing an object at another person could cause pain, and their choice to throw the object may provide information about their personal moral beliefs.

Kohlberg theorized that morality varied across age ranges; consequently, the **age ranges** associated with each of his stages of development are not absolute. In the first two stages, obedience and self-interest, people learn to obey commands in order to avoid negative experiences in their own self-interest. The next two stages, conformity and order, are stages in which people learn how to act within their society. These conventions and norms give rise to what a person may believe to be moral and ethical traditions. In the final stages of social contract orientation and universal human ethics, people understand and abide their own beliefs of what is moral and ethical rather than abiding by society or authority rules. Kohlberg believes not all people reach these stages, often as a result of the parameters of the society in which they live. Ultimately, Kohlberg utilized both environmental experiences and personal cognition as influential factors that work in tandem to shape a person's moral development.

Play and Its Influence on Cognitive Development

Play is a fundamental aspect of human development and has a significant impact on cognitive growth from birth through adolescence. Through play, children can actively explore, interact with their environment, and construct knowledge. Encouraging and supporting play in all its healthy forms is essential for promoting optimal cognitive development across different stages of childhood and adolescence. Below are some types of play, along with the average stages of life at which they are most psychologically relevant to development and the ways they influence cognitive development throughout one's life:

- Sensorimotor play (birth to two years): In the early years, most play is described as sensorimotor, involving cornerstone use of the senses and motor skills. Infants engage in exploratory play and use their senses to learn about objects, textures, and sounds. There is rarely any conscious intent to this kind of play; it is more instinctual than anything else, but it promotes cognitive

447

development by fostering sensory integration, object permanence, and cause-and-effect understanding.

- Symbolic play (two to seven years): Also known as pretend or imaginative play, symbolic play emerges during early childhood. Children create imaginary scenarios, use objects symbolically, and engage in role-playing. Symbolic play uses problem-solving skills, abstract thinking, creativity, and sometimes empathy. It helps children develop language, social understanding, and perspective-taking abilities.

- Constructive play (three to seven years): At its core, constructive play involves manipulating objects to create something new. Examples include building with blocks, assembling puzzles, or constructing models. This type of play enhances cognitive development by using spatial awareness, logical thinking, and planning skills. It helps develop problem-solving, fine motor skills, and creativity.

- Games with rules (seven years and onward): As children grow older, they begin to understand, tolerate, and seek baseline structure. As a result, they engage in games with rules, such as board games, sports, and organized activities. These games require attention, strategic thinking, decision-making, and rule-following to some degree. They foster memory skills, mathematical thinking, social interaction, and teamwork. Games with rules also help children develop self-control, patience, and sportsmanship in later years, usually right before or at the beginning of early adolescence.

- Social play (throughout childhood, adolescence, and onward): Play is inherently social and provides numerous opportunities for children to engage in social interaction, collaboration, and negotiation. Through cooperative play, children learn to communicate, share, and take turns, which develops their social and emotional intelligence. Social play develops this intelligence by promoting perspective-taking, empathy, and understanding of others' thoughts and feelings.

- Problem-solving play (throughout childhood, adolescence, and onward): This form of play is more complex than simple rule-following, as it presents challenges and problems that children need to solve without being told what to do in the moment. Whether it involves solving puzzles, strategizing, or building complex structures, problem-solving play heavily promotes mental development though critical thinking, reasoning, logical sequencing, and creativity. Problem-solving play helps children learn to approach problems from different angles, develop hypotheses, and experiment with solutions.

Theory of Multiple Intelligences

American developmental psychologist Howard Gardner (1943–) is a very well-known figure in the field of psychology. While he has written numerous articles and books throughout the span of his career, his most notable contribution consists of devising what has been dubbed the theory of multiple intelligences. The **theory of multiple intelligences** distinguishes human intelligence into distinctive modalities, as opposed to viewing intelligence as a single general ability. In other words, Gardner looked at the different types of

intelligence that people can possess. His theory consisted of eight different types of intelligence, each with multiple qualities in children that may reveal their areas of intelligence early in life:

- Musical-rhythmic intelligence relates to good or absolute pitch. An example is a musician who can sing, play instruments, and compose music. This can be identified early in the following ways:

- More quickly developing abilities to sing, play musical instruments, or compose music

- Keener sensitivity to rhythm, melody, and pitch

- Skill in recognizing and reproducing musical patterns

- Visual-spatial intelligence consists of the ability to solve spatial navigational problems, visualizing things from different angles, facial and scene recognition, and observation of fine details. Some examples of those likely to fall under this category would include architects, photographers, and physicists. This can be identified early in the following ways:

- Inherent tendency to visualize objects from different angles

- Quicker to recognize faces, scenes, and fine details than names, words, or phrases

- Passion for fields such as architecture, photography, and physics

- Verbal-linguistic intelligence outlines a penchant for words and languages. For example, a person with high verbal-linguistic intelligence is typically skilled at reading, writing, storytelling, and memorizing vocabulary. This can be identified early in the following ways:

- Earlier-than-average reading, writing, and storytelling abilities

- Skill in memorizing vocabulary and language patterns

- Rapidly growing vocabulary and effectiveness at expressing themself

- Logical-mathematical intelligence describes the use of abstractions, critical thinking, logic, numbers, and reasoning. For instance, a person proficient in this skill is able to successfully apply logic and reason to assimilate and accommodate new information and generally make sense of things. This can be identified early in the following ways:

- Early competence in understanding/manipulating numbers and abstractions more so than words and language

- Penchant for problem-solving and analyzing comparatively complex systems

- Bodily-kinesthetic intelligence consists of the ability to control one's bodily movements and skillful handling of objects. Some examples include athletes, dancers, actors, and soldiers. This can be identified early in the following ways:

- More intuitive control of body movements and coordination

- Skillful handling of objects and physical activities

449

- High aptitude in areas like sports, dance, and theatre

- Interpersonal intelligence involves the ability to be sensitive to how others think and feel and cooperate with others. Some examples of professions that typically rely on this type of intelligence include managers, teachers, administrators, and social workers. This can be identified early in the following ways:

- Early sensitivity to others' thoughts and feelings

- Strong social skills, as well as the ability to cooperate and collaborate

- Gravitation toward leadership and organization roles among groups

- Intrapersonal intelligence has to do with introspection and self-reflection. Consider a person who can predict their own emotional reactions to particular events, outline their strengths and weaknesses, and has a profound understanding of themselves. Such people would likely be theologians, entrepreneurs, and counselors. This can be identified early in the following ways:

- Early self-awareness and accurate understanding of one's own emotions, strengths, and weaknesses

- Ability to identify and predict one's own emotional reactions and motivations

- Naturalistic intelligence involves cultivating and conveying details about one's natural environment. Some examples here of those relying on this type of intelligence include hunters, gatherers, farmers, and scientists. This can be identified early in the following ways:

- Fixation on observing, understanding, and categorizing elements of one's surroundings

- Tendency to recognize and recall patterns and relationships in nature

- Passion for topics such as collecting, farming, and science

Social and Physical Development from Birth Through Adolescence: Social Development

Typical and Atypical Social Growth, Development, and the Socialization Process

Social development refers to the development of the skills that allow individuals to have effective interpersonal relationships and to contribute in a positive manner to the world around them.

Social learning is taught directly by caregivers and educators, but it is also learned indirectly by the experience of various social relationships.

Social development is commonly influenced by extended family, communities, religious institutions, schools, and sports teams or social groups. Positive social development is supported when caregivers do the following:

- Attune to a child's needs and feelings

- Demonstrate respect for others

- Teach children how to handle conflict and solve problems encountered during social experiences

- Help children learn to take the perspective of another person and develop empathy

- Encourage discussion of morals and values and listen to the child's opinions on those topics

- Explain rules and encourage fair treatment of others

- Encourage cooperation, rather than competition

Social development begins from birth as a child learns to attach to their mother and other caregivers. During adolescence, social development focuses on peer relationships and self-identity.

Typical and Atypical Emotional Growth and Development

Emotional development encompasses the development of the following abilities:

- Identifying and understanding the feelings that one experiences
- Identifying and understanding the feelings of others
- Emotional and behavioral regulation
- Empathy
- Establishing relationships with others

Caregivers who are nurturing and responsive enable children to learn to regulate emotions and feel safe in the environment around them.

- By age two to three months, infants express delight and distress, begin smiling, and may be able to be soothed by rocking.

- By three to four months, infants communicate via crying and begin to express interest and surprise.

- Between four to nine months, infants respond differently to strangers in comparison to known individuals, solicit attention, show a particular attachment for a primary caregiver, and have an expanded range of expressed emotions that include anger, fear, and shyness.

- At ten to twelve months, babies show an increase in exploration and curiosity, demonstrate affection, and display a sense of humor.

- Children at age twelve to twenty-four months often demonstrate anger via aggression, laugh in social situations, recognize themselves in a mirror, engage in symbolic play, and have a complete range of emotional expression.

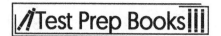

- Around age two, children begin using different facial expressions to show their emotions, begin to play cooperatively, and may transition from being calm and affectionate to temperamental and easily frustrated.

- At age three, children engage in more social and imaginative play, show interest in the feelings of others, begin to learn to manage frustration, and are often inconsistent and stubborn.

- Children at age four show improved cooperation, express sympathy, and may exhibit lying and/or guilty behavior.

- At age five, children can play rule-based games, often want to do what is expected of them, express emotion easily, and choose friends for themselves.

- Children at age six typically describe themselves in terms of their external attributes, have a difficult time coping with challenges and criticism, prefer routines, and show inconsistent self-control.

- Around age seven, children can typically describe causes and outcomes of emotions and show better regulation of emotions in most situations.

- From ages eight to ten, children have an increased need for independence, want to be viewed as intelligent, experience and better understand emotional subtleties, and may be defiant.

- During adolescence, children begin to master emotional skills to manage stress, increase self-awareness, develop identity, show increased ability for empathy, and learn to manage conflict.

Normal versus abnormal behavior is difficult to distinguish because each person is unique, so creating a standard of normal can be challenging. This standard also changes constantly as the culture evolves.

Normal behaviors are those that are common to the majority of the population, as related to emotional functioning, social interactions, and mental capacity. **Abnormal behavior** is generally considered that which is maladaptive, dysfunctional, and disruptive to life. These behaviors may be an exaggeration of a normal behavior or even an absence of a typical response. They do not conform to the accepted patterns or common behaviors of society. Sadness over the death of a loved one is considered normal, but disabling depression that interferes with school and work responsibilities is not.

Identity Development

Identity includes **self-concept** and **self-esteem**. Self-concept is the beliefs one holds about one's self. Self-esteem is how one feels about one's self-concept.

The physical changes of adolescence can have a strong influence on an adolescent's self-esteem. Adolescents also incorporate comments from others, particularly parents and friends, into their identity. Adolescents also undergo important emotional development and begin to hone the skills that are necessary for stress management and effective relationships with others. Some of the skills necessary for stress management are recognizing and managing one's own emotions, developing empathy for others, learning appropriate and constructive methods of managing conflict, and learning to work cooperatively rather than competitively.

A normal part of adolescence is a yearning for independence. Teachers can educate both parents and adolescents about the importance of positive peer relationships during this time. Peer groups help adolescents

learn about the world outside of their families and identify how they differ from their parents. Adolescents who are accepted by their peers and who have positive peer relationships may have better psychosocial outcomes in both adolescence and adulthood.

An increase in conflict with parents is normal during adolescence and seems to be most prevalent between girls and mothers. Parents may need reassurance that this conflict does not represent rejection, but rather a normal striving for independence.

Some theories seek to explain the prevalence of risk-taking behaviors among adolescents. One theory of risk-taking behavior explains that the need for excitement and sensation seeking outweighs any potential dangers that may come from sensation seeking. Another theory says that risk-taking often occurs within groups as a way to gain status and acceptance among peers. Additionally, adolescents who engage in risk-taking behavior may be modeling adult behavior that has been romanticized.

There are many ways in which teachers and parents can provide guidance to young people with regard to their risk-taking behavior. They should become comfortable discussing uncomfortable topics, so that adolescents can safely talk about their decision-making and peer pressure. Additionally, it is wise to steer adolescents toward healthy outlets that channel their talents or get them involved in positive activities.

Adolescent resilience and positive outcomes are associated with these factors:

- Having a stable and positive relationship with at least one involved and caring adult (e.g., parent, coach, teacher, family member, community member)

- Developing a sense of self-meaning, often through a church or spiritual outlet

- Attending a school that has high, but realistic, expectations and supports its students

- Living in a warm and nurturing home

- Having adequate ability to manage stress

Attachment and Bonding

It has become more important than ever to understand attachment and bonding, especially in relation to changes within the US culture's attitudes about child welfare over the last fifty years. Child Protective Service Teams have become more active in every city. The medical profession, the educational system, and the mental health profession are more informed about children at risk. As a result, more children are being taken from parents, sometimes as early as the day of birth. An older child victim may travel from relative to relative, back to the mother, then into foster or group homes. These children do not have an opportunity to form attachments with their caregivers, nor do caregivers have the opportunity to bond with the children.

Bonding refers to a mother's initial connection to her baby. This generally occurs within the first hours or days of the birth. Mothers who are able and willing to hold their child close to them shortly after birth generally have more positive relationships with the child. When a mother fails to bond, the child is at greater risk for having behavioral problems.

Attachment, on the other hand, refers to a more gradual development of the baby's relationship with their caretaker. A secure attachment naturally grows out of a positive, loving relationship in which there is soothing physical contact, emotional and physical safety, and responsiveness to the child's needs. The baby who has a

secure attachment will venture out from their safe base, but immediately seek their mother when fearful or anxious, having learned that mommy will be there to protect them. This type of secure relationship becomes impossible if the child is moved from home to home or has experienced abuse or neglect.

A child whose needs have not been met or who has learned through mistreatment that the world is unfriendly and hostile may develop an avoidant attachment or ambivalent attachment. An **avoidant attachment** is characterized by a detached relationship in which the child does not seek out the caregiver when distressed, but acts independently. A child with **ambivalent attachment** shows inconsistency toward the caregiver; sometimes the child clings to them, and at other times, resists their comfort. Establishing a secure, positive attachment with a caregiver is crucial to a child's life-long emotional and social success. The development of attachment disorder is often present in foster children or those adopted later in life and can create much frustration and heartache as the more stable parents step in and attempt to bond with them.

Autonomy

Autonomy refers to an individual's ability to act independently, make decisions, and exert control over their own behavior and actions. The development of autonomy plays a crucial role in shaping an individual's sense of self, personal identity, and psychological well-being.

The process of developing autonomy begins early in life as children start to assert their independence and explore their environment. They develop a sense of agency and a desire to have control over their actions and choices. For example, infants may exhibit autonomy by attempting to feed themselves or crawl toward objects of interest. As children grow, their autonomy expands, and they engage in activities such as dressing themselves and making choices about playtime.

Throughout childhood and adolescence, autonomy becomes increasingly complex. It involves not only physical independence, but also emotional and cognitive autonomy. Emotionally, children strive for a sense of self-reliance and self-regulation. They learn to identify and manage their emotions by choice, as opposed to being told to control their behavior. Cognitively, they develop the ability to think critically, make decisions, and set personal goals. Autonomy in adolescence often involves asserting independence from parents and establishing a sense of personal values and beliefs.

Autonomy contributes to the formation of a unique personality by allowing individuals to explore and better understand their own preferences, interests, and values. Children and adolescents who are encouraged to express themselves and make decisions based on their own internal motivations are more likely to effectively use their autonomy and develop a strong, clear, authentic sense of self. However, the development of autonomy is a gradual, complex process that can vary across individuals. Some children may exhibit a higher degree of autonomy at an early age, while others may require more support and guidance.

Social Development

Social development is a complex and dynamic process that involves a constant intake of social skills, the frequent development and shifting of relationships, and the formulation of a sense of identity within a given social environment context, which is often largely out of one's control. This development is influenced by a great many factors, including—but not limited to—cognitive abilities, emotional maturation, cultural norms, and behavioral differences within an individual and the people around them. Here is a general outline of the social development of children and young adolescents at various stages of life, along with additional considerations for individuals with special needs:

- During early childhood (ages zero to five), children begin to develop social skills, typically through interactions with family members, caregivers, and similarly aged peers. In this phase of life, children are most likely to engage in parallel play, where they play alongside but not necessarily with other children. They are still establishing an understanding of how their own mind and body react with the world around them. In early childhood, socialization is usually centered around the family, and children develop attachments to caregivers above anyone else.

- In middle childhood (ages six to twelve), socialization begins to meaningfully extend beyond the family. Children form friendships based on shared interests and activities as they begin to independently build on their sense of self to form the beginnings of a full identity. They engage in cooperative play, participate in group activities, and develop a sense of belonging within their peer group. Social skills such as sharing, taking turns, and resolving conflicts become more refined at this stage.

- Finally, during early adolescence (ages twelve to fourteen), peer relationships become especially influential. Adolescents prioritize seeking acceptance and validation from their peers, potentially over seeking acceptance from family and caregivers. Young adolescents tend to form closer friendships and begin exploring more intimate relationships as well. In this stage, they develop a fuller sense of identity and may experiment with different social roles and behaviors within their relationships.

It is important to recognize that individuals with **special needs** may have unique experiences and challenges in their social development that differ from person to person. Children with special needs may face challenges in social interactions and may benefit from structured social skills training and inclusive educational environments. Young adolescents with special needs may experience difficulties in socializing, establishing peer relationships, finding individual identity, and managing the social pressures of adolescence as their peers also begin to undergo heavy social change. However, it is important to recognize that individuals with special needs also have strengths and abilities that contribute to their social development and the formulation of their own identity. Below are some examples of supportive strategies for children and young adolescents with special needs in social development:

- Creating inclusive and supportive environments that foster acceptance, empathy, and understanding.

- Providing targeted social skills training and interventions that address specific challenges in the individual's personal social life.

- Encouraging peer interactions and facilitating inclusive play and learning opportunities in special needs-friendly environments.

- Promoting self-advocacy skills and empowering individuals to express their own needs and preferences.

- Collaborating with families and medical professionals to create individualized support plans for every necessary aspect of the individual's life.

Overall, the social development of children and young adolescents evolves and shifts dramatically throughout the different stages of development. There is no way to fully and reliably predict how an individual's social development will unfold. However, to ensure the healthiest and most well-adjusted development possible, it is

important to foster positive social experiences for children and young adolescents, provide them with appropriate support, and promote acceptance of their social individuality.

Impact of Play on Social Development

Play serves as a natural and essential platform for children to explore, interact, and learn about the social world around them. Through play, children develop crucial social skills, build relationships, and gain a deeper understanding of social norms and expectations. Below are some key ways that play influences social development:

- Play provides opportunities for children to practice and refine their communication and language skills. Whether engaging in pretend play, cooperative games, or group activities, children learn to express their thoughts, ideas, and emotions. They develop vocabulary, learn to take turns, negotiate, and listen to others.

- Play often encourages cooperation and collaboration among children and their peers. They learn to share, compromise, and problem-solve as they engage in joint play activities. Through cooperative play, children develop a sense of teamwork and learn to value others' contributions.

- Play also helps develop emotional regulation and offers a low-consequence space for children to explore and understand their range of emotions. They learn to manage conflicts, handle frustration, and control expectations during play scenarios.

- Children are also given opportunities to practice relational skills and empathy during play. They learn to read social cues, interpret non-verbal communication, and understand the impact of their actions on others. This nurtures a sense of empathy as children take on different roles, perspectives, and emotions.

- Self-identity and social roles are developed and experimented with through play as well. In play, children can pretend to be different characters, imitate adult roles, or engage in full fantasy play. By trying out these roles, children gain insights into different social dynamics and refine their own sense of self in contrast.

Development of Prosocial Behavior

Prosocial behavior refers to voluntary actions intended primarily to benefit others. It is influenced by multiple factors throughout childhood and adolescence that shape a child's understanding of empathy, moral reasoning, and their willingness to engage in prosocial activity. Below are several key factors that influence the development of prosocial behavior in children:

- The relationship children have with their parents and caregivers is crucial in shaping their prosocial development. Parents who model prosocial behavior, encourage sharing and helping, and provide opportunities for children to engage in acts of kindness contribute to the development of prosocial behavior.

- Socialization and peer interactions provide important opportunities for children to practice and develop good prosocial behavior. Through positive interactions with peers, children learn the importance of sharing, cooperation, and empathy, as well as experiencing the impact of their behavior on others.

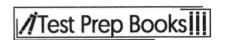

- Children learn much through observational learning and imitating others. They see the prosocial behaviors of significant adults, siblings, and peers and incorporate these behaviors into their own repertoire. Role models who engage in prosocial behavior, such as teachers, parents, and community members, can inspire and shape children's prosocial actions.

- Cultural and societal norms and values are among the greatest influences of prosocial behavior development. Cultural expectations, religious teachings, and community practices can all shape children's understanding of what is considered morally right and socially acceptable. Cultures that prioritize cooperation, interdependence, and community well-being may foster higher levels of prosocial behavior in children.

- Prosocial behavior is also heavily influenced by a child's schooling and educational context. Classroom environments that emphasize cooperation, empathy, and inclusivity can facilitate the development of prosocial behavior. Educational programs and curriculum interventions that teach social-emotional skills, conflict resolution, and empathy have been shown to positively impact prosocial behavior in children.

- Media and technology have an ever-expanding influence on the development of prosocial behavior, for better or for worse. Positive portrayals of prosocial behavior in media such as television shows, books, and internet content can provide children with role models and inspire prosocial actions. Exposure to violent, egocentric, or aggressive media can have the opposite effect, potentially reducing prosocial behavior.

Individual differences and the interaction of multiple influences contribute to theoretically infinite avenues of prosocial behavior development in many directions. Some children may have a natural inclination toward prosocial behavior, while others may require more guidance and support to develop these skills. Creating nurturing and supportive environments, providing positive role models, and fostering empathy and cooperation are all effective and controllable ways to positively impact a child's prosocial development.

Social and Physical Development from Birth Through Adolescence: Physical Development

Individual Differences in Physical Development

Individual physical differences in development from birth through adolescence are significant and influenced by various factors such as **genetics, nutrition, environment, and overall health**. These differences can be observed in the timing, rate, and extent of physical growth and maturation.

In terms of growth, children may vary in **height, weight, and body composition**. Some individuals may experience early or late growth spurts, leading to variations in physical stature compared to their peers that may not accurately reflect how their stature will differ as adults. Similarly, the onset of puberty can differ among individuals, as some will experience either **early or delayed sexual maturation**. Some children may excel early in certain complex physical activities, such as sports or dancing, while others may struggle with coordination or fine motor skills at the same age.

Children with special needs may exhibit especially unique patterns of physical development. Some individuals with developmental disabilities may experience delays or differences in motor skills, coordination, and muscle

strength. **Physical therapy and interventions** tailored to their specific needs can help address these challenges and promote optimal physical development.

It is important to recognize and support individual differences in physical development, including those with special needs. Adequate educational and developmental support can help individuals both with and without special needs overcome challenges and maximize their physical potential.

Indicators of Normal Physical Growth and Development

It is important to understand normal developmental milestones. While not all children progress at the same rate, one must know some benchmarks to determine if the child has any developmental delays that prevent him or her from reaching goals by a certain age.

Infancy Through Age 5

During the first year of life, abundant changes occur. The child learns basic, but important, skills. The child is learning to manipulate objects, hold their head without support, crawl, and pull up into a standing position. The toddler should be able walk without assistance by 18 months. By age two, the child should be running and able to climb steps one stair at a time. By age three, the child should be curious and full of questions about how the world works or why people behave in certain ways. The child should have the balance and coordination to climb stairs using only one foot per stair. By age four, the child is increasingly independent, demonstrating skills like attending to toilet needs and dressing with some adult assistance.

School Age to Adolescence

By age five, speech is becoming more fluent, and the ability to draw simple figures improves. Dressing without help is achieved. By age six, speech should be fluent and motor skills are strengthened. The youth is now able to navigate playground equipment and kick and throw a ball. Towards the end of this phase, around age 12, secondary sexual characteristics, such as darker body hair or breast development, may occur.

Adolescence

Adolescence is a critical period of physical development characterized by rapid growth and significant changes in various aspects of the body. It marks the onset of **puberty**, a process triggered by hormonal changes that ultimately lead to sexual maturation. Puberty involves the development of secondary sexual characteristics, such as breast development in females and facial hair growth in males. Adolescence also often includes a rapid **growth spurt**, typically occurring between the ages of ten and sixteen in females and between twelve and nineteen in males. During this period, adolescents experience a significant increase in height and weight as their skeletal systems grow and their muscles, organs, and tissues develop. This almost invariably results in **changes in body composition**, including an increase in muscle mass and bone density. However, there is also an increase in body fat, particularly in females, as a part of normal development.

Additionally, physical development during adolescence involves the **refinement of motor skills and coordination**. Adolescents gain greater control over their movements and enhance their ability to perform complex physical activities such as sports and dancing, as well as fine motor skills like writing or playing musical instruments. The **cardiovascular and respiratory systems** also undergo significant changes as the heart and lungs increase in size and efficiency, allowing for improved endurance and aerobic capacity.

Influences on Development from Birth Through Adolescence

Impact of Physical, Mental, and Cognitive Impairment on Human Development

Approximately 7 percent of US children have some type of disability. The most common physical disabilities that impact development are cerebral palsy, hearing issues, and visual issues. Learning disabilities are also common—these could be Down's syndrome or other developmental delays. Common psychiatric disabilities are ADHD and autism spectrum disorders. Others include mood disorders, oppositional disorders, anxiety disorders, and, in rare cases, schizophrenia. The impact upon the child and family corresponds to the family's ability to adapt to the condition and their ability to connect to community resources.

How the individual develops and copes with the disability depends greatly upon the social context and the child's own personal attributes. Raising a disabled child puts tremendous stress on parents and siblings. There are issues of stigma, financial burden, missed days of work for parents, and the time and energy needed to seek useful resources. Siblings may be called upon to take roles of parenting to help out. These siblings may be bullied by peers who make fun of their disabled family member. They may feel neglected by their parents. Additionally, there may be a need for special housing and special schools. Low-income families may face barriers to accessing services such as transportation, medical specialists, or assistance with childcare.

Potential Impacts on Development of Children and Young Adolescents

The development of children and young adolescents can be heavily impacted by demographic factors such as economic class and sex/gender. These factors can influence aspects of their lives such as access to resources, opportunities, and social experiences. Understanding and addressing these influences help promote equity, provide equal opportunities, and ensure the well-being of all children, regardless of those demographic factors.

Poverty and socioeconomic status can directly affect children's physical, cognitive, and socioemotional development. Limited access to quality healthcare, nutritious food, and safe living conditions can have detrimental effects on physical health and well-being. Poverty may also limit educational opportunities and lead to disparities in academic achievement. Additionally, children from low-income backgrounds may face increased stressors and have fewer resources for positive social experiences.

Additionally, **gender/sex** can lead to unique cultural challenges in a child's development. Gender norms and expectations often shape the experiences and opportunities available to children and adolescents. Girls tend to face barriers in accessing education or participating in certain activities due to cultural or societal beliefs, while boys are likely to face pressures to conform to traditional masculine ideals, which can potentially hinder their emotional development and mental health.

Furthermore, the **intersection of socioeconomic factors and gender** can result in even greater disparities in development outcomes, especially as they pertain to health. For example, girls from lower socioeconomic backgrounds may face challenges in accessing feminine or reproductive healthcare, which negatively impacts their physical, mental, and potentially social well-being, depending on how greatly each individual needs reproductive healthcare.

Effort should be made to reduce the impact of socioeconomic disparities, especially in the role of an educator. Examples include providing comprehensive health education, healthcare literacy, and social support programs

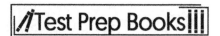

in adolescent learning spaces. Challenging gender stereotypes and promoting gender equality can also create an environment that allows all children to thrive.

Interaction of Nature and Nurture in Determination of Behavior

The **nature versus nurture debate** describes how particular behavioral features are a product of either genetic or environmental influences. While this debate persists, most psychological researchers are now aware of how both genes and environment play a vital role in an individual's growth and development. In psychology, **epigenetics** outlines how gene expression is influenced by environmental factors to help shape a person's behavior and general development. In other words, environmental factors can impact the expression of genes. Genes and one's environment communicate back and forth and work in tandem to create traits, and also influence our physical development. **Physical development** involves a process that begins in infancy and persists up into late adolescence. It focuses on the development of gross and fine motor skills, and also puberty. Physical development is related to numerous environmental factors. In fact, one of the most important factors that contribute to an individual's growth and development is their culture.

People raised in different cultures receive specific environmental inputs, ranging from language, parenting style, and social interactions. Every culture has their own rich tapestry of traditions, beliefs, values, laws, norms, and practices that set them apart from other cultures and contribute to a person's uniqueness. Culture also shapes an individual's perspective of the world around them, which, in turn, influences their behavior and perception of events. What is considered normal in one culture might be considered abnormal or taboo in another, and vice versa. Cultural identity can also affect one's physical development, such as how a child learns and develops both fine and gross motor skills, because parenting styles vary across cultures and are passed down from one generation to another.

For example, various Western societies encourage parents to make sure infants are sleeping on their backs in order to prevent the prospect of sudden infant death syndrome, which, in turn, causes them to spend less time on their stomachs and be slower to crawl or sit up. However, in Jamaican culture, parents tend to promote accelerated development as it relates to sitting by placing their infants' waist-deep in holes and supporting their posture with blankets.

As people progress through the years, their behavior can be affected by a combination of their genetic makeup and the environment in which they were raised. The nature side of this debate has stated that one's genes will impact their response to a situation regardless of their surrounding environment, which, in turn, affects their behavior, personality, and general perception of the world around them. But on the nurture side of this debate, how and where a person is raised, along with any cultural expectations, are said to influence how one behaves and the personality type they develop.

However, most research shows that genes and environment often interact with each other to influence an organism's growth and development. Most researchers have realized that it is the interaction of one's innate biological factors with their external environmental factors that influences and facilitates human growth and development. Cognitive, behavioral, and emotional advancements that typically occur at certain points in one's life warrant genetically-based changes and experiences in one's social environment. Culture is a prime example of how environment can affect a person's behavior and result in a certain personality type. Along with physical development, social development can also be influenced by one's cultural setting.

Social development describes how people form necessary social and emotional skills throughout the course of their lifespan. Childhood and adolescence tend to be particular areas of focus in one's development. A healthy

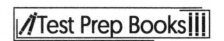

social development enables people to develop positive relationships with family, friends, and numerous other people they encounter in their lives. As people grow and mature, they learn to become better emotional regulators by managing their feelings and their needs, and by becoming more attune to the feelings and needs of others and responding accordingly. A child's personality, opportunities for socialization, observed learning experiences, and developmental disorders can each affect their social development throughout their lives. For instance, a child who is already quick to anger and bears witness to violent and aggressive behaviors could later end up having a particularly difficult time learning how to appropriately interact with others. Because people living in different cultures vary in how they perceive themselves and relate to others, they also tend to view things differently.

For example, when explaining a personal experience that stands out to them, European-American children will tend to focus more on details, remember specific events, and emphasize their views on them. However, Asian children will tend to pay more attention to describing everyone they met and how they seemed to relate to them.

Development During Adolescence

Adolescence is a period of development in which significant biological, psychological, and social changes take place.

In both sexes, biological changes stem from a shift in hormone production that results in physical growth spurts as well as the further development of sexual and reproductive characteristics. Males experience increased levels of testosterone, resulting in a visible Adam's apple, a voice that is deeper in pitch, an increase in lean muscle mass, the onset of facial hair, and the ability to ejaculate seminal fluid from the penis. Females experience increased levels of estrogen, which encourages fat deposits (e.g., breasts) and a wider hip structure. The increased amount of body fat is necessary for females to begin menstruation, which is a monthly release of an unfertilized egg from one of the two ovaries.

Both sexes also experience in an increase in body hair (although males typically grow more body hair than females), an increase in functioning sweat glands (and therefore body odor), and changes to the cardiovascular system. Due to these biological changes that encourage reproduction, both sexes may feel more desire for the opposite sex and the urge to engage in sexual behaviors. Females tend to experience puberty and maturation first, while males appear to lag some years behind.

A number of cognitive, psychological, and emotional changes also occur. These are also hormone-driven changes. The adolescent brain changes in physical composition and in its use of neural pathways, especially in areas that regulate mood and behavior. Adolescents also experience different interactions in their environment and with their primary peers that affect how their cognition is shaped. Compared to children's brains, adolescent brains are primed to think more critically, hold attention and focus for longer, and have better personal self-control; however, these abilities are not fully developed until the mid- to late-twenties in most people.

Some researchers believe that although increased cognitive abilities related to critical thinking and personal control are present, the social and emotional areas that also influence the outward presentation of these skills develop at a different rate. This imbalance may contribute to the stereotype of adolescent behavior (e.g., emotional, impulsive, moody). It is also believed that the adolescent brain favors high-risk situations and is more motivated by social and cultural reward. This may have an evolutionary basis; seemingly risky situations, such as leaving the family home, interacting with strangers, and seeking new experiences, often lead to a less

familial mate who provides more gene variation for higher reproductive fitness. However, these behaviors often come at a high cost in modern society, such as unsafe sex practices that result in disease transmission or teenage pregnancies.

Coupled with the biological changes of adolescence, as well as with cultural norms within specific environments, adolescents may appear to undergo tremendous changes in personality. This can be a rough adjustment for the adolescent's family of origin. Newly-formed cognitive skills, such as critical thinking and the awareness of other perspectives in the world, may contribute to the adolescent questioning or rebelling against family norms and values as the adolescent tries to form their unique identity. It may be difficult for parents to view emotional outbursts or unstable moods, as well as risky behaviors. Adolescents tend to favor the opinions of peers rather than that of family members or elder relatives; trying to balance peer pressure with family values can increase conflicts between parents and adolescents. Through these changes, the adolescent is ultimately preparing for independence and moving away from the family group.

Sources of Possible Abuse and Neglect

Abuse and neglect are serious issues that can have profound and long-lasting impacts in any stage of human development, but especially for children. Various sources of abuse and neglect as they pertain to children and young adolescents are discussed below.

Physical abuse involves the intentional use of physical force that causes any level of harm or injury to a child. This can include hitting, slapping, burning, or any other form of physical harm. This abuse can lead to physical injuries, impaired brain development, and emotional trauma. It can affect a child's sense of safety, trust, and overall well-being.

Emotional abuse involves the persistent emotional mistreatment of a child, including, but not limited to humiliation, rejection, and constant criticism. This form of abuse can have detrimental effects on a child's self-esteem, emotional regulation, and social development. Children who experience emotional abuse may struggle with forming healthy relationships and exhibit symptoms of anxiety, depression, or other mental health disorders.

Substance abuse, such as drug or alcohol addiction, is guaranteed to significantly impact a child's development when done by a child, but substance abuse from a parent or caregiver can heavily impact child development as well. Children who live in households where substance abuse is present may experience neglect, inconsistent treatment, and exposure to dangerous behaviors and situations. These circumstances can lead to physical and emotional abuse and neglect, impaired cognitive development, and increased risk of substance abuse from the child themself later in life.

Neglect occurs when a caregiver fails to provide adequate care, supervision, and support to meet a child's basic needs. It can manifest as physical neglect (lack of proper nutrition, clothing, or medical care), emotional neglect (lack of affection, attention, or emotional support), or educational neglect (lack of access to education or failure to address educational needs). Neglect can result in developmental delays, poor academic performance, social difficulties, and myriad other long-term psychological consequences.

It is crucial as an educator to understand these terms to identify and address cases of abuse and neglect promptly. Early intervention and appropriate support services can mitigate the negative impacts and promote healing and recovery. Providing a safe and nurturing environment, access to counseling and therapeutic interventions, and supportive relationships are essential for children to overcome the effects of abuse and neglect and develop into healthy and resilient adults.

Impact of Abuse and Neglect on Development

Abuse and neglect are serious issues that can have profound and long-lasting impacts in any stage of human development, but especially for children. Various sources of abuse and neglect as they pertain to children and young adolescents are discussed below:

- **Physical abuse** involves the intentional use of physical force that causes any level of harm or injury to a child. This can include hitting, slapping, burning, or any other form of physical harm. This abuse can lead to physical injuries, impaired brain development, and emotional trauma. It can affect a child's sense of safety, trust, and overall well-being.

- **Emotional abuse** involves the persistent emotional mistreatment of a child, including, but not limited to humiliation, rejection, and constant criticism. This form of abuse can have detrimental effects on a child's self-esteem, emotional regulation, and social development. Children who experience emotional abuse may struggle with forming healthy relationships and exhibit symptoms of anxiety, depression, or other mental health disorders.

- **Substance abuse**, such as drug or alcohol addiction, is guaranteed to significantly impact a child's development when done by a child, but substance abuse from a parent or caregiver can heavily impact child development as well. Children who live in households where substance abuse is present may experience neglect, inconsistent treatment, and exposure to dangerous behaviors and situations. These circumstances can lead to physical and emotional abuse and neglect, impaired cognitive development, and increased risk of substance abuse from the child themself later in life.

- **Neglect** occurs when a caregiver fails to provide adequate care, supervision, and support to meet a child's basic needs. It can manifest as physical neglect (lack of proper nutrition, clothing, or medical care), emotional neglect (lack of affection, attention, or emotional support), or educational neglect (lack of access to education or failure to address educational needs). Neglect can result in developmental delays, poor academic performance, social difficulties, and myriad other long-term psychological consequences.

It is crucial as an educator to understand these terms to identify and address cases of abuse and neglect promptly. Early intervention and appropriate support services can mitigate the negative impacts and promote healing and recovery. Providing a safe and nurturing environment, access to counseling and therapeutic interventions, and supportive relationships are essential for children to overcome the effects of abuse and neglect and to develop into healthy and resilient adults.

Practice Test

Subtest I

1. When children begin to negotiate the sounds that make up words in their language independently, what skill(s) are they demonstrating?
    a. Phonological awareness
    b. Phonemes
    c. Phoneme substitution
    d. Blending

2. What is phonics?
    a. The study of syllabication
    b. The study of onsets and rimes
    c. The study of sound-letter relationships
    d. The study of graphemes

3. Word analysis skills are NOT critical for the development of what area of literacy?
    a. Vocabulary
    b. Reading fluency
    c. Spelling
    d. Articulation

4. What area of study involves mechanics, usage, and sentence formation?
    a. Word analysis
    b. Spelling conventions
    c. Morphemes
    d. Phonics

5. How do the majority of high-frequency sight words differ from decodable words?
    a. They do not rhyme.
    b. They do not follow the alphabetic principle.
    c. They do not contain onsets.
    d. They contain rimes.

6. Reading fluency involves what key areas?
    a. Accuracy, rate, and prosody
    b. Accuracy, rate, and consistency
    c. Prosody, accuracy, and clarity
    d. Rate, prosody, and comprehension

7. When students study character development, setting, and plot, what are they most likely studying?
    a. Word analysis
    b. Point of view
    c. Literary analysis of a fictional text
    d. Fluency

8. When students use inference, what are they able to do?
    a. Make logical assumptions based on contextual clues
    b. Independently navigate various types of text
    c. Summarize a text's main idea
    d. Paraphrase a text's main idea

The next three questions are based on the following passage:

George Washington emerged out of the American Revolution as an unlikely champion of liberty. On June 14, 1775, the Second Continental Congress created the Continental Army, and John Adams, serving in the Congress, nominated Washington to be its first commander. Washington had fought under the British during the French and Indian War, and his experience and prestige proved instrumental to the American war effort. Washington provided invaluable leadership, training, and strategy during the Revolutionary War. He emerged from the war as the embodiment of liberty and freedom from tyranny.

After vanquishing the heavily favored British forces, Washington could have pronounced himself the autocratic leader of the former colonies without any opposition, but he famously refused and returned to his Mount Vernon plantation. His restraint proved his commitment to the fledgling state's republicanism. Washington was later unanimously elected as the first American president. But it is Washington's farewell address that cemented his legacy as a visionary worthy of study.

In 1796, President Washington issued his farewell address by public letter. Washington enlisted his good friend, Alexander Hamilton, in drafting his most famous address. The letter expressed Washington's faith in the Constitution and rule of law. He encouraged his fellow Americans to put aside partisan differences and establish a national union. Washington warned Americans against meddling in foreign affairs and entering military alliances. Additionally, he stated his opposition to national political parties, which he considered partisan and counterproductive.

Americans would be wise to remember Washington's farewell, especially during presidential elections, when politics hit a fever pitch. They might want to question the political institutions that were not planned by the Founding Fathers, such as the nomination process and political parties themselves.

9. Which of the following statements is logically based on the information contained in the passage above?
    a. George Washington's background as a wealthy landholder directly led to his faith in equality, liberty, and democracy.
    b. George Washington would have opposed America's involvement in the Second World War.
    c. George Washington would not have been able to write as great a farewell address without the assistance of Alexander Hamilton.
    d. George Washington would probably not approve of modern political parties.

10. Which of the following is the best description of the author's purpose in writing this passage about George Washington?
   a. To inform American voters about a Founding Father's sage advice on a contemporary issue and explain its applicability to modern times
   b. To introduce George Washington to readers as a historical figure worthy of study
   c. To note that George Washington was more than a famous military hero
   d. To convince readers that George Washington is a hero of republicanism and liberty

11. In which of the following materials would the author be the most likely to include this passage?
   a. A history textbook
   b. An obituary
   c. A fictional story
   d. A newspaper editorial

The next question is based on the following passage:

A famous children's author recently published a historical fiction novel under a pseudonym; however, it did not sell as many copies as her children's books. In her earlier years, she had majored in history and earned a graduate degree in Antebellum American History, which is the time frame of her new novel. Critics praised this newest work far more than the children's series that made her famous. In fact, her new novel was nominated for the prestigious Albert J. Beveridge Award but still isn't selling like her children's books, which fly off the shelves because of her name alone.

12. Which one of the following statements might be accurately inferred based on the above passage?
   a. The famous children's author produced an inferior book under her pseudonym.
   b. The famous children's author is the foremost expert on Antebellum America.
   c. The famous children's author did not receive the bump in publicity for her historical novel that it would have received if it were written under her given name.
   d. People generally prefer to read children's series than historical fiction.

Read the selection and answer questions 13–17:

[1]I have to admit that when my father bought an RV, I thought he was making a huge mistake. [2]In fact, I even thought he might have gone a little bit crazy. [3]I did not really know anything about recreational vehicles, but I knew that my dad was as big a "city slicker" as there was. [4]On trips to the beach, he preferred to swim at the pool, and whenever he went hiking, he avoided touching any plants for fear that they might be poison ivy. [5]Why would this man, with an almost irrational fear of the outdoors, want a 40-foot camping behemoth?

[6]The RV was a great purchase for our family and brought us all closer together. [7]Every morning we would wake up, eat breakfast, and broke camp. [8]We laughed at our own comical attempts to back The Beast into spaces that seemed impossibly small. [9]We rejoiced when we figured out how to "hack" a solution to a nagging technological problem. [10]When things inevitably went wrong and we couldn't solve the problems on our own, we discovered the incredible helpfulness and friendliness of the RV community. We even made some new friends in the process.

[11]Above all, owning the RV allowed us to share adventures travelling across America that we could not have experienced in cars and hotels. [12]Enjoying a campfire on a chilly summer evening with the mountains of Glacier National Park in the background, or waking up early in the morning to see the sun rising over the distant spires of Arches National Park are memories that will always stay with me and our entire family. [13]Those are also memories that my siblings and I have now shared with our own children.

13. Which of the following choices offers the best phrasing for sentence 11?
   a. Above all, owning the RV allowed us to share adventures travelling across America that we could not have experienced in cars and hotels.
   b. Above all, owning the RV will allow us to share adventures travelling across America that we could not have experienced in cars and hotels.
   c. Above all, it allows you to share adventures travelling across America that you could not have experienced in cars and hotels.
   d. Above all, it allows them to share adventures travelling across America that they could not have experienced in cars and hotels.

14. Which of the following examples would make a good addition to the selection after sentence 4?
   a. My father is also afraid of seeing insects.
   b. My father is surprisingly good at starting a campfire.
   c. My father negotiated contracts for a living.
   d. My father isn't even bothered by pigeons.

15. While studying vocabulary, a student notices that the words *circumference*, *circumnavigate*, and *circumstance* all begin with the prefix *circum–*. The student uses her knowledge of affixes to infer that all of these words share what related meaning?
   a. Around, surrounding
   b. Travel, transport
   c. Size, measurement
   d. Area, location

16. Word walls are used to:
   a. Allow students to share words they find interesting
   b. Present words utilized in a current unit of study
   c. Specify words that students are to utilize within writing assignments
   d. All of the above

17. Context clues assist vocabulary development by providing:
   a. A knowledge of roots, prefixes, and suffixes that are used to determine the meaning of a word
   b. Information within the sentence that surrounds an unknown word and is used to determine the word's meaning
   c. Content learned in previous grades that serves as a bridge to the new term
   d. Background knowledge to fill in a missing word within a sentence

Question 18 is based upon the following passage:

Four score and seven years ago our fathers brought forth on this continent, a new nation, conceived in liberty, and dedicated to the proposition that all men are created equal.

Now we are engaged in a great civil war, testing whether that nation, or any nation so conceived and so dedicated, can long endure. We are met on a great battlefield of that war. We have come to dedicate a portion of that field, as a final resting place for those who here gave their lives that that nation might live. It is altogether fitting and proper that we should do this.

But, in a larger sense, we cannot dedicate—we cannot consecrate—we cannot hallow—this ground. The brave men, living and dead, who struggled here, have consecrated it, far above our poor power to add or detract. The world will little note, nor long remember what we say here, but it can never forget what they did here. It is for us the living, rather, to be dedicated here to the unfinished work which they who fought here have thus far so nobly advanced. It is rather for us to be here dedicated to the great task remaining before us—that from these honored dead we take increased devotion to that cause for which they gave the last full measure of devotion—that we here highly resolve that these dead shall not have died in vain—that this nation, under God, shall have a new birth of freedom— and that government of the people, by the people, for the people, shall not perish from the earth.

Address by Abraham Lincoln, delivered at the dedication of the cemetery at Gettysburg, November 19, 1863

18. What message is the speaker trying to convey through this address?
  a. The audience should perpetuate the ideals of freedom that the soldiers died fighting for.
  b. The audience should honor the dead by establishing an annual memorial service.
  c. The audience should form a militia that would overturn the current political structure.
  d. The audience should forget the lives that were lost and discredit the soldiers.

The next question is based on the following passage:

Annabelle Rice started having trouble sleeping. Her biological clock was suddenly amiss, and she began to lead a nocturnal schedule. She thought her insomnia was due to spending nights writing a horror story, but then she realized that even the idea of going outside into the bright world scared her to bits. She concluded she was now suffering from heliophobia.

19. Which of the following most accurately describes the meaning of the underlined word in the sentence above?
  a. Fear of dreams
  b. Fear of sunlight
  c. Fear of strangers
  d. Anxiety spectrum disorder

20. The question is based on the passage below. Which option best expresses the symbolic meaning of the "road" and the overall theme?

Two roads diverged in a yellow wood,
And sorry I could not travel both
And be one traveler, long I stood
And looked down one as far as I could
To where it bent in the undergrowth;   5

Then took the other, as just as fair,
And having perhaps the better claim,

Because it was grassy and wanted wear;
Though as for that the passing there
Had worn them really about the same,   10

And both that morning equally lay
In leaves no step had trodden black.
Oh, I kept the first for another day!
Yet knowing how way leads on to way,
I doubted if I should ever come back.   15

I shall be telling this with a sigh
Somewhere ages and ages hence:
Two roads diverged in a wood, and I—
I took the one less traveled by,
And that has made all the difference.   *20*

"The Road Not Taken" by Robert Frost

a. A spot where the traveler had to choose between two paths
b. A choice between good and evil that the traveler needs to make
c. The traveler's feelings about a lost love and future prospects
d. Life's journey and the choices with which humans are faced

21. Which option best exemplifies an author's use of alliteration and personification?
a. Her mood hung about her like a weary cape, very dull from wear.
b. The building shuddered, swayed, shook, and screamed its way into dust under hot flames.
c. Driving past the still, silent house always sent a shiver down his spine.
d. At its shoreline, visitors swore they heard the siren call of the cliffs above.

22. Read the following poem. Which option best depicts the rhyme scheme?
A slumber did my spirit seal;
I had no human fears:
She seemed a thing that could not feel
The touch of earthly years.

Stanza from "A Slumber Did My Spirit Seal" by William Wordsworth

a. BAC BAC
b. ABAB
c. ABBA
d. AB CD AB

469

23. Read the following poem. Which option describes its corresponding meter?

> Half a league, half a league
> Half a league onward,
> All in the valley of Death
> Rode the six hundred.
> 'Forward, the Light Brigade!
> Charge for the guns!' he said:
> Into the valley of Death
> Rode the six hundred.
>
> Stanza from "The Charge of the Light Brigade" by Alfred Lord Tennyson

   a. Iambic (unstressed/stressed syllables)
   b. Anapest (unstressed/unstressed/stressed syllables)
   c. Spondee (stressed/stressed syllables)
   d. Dactyl (stressed/unstressed/unstressed syllables)

24. This work, published in 1922, was a modernist piece that was banned both in the United States and overseas for meeting the criteria of obscenity. Taking place in a single day (June 16th, 1904), the novel contains eighteen episodes reflecting the activities of character Leopold Bloom in Dublin, Ireland. Originally written as to portray an Odysseus figure for adults, the structure of the work is often viewed as convoluted and chaotic, as its author utilized the stream of consciousness technique. Its literary reception was vastly polarized and remains so to this day, although modern critics tend to hail the novel as addressing the vast panoramic of futility within contemporary history.

The above passage describes which famous literary work?
   a. James Joyce's *Ulysses*
   b. Anne Sexton's poem "45 Mercy Street"
   c. F. Scott Fitzgerald's *Tender is the Night*
   d. George Eliot's *Middlemarch: A Study of Provincial Life*

25. Jerome K. Jerome's humorous account of a boating holiday, Three Men in a Boat, was published in 1889. Originally intended as a serious travel guide, the work became a prime example of a comic novel. Read the passage below, noting the word in italics. Answer the question that follows.

> I felt rather hurt about this at first; it seemed somehow to be a sort of slight. Why hadn't I got housemaid's knee? Why this invidious reservation? After a while, however, less grasping feelings prevailed. I reflected that I had every other known malady in the pharmacology, and I grew less selfish, and determined to do without housemaid's knee. Gout, in its most malignant stage, it would appear, had seized me without my being aware of it; and *zymosis* I had evidently been suffering with from boyhood. There were no more diseases after *zymosis*, so I concluded there was nothing else the matter with me.
>
> "Three Men in a Boat" by Jerome K. Jerome

Which definition best fits the word *zymosis*?
   a. Discontent

b. An infectious disease
c. Poverty
d. Bad luck

26. Read the following poem. Which option best describes the use of the spider?

The spider as an artist
Has never been employed
Though his surpassing merit
Is freely certified
By every broom and Bridget   5
Throughout a Christian land.
Neglected son of genius,

I take thee by the hand.

"Cobwebs" by Emily Dickinson

a. Idiom
b. Haiku
c. ABBA rhyming convention
d. Simile

27. Which type of map illustrates the world's climatological regions?
a. Topographic Map
b. Conformal Projection
c. Isoline Map
d. Thematic Map

28. In which manner is absolute location expressed?
a. The cardinal directions (north, south, east, and west)
b. Through latitudinal and longitudinal coordinates
c. Location nearest to a more well-known location
d. Hemispherical position on the globe

29. Which of these is NOT a true statement about culture?
a. Culture derives from the beliefs, values, and behaviors of people in a community.
b. All people are born into a certain culture.
c. Cultures are stagnant and cannot be changed.
d. Culture can be embedded within families, schools, businesses, social classes, and religions.

30. Latitudinal lines are used to measure distance in which direction?
a. East to west
b. North to south
c. Between two sets of coordinates
d. In an inexact manner

31. Which of the following civilizations developed the first democratic form of government?
    a. Roman Empire
    b. Ancient Greece
    c. Achaemenid Empire
    d. Zhou Dynasty

32. Which of the following statements most accurately describes the Achaemenid Empire in Persia until the fourth century BC?
    a. Islam was the official religion.
    b. Achaemenid emperors constructed the entire Silk Road network.
    c. The Achaemenid Empire successfully conquered Greece.
    d. None of the above

33. The Silk Roads had which of the following results?
    a. Spread of Buddhism from India to China
    b. The devastation of European economies
    c. Introduction of the Bubonic Plague to the New World
    d. The Great War

34. What caused the end of the Western Roman Empire in 476 AD?
    a. Invasions by Germanic tribes
    b. The Mongol invasion
    c. The assassination of Julius Caesar
    d. Introduction of Taoism in Rome

35. Which of the following statements most accurately describes the Mongol Empire?
    a. The Mongol army was largely a cavalry force.
    b. Mongol rulers did not tolerate other religions.
    c. Mongol rulers neglected foreign trade.
    d. The Mongol Empire is known for its discouragement of literacy and the arts.

36. Renaissance scholars and artists were inspired by which classical civilization?
    a. Ancient Greece
    b. Ancient Egypt
    c. The Zhou Dynasty
    c. The Ottoman Empire

37. Which of the following was a consequence of increasing nationalism in Europe in the 1800s?
    a. The unification of Spain
    b. The unification of France
    c. Increasing competition and tension between European powers
    d. More efficient trade between nations

38. Which of the following led to the American Revolutionary War?
    a. The Stamp Act
    b. The Boston Massacre
    c. The Boston Tea Party
    d. All of the above

39. Which political concept describes a ruling body's ability to influence the actions, behaviors, or attitudes of a person or community?
    a. Authority
    b. Sovereignty
    c. Power
    d. Legitimacy

40. Which feature differentiates a state from a nation?
    a. Shared history
    b. Common language
    c. Population
    d. Sovereignty

41. Which of the following was a consequence of World War II?
    a. The collapse of British and French empires in Asia and Africa
    b. A Communist revolution in Russia
    c. The end of the Cold War
    d. The death of Franz Ferdinand, the Archduke of Austria

42. Which political theorist is considered the father of the social contract theory?
    a. John Stuart Mills
    b. Thomas Hobbes
    c. Aristotle
    d. Immanuel Kant

43. Which political orientation emphasizes maintaining traditions and stability over progress and change?
    a. Socialism
    b. Liberalism
    c. Conservatism
    d. Libertarianism

44. What was the name of the incipient revolt led by the oft-overlooked American settler, William Ide, in 1846, which led to the halfhearted creation of the "California Republic"?
    a. The Bear Flag Revolt
    b. The Asian Exclusionary Revolt
    c. The Mexican-American War
    d. The Dust Bowl

45. In what year did the Scottish-American settler James Wilson Marshall discover gold at Sutter's Mill?
    a. 1822
    b. 1848
    c. 1849
    d. 1879

46. Which of the following would be an example of a xenophobic policy in US history that affected race relations in California history?
    a. The Immigration Act of 1965
    b. The Civil Rights Act of 1964
    c. The Swing-Johnson Bill of 1928
    d. The Chinese Exclusion Act of 1882

47. In 1849, what geographic landmark was designated as the eastern line of demarcation for the state of California?
    a. The Salt Lake Basin
    b. The Central Valley
    c. The Sierra Crest
    d. The Redwood forests

48. In what years did California host its two major constitutional conventions?
    a. 1822 and 1849
    b. 1849 and 1911
    c. 1849 and 1879
    d. 1879 and 1911

49. Why did migrants travel to California during the Dust Bowl of the 1930s?
    a. They wanted to participate in the expansion of the aerospace industry.
    b. They wanted to participate in the Silicon Valley tech boom of this era.
    c. They wanted to find work in leisure industries such as Disneyland.
    d. They wanted to find work in the expanding agricultural economy of California.

50. The modern-day debate over illegal immigration in California is mostly a debate over which of the following categories?
    a. Politics
    b. Race relations and diversity
    c. Economics
    d. All of the above

51. Which of the following can be considered a shortcoming of Progressive Era politics in California and the United States in the early twentieth century?
    a. Progressive Era politics failed to bring about women's suffrage.
    b. Progressive Era politics failed to end Asian exclusionary laws.
    c. Progressive Era politics failed to support temperance and bring about prohibition.
    d. Progressive Era politics failed to attack urban plight.

52. California was ceded to the United States following what North American conflict?
    a. The Spanish-American War
    b. The American Civil War
    c. The Mexican Revolution
    d. The Mexican-American War

Subtest II

1. How many daughter cells are formed from one parent cell during meiosis?
   a. One
   b. Two
   c. Three
   d. Four

2. What does the Lewis dot structure of an element represent?
   a. The outer electron valence shell population
   b. The inner electron valence shell population
   c. The positioning of the element's protons
   d. The positioning of the element's neutrons

3. What is the name of this compound: CO?
   a. Carbonite oxide
   b. Carbonic dioxide
   c. Carbonic monoxide
   d. Carbon monoxide

4. What is the molarity of a solution made by dissolving 4.0 grams of NaCl into enough water to make 120 mL of solution? The atomic mass of Na is 23.0 g/mol and Cl is 35.5 g/mol.
   a. 0.34 M
   b. 0.57 M
   c. 0.034 M
   d. 0.057 M

5. Considering a gas in a closed system, at a constant volume, what will happen to the temperature if the pressure is increased?
   a. The temperature will stay the same.
   b. The temperature will decrease.
   c. The temperature will increase.
   d. It cannot be determined with the information given.

6. According to Newton's three laws of motion, which of the following is true?
   a. Two objects cannot exert a force on each other without touching.
   b. An object at rest has no inertia.
   c. The weight of an object is the same as the mass of the object.
   d. The weight of an object is equal to the mass of an object multiplied by gravity.

7. Which of the following is a balanced chemical equation?
   a. $Na + Cl_2 \rightarrow NaCl$
   b. $2\,Na + Cl_2 \rightarrow NaCl$
   c. $2\,Na + Cl_2 \rightarrow 2\,NaCl$
   d. $2\,Na + 2\,Cl_2 \rightarrow 2\,NaCl$

8. What effect changes the oscillations of a wave and can alter the appearance of light waves?
   a. Reflection
   b. Refraction
   c. Dispersion
   d. Polarization

9. The Sun transferring heat to the Earth through space is an example of which of the following?
   a. Convection
   b. Conduction
   c. Induction
   d. Radiation

10. What is 45 °C converted to °F?
   a. 113 °F
   b. 135 °F
   c. 57 °F
   d. 88 °F

11. What type of chemical reaction produces a salt?
   a. An oxidation reaction
   b. A neutralization reaction
   c. A synthesis reaction
   d. A decomposition reaction

12. If a reading is above the curve on a solubility curve, the solvent is considered to be which of the following?
   a. Unsaturated
   b. Supersaturated
   c. Stable
   d. Saturated

13. Which rock is formed from cooling magma underneath the Earth's surface?
   a. Extrusive sedimentary rocks
   b. Sedimentary rocks
   c. Igneous rocks
   d. Metamorphic rocks

14. Water that has seeped into rock cracks and freezes will most likely result in what process?
   a. Chemical weathering
   b. Mechanical weathering
   c. Erosion
   d. Deposition

15. Which soil is the least permeable to water?
   a. Pure sand
   b. Pure silt
   c. Pure clay
   d. Loam

16. Which of the Earth's layers is thickest?
    a. The crust
    b. The shell
    c. The mantle
    d. The inner core

17. Which level of protein structure is defined by the folds and coils of the protein's polypeptide backbone?
    a. Primary
    b. Secondary
    c. Tertiary
    d. Quaternary

18. What is the process called in which a tectonic plate moves over another plate?
    a. Fault
    b. Diversion
    c. Subduction
    d. Drift

19. What is transpiration?
    a. Evaporation from moving water
    b. Evaporation from plant life
    c. Movement of water through the ground
    d. Precipitation that falls on trees

20. Which of the following will freeze last?
    a. Freshwater from a pond
    b. Pure water
    c. Seawater from the Pacific Ocean
    d. Seawater from the Dead Sea

21. Which of the following is true of glaciers?
    a. They form in water.
    b. They float.
    c. They form on land.
    d. They are formed from icebergs.

22. What is the broadest, or least specialized, classification of the Linnaean taxonomic system?
    a. Species
    b. Family
    c. Domain
    d. Phylum

23. Which of the following is most abundant in the Earth's atmosphere?
    a. Carbon dioxide
    b. Oxygen
    c. Nitrogen
    d. Water

24. Dew point is a measure of which of the following?

     I. Pressure
     II. Temperature at which water vapor condenses
     III. Temperature at which water evaporates

    a. I and III
    b. I and II
    c. II and III
    d. All the above

25. The Coriolis Effect is created by which of the following?
    a. Wind
    b. Earth's rotation
    c. Earth's axis
    d. Mountains

26. Dark storm clouds are usually located where?
    a. Between 5,000 and 13,000 meters above sea level
    b. Between 2,000 and 7,000 meters above sea level
    c. Below 2,000 meters above sea level
    d. Outer space

27. What is the solution to the following system of equations?

$$x^2 - 2x + y = 8$$

$$x - y = -2$$

    a. $(-2, 3)$
    b. There is no solution.
    c. $(-2, 0)\ (1, 3)$
    d. $(-2, 0)\ (3, 5)$

28. How could the following equation be factored to find the zeros?

$$y = x^3 - 3x^2 - 4x$$

    a. $0 = x^2(x - 4), x = 0, 4$
    b. $0 = 3x(x + 1)(x + 4), x = 0, -1, -4$
    c. $0 = x(x + 1)(x + 6), x = 0, -1, -6$
    d. $0 = x(x + 1)(x - 4), x = 0, -1, 4$

29. What is the simplified quotient of $\frac{5x^3}{3x^2y} \div \frac{25}{3y^9}$?

   a. $\frac{125x}{9y^{10}}$

   b. $\frac{x}{5y^8}$

   c. $\frac{5}{xy^8}$

   d. $\frac{xy^8}{5}$

30. Mom's car drove 72 miles in 90 minutes. How fast did she drive in feet per second?
   a. 0.8 feet per second
   b. 48.9 feet per second
   c. 0.009 feet per second
   d. 70.4 feet per second

31. For the following similar triangles, what are the values of x and y (rounded to one decimal place)?

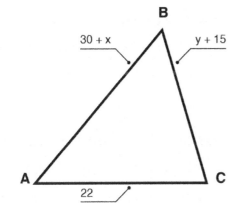
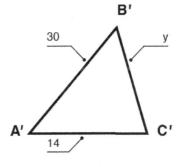

   a. $x = 16.5, y = 25.1$
   b. $x = 19.5, y = 24.1$
   c. $x = 17.1, y = 26.3$
   d. $x = 26.3, y = 17.1$

32. What are the center and radius of a circle with equation $4x^2 + 4y^2 - 16x - 24y + 51 = 0$?
   a. Center $(3, 2)$ and radius $1/2$
   b. Center $(2, 3)$ and radius $1/2$
   c. Center $(3, 2)$ and radius $1/4$
   d. Center $(2, 3)$ and radius $1/4$

33. If the point $(-3, -4)$ is reflected over the x-axis, what new point does it make?
   a. $(-3, -4)$
   b. $(3, -4)$
   c. $(3, 4)$
   d. $(-3, 4)$

479

34. If the volume of a sphere is 288π cubic meters, what are the radius and surface area of the same sphere?
   a.   Radius: 6 meters, surface area: 144π square meters
   b.   Radius: 36 meters, surface area a: 144π square meters
   c.   Radius: 6 meters, surface area: 12π square meters
   d.   Radius: 36 meters, surface area a: 12π square meters

35. Simplify:

$$\frac{4a^{-1}b^3}{a^4b^{-2}} \times \frac{3a}{b}$$

   a. $12a^3b^5$

   b. $12\dfrac{b^4}{a^4}$

   c. $\dfrac{12}{a^4}$

   d. $7\dfrac{b^4}{a}$

36. The area of a given rectangle is 24 square centimeters. If the measure of each side is multiplied by 3, what is the area of the new figure?
   a.   48 cm2
   b.   72 cm2
   c.   216 cm2
   d.   13,824 cm2

37. The perimeter of a 6-sided polygon is 56 cm. The lengths of three sides are 9 cm each. The lengths of two other sides are 8 cm each. What is the length of the final side?
   a.   11 cm
   b.   12 cm
   c.   13 cm
   d.   10 cm

38. A shuffled deck of 52 cards contains 4 kings. One card is drawn, and is not put back in the deck. Then a second card is drawn. What's the probability that both cards are kings?
   a. $\dfrac{1}{169}$

   b. $\dfrac{1}{221}$

   c. $\dfrac{1}{13}$

   d. $\dfrac{4}{13}$

39. For a group of 20 men, the median weight is 180 pounds and the range is 30 pounds. If each man gains 10 pounds, which of the following would be true?
    a. The median weight will increase, and the range will remain the same.
    b. The median weight and range will both remain the same.
    c. The median weight will stay the same, and the range will increase.
    d. The median weight and range will both increase.

40. A pair of dice is thrown, and the sum of the two scores is calculated. What's the expected value of the roll?
    a. 5
    b. 6
    c. 7
    d. 8

41. Which measure for the center of a small sample set is most affected by outliers?
    a. Mean
    b. Median
    c. Mode
    d. None of the above

42. Given the value of a given stock at monthly intervals, which graph should be used to best represent the trend of the stock?
    a. Box plot
    b. Line plot
    c. Line graph
    d. Circle graph

43. Before a race of four horses, you make a random guess of which horse will get first place and which will get second place. What is the probability that both your guesses will be correct?
    a. $\frac{1}{4}$
    b. $\frac{1}{2}$
    c. $\frac{1}{16}$
    d. $\frac{1}{12}$

44. In Jim's school, there are a total of 650 boys and girls. There are 3 girls for every 2 boys. How many students are girls?
    a. 260
    b. 130
    c. 65
    d. 390

45. Five of six numbers have a sum of 25. The average of all six numbers is 6. What is the sixth number?
    a. 8
    b. 10
    c. 11
    d. 12

46. What is the solution for the following equation?

$$\frac{x^2 + x - 30}{x - 5} = 11$$

a. $x = -6$
b. There is no solution.
c. $x = 16$
d. $x = 5$

47. If x is not zero, then $\frac{3}{x} + \frac{5u}{2x} - \frac{u}{4} =$

a. $\frac{12+10u-ux}{4x}$

b. $\frac{3+5u-ux}{x}$

c. $\frac{12x+10u+ux}{4x}$

d. $\frac{12+10u-u}{4x}$

48. A piggy bank contains 12 dollars' worth of nickels. A nickel weighs 5 grams, and the empty piggy bank weighs 1,050 grams. What is the total weight of the full piggy bank?
a. 1,110 grams
b. 1,200 grams
c. 2,250 grams
d. 2,200 grams

49. Karen gets paid a weekly salary and a commission for every sale that she makes. The table below shows the number of sales and her pay for different weeks.

Sales	2	7	4	8
Pay	$380	$580	$460	$620

Which of the following equations represents Karen's weekly pay?
a. $y = 90x + 200$
b. $y = 90x - 200$
c. $y = 40x + 300$
d. $y = 40x - 300$

50. The square and circle have the same center. The circle has a radius of r. What is the area of the shaded region?

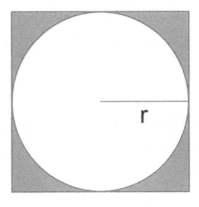

a. $r^2 - \pi r^2$
b. $4r^2 - 2\pi r$
c. $(4 - \pi)r^2$
d. $(\pi - 1)r^2$

51. What is the solution to the radical equation $\sqrt[3]{2x + 11} + 9 = 12$?

a. −8
b. 8
c. 0
d. 12

52. The hospital has a nurse-to-patient ratio of $1 : 25$. If a maximum of 325 patients may be admitted at a time, how many nurses are there?

a. 13 nurses
b. 25 nurses
c. 325 nurses
d. 12 nurses

Subtest III

1. Which of the following is NOT a general category of basic movement skills?
    a. Locomotor skills
    b. Sports-specific skills
    c. Non-locomotor skills
    d. Manipulative skills

2. In a kindergarten classroom, physical education should include a focus on all EXCEPT which of the following?
    a. Hitting targets
    b. Weight transfer
    c. Following objects with the eyes
    d. Running and stopping

3. Which of the following is NOT considered one of the five main components of health-related physical fitness?
    a. Muscular power
    b. Flexibility
    c. Muscular endurance
    d. Body composition

4. Ligaments connect what?
    a. Muscle to muscle
    b. Bone to bone
    c. Bone to muscle
    d. Muscle to tendon

5. Which of the following reflects the correct blood flow pathway (heart-valve-vessel)?
    a. Right atrium, left atrium, right ventricle, mitral valve, left ventricle, aorta
    b. Right atrium, mitral valve, right ventricle, systemic circulation, left atrium, left ventricle, aorta
    c. Right atrium, right ventricle, left atrium, tricuspid valve, left ventricle, aorta
    d. Right atrium, right ventricle, pulmonary circulation, left atrium, mitral valve, left ventricle, aorta

6. Which of the following terms means "movement away from the body's midline"?
    a. Abduction
    b. Adduction
    c. Pronation
    d. Supination

7. What muscle is the primary antagonist in knee flexion?
    a. Hamstrings
    b. Quadriceps
    c. Gastrocnemius
    d. Tibialis anterior

8. In what plane does shoulder flexion occur?
   a. Sagittal
   b. Frontal
   c. Transverse
   d. Coronal

9. What is the primary energy pathway for ATP production for an intense two-minute bout of activity?
   a. Aerobic metabolism
   b. Krebs cycle
   c. Glycolysis
   d. ATP-PC system

10. Which of the following is NOT an adaptation to chronic cardiovascular exercise?
    a. Increased heart chambers' sizes
    b. Increased stroke volume
    c. Increased cardiac output
    d. Increased submaximal heart rate

11. Pectoralis major is doing what type of contraction during a pushup?
    a. Isokinetic
    b. Isometric
    c. Isotonic
    d. Eccentric

12. Which of the following types of joints are correctly matched with the anatomic joint example given?

    I. Cartilaginous: pubic symphysis

    II. Saddle: thumb carpal-metacarpal

    III. Plane: sutures in skull

    IV. Pivot: radial head on ulna

    a. Choices I, II, and III
    b. Choices I, II, and IV
    c. Choices I, III, and IV
    d. All are correct

13. In considering the importance of fitness in different regions and time periods throughout history, which of the following statements is most accurate?
    a. After the prevalence of hypokinetic (lack of movement) diseases increased, organized fitness programs were finally implemented.
    b. Times of war often saw increases in organized fitness training programs, particularly for boys and men.
    c. Gymnastics is a relatively new sport but it is enjoyed in many areas around the world.
    d. The practice of yoga began in Ancient China in response to the philosophies and teachings of Confucius.

14. During what age range do infants typically begin to develop a sense of external curiosity?
    a. Three to four months
    b. Four to nine months
    c. Ten to twelve months
    d. Twelve to twenty-four months

15. The optimal physical education curriculum for five- to six-year-old children should focus on which of the following?
    a. Movement for enjoyment
    b. Sport-specific skills
    c. Hand-eye coordination
    d. Low intensity, endurance activities

16. Which of the following is true regarding classroom instruction of new movement skills for young children?
    a. It should occur in one long session at the beginning of the class, followed by time for children to play and attempt the skill.
    b. It should contain many small steps for the children to keep track of during play.
    c. It should be limited to short twenty-second stretches of instruction interspersed with long periods of play.
    d. It should be given in written form so children can read it at their leisure.

17. Which of the following is a healthy lifestyle habit for children?
    a. Getting eight hours of sleep every night
    b. Keeping their emotions to themselves
    c. Following safety procedures like wearing a seat belt
    d. Brushing their teeth once a day before bed

18. Educators should teach students about the importance of visiting a doctor for all EXCEPT which of the following reasons?
    a. Routine medical care and check-ups
    b. Consistent feelings of sadness, anxiety, loneliness, and stress
    c. Pains or aches that do not go away
    d. When insurance coverage changes

19. Health insurance status, safety and injury prevention education and care, nutritional meal planning and diet composition, social dynamics and stress, and culture around leisure time are all potential health behavior influences related to which factor?
    a. Family
    b. Peers
    c. School
    d. Media

20. Which of the following is true regarding motor skill development in children?
    a. Motor skill development shouldn't begin until after kindergarten.
    b. Sports skills are learned more readily than generalized body movements such as skipping.
    c. Gross motor skills are mastered before fine motor skills.
    d. Students benefit from formal movement training rather than free play.

21. What is the highest level of Maslow's hierarchy of needs?
   a. Prestige
   b. Accomplishment
   c. Self-esteem
   d. Self-actualization

22. A three- to four-year-old child would likely create a drawing emphasizing which of the following?
   a. The emotions expressed in their work.
   b. The figural accuracy of the drawing.
   c. The symbolic meaning of their work.
   d. The colors they use and how they look.

23. What term best describes a feeling of personal worth or value?
   a. Self-identity
   b. Self-concept
   c. Self-efficacy
   d. Self-esteem

24. Which of the following represents the concept of equilibrium as presented by Piaget's theory of cognitive development?
   a. Successfully assimilating new information
   b. Altering one's cognitive framework in order to adjust to new information
   c. The means by which one understands new information
   d. Forming a framework to organize information

25. Which of the following correctly lists the order of stages of cognitive development?
   a. Pre-operational, formal operational, concrete operational, sensorimotor
   b. Pre-operational, concrete operational, formal operational, sensorimotor
   c. Sensorimotor, pre-operational, formal operational, concrete operational
   d. Sensorimotor, pre-operational, concrete operational, formal operational

26. Which of the following is often experienced by foster children?
   a. Bonding disorder
   b. Attachment disorder
   c. Maslow's Hierarchy of Needs
   d. Altruism

27. Which of the following are the major categories of the arts that educators should focus curricular activities on?
   a. Music, dance, theater, visual arts
   b. Music, performing arts, visual arts, sculpture
   c. Painting, drawing, woodworking, visual arts
   d. Language arts, music, theater, visual arts

28. The youngest children just beginning in art tend to create art with a focus on which of the following?
    a. Self-expression
    b. Narrative storytelling
    c. Scientific and sensory observations
    d. Creative and artistic ideas

29. Which of the following is true of art education for children?
    a. Children should focus on learning about art from their own culture and time-period.
    b. It is important for children to see professional art before creating their own works.
    c. It is important for children to study art theory before beginning their own projects.
    d. Children should experiment with a variety of methods and materials to create art.

30. Which of the following is a way for young students to easily learn rhythm in music class?
    a. Have students memorize each song on multiple instruments.
    b. Have students sit still and focus intently on the music.
    c. Have students read the lyrics before they listen to the music.
    d. Have students accompany music with simple instruments like tambourines.

31. Which of the following is performed by teachers and students using curriculum material on social issues?
    a. Puppetry
    b. Participation Theater
    c. Reader's Theater
    d. Theater-in-Education (TIE)

32. The main skills in theatrical arts for children include all EXCEPT which of the following?
    a. Staging
    b. Literary
    c. Technical
    d. Performance

33. Which of the following is a technique used to make flat objects look as though they have depth?
    a. Balance
    b. Perspective
    c. Optical illusion
    d. Abstraction

34. Art serves all EXCEPT which of the following main functional categories?
    a. Religious functions
    b. Personal functions
    c. Social functions
    d. Physical functions

35. Which of the following is a principle in art that highlights the similarities in separate but related parts of a composition?
    a. Contrast
    b. Harmony
    c. Movement
    d. Balance

36. Balance is facilitated by _____ the base of support and _____ the center of mass.
    a. widening, lowering
    b. widening, raising
    c. lowering, widening
    d. raising, raising

37. Where did the waltz originate?
    a. Paris
    b. Copenhagen
    c. Venice
    d. Vienna

38. Which of the following is true regarding the origin of the tango?
    a. It has its roots in 19th century Buenos Aires.
    b. It began in Cuba in the 19th century.
    c. It is a recently developed dance from Argentina.
    d. It is a modern popular ballroom dance from Cuba.

39. Engaging in physical movements such as clapping, stomping, or dancing while listening to music is one way that educators can help students do which of the following?
    a. Learn about melody and harmony
    b. Figure out the key in which the song is played
    c. Learn about rhythm and tempo
    d. Learn about instruments and chords

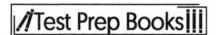

Subtest I Constructed-Response Questions

Constructed-Response Assignment #1

Read the excerpt below from *The Chinese Exclusion Act (May 6, 1882)*; then, complete the exercise that follows.

An Act to Execute Certain Treaty Stipulations Relating to Chinese

SEC. 11. That any person who shall knowingly bring into or cause to be brought into the United States by land, or who shall knowingly aid or abet the same, or aid or abet the landing in the United States from any vessel of any Chinese person not lawfully entitled to enter the United States, shall be deemed guilty of a misdemeanor, and shall, on conviction thereof, be fined in a sum not exceeding $1,000 and imprisoned for a term not exceeding one year.

SEC. 12. That no Chinese person shall be permitted to enter the United States by land without producing to the proper officer of customs the certificate in this act required of Chinese persons seeking to land from a vessel...

SEC. 13. That this act shall not apply to diplomatic and other officers of the Chinese Government traveling upon the business of that government, whose credentials shall be taken as equivalent to the certificate in this act mentioned and shall exempt them and their body and household servants from the provisions of this act as to other Chinese persons.

SEC. 14. That hereafter no State court or court of the United States shall admit Chinese to citizenship; and all laws in conflict with this act are hereby repealed.

SEC. 15. That the words "Chinese laborers," wherever used in this act, shall be construed to mean both skilled and unskilled laborers and Chinese employed in mining.

Approved, May 6, 1882.

Write a response in which you:

Use the excerpt to describe the ways in which xenophobia is embedded into the sections of the document.

Explain the ways in which common US citizens were also affected by the Chinese Exclusion Act.

Be sure to cite specific evidence from the text.

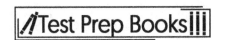

Constructed-Response Assignment #2

A fifth-grade student attempts to list important dates in California history. Shown below are the student's answers on a matching section of the quiz. Write a quick response in which you correct student errors and provide feedback. Cite specific historical materials to support your conclusions.

WORD BANK
First California Constitutional Convention Women's Suffrage Second California Constitutional Convention "Discovery of Gold" at Sutter's Mill The Chinese Exclusion Act Creation of the Mexican Republic

Student directions: Please use the word bank above to fill in the proper event to match the appropriate year.

1822	Creation of the Mexican Republic
1848	"Discovery of Gold" at Sutter's Mill
1849	The Chinese Exclusion Act
1879	First California Constitutional Convention
1882	Second California Constitutional Convention
1911	Women's Suffrage

Write a quick response in which you correct student errors and provide history-based feedback.

Constructed-Response Assignment #3

Complete the exercise that follows.

In the 1920s and 1930s, the US and California governments joined forces in public works projects to create an expansive water delivery system in the West.

Using your knowledge of US and California history, prepare a response in which you:

- Identify three important causes that led to the creation of the water delivery system.

- Select one of the causes you have identified.

- Explain why this cause was a decisive factor in the creation of modern dams, canals, and aqueduct systems in California.

Constructed-Response Assignment #4

Complete the exercise that follows.

In the twentieth and twenty-first centuries, Californians have become enmeshed in the ongoing debate over undocumented labor and illegal immigration.

Using your knowledge of California history, prepare a response in which you:

- Identify four important focal points (social, political, economic, cultural) of the ongoing debate over undocumented labor and illegal immigration.

- Select one of the focal points you have identified.

- Explain the contentious arguments (on both "sides" of the debate) that have stemmed from this particular focal point.

Subtest II Constructed-Response Questions

As mentioned, constructed-response questions allow CSET test takers to break free from the monotonous, restrictive limitations multiple-choice questions place on one's knowledge. They provide a platform for writers of any skill level to openly display their content knowledge and test-prep capabilities. Subtest II of the CSET: Multiple Subjects exam includes four constructed-response questions—two assignments each for science topics and mathematics topics. Test takers are provided with a prompt and must prepare and produce a written response of at least 100-200 words that addresses the assignment tasked in the prompt.

The primary goal of the constructed-response assignments is for test takers to demonstrate their ability to integrate their knowledge of different concepts and communicate their understanding of the subject matter in a concise and coherent manner. Rather than simply regurgitating memorized factual information, test takers are expected to connect concepts, analyze ideas, and otherwise use the written response assignment to demonstrate a deep understanding of the applicable concepts in the subject area.

The constructed-response assignments, which contribute 30% of a test taker's grade for the subtest, are evaluated using a rubric based on the following three criteria:

Purpose: how well the response fulfills the assignment's intent in accordance to the CSET Multiple Subjects content requirements

Subject Matter Knowledge: the degree to which the test taker has correctly and appropriately applied their knowledge and understanding of subject knowledge

Support: the effectiveness, correctness, and relevance of the supporting evidence the test taker has included to substantiate their ideas and claims

Although it is recommended that test takers take time after carefully and fully reading the assignment to brainstorm and outline content and organization ideas using the provided erasable booklet, the final response must be either typed into the computer's on-screen response box, written on an official response sheet and scanned in via the workstation's scanner, or a combination of both. For example, if text is accompanied with calculations and sketches, it is acceptable to type the text portion into the on-screen response box and then hand-create and scan in the accompanying graphics using the paper response sheet and scanner.

Test takers should gear their responses to be appropriate for an audience comprised of educators in the field. Although constructed-response answers are only graded on content and not on the quality of the writing, the writing should be clear, formal, and conform to the standard American English conventions. All work must be written in the test taker's own words, pertain to the assigned topic, and be developed and created without the use of any reference materials. It is strongly encouraged that test takers read through, edit, and revise their final response before submitting it for scoring. This will help ensure the response is as organized, sound, complete, and polished as possible.

It is important to note that responses must be fully scanned in or submitted via the on-screen box prior to the conclusion of the testing session. For that reason, it is crucial for test takers to monitor the amount of time remaining in the testing session so that ample time is left to ensure the written response is submitted before time runs out. Any time spent planning, organizing, drafting, revising, and scanning response sheets counts towards the test taker's testing time. Materials written, typed, or created that are not scanned in during the

testing time will not be reviewed or scored. Any hand-written content must be neat and legible, or it will not be scored.

In order to best prepare for the constructed-response assignments, test takers should try and attain a thorough understanding of the topics in all content areas on the exam. In addition, test takers should practice generating 100-200 word responses on different topics under similar time constraints.

Constructed-Response Assignment #1

Some mosquitoes carry a gene that makes affords them resistance to the pesticides humans spray in hopes of controlling the spread of malaria. Prepare a written response that accomplishes the following:

a. Explains a process that might cause certain mosquitoes to carry the new pesticide-resistant gene.

b. Describes how over time, the pesticide-resistant gene would either propagate through the mosquito population in a certain area or die out.

c. Explains a viable alternative method of controlling the spread of malaria that would prevent the development of a genetic variant that made certain mosquitoes resistant to pesticides.

Constructed-Response Assignment #2

A student is interested in researching some different flowering plants. She asks each of her friends for the common name of one of their favorite flowering plants. She then looks up the scientific name and adds it to a chart.

a. Use the chart below to identify the two plants that are most closely related. Explain to the student how you arrived at this answer.

b. Describe two different types of scientific evidence biologists use to classify plants in the taxonomic system used today.

c. Explain how biologists could use each of the two types of evidence identified in part (b) to determine which two flowering plants in the chart are more closely related to each other than the others.

Scientific Name	Common Name
Gossypium sturtianum	Sturt's Desert Rose
Ipomoea batatas	Sweet Potato
Digitalis purpurea	Foxglove
Helleborus niger	Christmas Rose
Syringa vulgaris	Lilac
Echinacea purpurea	Purple Coneflower
Ipomoea nil	Japanese Morning Glory

Constructed-Response Assignment #3

A math teacher gave students the following problem on a quiz:

On Friday, the auditorium seats where the high school performance of *My Fair Lady* was taking place were 70% full. 126 tickets were sold that night. For the matinee on Saturday, 27 more tickets were sold than on Friday night. What percentage of the seats were filled on Saturday afternoon?

Tommy wrote the following response:

There were 27 more tickets sold on Saturday, so 126 + 27 = 153 tickets.

$$
\begin{array}{r}
0.82 \\
153\overline{)126.00} \\
1224 \\
\hline
360 \\
306 \\
\hline
54
\end{array}
$$

Therefore, approximately 82% of the seats in the auditorium were filled on Saturday.

Use your mathematics knowledge to demonstrate how you would respond to Tommy. Your response should analyze his work and include the following:

   a. Corrections of any mistakes in Tommy's work along with a thorough explanation about why his response is not mathematically correct.

   b. The correct solution and how you would derive that answer.

   c. An explanation of an alternative method to solve the problem that could improve Tommy's understanding of the percentages in the context of the problem.

Constructed-Response Assignment #4

A water therapy tank in a physical therapy office is shaped like an isosceles trapezoidal prism. The therapy tank is 24 inches across the top and 18 inches deep. The base is 16 inches, and is 6 feet long. The base and top of the tank are both parallel to the floor. The tank initially contains water that is 8 inches deep. Water will be added to the tank at a rate of 200 cubic inches per minute.

Apply your knowledge of geometry in two and three dimension, functions, and operations to prepare a response that analyzes the situation described. The response should show all work and explain your reasoning. It should also include the following:

    a. a labeled diagram that clearly depicts the provided information and any necessary variables
    b. calculations for the initial volume of water in the tank
    c. an equation that correctly expresses the tank's total volume of water as a function of time
    d. a rough sketch of the equation in part (c) graphed with an explanation of the meaning of the slope and the y-intercept of the graph in the context of the problem
    e. calculations and a solution for how long it will take to completely fill the tank

Subtest III Constructed-Response Questions

Subtest III of the CSET: Multiple Subjects exam contains three constructed-response questions, one each for Physical Education, Human Development, and Visual and Performing Arts. As mentioned, for these constructed-response questions, test takers are provided with a prompt and must prepare and produce a written response of at least 100-200 words that addresses the assignment tasked in the prompt.

The primary goal of the constructed-response assignments is for test takers to demonstrate their ability to integrate their knowledge of different concepts and communicate their understanding of the subject matter in a concise and coherent manner. Rather than simply regurgitating memorized factual information, test takers are expected to connect concepts, analyze ideas, and otherwise use the constructed response assignment to demonstrate a deep understanding of the applicable concepts in the subject area.

The constructed-response assignments, which contribute 30% of a test taker's grade for the subtest, are evaluated using a rubric based on the following three criteria:

1. **Purpose:** how well the response fulfills the assignment's intent in accordance to the CSET Multiple Subjects content requirements

2. **Subject Matter Knowledge:** the degree to which the test taker has correctly and appropriately applied their knowledge and understanding of subject knowledge

3. **Support:** the effectiveness, correctness, and relevance of the supporting evidence the test taker has included to substantiate their ideas and claims

Although it is recommended that test takers take time after carefully and fully reading the assignment to brainstorm and outline content and organization ideas using the provided erasable booklet, the final response must be either typed into the computer's on-screen response box, written on an official response sheet and scanned in via the workstation's scanner, or a combination of both. For example, if text is accompanied with calculations and sketches, it is acceptable to type the text portion into the on-screen response box and then hand-create and scan in the accompanying graphics using the paper response sheet and scanner.

Test takers should gear their responses to be appropriate for an audience comprised of educators in the field. Although constructed-response answers are only graded on content and not on the quality of the writing, the writing should be clear, formal, and conform to the standard American English conventions. All work must be written in the test taker's own words, pertain to the assigned topic, and be developed and created without the use of any reference materials. It is strongly encouraged that test takers read through, edit, and revise their final response before submitting it for scoring. This will help ensure the response is as organized, sound, complete, and polished as possible.

It is important to note that responses must be fully scanned in or submitted via the on-screen box prior to the conclusion of the testing session. For that reason, it is crucial for test takers to monitor the amount of time remaining in the testing session so that ample time is left to ensure the written response is submitted before time runs out. Any time spent planning, organizing, drafting, revising, and scanning response sheets counts towards the test taker's testing time. Materials written, typed, or created that are not scanned in during the testing time will not be reviewed or scored. Any hand-written content must be neat and legible, or it will not be scored.

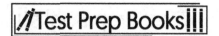

Constructed-Response Assignment #1

A second-grade physical education class includes the following year-long goal:

Students will demonstrate an improved ability to control their bodies during locomotion and make more precise and rapid changes of direction.

Using your knowledge of kinesiology, physical activity, motor development, and motor learning, prepare a written response that accomplishes the following:

a. Identifies the component of fitness described in the goal and explain why it is an important skill and how it helps the child

b. Identifies motor learning principle that could help promote students' acquisition of this fitness skill

c. Describes one activity that would primarily address that principle of fitness and motor learning identified in part (a) and part (b)

d. Explains why you believe that the activity and motor learning strategy would be effective in helping students increase their proficiency in this physical activity skill.

Constructed-Response Assignment #2

Using your knowledge of child development and strategies to support healthy development, develop a written response that:

a. Identifies one change that typically occurs in a child's emotional growth somewhere between the ages of 5 and 10

b. Explains the significance of that change on a child's daily life and functioning

c. Describes one classroom activity that could help foster the development of that change

Constructed-Response Assignment #3

Artists, regardless of medium, typically rely on six main principles in art: emphasis, rhythm, balance, contrast, harmony, and movement. Prepare a written response that:

- describes two of the above six principles and how they can manifest in the following four types of art:
  - music
  - dance
  - theater arts
  - visual arts
- describes a classroom activity for each of the four types of art that can help students develop an understanding of the two selected principles of art. Please note, both principles should be addressed in the activity. For example, if balance and rhythm are selected, a musical activity must be geared toward both balance and rhythm.

498

Answer Explanations

Subtest I

1. A: Phonological awareness refers to a child's ability to understand and use familiar sounds in their social environment in order to form coherent words. Phonemes are defined as distinct sound units in any given language. Phonemic substitution refers to the ability to substitute specific phonemes for others. Blending refers to the ability to construct or build words from individual phonemes by blending the sounds together in a unique sequence.

2. C: When children begin to recognize and apply sound-letter relationships independently and accurately, they are demonstrating a growing mastery of phonics. Phonics is the most commonly used method for teaching people to read and write by associating sounds with their corresponding letters or groups of letters, using a language's alphabetic writing system. Syllabication refers to the ability to break down words into their individual syllables. The study of onsets and rimes strives to help students recognize and separate a word's beginning consonant or consonant-cluster sound, the onset, from the word's rime, the vowel and/or consonants that follow the onset. A grapheme is a letter or a group of letters in a language that represent a sound.

3. D: Word analysis involves breaking down words into their individual parts and studying prefixes, suffixes, root words, rimes, and onsets. When children analyze words, they develop their vocabulary and strengthen their spelling and reading fluency.

4. B: Spelling conventions is the area of study that involves mechanics, usage, and sentence formation. Mechanics refers to spelling, punctuation, and capitalization. Usage refers to the use of the various parts of speech within sentences, and sentence formation is the order in which the various words in a sentence appear. Generally speaking, word analysis is the breaking down of words into morphemes and word units in order to arrive at the word's meaning. Morphemes are the smallest units of a written language that carry meaning, and phonics refers to the study of letter-sound relationships.

5. B: The alphabetic principle relies on specific letter-sound correspondence. Although some high-frequency sight words are decodable, the majority of them are not High-frequency sight words appear often in children's literature and are studied and memorized in order to strengthen a child's spelling and reading fluency. High-frequency sight words, as well as decodable words, may or may not rhyme and may or may not contain onsets and rimes.

6. A: Reading fluency involves how accurately a child reads each individual word within a sentence, the speed at which a child reads, and the expression the child applies while reading. Therefore, accuracy, rate, and prosody are the three key areas of reading fluency.

7. C: Literary analysis of a fictional text involves several areas of study, including character development, setting, and plot. Although point of view refers to a specific area of study in literary analysis, it is only one area. Word analysis does not involve the study of elements within a fictional text.

8. A: When a person infers something, he or she is demonstrating the ability to extract key information and make logical assumptions based on that information. The information provided is not direct, but implied. Being able to navigate a variety of texts independently has nothing to do with inference; it demonstrates a student's

reading comprehension and fluency. Successfully summarizing and paraphrasing texts are advanced literacy skills that demonstrate a student's reading comprehension and writing proficiency.

9. D: Although Washington was from a wealthy background, the passage does not say that his wealth led to his republican ideals, so Choice *A* is not supported. Choice *B* also does not follow from the passage. Washington's warning against meddling in foreign affairs does not mean that he would oppose wars of every kind, so Choice *B* is wrong. Choice *C* is also unjustified since the author does not indicate that Alexander Hamilton's assistance was absolutely necessary. Choice *D* is correct because the passage states that Washington's farewell address clearly opposes political parties and partisanship. The author then notes that presidential elections often hit a fever pitch of partisanship. Thus, it follows that George Washington would probably not approve of modern political parties and their involvement in presidential elections.

10. A: The author finishes the passage by applying Washington's farewell address to modern politics, so the purpose probably includes this application. The other descriptions also fit the passage to some degree, but they do not describe the author's main purpose, which is revealed in the final paragraph.

11. D: Choice *A* is wrong because the last paragraph is not appropriate for a history textbook. Choice *B* is false because the piece is not a notice or announcement of Washington's death. Choice *C* is false because it is not fiction. Choice *D* is correct. The passage is most likely to appear in a newspaper editorial because it cites information that is relevant and applicable to the present day, a popular subject in editorials.

12. C: We are looking for an inference—a conclusion that is reached on the basis of evidence and reasoning—from the passage that will likely explain why the famous children's author did not achieve her usual success with the new genre (despite the book's acclaim). Choice *A* is wrong because the statement is false according to the passage. Choice *B* is wrong because, although the passage says the author has a graduate degree on the subject, it would be an unrealistic leap to infer that she is the foremost expert on Antebellum America. Choice *D* is wrong because there is nothing in the passage to lead us to infer that people generally prefer a children's series to historical fiction. In contrast, Choice *C* can be logically inferred since the passage speaks of the great success of the children's series and the declaration that the fame of the author's name causes the children's books to "fly off the shelves." Thus, we can infer that she did not receive any bump from her name since she published the historical novel under a pseudonym, which makes Choice *C* correct.

13. A: The sentence should be in the same tense and person as the rest of the selection. The rest of the selection is in past tense and first person. Choice *B* is in future tense. Choice *C* is in second person. Choice *D* is in third person. While none of these sentences are incorrect by themselves, they are written in a tense that is different from the rest of the selection. Choices *C* and *D* additionally begin the third paragraph with a pronoun. Ideally, since a paragraph introduces separate ideas, it should reintroduce its nouns. Only Choice *A*, the original sentence, maintains tense and voice consistent with the rest of the selection.

14. A: Choices *B* and *D* go against the point the author is trying to make—that the father is not comfortable in nature. Choice *C* is irrelevant to the topic. Choice *A* is the only choice that emphasizes the father's discomfort with spending time in nature.

15. A: The affix *circum–* originates from Latin and means *around or surrounding*. It is also related to other round words, such as circle and circus. The rest of the choices do not relate to the affix *circum–* and are therefore incorrect.

16. D: A love of words can be instilled when students share new and interesting words that they encounter through independent reading or that are taught by a teacher. These words can be kept in either word lists or

500

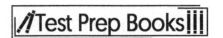

word walls. Word lists and walls help to personalize vocabulary instruction while improving students' flexibility and fluency. Additionally, there are thousands of online word blogs and word clouds that encourage students to share the words they love. If a lack of technology is an issue, students can share new words on a word bank displayed on a wall within the classroom or a word list contained within a notebook. The list of new words should be referred to often in order to increase students' exposure to new words. Students should be required to utilize the words within writing activities and discussions.

17. B: When using contextual strategies, students are indirectly introduced to new words within a sentence or paragraph. Contextual strategies require students to infer the meaning(s) of new words. Word meaning is developed by utilizing semantic and contextual clues of the reading in which the word is located.

18. A: The audience should perpetuate the ideals of freedom that the soldiers died fighting for. Lincoln doesn't address any of the topics outlined in Choices *B*, *C*, or *D*. Therefore, Choice *A* is the correct answer.

19. B: The passage indicates that *Annabelle* has a fear of going outside into the daylight. Thus, *heliophobia* must refer to a fear of bright lights or sunlight.

20. D: Choice *A* is literal, not symbolic. Choice *B* is incorrect because the traveler deems both roads to be equally "fair" or pleasant. Choice *C* deals with the past and the future, but the traveler is considering two paths forward.

21. B: Only Choice *B* uses both repetitive beginning sounds (alliteration) and personification—the portrayal of a building as a human crumbling under a fire. Choice *A* is a simile and does not utilize alliteration or the use of consistent consonant sounds for effect. Although Choice *C* does use alliteration, it does not use personification to describe the house. Choice *D* describes neither alliteration nor personification.

22. B: The correct answer is ABAB because the first line rhymes with the third while the second line rhymes with the fourth. Choice *A* is not a valid rhyme scheme. Choice *C* would require the second and third lines to rhyme, so it is incorrect. Choice *D* would require the first and fifth lines rhyme, then the second and sixth. This is also incorrect as the passage only contains four lines.

23. D: If read with a combination of stressed and unstressed syllables as Tennyson intended and as the poem naturally flows, the reader will stumble upon the stressed/unstressed/unstressed rhythmic, dactyl meter similar to a waltz beat. Choices *A*, *B*, and *C* describe meters that do not follow the dactyl pattern.

24. A: The correct answer is *A* as it is the only option that utilizes stream of consciousness technique in a novel format. Choice *B* is a poem by poet Anne Sexton, not a novel. Although Ms. Sexton's works were often criticized for their intimate content, this answer does not meet the question's criteria. Choices *C* and *D* are both incorrect. Both are novels, but not of the appropriate time period, country, or literary content.

25. B: The correct answer is an infectious disease. By reading and understanding the context of the passage, all other options can be eliminated since the author restates zymosis as a disease.

26. D: The correct answer is a simile, because the use of the word "as." Choice *A* is incorrect because the poem does not contain an idiom. Choice *B* is incorrect since the poem is not haiku. Choice *C* is incorrect as it does not use the ABBA rhyming convention.

27. D: Thematic maps create certain themes in which they attempt to illustrate a certain phenomenon or pattern. The obvious theme of a climate map is the climates in the represented areas. Thematic maps are very

extensive and can include thousands of different themes, which makes them quite useful for students of geography. Topographic maps, Choice *A*, are utilized to show physical features, conformal projections, Choice *B*, attempt to illustrate the globe in an undistorted fashion, and isoline maps, Choice *C*, illustrate differences in variables between two points on a map.

28. B: Latitudinal and longitudinal coordinates delineate absolute location. In contrast to relative location, which describes a location as compared to another, better-known place, absolute location provides an exact place on the globe through the latitude and longitude system. Cardinal directions (north, south, east, west), Choice *A*, are used in absolute location, but coordinates must be added in order to have an absolute location. Using other, better-known locations to find a location, Choice *C*, is referred to as relative location, and absolute location is far more precise than simply finding hemispherical position on the globe.

29. C: Each statement about culture is correct except for Choice *C*. Cultures often will adapt to the settings in which they are found. Improvements in technology, changes in social values, and interactions with other cultures all contribute to cultural change.

30. B: Lines of latitude measure distance north and south. The equator is zero degrees, and the Tropic of Cancer is 23 ½ degrees north of the equator. The distance between those two lines measures degrees north to south, as with any other two lines of latitude. Longitudinal lines, or meridians, measure distance east and west, even though they run north and south down the Globe. Latitude is not inexact, in that there are set distances between the lines. Furthermore, coordinates can only exist with the use of longitude and latitude.

31. B: Ancient Greeks created many of the cultural and political institutions that form the basis of modern western civilization. Athens was an important Greek democracy, and all adult men could participate in politics after they had completed their military service. The Roman Empire, Choice *A*, evolved from the Roman Republic, but it was not democratic. The Achaemenid Empire and Zhou Dynasty, Choices *C* and *D*, were imperial monarchies that did not allow citizens to have much, if any, political voice.

32. D: During the Achaemenid Empire, Persians practiced the Zoroastrian faith and worshipped two gods. Islam only came about one thousand years later. The Achaemenids built a Royal Road that stretched across their empire, but the Silk Roads expanded throughout Asia. The Achaemenids twice tried to conquer Greece but failed both times.

33. A: The Silk Roads were a network of trade routes between Asia and the Mediterranean. Merchants and Pilgrims traveled along the Silk Roads and brought new ideas and technologies, as well as trade goods. For example, Buddhism spread from India to China. Chinese technologies also spread westward, including gunpowder and the printing press. The Silk Roads also spread the Bubonic Plague to Europe, but it did not arrive in the New World until Columbus landed there in 1492.

34. A: Large numbers of Franks, Goths, Vandals, and other Germanic peoples began moving south in the fifth century AD. They conquered Rome twice, and the Western Roman Empire finally disintegrated. The Mongol invasion, Choice *B*, pushed westward in the thirteenth century, long after the western Roman Empire was gone. The assassination of Julius Caesar, Choice *C*, led to the end of the Roman Republic and the birth of the Roman Empire. Taoism never spread to Rome, making Choice *D* incorrect.

35. A: The Mongols were a nomadic people who trained as horsemen from a young age. They used their highly mobile army to build a huge empire in Asia, the Middle East, and Eastern Europe. Mongol rulers were relatively tolerant of other religions because they wanted to reduce conflict within their empire, making Choice *B*

incorrect. They also encouraged trade because they produced few of their own goods, making Choice C incorrect. The Mongol rulers also encouraged literacy and appreciated visual art, making Choice D incorrect.

36. A: Renaissance scholars and artists sought to emulate classical Greek and Roman culture. They translated Greek and Roman political philosophers and literature. They also copied classical architecture. Europeans had little direct contact with China until the thirteenth century, which was long after the Zhou Dynasty collapsed, making Choice C incorrect. The Renaissance Era occurred within the continent of Europe and drew from other European styles, so nations of northern Africa and the Middle East, such as ancient Egypt and the Ottoman Empire, had little to no inspiration on Renaissance scholars and artists at that time. Therefore, Choices B and D are incorrect.

37. C: In the 1800s, nationalists in different parts of Europe encouraged their countrymen to take pride in their shared backgrounds. This led to tension between different nations, as each sought to increase its status and prestige. The French and British nearly came to blows in Africa, and nationalism ultimately led to World War I in 1914. France and Spain were unified several centuries before the 1800s.

38. D: All three events led to increasing tension and conflict between the colonists and the British government, which finally exploded at the Battle of Lexington and Concord in 1775. The Stamp Act of 1765 imposed a tax on documents. It was repealed after colonists organized protests. The Boston Massacre resulted in the death of five colonists in 1770. The Boston Tea Party was a protest in 1773 against a law that hurt colonial tea merchants. The British responded to the tea party by punishing the colony of Massachusetts, which created fear among the other colonies and united them against the British government.

39. C: Power is the ability of a ruling body or political entity to influence the actions, behavior, and attitude of a person or group of people. Authority, Choice A, is the right and justification of the government to exercise power as recognized by the citizens or influential elites. Similarly, legitimacy, Choice D, is another way of expressing the concept of authority. Sovereignty, Choice B, refers to the ability of a state to determine and control their territory without foreign interference.

40. D: Sovereignty is the feature that differentiates a state from a nation. Nations have no sovereignty, as they are unable to enact and enforce laws independently of their state. A state must possess sovereignty over the population of a territory in order to be legitimized as a state. Both a nation and a state must have a population, Choice C. Although sometimes present, shared history and common language are not requirements for a state, making Choices A and B incorrect.

41. A: Devastated by World War II, Britain and France were unable to maintain their empires. Japan and Germany were also weak, which left only the United States and USSR as superpowers. The Russian Revolution had occurred during World War I, in 1917, making Choice B incorrect. Ideological and economic conflict between the US and the USSR led to the start of the Cold War shortly after World War II ended, making Choice C incorrect. Choice D is also incorrect; the death of Franz Ferdinand marked the beginning of World War I.

42. B: Thomas Hobbes is considered the father of social contract theory. In his book *Leviathan,* Hobbes advocated for a strong central government and posited that the citizens of a state make a social contract with the government to allow it to rule them in exchange for protection and security. John Stuart Mills, Choice A, is most commonly associated with the political philosophy of utilitarianism. Aristotle, Choice C, believed that man could only achieve happiness by bettering their community through noble acts, while Immanuel Kant, Choice D, promoted democracy and asserted that states could only achieve lasting global peace through international cooperation.

43. C: Conservatism emphasizes maintaining traditions and believes political and social stability is more important than progress and reform. In general, Socialism, Choice *A*, seeks to establish a democratically elected government that owns the means of production, regulates the exchange of commodities, and distributes the wealth equally among citizens. Liberalism, Choice *B*, is based on individualism and equality, supporting the freedoms of speech, press, and religion, while Libertarian ideals, Choice *D*, emphasize individual liberties and freedom from government interference.

44. A: The answer is Choice *A*, the Bear Flag Revolt. The Bear Flag Revolt has long been the part of the historical mythos of California history; however, the skirmish, which was led by William Ide in 1846, affected the history of the state in only a minor way, paving the way to the engineering of California's infamous "Bear Flag," which still serves as the state flag. Choice *B*, the Asian Exclusionary Revolt, is a fictitious event, although California has had a long history of Asian exclusion. Choice *C*, the Mexican-American War, was a much larger North American conflict that led to the cession of California to the United States by Mexico. Choice *D*, the Dust Bowl, was not a military conflict, but rather an environmental disaster during the 1930s that brought many farmers and migrants to California's lush Central Valley.

45. B: The answer is Choice *B*, 1848. This is the year the Scottish-American settler James Wilson Marshall discovered gold at Sutter's Mill. Test takers may be tempted to choose Choice *C*, 1849, because of the association of the gold rush with the so-called forty-niners, but the discovery actually began a year prior to this rush. Choice *A*, 1822, is the year that California became a part of the new Mexican Republic. Choice *D*, 1879, is the year of the second California state constitutional convention.

46. D: The answer is Choice *D*, the Chinese Exclusion Act of 1882, a xenophobic law that restricted the immigration of Asians, and specifically Chinese Asians, to the United States based solely on US citizens' prejudice and fear. Choices *A* and *B*, the Immigration Act of 1965 and the Civil Rights Act of 1964, are incorrect because they actually encouraged diversity and inclusion. The Immigration Act of 1965 opened the gates to more immigrants from Asia and other parts of the world. The Civil Rights Act of 1964 helped end legal segregation by protecting ethnic and racial minorities and their civil rights as citizens of the United States. Choice *C*, the Swing-Johnson Bill of 1928, is the furthest from the mark because it has nothing to do with immigration or civil rights. The Swing-Johnson Bill of 1928 helped make the construction of the Hoover Dam a reality.

47. C: The answer is Choice *C*, the Sierra Crest. The delegates at the first state constitutional convention in California debated whether the eastern line of demarcation should be placed along the Sierra Crest or the Salt Lake Basin, Choice *A*. Ultimately, they decided on the former, leaving the deserts to the east of the Sierra Nevada mountain range to the territory that would later become the state of Nevada. Choice *B*, the Central Valley, is the region in the center of the state known for its agricultural production. Choice *D*, the Redwood forests, are the ancient woodlands located along the northwest coast of California.

48. C: The answer is Choice *C*, 1849 and 1879. The initial state constitution was drafted and ratified in 1849, and it was later rewritten as an extended code of laws in 1879, as the railroad industry and rampant urbanization shifted the labor and political scenes in California. Choice *A*, 1822 and 1849, is incorrect because 1822 is the date when California fell under Mexican independence. Choices *B* and *D* are incorrect because they include the date 1911, which is the year suffrage was extended to women.

49. D: The answer is Choice *D*, "They wanted to find work in the expanding agricultural economy of California." The Dust Bowl of the 1930s devastated farmlands in the Midwest and Great Plains, forcing farmers and their families to move west to California, known as the "Land of Milk and Honey." In California, they became part of

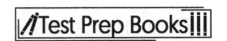

a burgeoning agricultural economy that avoided most of the environmental plight of the Depression era. Choices *A, B,* and *C* are incorrect because the leisure industries (i.e., Disneyland) and the aerospace industry did not take root in California until the economic boom of the early Cold War. The tech boom—Choice *B*—in Silicon Valley did not occur until the advent of personal computers and the internet in the 1980s and 1990s.

50. D: The answer is Choice *D*, all of the above. The modern-day debate over illegal immigration in California extends into all aspects of society, including politics, Choice *A*, race relations and diversity, Choice *B*, and economics, Choice *C*. Liberal political proponents of undocumented immigration point out the ways in which undocumented immigrants increase diversity structures in the United States and bolster the economy. Conservative political opponents of illegal immigration claim that illegal immigrants threaten the cultural character of the nation and place a strain on welfare and the economy.

51. B: The answer is Choice *B*, "Progressive Era politics failed to end Asian exclusionary laws." In fact, critics of Progressive politics claim that the Progressive Era fell short in its reforms by reinforcing xenophobia and racism in spite of the apparent moral and political gains. Choices *A, C,* and *D* are incorrect because Progressive Era politics actually helped bring about women's suffrage, Choice *A*, and temperance/prohibition, Choice *C*. Additionally, Progressive Era politics can be categorized as a direct response to the "ills" of urbanization and urban plight, Choice *D*.

52. D: The answer is Choice *D*, the Mexican-American War. Following this North American conflict, the California territory of the Mexican Republic fell into US hands. Choice *A*—the Spanish-American War—also led to some territory changes in the Caribbean and the Pacific but occurred well after California statehood, at the turn of the twentieth century. Although California became a player in the divisive politics of the American Civil War, Choice *B*, as a "free state," it was already in US hands by the time shots were fired between the Union and the Confederacy. The Mexican Revolution, Choice *C*, brought California under the control of the newly founded Mexican Republic, not the United States.

Subtest II

1. D: Meiosis has the same phases as mitosis, except that they occur twice—once in meiosis I and once in meiosis II. During meiosis I, the cell splits into two. Each cell contains two sets of chromosomes. Next, during meiosis II, the two intermediate daughter cells divide again, producing four total haploid cells that each contain one set of chromosomes.

2. A: A Lewis Dot structure shows the alignment of the valence (outer) shell electrons and how readily they can pair or bond with the valence shell electrons of other atoms to form a compound. Choice B is incorrect because the inner shell does not help us understand how likely an atom is to bond with another atom. The positioning of protons and neutrons concerns the nucleus of the atom, which again would not relate to the likelihood of bonding.

3. D: The naming of compounds focuses on the second element in a chemical compound. Elements from the nonmetal category are written with an "ide" at the end. The compound CO has one carbon and one oxygen, so it is called carbon monoxide. Choice B indicates that there are two oxygen atoms. Also, Choices A, B, and C incorrectly alter the name of the first element, which should remain "carbon."

4. B: To solve this, the number of moles of NaCl needs to be calculated:

First, to find the mass of NaCl, the mass of each of the molecule's atoms is added together as follows:

$$23.0 \ g \ Na \ + \ 35.5 \ g \ Cl = 58.5 \ g \ NaCl$$

Next, the given mass of the substance is multiplied by one mole per total mass of the substance:

$$4.0 \ g \ NaCl \times \frac{1 \ mol \ NaCl}{58.5 \ g \ NaCl} = 0.068 \ mol \ NaCl$$

Finally, the moles are divided by the number of liters of the solution to find the molarity:

$$\frac{0.068 \ \text{mol NaCl}}{0.120 \ \text{L}} = 0.57 \ \text{M NaCl}$$

5. C: According to the *ideal gas law* ($PV = nRT$), if volume is constant, the temperature is directly related to the pressure in a system. Therefore, if the pressure increases, the temperature will increase in direct proportion. Choice A would not be possible, since the system is closed and a change is occurring, so the temperature will change. Choice B incorrectly exhibits an inverse relationship between pressure and temperature, or $P = 1/T$. Choice D is incorrect because even without actual values for the variables, the relationship and proportions can be determined.

6. D: According to Newton's second law of motion, $F = m \times a$. Weight is the force resulting from a given situation, so the mass of the object needs to be multiplied by the acceleration of gravity on Earth: $W = m \times g$.

Choice A is incorrect because, according to Newton's first law, all objects exert some force on each other, based on their distance from each other and their masses. This is seen in planets, which affect each other's paths and those of their moons. Choice B is incorrect because an object in motion or at rest can have inertia; inertia is the resistance of a physical object to change its state of motion. Choice C is incorrect because the

mass of an object is a measurement of how much substance there is to the object, while the weight is gravity's effect on the mass.

7. C: The number of each element must be equal on both sides of the equation, so Choice *C* is the only correct option:

$$2\,Na + Cl_2 \rightarrow 2\,NaCl$$

$2\,Na + 2\,Cl$ does equal $2\,Na + 2\,Cl$ (the number of sodium atoms and chlorine atoms match)

Choice *A*: $Na + Cl_2 \rightarrow NaCl$

$1\,Na + 2\,Cl$ does not equal $1\,Na + 1\,Cl$ (the number of chlorine atoms does not match)

Choice *B*: $2\,Na + Cl_2 \rightarrow NaCl$

$2\,Na + 2\,Cl$ does not equal $1\,Na + 1\,Cl$ (neither the number of sodium atoms nor chlorine atoms match)

Choice *D*: $2\,Na + 2\,Cl_2 \rightarrow 2\,NaCl$

$2\,Na + 4\,Cl$ does not equal $2\,Na + 2\,Cl$ (the number of chlorine atoms does not match)

8. D: Polarization changes the oscillations of a wave and can alter the appearance in light waves. For example, polarized sunglasses remove the "glare" from sunlight by altering the oscillation pattern observed by the wearer. Choice *A*, reflection, is the bouncing back of a wave, such as in a mirror; Choice *B* is the bending of a wave as it travels from one medium to another, such as going from air to water; and Choice *C*, dispersion, is the spreading of a wave through a barrier or a prism.

9. D: Radiation can be transmitted through electromagnetic waves and needs no medium to travel; it can travel in a vacuum. This is how the Sun warms the Earth and it typically applies to large objects with great amounts of heat, or objects that have a large difference in their heat measurements. Choice *A*, convection, involves atoms or molecules traveling from areas of high concentration to those of low concentration and transferring energy or heat with them. Choice *B*, conduction, involves the touching or bumping of atoms or molecules to transfer energy or heat. Choice *C*, induction, deals with charges and does not apply to the transfer of energy or heat. Choices *A*, *B*, and *C* need a medium in which to travel, while radiation requires no medium.

10. A: Review the following conversion:

$$°F = \frac{9}{5}(°C) + 32$$

$$°F = \frac{9}{5}(45) + 32$$

$$°F = 113\,°F$$

Choices *B*, *C*, and *D* all incorporate a mistake in the order of operations necessary for this calculation to convert degrees Celsius to degrees Fahrenheit: divide by 5, multiply by 9, and then add 32.

11. B: A solid produced during a reaction in solution is called a precipitate. In a neutralization reaction, the products (an acid and a base) react to form a salt and water. Choice *A*, an oxidation reaction, involves the transfer of an electron. Choice *C*, a synthesis reaction, involves the joining of two molecules to form a single molecule. Choice *D*, a decomposition reaction, involves the separation of a molecule into two other molecules.

12. B: When a solution is on the verge of—or in the process of—crystallization, it is called a *supersaturated* solution. This can also occur in a solution that seems stable, but if it is disturbed, the change can begin the crystallization process. To display the relationship between the mass of a solute that a solvent holds and a given temperature, a *solubility curve* is used. If a reading is on the solubility curve, the solvent is *saturated*; it is full and cannot hold more solute. If a reading is above the curve, the solvent is *supersaturated* and unstable from holding more solute than it should. If a reading is below the curve, the solvent is *unsaturated* and could hold more solute. Choices *A*, *C*, and *D* are all stable, whereas Choice *B* is unstable.

13. C: Igneous rocks are formed from the cooling of magma, both on and below the Earth's surface, which are classified as extrusive and intrusive, respectively. Sedimentary rocks are formed from deposition and cementation on the surface, and metamorphic rocks are formed from the transformation of sedimentary or igneous rocks through heat and pressure.

14. B: Freezing water expands because ice is less dense than liquid water. This expansion can break up solid rocks, which describes a form of mechanical weathering. Chemical weathering occurs when water dissolves rocks. Erosion is the movement of broken rock, and deposition is the process of laying down rocks from erosion.

15. C: Pure clay has small particles that pack together tightly and are impermeable to water. Sand is the most permeable type of soil because it has the largest grains. Loam is a combination of all three types of soil in relatively equal proportions.

16. C: The mantle is the Earth's thickest layer; it holds most of the Earth's material. The crust is thin, and the inner core is also small compared to the mantle. There is no such thing as Earth's shell.

17. B: The secondary structure of a protein refers to the folds and coils that are formed by hydrogen bonding between the slightly charged atoms of the polypeptide backbone. The primary structure is the sequence of amino acids, similar to the letters in a long word. The tertiary structure is the overall shape of the molecule that results from the interactions between the side chains that are linked to the polypeptide backbone. The quaternary structure is the complete protein structure that occurs when a protein is made up of two or more polypeptide chains.

18. C: Subduction occurs when one plate is pushed down by another. A fault is where two plates meet. Diversion occurs when two plates move apart. Drift isn't a term used with tectonic plates.

19. B: Transpiration is water that evaporates from pores in plants called stomata. Evaporation of moving water is still called evaporation. Infiltration is the process of water moving into the ground, and precipitation that falls on trees is called canopy interception.

20. D: Water with a higher salinity has more dissolved salt and a lower freezing point. Water from the Dead Sea has the highest salinity of the answer choices.

21. C: Glaciers are formed only on land and constantly move because of their own weight. Icebergs are formed from glaciers, and they float.

22. C: In the Linnaean system, organisms are classified as follows, moving from few and general similarities to comprehensive and specific similarities: domain, kingdom, phylum, class, order, family, genus, and species. A popular mnemonic device to remember the Linnaean system is "Dear King Philip came over for good soup."

23. C: Nitrogen is the most abundant element in the atmosphere at 78%. Carbon dioxide and water don't make up a large percentage. Oxygen makes up only 21% of the atmosphere.

24. C: The dew point is the temperature at which the water vapor in a sample of air at constant barometric pressure condenses into water at the same rate at which it evaporates. It isn't a measure of pressure.

25. B: The Coriolis Effect is created by Earth's rotation. As wind moves toward the equator, the Earth's rotation also makes the wind move to the west. The Earth's axis and mountains don't play a part in the Coriolis Effect.

26. C: Dark storm clouds are considered nimbostratus clouds, which are located below 2,000 meters above sea level. There are no atmospheric clouds in outer space.

27. D: This system of equations involves one quadratic equation and one linear equation. One way to solve this is through substitution.

Solving for y in the second equation yields:

$$y = x + 2$$

Plugging this equation in for the y of the quadratic equation yields:

$$x^2 - 2x + x + 2 = 8$$

Simplifying the equation, it becomes:

$$x^2 - x + 2 = 8$$

Setting this equal to zero and factoring, it becomes:

$$x^2 - x - 6 = 0 = (x - 3)(x + 2)$$

Solving these two factors for x gives the zeros:

$$x = 3, -2$$

To find the y-value for the point, each number can be plugged in to either original equation. Solving each one for y yields the points $(3, 5)$ and $(-2, 0)$.

28. D: Finding the zeros for a function by factoring is done by setting the equation equal to zero, then completely factoring. Since there is a common x for each term in the provided equation, that should be factored out first to get $x(x^2 - 3x - 4)$. Then the quadratic that is left can be factored into two binomials, which are $(x + 1)(x - 4)$. This gives the factored equation 0=x$(x + 1)(x - 4)$.

29. D: Dividing rational expressions follows the same rule as dividing fractions. The division is changed to multiplication by the reciprocal of the second fraction. This turns the expression into:

$$\frac{5x^3}{3x^2y} \times \frac{3y^9}{25}$$

509

This can be simplified by finding common factors in the numerators and denominators of the two fractions.

$$\frac{x^3}{x^2 y} \times \frac{y^9}{5}$$

Multiplying across creates:

$$\frac{x^3 y^9}{5x^2 y}$$

Simplifying leads to the final expression of:

$$\frac{xy^8}{5}$$

30. D: This problem can be solved by using unit conversion. The initial units are miles per minute. The final units need to be feet per second. Converting miles to feet uses the equivalence statement 1 mi = 5,280 ft. Converting minutes to seconds uses the equivalence statement 1 min = 60 s. Setting up the ratios to convert the units is shown in the following equation:

$$\frac{72 \text{ mi}}{90 \text{ min}} \times \frac{1 \text{ min}}{60 \text{ s}} \times \frac{5,280 \text{ ft}}{1 \text{ mi}} = 70.4 \frac{\text{ft}}{\text{s}}$$

The initial units cancel out, and the new units are left.

31. C: Because the triangles are similar, the lengths of the corresponding sides are proportional. Therefore:

$$\frac{30 + x}{30} = \frac{22}{14} = \frac{y + 15}{y}$$

Using cross multiplication on the first two terms results in the equation:

$$14(30 + x) = 22 \times 30$$

When solved, this gives:

$$x \approx 17.1$$

Using cross multiplication on the last two terms results in the equation:

$$14(y + 15) = 22y$$

When solved, this gives:

$$y \approx 26.3$$

32. B: The technique of completing the square must be used to change the equation below into the standard equation of a circle:

$$4x^2 + 4y^2 - 16x - 24y + 51 = 0$$

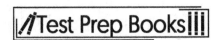

First, the constant must be moved to the right-hand side of the equals sign and each term must be divided by the coefficient of the x^2-term (which is 4). The x- and y- terms must be grouped together to obtain:

$$x^2 - 4x + y^2 - 6y = -\frac{51}{4}$$

Then, the process of completing the square must be completed for each variable. This gives:

$$(x^2 - 4x + 4) + (y^2 - 6y + 9) = -\frac{51}{4} + 4 + 9$$

The equation can be written as:

$$(x - 2)^2 + (y - 3)^2 = \frac{1}{4}$$

Therefore, the center of the circle is $(2, 3)$ and the radius is:

$$\sqrt{\frac{1}{4}} = \frac{1}{2}$$

33. D: When a point is reflected over an axis, the sign of at least one of the coordinates must change. When it's reflected over the x-axis, the sign of the y coordinate must change. The x value remains the same. Therefore, the new point is $(-3,4)$.

34. A: The volume of the sphere is 288π cubic meters. Using the formula for sphere volume, we see that:

$$\frac{4}{3}\pi r^3 = 288\pi$$

This equation is solved for r to obtain a radius of 6 meters. The formula for surface area is $4\pi r^2$, so:

$$SA = 4\pi 6^2 = 144\pi \text{ square meters}$$

35. B: The first step is to make all exponents positive by moving the terms with negative exponents to the opposite side of the fraction. This expression becomes:

$$\frac{4b^3 b^2}{a^1 a^4} \times \frac{3a}{b}$$

Then the rules for exponents can be used to simplify. Multiplying the same bases means the exponents can be added. Dividing the same bases means the exponents are subtracted. Thus, after multiplying the exponents in the first fraction, the expression becomes:

$$\frac{4b^5}{a^5} \times \frac{3a}{b}$$

Therefore, we can first multiply to get:

$$\frac{12ab^5}{a^5 b}$$

511

Then, simplifying yields:

$$12\frac{b^4}{a^4}$$

36. C: Because area is a two-dimensional measurement, the dimensions are multiplied by a scale factor that is squared to determine the scale factor of the corresponding areas. The dimensions of the rectangle are multiplied by a scale factor of 3. Therefore, the area is multiplied by a scale factor of 3^2 (which is equal to 9):

$$24 \text{ cm}^2 \times 9 = 216 \text{ cm}^2$$

37. C: The perimeter is found by calculating the sum of all sides of the polygon:

$$9 + 9 + 9 + 8 + 8 + s = 56$$

where s is the missing side length. Therefore, $43 + s = 56$. The missing side length is 13 cm.

38. B: For the first card drawn, the probability of a king being pulled is $\frac{4}{52}$. Since this card isn't replaced, if a king is drawn first, the probability of a king being drawn second is $\frac{3}{51}$. The probability of a king being drawn in both the first and second draw is the product of the two probabilities:

$$\frac{4}{52} \times \frac{3}{51} = \frac{12}{2,652}$$

To reduce this fraction, divide the top and bottom by 12 to get $\frac{1}{221}$.

39. A: If each man gains 10 pounds, every original data point will increase by 10 pounds. Therefore, the man with the original median will still have the median value, but that value will increase by 10. The smallest value and largest value will also increase by 10, so the difference between the two (the range) will remain the same.

40. C: To find the expected value, take the product of each individual sum and the probability of rolling the sum, then add together the products for each sum. There are 36 possible rolls.

The probability of rolling a 2 is $\frac{1}{36}$.

The probability of rolling a 3 is $\frac{2}{36}$.

The probability of rolling a 4 is $\frac{3}{36}$.

The probability of rolling a 5 is $\frac{4}{36}$.

The probability of rolling a 6 is $\frac{5}{36}$.

The probability of rolling a 7 is $\frac{6}{36}$.

The probability of rolling an 8 is $\frac{5}{36}$.

The probability of rolling a 9 is $\frac{4}{36}$.

The probability of rolling a 10 is $\frac{3}{36}$.

The probability of rolling an 11 is $\frac{2}{36}$.

Finally, the probability of rolling a 12 is $\frac{1}{36}$.

Each possible outcome is multiplied by the probability of it occurring. Like this:

$$2 \times \frac{1}{36} = a$$

$$3 \times \frac{2}{36} = b$$

$$4 \times \frac{3}{36} = c$$

And so forth.

Then, all of those results are added together:

$$a + b + c \ldots = expected\ value$$

In this case, it equals 7, which makes sense considering it is the value that has the highest probability of being rolled.

41. A: An outlier is a data value that is either far above or far below the majority of values in a sample set. The mean is the average of all the values in the set. In a small sample set, a very high or very low number could drastically change the average (or mean) of the data points. Outliers will have no more of an effect on the median (the middle value when arranged from lowest to highest) than any other value above or below the median. If the same outlier does not repeat, outliers will have no effect on the mode (value that repeats most often).

42. C: The scenario involves data consisting of two variables: month and stock value. Box plots display data consisting of values for one variable. Therefore, a box plot is not an appropriate choice. Both line plots and circle graphs are used to display frequencies within categorical data. Neither can be used for the given scenario. Line graphs display two numerical variables on a coordinate grid and show trends among the variables, so this is the correct choice.

43. D: The probability of picking the winner of the race is $\frac{1}{4}$, or $\left(\frac{\text{number of favorable outcomes}}{\text{number of total outcomes}} \right)$. Assuming the winner was picked on the first selection, three horses remain from which to choose the runner-up (these are dependent events). Therefore, the probability of picking the runner-up is $\frac{1}{3}$. To determine the probability that multiple events all happen, multiply the probabilities of the events:

$$\frac{1}{4} \times \frac{1}{3} = \frac{1}{12}$$

513

44. D: Three girls for every two boys can be expressed as a ratio: 3 : 2. This can be visualized as splitting the school into 5 groups: 3 girl groups and 2 boy groups. The number of students that are in each group can be found by dividing the total number of students by 5:

$$\frac{650 \text{ students}}{5 \text{ groups}} = \frac{130 \text{ students}}{\text{group}}$$

To find the total number of girls, multiply the number of students per group (130) by the number of girl groups in the school (3). This equals 390, Choice *D*.

45. C: If the average of all six numbers is 6, that means:

$$\frac{a + b + c + d + e + x}{6} = 6$$

The sum of the first five numbers is 25, so this equation can be simplified to $\frac{25+x}{6} = 6$. Multiplying both sides by 6 gives $25 + x = 36$, and x, or the sixth number, is found to equal 11.

46. B: We can try to solve the equation by factoring the numerator into $(x + 6)(x - 5)$. Since $(x - 5)$ is on the top and bottom, that factor cancels out. This leaves the equation $x + 6 = 11$. Solving the equation gives the answer $x = 5$. When this value is plugged into the equation, it yields a zero in the denominator of the fraction. Since this is undefined, there is no solution.

47. A: The common denominator here will be $4x$. Rewrite these fractions as:

$$\frac{3}{x} + \frac{5u}{2x} - \frac{u}{4}$$

$$\frac{12}{4x} + \frac{10u}{4x} - \frac{ux}{4x}$$

$$\frac{12 + 10u - ux}{4x}$$

48. C: A dollar contains 20 nickels. Therefore, if there are 12 dollars' worth of nickels, there are $12 \times 20 = 240$ nickels. Each nickel weighs 5 grams. Therefore, the weight of the nickels is $240 \times 5 = 1{,}200$ grams. Adding in the weight of the empty piggy bank, the filled bank weighs 2,250 grams.

49. C: In this scenario, the variables are the number of sales and Karen's weekly pay. The weekly pay depends on the number of sales. Therefore, weekly pay is the dependent variable (y), and the number of sales is the independent variable (x). All four answer choices are in slope-intercept form, $y = mx + b$, so we just need to find m (the slope) and b (the y-intercept). We can calculate both by picking any two points, for example, (2, 380) and (4, 460).

The slope is given by $m = \frac{y_2 - y_1}{x_2 - x_1}$, so $m = \frac{460 - 380}{4 - 2} = 40$. This gives us the equation $y = 40x + b$. Now we can plug in the x and y values from our first point to find b. Since $380 = 40(2) + b$, we find $b = 300$. This means the equation is $y = 40x + 300$.

50. C: The area of the shaded region is the area of the square minus the area of the circle. The area of the circle is πr^2. The side of the square will be $2r$, so the area of the square will be $4r^2$. Therefore, the difference is:

$$4r^2 - \pi r^2 = (4 - \pi)r^2$$

51. B: First, subtract 9 from both sides to isolate the radical. Then, cube each side of the equation to obtain:

$$\sqrt[3]{2x + 11} + 9 = 12$$

$$\sqrt[3]{2x + 11} = 3$$

$$2x + 11 = 27$$

Subtract 11 from both sides, and then divide by 2.

$$2x = 16$$

The result is $x = 8$. Plug 8 back into the original equation to check the answer:

$$\sqrt[3]{16 + 11} + 9 = 12$$

$$\sqrt[3]{27} + 9 = 12$$

$$3 + 9 = 12$$

52. A: 13 nurses. Using the given information of 1 nurse to 25 patients and 325 patients, set up an equation to solve for the number of nurses (N):

$$\frac{N}{325} = \frac{1}{25}$$

Multiply both sides by 325 to get N by itself on one side:

$$\frac{N}{1} = \frac{325}{25} = 13 \; nurses$$

Subtest III

1. B: The general categories of basic movement skills include locomotor skills like walking, running, and skipping; non-locomotor skills such as squatting and twisting; and manipulative skills such as throwing and catching.

2. A: In a kindergarten classroom, hitting targets is not an appropriate focus for physical education because children at this age have not mastered the fine motor abilities and complex skills to aim and hit targets. Hitting targets is more appropriate for fifth grade students. In kindergarten, activities should focus on foundational skills such as weight transfer, balance, following objects with the eyes, and basic skills like jumping and skipping.

3. A: The five main components of health-related physical fitness are cardiovascular fitness, muscular endurance, flexibility, body composition, and flexibility. Muscular power is related to exercise performance and is a measure of strength to speed. It isn't one of the five components of fitness that directly relates to health.

4. B: Ligaments connect bone to bone. Tendons connect muscle to bone. Both are made of dense, fibrous connective tissue (primarily Type 1 collagen) to give strength. However, tendons are more organized, especially in the long axis direction like muscle fibers themselves, and they have more collagen. This arrangement makes more sense because muscles have specific orientations of their fibers, so they contract in somewhat predictable directions. Ligaments are less organized and more of a woven pattern because bone connections are not as organized as bundles of muscle fibers, so ligaments must have strength in multiple directions to protect against injury.

5. D: Blood returning to the heart from the body enters the right atrium and then moves through the tricuspid valve into the right ventricle. After filling, the right ventricle contracts, and the tricuspid valve closes, pushing blood through the pulmonary semilunar valve into the pulmonary arteries for pulmonary circulation, after which it enters the left atrium. Contraction of the left atrium moves blood through the bicuspid valve into the left ventricle (the largest heart chamber). When the bicuspid valve closes and the left ventricle contracts, blood is forced into the aortic valve through the aorta and on to systemic circulation.

6. A: Abduction is movement away from the body's midline (out to the side). Side-lying leg raises is a common exercise used to strengthen the gluteus medius and is an example of abduction. Adduction is the opposite—movement towards the body's centerline. Pronation is rotating up or inward, while supination is rotating down or outward. These latter two terms often describe movement of the forearm or ankle.

7. B: Antagonists are muscles that oppose the action of the agonist—the primary muscle causing a motion. Hamstrings are the primary knee flexors—the agonists—and the quadriceps fire in opposition. The gastrocnemius does cross the knee joint, so it is a knee flexor, although secondary to the hamstrings. The tibialis anterior is on the shin and is involved in dorsiflexion.

8. A: Shoulder flexion occurs in the sagittal plane (as does most flexion from anatomical position). Shoulder flexion is bringing the arm forward up towards overhead. The sagittal plane is viewing the body from the side, dividing the body into right and left sections. Abduction and adduction occur in the frontal plane and in rotation, such as trunk twists, and typically occur in the transverse plane.

9. C: Glycolysis is one of the anaerobic (without oxygen) metabolic pathways for producing ATP. It generates ATP from carbohydrate (glucose) metabolism that is used for two to three minutes of high intensity activity. The ATP-PC system is the other anaerobic pathway. It uses ATP stored in muscles; however, there is very little, so it is sufficient only for about ten-second high intensity bouts of activity at a time. The aerobic pathway involves the Krebs cycle. ATP is generated through the breakdown of carbohydrates and fats and, to a lesser degree, proteins. It supplies energy during long-duration endurance activities and is used when the other energy systems are depleted or insufficient, but this takes a relatively long time and would be inefficient for short bursts of energy.

10. D: Increased submaximal heart rate is not a chronic adaptation to cardiovascular exercise; in fact, heart rate decreases at a given submaximal workload due to improvements in cardiorespiratory economy. Heart chamber size increases as does preload (the amount of blood that fills a chamber before it contracts to eject it), resulting in a higher stroke volume per heartbeat. This means that more blood, oxygen, and nutrients get moved per pump of the heart. Blood volume and hemoglobin content of the blood also increases.

11. C: In isotonic contractions, the muscle exerts constant tension such as in a pushup or squat. Isometric contractions, like planks, are ones in which there is no change in muscle length. The body is static, and muscles are contracting to stabilize and hold the body stable against gravity. Isokinetic contractions are ones that move through the range of motion at a constant speed, but they are rarely used in practice due to the limited manufactured isokinetic equipment (some Cybex machines are isokinetic as are dynamometers). Eccentric are lengthening contractions, such as the lowering phase of a biceps curl.

12. B: Choices *I*, *II*, and *IV* are correct. Here are examples of correct matches:

- Fibrous: sutures in skull
- Plane: intercarpal
- Saddle: thumb
- Hinge: elbow
- Condyloid: wrist
- Pivot: radial head on ulna
- Cartilaginous: pubic symphysis

13. B: Times of war or conflict often spurred nations to organize regimented fitness training programs for young boys and men to prepare them to be strong soldiers. This can be seen as early as 4000 BCE in the Persian Empire as well as later in Ancient Greece and Sparta and all the way into the twentieth century in the United States in preparation for the World Wars. Choice *A* is incorrect because although the attention given to fitness increased with the awareness of the danger of a sedentary lifestyle in the 1950s and 1960s, people recognized the importance of fitness around the world well before that time. Choice *C* is incorrect because gymnastics dates back all the way to Ancient China with Kung Fu gymnastics and Choice *D* is incorrect because yoga originated in India.

14. C: At ten to twelve months, babies show an increase in exploration and curiosity, demonstrate affection, and display a sense of humor. Infants around three to four months old typically begin to communicate by crying and express interest and surprise. Between four to nine months old, infants begin to respond differently to strangers compared to known individuals, solicit attention, show attachment to their primary caregiver, and show an expanded range of emotions including anger, fear, and shyness. By twelve to twenty-four months, infants typically demonstrate anger through aggression, laugh in social situations, recognize themselves in a mirror, engage in symbolic play, and have a complete range of emotional expression.

517

15. A: The optimal physical education curriculum for five- to six-year-old children should focus on movement for enjoyment. Children at this age are motivated by fun and playing and will be active if it is fun. They are not necessarily ready to focus on sports-specific skills requiring significant hand-eye coordination. They do best with moderate- and high-intensity activities with adequate rest.

16. C: When teaching new skills, especially to toddlers and young children, instructions lasting longer than twenty seconds or containing more than just a couple of steps or cues will lead students to losing interest or getting overwhelmed. It is typically advantageous to have very short instructional periods interspersed between longer breaks to play and try out the introduced skills. Reading material is likely not appropriate for this age group, many of whom do not yet know how to read.

17. C: Following safety procedures like wearing a seatbelt is the best choice. Experts recommend that children get over nine hours of sleep per night. Also, children should brush their teeth after every meal, not just before bed. Finally, it is important for children to learn how to express their emotions in a healthy way and let a trusted adult know if they are struggling with persistent feelings of sadness or anxiety.

18. D: Teachers should educate students on the importance of visiting doctors for routine medical care and check-ups (every six months or so); consistent feelings of sadness, anxiety, loneliness, and stress; and pains or aches that do not go away. Research has found that even at the preschool level, talking about the importance of visiting the doctor can positively impact health behaviors in adulthood.

19. A: Family influences on health behaviors include health insurance status, safety and injury prevention education and care, nutritional meal planning and diet composition, social dynamics and stress, and the family's culture around leisure time.

20. C: Gross motor skills are mastered before fine motor skills. Students begin developing basic motor skills like walking, balancing, and manipulating objects from a very early age. They master gross motor skills before they move on to fine motor skills. Sports skills are not learned more readily than generalized body movements, because sports skills require more fine motor skills, complex motions, and cognitive abilities (e.g., locating and aiming for targets). Also, what looks like play actually helps children develop movement patterns and abilities.

21. D: The highest level of Maslow's hierarchy of needs is self-actualization, in which one achieves their full potential, including creative pursuits. Prestige, a feeling of accomplishment, and self-esteem are all part of the esteem needs, one level below the top and part of the psychological needs section.

22. D: A three- to four-year-old child's drawing usually emphasizes their color choices. At this young age, children typically do not use art for self-expression, symbolism, or realistic figural accuracy. These are all artistic skills that students develop when they are older. Young students tend to focus on sensory exploration involving color, shape, and texture.

23. D: Self-efficacy refers to a person's feelings of competency to perform or achieve a particular task. Self-identity and self-concept have to do with one's overall view of self.

24. A: Equilibrium is represented by the successful assimilation of information into the individual's schema. In contrast, failure to assimilate information is termed disequilibrium. Altering one's cognitive framework to adjust to new information is termed accommodation, which follows after disequilibrium. When information is understood and internalized, this is known as assimilation. The mental framework in which information is organized is called a schema, which is not consciously formed but rather is organically developed through encountering new information.

25. D: The stages of cognitive development in the order in which they occur are sensorimotor, pre-operational, concrete operational, and formal operational. The first stage, sensorimotor occurs from birth to around approximately age two and is when the child develops object permanence. In the pre-operational stage, from two to seven years of age, children engage in symbolic play and can use logic. The concrete operational stage is from around age seven to eleven years. Children use inductive reasoning to make generalizations by drawing conclusions from what they observe, yet they are generally unable to use deductive reasoning or come to a conclusion. The formal operational stage occurs from adolescence through early adulthood. People develop abstract thought, metacognition, and problem-solving ability.

26. B: Establishing a secure, positive attachment with a caregiver is crucial to a child's life-long emotional and social success, and foster children of those adopted later in life can develop an attachment disorder as a result of an inconsistent or lacking caregiver. While bonding is the initial relationship between a mother and a baby just after giving birth, attachment grows more slowly over time as the relationship with the caregiver develops into a trusting and loving, dependable bond. Children who lack this stability or care can develop an attachment disorder. Maslow's Hierarchy of Needs is thought to apply equally to all people, and altruism is a somewhat controversial construct in which people show an unselfish care or concern for the needs of others.

27. A: Educators should focus curricular activities on the major categories of arts: music, dance, theater, and visual arts (painting, drawing, sculpture, pottery, etc.).

28. C: The youngest children tend to create art with a focus on the scientific and sensory aspects of the project rather than artistic creativity, self-expression, or conveying a narrative or story. They enjoy art more as a means to which explore the textures they make (for example, making texture rubbings with crayon on paper), the contrast of colors they use, and the various shapes they make as they move the drawing utensil around (although they are not making shapes for symbolic reasons, they are simply enjoying and exploring what they make when they use the supplies).

29. D: Children should experiment with a variety of methods and materials to create art. Educators should provide children with a wide range of materials like finger paint, glitter, and felt so that children experiment with different textures. Choice *A* is not the best answer because art education should expose students to the historical and cultural context of art beyond that of their everyday experiences. Students can learn about famous artists and art history, but those lessons can be incorporated into creative coursework; they are not a prerequisite for student experimentation.

30. D: Have students accompany the music with simple instruments like tambourines. Students can easily beat along to simple songs using rhythmic instruments like tambourines, maracas, or small drums. Young children enjoy moving around more than sitting and focusing on one thing for an extended time, so learning rhythm through actions like shaking rhythmic instruments or stomping and clapping is more effective for students at this age. Also, *C* is not the best answer because many young children are not yet strong readers.

31. D: Theater-in-education (TIE) is performed by teachers and students using curriculum material on social issues. Participants take on roles, which enable them to explore and problem-solve in a flexible structure, yet in an educational theatrical way. In Readers' Theater, readers perform a dramatic presentation sitting on stools reading their lines, typically from children's literature, enabling performance opportunities in the absence of elaborate staging or script memorization. Puppetry can be used for creative drama with either simple puppets and stages made of bags, cardboard, socks, or more elaborate, artistic materials.

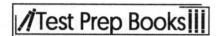

32. A: The main skills in theatrical arts for children include literary (reading and writing the script and memorizing lines), technical (includes the staging, lighting, sound effects, etc.), and performance elements (such as the set design and the musical score). Staging is part of the technical elements.

33. B: Perspective is a technique used to make flat objects look as though they have depth. Balance is using size, position, color, shape, and lighting in the artwork so that all of the elements are equally present with no particular component overpowering the others. Abstraction is unrealistic artwork that typically has geometric lines or patterns.

34. A: Art has personal (self-expression, gratification, narrative functions), social (collective meaning for a group of people such as symbolic art honoring a god or political art), and physical functions (such as a pottery mug for tea) that often overlap in a project. Religious functions fall under the realm of social functions.

35. B: Harmony is a principle in art that highlights the similarities in separate but related parts of a composition to show how different things can actually be similar and blend together. Balance is positioning objects or using size, color, shape, and lighting in a way that makes all of the elements equally present. Contrast is exemplifying differences between two unlike things such as loud and soft music, major and minor tones, fast and slow dancing movements, and light and dark colors.

36. A: Balance is the ability to control the center of mass within the base of support without falling. The wider the base of support and the lower the center of gravity, the easier it is to maintain balance. Center of gravity is the location of a theoretical point that represents the total weight of an object. Base of support is the part of an object that serves as the supporting surface, often thought of as feet in contact with the ground. The base of support also refers to the area between the feet as well, not just the physical structures of the body in contact with the supporting surface. Choice C is incorrect because a person cannot easily widen the center of gravity of the body. The center is a fixed point, so it can be moved, but not expanded. Choices B and D would make it harder to balance if the center of mass is raised.

37. C: Waltzes first appeared in Venetian ballrooms in the 13th century.

38. A: The tango is an energetic ballroom dance originating in the suburbs of Buenos Aires in the late nineteenth century. It quickly gained popularity in other cultures.

39. C: Teachers can help students learn about the rhythm or tempo of a piece of music by accompanying the listening experience with physical movements such as clapping, stomping, dancing, or following the beat with percussive instruments like tambourines or small drums. The other answer choices pertain to the melodic arrangement of the particular pitches or sounds so stomping or clapping (a rhythmic activity) would not facilitate learning these concepts.

Dear CSET Multiple Subject Test Taker,

Thank you again for purchasing this study guide for your CSET Multiple Subject exam. We hope that we exceeded your expectations.

Our goal in creating this study guide was to cover all of the topics that you will see on the test. We also strove to make our practice questions as similar as possible to what you will encounter on test day. With that being said, if you found something that you feel was not up to your standards, please send us an email and let us know.

We would also like to let you know about other books in our catalog that may interest you.

CSET English

This can be found on Amazon: amazon.com/dp/1628458941

CSET Mathematics

amazon.com/dp/1628459158

CBEST

amazon.com/dp/1637752636

NES Elementary Education

amazon.com/dp/1628459239

We have study guides in a wide variety of fields. If the one you are looking for isn't listed above, then try searching for it on Amazon or send us an email.

Thanks Again and Happy Testing!

Product Development Team

info@studyguideteam.com

FREE Test Taking Tips Video/DVD Offer

To better serve you, we created videos covering test taking tips that we want to give you for FREE. **These videos cover world-class tips that will help you succeed on your test.**

We just ask that you send us feedback about this product. Please let us know what you thought about it—whether good, bad, or indifferent.

To get your **FREE videos**, you can use the QR code below or email freevideos@studyguideteam.com with "Free Videos" in the subject line and the following information in the body of the email:

     a. The title of your product

     b. Your product rating on a scale of 1-5, with 5 being the highest

     c. Your feedback about the product

If you have any questions or concerns, please don't hesitate to contact us at info@studyguideteam.com.

Thank you!

Made in the USA
Las Vegas, NV
15 February 2024

85836555R00293